U2

BONO, THE EDGE
ADAM CLAYTON
LARRY MULLEN JR

BY

U2

U2

**BONO, THE EDGE
ADAM CLAYTON
LARRY MULLEN JR**

BY

U2

with NEIL McCORMICK

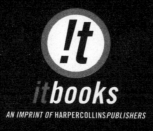

itbooks

AN IMPRINT OF HARPERCOLLINS PUBLISHERS

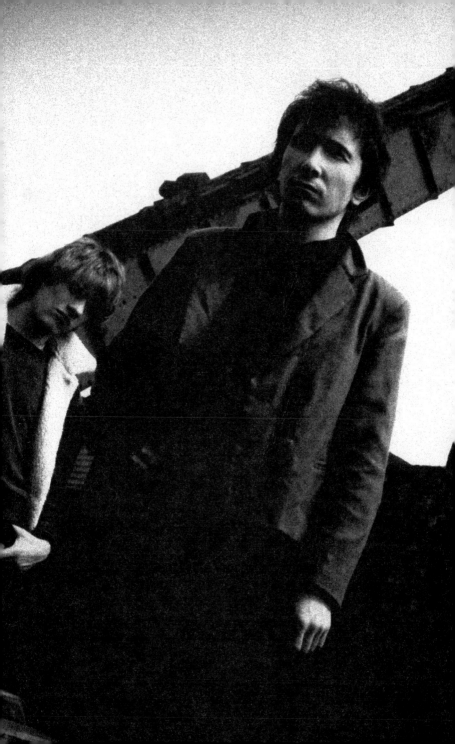

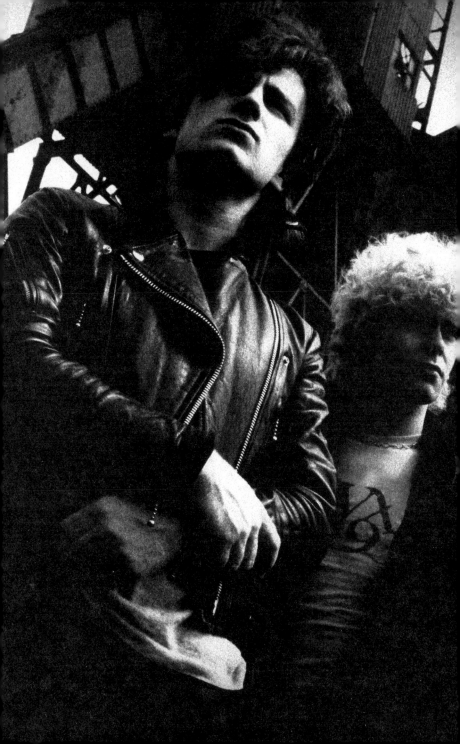

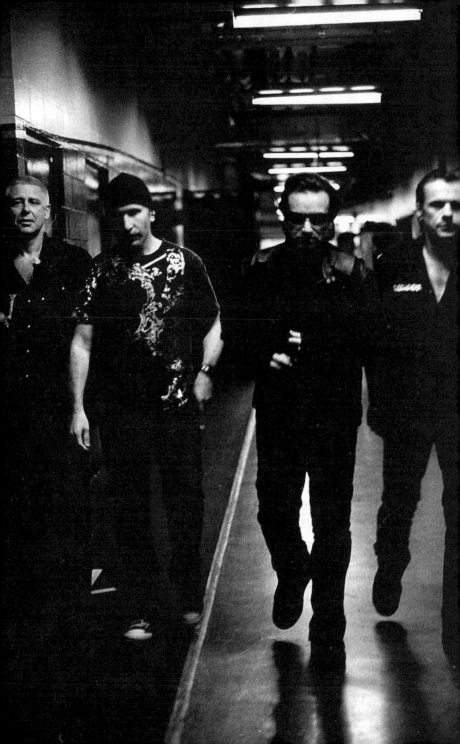

Contents

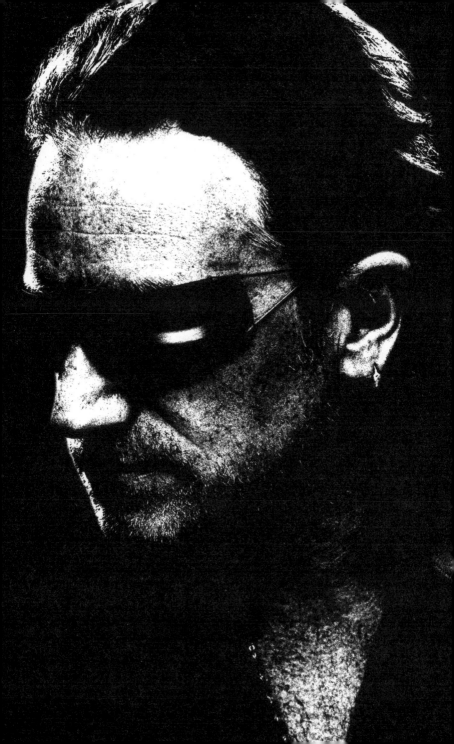

Bono

SOMETIMES IT COMES ACROSS AS IF I GOT INTO U2
TO SAVE THE WORLD. I GOT INTO U2 TO SAVE MYSELF.
I MEET PEOPLE OUT ON THE STREET WHO APPROACH
ME LIKE I'M MAHATMA GANDHI.

And when someone says, 'Hail, man of peace,' I can hear Larry laughing under his breath: 'You're lucky he didn't nut you.' The band are very bemused by my attraction to non-violence, because they know you couldn't get further from the songs than the singer. They understand the reason I have been so attracted to these characters, the subjects of the songs – because in my life and temperament I am so far from them. There is a rage in me and it is not all injustice. I have developed good manners to disguise it.

I am better at it now, but it used to be difficult to talk to me after a show, because I would be very hyped-up for about an hour, and, if the show hadn't gone well, I would feel cheated and raw. Backstage at a U2 concert, it's more like a dressing-room after a boxing or soccer match than a rock gig. You have to remember, for U2 every night has to be the best night. And if it isn't, there has to be a reason. We have very high standards and we always remember who pays our wages. Our audience deserves the best possible set of songs, not just running through some jukebox to keep ourselves amused. I can feel if the crowd are losing interest and I might just throw a firecracker into that part of the crowd, and the firecracker would probably be me. Light the fuse, see what happens.

To sing those songs, to hit those high notes, takes an incredible concentration and commitment. You have to step inside and live the songs. So you're right in the middle of Derry performing 'Sunday, Bloody Sunday', or you are in Memphis at a civil-rights rally with Dr King, singing 'Pride in the Name of Love'. I'm right up there. Your mate is ruining his life with a bag of smack. It's 'Bad'. You're in those emotions. And I think the band have been very good about realizing that I get to that spot. At times it must have been very difficult for them, because the singer would be right out there.

Your nature is a hard thing to change; it takes time. One of the extraordinary transferences that happen in your spiritual life is not that your character flaws go away but they start to work for you. A negative becomes a positive: you've a big mouth: you end up a singer. You're insecure: you end up a performer who needs applause. I have heard of people having life-changing, miraculous turn-arounds, people set free from addiction after a single prayer, relationships saved where both parties 'let go, and let God'. But it was not like that for me. For all that 'I was lost, I am found', it is probably more accurate to say, 'I was really lost, I'm a little less so at the moment.' And then a little less and a little less again. That to me is the spiritual life. The slow reworking and rebooting of a computer at regular intervals, reading the small print of the service manual. It has slowly rebuilt me in a better image. It has taken years, though, and it is not over yet.

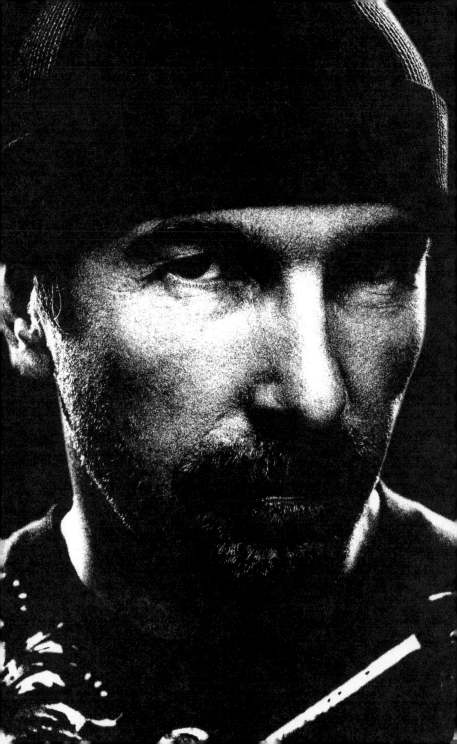

Edge

ROCK 'N' ROLL IS PARTICULAR TO THIS PERIOD OF TIME. THERE WAS NO PRECEDENT IN MUSICAL HISTORY, BECAUSE IT IS COMPLETELY ABOUT ELECTRICITY.

When you play an electric guitar through a Marshall amplifier in a studio with the volume turned up so loud it reaches the point where it has stopped being able to accurately reproduce the sound, you create the effect of compression. It is as if the sound is too explosive to be contained by the speakers. You get a sense of everything caving in, which is actually what happens to the eardrum when it is being assaulted by an incredibly loud sound – it has a natural tendency to close down. That sonic excitement is what people love about rock and roll. You don't get that with an acoustic guitar.

There is a certain strange magic in the sound of an electric guitar. Stratocasters, Telecasters, Les Pauls, Explorers: they are really just chunks of wood with a neck and strings and pick-ups, yet there is a remarkable amount of variation and they all react differently to effect units and amplifiers. I don't have a relationship with a particular guitar, I am not that sentimental. I just see the different possibilities they all present. I am absolutely fascinated with sound and how it can be sculpted using the technology of the day.

It seems impossible now to contemplate an existence outside of music but I honestly don't know if I would have even become a professional musician if U2 hadn't made me believe it was possible. We have been together all of our adult lives, which demonstrates an incredible level of commitment and solidarity between four people who decided to form a band in 1975. All the reasons why it was a great idea at the time still hold true. On our day we can still make great music together, come up with original ideas and perform emotional, exciting, spiritual shows bursting with the possibility that anything might happen.

On a certain level, U2 are a very dysfunctional band. We became the band we are because we weren't particularly capable musicians. We couldn't play other people's songs so we had to create our own. That musical dysfunction can still creep up on us. Sometimes when we are getting ready to go out on the road, I listen again to our old records and I am left scratching my head, wondering, 'What did I play there? That's kind of weird, how did I do that?' Yet somehow we have managed to turn weakness into strength. We may not be the most musically accomplished band in the history of rock and roll but I think we are amongst the most original.

The chemistry of the personalities is a big factor. Bono is chairman and founding-member of Over-Achievers Anonymous. He has an irrepressible drive to be great and a lust for life. He wants to experience it all, which actually makes him very vulnerable. I sometimes worry that the media has created a myth about who he is and what he stands for. I hope the hype doesn't stop people realizing that he is just a man who is trying to find himself. It's part of everyone's struggle to figure out what they're doing and where they want to go. U2 write songs about the struggle but we are just as confused as anyone else.

I am driven in different ways to Bono. I have a curiosity which compels me to want to find ways to make music that are fresh and new, and I have the focus to keep going until we realize our goals. If Bono should be attending Over-Achievers Anonymous, I might have to take the 12 steps at Workaholics Anonymous. The two of us together really feed off one another's determination and concentration and energy.

Adam and Larry are the counterpoints to Bono and myself. Adam has an incredible soul, the unlikely conscience of the band. During the early days, when the rest of us were at the height of our Christian fervour, Adam was actually the most Christian in his tolerance and humanity. In some ways, because he is the one who doesn't have to worry so much about the music or the lyrics, he has a freedom to contribute things you would never have thought of, to throw in something that is way outside of the discussion. He is our wild card, naturally avant-garde. Larry is the nuts and bolts of the band, a practical, solid and deeply cautious person who is always going to rein us in when we get too excited. He is always there to steady the ship when it is heading for the rocks and I have my telescope pointing the other direction, Bono is hanging off the rigging and Adam is pottering about in the engine-room.

We grew up together, we learned how to play music together. In many respects the way we think is almost telepathic. When Bono is singing I will feel where he wants to go with the chords. Even if I'm writing on my own, I hear his voice as I'm going through ideas. But the really interesting thing is when those songs go to the next stage and Adam and Larry come in and play with us – a whole other evolutionary thing takes place. I guess, in the end, that is the strength of a band, when you are able to take advantage of four different perspectives. It is something far greater than any of us could achieve on our own.

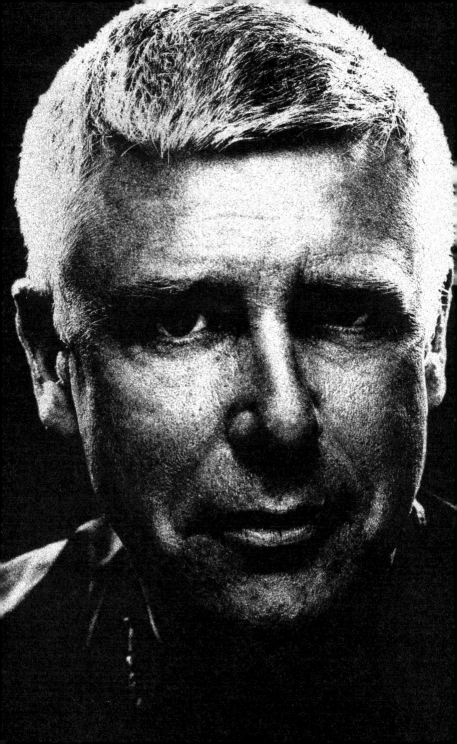

Adam

I ALWAYS WANTED TO BE A ROCK STAR. WHEN I GOT
MY FIRST BASS GUITAR AT THE AGE OF FIFTEEN,
THAT WAS IT FOR ME. I DIDN'T HAVE A WHOLE LOT
ELSE GOING ON IN MY LIFE.

If U2 hadn't worked out, God knows where I would have ended up. Not that I
ever worried about it, as I had an enormous amount of ambition and energy
which I focused on becoming the kind of person I thought I ought to be. I
embraced all that life had to offer and when the opportunity came I really lived
it. And then I moved on, I disposed of the cars, I got rid of certain aspects of
the way I was living. I settled down with my partner, Susie. I discovered that I
am actually a much simpler and more low-key person than I ever would have
imagined. I came to realize that it wasn't the trappings of rock and roll that
sustained me on this journey. It was the music and the comradeship.

I wouldn't describe it as fun recording with U2; it is work. Sessions are
not exactly filled with laughter and joviality. Frequently we're being told how
crap we are by Bono – and he includes himself in that assessment. There's a
tense atmosphere in the studio. We have to evaluate things very quickly, and

unless it's brilliant, it is not good enough. That can be a hard environment to work in, you have to be prepared to defend your corner or stand back as your idea is shot down in flames. The creative process is exhausting. It is as if we have to try all possibilities and explore every avenue before settling on a final version. Songs go from A to Z and frequently all the way back again. We are trying to pin down something elusive, something that represents where we are, emotionally, physically, spiritually, but is also fresh and exciting. If it is not absolutely the best it can be, then why bother?

Without a doubt, Bono is the driving force. No matter how you might try to describe Bono, the words would be inadequate because there's so much more to him. To say he is a mass of contradictions barely does him justice. He is hugely intelligent and capable as a strategist with relentless logic but he wouldn't know how to boil an egg. But that's OK, I suspect he's not interested in boiling an egg. He has what you might describe as classic Alpha Male programming. He has no difficulty in deciding what he wants and he goes and gets it. He doesn't see limitations, he only sees possibilities. In some ways he is the psyche of U2, he represents things that are a part of all of us.

Edge is also very ambitious and driven but you might not see that unless you know him well because it is slightly obscured by his humanity and kindness. He always puts other people first. He is quite likely to be up in the middle of the night doing his own work but if you ask for help with something he will devote his full attention to solving whatever your particular problem is. He is an amazing friend and colleague, with a razor-sharp brain. Bono is results-oriented whereas Edge is much more into detail. That makes for a powerful combination of creative forces.

Larry is a very sensitive guy and a very loyal friend. He is also very black-and-white. He thinks about the world the same way he thinks about drumming: something is either in time or out of time, it can't be slightly in time or slightly out of time. It is usually me that is out of time, by the way. But Larry is a hugely gifted drummer. It is hard to figure out how Larry does it because he just turns up and plays. He might come in from the gym, sit down at his kit and he's off. He makes it look terribly easy.

I can't say what it is I bring to U2. It is not necessarily my bass-playing. Sometimes Edge might play bass, sometimes Bono. It's not particularly my territory. The best idea survives, no matter who has it. But something takes place when the band plays together. It is something unquantifiable but it has always been the thing that excites me the most. It's the thing that we built U2 on, the spark of excitement and energy between us, and you have to be there for that to happen.

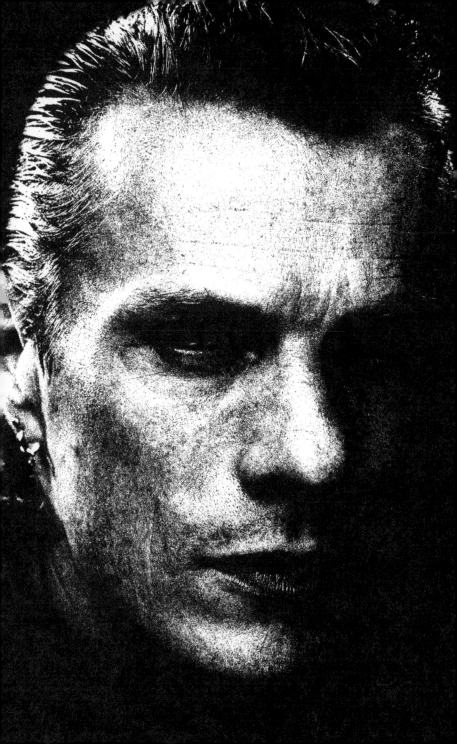

Larry

I WAS NEVER PARTICULARLY COMFORTABLE WITH
THE CELEBRITY OR FAME THING. I DON'T LIKE TO
DRAW TOO MUCH ATTENTION TO MYSELF.

You might say I chose the wrong career, and you may be right. Playing drums
and being creative in the studio are my drugs of choice. When I started out
doing this, any idea of becoming a rock star was laughable.

I have read a lot of rubbish about U2. Sometimes when I see us
described in some mythic sense or called corporate masters of our own
destiny, I have to laugh out loud. Being in U2 is more like riding a runaway
train, hanging on to it for dear life.

Over the years the band has really struggled with musical deficiencies, so
just playing together can be a challenge. Live shows can be a bit like an obstacle
course and occasionally we fall over. So I try to be rock-solid. I would like to
think that if there is any confusion about where anybody is in a song, they would
know that, as their drummer, I would be on top of it. Easier said than done.

Adam and I rely on each other a lot. Edge always has a lot to do on
stage, pushing various buttons, to get different sounds. Bono could be

climbing up scaffolding, diving into the audience – there were times we'd have no idea where he was. Occasionally it's been just myself and Adam on stage, so we've learned how to interact and communicate with each other in a way most rhythm sections don't.

You could say U2 are a democracy. The decision-making process is the same now as when we started. Those with the ability to debate, argue and articulate their views win the day. If you are in a band with someone as talkative, argumentative and persuasive as Bono, well, things can be kind of difficult for the rest of us.

We are four very, very different people with diverse personalities. All of us have various needs, both professionally and privately. We are one but we are definitely not the same. If there is something special about U2, it has nothing to do with us as individuals. It's what happens when we get together on stage or in the studio. It's very hard to describe and even harder to explain. However, it's the only reason we are still doing this. When we play music together, something happens.

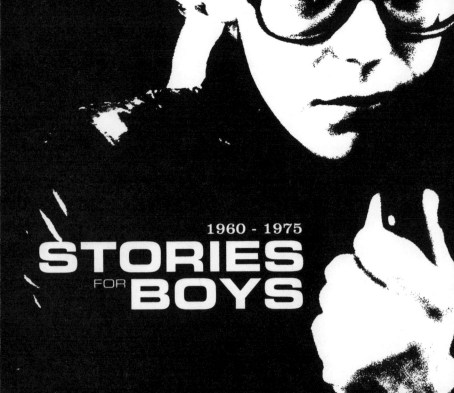

1960 - 1975

STORIES FOR BOYS

Adam Clayton

I WAS BORN INTO A HOUSE FULL OF WOMEN AND FULL OF MUSIC: TWO FORCES WHICH HAVE PRETTY MUCH DICTATED THE SHAPE OF MY SUBSEQUENT LIFE. IT WAS IN MY GRANDPARENTS' HOUSE IN AN OXFORDSHIRE VILLAGE CALLED CHINNOR ON 13 MARCH 1960.

My father had a career in aviation and it always seemed he wasn't there very much. Even now that he has retired, he spends a lot of his time fishing, which is a very solitary activity, away from the family.

My grandfather was a PE instructor in the RAF, so he wasn't often around. But my grandmother, her mother, my mother and her two sisters all lived in this house. I was the first child, a boy, fussed over by this group of women. My grandmother was a piano-player in a dance band. She was always off gigging at weekends and I was left with my mum and the two sisters. I remember listening to Forces radio and also being aware that my aunts had music they'd play on reel-to-reel tapes. Later there was a record-player and a lot of singles.

My youngest aunt was into Elvis and then The Beatles, when all that kicked off. I remember being aware of black and white *Top of the Pops* and really being intrigued by the outfits and instruments. I think even then I kind of knew the shape and shine of electric guitars, although strangely enough Ringo was my favourite Beatle.

My dad was an RAF pilot and when he was demobbed he started picking up work as a flying instructor at Biggin Hill, and then gradually he moved into civil aviation. My mum did a little bit of moonlighting as a stewardess and dad was the pilot on the small planes that eventually became BA (British Airways).

When I was four years old, dad found work in Kenya flying for East African Airways. We were based in Nairobi: this was definitely the happiest period I can remember from my early life; the heat and the freedom. My parents would have been living relatively comfortably compared to before, with regular work, a decent-sized house, someone to clean and help, that sort of stuff. Mostly I remember the sunshine and the smells. I have kept a lot of things African with me over the years, and whenever I've been back there it has always seemed very familiar.

Kenya had become an independent country as recently as 1963, throwing off British rule, and the situation there was still volatile. By 1965, it was getting quite dangerous to be a white person there. My dad had job offers in Ireland and Hong Kong but Ireland seemed closer to the family, so we came here, settling in Malahide, a suburban coastal town about eight miles from Dublin. I went to the local National school and that was pretty much where it stopped making sense for me. I arrived into an Ireland that was subtly repressive. The sky was grey and grim and at school there was a lot of instruction in Irish, a language I didn't understand. I found it difficult to fit into that system.

It was there that I met David Evans, The Edge, for the first time, although I have no real memory of it. His parents were part of that same community, which, unusually for Ireland, had a lot of Protestants and British ex-pats. The Evanses were amongst a group of parents who would occasionally call by the house, or we might visit their house and I'd meet Dave and his brother and sister. We didn't really bond until we came to know each other again in the band.

I have a sister, Sindy, who is four years younger than me, and a brother Sebastian, who is ten years younger. But it is hard for me to remember us as a family much of the time. Dad always seemed to be away working. Because he was doing a lot of the Atlantic runs for Aer Lingus when I was growing up, invariably he would be away three or four days at a time. Then, at the age of eight, I was sent to boarding school, which just disrupted things even more. Sindy was four when I went away and so I would see her only at weekends and holidays and we never developed an intense relationship until we were much older, we were simply not close enough in age to share common experiences. It's funny, but even though there is a bigger gap with my brother, for some reason we clicked, perhaps because by the time I'd finished school he was six or seven so I had the chance to get to know him better.

The boarding school was called Castle Park, in Dalkey, way over on the other side of Dublin Bay. In retrospect, I can understand that my parents were in a foreign country (as they would have seen it) and they didn't really know what would be an appropriate way to educate a child. Castle Park was a prep school along the lines of the English system and some of their friends had kids there, and they would have probably seen it leading on to a good English public school, like Eton or Harrow, and then a degree from Oxford or

THERE WAS A BOY WHO PLAYED CLASSICAL GUITAR IN THE DORMS. WHENEVER HE PLAYED I ALWAYS HAD AN EMOTIONAL CONNECTION. IT SPIRITED ME AWAY FROM THE CONFINES OF SCHOOL. ADAM

Cambridge. That was the plan, anyway. It didn't quite work out.

I didn't respond to boarding school particularly well. I wasn't sports orientated, I wasn't a hugely social character. I just kept my head down. Even then, I was keen on music, but we weren't allowed to listen to pop or watch television. Sport was the thing! But there was a boy who played classical guitar and he was allowed to have a guitar up in the dorms. Whenever he played I always had an emotional connection. In some way it spirited me away from the confines of school. I consequently joined the Gramophone Society, which used to meet a couple of afternoons a week and listen to classical music. Again, that just led me into a completely different world. At some point, I tried piano lessons, but I couldn't really match the aspiration and the coordination. I thought because of my grandmother that it would come easily but I guess I never came to terms with the hard work. I never made the mental jump that if you practised you might get the desired results!

About the age of ten or eleven, I started to fall in with people who would tape the Top Twenty on Radio Caroline on a Sunday night and then play it back, all undercover, of course. You weren't actually allowed to listen to the radio in school but certain music was tolerated. You could listen to rock opera like *Jesus Christ Superstar* and *Hair* and things that were midway between classical and popular music. So that was really my early awakening and maybe, in the very back of my mind, I began to think, 'I'll pick up the guitar', but it was always just a background notion, I never quite knew how I was going to get to that point.

I moved school when I was thirteen, again to an Irish public boarding school, St Columba's College in Rathfarnham. The buildings were old, there were no curtains and it was cold up there, the kind of cold that you never really forget. I can't say I was hugely enthused about the move. But fairly early on I fell in with a boy called John Leslie, who could play guitar. John had cassette tapes and we would listen to The Who, The Grateful Dead, Kris Kristofferson, Carole King, Neil Young, people that were around at that time, singer-songwriter things and some far-out stuff, Hawkwind, The Edgar Winter Group, Edgar Broughton. And then the prefects at school would listen to Rory Gallagher, The Beatles, The Stones, Eric Clapton, so we'd hear a bit of that,

SO THERE I WAS, FIFTEEN YEARS OLD, WITH A DARK BROWN IBANEZ-COPY BASS GUITAR AND NO AMP. I HAD NO IDEA WHAT I WAS SUPPOSED TO DO WITH IT. ABSOLUTELY NONE. NOT A CLUE. IT JUST SOUNDED GOOD TO ME. DEEP AND FAT AND SATISFYING. ADAM

and some American performers like the Doobie Brothers. So I was getting pretty turned on to music and it always seemed to change my mood; it somehow made it bearable to be in that school situation.

I remember reading that Clapton hadn't started playing guitar until he was fifteen or sixteen and I thought, 'Well, there's still time for me!' So I bought a £5 acoustic guitar from a junk-shop down Dublin quays and I started learning chords and collecting songs. There was a guy in school who had a bit of a band going. He had an electric guitar and the school gave him a room to practise in; there was a bass player and a drummer and the sound was amazing to me. I just loved it. I don't know what it was like objectively, four teenage schoolkids struggling to play a song, probably, but the sound of drums and guitar and bass felt primal to me. I started to see that not only did this make me feel good but you got a bit of attention if you did it, too. You could meet girls and these people were considered cool. I suppose that was when I really made my decision that this was what I wanted to do. I had no interest in sports. I didn't want to be academic, particularly, and at any rate was showing little aptitude. I liked the creative things, such as painting and music; I found that community of people more interesting.

So John persuaded me that we could start our own group. He wanted to play electric guitar, so he said I should play bass. I don't remember being particularly convinced at first. I knew that you needed bass and drums to make that rock sound but I didn't really know anything about music which would have qualified me to be a bassist. But John said he'd teach me what I needed to learn. I'd been taking some classical guitar lessons, and there was a folk guitar teacher who used to come by as well, so I picked up a few rudimentary things and decided to go for a bass. I talked my parents into buying it for me. I had to make a solemn promise that I was going to stick at it and all this kind of carry-on. Now that I look back it was an amazing thing for my parents to do, quite out of character. It was more my mother, I suppose. She had something of the romantic in her and probably thought it wouldn't do any harm. I guess there was enough music in the family that she could relate to it.

So there I was, fifteen years old, with a dark brown Ibanez-copy bass guitar and no amp. I had no idea what I was supposed to do with it. Absolutely none. Not a clue. It just sounded good to me. Deep and fat and satisfying. Presumably, in the big picture, someone like me would have been expected to have a couple of years of amateur rock and roll and then move on to something more sensible. But it was all that I had. I didn't have anything else.

My grades were so bad the following year that my parents said they were not prepared to keep me at this expensive school. That was pretty bad news for me, or so it seemed at the time, because we were just getting a band going. John Leslie and I had started writing an Irish rock opera based on the Celtic myth of the Children of Lir, in which children are turned into swans by their wicked stepmother. But I had to leave before having the chance to establish myself as Ireland's answer to Andrew Lloyd Webber.

I thought that was it, the musical career was over. And so I was dispatched to Mount Temple, a comprehensive school in north Dublin, which was not a place where I felt comfortable at all, to contemplate a future without much in the way of career prospects.

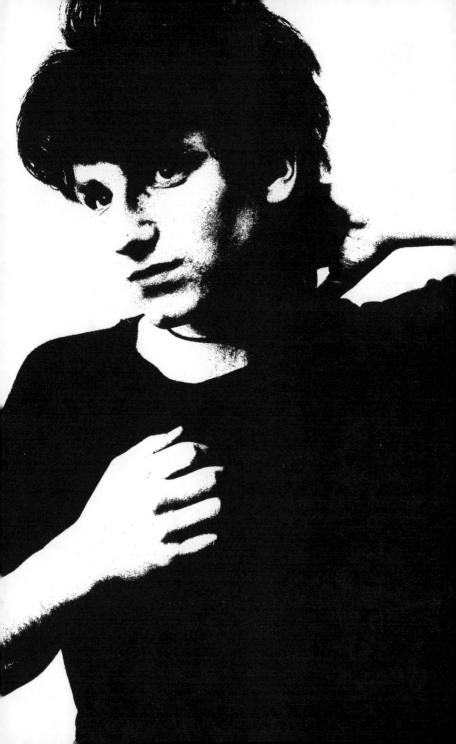

Bono

YOU DON'T BECOME A ROCK STAR UNLESS YOU'VE
GOT SOMETHING MISSING SOMEWHERE, THAT IS
OBVIOUS TO ME. IF YOU WERE OF SOUND MIND OR
A MORE COMPLETE PERSON, YOU COULD FEEL
NORMAL WITHOUT 70,000 PEOPLE A NIGHT
SCREAMING THEIR LOVE FOR YOU.

Blaise Pascal called it the God-shaped hole. Everyone's got one but some are blacker and wider than others. It's a feeling of being abandoned, cut adrift in space and time.

Sometimes this stuff follows the loss of a loved one. With me, I was like the character in that old blues song: 'sometimes I feel like a motherless child'. So many years later, my own hole can still open up. I don't think you can ever completely fill it in this life. You can try to fill it up with songs, family, faith; by living a full life, but when things are silent you can still hear the hissing of what's missing.

I don't have very many memories from my early life. I've talked about this with my brother because he doesn't have many either. The only explanation we can come up with is that when my mother died, my father didn't talk about her, at all, ever. So as a result of her being erased from memory, simply through not wanting to go there, I think a lot of other stuff went with her. It's a real singer's thing, missing mothers. Johnny Lydon, John Lennon, it seems to be the very heart of rock and roll, as missing fathers are to hip hop.

My grandfather Hewson, on my father's side, was a comedian. He played the Dame at Saint Francis Xavier Hall, in the centre of Dublin city. I didn't get to know him. Some said he died of TB but it is hard to be definitive, there was a terrible stigma back then. People used to put weights in their shoes to disguise the fact that they were wasting away. It's a very Irish story. Ireland was like Africa back then, it was a Third World country. There was a TB epidemic, so the workers, if their weight went down, used to put lead in their boots to get past the weigh-in. My father told me this story. Whatever the truth, he was by all accounts, a morose man. In the only picture I have of him he looks very cross, as I guess you would be if you were dying of TB. But, oddly enough, he got the footlights thing going. I think it's interesting that this man played the Dame, dressing up as a woman for laughs, but was so downbeat, even melancholic, as a man. I think this peculiarity of laughing a lot and then biting one's own tongue is something that runs in the family.

The Hewsons are a very interesting breed, very intelligent, quick with the crossword puzzles, a little wired in the sense that they are really aware of what's going on in the room. Only my father drove a car. I don't know what that says about the family but I know there are a few people who wish that I wouldn't drive. But there's melancholy in us that I think comes from my granddad. My father, Bob Hewson, didn't particularly give in to it as a public person but I think, if he was on his own, he felt it. You can taste that bittersweetness, the happy sad feeling in U2's music.

My grandmother Rankin, on my mother's side, was a really big laugh, which disguised the fact that beneath her dress, she had a big stick with which she reared, I think, eight kids. Contraceptives were banned in Ireland and people tried to get them from the UK. She used to joke that the parcels were intercepted at the post office and – too late! – another kid was born, another mouth to feed. They were a very close family. They lived in inner-city Dublin, 10 Cowper Street, two-up, two-down, outside toilet. My grandmother's house was very exciting, always buzzing with activity. They'd have sing-songs and my grandmother would play piano. A brilliant, brilliant place, number ten. We called my grandfather 'Gags' Rankin. He fought in the trenches in the First World War where gas left him coughing his guts up for the rest of his life. My mother, Iris, was the oldest of her family and quite petite, really a delicate flower, but she took on the responsibility of bringing up the younger kids. Her closest sister and best friend was Ruth, still the historian of the family. And there was my Uncle Jack, I loved him. Wherever you went, Jack knew everybody; you couldn't go to a place where he wouldn't meet somebody he knew. People were always coming up and shaking his hand. I used to think this was Godlike. He is a very up, generous person and it was a thrill to be around him. Jack was a travelling salesman, as many of my uncles were, and they came from a long line of travelling salesmen. And in fact I am a travelling salesman. I sell songs for U2, door to door, city to city, and I promote ideas like debt cancellation or fair trade at the market, and I reckon I must have got it from the Rankins – which, by the way, is usually a Jewish name. They all looked Jewish too. I've heard it said that the Rankins were Jewish at one point when they were based in Scotland, then they came over to Ireland and they weren't Jewish any more, which I think used to happen a lot. I don't know if that is true, but I'd like it if it were.

I CAME INTO THE WORLD CRYING AND APPARENTLY I CRIED FOR THREE YEARS. THE CRYING STOPPED ON THE FIRST DAY I WENT TO SCHOOL. I REMEMBER THAT DAY. A BOY CAME UP TO MY BEST MATE AND BIT HIS EAR, AND I TOOK THAT KID'S HEAD AND BANGED IT ON SOME IRON RAILINGS. BONO

My mother and father lived round the corner from each other. My mother was a Protestant, and my father was a Catholic and their love affair was practically illicit at the time. Ireland was just being born as a country and everything was at fever pitch. The country was almost at civil war along religious lines, with a Catholic power base running this new nation while Protestantism was seen as the faith of our former masters, the invaders' religion. But my parents faced the flak and got married.

I was born on 10 May 1960. I think I wrote a song about this: *One dull morning woke the world with bawling, they were so glad, I was so sad.* Not a great rhyme, but there you go. That was 'Out Of Control', U2's first single. I did come into the world crying and apparently I cried for three years, non-stop. I have a vague memory of being in hospital, aged three, for tests to find out what was wrong with the screaming child. It was a strange thing, they seemed to think it might be something to do with my heart. I have a kind of memory of that, and of a red-headed nurse I think I rather fancied even then. My heart is still beating in its own unique fashion. I recently had to have my unusual heartbeat re-diagnosed and the doctor sat down and said: 'You're as healthy as you would want to be but you have what's known as an eccentric heart.' I said, 'I could have told you that!' I had to go to the best specialist money can buy to be told what everyone who knows me has long since figured out.

The crying stopped on the first day I went to school. I remember that day. A boy came up to my new best mate, James Mahon, and bit his ear, and I took that kid's head and banged it on some iron railings. It is terrible, but that is the sort of thing I remember. The little pieces that I can put back together are, if not violent, then aggressive. I never liked bullies. But maybe that was just my excuse for bad behaviour.

I remember having my photograph taken with my brother, Norman (who is eight years older than me) and not liking it. I was around three years old. We had two little china leopards standing as ornaments on the mantel and at the end of the session there was only one leopard left. And I was put away for that!

I was a freckle-faced kid who was difficult to tie down from the very beginning, a messer full of life and mischief, noisy, maybe a little too much testosterone. I should admit to my first family nickname: the Antichrist. It wasn't completely wide of the mark. I haven't met many other kids who were nicknamed the Antichrist! I'd come round to my aunties and just buzz about wrecking their houses. But now I look back on it and I think I was just a bit wide-awake, a bit bright, a bit experimental, that's all. But it still comes up, to this very day. When I told my dad that Ali, my wife, was pregnant for the first time, he burst out laughing. Tears welled up in his eyes, but this was not at all sentimental, they were tears of laughter. He just looked at me and instead of congratulations offered the word: 'Revenge!'

I wish I had more of a sense of my mother. I forget what she looked liked. I have just a few vague memories. My father used to make things, he was good at DIY and he'd be building presses and wardrobes and whatever. I remember he was upstairs in the bedroom and he was using an electric drill and there was a scream, a wild, mad sound. Mother and I ran out to the bottom of the stairs and we looked up. My dad had been drilling a piece of wood while holding it between his legs and the electric drill had slipped out of the wood and gone right into his crotch. He was standing holding it with an 'I've castrated myself!' kind of look on his face, and I remember my mother literally crying with laughter. At that point, of course, we didn't know if he had castrated himself or not, but as serious as she must have known it was, she couldn't stop laughing. She had a real dark sense of humour.

I have a couple of memories of her laughing like that. I remember her chasing me with a wooden cane after I had done something bad. I was running away from her, terrified, but when I looked around I saw her laughing her head off again. She couldn't take discipline that seriously. That's a nice snapshot to have.

My father was a very strict man but his severity was wasted on me. He was a good father in all the ways you could reasonably expect but we clashed a lot. I'm sure it was my fault most of the time but in nature there is always some young elk in the herd that is going to challenge the head male for supremacy and maybe that's what it was. Perhaps he saw me as challenging his position. I don't remember it like that but then I don't remember very much. But I know we didn't get on very well. I have a memory of having one particular row with him and he locked me in the box-room. So I went up, I pulled up the blind, opened the window, and I was sitting on the window sill with my feet out, talking to my mates who were down on the street below. I was ten years old. I'm telling them what an absolute ass my father was and suddenly they fell very quiet. The old man was standing right behind me listening to my abuse, yards

MY DAD WAS AN AUTODIDACT AND A VERY BRIGHT
FELLAH. HE TAUGHT HIMSELF SHAKESPEARE AND
LISTENED TO OPERA ALL THE TIME. HE WAS A
BEAUTIFUL TENOR WHO WOULD STAND THERE IN
FRONT OF THE SPEAKERS, CONDUCTING THE MUSIC
WITH MY MOTHER'S KNITTING NEEDLES. I REMEMBER
THE LOOK ON HIS FACE, JUST LOST TO MUSIC. FOR
SOME REASON, HE NEVER IMAGINED MUSIC MIGHT BE
HANDED DOWN THROUGH THE DNA LIKE HIS BAD
BACK AND QUICK TEMPER. BONO

and yards of expletives, cruel descriptions all now on his record. As I think of it now, he had a lot to put up with.

Bob worked in the post office, where he was an overseer. He would always be in a very bad humour at Christmas because he did a lot of overtime then; he'd have to get up at six in the morning and didn't come home until nine in the evening. It was an invisible world to me. Trying to talk to my old man was like trying to talk to a brick wall. The first time he really spoke to me was the night of his retirement from the post office, when I went to his send-off party. I used to hear all the names, Gerry O'This and Gary O'That, but I never knew who they were; and I didn't really know what he did. But at this party in 1985, I met all these people, and they were amazing. It was at a pub in the city centre, and there was a guy with a fiddle, and they were all singing songs. A man who had painted on a Hitler moustache introduced me to his daughter and I asked, 'Who are you?' and she said, 'The Hitler youth.' It was like a Fellini movie, very surreal, very evolved Dublin sense of humour. Afterwards, he showed me the place he worked, where I had never been, and he pointed out the seat that he used to sit in. Already someone else had moved into that seat. And that night, I got to talk to my old man for the first time. We had a glass of whiskey, and he began to tell me a few things about what it was like growing up. I made a mental note not to be so easily replaceable.

Our house was 10 Cedarwood Road, regular, middle-class, three bedrooms with a garage, and I slept in the box-room, which was a tiny room about the size of a cupboard. At the back of the house were fields and trees, which was incredible. You could go out and climb up trees and stay for a whole day, just disappear into the forest. Well, it wasn't really a forest but there were lots of trees, so it was a forest to me. I remember a little bit of fear, because there were gangs that used to wander through 'the fields' and if you were caught, as we occasionally were, they'd beat the crap out of you, or threaten to string you up and generally terrify you. It was an interesting place, exciting but a little dangerous. Then they tore down the trees and built these things called the seven towers, the Ballymun Flats. I don't know why they're called flats because they're the first high-rise projects in the country. When everyone else in Europe had figured out that people don't really like living on top of each other, they decided to start the experiment in Ireland. So they built the towers and at first you thought it was really modern, watching these buildings arise; this was incredible, gosh, a high-rise project, wow, with lifts! But they took people out of the inner city and forced them to live there and broke up communities and there was a lot of unhappiness and trouble. The towers housed some very heavy gangs, so even though we lived on a nice little road we had two fairly rough neighbourhoods on either side of us, West Finglas one way and Ballymun the other. It was like being stuck between cowboys and Indians, rumbles between the top end of the street and the bottom end of the street, between bootboys and skinheads. Occasionally you would be wandering down a road and there'd be gangs coming down the street and they'd say: 'Where you from?' Oh fuck, you'd be thinking, are this gang from Finglas or are they from Ballymun? If you gave the wrong answer there was murder so we had to become quite good at violence, me and my friend Guggi. Street fights were just the way it was. I remember picking up a dustbin in a street fight and thinking to myself, 'This is mad. Am I really going to hit someone with this?' And right then, some skin was up on me with an iron bar trying to smash my skull in. I used the lid to protect myself. I would have been stone dead if I hadn't had that thing. It's not like the violence I hear about now – there were no guns, just sticks, bottles, knives … and, now that I think about it, a few hammers and saws. I don't want to exaggerate here but it's how I remember things.

When you're singing songs, people think you are like the songs you sing. But the reason that I'm attracted to people like Gandhi and Martin Luther King is because I was exactly the opposite of that. I was the boy who wouldn't turn the other cheek. But I never liked the violence. Never. I would worry myself sick about having to go out on the street, in case another teenager I had been in a mill with would come back for more. I remember, some years later, talking to my old man about the violence of those early years, which was such a big part of my growing-up, and he was offended, protesting, 'Our street was very nice!' And it was a nice little street, it was just if you turned left or right!

My dad was an autodidact and a very bright fellah. He taught himself

Shakespeare and listened to opera all the time. He was a beautiful tenor who would stand there in front of the speakers, conducting the music with my mother's knitting needles. I remember the look on his face, just lost to music. For some reason, he never imagined music might be handed down through the DNA like his bad back and quick temper. I asked him years later, 'What are the things you regret the most?' He said, 'Not being able to play music.' And I said, 'Why, therefore, would you not think of teaching your kids music?' I'd ask for lessons and it'd be like, shut up, a complete blank. I would have loved to have learned the piano.

My grandmother had a piano and that is one of my earliest and best memories. I don't know how old I would have been but my head was certainly below the keys. I remember being underneath that piano and listening to the music reverberate and being lost in the wonder of it. So even though I couldn't see the keys, I remember putting my hand up and pressing the keyboard and hearing a note, and then pressing another note, playing with it the way kids do, just making noise – but it is not really noise, it is making music. I could almost, even then, hear the melodies in the air. I would be picking out tunes, because you play one note and then you hear a rhyme for it in your head, then you have to find that note and then you hear another note. It's a strange thing being a songwriter, it's like each step is a question of faith, really. You believe that you're going to hear the next note until you do and they all tumble together into a melody.

Much later, when I was about fifteen, I remember going into a bit of a tormented-teenager phase. One of the things that really would still my soul was playing piano. I couldn't actually play it but I used to put my foot on the pedal and hit keys and I remember how the room would change shape, because the note would get this cloud of reverb around it, become cathedral-like. I remember those icy notes at the top of the keyboard really made me feel better. I think I have held on to music very tightly while my head was exploding.

I remember when they were selling my grandmother's piano. There was no room in the house now that there were more grandchildren than money. I kept asking could we have it? I knew even then I had some music in me. And my mother said, 'No, we've no room for it in our house.' I said, 'We have, we could … we could put it there!' 'Ach, go on away with you!' What was so remarkable about my mother was that she was very funny, I mean she had a real black sense of humour, but she was not in the least romantic. Playing music would not have been practical to her. What do you want to play that for? So they wouldn't let me have a piano. That really bothers me even now. Trying to write on the piano is difficult for me.

It's so odd, it's the thing I can't figure out. It was almost like my father's whole attitude was: don't dream. This was his unspoken and sometimes spoken advice. To dream is to be disappointed, that was the running theme, and I think that was perhaps because he had given up his dreams. So he didn't want me to fill my head with mine. But to say to me before he died that the single greatest regret of his life was that he didn't become a musician, you would think that the first thing he would do is make sure his kids have that opportunity. But no – sell the piano. Sell the fucking piano. It's amazing. If you were a kid like me, that is like somebody taking away your oxygen tank. You can't breathe.

There's a lot in that. I think the seeds of ambition were sown, paradoxically by this repression of the spirit. If you keep telling somebody not to do something then that might just be what they become driven to do. Megalomania might have started right here. I was going to have my revenge on the world. Everyone was going to have to listen to me! Of course, I didn't know what it was I was actually going to say or play, but the world was going to have to listen. Which, of course, is really psychological shorthand for 'my father would have to listen'. When it gets down to it, there's only ever really one person in the audience, no matter how big the crowd. It could be your father on earth, your father in heaven, your lover, a friend, it may switch, but you are usually singing to one person.

It's fair to say I was promiscuous with my ambitions, flirting with all kind of things. One day I'd wake up and want to be a chess player. I'd read a book on it and become fascinated. At twelve I joined an adult chess club, studied the grandmasters and played blindfold chess with my mate Joseph Marks. The next year I'd think, 'No, I'll be a painter.' I'd skip school to go and see Louis Le Brocquy's paintings hanging in the Municipal gallery. So I was just wandering. I still have the wanderlust. Intellectual curiosity is what adults call it. At one point I think I felt I wanted to be on stage. I knew I had that in me. My friend Reggie Manuel was always telling me I should be an actor and I remember trying to find a drama school, so I must have been serious about it. But then I didn't find one, so perhaps I wasn't all that serious.

As a junior, I went to a school called The Inkwell, a little Protestant Church of Ireland school that backed on to the Tolka river. The headmaster was a very sweet man. We used to play football at break and if it was a fine day we'd kick the football into the river and then we'd have to climb over the railings and chase it downstream. The headmaster would come with us. Looking back, he was probably delighted to get away for an hour. We'd chase the ball down to the Botanic Gardens in Griffith Park, an amazing place. We used to go there after school and hang out. It was a beautiful spot, a real oasis.

We'd take girls there and go for walks.

In a mixed marriage the children were supposed to be brought up as Catholics. The Protestants made up only about ten percent of the population at the time, and it was anathema to them. My mother decided to bring us up in the Protestant Church, and my old man went along with this. So on Sunday he would drop us off at one place of worship, a little Church of Ireland church, and then go to Mass by himself. And then when we came out he'd be waiting for us. He must have been a very cool man to show that tolerance but I was always fighting with him, always fighting. We were just too alike. He was very measured politically. He could pick and choose between the offerings of left and right, a third-way man before that term was invented, and long before I had to live it. Our house was ambidextrous, politically and religiously.

These days, I take my kids to Mass, to church, I take them to wherever I feel there's life. But in those days there was a huge divide along religious lines so I guess it was a big deal and my father was incredibly respectful of my mother's Protestantism. But I didn't feel anything about God and church, it just didn't reach me. Now, my friend Guggi (pronounced Googi), his father was a real Bible-basher and if I went with Guggi to his church I used to hear powerful preaching and I remember being very taken with that, thinking, 'Wow this is a bit different to what I'm used to.' At the Church of Ireland, they're amazing people and you couldn't not like them but if you're not careful it can be death by niceness. My impression of it was that it was really a community thing. We worshipped God but I'm not sure we knew what God was. The service was not usually very lively, although in Finglas we were lucky enough to have a young reverend running the show called Sydney Laing, who was fun and active.

I became friends with Guggi when I was still plain Paul Hewson and he was Derek Rowen. He said he didn't like me very much but he wanted to have a go on the swing in our back garden. He was four, I was three, and in very many ways he is still four and I am still three. He was and is an incredible person. Guggi came from a very big family. I think there were twelve of them. They were interested in motorbikes and cars and they had collections of bikes and scooters all over the place. Everything that Guggi had, he used to give me half. If he got a pound, he'd give me fifty pence. He really did teach me a lesson, which I've held on to and try to pass on to my kids. It is an amazing thing, the gift of sharing, because he didn't have very much but he would share whatever he had. And when I was broke and in a rock and roll band, Guggi and my friend Gavin and my girlfriend Ali, people like this, paid my way for years. That is a kind of friendship you don't take lightly.

There was music all around, growing up. My old man's opera

permeated the house. It was like heavy metal to me. I like those bawdy opera songs: the king is unfaithful to the queen, then he gets the pox, they have a son, the son grows up and turns into an alligator, and in the end they kill the alligator and make shoes for the king. But because it's sung in Italian, people think it's very aloof – not at all. I was interested in Irish folk music because of all the sing-songs at my grandmother's house. My brother had a reel-to-reel tape-recorder and he had impeccable taste in music; I didn't really go through a pop-music phase, as a result. Most kids get into rock and roll in their mid-teens but from ten years old I was listening to Jimi Hendrix, The Who, The Beatles and John Lennon. I remember listening to 'Imagine' at twelve years old and it kind of blew my mind. One thing I really liked on the reel-to-reel was a folky duo called *Hunky Dory*. I loved that duo. It was years later I discovered it was David Bowie and Hunky Dory was the name of the album. My brother played guitar and he had The Beatles song book, so I started trying to play the guitar by myself. My brother showed me a few chords. He used to play 'Ruby, Don't Take Your Love to Town'. I'm still fascinated by that song. 'If I Had a Hammer' was another one, a gospel protest song. In so many ways I have been writing those two songs ever since.

I never thought of singing as a career but I remember singing hymns and it stirring up this really strong feeling of being moved by the music. And I could sing them quite well. But when it was time for me to go to secondary school, I must have been twelve years old, my mother took me down to be interviewed by the headmaster of St Patrick's grammar school. It was linked to St Patrick's cathedral and it was well known for its boys' choir. So I was sitting there and the headmaster says, 'Well, you know, we've got a boys' choir here that's very famous around the country and it's something we take very seriously. Will you be at all interested in being part of the choir?' And before I could open my mouth my mother says, 'No, no, he wouldn't be interested in that.' There was nothing dark about that, no malign intentions. She just genuinely didn't think I'd be interested and was filling in the blank for me. And, of course, I was embarrassed about the idea of wanting to be in a choir. I didn't really want to speak up because I thought he might ask me to sing something on the spot.

I spent a year at St Patrick's, not being happy, and basically they asked me to leave. I was caught throwing dog shit at the Spanish teacher. Her nickname was Biddy and we did not see eye to eye. I did not have a high opinion of her and I suspect the feeling was mutual. One Monday, a few boys and I climbed over the railings into the park next to the cathedral. She was there eating her lunch. We found some dry dog shit and started lobbing it at her and we were caught. So I left St Patrick's and went to Mount Temple

Comprehensive. There was a very different feeling in that school. I remember cycling there on the first day with my friend Reggie Manuel. It was about three and a half miles, which was quite a cycle ride at twelve years old, but it was such an adventure. The moment I arrived I felt alive. St Patrick's was a boys' school, Mount Temple was mixed. It had girls, and that was reason enough to want to go there. I loved being around the school itself. It was very progressive, co-educational and non-denominational. There were only two such free schools in the country. It was an amazing place, and we all felt privileged to go there. We didn't think of it as like any other school. I was having the time of my life. I was good fun to hang out with, girls liked me, boys liked me, it all worked. And then it kind of stopped working. As Austin Powers says: I lost my mojo.

It was my grandparents' jubilee wedding anniversary, September 1974. All the family had gathered from wherever they were and there was a big hooly. They rented a room in a hotel, so it was a very big deal. My grandfather was dancing, kicking his legs up to Dicey Reilly and just the happiest man on earth with his wife and his family all around him. The drink was flowing, in fact, so flowing was it that they put him to bed and put a bucket beside the bed in case he couldn't make it to the outside bathroom. I'm sure you've heard the expression kick the bucket. Well, Alec Rankin had a heart attack in the middle of the night and nutted the bucket. I remember waking up and my mother wasn't around. I asked, 'Where is she?' I was told, 'Something has happened with your grandfather.' Then she came back to the house and said, 'Your grandfather's dead.' He went out on a high. But she was shaken. We were all a bit shaken. And then she went off, because she was the eldest sister, she was the organizer of the family. The next time I saw her was at the graveside, watching her father being buried. And then she collapses. And I see my father carrying her. Everyone's asking, 'What's happened?' 'She fainted!' 'Oh my goodness, she fainted, your mother's fainted!' So everyone's in a bit of shock but we all go back to number ten. We didn't really know what was going on. I suppose they were trying to keep it from the kids. And then I remember my uncle arriving at the door and wailing, just like a little child. It was such a strange thing. I knew something terrible had happened.

She had suffered a brain haemorrhage. She stayed alive for about four days, I think. Some powerful things happened in those few days, very powerful things. I read the Bible and I prayed to God not to let my mother die.

We were brought in to say goodbye to her: my old man, Norman and me. And then they turned off whatever technology was keeping her alive. That was really extraordinary. They have a choice, they can keep you alive or they can allow you to die – the decision must have been made to allow her to die.

IN DESPAIR, I DID PRAY TO GOD. AND I DISCOVERED THAT, EVEN SOMETIMES IN THE SILENCE, GOD DOES ANSWER. THE ANSWER MAY NOT BE THE ONE YOU WANT TO HEAR BUT THERE'S ALWAYS AN ANSWER, IF YOU ARE SERIOUS, IF YOU ARE READY TO LET GO. BONO

They just came in, we all said goodbye and then they pulled a switch. I remember the doctor was very moved. The clergyman, the same Sydney Laing, was a beautiful man, very elegant and great with my dad, who didn't go to our church. And that was it. I had a feeling of the house being pulled down on me. My mother died and then there were just three men living on their own in a house. That is all it was then, it ceased being a home. It was just a house, with three men killing each other slowly, not knowing what to do with our sense of loss and just taking it out on each other. Things could get to a very, very high pitch.

I was just an average kid in a now not average family, losing interest in anything except girls and music. School work went down the toilet. I didn't want to do anything like that at all. I didn't really know that I was heading for any kind of crash, but there were a few incidents that might have sounded alerts, like putting a teacher up against the wall in class. That was one of the more interesting ones. He was being a bit of a bully but at the same time attacking your teacher is not the sign of a person in a reasonable state of mind. There were a couple of other incidents that gave the school some concern. I was having very vivid dreams, even when I was awake. I thought I was going mad.

Mount Temple was very understanding of these outbursts. They actually gave me free leave of school. I could walk in and out when I wanted. My mind was speeding, not from drugs, just from all the pressures, things I couldn't figure out. From an early age, I instinctively believed in God but wasn't sure that God believed in me or anyone. Why? How? Where? All the big questions started to intensify. I went to church, but there just seemed to be people there, singing psalms of glory but not much glory present in the house. It wasn't enough for me. Religion felt all wrong. Yet outside, when I looked around me, I would see clues that God might exist, and might be interested in us. Then I'd lose hope again.

There was a beautiful woman teaching religion at the time, Sophie Shirley, and she would say things like, 'Yes, it's a fallen world but it's still beautiful. God's fingerprints are everywhere if you want to see them.' So there

I'd be, standing on Dollymount Strand, staring at the sea, watching the waves, looking at a storm on the horizon, and wondering who chose the colour of the sky? Who makes the earth turn at this speed? Who invented gravity and who designed girls' laughter? Is it all cold science? Cosmic accident or creation? Is it love or survival of the fittest?

Those questions filled my teenage head. My mother's death just threw petrol on the fire. The big questions built to a crescendo. I felt hopeless. I thought about suicide. I was thinking too hard about everything. It still amazes me how much you can fit into a fourteen-year-old's head. But something had to give and it did. My mind slipped. Literally, for two weeks, I forgot everything. I couldn't remember what I had done.

I was working on a project for history class, and it became very important to me. It was on the oldest street in Dublin, Church Street, and I was going round the churches and the schools and interviewing people who lived on Church Street. Then I couldn't find my notes of the conversations. And I started wondering had I actually done the interviews or was I somehow imagining it? It was very upsetting. You could call it a sort of electrical storm, overloaded brain cells. I turned over a few chairs and tables in the class and threw a bit of a tantrum.

I didn't know what to do. So I went to see Jack Heaslip. He was a young, progressive, liberal teacher, not a believer at that point. He later became an Anglican priest and indeed married myself and Ali and has been a source of inspiration and calm for us over our lives. He has baptized our children and is still a very good friend. But back then he was just the English teacher and the Guidance Counsellor. There were some very important people in the school at that time, such as Donald Moxham, the History teacher, who seemed to see the lives that they were entrusted with as having some value that they could nurture. Jack was one of those people and I liked him – more than liked him, I trusted him, and so I went in. By all accounts I talked for hours and hours. It was like nine to five. It just went on and on and on.

And he thought, maybe this kid's having a breakdown; something's going on. So he sent me to a psychologist who lived round the corner, and she was very cool. She listened to me. She was an atheist and perhaps even a communist at that time, so she couldn't get a handle on some of the religious stuff I was going through. But she used to start talking to me about her problems. She would tell me all about her kid. I only realized later that it was a technique; taking me out of myself and getting me thinking about her and other people was very clever. And after a few weeks she said, 'I really don't think you need to come back here. You're fine. You just had some kind of trauma.' I guess that's not an unreasonable thing for somebody who's been through that kind of upset in their life. I wouldn't think it's that peculiar. But that's the way it manifested itself in me: a slightly violent, aggressive outpouring and some kind of religious experience following on. Because in this despair, I did pray to God. And I discovered that, even sometimes in the silence, God does answer. The answer may not be the one you want to hear but there's always an answer, if you are serious, if you are ready to let go. Anyway, I had to follow these feelings, or instincts, to see where they led.

It was 1976, and I wasn't the only one going through a religious experience in the school. It felt like the whole place was going off. It was early days in what would become known as the 'Charismatic' movement, Catholics and Protestants in Ireland worshipping God together in a kind of hippy rave format, minus the beats per minute. In Mount Temple more than a few pupils would get together and study the Bible and people were having very profound, life-changing experiences. It was an interesting thing. In the deep South, they call it a Revival. People who are in the religion business will tell you that these things happen in waves. In history you read about the John Wesley revival that brought Methodism. It's like something just breaks out and for a couple of years sweeps across the country, like a fire, and people have very deep religious experiences. Then it goes away for fifty or sixty years. I suppose that was what was happening in 1976, because it was happening to a great many people. Bob Dylan was at one end of the spectrum in LA and a little school in Clontarf, Dublin was at the other. A lot of people who were aged sixteen at the time have told me about similar experiences. They may have moved away from it since, but it is in their work, I heard and I can hear it. The maddest one was Michael Hutchence. We were sitting one night, completely wasted, on a beach, and I was trying to explain to him where all this stuff came from, and he turned to me and said, 'You know, myself and Andrew (his songwriting partner) both had similar experiences that year.' I said, 'What!?!?!?!' This was like having Casanova tell you he was pledged to Christ. But I believe there is some sort of connection between the disturbing energies of creative activity and your spiritual life. Or maybe I was just having these electrical storms because I couldn't finish my homework. Make of it what you will. It was pretty powerful.

So I have these fireworks going off. I get to a place in my life where I want to make some sort of spiritual sense of the world. I put out those prayers because I really did think that my head was going to explode, and two things happened in the same few weeks and they both saved my life. And it turned out to be a very good year for me. A very, very good year.

The first thing is that I had a vision of my future. I remember I'd seen this girl when she first came to the school, very early on, and thought she looked Spanish, a rose for sure, dark with blood-red lips. But later, on one of those days when my head was exploding, Reggie Manuel the Cocker Spaniel was taking me out of school on the back of his motorbike. I looked around and saw the same quiet, mysterious girl who was so unselfconscious, she was completely unaware that she was even attractive. There was a heat haze coming off the back of Reggie's bike, and she looked like she was in a pool of water, walking through it. There was something so still about her, and to a person who is not still, it was the most attractive thing in the world. And that was Ali, who within a few weeks would become my girlfriend, and within a few years my wife.

And then another amazing thing happened. I joined a band. Nothing much has changed since then. I'm still with Ali, and I'm still with the band.

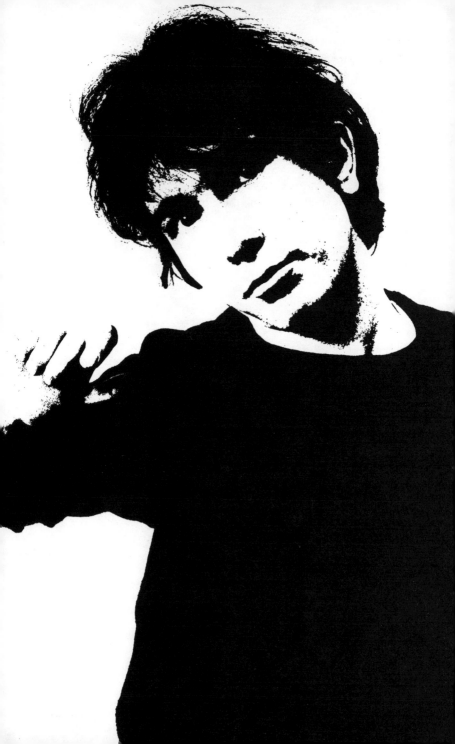

The Edge

JUST ABOUT EVERYBODY CALLS ME EDGE, OR 'THE EDGE' IF IT'S A FORMAL OCCASION. I'M ONLY DAVID EVANS TO PEOPLE WHO DON'T KNOW ME VERY WELL, IMMIGRATION OFFICERS AND THE LIKE.

I was born 8 August 1961 in a maternity hospital in Barking, on the eastern fringe of London, and so in some small way I could be considered an Essex Lad.

My parents are Welsh, both from Llanelli, a town in the heart of the industrial south. Llanelli is all tin-works and rugby; everything about it is tough and grey. They moved to London as newlyweds in the mid-fifties, and started a family. First they had my brother, Richard (who many people know as Dick), and then me. My father, Garvin, an engineer, started out working for the local electricity board and then took a job with an electronics company called Plessey's. We lived in Chadwell Heath at the time but I have no memory of the place whatsoever. Then some time around the beginning of 1962 my father was offered a promotion, and a transfer, and so my parents made the decision to leave Chadwell Heath and start a new life across the Irish Sea. They made the move to Ireland when I was one. All of my earliest memories are of our family home in the small coastal village of Malahide, then a sleepy little suburb of Dublin city. It was a place of sanctuary and nurture, but a place I used to try and escape from at every opportunity. As soon as I could walk all I wanted to do was get out. I was extremely inquisitive and I had a friend, Shane Fogarty, who I would always try and find. I wasn't sure where he lived and my mother would catch me, aged two, down in the town looking for his house. To successfully escape I had to time things perfectly. I would wait until my mother was having a nice little sit-down, then I would drag a stool over to the front door, turn the latch and out I went. The village was down the hill so my small tricycle was a very effective mode of transport. If I managed to get to the end of the driveway I could easily out-pace my mother, who was heavily pregnant at the time. Growing up I had two different accents, one I would use to communicate with my family, a soft Welsh lilt, the other for my friends, featuring the elements of my Welsh accent I could do nothing about, mixed with my best approximation of the local Irish accent. I think it must have been a very weird combination. The reason for this dual identity was mainly to be understood by my peers, but also to be accepted. I later discovered that my father had done exactly the same thing as a four-year-old living in London. He oscillated between broad Welsh and broad cockney.

I was a very cute toddler; I've seen the photographs. But then at around the age of five something started to happen that radically changed my appearance. We are not talking here about some accidental injury or anything medical, but a gradual transformation. And I don't mean to suggest that I became one of the obviously ugly kids, more that my appearance started to inspire a certain mild alarm in adults who caught sight of me for the first time, and to elicit sympathetic and vaguely disappointed looks from my parents. My head grew, quite quickly, to an unfeasibly large size. It was not a disagreeable head, in certain contexts it was quite handsome, but from the age of five as a result of this unusual development I started to look unnervingly like the kid on the cover of *Mad* magazine. Along with the head came the teeth, or specifically my two big front teeth. When they first appeared sprouting out of my gums, I knew there was something up. Their size was obvious from the beginning, and they grew in with a kind of terrible inevitability. No matter what form of mouth management I employed there was just no hiding them, so by aged seven the full '*Mad* magazine' look was complete. This was made all the more difficult by the fact that my best friend Shane, a person from whom I was pretty much inseparable from the age of two, was a dead ringer for a young Paul Newman, complete with cornflower-blue eyes and perfect teeth. He knew it, as did everybody else. A year older than me, Shane was super-popular, a great athlete and in many ways my nemesis. It's funny how even as a young kid you pick up on these things. I went through some very formative years as the proverbial ugly duckling with my mate Shane a constant reminder that I was nothing special. The upshot was that I grew even more shy and awkward. I think that kind of experience is either the making or the breaking of you. And in my case having a very supportive home life helped a lot, but I didn't see that at the time.

My parents had a very strong cultural connection with Wales. My mother, Gwenda, did most of the hands-on rearing of us kids and we were brought up with all the classic Welsh influences: singing, rugby, chapel on a Sunday, a certain frugality, and very bad dress sense – it was all very family-orientated. But growing up, I really did assimilate and become Irish, and so did my parents in many ways.

What brought the family to Ireland in the first place was my parents appreciation of the Irish attitude to life: what is known locally as 'the craic' or put simply 'knowing how to have a fun time'. There wasn't very much 'craic' to be had in the Welsh valleys, or Llanelli town. Chadwell Heath wasn't a bundle of laughs either. But my parents had spent some time in Northern Ireland in the early fifties while my father was doing his National Service, stationed in Eglinton, attached to the navy Fleet Air Arm, and they had a really great time. Such a great time that when my father was offered a promotion and a choice of managing a Plessey's plant in Dublin or Manchester, they decided without hesitation to go to Dublin on the grounds that Dublin would be way more 'craic' than Manchester. They certainly got that right.

Not a man to waste time, on the first Saturday after starting his new job my father went out and bought the house we were all to live in for the next forty years. Quite decisive, I think you'll agree.

My parents are pretty easy-going in most respects, not interested in the trappings of the petit bourgeois life-style. They both suffer from a bit of angst, which is a Welsh disease, but generally speaking they are positive folk. My father is very competitive, he works very hard and likes to be busy. He never really enjoyed holidays. He tried, but it was always obvious that he would have preferred to be at home designing some shopping centre air-conditioning system. He could never sit still. Sunbathing on a beach would have been an indescribably hideous form of torture for my father. My mother on the other hand is much more chilled out and has been known to bring out a sun lounger, but once in a while, growing up, the Welsh angst would get the better of her and she would blow her top. So, when we were kids, there wasn't a particularly strict disciplinarian atmosphere about the place, but occasionally we'd overstep the mark and there'd be some heavy retribution. Generally speaking, we couldn't have been more happy and supported. My sister, Gillian, was born in 1963 into our male-dominated household. It took us a while to get used to her. I think my nose was put seriously out of joint when she arrived. I was the apple of my mother's eye up until that point, or certainly until I started to grow the large head. I wasn't always terribly nice to Gill, for the first few years it was more begrudging acceptance. I got over it, and as time went on we started to get on a lot better.

My brother and I always had a very close rapport, and very similar sense of humour and general outlook. We hung out together, created various types of homemade explosives, petrol bombs, built bonfires, went on joyrides with our friends in dumper trucks borrowed from local construction sites, all the usual sort of stuff. And if other people didn't quite understand us, we understood each other. We were a bit of a handful but very good-natured. It was the combination of curiosity, wildness, lack of strict parental control, and access to a fully stocked school chemistry lab that led to our experiments, anything really to break the tedium of the Dublin suburbs of the 1970's.

Ours was the classic 1960's suburban house, three bedrooms and one and a half bathrooms. My father fancied himself as a bit of a handyman, and with some help he built on a couple of small additions. One, at the end of the garden, was used as a garden shed, later to become our band rehearsal room. It was a small space, about ten feet by ten feet. This was where one of the Evans brothers early experiments with a petrol bomb went a bit wrong. My brother still bears the scar. The other was a small workshop off the house, full of bits and pieces of old electronics, pieces of wood, tins of bolts, washers, nuts and screws. We would spend hours taking things apart or building something. My brother was a bit of an electronics prodigy. He eventually built a pretty good electric guitar from scratch with Barry O'Connell, a friend from down the road, following plans found in an electronics magazine. This guitar was the culmination of our twin fascinations: rock and roll and electronic gadgetry.

Music was big in our house. I used to love listening to any music that I could, from any source. When I was aged two my mother used to turn on the TV test-card so I could play drums along to the soundtrack (knitting needles and a few biscuit tins). I vividly remember the profound goose-bump raising shock of hearing for the first time a fully attended Welsh chapel open up in perfect four-part harmony one Sunday morning during one of our annual pilgrimages to Wales. It was a truly religious experience communicated through music. Unfortunately our own church in Malahide managed to preserve all the most tediously boring aspects of the Presbyterian service, and in spite of the best efforts of my parents (a respectable alto, and more than decent tenor) and the rest of the small but enthusiastic choir, the music just never came close. My first exposure to rock 'n' roll came one Christmas watching The Beatles movie *A Hard Day's Night* on TV. I was very impressed and I thought that they would go far. This coincided with my brother getting a small mono record-player. He and I started buying records together. The first album we bought was *Sgt. Pepper's Lonely Hearts Club Band*. The second album we bought was *A Hard Day's Night*. I then wanted to get another one of The Beatles early records; Richard wanted to get one of the later ones. We had a standoff and as a compromise we agreed to get Ringo Starr's newly released *Sentimental Journey*. This was when the penny dropped for me that some records are better then others.

My mother must have suspected I had an ear for music because she bought me a little Spanish guitar when I was seven years old. For me, this was completely fascinating. I couldn't tune it, I didn't even know how to hold it, but it was so cool – that much I did know. I would wave it around and pretend, to the gullible youngsters on our street, that I could play. That first guitar of mine was really little more than a toy. The first proper guitar that came into our house was bought by my mother at a jumble sale for a pound. Never in the history of the Malahide parish bring-and-buy sales has one pound been as well spent, and given back as much value. I think she might have bought it for my brother, but the two of us would practise on that guitar for hours. It was rough, but it played in tune, and when we replaced the rusty wire strings with some nylon Spanish guitar strings it sounded decent enough. I learnt my first open chords on that guitar, tutored very effectively by Richard, and pretty soon I started working out how to play whole songs. I was interested to discover that I could do a lot with that instrument, and I drove everyone in the house mad by playing it at all times, while doing all manner of other tasks. I could eat toast and play guitar, get dressed without missing a note. I would play along every evening while the family watched TV, providing a kind of silent-movie-era soundtrack. My poor mother gave up shouting at me to stop, and used to just hit me with a large stick. Even that didn't work. I was twelve or thirteen by then, and our record collection had expanded to include some 45's by Slade and Alice Cooper.

Along with our Beatles LP's we got some by Led Zeppelin, Creedence Clearwater Revival, The Rolling Stones, Jimi Hendrix, David Bowie, Yes, Rory Gallagher and Taste. I discovered Derek and the Dominos while staying with my older cousins in Blackpool. It is hard to explain the significance of music for all of the kids in our area. There was nothing else nearly as important in terms of establishing your identity. I would have huge arguments with my friends about who was the best band in the world, or what was the best record ever made. The TV music shows *Top of the Pops* and *The Old Grey Whistle Test* were considered unmissable. The British music papers NME and Sounds were read from cover-to-cover, mostly courtesy of our friend Fergus Crossan who had a part-time job and could afford such luxuries. Around this time I took some piano lessons, but it wasn't for me. I couldn't get excited about sight-reading when I could pick up the guitar and learn by ear. With only a few chords I was able to play my favourite tunes by Slade, T. Rex and The Beatles.

We would hang out with our mates from the area, Shane and the O'Connell brothers, and play music. We would meet up at the end of our street, literally hanging out on the corner with some guitars playing and singing Beatles songs, Simon and Garfunkel, T. Rex or whatever anyone had learned. There were always a few girls around to keep it interesting.

All of this was considered a very positive development. At least we were no longer blowing things up.

I SAW BONO ON ONE OF THE LUNCHTIME BREAKS, SITTING DOWN WITH A GUITAR TRYING TO IMPRESS SOME GIRLS. WE DIDN'T HIT IT OFF PARTICULARLY, BUT I COULDN'T HELP BUT OBSERVE THAT I WAS A BETTER PLAYER AND YET HE WAS MORE POPULAR. I MADE A MENTAL NOTE THAT PERHAPS THE WAY YOU CARRIED YOUR GUITAR WAS AS IMPORTANT AS HOW WELL YOU COULD PLAY IT. EDGE

My early education came courtesy of St Andrew's National school, a mere five minutes' walk from our house. My brother was extremely bright and always did well. My sister could spell and was good at Irish. The teachers had high hopes for me too, but I was not exactly an over-achiever. I was just restless and always seemed to be doing stupid things. I sat on an old desk on the fringe of the classroom and exhibiting serious stupidity one day carved my name into the top. I think I was even a little surprised by my teacher's unforeseen talent as a sleuth when I was immediately identified as the culprit and punished. I was in St. Andrew's for a very brief period with Adam. He had a very short haircut, glasses and a set of unusually large front teeth like my own. Adam was a year and half older than me and in a class ahead, but I was vaguely aware of him because Malahide was a small town. Then he was shifted out to a posh prep school. So he disappeared off the radar when I was about seven and we didn't meet again until he appeared in Mount Temple.

My best friend Shane was in my class at St Andrew's. I was a year younger than the rest of the class and it was decided during my final year that I wasn't old enough to graduate. Shane went ahead into the big school and we sort of lost touch with each other. I met him one day soon after he had started at Mount Temple and he told me about this wild kid in his class called Paul Hewson. He seemed to share our interest in high-explosives: there was some story involving a small fire, and some rivet-gun caps, taken from the building site that was to become our new school. So I heard about Bono a couple of years before I even met him. You could say his reputation preceded him.

Mount Temple was a big change from the small village school I was used to. It was a big, multi-denominational, co-educational school with a catchment area that included some very rough neighbourhoods. I'd been hanging out with some of the tough kids in my area but there was a whole new level of tough to be negotiated in the big school. That was like my first entry into the greater 'world out there', and a few lessons had to be learned about not judging people by their appearances. The tough-looking kids weren't always the tough kids. Thankfully the head and front teeth had started to balance out by then. I fitted in reasonably well but being a bit shy and having a massive superiority complex I think of my first few years at Mount Temple as my 'loner period'. I discovered that being a loner and having a superiority complex works quite well, as your distorted self-image is never challenged by engaging in any way with the rest of humanity. In spite of my solitary instincts I did make a few good friends, particularly John Lawlor, and Stephen Balcombe. Steve was a talented soccer player and ended up playing briefly for Leeds United. John was not so driven but widely acknowledged as a really great bloke. They invited me to Skerries one time to go to a concert by Horslips, a folk-rock band who were hugely popular in Ireland. It was the first live show I'd ever attended and it was breathtaking to see a band on stage. Johnny Fean played a Les Paul through a Marshall stack and I couldn't take my eyes off him the whole night. Another friend from Mount Temple was David 'Barney' Barnett, a drummer who told me he played in a garage band. When I went over to Barney's house and saw them practise I was absolutely stunned. I knew I had to get into a band. I felt like I had found my niche.

That's how I got to know Bono a little bit. I'd been playing guitar for a while and I saw him somewhere, on one of the lunchtime breaks, sitting down with a guitar and a Beatles song book trying to impress some girls. When they drifted off we had a short conversation about chords and what tunes I could play. That was in the second year. He would have been about fifteen and I would have been fourteen. We didn't hit it off particularly, but I couldn't help but observe that I was a better player and yet he was more popular. I made a mental note that perhaps the way you carried your guitar was as important as how well you could play it.

Before the new school year, during the summer of 1976, my mother said, 'You remember Adam Clayton? He is going to your school this year.' So I was actually looking out for Adam but it was literally about halfway through the term that I realized this weird hippie kid who was sporting a very brave Afro hairdo (which made him look like an albino Bootsy Collins) and an Afghan coat was, in fact, the kid with the big teeth I had known when I was seven. I had seen him around but I thought he was in the year ahead because he was always hanging out behind the science labs with the rest of the sixth-form smoking fraternity. It was all very bohemian back there, and very cool. Anyway, I didn't realize he was in my year until after we formed the band. Larry, I had seen around. You might not know everyone's names in the classes below you, but I knew who he was. Then one day my music teacher, Albert Bradshaw, told me that Larry Mullen played drums, and wanted to form a band.

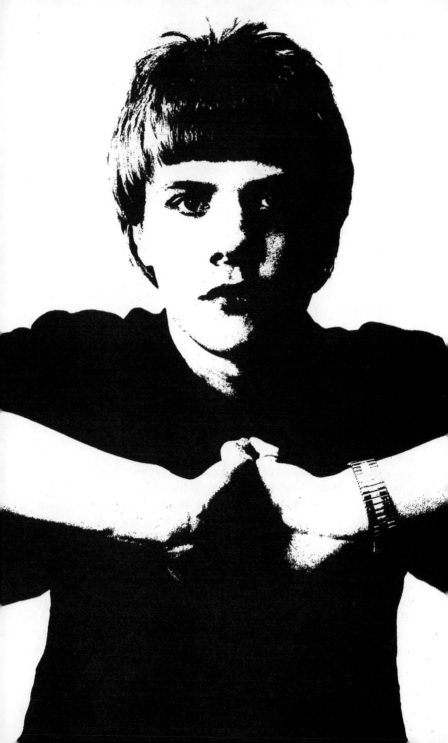

Larry Mullen Jr

I HAVE AN AVERAGE BACKGROUND. MY FATHER
WAS A CIVIL SERVANT, MY MOTHER A HOMEMAKER.
I WAS BORN 31 OCTOBER 1961, THE MIDDLE CHILD
OF THREE. I HAVE AN OLDER SISTER, CECILIA, AND
HAD A YOUNGER SISTER MARY.

Everything about my life was pretty normal for a while. My sister died in 1973 and then my mother died in 1976. In some ways, both events defined the kind of person I've become. My mother's death certainly catapulted me in the band's direction.

We lived on Rosemount Avenue in Artane, north Dublin. It was my home until my early twenties. Nothing special, three-up, three-down sort of house. My mother, when she was younger, was a very good concert pianist. Oddly it wasn't a particularly musical household, unlike some of my friends' houses which were full of music. I started piano lessons at the age of eight. I wasn't very good, not being academically-minded and all that, the idea of having to study scales and the theory of music didn't appeal to me. I wanted to get behind the piano and figure it out for myself.

My father, Larry Mullen Senior, was the disciplinarian – as all fathers were back then. My mother would have been a soft touch, she would always give in. You didn't mess with dad. It was a tough relationship. He would go to work in the morning, maybe drop you to school on the way, and then he'd come home at six o'clock, read the newspaper, watch the news. My dad was an academic. He was well educated and he valued schooling. I think he was a little disappointed that I wasn't academically-minded and wasn't arsed about sport. He was a very successful sportsman when he was younger. He played hurling and Gaelic football for St Vincent's, a well-known GAA club on the north side of Dublin. He went to St Joseph's Christian Brothers School in Marino. He was one of those really bright, smart kids who came from very little, the only thing they had was their brains, and they used them to excel in academics and sport. I was sent to an Irish school, where I was taught all subjects through the Irish language. I think I was subconsciously rebelling against him by not doing the things he thought I should.

I started playing the drums when I was nine. I had been going to the School of Music in Chatham Row to learn piano but it wasn't deemed a great success. One memorable day the teacher said, 'Larry, stop hitting my piano.' She suggested I try something else. I was delighted. So as I was coming from the piano lesson with my mother, I heard somebody practising on a drum. I just said, 'You hear that? I'd really like to do that.' They had spent a fortune on piano lessons, so they said if I wanted to learn how to play the drums I had to finance it myself. So I did. It was nine pounds a term. I mowed lawns and washed cars and I earned enough to pay for the first term myself, and my father (thankfully) paid for the second and third.

I never had any real interest in drums before I heard this guy playing. It was military-style drumming, and there was something about the sound that made me take notice. So I joined Joe Bonnie's drum class in 1971. He was an old-school theatre drummer, part of the orchestra pool, playing in the Gaiety Theatre and the Olympia and those kind of places. He was a well-respected drummer. He must have been in his sixties when I went to him. What impressed me most as a nine-year-old was when he took the pad off the drum. Normally you weren't allowed to play on the drum head, it was very loud and the building wasn't soundproofed. On special occasions he would remove the pad. And that's when I just so happened to be walking by. I remember the sound he made with that drum, the crack of it, and the way it made you feel. It just seemed so unmusical on one level but the way Joe played looked and sounded so skilful. I'd never seen or been close to it before. It was very exciting.

So I started lessons. I was really into it at first and then it started to wear off because I could only play on that bloody pad. My father had a pad made for me, a piece of thick rubber mounted on plywood, and I practised on it at home. Lots of practice. I ended up hating that pad. And then I had to study the theory of music again. I hated it, I couldn't figure out what it had to do with hitting something. It didn't make any sense to me, and sadly I gave up doing theory. I regret that because later on I could have really done with it. It was a mistake but it was the same thing as the piano: I just wanted to play! I wanted to get behind a kit and bash it. But I couldn't. I had to learn the rudiments, practising paradiddles and all that stuff. I got bored. Then my teacher died. Joe's daughter took over from him but I had lost interest, I stopped going to lessons and started to play on my own. I remember my father asking if I still wanted to play. I said, 'Yeah, but I want to play in a band. I want to physically hit the thing.' He suggested the Artane Boys Band, which I joined … for about three weeks. I didn't like that much either; far too much learning how to read music, too little time hitting things, so I lost interest again. I thought that you joined the Artane Boys Band, they gave you a drum, and they showed you what to play and you marched in Croke Park.

Then there was an issue about my appearance – they told me to get my hair cut. At the time, I had shoulder-length golden locks. Reluctantly, I cut a few inches off. They told me to cut more. That was it. I left and never went back.

I suppose my interest at that time was to play either in a marching band, become a theatre drummer or join the army band. The only music on the radio at that time was traditional Irish music, country and western or showband music. However my sister Cecilia was bringing records home. She was into the Stones, Bowie, The Eagles, David Essex and Bruce Springsteen. I started listening to drummers, looking at TV watching out for drummers, all different types of drummers. My parents would take me to various shows to look at different players. Buddy Rich, Gene Krupa and Sandy Nelson records started to arrive. My favourite was Nelson's 'Let There Be Drums', which my father bought for me. I also became a huge fan of glam rock bands Sweet, T.Rex and The Glitter Band, who had two drummers. I would mimic those guys and try to play along with the records. A friend of my sister was selling a drum kit made by a Japanese toy company. It was twelve pounds and I saved and saved, and eventually my dad took pity and helped me out. We bought this little drum kit. Drums became my world and took up every moment of my day. It was set up in my bedroom, this little boxroom with a bed and a drum kit. I could only practise at certain times. We didn't want to piss the neighbours off.

Then my father got me into the Post Office Workers Band. They played a lot of orchestral stuff with percussion, along with marching band standards. This was much more interesting. There were girls in the band, which was a big part of the attraction because I was just discovering girls. So you'd be drumming your little heart out trying to impress the girls and forgetting what you should have been playing. I had a lot of fun in that band. We used to play on the bandstand in Stephen's Green or on the one at Dun Laoghaire pier during the summertime. We entered competitions all around the country and marched at all kinds of different events. The uniform never fitted quite right because it was never designed for me, it was handed down from somebody who had left the band who was twice your age and usually twice your size. A lot of sewing went on in the Mullen household. There was something very cool about having a side drum strapped to you as you were marching down the street. At least I used to think so.

I was about to start school at Mount Temple. My father had wanted me to go to Chanel College or St Paul's, schools where I would have to excel in academics and sport. I took the exams for both schools but I just wasn't

I PUT THE NOW-LEGENDARY NOTICE UP. I THINK THE WORDING WAS SOMETHING LIKE: 'DRUMMER SEEKS MUSICIANS TO FORM BAND'. I JUST THOUGHT OF IT AS A GROUP OF PEOPLE COMING TOGETHER TO HAVE A BIT OF FUN, IT WAS NEVER ANYTHING ELSE. NO IDEAS, NO EXPECTATIONS. LARRY

interested. It wasn't even laziness, it was just a different world to me. It was his world, not mine. Then my sister Mary died. She was nine years old, it was very traumatic for everybody. I think my father gave up pushing me after that. I was sent to Mount Temple. It was close by and it had just opened up to the general public. They didn't put the same emphasis on academic achievement. I got on quite well in Mount Temple, funnily enough. I wasn't a genius but I really developed in subjects that I had never been good at before. I did quite well at Maths; I was good at Art and English. My father had just backed off. There was just no point pushing any more. Ironically now that I have my own children in school I really understand why he felt he needed to push so hard. He wasn't wrong about the importance of school or many other things for that matter. It was my father who suggested I put a notice up on the school board for fellow musicians. We didn't always see eye to eye but through it all he was still watching my back, he was figuring, 'OK, the kid wants to play drums, how do I help him survive and navigate this because he's never going to be a brain surgeon.' I had started taking lessons with Johnny Wadham, a jazz drummer in town, but I was getting bored and I wanted to play in a rock band. Then the old man stepped in with the school notice. It was him – it wasn't even my idea.

So I put the now-legendary notice up. I think the wording went something like: 'drummer seeks musicians to form band'. I just thought of it as a bit of fun, it was never anything else. No big ideas, no expectations, really. I had a school friend, Peter Martin, who had an electric guitar and an amplifier, although he couldn't play. We borrowed his gear for our rehearsal. He knew Ivan McCormick, who was in the year below us. He had an electric guitar that apparently he could play. Ivan made it to our first get together. After the notice went up, people asked if I knew, 'Yer man Paul Hewson, he plays guitar.' I said I didn't but it turned out everybody knew who he was and what he did and who he was going out with, so it didn't take long for me to discover who I was going to have to deal with. Edge and Dick were basically like one person, they were into inventing things and they played a yellow guitar that they had made together, so it took a while to work out which of them would be in the band. I knew of Adam, he used to wear a long sheepskin Afghan coat, he had tinted glasses and he smoked. Some people were saying to me, 'You know that weirdo in the Afghan coat? He has a bass.' It didn't matter if he could play it. Adam was in. So on Saturday 25 September 1976, this odd group of people convened in my kitchen in Artane. And that's where it started.

ANOTHER
TIME ANOTHER
PLACE
1976 - 1978

Adam

THE SUMMER BEFORE I WENT TO MOUNT TEMPLE,
I SPENT SOME TIME IN PAKISTAN WITH A SCHOOL
FRIEND AND I DISCOVERED HASHISH AND BOB
MARLEY AND HANGING OUT. THERE MAY HAVE BEEN
THE ODD MOMENTS OF DRUNKENNESS AS WELL.

I was staying with my good friend Gordon Petherbridge, whose father was
the Australian ambassador to Pakistan and Afghanistan, and he had left
school under similar circumstances to me and had gone to the international
school in Pakistan.

When I was leaving Columba's in disgrace, rather than spend the
summer at home being miserable he invited me out to Pakistan. I stayed about
a month and we went up to Kabul for a week of that, which was part of the
hippie trail, so there was a whole education that went on of buying Afghan
coats, cheesecloth and drinking tea with the locals. There was a lot of hash
being smoked and that connected me with much of the music that I'd been
listening to and gave me a sense of who I was. By the time I came to Mount
Temple the spirit of rebellion was upon me, and maybe I thought the best
form of defence was attack: go in there with attitude and people wouldn't
mess with you.

With my background and experiences, a north Dublin comprehensive
school was not a place I felt comfortable. I was arriving in the middle of it, so I
suppose I needed as many props as I could get to shore myself up. I had the
Afghan coat, mirror sunglasses and I would carry a flask of coffee. I found
lessons really quite tedious and it was a form of protest to get your lunch out
or drink coffee in class. It was a way of not being there. There was little
likelihood that I would suddenly develop a huge academic interest so it was
quite difficult to settle in. I gravitated towards the smokers and that became
my community: I started smoking cigarettes and dope.

Two or three weeks into my first term I heard that Larry Mullen had
put up a note about starting a band. My only qualification was that I
actually had a bass, but that was enough to get me invited to the first
meeting in Larry's kitchen.

BONO: It was my friend Reggie Manuel, the Bad Dog, who persuaded me to go to that first meeting. He really did believe in me in a way that I can't quite figure out. When anyone else was saying, 'You should be a door-to-door salesman', he was saying: 'No. You've got something else to do and this might be it.' And so I said, 'I couldn't do that. I wouldn't hang out with that lot anyway. They're very uncool.' And I wouldn't have gone, because I was in a very self-conscious teenage phase. I had lost all kind of confidence. But the Bad Dog said, 'I really think you should go to this. I'll drive you there.' And he did. I turned up at Larry's house in Artane on the back of Reggie's bike. I don't think I even brought a guitar, because I couldn't carry it on the bike. But that didn't mean I was going to sing, that's for sure. It was all about guitars, at that moment in time. I probably figured I would suss the situation out, maybe play somebody else's guitar. I had to big myself up, put the front back on for the young people. I had worked out a little solo from Santana's *Abraxas*. At least I thought I could play it, until Edge played it, and then it sounded a little different.

EDGE: One of the music teachers told me some kid wants to form a band. So I thought, 'Well, that would be cool. If there's another garage band starting may as well check this one out rather than try to start my own.' So myself and my brother showed up, and Adam was there and then Paul arrived and a couple of others. My brother had left school by then but we did a lot of musical stuff together, so we kind of came as a pair. We brought along the yellow Flying V guitar that Dick had made in the garden shed. It was a very rough and ready piece of gear altogether but it made a noise and that was the main thing.

ADAM: I remember meeting David and Dick with their yellow guitar. It was interesting; neither of them really wanted to give it up, it was like they had it between them. It was all pretty daunting for me. I'd been secluded until the age of sixteen. I wasn't used to getting around on buses and so it was a big deal to go to someone's house like that. I remember Larry's mum and dad and sister Cecilia were there, and his drum kit was set up in the kitchen. I didn't know whether it was Larry or his parents who were auditioning us.

LARRY: We set up in the kitchen, the fireplace had been removed during renovations. This gave us some extra space. We folded the kitchen table down, piled the chairs on top and pushed it against the wall; I could just about fit the drums into a corner. Everybody else squeezed in around me, about seven people. There was very little playing, just an awful lot of tuning up. I think we may have attempted to play one song that nobody knew. It was basically a jam that went on all afternoon.

BONO: Larry was incredible because he could really play the drums and they sounded amazing. I mean, playing drums in the kitchen is like singing in the bath. The kitchen was only the size of the drum kit. I don't know how the rest of us got in. I thought that Edge had an extraordinary head – he looked like an Apache Indian. I had heard him play before, because he was in Ali's class, and I knew he could play pretty well. The only thing that sounded better than Reggie Manuel's motorcycle was a power chord on an electric guitar. When Edge opened the throttle, there was quite a roar. Adam was there and he really looked the part; I don't know about his playing, but he had the look right.

ADAM: I don't think we played very much, it was more talk. I don't think Bono even turned up with a guitar, but that didn't stop him taking charge pretty much immediately.

LARRY: It was the Larry Mullen Band for about ten minutes, so as not to hurt my feelings. It was also my kitchen. Then Bono came in and that was the end of that. He blew any chance I had of being in charge.

BONO: Larry seemed very young but he had some excitement going, even then, because in the middle of rehearsals there was screaming outside and girls trying to climb over the garden wall. And I remember him doing a rather novel thing – he took the hose to them! Which he has been doing ever since. You know, he was like: 'Go away, we've got some real stuff to do!'

EDGE: It wasn't a particularly auspicious beginning. There was a lot of talk, a lot of people playing songs they knew very badly trying to impress one another, trying to figure out if we had similar musical tastes. They were pretty broad but I think we managed to establish certain intersections. Everybody liked T. Rex and Bowie but I might have been playing some Rory Gallagher badly and that didn't seem to impress Larry. Somebody else might have been playing the Eagles because that was very big at the time.

BONO: Edge was into Taste, Rory Gallagher's group. I was listening to the Beach Boys and early rock and roll at the time. I could play that, it was simple twelve-bar stuff. Larry was into the Eagles, as his sister was.

EDGE: I remember thinking that I liked everybody, which was the most important thing. Just a sense that actually these are cool people.

LARRY: I didn't know these people, they didn't know me, I never thought it would happen, getting four or five strangers into a room playing music together. Now anything seemed possible. We organized our second rehearsal before we left the first one.

ADAM: The strategy was to find a rehearsal room at school. I think it was a way of getting kudos at school, really. Let everyone know we were in a band.

LARRY: Mr McKenzie, our Music teacher in Mount Temple, let us rehearse in his classroom on Wednesday afternoons. Donald Moxham, one of the History teachers, and a good friend to us, was instrumental in getting the school to help us out.

ADAM: Wednesday was a half-day at Mount Temple, so it was something to do after school. I don't think there was much going on for anyone, so it was easy to arrange. It was really a doss for those first few rehearsals. There was a huge amount of enthusiasm. There were bits of cobbled-together gear. We would beg, steal and borrow guitars off anyone. Peter Martin was weeded out quite early on. He had a guitar and an amp but he couldn't play, and he was a different age group, as was Ivan McCormick, so it was probably on that basis. Ivan lasted a few weeks.

EDGE: Larry and I could play a bit, as could Ivan, but Adam really couldn't play, he kind of pretended. But by virtue of owning a bass there was no doubt he was going to be the bass player. Bono didn't even have a guitar but he seemed to think he was lead guitarist.

LARRY: It was obvious from the beginning that Bono was going to be the singer, not because of his great voice but because he didn't have a guitar, an amp or transport, what else was he going to do? He had delusions that maybe he was a guitarist but without the equipment it wasn't possible. He could strum a guitar but he was no guitar player and it could be argued that he's still no guitar player.

BONO: I had a few chords, a few songs I could play. The idea of wanting to sing, I don't remember when that happened. I mean I had always wanted to but I don't remember owning up to it.

EDGE: No one really wanted to sing because it was too revealing or it made you vulnerable. I certainly never felt comfortable standing out there and singing.

ADAM: Bono wasn't sure whether he was going to play guitar or sing at that point. We didn't even have microphones from what I remember. We had two guitars, a bass, a drum kit and half an amplifier that we were all going through.

EDGE: There was always a lot of tuning because the guitars weren't particularly well maintained and the strings would have been very old and there were no electronic tuners in those days. So we would play for maybe two minutes and then tune for anywhere between fifteen and forty-five minutes. Progress was slow and for a very long time we tried unsuccessfully to play a song, any song, from start to finish. I'm sure it was very comical but we thought we were very cool.

ADAM: It was pretty shambolic.

LARRY: Everybody was making suggestions about music and songs I'd never even heard of. I would just play along. I remember a guy from Bono's class, one of the older guys with a cool faded denim jacket, coming into rehearsal, listening for a while and asking, 'What song are you playing?' Obviously, he was having difficulty working it out for himself. When we told him he said, 'It sounds nothing like that! And the drums are completely wrong!' There was the slow realization that before you play a song, it might be an idea to learn it first. We never quite got that one down.

EDGE: We were all learning how to play together – we really didn't have a clue. There was a glimmer of ability but it was so hard to spot in amongst the lack of experience and coordination and whatever.

LARRY: We had a name for the band before we really had anything else. 'Feedback'. Terrible name. Ask Edge about it.

EDGE: It was one of the only technical terms we knew at the time. I remember Adam casually throwing in the word 'gig', which fooled us into thinking he knew what he was doing, and knew how to play bass. Adam had some jargon, and was already talking with great confidence about 'PAs' and 'mixing desks' and then somebody came up with the term 'feedback', probably Adam, and I think that stuck just because there was so much of it around during our early rehearsals, it seemed appropriate.

ADAM: Feedback seemed a rock sort of name. I don't know who came up with it.

BONO: Guilty, your honour.

EDGE: It didn't take long for the band to start to coalesce around the people that looked right together. That was the four future members of U2 and my brother Dick. He was just as good a guitar player as I was, a little more eccentric maybe but a very accomplished player in his own way. But then, after a little while, it started to become obvious that we made more sense as a four-piece. Larry knew this instinctively from fairly early on. He would come up to me in the corridor occasionally and say, 'Is Dick in the band?' And I'd go, 'Well, yeah, I think so, why?' 'I don't know. I just was wondering, you know. He's not like in school and he's kind of a bit strange, isn't he?'

ADAM: There was going to be a talent show in the school gymnasium at the end of term, and that was where it was decided we would make our debut. The gig was really the thing that we worked towards.

LARRY: I think we only had two songs, so that was our set. Peter Frampton's 'Show Me The Way' and, as a joke, 'Bye Bye Baby' by the Bay City Rollers.

EDGE: I was rather embarrassed to be playing 'Show Me The Way', actually. And I was so embarrassed to be playing 'Bye Bye Baby' that I had successfully erased it from my mind until now. But I think the truth is they were the only songs we could play all the way through. As much as we would have loved to play Rory Gallagher's 'Blister on the Moon' or something with a bit more credibility that we used to try at rehearsals, it was actually not going to happen, it was just not possible. Those two songs were simple enough that we could actually get by.

LARRY: I remember rehearsing 'Show Me The Way'. I always thought it was Bono's idea. He seemed to relate to the lyric.

BONO: I remember trying to do some rock-type numbers and not being able to sing them, my voice not sounding very good. Adam was a big fan of Peter Frampton and he played this song: 'I want you, show me the way'. And my voice, whatever configuration of chords, I could sing that, I could sing it really well. So that was an odd thing to discover that you did have a voice, in a certain context. But because of everything I was going through, I turned this pop song into a prayer. That's how I sang it. I'm not singing it for a girl. I mean, I look back and think, 'How did that happen?' I was starting to use music as a way of really expressing what was going on in my head. But taking,

WE WALKED ON THAT STAGE, I WAS PLAYING GUITAR, AND WHEN I HEARD THAT D-CHORD, I JUST STARTED TO LEVITATE. BOUNCING OFF THE WALLS I KNEW I HAD MY 'GET OUT OF JAIL FREE' CARD. BONO

you know, any old pop song. But of course there's no such thing as any old pop song. They're amazing things. The littlest pop ditty can be an opus if it's what you're feeling.

I actually met Peter Frampton in 2003, at an AIDS event, in an HIV/AIDS care centre in the outskirts of Chicago. There were a lot of people from different communities and different backgrounds and there's this fellow working with them, a most unassuming man. I'm not talking celebrity appearances, I'm talking roll-your-sleeves-up, out-on-the-frontline work. People say, Peter Frampton's disappeared off the face of the earth. Well it turns out he hasn't. He's actually arrived on the face of the earth with a real purpose, working for people who have absolutely nothing going for them. It was just beautiful. And I got to tell him how I discovered my voice on his song.

EDGE: I think the Bay City Rollers was Larry's suggestion.

LARRY: We were goofing around. We did it for a laugh.

BONO: We thought that was really funny. It came out in rehearsals, taking the piss, because girls would be going by when we were rehearsing and be pressing their faces up against the door. So we used to play that just to make them laugh. They would start screaming, because that was the big craze at the time.

ADAM: The gig was in daytime, there were no lights. We were playing on some tables set up in the gym. It was just the four of us. Dick was at college.

LARRY: There was a lot of excitement and a lot of nerves. I was very self-conscious. I was afraid we were going to be crap. How would I deal with the slagging from my classmates?

BONO: We walked on that stage, I was playing guitar, and when I heard that D-chord, I just started to levitate. When I heard that D-chord bouncing off the walls I knew I had my 'Get Out of Jail Free' card, and the audience went wild! Forget about what we played, because that's not important. I was singing, it was emancipation. That was a very special concert.

THE GIG WAS ALL OVER IN A FLASH BUT IN THAT TEN MINUTES A WORLD OPENED UP OF HOW THINGS COULD BE. AT THE TIME I THOUGHT A RIOT HAD TAKEN PLACE – AND MAYBE IT HAD. ADAM

EDGE: What was surprising to me was getting up there and playing 'Show Me The Way', which was really a fairly simple tune, and suddenly something happened, particularly in Bono as a performer and just generally the thrill of being on stage, I suppose, the reaction of people watching us. There was something about it that really worked between us, that even as inept as we were, when we hit it, stuff went off in a very visceral and very primitive way. If the performance bug is contagious, we definitely caught it that day.

BONO: It was really a feeling of liberation. It's like you've jumped into the sea and discovered you can swim.

LARRY: I remember looking into the crowd and seeing them start to clap and stand up and move towards us. Some of the teachers even stayed. I remember the feeling of relief. And then playing 'Bye Bye Baby' and thinking: 'Oh, maybe we've blown it here!'

ADAM: It was all over in a flash, and that may relate to just general stage fright and nervousness. But it was one of the most amazing buzzes, a huge shot of adrenalin. In that ten minutes a world opened up of how things could be. I had a great sense of power, being in front of an audience and seeing that there was a relationship, there was something that went off, an energy. At the time I thought a riot had taken place – and maybe it had.

LARRY: After that, I think we were a band. We had actually managed to play in public together without totally disgracing ourselves. It was as if my identity changed. I was no longer the blond kid hanging out in the corridor, I was now the kid in the band.

BONO: Everything changed for me, because now I knew what I wanted to do for the rest of my life. There it was, the thing I didn't know. And that happened so quickly. Suddenly you have a reason to be. I felt great relief, and thought it doesn't really matter now if you flunk your exams. And I was hanging out with some very smart people, so I wasn't looking forward to flunking. My friends were all going on to university. I still had to make a half-stab at doing that but in my head, I was never going to. This is what I was going to do, so it simplified my life, gave me clarity.

LARRY: I think if you asked Bono, Edge or Adam how they felt, they would say basically the same thing: that this had changed the way they thought about their future. Music and the band was it for them. I didn't think that way. I was a shy fourteen-year-old who hadn't figured many things, never mind the band or my future. All I knew was it was a lot more fun than playing alone in your bedroom.

ADAM: At the time I would definitely have found Bono the most mysterious. The Edge and I would travel to and from rehearsals together, so we started to get to know each other and spend time together. Larry's mum or dad would drop his drums off at the school in their car, so we'd meet them, have a little chat. Larry was that little bit younger but he was the drummer so he set up his stuff and we had a sense of him. But then Bono, you'd just never know when he was going to turn up. Sometimes he'd come on a bike, or Guggi would drop him over in a car, or maybe he'd get the bus if he had bus fare. It was always a bit more of an entrance with him. Sometimes he'd have a guitar and sometimes he wouldn't. I think we had cobbled together a few bits of gear at that stage. Edge had got a home-made combo, I bought a Marshall top that we could put everything through. We bought a microphone that Bono could sing through. It was slowly developing. But with Bono, I was always aware that he had some other life out there. He had a school life where he obviously was part of a scene and a nucleus of a lot of people and then he had another life in Cedarwood with Gavin and Guggi, the people that ultimately made up Lypton Village and the Virgin Prunes. I can't really remember how much of a driving force he was in terms of thinking big but definitely Bono had an energy.

EDGE: Bono was a great personality but I also knew he was a chancer, so on one level I was impressed but on another I knew he didn't always have the ability to back it up. But that was fine. Once I realized that was what I was dealing with, I didn't have a problem with it. I thought we were all chancing our arm to a greater or lesser degree.

LARRY: I was always the baby and I was treated as such. They would keep an eye out for me. I wasn't much younger in age but as far as being worldly wise or roadworthy, I was naïve. I was a couple of classes below and I was still struggling academically. But I could keep a beat and that went a long way. It was a little odd spending time with guys who were older and more advanced

IT WAS PRETTY OBVIOUS THAT THERE WAS A
DISCREPANCY IN WHAT YOU MIGHT CALL MUSICAL
PROWESS BETWEEN THE MEMBERS, BUT IT DIDN'T
MATTER BECAUSE WE WERE ALL PRETTY CRAP. DURING
ONE REHEARSAL, BONO, IN DESPERATION, ASKED HIS
FRIEND MAEVE TO COME DOWN AND LISTEN. SHE
BASICALLY LAID IT ON THE LINE: THAT FELLA ADAM
HAS NO IDEA WHAT HE'S DOING. EDGE

than me. Everybody know Bono, he was very popular and active in school. They knew Adam for different reasons, drinking coffee in class, dressing unusually and generally being eccentric. Edge was one of the bright sparks, destined for college. It was a little intimidating at first but I was eager to learn.

EDGE: It was really just great craic being in a band. There was really no other reason to play together because there was very little indication of any major talent. We were the world's worst covers band. Rehearsals would always break down halfway through a song, somebody would play the wrong thing. We never seemed to manage to get to the end of anything.

ADAM: The penny dropped that we weren't getting any better rehearsing for an hour once a week and it then became Saturdays as well, and that was a big shift because everyone had to give up free time, real weekends to get into school on a Saturday, so that was another level that we stepped up to. Then we got a gig at a disco in St Fintan's, a school at Sutton in north Dublin. There were going to be a few bands playing. It was during the Easter holidays in 1977 and my parents were going away, so we rehearsed at my house.

BONO: Adam lived in what I thought was a palace out in Malahide. I thought it was the most beautiful bungalow I had ever seen, and it was kept immaculately. His mother was very glamorous. I remember her walking out of the shower, walking past us with a towel on. She had a tan, she was blonde, and I thought: 'Wow, that's your mother!' It was one of those moments. And then they were away and we were all up in the house.

LARRY: Adam had an original style. He just came up with the coolest shit. He could play out-of-time-in-time for ages. Quite extraordinary. But that's what makes him a great bass player. He's not a virtuoso, however he's a very innovative player. And that comes from his disability, not being able to play perfectly in time. I'm not a virtuoso either, however my timing, thankfully, is good. If it wasn't we'd be in trouble. Adam made it into U2 because of his Afghan coat, those very cool sunglasses, bass guitar and a curly mop of sandy hair. Could he play? I didn't give a shit. He looked great. And that counts.

EDGE: It was pretty obvious that there was a discrepancy in what you might call musical prowess between the members, but it didn't matter because we were all pretty crap. During one rehearsal, Bono, in desperation almost, asked his friend Maeve O'Regan to come down and listen to us to find out what was up. She came and listened and just basically laid it on the line: 'Larry's pretty good, David seems to be OK, but that fella Adam has no idea what he's doing, he's completely out of time and out of tune.' We obviously weren't really together enough ourselves to even know the difference but she spotted it. This would have been a bombshell to most other groups but not to us. What Adam didn't have in terms of natural talent, he made up for in heart and commitment. We never considered finding a more able bass player. We knew he was our bass player, because we were a band. A band of chancers, but a band.

ADAM: I was blissfully ignorant; I had no idea how little I knew and, you know, it's a wonderful buffering situation to be in. I think that cocoon probably lasted up to our first record, maybe through to our second record. After that, lack of ability and technique really began to hit home. Back then, I honestly did just think it was a laugh, that it was easy and that I was brilliant. It's extraordinary when you read now about seminal bands like The Beatles or The Stones who were highly accomplished musicians before they became bands and songwriters. They really knew what they were doing – we did not come from that background at all. We never got to finish a song in rehearsals, so once we started to play in front of an audience we didn't know how to end a song. I think Larry was probably the most disciplined but even that kind of discipline was pretty wild. He at least had some idea of beginning, middle and end. Maybe Edge did as well, but I think he was just concentrating so hard on making the sounds that I'm not sure he was focusing on structure too much. Bono never knew the words of anything. We had tuning problems. We were all doing our best but it was pretty undisciplined and unformed.

EDGE: We had a slightly larger repertoire at Saint Fintan's but I realized, in a moment of panic about twenty minutes before starting that show, that we'd actually never managed to finish playing any of the numbers, therefore there was no ending. We hadn't got to an end of anything ever. I remember sitting on some steps and trying to talk Larry and Adam through ending some songs.

BONO: I don't think we were very good. I don't think we were very good for quite a while.

EDGE: Bono had brought a couple of girls in, Orla Dunne and Stella McCormick. He probably thought it would flesh out the sound a bit.

ADAM: Bono basically decided the band needed a couple of sexy backing singers.

BONO: I think it was just that the band needed sex! That might have been it. They were in my year at Mount Temple, sang in the choir and they were both kind of hippie chicks. It was sexy; they were singing and Orla was playing the flute. Everyone in the band got a choice of material. Adam's was the Eagles, Edge's was Rory Gallagher, but my uncool choice was the worst of all. I was responsible for 'Nights In White Satin' by the Moody Blues. I thought it would be great with the sexy backing singers and the flute but it was a disaster. It was far too complicated for us – it had more than four chords.

EDGE: Orla and Stella came up to me before the show saying, 'David, will you sing? Because Bono can't really sing very well!' I did the only thing I could do, I lied. 'I think he sings great,' I said. 'What are you talking about? You're so wrong. He's a great singer.' I knew they had a point but there was no way I was going to get up there and sing. They insisted, 'He just shouts all the time and people can't hear the words.' 'What are you saying?' I countered. 'I love his singing.' Then I mumbled something about having to change my strings and made a run for it. Bono, in the early days, used pure volume and energy as a kind of shock tactic to get people's attention. It wasn't particularly subtle but he scored big time on commitment. Of course, it might have helped if we had a proper PA, instead of putting his voice through a guitar amp.

ADAM: There was another group called Rat Salad playing. They were pretty scary.

LARRY: There was an argument about who was going to open and who was going to close the show. We lost and went on first.

ADAM: It felt like a proper stage and I don't think we'd been on a proper stage at that point; and it was a nice room, good proportions. I think the Lypton Village support crew were starting to come around, so we felt rather like a gang. I remember attempting 'White Satin' and feeling it was great having backing singers and a flute player. It felt like we were versatile – but it all started going horribly wrong.

LARRY: I was embarrassed and humiliated. We were completely out of time with each other.

EDGE: Even though we were probably incredibly inept just the thrill of playing in front of an audience was enough for me. I was thinking, 'Man, this is cool! Girls are talking to me and I like doing this.' We were opening up for this other group, and even at that point, even though they could play, I knew that they were not really interesting. There was a lot more to be discovered out there. Music should be more than bar-room rock.

LARRY: We were crap, people booed and Rat Salad were laughing at us. It was awful.

BONO: I wrote my first song while we were rehearsing at Adam's house. That was interesting because it happened very quickly. I don't know where I got the guitar or whose guitar it was, but I remember figuring out minor chords, and moving between them. It was a chord I made up; it's not that hard.

ADAM: I think the first chord would be a B major seventh and then it was followed by an A major, and he just moved between those two chords and that became the song. There was a kind of a magic about them. They had a mood and tone.

BONO: I got a chorus almost immediately – 'What's Going On?' I thought that was very original!

ADAM: We hadn't heard of Marvin Gaye in those days, so we weren't aware the title had been used before. But it just had something.

LARRY: I thought it was called 'Wednesday Afternoon', because we used to rehearse on Wednesday afternoons. We got so frustrated trying to do cover versions. One afternoon Bono just started strumming away on a few chords. After a while it started to sound like music.

BONO: Everyone was trying to figure out how to play 'Brown Sugar' or 'Jumping Jack Flash'. But I thought: 'Gosh, this is interesting, look, you can write songs really easily.' And I just presumed everyone could, but maybe they couldn't.

LARRY: That was really interesting because nobody was saying: 'Well it doesn't sound like the original.' There was no original. It was a landmark in U2's development. Once we had written the first song, we spent the rest of our time trying to write better songs and drop the covers from our set.

ADAM: When we were planning our sets and looking at different material, I remember feeling that this music we were trying to play was part of another generation, it didn't really connect with us. We were very unschooled musicians who were just ripe for the energy of punk when it came along. We were just exuberant enthusiasts and who knows where that flame would have gone without punk?

BONO: There were only about a hundred people in the country into punk rock at this point, at least it felt like that. I was very bored with music at that time. If that was the summer when London was burning, well, I wouldn't know about London burning – but I was burning. I remember all I used to listen to was The Rolling Stones' *High Tide and Green Grass*, a collection of their early hits. That's what I was at. And *The Idiot* by Iggy Pop. But even before that, I always liked rock 'n' roll: Eddie Cochrane rock 'n' roll, Elvis rock 'n' roll, The Beatles rock 'n' roll, The Beach Boys. I didn't really like heavy rock, I was genuinely looking for something different, I think a lot of people were. And then I remember hearing The Radiators From Space. They were Ireland's first punk band. They had a single that went, *I'm gonna put my telecaster through the television screen because I don't like what's going on.* When I heard it my ears pricked up. It was the same as The Beach Boys' version of 'Johnny B Goode'. Straight twelve-bar rock 'n' roll, but through a fuzz box, and I said, 'We can play this. And we really can play it. And not only can we play it but this is the kind of shit I like.' So we were off then.

ADAM: Punk opened the door. It created a language, although it wasn't particularly accessible to us at the time. This was 1977, it was just kicking off in England. I think the odd single is all that we might have heard. A neighbour of mine was the first punk in Malahide and he had the Sex Pistols' singles and we would go round to his house to listen to them along with anything else that was coming out: The Buzzcocks, The Damned, Slaughter and the Dogs, The Stranglers, The Clash.

EDGE: I suppose a watershed moment would have been seeing The Jam on *Top of the Pops* and realizing that actually not knowing how to play was not a problem, in that music was more about energy and trying to say something and not necessarily about musicianship. So it was a great encouragement to hear these bands were playing very simple stuff, the way we naturally played, with total commitment, ten times as fast as was appropriate and with very little in the way of subtlety, just bashing it out. Which is what we were doing to everything anyway, so it fitted perfectly.

ADAM: In the summer of 1977, I had a school-holiday job in London, working for a couple of months in Billingsgate fish market.

EDGE: The band was put on hold while Adam was away. This was because, since he did not seem to be doing any work in Mount Temple, his parents told him they would no longer support him. So they encouraged him to go to London and get a job because they thought he was going to be a complete waster unless he learned to support himself financially. Adam's parents were really unsure about music for Adam, one of the reasons being they thought that his musical abilities were quite meagre and that to be successful you had to be talented, or at least have the basics of singing in tune and playing in time, things which were a big challenge for Adam. Larry's parents were very supportive because he was actually quite a promising young drummer. My parents also, because they probably thought I had some flair and it was a nice hobby. Bono and his dad, well, that was another story but Bono was going his own way, whatever.

ADAM: Trading at Billingsgate started at six in the morning. I had to be in there at five to lay out the stalls. Business would be over at eleven and I would go up to Oxford Street or Soho and buy records and walk around and look at people. It was a little bit precocious in certain ways, I suppose, I had this ability to put myself forward. I don't have that same energy now. Mixed up in it would also have been going out drinking with people, a little bit of drugs, so I was out there feeling pretty grown-up. I suppose I saw it as trying to gain as much worldly wisdom as possible, to figure out how to have a career and how to get somewhere. I'd buy records in London and then bring them back; so that particular summer I'd bought Patti Smith's *Horses*, Television's *Marquee Moon*, the first Clash album, The Stranglers as well as a Ted Nugent record and a heavy metal album by a group called Lonestar, that didn't go down so well. When I came back I think the rest of the guys had been listening to things like Richard Hell, so everyone latched on to the same kind of music.

EDGE: Adam came back from London with some very interesting records … and one awful heavy metal one. We were all broke so this was the prize, I suppose, for having spent the summer in the fish market. It was very exciting. *Horses* made a big impression and I went out a week afterwards and bought my own vinyl copy. It was a music that was completely fresh and different to everything else that was happening, alongside the Pistols and The Clash and The Stranglers. Patti Smith's music had that confrontational aspect. What was different was that it's poetry. Punk had all the anger but none of the poetry. My friend Stephen Balcombe wasn't really a music fan but I was so excited by this album I wanted to play it to everybody. He came over to my house and I put it on and we listened to the first minute and a half of 'Gloria': *Jesus died for somebody's sins but not mine.* Stephen turned round and said, 'Man, this makes me want to get sick!' He just found it much too heavy and confrontational to have this strange, sexually ambivalent creature spewing out lyrics that challenged his whole faith. I thought it was fantastic and I liked the simplicity of the production, the guitar playing was great. Tom Verlaine played on one of the songs and he became a big influence on me with his group Television. We'd heard Richard Hell and The Voidoids (Verlaine's original sparring partner), we knew a little bit about the New York scene. The dark beauty of Patti Smith was just so compelling and inspiring.

ADAM: While I was away I'd saved my money and I'd bought a fifteen-inch speaker to work with my Marshall amp and I bought a four x twelve cabinet on behalf of Edge, so he finally got something to play through; so we were gradually getting bits of equipment together.

BONO: I was off to UCD (University College Dublin) to study English and History, an arts degree. But it turned out I had falsely matriculated because I failed Irish, and if you failed Irish, you failed everything, that was the order of the day, so I shouldn't have been offered the place. I went back to Mount Temple to repeat a year, which was fine by me, because the band was there.

I'd been working in a shoe shop in town called Justin Lord's. Myself and Guggi got a gig there over the summer, so we got a little bit of money. We were into punk rock; and we got jackets like Iggy Pop on the cover of *The Idiot*, with sleeves too short, and we had these mad-looking psychedelic winklepicker shoes. We chopped our hair. I walked into school one day with a safety pin stuck in my cheek to wind everyone up, which of course it did – I think a riot broke out. Ali broke up with me, so I gave up the safety pin for love.

EDGE: I started wearing this military naval jacket, which actually was my father's from his National Service. It was a good fit. You had to improvise to get your punk look together – I wasn't particularly flush with money for fashion purchases. Around that time we came up with a new name that reflected our shift in emphasis to this new power music.

ADAM: It was pretty obvious that Feedback was not going to be part of the punk movement and that The Hype was. It may have been helped a little bit by the fact that it was Bowie's first band name. I don't know who came up with it.

BONO: Guilty, your honour.

LARRY: I remember being asked, 'Why are you called The Hype? Is that all this is or can you really play?' Feedback made more sense because there was an awful lot of it.

EDGE: We learnt some Ramones songs, those would have been the first punk numbers we played. I think 'Glad To See You Go' was the first.

ADAM: Punk was simple songs played very fast. People called it rhythm and blues but just speeded up, which some of it was. There was The Radiators From Space, which was an Irish punk band, and The Boomtown Rats, so suddenly it was coming closer to home, there was some way we could aspire to playing gigs and getting record deals. We started to add some punk material, some Ramones numbers, a couple of Sex Pistols, possibly something by Wire, a couple of Stranglers numbers.

LARRY: Bono was a huge fan of The Stranglers and he wanted to rehearse 'Go Buddy Go'. That was OK but I was still unsure about some of the punk stuff.

BONO: There was a great moment when I was there with the safety pin and the mental, winklepicker shoes. And Larry was saying, 'Now, we're not a punk band,

'No, no, we're not, Larry, no.'
'This is The Stranglers we're listening to,
Isn't it? They're punk, are they?' 'Yeah.'
'We're playing one of their songs.' 'Yeah.'
'But we're not a punk band?' 'No, we're not.'
'Because I don't want to be in a punk band.'
'OK, then, we're not in a punk band.
This isn't a punk band.'

are we?' That was his big line at the time: 'We're not in a punk band, are we?' I think what was going on was that he was getting hell at home from his old man, who had spent all this money on jazz lessons. It was hard enough for his father to accept that Larry was playing in anything other than a jazz band, but the idea that we were punk rock was beyond the pale. So I think he made Larry promise that he wasn't in a punk rock band.

LARRY: Being in the band meant I'd started to think about music differently. I began to pick up some of my sister's records, Steely Dan, Bruce Springsteen. I was listening to David Bowie. Then punk happened. I was just a little too young to get it. I didn't know much about the music punk was meant to be rebelling against. Images of The Sex Pistols gobbing on their fans and being gobbed at were disgusting. Musically, however, *Never Mind The Bollocks* is one of the great albums. But I wasn't even seventeen. I had my long hair and my denims. I wasn't quite ready for rebellion. I hadn't quite reached that phase.

I remember meeting Bono's friend Gavin Friday on the way to a Boomtown Rats gig. He looked the part. He was wearing a jacket top, drainpipes and brothel creepers, a tight haircut and a scowl.

BONO: Guggi and I met Gavin when we were about thirteen. We all lived on Cedarwood Road. I think he came to a party that he wasn't invited to, a free house, and he showed up with a friend, and we caught them trying to steal something from the house. There was a bit of a fracas, just classic teenage stuff. But we became friends. He was cool; his name then was Fionan Hanvey, and he was kind of hippie. He used to listen to T. Rex, he looked like Marc Bolan and he was always getting beaten up by the skinheads and bootboys because he had long hair. They used to call him Handbag Hanvey and later, for revenge, he used to carry an enormous handbag. Gavin really embraced punk rock. I think he clung even tighter to music than I did. He would walk around like 'I dare youse!' He'd have these military stormtrooping boots and then an Eraserhead haircut, huge, high, mad-looking hair. It was so offensive to some people they would just see him and want to kill him, and the more they wanted to kill him, the more outrageously he would dress.

EDGE: Bono had this other scene going, the Village thing with Gavin and Guggi, a whole other set of relationships. I remember he told us a lot about this guy Derek Rowan, who was one of his best friends. The way Bono described Guggi as this really tough but funny, brilliant guy, I imagined a physically larger person. So I was quite taken aback by this delicate little Iggy Pop lookalike with blond hair, but we very instantly connected on a humour level. I liked most of the people Bono brought to the rehearsals. I thought Gavin was a very cool guy and brought a lot along in terms of knowing music, good ideas, better record collection than me. I thought we can work with this if he comes along.

BONO: I might have come up with Lypton Village but from where, who knows? We were inventing names, mythical places, even our own language. We just didn't like the world we were living in so we started re-imagining it, and I'm sure it was very arrogant and exclusive. We used to do these kind of art attacks, where we would go into Grafton Street, get on the number nineteen bus and bring stepladders, a drill, a few saws, a bunch of bananas. We would climb the stepladder, set up these little performances and try to get the crowd interested in us, and then run off. I don't think there was much art involved – it was just the idea of using humour as a weapon. It was all very Monty Python. We never missed Monty Python. Name-giving was a part of the process; there were many different names and a whole range of characters. Strongman, Pod, Day-Vid. My first name was Steinhegvanhuysenolegbangbangbang. Imagine that on an album sleeve! Then that got shortened to Hausman, and then it was Bono Vox.

LARRY: One weekend we were walking up O'Connell Street. As we pass a sign over a hearing-aid shop, Bono points and to it and says, 'That's me.' It said Bono Vox.

BONO: The idea was that if you don't want the life you've been given, perhaps you don't want the name that you were given to live with. It is probably the ultimate form of rebellion against your father – you won't take his name. But you still weren't allowed to choose your new name, that was a part of it. Edge almost became Inchicore, which is a place on the Dublin outskirts. I have no idea why. I'm not sure that would have worked. 'On guitar … Inchicore!' I wasn't sure about the name Bono Vox actually, it was a bit of a mouthful. I mean I've had it now probably since I was about fifteen. So the decision to go with it as a stage name was interesting, because Bono was a private name. Only my closest friends called me Bono – my name was Paul Hewson. Then one day I said to the band would they mind calling me Bono from now on? 'Sure Paul!' But to their credit they did, it just took them a while.

ADAM: I liked the Village enormously. In terms of my own rebellion, trying to get away from my own middle-class roots and rebelling against my parents, I think they were naturally the people I was drawn towards. Also they were very generous, Gavin and Guggi in particular, they always had money in their pockets and they always had cigarettes and they'd buy you a cup of tea or whatever. They became a sort of support group. And I guess as punk started to take a grip on the Village and people wore more and more outlandish clothes, it was really just a way of self-expression. It didn't have anything of the violence of how inner-city punk expressed itself. There wasn't much drink around at that time so it didn't have that kind of alcohol-fuelled craziness either. It was very moderated.

BONO: Adam always had a very strong sense of the surreal. He used to sit beside me in German class. He'd arrive in German, sit down, take out a flask of coffee, set it up. I mean, no one drank coffee. And then he'd just take out a novel and read it. But with impeccable manners; so if somebody asked, 'What are you doing?' he'd say, 'I'm terribly sorry, it's just I have this book and I don't think I'm going to be speaking German.' He was a surrealist from the word go, and Edge and Dick used to blow up their garden shed – they were all kinds of misfits really, and that's what the two sets of people had in common.

LARRY: They were strange and could be intimidating, but they never bothered with me, really.

EDGE: We did a couple of gigs in Sutton in October 1977. There was one at the Marine Hotel. I think our stage was a bunch of tables pushed together. It was really basic stuff, there was no sound mix, the balance was just whatever noise we were capable of making. It was very loud. It was the beginning of our punk phase and so it was a completely different sort of intensity to the early more pastoral stage that we went through.

LARRY: We did some Stranglers covers and a couple of originals. The audience was made up of friends. It was very hot and sweaty. Our friends were very generous, clapping and jumping up and down.

BONO: I cut my finger. I dropped my plectrum, but I kept playing, and blood kept spraying. There was blood all over this white Telecaster, Peter Martin's guitar, which in my head I was trying to put through somebody's TV screen. I heard people shouting: 'There's blood on there!' It was exciting.

EDGE: Bono may have been playing guitar, but I'm not sure it would have been plugged in. Dick was playing with us, so there really wasn't any need for three guitars. Did Bono even own a guitar in those days? I don't think so.

BONO: I think the band said to me, 'You're better at starting a riot than you are at being a musician.' I can't remember if my feelings were hurt or not but they had their way. I remember thinking if I was going to be frontman then I had to develop a persona. There were a few songs I was writing, one of which was a song called 'The Fool'. We studied theatre in school and there was a Shakespearean thing going on in my head. I wanted to create this personality that was the opposite to Ziggy Stardust, that wasn't super-cool, that was maybe super-uncool and childlike and could get away with saying things. The lyrics were changing every time I sang that song but when I had to write them down to do a demo I realized they were kind of shite. 'Alive in an ocean, a world of glad eyes, insane!' – that was one line. 'They call me the Fool, I'm gonna break all the rules.' Oh dear!

ADAM: I suppose if punk hadn't happened we would have had to have got better at cover versions but punk happened and we were able to get the very essence of three-chord songs and make something of them, and then that very quickly shifted to us being able to write our own tunes. Not terribly good tunes at the time, but certainly energetic and experimental.

EDGE: I was becoming more interested in writing our own songs. Bono had two and then I went off and wrote something called 'Life on a Distant Planet'. I suppose the process was really finding a collision of melody and guitar that just inspired me and set me off. Even though we ended up playing the song on Irish TV, it never really got beyond the initial inspiration to become a full-fledged tune. It was really just two or three ideas put together. I was actually thinking about it the other day. I should probably finish it. So that was my first tune with the band although I had written some material years before with my brother, sort of comedy stuff, goofing around with tape-recorders. It was inspiring to suddenly see Bono write some tunes and then to discover that I could do it too.

LARRY: I know we were trying to write songs but we found it difficult to finish many of the ideas. There was a lot of strumming on guitar, Adam and I would just play along. And after days or even weeks of strumming, maybe a verse or a chorus would appear, and then maybe some lyrics. It was all pretty uneventful … and then something would go off out of nowhere and the ideas would come together. The process can be the same, thirty years later.

ADAM: By time we were rehearsing Wednesday afternoons, Saturdays and Sundays, just to try and get to the end of a song. Sometimes we would rehearse up in Edge's house because his parents were pretty tolerant, we could hang out all day and drink as much coffee as we wanted. It was easy for me and Edge to get together there, and sometimes Larry would come out. He always had issues with his parents about whether he was allowed out at certain times and he always needed a car to transport the drums. Then Bono would drop out depending on whether he could get transport, whether he could come out on the back of a bike or in somebody's car. That was where we came up with 'Street Missions', which became our big set-piece. Edge and myself came up with the basic verse and then on one of Bono's trips out he came up with the chorus and the idea for the lyric.

Oh no man, I just got here You got me thinking
I'm about to leave Someday, maybe tomorrow
New direction, hello Oh no no no
I walk tall, I walk in a wild wind
I love to stare I love to watch myself grow
Someday, maybe tomorrow
New direction, hello
Oh no no no no no no no
Street missions ...

EDGE: Fantastic! It means absolutely nothing! I don't know whether Bono was ever really writing it about anything. I think he was just improvising vocal melodies over these riffs and these were the sounds that he used at the time and he used to weave those sounds into words and eventually meanings would arrive. It's like speaking in tongues, maybe not divinely inspired but from your own inner jumbled-up psyche.

BONO: What was interesting about 'Street Missions' was that it ended with this huge guitar solo in a completely different time signature. Everyone says there were rules that came up with punk, such as no guitar solos. But we said, 'Of course we can play a guitar solo if we want to.' We were never going to be a punk band really, because there were just other things that we were interested in, like the lyricism of Edge's playing.

ADAM: The first half was quite punky and energetic. Then, because we didn't know how to end it, we decided to have a guitar solo. It didn't really make much sense but, in a way, it worked live. It gave a bit of an instrumental break for Bono before he came back to sing the final bit.

BONO: Edge really did have something, even then. When he started to play you watched him. He was remarkable, and he stood so still at that point. He didn't move. He was running around playing chords, but when he played the solo he would stand so still and then *everything* just became still. It was as if everything stopped, time itself stopped. He was a storyteller in his guitar solos. They were little journeys.

EDGE: A lot of our songs had those strange twists, 'Turn left at Greenland!' Sometimes they didn't work out, it has to be said. Then occasionally you'd just go 'Wow'. Not many bands have ever done that, shown the sheer imagination to go to this other place. I think that came out of writing the way we did, in a rehearsal situation with everybody playing at full throttle, and then you are open to massive changes of mood and direction within a song because you can do that when everyone is present at the same moment. Everybody hits this completely different thing together and you get an instant realignment of the instruments. It's very hard to write that sort of thing because you never go there really if you were to sit down on your own. I think the strength of the band is shown in the ability to make those kind of radical moves.

ADAM: In keeping with the punk ethic of non-musicianship, our early song-writing was characterized by a lack of virtuosity. So we would always try and bolt on an unexpected bit, some sort of change that would in some way get us over the fact that we weren't doing it very skilfully. I suppose we were looking for drama in what we were doing. And when you're not a virtuoso, it's very hard to create that drama except by hard cuts; it's either a drum break or something very fast or something unharmonious or whatever. We tended to find those bits and just stick them together. We were very proud of 'Street Missions'. We used to start and end our sets with it. It was our 'Freebird'.

LARRY: We played a gig during a break at a school disco, in the basement of the old school building. It used to get really hot and sweaty down there, and the walls would drip with condensation. As we were playing, The Edge decided to run up the wall. He slipped and fell flat on his arse. I wasn't sure whether to laugh or cry.

EDGE: In a moment of pure adrenalin, I tried to run up the wall, not realizing that this move might have been OK earlier on in the day but was now lethal, as the walls were dripping with sweat from a few hours of heaving disco. So I take a run at it and try to step up the wall but fail to get any traction whatsoever and my shoe slips and 'whack!', I end up flat on my back in the middle of the stage, still playing, in agony but pretending that it hadn't hurt at all.

We had a gig lined up at the Nucleus, a little club in Raheny, but we played so badly at the school disco that the DJ who worked at the Nucleus, who was also from Mount Temple, wouldn't put us on. He insisted on coming to an audition. We played him some songs and very begrudgingly he put us on at the Nucleus. Before the show we decided to go and get drunk, because we knew that was what you did when you were in a rock band. So, as appalling as we normally were, we were just indescribably bad, and the sound was atrocious. We were in this tiny little prefab scout hut and we couldn't afford a proper PA. We recorded the show and a couple of days afterwards we listened to it in utter disbelief at what we were hearing. Bono was just bellowing and all you could hear was this really distorted noise that sounded like the early Stooges. Unfortunately I think we were playing an Eagles song. That was the same occasion when Bono introduced 'Jumping Jack Flash' and my brother started playing 'Brown Sugar', getting his Stones mixed up. It was truly one of the absolute low points. Everyone was out of tune. On the recording you can hear the DJ leaning in when we're halfway through the set saying, 'Would you ever just stop? Please stop! They're all sitting outside.' Listening back to that show, it was the first time I thought 'Oh God, no! This isn't going to work.' We were so hopelessly inconsistent. One show would have that moment of promise and coming together and then the next three would be utterly crap.

BONO: Dick was a very innovative guitar player. He was a bit of a genius, and the government were paying for him to go to college. They did not just give him a grant, they actually paid him. He had some mad idea at the time, he was talking about computers, saying they were going to take over the world and change the way we all live. His head seemed full of all that stuff. It could be very, very funny with Dick in the band, because you'd call out for one song, and the two Evans brothers would play two different ones – it was a cacophony. And I remember Larry, in a very Larry-like way, used to keep asking the question: 'Is Dick really in the band?' I remember him saying to Edge: 'Are you sure Dick really wants to be in the band?' And then we realized what Larry was saying was: 'Does he really have to be in the band?' Because there's nothing more terrifying for a drummer than the sound of people tuning their instruments – and loudly. It's still an extraordinary thing to me that Edge won't turn down when he's tuning up. Luckily he has somebody now to tune up for him.

BONO: Our rehearsals at this point were just people screaming at each other from beginning to end. The first television show we did came out of a row about how to end something.

ADAM: As usual, this was very much driven by Bono. He had heard that an RTE producer was coming to meet music teacher Albert Bradshaw about getting the choir for his children's youth programme, *Youngline*.

EDGE: We let it be known that we'd like to be considered for the show.

ADAM: Bono got Albert Bradshaw to agree to bring this guy via our rehearsals. The idea was that we were going to allegedly be this young band that was writing and performing their own songs. Except that particular rehearsal, not unlike most rehearsals, we'd spent most of it rowing and hadn't rehearsed anything and couldn't play anything because we were too busy arguing.

BONO: We were like: 'Wow, this is somebody from the world of show business and television coming to see us!' So we were particularly wired and especially difficult, and when he knocked on the door we were in the middle of a shouting match. We stopped, and we just didn't know what to do because we couldn't play the songs we wanted to play, our own songs. So he said, 'I believe you write your own songs?' I said, 'Yes, we do, yeah.' He said, 'Can I hear one?'

ADAM: Bono told us to play Ramones songs because they were melodic and we could get through them reasonably easy.

BONO: So we played him The Ramones 'Glad to See You Go'. He said, 'That's amazing. Did you write that?' And I said 'Yeah.' And they're all looking at me – we wrote that? 'Yeah, we wrote that.' And then we played him another Ramones song. And he said, 'You wrote that too?' And I told him, 'Yeah.'

ADAM: The producer was saying, 'Gosh, they're amazingly good songs for young people to write.' And we were saying, 'They just come out.'

BONO: And then we got the gig, and when we got to the TV studio we had our own songs. He didn't notice.

LARRY: We played 'Street Missions' and 'Life On a Distant Planet'. It was like being brought into the cockpit on a plane, having never been in a TV studio before. It was much smaller than I thought it would be. It was white, with lights hanging from the ceiling. There was no audience. It was a really amazing and weird experience, coming from my kitchen into a TV studio. It was another milestone. We couldn't believe that we were actually going to be on TV. Nowadays it's not such a big deal, everybody's on TV. For an Irish punk

STEVE AVERILL GAVE US A LIST OF NAMES FOR THE BAND, SOME OF THEM WERE A LITTLE TOO ADVANCED FOR ME THEN... AS THEY ARE NOW. FLYING TIGERS, THE BLAZERS. OH DEAR, OH DEAR. WHERE WOULD ROCK 'N' ROLL BE WITHOUT PUNS? U2'S APPEAL WAS ITS AMBIGUITY. IT HAD OPEN-ENDED INTERPRETATIONS. I HATE THE NAME, BY THE WAY. SOON AFTER IT CAUGHT ON, I STARTED REALIZING THAT IT TOO WAS AN AWFUL PUN. BONO

band in the Seventies, it was a huge thing. And in a very unpunk moment, I polished the drum kit and cymbals thinking it would look professional.

EDGE: We did the audition for RTE as The Hype, but by the time we did the show we had become U2.

BONO: I liked the name The Hype. But it was the name of a punk rock group in our heads, and it was clear that wasn't where we were going. We were bound for somewhere else. I don't know who became dissatisfied with it or who even thought about changing it, but we went to Steve Averill, or at least Adam went to see him, and he came up with some names.

ADAM: I was hanging off the shirt-tails of anyone that could help us in any way. Steve Averill was the son of a friend of my parents. He had been in The Radiators From Space, a very early punk band who made one album and then he left. They were over in six months and he'd gone back to his day job as a graphic designer. But he was someone who knew the ropes. He would have been probably ten years older than us. I would walk over to his house in Portmarnock. His wife would normally give me coffee or something to eat and we'd listen to music and talk. It's amazing now when I look back, a guy that age talking to a teenager for a few hours on his night off after he's been at work. That was a very generous thing to do. At that stage he was into synthesizers, Devo and Kraftwerk and all that, which I didn't really understand because I preferred the energy of punk. But it's been a long friendship. Steve thought The Hype wasn't a serious name. He started to suggest that we think about what we wore, told us we needed to get some photographs done and he subsequently designed our first poster and some button badges as well.

EDGE: We looked up to Steve Averill because he was part of The Radiators from Space and then discovered that he's a great commercial artist as well. Steve gave us a list of about six possible names, none of which we really liked, to be honest.

BONO: Some of them were a little too advanced for me then … as they are now. Flying Tigers was one. The Blazers. Oh dear, oh dear. Where would rock 'n' roll be without puns? I didn't notice that The Beatles was a pun until very recently, I really didn't. I suppose in my mind they were such great men, the idea that they were merry little punsters hadn't occurred to me.

ADAM: U2 was on there, like the spy plane, which I'd heard about because I came from a flying background. I don't know if the others saw it that way. It wasn't an obvious name, it didn't jump out. It was almost kind of the one that everyone disagreed with the least.

BONO: U2's appeal was its ambiguity. It had open-ended interpretations. In my mind's eye, I was thinking more of a U-boat than I was of Gary Powers and the spy plane, and I quite liked that. Strangely, it turns out that the train line in Berlin that took you to Zoo Station was called the U2 line. You see it everywhere you go in Berlin.

EDGE: It was the least bad of the bunch. We thought about it for a few days and said, 'Well, it's better than The Hype, why don't we just go for it for the moment?' So we picked U2. As time went by we started to like it more and more. The graphic nature of it was very strong. It meant nothing in particular, so we started to like the idea that it didn't have any major connotations. And it also separated us from The Whatevers, you know, The Jam, The Clash, all the bands whose names started with The at that time. Our name was a bit different, but it was by no means a Eureka moment, 'That's the best name we've ever heard!' It was more like, 'It will do'.

ADAM: I think people acknowledge that it was multi-faceted. It was an inclusive name. Also it was only a letter and a number so it could be very big on a poster. And it could be part of normal conversation, so you could slip it into advertising slogans and things like that, so there was a general savviness with how it could work for us.

BONO: I hate the name, by the way. Soon after it caught on, I started realizing that it too was an awful pun. That hadn't dawned on me either. You Too. Oh no!

EDGE: There were lots of puns, bad and good, that the name suggested but we were just interested in the openness of it. We had a series of band badges, 'U2 could happen to anyone' which we had made at the time. Each badge had one word with the name U2 on each one: U2 COULD; HAPPEN; TO; ANYONE. A four-badge set, which only really worked if we were all standing in line in the right order. But it was good for that kind of thing, playing around with different ideas.

LARRY: The first time it was printed in a newspaper, it called us U2 Malahide. They meant to say 'U2 from Malahide', which, of course, wasn't correct either.

EDGE: By this time, Adam had, shall we say, opted out of school.

ADAM: There had been a couple of incidents at Mount Temple. There was no uniform policy at school and I think there had been some talk about whether a boy could get away with wearing a skirt. As I had become a smoker, money was increasingly important because you could buy cigarettes with it. So I had persuaded a number of people to bet me fifty pence each that I wouldn't wear a skirt in school. That was the first incident.

LARRY: I believe there was a streaker in Mount Temple and Adam's name was mentioned. But I didn't see it myself.

ADAM: I have no recollection of a streaking incident, per se. But it is not implausible.

BONO: Adam was known to take off his clothes and walk naked through the school corridors.

ADAM: Around that time it was beginning to become clear to my housemaster, Donald Moxham, that although I was a very reasonable and decent character, I wasn't terribly interested in school. He was a man of a fiery temperament and eventually I think this got to him. I would get caught up in minor incidents but they were matters of great irritation to him. I must say, from where he was standing, he was very tolerant because he was very committed to being a teacher and giving people chances and opportunities, and he had helped us out with rehearsal space and a number of other things. So in a sense we were on the same page but eventually he did say to me that he felt I'd 'outgrown' the school system and there wasn't a whole lot of point in me being there and using up valuable resources, which was a very reasonable way to say 'On your bike'. I suppose I could have protested and maybe could have stayed on. But he gave me the choice. He said, 'The Leaving Certificate exams are coming up and, if you want to, you can come to the school and do your exams.' And with high dignity I said, 'I don't want to do that crappy exam anyway!' It was absolute bluff because I knew I wouldn't do very well. It was all youthful arrogance.

EDGE: Adam became our manager and had cards printed up. For a while, Adam and Bono were certainly the two most vocal characters in the group, myself and Larry being a bit younger. Adam's understanding of such exotic terms as gig and riff gave him a certain authority. I think we were using the word 'rift' until Adam put us right. We were suitably impressed.

ADAM: Even though I was managing the band, whatever that meant, I think I was pretty much being coaxed by Bono. He always had a vision of what he wanted and what he felt the band could do. But I guess I had a lot more time than anyone else, and also the phone rules were a little bit more relaxed in my house. I don't think Bono could make calls from his house. His dad was pretty heavy. So I would call up anyone I thought might be able to help. There was a place called The Spinning Wheel on Mary Street that used to have afternoon gigs that you could go to on Saturdays and Sundays, and I would hang out there talking to people. I was just a brazen spoofer at the time and any kind of titbit of information or contact with show business on any level was enough to keep me going for days.

EDGE: The issue of whether my brother was in the band was starting to come to a head. It was becoming obvious that the four-piece unit had a certain ease. Because we were getting into writing songs as a four-piece there was a natural way of playing with each other that started to develop. But it was a difficult time because I was obviously quite resistant to the idea of Dick not being part of the group. I was somewhat in denial for a while about the good sense of it.

LARRY: Dick was a scientist, and I didn't understand why we had a scientist in the band. I was young and naïve and not very diplomatic. Sorry Dick.

ADAM: We were very sensitive to the fact that we had two brothers in the band. And one of them you went to school with and was, you know, one of the gang. Which I think, in those early days, so much of it is actually just about that: 'Are we a band? Who's in the band? What does it mean?' Dick was obviously a different generation. He was already at Trinity, he didn't really have the same drives as we did. He was an honours student, so it was very hard to feel that his commitment would be the same as anyone else's. He couldn't always get to rehearsals, he couldn't always make various things that were going on and be there for key discussions. There was also something attractive about slimming down to a three-piece music section. It was more the energy of the day, one guitar player doing power chords and you didn't have any excess. We were becoming a bit more finely tuned towards image. We had an inkling of magazines like *Hot Press* and *NME*, some of the punk groups, we were beginning to see their artwork, and I guess it was clear that perhaps Dick didn't really fit into that. The beard may have been a little bit of a problem.

LARRY: It became messy. One time there was a bit of a stand-off. Surprisingly, Dick just turned round and whacked me in the stomach. I think that was the final straw.

ADAM: It was a difficult transition in terms of not really wanting to offend anyone. Edge didn't necessarily have a vote, because of conflict of interest. I don't think he took a position. It was something that myself, Larry and Bono would have been more involved in.

BONO: I have no memory of how that whole thing played out.

EDGE: I rang Dick and broke the news. I fudged it somewhat. I said there was this new thing called U2, which has just four members. That The Hype was being phased out.

ADAM: The exact point of becoming U2 was a talent competition sponsored by Harp Lager in Limerick, on Saint Patrick's Day in March 1978. There was prize money of £500 and a record deal. We had entered as The Hype, and we realized that if we won it, then we would be stuck with The Hype. So we had to change the name before the competition.

BONO: The Hype did a midnight gig at The Project Arts Centre for Paddy's Day. A real gig in a proper Dublin venue! There may have been some celebrating after. I don't think there was much sleep being had. Then we had to be up in the morning to catch a train to Limerick. Some of the Village came along. It was very exciting to be on a train with your mates, going somewhere to play in front of the music business. It was rock'n'roll!

LARRY: My old man and me arrived at Connolly Station at twenty to two to realize that the only train to Limerick left from Houston Station at two o'clock. I remember the old man muttering underneath his breath, 'Oh, what kind of bloody idiot are you!' as we ran back down the platform back to the car. We just about made the Limerick train.

ADAM: There was quite a party. Gavin, Guggi, Strongman and Pod were there. And Maeve O'Regan.

LARRY: I'd never stayed in a hotel before. I think I shared a room with Pod and Strongman. Bono shared a room with Maeve O'Regan. I thought this was mad! He's sharing a room with a girl. I was completely intrigued but I knew my parents wouldn't approve.

BONO: I've always had girlfriends who weren't my girlfriend. At the top of the list was Maeve. We were real soulmates, and we would discuss life and poetry, and sex and faith, and love and fear, and 'all the things that keep us here in the mysterious distance between a man and a woman'. I remember I really wanted to talk to her. I think I had something on my mind. But we were friends, so there'd be no, you know, funky stuff. But then she went off for a walk with Adam and didn't come back for us to have our discussion on poetry and politics and whatever. My feelings were hurt and I realized the power of the Afro, even if it was a reverse Afro. Adam had hair Michael Jackson would be proud of. And he knew how to light up cigarettes and how to tap the cigarette off the box. At the time, I was probably more likely to set myself on fire.

I probably looked like a very confident person. And I had been when I was younger, but there's only so far self-confidence can get you as it turns out. And nothing great ever came out of it. I think art is an attempt to identify yourself. If you're sure of who you are in the world, there's no reason to try and find out. I had been a very confident person and then my mother died and that shook my confidence. When I was seventeen I was kind of getting it back a little bit, because I had discovered now what to do with my life. I might even have been getting right up to annoying levels again. But not quite. Because now you know how far you can fall, so that's always in the background. I was still trying to manage that somehow. But I looked confident on stage. Have you ever seen someone awkward, sort of clumsy, who can swim beautifully? Normally they're just a clod, walking into tables and chairs and tripping over bags but put them in the water and suddenly they are at ease. That's a bit what it's like. So you get to do the thing that you do. And it's an amazing feeling. I gained a lot of confidence from the music.

ADAM: The contest was in a room with a big stage with a PA and lights and all these various seasoned showband musicians doing their stuff, everyone looking to get the record deal, and a couple of other younger more punky types of things, and us.

LARRY: It was an early show starting at six o'clock in the evening. The place was jammed. We watched our competition, not feeling very confident.

EDGE: I had no idea what they were looking for at this show. I thought to myself this could be like some dreadful amateur free-for-all that we're walking into and it'll be won by some guy who's able to sing 'Auld Lang Syne' and drink a glass of water at the same time. But when we arrived we found Jackie Hayden, the judge from CBS Ireland, to be this pretty hip character, so there was a sense that it might be better than we feared. Then we saw some of the acts that went on before us and they were all pretty good musicians. A lot of them were doing covers but some were doing original material. I don't think the songs were much good but they could all play and sing in tune. I was a bit nervous and thought, 'Oh shit, we might just fall at the first fence.'

BONO: There were bands there that could play in time and in tune and with great confidence, all of which we couldn't pull off. But, you know, some bands have everything but *it*. We had nothing but *it*.

EDGE: I think we played three of our songs. All like three minutes, really simple stuff.

LARRY: We did 'Street Missions' and a couple of others.

ADAM: I think we did 'Life On A Distant Planet' and something called 'The TV Song', so named because it sounded a bit like the band Television. It was kind of a melodic, mid-tempo thing whose chief appeal was that we could actually get to the end.

EDGE: I just remember we hit it. Sometimes something goes off in the room. It reminded me of the first gymnasium concert in Mount Temple and I could tell from everyone's face out in the hall that we'd really connected. So that made me feel great, but we still really weren't imagining that we'd won.

LARRY: Everybody with us in Limerick thought we'd done well up there. We didn't get much of a reaction from the crowd but we were the only band to play all original material in the competition. Afterwards we sat in the audience. A few more acts performed then there was a long break while the voting got underway. I can't remember what the voting process was, I don't think it was particularly complicated but I was so excited I couldn't get my head around it. The East Coast Angels came in third. Maeve O'Regan turned to me and said we were going to come first or second. I was telling her she had got the voting system wrong, then an all-girl folk group came in second. I was convinced we'd lost. Maeve said we had won. She was right. We couldn't believe it. Five hundred quid and a chance to record a single. It couldn't get any better than this.

ADAM: This was one of the few occasions when my dad was actually around. He was in Shannon on a stopover and he'd come to the show. It was just unbelievable that we could have won such a thing. I mean, in the way that you think maybe you can win the lottery or something, that was the way I thought about it. And then to have actually won it was the most amazing buzz. I remember grabbing the chair in front of me and slamming it down. I slammed it down on my dad's foot. And he didn't really know why, because he hadn't realized that we'd actually won.

EDGE: Our row just went ballistic. Pod jumped about a foot in the air and landed on top of me, nearly breaking my leg in the excitement. Because of the way the competition was run it was more than likely that we hadn't been placed at all, so from the jaws of utter defeat and ignominy we plucked victory. We couldn't believe it. I was completely shocked. We weren't of an age to go out partying as such but I don't think anyone slept that night. Adam, as the eldest and the person who seemed to communicate better with the grown-ups, went and picked up the cheque. Adam's father happened to be around so he took the cheque off us for safe-keeping and that was basically it. Really it was just a great affirmation to win that competition, even though I've no idea how good we were or what the competition was really like. But to win at that point was incredibly important for morale and everyone's belief in the whole project.

LARRY: There was some kind of parade on the next morning, we watched from the balcony of the hotel. We had to spend the day in Limerick because of the train schedules. We were still too young to get served in the pubs, so we spent the afternoon killing time at a local fairground. We had no real idea how winning in Limerick would change our lives.

ADAM: In a sense that set us off on another course. It was all very amateur but we thought it was the real thing, and the record deal wasn't really a proper record deal when we looked into it, there was nothing to favour the artist. But it got us a little bit further down the line.

BONO: Somebody tried to throw the trophy out of the window of the train on the way back, because it looked like a golfing trophy.

ADAM: There was one more gig for the five-piece Hype after that, in which we bade farewell to Dick. It was in the Presbyterian Church Hall in Howth. It had the whole atmosphere of having tea with the vicar about it. It didn't seem very rock 'n' roll. It was a fun-packed night, though, something for everyone.

BONO: There were actually four bands on that night and Adam was in all of them! He played with The Hype, then he and Edge backed Gavin and Guggi in the first Virgin Prunes show, then he did a couple of songs with Steve Averill's new synth band, The Modern Heirs. And U2, of course. What was so great about Adam was he always knew what he wanted and was brave enough to say it. And what he wanted was to be in a band and go all the way.

EDGE: It was a pivotal moment. We did cover versions as The Hype, then came back on and did a set of originals as U2.

Dick was obviously a bit disappointed that this was the end but I think he accepted it with a certain fatalism. There were no tears, no heavy scenes. But there was a certain sadness from my point of view. He was my mate and my brother. We had been really close for so many years and had been real partners in music, and this was the parting of the ways. But I had to acknowledge that it was the right thing for everybody. As a four-piece I think there was a sense of real excitement. That stripped-down outfit had a tightness and a focus which was really appealing. We were looking forward to the next songs, the next gigs. We'd really caught the fever.

These days Dick is busy mostly doing research in the computer science world. I see him regularly and he still plays guitar and remains involved in music. I'm sure he harbours some regrets about the train leaving the station without him. He would have loved being part of it all. But I'm sure he doesn't have any question in his mind about whether it could have been different. Even then there was a symmetry to U2 that The Hype never had. It wouldn't have worked in the same way with two guitar players. His playing was so quirky, so unique. He's so brilliant. At the beginning he was a much better guitar player than me, he taught me how to play, but his natural style was always different. He is more of a cerebral character and that really came through in his playing.

ADAM: I remember the significance of us becoming U2 that night, of it just being the four of us. It was a feeling of OK, now we're where we should be, playing our own material and everything is in place. Next week: *Top of the Pops*!

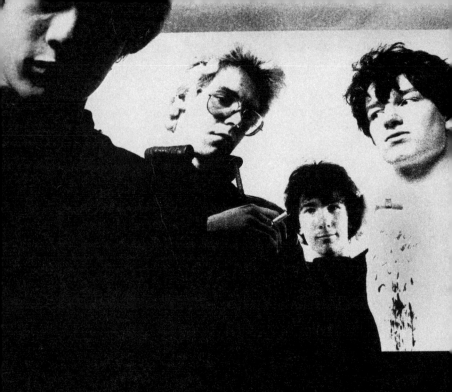

1978 - 1980

STARING
AT THE SUN

Edge

IT WAS A VERY SLOW PROCESS FOR ME TO FINALLY COME TO THE CONCLUSION THAT THIS WAS WHAT I REALLY WANTED TO DO WITH MY LIFE.

Maybe it occurred to Adam first because, at that point, he was adrift and music was a life-raft. But I wasn't in that position. I had lots of options. I just didn't have any real interest in anything other than music.

I was waiting to find the thing that would become my life's work – and it found me. I fell into it and eventually, when the band started getting good and we started writing songs, I realized this was what I wanted to do. It wasn't that I had always harboured a secret ambition to become a rock star. That came later. I wouldn't have wanted to be in any other band. At first we were all going nowhere, and decided to go there together. Then something very special started to develop between us. It was a kind of brotherhood, with a loyalty to each other and a belief that we could go all the way. Before we could play, before we could write songs, before we could perform, we believed in ourselves as a band. If I hadn't stumbled into Bono, Adam and Larry, I would probably have gone to college, tried to get a degree in something or other and figured it out from there. I really have no idea where I would be without U2.

LARRY: I was surprised how far we had come. But I didn't want to get too excited about it yet. For now, it was a bit of fun. I wasn't ready to jack everything in for the band. Things at home weren't that simple. I just couldn't do whatever I wanted.

ADAM: The band was it for me, all my eggs were in this particular basket. I didn't really have any other options.

BONO: We were still at school but in my head Mount Temple had become a rehearsal room. I have great feelings of affection for it as a place that helped shape me, myself, my friends and my band, a real sense of pride that we were a part of something progressive.

I really believed U2 were capable of becoming something extraordinary, I am not sure why. But if you look back through the detritus of poor ideas, there were always a few good ones in there. I think the first concept that we had of value was that people who live ordinary lives had extraordinary things in their heads sometimes – most of the time, actually, and that people *are* extraordinary. I think of Patrick Kavanagh saying, 'Nobody need be a mediocrity if he is himself. God creates nothing but geniuses.' Rock 'n' roll tended to simplify the real, reducing all the complicated thoughts and imaginings of a teenager into just 'you want to be rich and you want to get laid'. That is rock 'n' roll. But everyone I knew was more complicated than that. They all had mad thoughts in their head as they were growing up, and they became less mad as they grew older. And that's a shame. Young people are dealing with big concepts like death and the elusiveness of being a man or a woman. I wanted to write about all of those things. The sneer of punk just didn't explain enough to me, and the power chord didn't say enough to me about whatever it was that was going on in my head and my life.

I was surrounded by extraordinary people. Guggi always had a different way of seeing the world. My father used to stand over us when we were both drawing and he'd look down and say: 'You've really got a talent ... Guggi!' And he really did. Even as a kid using biros he was an amazing visual artist, a prodigy. His family knew he was gifted and they wanted everything to work out for him but they weren't equipped to know what to do with an arty child. On our street, I don't think any family was. So Guggi and Gavin formed the Virgin Prunes but Guggi was never really interested in music. For him the Prunes was a way into becoming a performance artist.

But I always knew he was great. Not just because he could draw a likeness but because he saw things that other people didn't see. Even if it was just money on the ground – which it often was, by the way. He could spot a fifty-pence piece at a hundred yards.

He had an incredible eye for adventure and opportunity. We used to go to all the amusements when we were in town, because people who win are so excited they never collect all the money, there's always something that falls out. There is a great moment when all the coins shoot out and it feels like somebody jumping in a swimming pool made of silver. We could always live on our wits around town, and we used to describe the people we'd meet by sounds rather than words. He'd be looking at the queue outside the Harp Bar and he'd look at me and give a high-pitched tweet. And I'd say: 'Oh that guy, the red-haired guy with the tiny head. Yes!' I always knew who he meant. We developed this sort of code, a way of reinterpreting the world.

We followed one fellow from the amusements all around town, he was just so interesting to us. He had a Mohican haircut, a blanket over his head, and he had a big staff. We'd never seen anything like this in our lives. We

ADAM WAS VERY PERSUASIVE. HE HAD PRINTED UP CARDS WITH 'ADAM CLAYTON, MANAGER OF U2', AND HE WAS CALLING PEOPLE. THIS WAS THE POST-GELDOF WORLD IN WHICH IT WAS OK TO HUSTLE AND HASSLE FOR A PLACE AT THE FRONT OF THE QUEUE. BONO

followed him round the back streets up to the Project Arts Theatre. That was Mick Mulcahy, the rightfully acclaimed artist – I think he might have been on mushrooms at the time. We walked into the Project, a place where arty, middle-class people were hanging out, and there was a naked man crawling around on his belly in flour. This was Nigel Rolfe the slightly less acclaimed artist! He had laid out white and black powder and then he crawled across it. Myself and Guggi were laughing so much there were tears. These people were into performance and into Dada – we didn't even know what Dada was. But we were both having daddy problems, so we liked the sound of it!

We met Jim Sheridan around this time, the playwright who became a great film-maker. And Mannix Flynn, who had been in and out of borstal and had written some very powerful pieces about it. He had great energy, and his eyes were full of laughter and mischief. He was talking about the theatre and how to use the space of being on a stage, how to move your body and make people believe you when you're pretending. He started giving myself, Gavin and Guggi classes in mime. With U2 and the Prunes and all this interesting new stuff going on, it really felt as if something special was unfolding.

EDGE: The Virgin Prunes presented an opportunity for Dick, right at the moment when The Hype morphed into U2. Gavin and Guggi wanted to put a band together, because at that point U2 (minus Bono) were their backing band. Bono saw Dick as a perfect foil to Gavin and Guggi's naturally avant garde approach, I thought it was a brilliant idea so I called Dick and he seemed cautiously optimistic. Next thing they were in rehearsal and it was as if they had been together for years. I have to say I felt a little off the hook when that worked out. I really didn't like the idea of leaving him stranded.

BONO: I always liked Dick. I thought he was experimental and extraordinary. I think he was actually better suited, with that experimental head, to the Virgin Prunes.

ADAM: So Gavin and Guggi put their own band together with members of the Village and my days as an honorary Prune came to an end. I liked the

Prunes, we all did, even though they were almost the opposite of U2. But I had no difficulty with the concept, the exhibitionism of Gavin and Guggi and the fact that it was about making a noise and offending people. I was always happy to make as much noise as possible.

LARRY: We spent the £500 Limerick prize-money on a few things. We did our first photo shoot. Bono, Adam and Edge took a trip into Ireland's only punk clothing shop, No Romance, owned by the Moylett sisters, Regine and Susan. They got fitted out in some new gear.

BONO: We had a very clear idea about what we wanted. I had in my head a white background and we were trying for this kind of early Sixties junior Velvet Underground look. And everyone had to wear drainpipes, because that's what you did if you were in punk rock. Larry refused and came to the photo shoot in flares. Flares were the enemy, they were a hippie leftover, so we tried to hide him at the back.

ADAM: Steve Averill had organized the photo session with the intention of making a good poster. It was a big deal for us to get a poster with colour, a big red U2 on it, and a picture of us all. These status things really meant a lot in those days. Looking at it now, we look like kids. The photos were taken by a girl called Phil Sheehy and they were the first pictures of us printed in *Hot Press* magazine.

EDGE: *Hot Press* was *the* Irish music magazine and we all read it. Bill Graham was one of the writers that we really respected. He had a remarkable way of writing which could be quite impenetrable at times but nonetheless he had a heart and soul for music which came through in his work so clearly. We were big fans, and somehow Adam persuaded him to come and meet us.

BONO: Adam was very persuasive. He had printed up cards with 'Adam Clayton, Manager of U2', and he was calling people. This was the post-Geldof world in which it was OK to hustle and hassle for a place at the front of the queue. Suddenly climbing Mount Everest by helicopter was all the rage. You could get away with things if you were smart. There was a little bit of that in us: who can we rope in? And Bill knew that and let us put the lasso around his neck.

ADAM: I was managing the band inasmuch as I was making the phone calls and trying to get gigs out of people. Really all that meant was ringing them two or three times a week and eventually they'd give in. But Bono's natural street suss of just getting connected, of knowing where to look for gigs and what things to do next would all have qualified him as being very functioning in that leadership role. It was Bono's idea to ring *Hot Press* and arrange to meet with Bill. The idea was to bring him out to a rehearsal in Mount Temple, play him a few songs live, and then go down to the local pub, the White Horse, and get some information from him. We never went to pubs, so it all seemed very grown-up.

Fair dues to Bill, he did come out and sit through us thrashing out some songs. He was a very open-minded, curious guy. We were schoolboys at the time, knowing nothing really and barely able to play our instruments. But he sat in the pub with us and gave us some pearls of wisdom.

EDGE: Bill's most useful advice was, 'Find a good manager.' We said, 'That sounds good. Do you know any?' And he said, 'There's one guy. He's managing a band called Spud at the moment. His name is Paul McGuinness.' Bono said, 'Can you get me his phone number?' And that was it. As a result of that first meeting I think we got a few column-inches in *Hot Press*, really just a tiny little mention that Bill put in with a photo. But it was typical of him to do that. He saw a spark in us and was ready to fan it in any way he could. That's what he was about. He loved to get a feel for what was happening in the various garages across suburbia. He was willing to come out to Clontarf to meet a bunch of schoolkids because there was just a small chance that something interesting might be going on.

BONO: Some people are given the gift of seeing what's wrong with the present. A few people are given the gift of thinking what might be in the future. Bill was in the latter group. He was never so pissed off about where things were because he knew what might be round the corner. He was great at that. It's a rare thing, you know.

PAUL MCGUINNESS: I was born in an army hospital in Germany in 1951, where my father was stationed with the RAF. I spent only a year there, then we moved to a succession of other RAF bases. My father was from Liverpool, which is known as the biggest Irish city outside Ireland. My mother was a school-teacher from Kerry. They decided, I think, for cultural or perhaps even religious reasons, to send me to boarding school in Ireland. So in 1961, from the age of ten, I attended Clongowes Wood College, run by the Jesuits.

I thought Ireland was a very strange place when I came here first. I found it hard to understand what people were saying. But I made the best of it and by the time I left school, I thought of myself as Irish. I went to Trinity College in Dublin to study psychology and philosophy. I lost interest in psychology almost immediately. It was a very extreme form of psychology that was being promulgated at the time; they were all behaviourists and there were a lot of white rats and not much discussion about the inner life of the mind. I carried on with the philosophy, although to be fair to my tutors, I wasn't doing very much work. I quickly became friendly with a bunch of people who were more interested in listening to records and getting to know girls and smoking joints. That was our way of life. I was involved in the theatre with the Trinity Players, did a bit of acting (not very well), directed a few plays and edited the college magazine for one term. I had a bit of fun with that, too much fun as it turned out. I insulted Brendan Kennelly, the Junior Dean, on a fairly regular basis, which really got up his nose. At the end of my third year, I got a letter from Kennelly saying I wasn't able to sit exams because I hadn't been to any lectures. This kind of proscription was unheard of, since it was customary for students to avoid lectures, but it was Kennelly's revenge, so that was the end of that. I had to leave Trinity.

My parents insisted on my enrolling at the University of Southampton, near where they lived in Bournemouth. The idea was that I would stay somewhere where they could keep an eye on me. But that didn't appeal to me at all and after a week or two, I caught the train to college and just stayed on all the way to London. I did various jobs: mini-cab driver, working in a book warehouse, travel guide on pilgrimages to Lourdes. At the end of that year I had earned enough money to return to Trinity and repeat my third year. I was only halfway through the year when I was offered the job of location manager on a movie, John Boorman's *Zardoz*. My only qualification was that I knew the production manager and he knew I wanted to move into the film business. All the job really involved was getting the trucks parked in the right location and making sure the catering tent wasn't in shot, that kind of thing, just servicing a small, military-style filming operation. But I took the job and made a little bargain with myself that if I was still working in films by the time the exams came round I wouldn't bother doing them.

Looking back on that period, I wanted to be either a film producer (I never wanted to be a director, funnily enough) or the manager of a big rock and roll band. I knew of people like Brian Epstein (manager of The Beatles), Andrew Oldham (manager of The Rolling Stones) and Albert Grossman (manager of Bob Dylan) and I thought this was a great job to have if you can get it, involving a great deal of creativity of the most interesting kind – getting together with a small group of people and building something that had cultural impact. I was never a musician or even a frustrated musician. I just

BILL AND I WOULD TALK ABOUT THIS IDEA OF THE 'BABY BAND'. WHAT IT REALLY MEANT WAS STARTING FROM SCRATCH, NOT WITH PEOPLE WHO HAD BEEN IN LOTS OF OTHER BANDS AND WERE JADED. IT SEEMED TO ME THAT A YOUNG, AMBITIOUS BABY BAND COULD USE DUBLIN AS A BASE TO TAKE OVER THE WORLD. PAUL

couldn't play anything, a fact that was obvious to me. But I was a music fan. I bought records when I could afford them and read the music press, and as students, a few of us ran a mobile disco for a while, and put on concerts.

One of my friends, Michael Deeny, was managing Horslips, a folk-rock band formed by some smart and talented men who were all working in ad agencies and jobs like that. They became hugely popular in Ireland. At the time, I was still a student and they were all a bit more grown-up than me, but they were my friends and I saw a lot of them. I noted how they went about starting a group and getting a record deal and acquiring vans and roadies and filling out carnets (customs forms) and I developed a taste for it. So I started to look for a band to manage. I experimented a little; there was a composer called Shaun Davey whom I managed to get a hit single for. He did the music for a television commercial for the National Dairy Council. It was called 'The Pride of the Herd'. We released it on CBS and the Council bought thousands of copies to give to farmers and it went to number one.

An old Trinity friend called Don Knox had a quite well-known local folk group, who rejoiced in the name Spud. They probably thought that some of what was making it work for Horslips might rub off on them, so they asked me to manage them. They were a five-piece group with a drummer and they were playing cabaret in tiny bars around the country. Horslips had opened up the ballrooms for a folk-tinged rock band and so I started booking them to the same promoters. But it was difficult – I think it's fair to say they weren't as charismatic as Horslips and they were also less ambitious. It was very difficult financially working with them because they had families and they needed the money, so there was very little leeway to do the sort of things you needed in terms of posters and stageclothes and so on. Their sights were set fairly low.

They used to go to Sweden a few times a year, where the difference between the exchange rates meant they could make quite good money. They'd been dropped by their record label, Polydor, and so we made up a label called Break Records and recorded an album which Sonet, a Swedish record company paid for. I licensed that to the showband label Release in Ireland. So

I was learning how you assemble the finance to do something more businesslike than just be a band and rent gear and a van and always be broke. I tried to be quite professional but they were always trying to fire each other, in different combinations. Two of them would come and see me in the morning and say, 'You've got to get rid of the other three.' Then, in a different permutation, some of them would come back in the afternoon and say, 'No, no, we don't want to get rid of the ones we were talking about before. We've got to dump the other guys.' So they weren't very loyal to each other.

Bill Graham was a friend of mine at Trinity. He seemed to know a great deal about music and always had a couple of interesting albums under his arm. We often used to listen to music together, and as time went by, when I was managing Spud and he was working for *Hot Press*, we used to go to nightclubs and dream about the idea of taking an Irish band to the very top. Horslips had already shown that they could get themselves signed abroad from a Dublin base. They had a number of record deals over the years, with Atlantic, RCA, Mercury. It's true they were frequently dropped but they made ten albums and had four or five record deals. But they always had their own label in Ireland. They made quite good money here and used to invest their profits in loss-making tours of Germany or Britain or even America, where they would try and gain a toehold.

Bill and I would talk about this idea of the 'baby band'. What it really meant was starting from scratch, not with people who had been in lots of other bands and were jaded. Youth is important. I don't think there's much point in trying to make it if you're twenty-seven or twenty-eight. It seemed to me that a young, ambitious baby band could use Dublin as a base to take over the world, rather in the way that Horslips had tried but failed to do. So I used to look around at all the bands. I was asked to manage a few but turned them down. I was a freelance film technician, which was reasonably well paid when there was work, and though I made very little money from the music side of things, I was married by then, to Kathy Gilfillan, whom I met in college. My wife was supporting me to some extent but my needs were modest. I drove an old banger and we lived in a two-roomed flat in Ballsbridge.

I think Bill mentioned U2 in March 1978. The way I recall it, they hustled him into going to a rehearsal and played some songs and he said, 'But those are Ramones songs!' They were embarrassed that he knew they were Ramones numbers and not theirs, but they did have a song or two of their own and he must have seen something in them. He told them they needed a manager and it should be me. I then started to get phone calls from Adam. Eventually, after a couple of missed opportunities, he came round to see me with a demo tape, which may have just been a recording of a rehearsal. I didn't even have a tape deck, so we played the cassette on my telephone answering machine. I was

U2 WERE DOING THEN, BADLY, WHAT THEY NOW DO WELL. BONO WAS AT THE FRONT OF THE STAGE TRYING TO ENGAGE THE AUDIENCE, EDGE WAS PLAYING A KIND OF JANGLY GUITAR, ADAM LOOKED AS IF HE KNEW EXACTLY WHAT HE WAS DOING AND THEY WERE ALL STANDING IN THE SAME POSITIONS AS THEY STAND ON STAGE NOW. PAUL

pretty naïve about music myself at that stage. I wasn't a musician, so I really couldn't tell how coarse it was. Listening to it subsequently it really was pretty rough but it must have had something, because I agreed to go and see them.

ADAM: I think we met him at the entrance of the Project Arts Centre. He is about ten years older than us, so he would have been twenty-seven. It's a big age difference if you are seventeen. He struck me as a grown-up but definitely quite cool, in leather jacket and jeans. He had a certain authority.

PAUL: They were opening at the Project for a band called the Gamblers, who were managed by my kid sister. U2 were the support and were clearly better. They were doing then, badly, what they now do well. Bono was very unusual in that he was at the front of the stage trying to engage the audience, to get them to look in his eyes. Most other singers at that time were looking anywhere but at the audience. Edge was playing a kind of jangly guitar but it was notes rather than chords and you could kind of make out what he was trying to do, even if he wasn't quite getting one hundred percent. Adam looked as if he knew exactly what he was doing. I wasn't really looking at it from a musical point of view at all – I just thought he looked like a proper bass player. Larry was bashing away at his drum kit, and they were all standing in the same positions as they stand on stage now.

I met them afterwards and we went into the Granary Bar next door and I bought them drinks, which, of course, they were too young for.

EDGE: In Ireland there was still a folk memory of the days of 'British rule' that would come out in odd ways. If you had a 'west Brit' accent like Paul, people would sit up and take notice. It was unconscious but I saw it often happen. He was only twenty-six but he definitely commanded everyone's respect. In fact hard men, some of them we hung out with, were terrified of Paul. His first job for U2 was getting us served in the Granary Bar, which was notoriously difficult. We'd been thrown out many times before, but he organized drinks and suddenly everyone is thinking if he can get a round of drinks in here then probably he is the right sort of guy to represent us.

LARRY: Paul made a big impression with his refined accent and well groomed look. He had cool shades on, though they might have been tinted bi-focals. I remember he was very taken with Bono's stage presence. And I assume he must have thought the rest of us were OK, because we talked about management.

BONO: Paul had an air of confidence about him, as he does now. One of his great gifts is he makes something normal by saying it. An idea that seems a little difficult to envision becomes possible because he's talking about it. He would have been saying:

'The way it is, you know, is you work up a few songs, you try them out live, you then record them.' 'Then you may buy a van?' I think was my response. He said: 'No, no, then you've got to go to a record company. And then you make your first album and then you start to tour.' 'And then you may buy a van?'

All we wanted was to get our hands on a van because then we could pay our way. One night we went to Kerry to play a bar where you slept upstairs to save having to get a guesthouse. The owner of the bar appeared generous: 'Sandwiches, teas, coffees, whatever you want, take it, don't be shy.' So, of course, we ate every sandwich in sight and drank everything we could. That night after the gig, where only seventy people turned up, he was to give us our fee, a hundred pounds, less the sandwiches, and the accommodation. We ended up with thirty quid … but the van was forty! So there was a feeling that if we got the van we might actually make some money. Somehow if the manager could subsidize our van … and he looked like he might have a few bob with that accent of his. But his line was: 'It's all there. You've just got to get better at it. But it's all there.'

LARRY: I was cautious of Paul. Even at our stage, there were stories of managers and record companies ripping bands off. Paul had some experience of management from his time with Spud. It seemed an odd choice for a man who was obviously bright and intelligent. But what would I know, I was still a snot-nosed kid.

EDGE: I don't think Paul was ready to start managing somebody else. The Spud experience had not exactly been a triumph. He had then got involved with promoting various other bands in Sweden, some of whom had declined to pay his commission because he was in Dublin, they were in Sweden and they weren't coming home, so feck off. He was a bit sore about that. Anyway, we got on pretty well with him but he didn't say there and then whether he would be interested in managing us.

ADAM: Initially, out of that first meeting, he said, 'You guys seem to be doing pretty well as you are. You're managing to get gigs, you're improving all the time, you know, stay in touch.' And we were going, 'But, no, we want more gigs. We want to make a demo tape, we want to make a record.' His attitude was very much, 'You're not really ready yet.' Which I understand now, but at the time it was like a form of rejection, and also we did want a manager to start solving some of the problems, such as money and buying reliable gear and having a van to get to and from gigs. So nothing happened for a while.

PAUL: I thought, well, this could be the band, but we spent a few weeks, maybe months, kind of skirting around each other, inspecting each other and having meetings and just trying to find out whether the other people were smart or committed or on the same wavelength. And we were. They had a great group of followers who used to come to support them and they were ingenious and ambitious and very bright.

BONO: I remember my eighteenth birthday. We went to McGonagles, as I often did with Guggi and Gavin and the Village. It was the Crystal Ballroom when my mother and father used to go there. Now it hosted punk rock gigs. We'd dress up in the most outrageous things we could find in our mothers' wardrobes, or big brother's, and bum into McGonagles. We never had the fare for taxis, so we used to walk most of the way home and get a taxi at the latest point possible, so it would be cheaper. I remember being in O'Connell Street, just lying down, having had just a few drinks, not too many. You know, being drunk was the height of uncool. It really was for losers, the kind of people you didn't want to be. As I say, 'What you mock will overtake you.' I remember lying down and staring up at the sky, and thinking this is a great feeling, to be in a band, to be in this very small scene, to be dressed like a bad extra on *Star*

Trek. And, as I was looking up, a face lowered into my field of vision, the face of a big Garda (Irish policeman). And he was saying: 'Would you get up out of that now? You can't be sleeping out here, this is O'Connell Street!' When we got home, we'd stay up and talk. We'd go into my kitchen and just talk and talk, all about music, talking and talking till the sun came out. It was the morning after my eighteenth birthday I wrote 'Out Of Control'.

Monday morning, eighteen years dawning, I said how long? / It was one dull morning, I woke the world with bawling. They were so glad, I was so sad. There is a birthday song for you: objecting to being born. It is funny, it is teenage, I know, but it is an interesting idea for a song. And realizing that you have no say in the two most important things that happen to you: when you arrive and when you depart the planet. 'I was of the feeling it was out of control...'

EDGE: Bono came in with the idea for 'Out Of Control' and we kicked it around for a while. In the beginning we were such bad musicians that really our songwriting developed out of just finding things that we could play, and so they were very simple riffs, simple ideas, simple chord changes and Bono was always looking for melodies over our jam sessions. 'Shadows And Tall Trees' came out of that kind of situation. Bono or I would sometimes come in with something we had prepared earlier but in the end songs would really succeed or fail based on whether we could play them. I'm not suggesting there were any fantastic gems that didn't see the light of day but if the rehearsal didn't work out, a song wouldn't end up going very far. That was kind of the crucible in which these ideas were tested. And I suppose listening to a lot of music, as we were at that point, our songwriting was influenced by Patti Smith, The Jam, The Clash, Siouxsie and the Banshees, Bowie, Magazine, The Buzzcocks: everything that was around was thrown into the pot and these songs would come out. We were just trying to figure out how to do it properly. So there were many false starts and much trial and error. It was very innovative stuff sometimes but it was far from finely honed. It was really rough and quite eccentric, eclectic and schizophrenic, but the principal thing was just the force, the pure vitality of it. A lot of energy and enthusiasm went into it.

'Out Of Control' was really the point where the songwriting started to become more exciting. It was still effectively the same process, but there was just more form to it. Generally there would be a big jam session and riffs would come out of that, we'd start building ideas around those riffs. There were endless arguments with Larry in rehearsals – 'You've changed your drum part. That's not the drum part you used to play!' – so we devised a system where we would record rehearsals and whenever something was really good we would keep that and it would be our benchmark for whatever aspect of the song it was, the drum or guitar part or vocal melody. That became a big feature in those early rehearsals, working out songs with a little cassette machine.

It was hard to hear Bono, so lyrics were not a major priority. Bono never really talked much about the words; even if there was a song going in full flight you were never really sure if there were any lyrics. They were sort of half-written, so that the odd line here or there really did make sense, then came whole sections that were just 'Bongolese', as we came to call it.

If I wrote a lyric, which sometimes I would do, I'd have to persuade him to sing it, which is always a little bit difficult. There was a song called 'Cartoon World' that I wrote, but Bono collaborated on the lyrics. *Jack and Jill went up the hill / They dropped some acid and they popped some pills! I'm sure that was one of his!*

BONO: I was trying to find our sound through childish things, nursery rhymes. There was a song called 'Concentration Cramp' built around a kid's word game: 'Let's go, concentration, let's go.' All that. 'Cartoon World' was the same. We were trying to figure out our language. It was all very healthy – I think even then we knew we had to find some new kind of cool, based on uncool.

ADAM: We did our first demo at Keystone Studios, which was part of the Limerick competition prize. Jackie Hayden from CBS Ireland was overseeing it, although I think Jackie would be the first to admit he is not a producer. It was horrible, because nobody told us anything. We just sort of set up there, we had no idea what we were doing. We could only just about play together in the same room or on a stage. But put us in a recording studio, where we were spread out and everything was baffled off and you couldn't really communicate, and it was going to sound shit and we were going to play crap. It was absolute hell.

BONO: Never having been in a recording studio in my life, I walked down into the basement of Keystone and there was the most beautiful girl in the world, with the most beautiful voice, sitting in reception. I thought: 'Wow! Do all recording studios have people like you working in them?' It was Mariella Frostrup (later to become a well-known British TV presenter). I remember the excitement of looking at the equipment. It was all very serious. I think we might have been a little tetchy with each other and not very good. The sound in my head wasn't coming out of the speakers. It seemed really lightweight. We were used to the sound in the rehearsal room; the volume of the drums and the cymbals and the rumble of the bass and guitar can cover up a lot of problems.

IT WAS HARD TO HEAR BONO, SO LYRICS WERE NOT A MAJOR PRIORITY; EVEN IF THERE WAS A SONG GOING IN FULL FLIGHT YOU WERE NEVER REALLY SURE IF THERE WERE ANY LYRICS. THEY WERE SORT OF HALF-WRITTEN, SO THAT THE ODD LINE HERE OR THERE REALLY DID MAKE SENSE, THEN CAME WHOLE SECTIONS THAT WERE JUST 'BONGOLESE', AS WE CAME TO CALL IT. EDGE

EDGE: We had no idea what we were doing. I completely misjudged the guitar sounds; I had my guitar at an inexplicably low volume and so when we heard it back it was like a toy guitar. It was literally just not knowing that in a recording studio you can be quite loud.

BONO: And then Larry Mullen Senior arrives and pulls Larry Mullen Junior out of there because he was only fifteen.

LARRY: I had exams the next day, so we could only record for a few hours, then my dad came through the door and said: 'I've got to take him home. He's at school tomorrow'. And I was gone.

ADAM: We were booked in to work through the night, because that was the cheapest time. Then Larry had to go at eleven o'clock. We only just got backing tracks down. Jackie wanted us to record our whole set but I think we only came out with one song finished, a track called 'Inside Out'. It was great to hear yourself recorded but also it was a bit of shock to realize that it really didn't sound that good. It didn't sound like the records we were hearing on the radio.

BONO: I had a problem with my singing voice. I had become a big Siouxsie and the Banshees fan, and whilst that in itself was not a problem, in fact it was one of the great things that could ever happen to you, it is not a great thing to adopt her accent. I was a mimic so I had to be very careful what I listened to because my voice would change shape. Many singers turn out to be really good mimics. David Bowie is a great mimic, as is Mick Jagger. John Lennon was a great mimic, apparently. It makes sense, it's an ear thing, an ability to speak like someone else, take on their accent. It's like being able to draw – that's your eye, this is your ear. So the recordings were preposterous. I developed an English accent. Oh dear, oh dear, oh dear.

When playing live, sheer volume could cover a multitude of sins. In performance, you were lost in the moment, you managed to connect with people. Gavin was a huge David Bowie fan; I was too. But he had it coming out of his ears and all that came with it, Kraftwerk, Brecht, Oscar Wilde. And the archness to my singing, I think, came through him. Whereas when I sang 'Show Me The Way' in the school gym, that wasn't arch at all, I was ringing true. So now you enter into a period of putting on your mother's lipstick and wearing her shoes, which are far too big for you, and you trundle down into the kitchen and all the relatives laugh. It was kind of that: just trying on other people's clothes, but you have to do that to find out what fits. I truly believe U2 is one of the great groups, and I always believed it from early on, but it would have been nice if you could point to our first recordings as evidence. It took me a long time to find my own voice.

LARRY: I thought it sounded amazing! In comparison to what we sounded like in rehearsal, when they played it back through the big speakers and put reverb on, I was completely blown away. I don't remember any difficulty in recording and I wasn't as disappointed as the others with what came out of Keystone. I thought it sounded all right ... sadly.

EDGE: School came to an end. We did a gig in the school car park, our farewell to Mount Temple, and then it was time to decide what to do.

My parents had a kind of *laissez-faire* attitude to parenting, which I can say worked very well in retrospect. They just let us get on with it, whatever it happened to be, and sometimes that wasn't a very good idea but most of the time it was fine. We pretty much decided things ourselves. So I did a deal with my parents. I said, 'Look, this band is getting serious. I don't know where it's going but I'm really enjoying working with these people and what we're doing and I'd like to give it a year and see how we get on. And if, after a year, there's nothing happening and we haven't got a record deal then I will go to college.' I had no real intention of going to college but I knew it would buy me some time. To their credit they agreed and instantly our house became the band hub. That year we did a lot of songwriting in the shed at the bottom of our garden. We turned it into a rehearsal room. There was a drop ceiling which we filled with sandbags and we had a huge mattress on the door and basically stuffed everyone into this space, which if you saw it you would die laughing. It was about ten feet square and we managed to get all of the sound insulation and everybody in to work there. It was great until it rained and the sand got wet and the whole ceiling caved in on us.

NOW YOU ENTER INTO A PERIOD OF PUTTING ON YOUR MOTHER'S LIPSTICK AND WEARING HER SHOES, WHICH ARE FAR TOO BIG FOR YOU, AND YOU TRUNDLE DOWN INTO THE KITCHEN AND ALL THE RELATIVES LAUGH. IT WAS KIND OF THAT: JUST TRYING ON OTHER PEOPLE'S CLOTHES, BUT YOU HAVE TO DO THAT TO FIND OUT WHAT FITS. BONO

BONO: My dad gave me a year. He said, 'Right, you can live at home for one year. But if, by the end of the year, you can't pay your way you've got to get a job or get out of the house.' I thought that was very generous of him. My brother had gone by then, so there was just me and him. It was the Bono and Bob show, and quite a show it was. He was still trying to be the sergeant-major, and I was not a very good private.

LARRY: I left school in 1978. The first and second years of school were a struggle. I took my Intermediate Certificate exams around 77-78. I did quite well to everyone's surprise, including my own. The school offered me a place and a chance to complete my Leaving Certificate exams. However, at that time the economic situation was so bad, people were leaving school with good qualifications and not getting jobs. My sister was working for an American company in Dublin, and they were looking for a junior to join the purchasing department. The company were involved in oil exploration off the coast of Ireland. I ended up working there for a year in the purchasing department, with the prospect of eventually becoming a computer programmer in their geology section.

ADAM: I was still managing the band but we definitely needed someone with more authority. But because Paul McGuinness wouldn't commit, we were always trying to think of someone else to put in that position. There are various people around the Irish music business who probably don't like to remember how they spurned our advances.

PAUL: There was a period at the start of the summer where we circled each other. They went to considerable lengths, looking back on it, to conceal the extent of their Christian belief because I think they felt that if I got wind of that I would run a mile, and they might have been right. That was certainly not explicit and would have worried me.

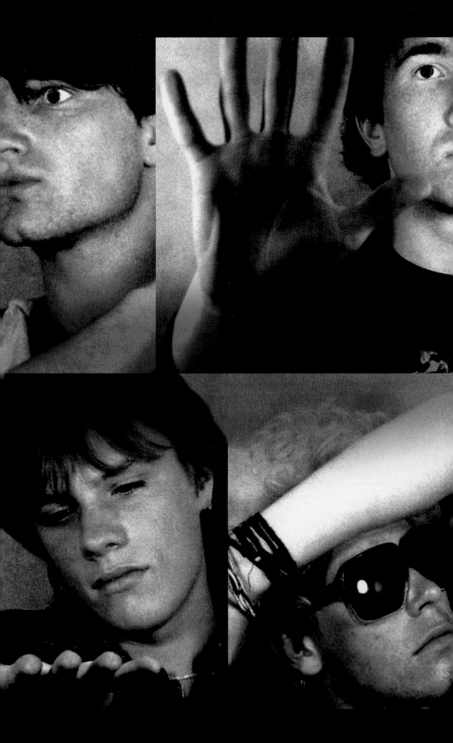

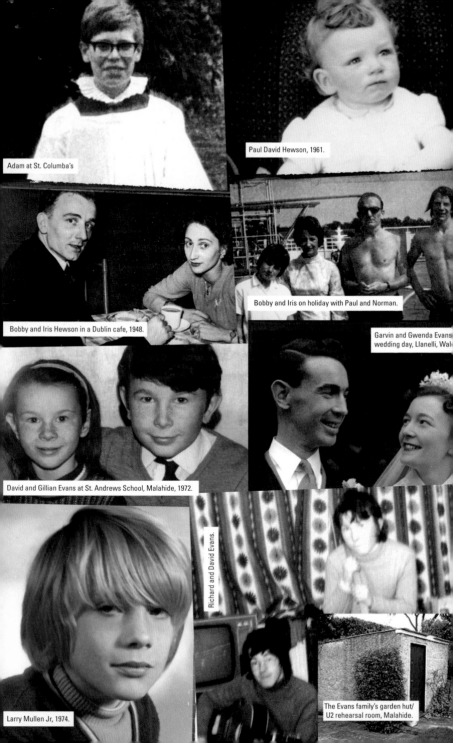

Adam at St. Columba's

Paul David Hewson, 1961.

Bobby and Iris Hewson in a Dublin cafe, 1948.

Bobby and Iris on holiday with Paul and Norman.

Garvin and Gwenda Evans wedding day, Llanelli, Wales.

David and Gillian Evans at St. Andrews School, Malahide, 1972.

Richard and David Evans.

Larry Mullen Jr, 1974.

The Evans family's garden hut/U2 rehearsal room, Malahide.

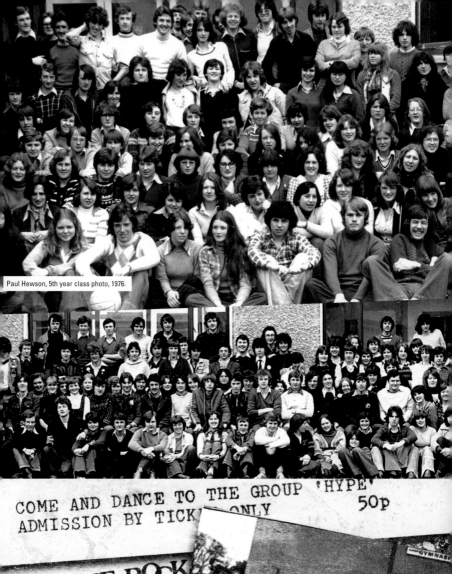

Paul Hewson, 5th year class photo, 1976.

COME AND DANCE TO THE GROUP 'HYPE'
ADMISSION BY TICKET ONLY   50p

LIVE ROCK
CONCERT

at
ST FINTANS Assembly Hall
on
EASTER MONDAY 11th April
Commencing 8 pm till 12 Midnight
dmission guaranteed after 9.30 pm   Adm 50p

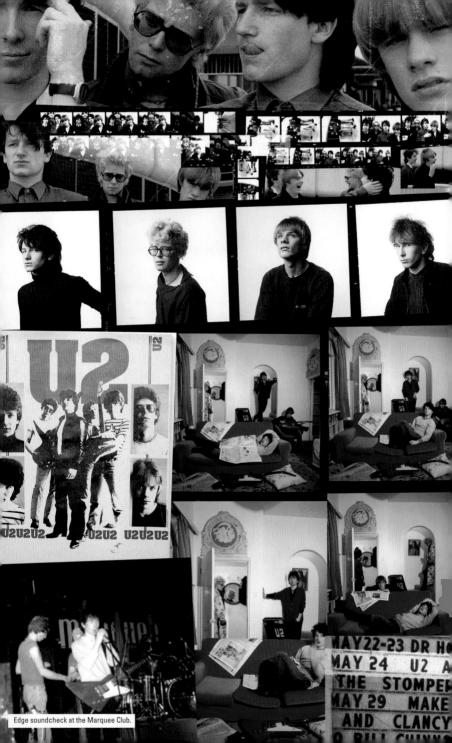

Edge soundcheck at the Marquee Club.

MAY 22-23 DR HO
MAY 24 U2 A
THE STOMPE
MAY 29 MAKE
AND CLANCY

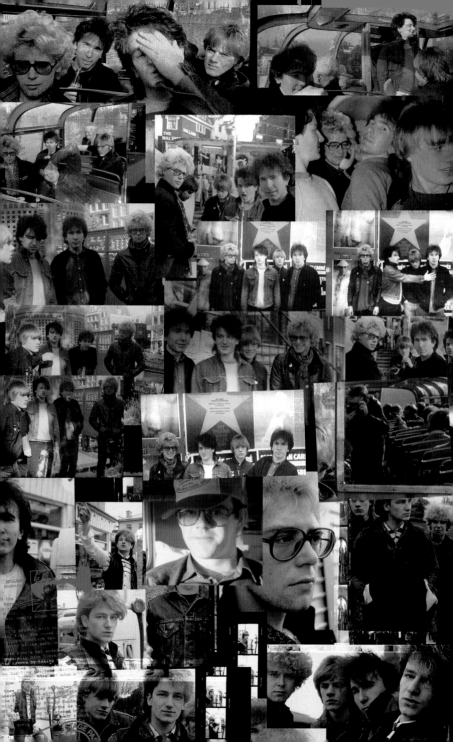

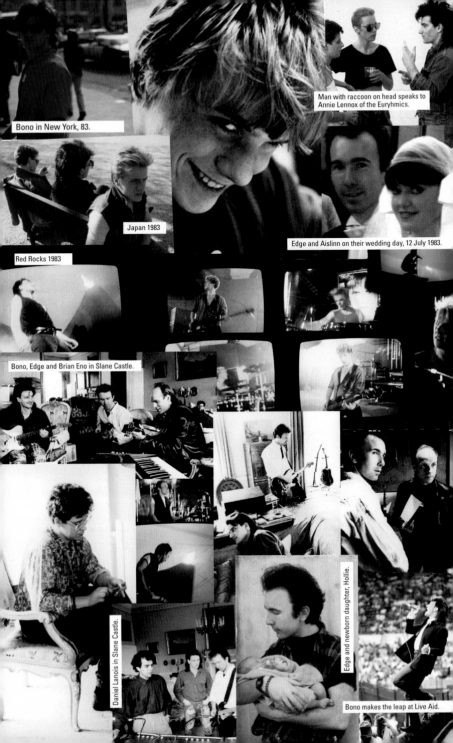

Bono in New York, 83.

Man with raccoon on head speaks to Annie Lennox of the Euryhmics.

Japan 1983

Edge and Aislinn on their wedding day, 12 July 1983.

Red Rocks 1983

Bono, Edge and Brian Eno in Slane Castle.

Daniel Lanois in Slane Castle.

Edge and newborn daughter, Hollie.

Bono makes the leap at Live Aid.

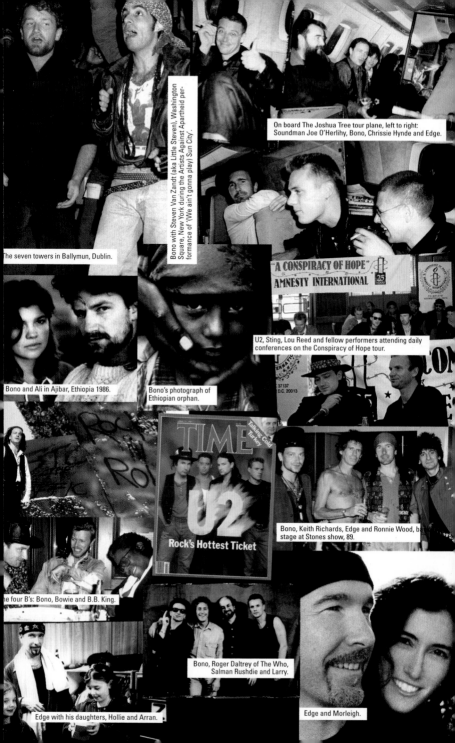

On board The Joshua Tree tour plane, left to right: Soundman Joe O'Herlihy, Bono, Chrissie Hynde and Edge.

Bono with Steven Van Zandt (aka Little Steven), Washington Square, New York during the Artists Against Apartheid performance of '(We ain't gonna play) Sun City'.

The seven towers in Ballymun, Dublin.

"A CONSPIRACY OF HOPE"
AMNESTY INTERNATIONAL

U2, Sting, Lou Reed and fellow performers attending daily conferences on the Conspiracy of Hope tour.

Bono and Ali in Ajibar, Ethiopia 1986.

Bono's photograph of Ethiopian orphan.

TIME
U2
Rock's Hottest Ticket

Bono, Keith Richards, Edge and Ronnie Wood, backstage at Stones show, 89.

The four B's: Bono, Bowie and B.B. King.

Bono, Roger Daltrey of The Who, Salman Rushdie and Larry.

Edge with his daughters, Hollie and Arran.

Edge and Morleigh.

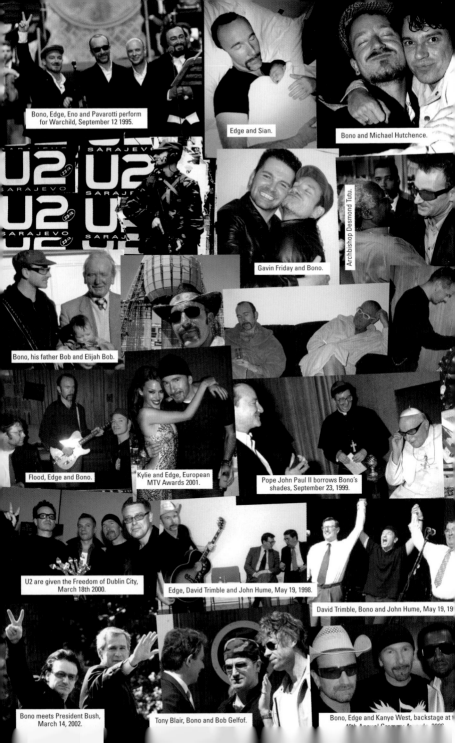

Bono, Edge, Eno and Pavarotti perform for Warchild, September 12 1995.

Edge and Sian.

Bono and Michael Hutchence.

Archbishop Desmond Tutu.

Gavin Friday and Bono.

Bono, his father Bob and Elijah Bob.

Flood, Edge and Bono.

Kylie and Edge, European MTV Awards 2001.

Pope John Paul II borrows Bono's shades, September 23, 1999.

U2 are given the Freedom of Dublin City, March 18th 2000.

Edge, David Trimble and John Hume, May 19, 1998.

David Trimble, Bono and John Hume, May 19, 19

Bono meets President Bush, March 14, 2002.

Tony Blair, Bono and Bob Gelfof.

Bono, Edge and Kanye West, backstage at

EDGE: I guess I started to become spiritually aware around the age of fifteen. We had a religion teacher called Sophie Shirley, who was the first born-again Christian I had ever met. She was really tormented by our class for being naïve, and not very cool but I was always quite interested. I had respect for what she was saying because there were other people in my life who had a similarly strong Christian faith, my maternal grandmother particularly. Then when Bono started talking about it, it struck a chord with me and I was quite interested in seeing what he was exploring. He told me there would be a guy coming down to Guggi's house, which he shared with two of his brothers in Glasnevin, opposite the cemetery. The Willows was the name of the house, and this fellow Shane O'Brien came down and there were about six or seven of us and we sat round drinking cups of coffee, talking about what it was to be a Christian, reading the Bible and praying for some divine inspiration or a clue. That was the first meeting. I know Bono had spoken to Adam about his beliefs but Adam had a completely opposite reaction. He was extremely negative towards any religious organization or anything spiritual. Adam thought this was dangerous and a real affront almost. He came to me one day and said, 'What are you doing? You're just doing this because of Bono. It's not you.' I guess Adam's perception was that through force of personality Bono was turning the group into a Christian group, and he was terrified of that idea. It upset him; he didn't get it.

ADAM: I don't think God was alluded to very much or brought out into the open. I suppose it would have been on my radar because these people used to turn up at gigs, and they were a little bit different. They weren't music people. I don't think the way these guys were selling themselves really rang true to me. That's all I can say. It seemed a little bit too culty and cliquey.

PAUL: The band used to come round to my flat in Waterloo Road and we would have lots of meetings about how to take over the world. I wasn't aware of this at the time but there was a big jar full of coins where I used to dump whatever change I had in my pocket, and this was actually what was financing the band. This is where bus fares and things like that came from.

BONO: That is so sad. But somewhere in the background, we thought Paul must have money, simply because of the way he spoke – and he had a job in the film business. So we would go to his house; first of all we would try to have meetings as close to lunch as possible, so we could get something to eat. And then he had a change jar. Now I don't think we ever robbed out of the change jar. I mean, we might have borrowed and not been serious about putting it back. But I'm sure we told him. I think he said: 'Look if you're stuck there's some change over there.'

ADAM: There are many layers to Paul but back then what really stood out about him was that everything was completely straightforward. He saw life in black and white and things were either honourable or not honourable. He was very much on the side of the artist against big business. I don't know where that came from; perhaps it was because he'd done a bit of theatre and saw actors as people who needed to be looked after. Or maybe it came from later on when he was in the film business. But that was what he brought to it, and a very practical sense of how good we were in terms of presenting a show and our polish and our focus. He was always very generous to us, which is a kindness I gratefully remember now. We never had any money and he was always buying us meals or coffee, and if we were in a pub he would pay for the drinks.

BONO: Paul was not a warm, fuzzy feeling. He was in the film business, and he was getting a little bit of stick from Kathy for spending time on this fanciful idea of breaking a baby band. She was a serious woman and was first bemused, then worried, by Paul spending more and more time on this project. The most striking thing about Paul was: 'I don't want to be your friend. I'll be your manager.' There was no attempt to play at friendship. Very interesting. And so the Village immediately hated his guts, because if he didn't want to be our friend he certainly didn't want to be theirs. He became public enemy number one. I don't think he wanted that sort of 'we're all in this together' relationship. It would be like your doctor or your accountant being too friendly. It was professional, and we were his clients. I think that was the way he saw us.

ADAM: One of the first things Paul did for us was a bit controversial. We were playing a gig in McGonagles with Steve Averill's band The Modern Heirs and another Dublin band called Revolver and we were bottom of the bill, but he made Modern Heirs go on first. I think his argument was that he had someone coming to see us. There was a nasty vibe in the air, and I know Steve was a bit freaked by that. Paul was capable of doing things like that, which you didn't feel very comfortable about, but you liked the fact that there was someone out there defending your position. That would have been the beginning of our ascent.

BONO: My old man met Paul. Paul speaks with the low hum of the British ascendancy, so that means my dad immediately doesn't trust him. He was saying, 'Watch that fellah.' Of course, my dad trusted no one. You know, every person knocking on the hall door after midnight is an assassin, every girl is a groupie. Every friend is a weirdo. Every record-business person is a hustler and a thief. Now how could he have known all of this?

EDGE: Having Paul on board didn't change things very much at first. He just told us to carry on writing songs and doing gigs. There was an underground scene developing in Dublin city with bands such as Revolver, The Vipers, The Atrix, DC Nien, The Blades, The New Versions and Berlin. It was always a hustle to get anything and Adam was doing most of the hustling. It could get quite frustrating. I remember going to McGonagles with Adam to talk to Terry O'Neill, who managed the club, about a second-on-the-bill support slot, only to discover we were being demoted to bottom of bill, behind a new all-girl band called The Boy Scoutz. When we pointed out that it was their first live gig, Terry said, 'It doesn't matter if they're crap because people just want to see chicks in a punk band.' And so the summer went by with a few support slots in McGonagles and the Project and some of the bars around Dublin. Our road crew at this point was 'Tiger Hunter' aka Lep Murphy, one of my brother's best friends from school. Before Tiger we had help from Stephen Milburn, Adam's neighbour.

LARRY: Because of my job, it wasn't possible to do all of the gigs during the week. I was friendly with a guy called Eugene who played drums in a north Dublin rock outfit called Stryder. He was a nice fellah and he filled in for me on the gigs I couldn't make.

BONO: Larry arranged his first stand-in, a guy from some metal band. But then a second drummer was brought in behind his back – I think Larry was deciding whether or not to be in the band. This was going on and on. Larry wasn't turning up for photo sessions, so Guggi would step in. They couldn't look less alike but because he had blonde hair, Guggi could stand at the back and pretend to be the drummer. Then Larry had an accident; he's working as a courier and he runs over his own toe whilst riding a motorbike. No one can figure out how he did it, but it meant he couldn't do gigs, so we found this guy called Eric Briggs. He wore a leather jacket, he was dark, kind of good-looking, and easy to hang with. We actually went out and talked to this fellow about being the drummer in U2. The question was: is Larry serious or is he not? This guy, Eric, is serious. We are serious … Larry is too serious! But not necessarily about wanting to be in the band. I think there was an element of bluff involved – any more guff out of you and we're bringing this guy in.

LARRY: I was as committed to the band as I could be at that stage. I did a deal with my parents to work for a year and have something to fall back on in the event things didn't work out in my musical life. Also, they didn't have the resources to look after me, so I had no choice. Bono did odd jobs, painting and decorating, he worked at a shoe shop for a bit. It was just him, his dad and brother, and I think there was a certain tolerance of his lifestyle because of his character. Edge and Adam had a lot more resources. I'm not saying they could always fall back on their parents but they knew they weren't going to end up on the street. There was pressure on me to at least try to get some experience doing something else. I'm not sure that the band understood but I stuck to the deal I made with my parents.

ADAM: Larry was moving away from us. Playing gigs didn't seem to be that important to him, and the rest of us were trying to rehearse, we were trying to write. So we did have another drummer, and he did a good job of filling in. But ultimately, I suppose, he wasn't a Beatle.

I was under pressure from my parents to get a job. I managed to stave it off for a while. Eventually I decided to find work where I thought I might be able to have the use of a van. I was delivering china products for a small retailer out of Malahide, which involved driving a VW van all over the country. I thought: 'At least I'll be able to use the van in the evening for moving gear.' But that was a bit naïve. My employer didn't like the idea of it being used as a band wagon at night.

But it was kind of interesting to drive the byways of Ireland delivering tea sets to shops in Tralee and Cork. I liked being out and about, because you could listen to the radio and nobody could monitor you, but the hours were extremely long, the money wasn't great and the van wasn't such a fun thing to drive. And I eventually crashed it. It had been a long day and I was coming back up to Dublin about 9.30 at night, trying to get back to the city for a rehearsal. Only one of the headlamps was working. I was coming into a corner a bit too fast and I just couldn't see where the kerb was. So that was the end of my driving career.

EDGE: We landed the opening slot for The Stranglers at The Top Hat Ballroom. It was our first exposure to playing alongside a hit band and a slightly disillusioning moment to realize that the punk ethos didn't extend to giving your support band a dressing-room or a few beers.

MY DAD TRUSTED NO ONE. YOU KNOW, EVERY PERSON KNOCKING ON THE HALL DOOR AFTER MIDNIGHT IS AN ASSASSIN, EVERY GIRL IS A GROUPIE. EVERY FRIEND IS A WEIRDO. EVERY RECORD-BUSINESS PERSON IS A HUSTLER AND A THIEF. NOW HOW COULD HE HAVE KNOWN ALL OF THIS? BONO

ADAM: Paul had gone to a wedding, so he couldn't be our manager and fight for us. We had to make sure that we had a soundcheck and lights and a dressing-room, and that we were treated fairly and paid at the end of the gig. But I don't think we got a soundcheck, and they had taken all the dressing-rooms, so we had to hang out backstage behind the speaker stacks. I know this was the root of what infuriated Bono later. Then we went on and did the show and the first or second number Edge broke a string and never fully got his guitar back into tune after that. I think Bono just felt the hostility of the audience, which was a hardcore punk audience who didn't have any tolerance for us. At the end of our set Bono went into The Stranglers' dressing-room and got into an argument about heroes and how you treat people.

BONO: I had a little argument with Jean-Jacques Burnel (The Stranglers' bassist). I'm sure he'd never remember but it was a giant moment for me.

LARRY: The Stranglers' big song was 'No More Heroes' and that was Bono's argument with them: if there are no more heroes, how come you treat the support band like shit?

BONO: The Stranglers had a presence – very male, very mannish. Not the usual skinny-boy, UK, punk-rock thing. I asked JJ would he wear a U2 badge on his bass? And he said, 'Why should I? Wear your own fucking badge.' He was acting out the punk-rock thing, and we decided he's an arsehole and that he doesn't understand what punk rock is. Not only are they not punk rock, they're the enemy of punk rock. So we refused to watch them on stage. Instead we broke into the dressing-room during the gig and stole their wine. I was full of righteous indignation, and fearlessness. It was a kind of anger that was in me, always picking fights with people who were much bigger.

EDGE: Bono went into the dressing-room and came back with a bottle of wine by way of protest and so we drank that in a disgruntled manner behind the loudspeakers. But it was good to see them doing the soundcheck. They were old, that was the thing that struck me. Jet Black, the drummer, was probably in his thirties but it might as well have been his fifties as far as we were concerned.

ADAM: We did a double bill with the Virgin Prunes at the Project. I think by this point Paul McGuinness was starting to get a bit upset with the Prunes.

PAUL: The Prunes became our obligatory opening act. We even had posters printed which had U2 and then at the bottom it said 'and the Virgin Prunes'. I would have to admit I wasn't a major fan – my dislike of some of the things they got up to was no secret.

EDGE: Gavin's approach was extreme, he was into Dada and performance art way ahead of his time. His attitude to an audience was much more confrontational than ours. Whereas Bono presented a charm offensive, Gav was just offensive. When McGuinness became our manager, that was the one thing he hated, that the Prunes were a fixture and they were always around.

PAUL: I would actually be watching the Virgin Prunes while U2 would often be backstage. Bono would say, 'I can't understand why the audience are in such a bad mood.' And I would say, 'It might be because your friends in the Virgin Prunes have just thrown a lot of pigs offal at them.'

EDGE: Paul would point out that we were literally paying these people to piss off our audience. Our loyalties to the Prunes were such that we were happy to give them the opportunity to play. We really liked what they were doing, although I don't think we realized just how great they were. At that time, you couldn't see anything like it in London or New York, let alone Dublin. Looking back they were really cutting-edge and extraordinary.

BONO: The Prunes came up with a name for Paul. He was The Goose.

EDGE: The nicknames weren't necessarily designed to make you sound as if you were the member of a cool rock band. They were actually given as ways of slagging people off. So Bono Vox of O'Connell Street, to give him his full name, was used to slag off Bono. As for The Edge, I suppose they were somehow hinting at my interesting head. Adam was Mrs Burns because he did come over like an old woman sometimes, and Larry was known as The Jam Jar. Bill Graham was Burgundy. There's some fantastic ones, very Joycean, like

Little Biddy One Way Street and Gook Pants Delaney. But Mrs Burns and The Jam Jar and The Goose weren't used so much, they were a bit too heavy. There was all manner of insult wrapped up in these names. For a while Bono was Bon Smelly Arse. I was glad that didn't stick, or things might have been different. I don't know if the band would have got very far with a singer called Bon Smelly Arse.

ADAM: The names that tended to stick were the ones that really summed up people's appearances. Because Edge had a very big, angular head, that seemed to fit. And Bono Vox of O'Connell Street just suited him – it was a hearing-aid shop. Not that he's hard of hearing ... or other people would be hard of hearing him! But it did fit.

BONO: Rehearsals at that point were really just screaming arguments, one long row after another. I was probably most responsible for this – but, you see, I'd come from a house where everyone screamed at each other, so I thought that was normal discourse. My father and my brother would watch the rugby, standing in front of the television with my dad shaking his fist at the referee, screaming 'I'll kill you!' My brother too. They were loud, and I guess I was too. I'm not now. In our house, I rarely raise my voice; I can raise the temperature in other ways. But, back then, that's how I thought you talked to people. So there was a lot of very, very aggressive stuff, and because we were dysfunctional as a band, it was very hard. Because I wasn't master of any instrument, I was relying on Edge, and he was relying on Adam and Larry, and none of us were good enough to be relied on. You'd hear the melody coming in, you're going to just grab it, it's going to be great, and then the fucking thing falls over. Somebody hits a clanger, and you want to kill them. And in my case that is: 'I will fucking kill you if you do that again!'

LARRY: Bono was – and is still – a bundle of contradictions. He has a very clear idea in his own mind of how the music should be and how it should sound and how it should feel, and he's got very high expectations. I think it was frustrating for him to go on stage and give one hundred percent and to feel the band weren't able to provide him with the back-up. He felt he was out there with his arse out the window, jumping around like a man possessed. His sound wasn't good on stage, he couldn't hear the drums and he would get it into his head that maybe it was because somebody wasn't playing hard enough – i.e. me. So he would get frustrated, the frustration would build, and then suddenly he would explode.

BONO: It wasn't that they didn't care, or they weren't paying attention. They were just fucking up, making ordinary mistakes. But it was awful, there'd be rows and screaming in the dressing-room, yelling in the rehearsal-room. But there'd be laughs too. Because I never had anything to eat, I'd always eat their lunch. Larry would be organized, he'd bring stuff. We had a heater in the rehearsal-room, and on that he would toast his cheese sandwiches. He'd go out to take a piss and he'd come back and they'd be gone, so he'd start bringing more. Things like that. I'm used to being in a gang but myself and Guggi and Gavin, we didn't scream at each other. So in some senses that must suggest the band were more like immediate family, which implies a set of rules different to those of friendship. But then we started to become friends in the band. We started hanging out more, and there were some good times.

PAUL: I remember a ferocious argument once with Bono that took place on O'Connell Street in the rain while he was waiting to get on a bus. The argument was probably about whether we were going to do a particular thing next, like play some gig. We used to take decisions together. I was making recommendations much of the time and they would very often follow them but it certainly wasn't a case of me ordering them around and there were many disputes and disagreements. There was a mad theory at one point that we were so broke they would start a second band that would perform under a different name and play covers, and would actually earn a living that would support U2, who would continue to perform their own material.

BONO: That's a very good idea. That is very practical.

PAUL: There were a number of bands around Dublin at the time that were doing significantly better financially than we were. There was a group called The Lookalikes and nobody ever knew who they were supposed to look like, but they had an amazing series of residencies at places like the Baggot Inn and the Crofton Airport Hotel. They were clearly making a lot of money, and we were making none. So there was a suggestion at one point we should get residencies and put the thing on a financial basis.

BONO: 'How are we going to afford a van?' That was the question. This is the year of the van, and we don't have one. The Lookalikes have their own van. They've not only their own van, they own a PA

Because my dad was about to ask me for some money, there were a few weeks where we thought about learning other people's songs and doing a 50/50 set like we'd done before, but doing it properly this time so we could get a van.

'They don't.' 'They do.' 'They lease it.'
'They don't, they own it.' 'They lease it.'
'I'm telling you, they own their own
Fucking PA and lights and van.'
'How do they do it?' 'They're getting loads of gigs around the country.'
'How?' 'They play other people's songs.'
'Fucking sell-out! Should we learn
Some other people's songs?'

ADAM: We were always looking for gigs that actually paid something. So we thought we would try doing a couple of nights at the Crofton Airport Hotel. It didn't work because the bands that were actually making money there were almost showbands, doing cover versions. I think six people turned up, and that was only because they thought another band was playing.

LARRY: We did a lot of gigs in the Arcadia ballroom in Cork. We had our first real fan base in that great city. It's the first city we ever sold out.

EDGE: Cork had a real music scene. It was a university gig so there was a guaranteed audience on the weekends. People would come along to drink and they didn't know who the hell we were but we connected. Next time we went back down, people were actually there to see us and it really took off. For quite a while we were bigger in Cork than we were in Dublin.

LARRY: Cork is where we met Joe O'Herlihy. He was the house sound engineer in the Arcadia ballroom. Joe was a real professional, lots of microphones. He was the best around at that time and eventually, when we could afford him, he became our sound engineer. Nearly thirty years later, he's still with us.

EDGE: We managed to persuade Paul that we needed to do another demo session. We knew we'd have to do better than before. We would have to get more involved, you couldn't really leave it up to engineers to dictate sounds. We had to learn a bit more about the recording process.

ADAM: Paul talked Barry Devlin from Horslips into producing it. I think Paul didn't fancy the idea of being in the studio with us, with nobody knowing what the fuck was going on. So he thought: 'At least if I have Barry there, he'll know how sessions run and what's meant to happen.' We thought we'd be making a hit record but it didn't really work out that way. It cost what seemed an awful lot of money to us at the time, and took a long time to record.

LARRY: It was much harder than we'd expected and again we hadn't prepared as well as we should have before going into the studio, but in the end we were happy enough.

EDGE: We recorded 'Street Missions', 'The Fool' and a new one, 'Shadows And Tall Trees', which was ultimately the only song to survive.

ADAM: I don't think we realized how rough the demos were.

PAUL: It took us a long time to secure a record deal, which I found frustrating and puzzling because I thought U2 were so good, though probably those early tapes weren't very impressive. I was certainly naïve myself and didn't discern the lack of expertise. I started sending tapes to A&R men in London particularly but also in America and sometimes they would reply and sometimes they wouldn't. Occasionally we would get somebody to come over and see the band but something would always go wrong. There were a lot of false starts – it was a tough period.

LARRY: My mother's death in a road traffic accident in November 1978 was, in the end, what made my mind up with regard to the band. I am not saying I wouldn't have jumped had she lived but, after her death, there was nowhere else I wanted to be.

EDGE: In a weird sense, the death of Larry's mother was such a massive shock to everybody that it brought us all together. The bonds of friendship became really strong, and it was really around that time that things started to happen. Larry sort of had one foot out of the band and was destined to join the oil business but suddenly it was back on, and he threw himself into the band and the job went by the board.

LARRY: After my mother's death I found it hard to concentrate on anything. Everything in me just shut down. Bono started to call round my house and try to get me to go out and forget my troubles. One afternoon, while standing on my front doorstep, he told me about losing his own mother when he was fourteen. I had no idea. I felt I had found someone who understood, we developed a bond and after a time we became close friends and I felt ready to get back into the band. Things were different now. I was no longer in a group I was in a band, and the band would become my way out. I was running away with the circus.

BONO: I'd gone through something similar. We became very close friends at this point, and what had been a kind of precocious drummer who brought problems to every solution you could offer, became one of my best friends. And what I understood then about Larry was the reason why he agonized over everything, over every commitment, including a commitment to the band, it was because he takes these contracts – verbal, emotional or otherwise – very seriously in life. He is not a messer, he takes his word very seriously. It's an amazing strength to be in a room with somebody who couldn't tell a lie. It gives them a lot of power. So to maintain this position, he moves very slowly in any direction but rarely has to retreat, when he wins ground he keeps it.

PAUL: Larry is the squeaky wheel in U2 that always has to be serviced and oiled before you can roll along. He is the voice of doom, always questioning the wisdom of what we are planning. He is not always right, but he's right often enough to make him worth the effort.

BONO: In one sense it's a voice I'm familiar with, through my own father. Larry is Mr What-Can-Go-Wrong – but things can, and do. And so Larry is the brakes of the band, and when the rocket is on the wrong trajectory you're very glad of that.

ADAM: The Greedy Bastards played the Stardust ballroom and we opened for them. This was real rock 'n' roll. It had the smell of rock 'n' roll, the look of rock 'n' roll. It had the swagger. The Bastards were members of Thin Lizzy and the Sex Pistols. Phil Lynott was at his peak then. Somehow, though a melodic, hard-rock guy he was able to fit into this punk stuff. You could tell he was having a blast. That was a very exciting time.

They were in town the night before and got up and did a jam at the Baggot Inn or McGonagles, and Steve Jones, the Pistols' guitarist, played Edge's Explorer. Edge was like: 'If this guy fucks the guitar, I can't do the gig tomorrow!' So he was kind of standing underneath Steve Jones the whole time, hoping he wasn't going to drop the guitar.

LARRY: There was a lot of backstage action. It looked glamorous to us, and we were treated a lot better than we were with The Stranglers. They all seemed to be having far too much fun though. Sex, drugs and rock and roll, I suppose.

ADAM: I don't know that we were hanging out, I think we were just brushing the coat-tails of these people, who really didn't want to be around a bunch of kids. I think they wanted to take drugs and chase girls. But it was interesting for us to be around that atmosphere, albeit in a voyeuristic way – seeing things like flight cases and equipment and roadies and lighting rigs. It was all that you aspired to have in the future.

BONO: Phil was a big star, he carried himself with a certain swagger and elegance, the like of which I had never seen before. But there were knowing glances between them which disturbed me, without my understanding what they were. Somebody was in the dressing-room, and one of the Greedy Bastards came off stage, walked straight through the door, threw up into the room, and then immediately walked straight back on stage. There was a mood around them that was so far from our mood. It was as if our two bands couldn't have been further apart.

Phil was at the end of Thin Lizzy and about to slide down the hill into the abyss. The same with the Sex Pistols, they'd finished, it had all turned bad. And here we were, only a promise and just trying to figure out the delivery. It was a strange moment. But we really didn't know how dark it could get for guys in a rock band. They had started playing with fire, and suddenly it turned around and fire was now playing with them. They were just being consumed and licked by the flames of all that is awful about sex and drugs and rock 'n' roll. Of course, Phil became my next-door neighbour in Howth, a few years later, and I didn't know what to do, because he had this look. And he was so kind to me and gentle about our band. He'd say, 'Do you want to come down for dinner?' And I didn't go down for dinner, because I didn't know what to do. I wish I had gone round now because he was so great. Heavy metal is one of the most empty-headed formats lyrically, with the poorest singers across the spectrum of pop, yet here was a guy with a certain lyrical dexterity and a voice that was so elegant and liquid. But we thought the Greedy Bastards were uncool – it was a strange thing.

ADAM: There was a time when I would have thought that being in a band meant sex, drugs and rock and roll. It would have been an aspiration originally. But, in a way, once I found myself in that situation, I wasn't so keen on it. I wasn't so sure that I wanted to be laid by that particular person or take those particular drugs, so there was comfort in the fact that the other three people in the band were actually kind of sane on that level. It did take the pressure off me, because I think for all my front I wasn't so comfortable with that kind of situation.

LARRY: I'd been an altar boy. I have a traditional Catholic background. I stopped going to church after everything that had happened, I didn't see myself going back. Bono, on the other hand, had a very strong faith, and, for the first time, he talked about it openly to me after my mother passed away.

BONO: I'd met some new people who'd reawakened that thing that's always been dormant in me, and I think in Edge and Larry and a few other people that we knew. We met these people through a group called Shalom. They're a community, the like of which we'd never seen before. They were on the street, living like first-century Christians. They believed in miracles as a daily business, and they lived the life of faith. They were fascinating. There was a touch of Pentecostal madness about them, which meant I was never fully comfortable, but it was certainly worth having a closer look. There was a fellow who led the group, who'd come from a mission in China as a kid. He was really an on-fire preacher, extraordinarily gifted, with scholarly insights into the nature of the scriptures which I still hold on to really tightly. I was attracted by that – it almost excused some of the others' lunacy because there was a bit of that too. But there always is. They would justify it by saying that when the Holy Spirit fell on the Apostles they all started speaking in tongues, and people thought they were drunk, or mad.

EDGE: Originally our spiritual search was something completely independent. We called it the Monday Night Group because we met on Monday evenings, initially in Guggi's house and then eventually in a room in Mount Temple. There was no hierarchy whatsoever, no rules or regulations. Open to all comers, no doctrines, just a group of kids taking an interest in spiritual matters, trying to figure out the big questions, really. Then, as the group gained a certain size, up to about forty or fifty people, members of this more mature group, Shalom, became involved. It was a great thing to spend time reading the scriptures and find out about this whole system of belief, Christianity, what it really means. We later found out that the Rasta movement had a similar fascination with scripture, and they would sit around smoking weed and discussing Bible references in sessions they called 'reasoning'. We did the same really, but without the weed.

Those Monday-night gatherings provided a kind of support system and that fed into the developing relationships in the band. We were going through a lot together, and there were deep bonds of friendship and respect between us.

We had a little rehearsal space on Malahide Road. It was a condemned lodge house, so we got it for a fiver a week or something. I don't know why they even bothered renting it to us. It was a real dump but perfect for what we needed.

EDGE ACQUIRED HIS ECHO UNIT, AND THAT CHANGED
EVERYTHING. IF YOU KNOW THE PRECISION OF HIS
PLAYING, THIS IS AN EFFECT THAT HE IS GOING TO
MASTER LIKE JIMI HENDRIX DID WAH WAH. IT WAS
PUNK ROCK WITH A SYMPHONY – SUDDENLY YOU'RE
IN OUTER SPACE INSTEAD OF SUBURBIA. BONO

BONO: Edge acquired his echo unit, and that changed everything. We were looking for that otherness which we just couldn't get out of power chords. So I said to Edge, 'Have you heard the start of Pink Floyd's *Animals*? You've got to get one of these echo units. The Cure are playing with one, but I think there's more to get out of it.' And he bought a thing called a Memory Man. If you know the precision of his playing, this is an effect that he is going to master like Jimi Hendrix did Wah Wah. It was punk rock with a symphony – suddenly you're in outer space instead of suburbia.

EDGE: The Memory Man was a really low-tech analogue delay unit. It didn't have any digital read-out, so you couldn't tell what your setting was, which was a bit of a disadvantage because quite quickly we realized that the echoes I was using were actually setting the tempo of the song. So I had to cover the Memory Man with little chinagraph marks on the speed knob, representing different songs. It had to be just right or else the song would be way off tempo. But in those days we only did one tempo: way too fast!

LARRY: How myself and Edge managed to stay in time is beyond me. In fact, I don't know that we did stay in time. We were all over the place. Making music by accident is what it's called.

EDGE: Adam was another reason my guitar playing developed the way it did. He was such an unorthodox bass player, and Larry and myself, in an attempt to make it work, developed our mutual styles to accommodate Adam's approach. In some ways Larry and I were like the rhythm section and Adam's really forceful bass playing was almost like the lead, it was very much out in the forefront.

BONO: Adam was bringing a lot of panache to proceedings, and he was starting to produce a really great bass sound, even though he was a very eccentric bass player. He could play really complicated things easily and then be unable to clap in time, and you'd just be left scratching your head.

LARRY: A bass player's job in the band is usually down in the engine room with the drummer, the other half of the rhythm section. But Adam took a much more musical approach. He always finds ways of making the instrument work for him.

EDGE: Our chord construction was interesting. We didn't like major chords because they sounded too happy, and minor chords sounded too down, so we stripped things back to absolute fundamentals, with fifths and root notes, no frills whatsoever. The third became our enemy. The third is the note that gives the sex of the chord in major or minor terms and if you leave out the third note, the key becomes ambiguous and much more open to different melodies. I came up with chord voicings where there was no third; basically you play the root with a fifth and the octave of the root, with maybe some other intervals in there. It worked quite well because it kept the canvas completely open. And when we came to recording, that ambiguity gave me the ability to play around with overdubs. You could really change things a lot because you weren't setting down the chords in a very clear fashion.

I guess we replaced virtuosity and songwriting chops with a very good sense of dynamics, being able to create quite different textures in a very simple way. That was one of our secrets; many of our songs featured breaks and sections where the musical landscape would change completely. And harmonics were one of the ways that we did that. It was a sound that people hadn't really explored much. The Police had touched on it a little, but very few other bands.

Harmonics create the sound for the electric guitar pick-ups, just the vibration of the string. The string is moving backwards and forwards, and if you touch the exact middle point of the string as you're hitting it, you actually get the string to vibrate in two halves, a kind of sympathetic vibration that gives you the note and its exact octave. There are also other areas where if you hit it in a certain place you'll get maybe a quarter of the string vibrating or a third of it, so you get subdivisions of the full string and that gives the corresponding interval. If it's a quarter of the string then it's two octaves up. A third of the string would probably be a fifth. In terms of what it sounds like, it has different harmonic characteristics, not exactly like a regular note, because you've touched the string to get this vibration occurring, so it's more of a subtle sound.

In the live context our ideas really came into focus. Many of the breaks were improvised live and after you'd used a certain idea a few times it would enter the repertoire for that song and kind of get written in. We'd be doing the song then Bono would wave the left hand, which meant 'Let's go somewhere else' and we'd all home in and take it right down. We were very good at playing without a script and the harmonic breaks were one of the things we became particularly adept at.

LARRY: Bono hated the idea that the songs and set would be so formalized. He wanted it to be like jazz, to be able to turn on a sixpence, stop and try something in a different timing, and then come back in where you left off. Of course, we hadn't got a clue. Then there was the famous left hand waving, giving directions to stop or slow down. For health and safety reasons, I had to learn this new sign language and figure out what he wanted. I learnt very quickly. To this day, he still does it.

ADAM: Improvisation implies some kind of musical knowledge, in the jazz sense. I think there was a lot of flying by the seat of our pants and making plenty of noise. There was soft, medium and loud, and we moved between those three tones, but I don't think we had enough knowledge to expand it further. It was more about each one of us learning how to do what we did; it was more practice in public than improvisation.

PAUL: We were trying to build the status of the band in Ireland and at the same time attract interest from record companies in London. People like Charlie Eyre at A&M, Chris Briggs and Tom Nolan at EMI, Chas De Whalley and Muff Winwood from CBS and Tarquin Gotch from Arista would occasionally come over to see a U2 gig and we would get very excited and think they were going to offer us a record deal, but they never did. So there was a lengthy period of arranging gigs and having disappointing responses from A&R men.

LARRY: We were hit and miss. We could have three great gigs in a row and then two shite ones, the record companies would always make it to the shite gigs. We were inconsistent. There was a gig at the Baggot Inn when some UK record company guys came to see us, heard two songs and then left to watch The Specials on some TV show. We really thought we were going to get signed there and then. That night myself, Bono and our friend Pod walked to the bus stop feeling totally dejected.

ADAM: We were turned down by every record company at least twice. We could not figure out why these people didn't realize what an important signing we were for them. It was always a disappointment, just because it meant that we had to wait a little longer to prove ourselves. To us it seemed the scene was moving quickly, and we didn't want to be left behind, so we had to go back in there and keep rehearsing, and write more songs. We did more demos in a small radio studio called The Eamon Andrews Studio. Dave Freely was the house engineer. It was very cheap because it was just a four-track studio. So we could spend more time and rehearse the numbers and put them down live. That was a more successful session.

BONO: They're quite creative, those demos. That's when our U2 sound started to develop, with songs like 'Alone In The Light', 'Another Time, Another Place'.

LARRY: Some of the other studios we had been in at least looked professional. This was a tiny room with a really tiny desk. The engineer, who was a nice fellah, asked: 'Who do you want to sound like?' He had a record collection there for us to choose from. We said: 'We don't want to sound like any of them.' And by the time we had finished recording, we didn't even sound like ourselves.

EDGE: Paul was taking the first demos around with mixed success. I thought he felt himself at the time we weren't necessarily ready but Bono was absolutely adamant that with the second set of demos he wanted to go and get a deal sooner rather than later.

BONO: Paul was not coming up with the van, and I'm just getting a bit tired of this. 'Oh yeah. All these big ideas. But where is the fucking van? Where are the gigs? Adam's finding the gigs. What are you doing? You're supposed to be the manager.' Despite Paul's protestations that the demos weren't good enough to go to London, I can't wait. Because I'm running out of time. My old man is pointing out that my year at home is almost up. The heat is on. I can't afford not to get a record deal, so I want to go to London and stir up interest. Paul is saying: 'Wait. Get better. We'll do this in a programmatic fashion.' I'm saying: 'We can't wait. And by the way, if we want to do well in Ireland, we should do well in the UK. Then they'll listen to us in Ireland.' So that was the plan I had.

I went to London with Ali. It was a big deal in my own mind because I was taking this beautiful girl on a trip, and I was supposed to be in charge but I didn't know what I was doing or where I was staying. I'd never been to London before. We were not married but we were going to sleep in the same room with the agreement that we wouldn't sleep in the same bed. Her old man had looked me in the eye and, you know, I'm going away for a week with his daughter. So I had to keep the promise, which was very, very hard.

We went to see Phil Chevron from The Radiators, the band that had mutated out of The Radiators From Space, who were now based in London.

He was very helpful and pointed us in the direction of a couple of music journalists he thought were good. And I had a couple of journalists that I thought were promising. I'd find the address, get the Tube, locate the *NME* or *Sounds* magazine or *Record Mirror*, go in, find the journalist we thought was the most open to new music, ask for them at reception. Which is very interesting, because if you get a call, 'somebody at reception for you', you don't think: 'Tell them to fuck off, I don't know these people.' You just kind of wander out, and you'd see me and my girlfriend. And I'd be saying: 'Listen, we're from Dublin, a band called U2, and we'd really like you to listen to this demo.' I had perfect manners. And they'd kind of look at this wide-eyed kid and I'd say:

'Good, well I'll be back in an hour.' They'd go: 'What?'

'I'll be back in an hour.' 'I've got

a fucking column to write!'

'Well I'm only here for a day or two.'

At this point a journalist called Dave McCullough at *Sounds* was very helpful. And a fellow named Chris Westwood from *Record Mirror* was extremely generous and was the first person to put us on the cover. He had very esoteric tastes but an ear for pop too. He was the most encouraging of them all and said: 'You should try this record company, you should try that record company. The guy who signed the Sex Pistols has his own label now, you should go and see him.'

So I went along knocking at his door – Automatic Records, they were called. And I said:

'Chris Westwood from *Record Mirror* told us we should see you.'

'Oh, yeah, you're with *Record Mirror*?'

'No, I'm with a band.' 'What do you mean, a band?'

I said: 'Would you listen to our song? The guy from

Record Mirror said you'd like it.' And I made him listen to it in front of us.

He said: 'Have you got a manager?' 'Yeah.'

'Why isn't he here?' 'He's at home trying to figure out how we'll get a van.

I'm the advance party but he can call you tomorrow.'

Ali paid for all this, by the way. I had no money.

EDGE: We played something called The Dark Space Festival at the Project Arts Centre, an all-night event with performance artists and strippers and comedians and most of the local post-punk bands. It felt like we were part of an interesting, rising scene. There was a huge level of excitement amongst those who were cognizant of what was going on in musical terms, but there was nothing actually there that blew my mind. It all seemed a bit second-rate, to tell you the truth. Of the bands that were around Dublin, I thought we were the best. Looking at the bands putting out records in England at the time, I thought we were as good as any of them. The Mekons were playing and they were an English band that had some kind of credibility with the subculture. I remember standing next to Bill Graham watching them and he turned round to me and said, 'The only thing remarkable about this band is their more highly developed sense of pose.'

I think we understood that climbing on stage was a pose in itself and to that end you had to have some element of self-awareness, but at the same time our focus was elsewhere. It was something I noticed when we met bands from London, they were almost defined by their pose, the image they projected. It was a very external thing, whereas in Ireland it was much more balanced between that and what you had to say, what you stood for in terms of politics and ideas. It might be a parochial versus big city thing. We probably thought we were quite stylish, which was patently untrue. I don't think we understood that language, but we also thought it was an aspect of rock 'n' roll that was overvalued. It wasn't that we were against it, it wasn't some kind of ethical issue, it was just that we were more interested in other things.

ADAM: Most of the London or New York bands were very image-conscious. But they tended to be older than us; we were just trying to play our instruments and write songs, and we didn't realize you had to present a visual analogy of how that music sounded and where it was coming from, hence the interesting fashion statements from that period.

I have never really liked photo sessions, or videos for that matter, though they are obviously key parts of commercial music. I think we had to get more involved in recognition of the harm it can do if you get it wrong, because in our early years we got it so wrong that it took us a long time to recover.

EDGE: Bono with chequerboard pants and polo-necks with one nipple cut out. That was probably the silliest it got.

ADAM: I had a two-tone orange and black wool jumper, very New Wave colours, which my girlfriend, Donna, knitted for me. And Larry still had his flares, of course.

EDGE: I played an Explorer guitar, which I bought in New York on a brief holiday. I had a shortlist of guitars I wanted to try – Les Paul, Rickenbacker – but I saw the Explorer in the window of the first guitar shop and thought 'Wow!' I played it for a while and really liked it. It was the zig-zag shape that set it apart but the sound and the feel were great too. Everyone was playing the same kinds of guitars and I thought, we sound different, let's look different.

LARRY: The Dandelion Market Car Park gigs started in May. A gig every Saturday afternoon for six weeks, fifty pence in, all ages welcome. People talk about these gigs as being legendary. They were. The Dandelion was where we really hit our stride.

EDGE: It was kind of an apocalyptic setting, this subterranean car park in the basement of an eighteenth-century district of Dublin, so you really felt like you were in the bowels of some hellhole. The stage had to be built every weekend and we'd bring the PA and lights in. The sound wasn't bad for such a shithole.

LARRY: There was a backdrop with the U2 logo on it. People were starting to look the part, the band were beginning to wear clothes that reflected the time, our audience likewise. And they were *our* audience, they were our contemporaries.

ADAM: It was our policy to actually get out from under headline acts and find our own venues and build our own audience. Those lunchtime gigs were just fantastic. They were very cheap to get into and there were always a lot of people in town on a Saturday afternoon with nothing to do, and they just built over successive weeks.

LARRY: The first gig was a little sparse, a little busier for the second. The third was looking good – the fourth was amazing. We were coming together as a musical force. We felt like we had refined what we did musically. This was the start of Bono climbing and running around like a caged animal.

BONO: We started applying lessons of performance art but in a pop way, and it all started gelling. You could feel the energy, you knew something was going on. That was our Beatles-in-the-Cavern moment.

ADAM: There was one show Edge missed. He was feeling really sick and after we'd set up they took him into Mercer hospital round the corner. A doctor took one look at him and said: 'You've got meningitis.'

EDGE: I said: 'Can I have some painkillers and come back to hospital after the gig?' The doctor said, 'If you leave this building I will not be held responsible for your life.' So I said, 'Which one is my bed?'

ADAM: The punters were in by then, so the show must go on.

BONO: I played guitar, which is generally not a good idea.

LARRY: We played a Lou Reed song, 'Sweet Jane', over and over again. I couldn't remember the drum part but I played along anyway, as I had done so many times before to songs I didn't know.

BONO: Then we started doing The Jingle Balls. We had this big idea, let us decide when Christmas is, and let's make it the middle of July, do up McGonagles and have a Christmas tree and decorations. It was a way to be in a pop band and still be surreal. It's a long way from *Zoo TV* but the inspiration is the same: everything you know is wrong.

ADAM: That was a pretty weird thing to do, I have to say. But we were aware that we had to create something to remember. And with our very limited resources, we always tried to think outside the box and maximize what was possible.

EDGE: We had a screen up at the side of the stage, which Bono and my sister Gill disappeared behind during a song called 'Boy/Girl' and their silhouettes were projected on it, taking their clothes off.

BONO: She had a gorgeous figure. And she looked as great behind the screen as she did in front. That was a good idea.

ADAM: Bono had his cigarette routine, from which he extracted considerable mileage. Several years' worth, I think. Actually, it was more of a lighter routine, repeatedly striking the lighter to try to light a cigarette he had bummed from the audience. That was to compensate for the fact that we couldn't afford a strobe light – it was the Irish version of a strobe.

BONO: I didn't smoke then. But I used to pick up a smoke, and it was a sort of post-coital smoke, at the end of some breathy moment in a song. And I'd be looking for a light, and wouldn't be able to get it. The lights would go down, and I'd start playing with the lighter like it was a revolver. I was like Jesse

James, I could make the lighter flash like a six-gun cracking, little theatrical things. I discovered round about then that out of the fifteen songs played, people would only remember a handful of moments, two of them might be musical, but three of them would be dramatic. It was a way of drawing people's attention to the music. Drama was working for us. Or if the songs weren't good, drama would take you away from them and they'd just become soundtracks to stage action. You become practised in the art of distraction.

This is the summer where it all went off. This is where *Hot Press* started becoming incredibly supportive. And the philosophy of the editor Niall Stokes and journalists of *Hot Press* started to feel more believable to us than, for example, the *NME*. When we look at it now, a kind of Maoist, cultural revolution was going on in England. Two legs bad, four legs good. Fashionista. Whereas *Hot Press* felt rounded, there was real politics involved. There was also a sense of music being part of Ireland's coming of age. I couldn't underestimate the importance of *Hot Press* and Bill Graham and Niall Stokes and Liam Mackey. They were coming to see us all the time. There were good feelings about the band – they could be important. Something could happen here.

ADAM: As we moved from being outside contenders to most likely to succeed, you could feel people getting around you. Between RTE, *Hot Press* and pirate radio there was a lot of support. Dave Fanning was important, he was the leading rock DJ on the pirate station Radio Dublin and was always on the lookout for Irish bands to play. He would do interviews and publicize gigs. Even equipment companies became more helpful, because you'd be looking for favours and cutting good deals so that you could get things done. Record companies were coming to see us but it was nerve-racking because there was always a hitch.

PAUL: I thought the evidence was pretty clear that U2 had the ammunition and the equipment to be a big band. I certainly didn't have any doubt about that. But it was very dispiriting that it wasn't clearer to the A&R people who were coming over. Jackie Hayden and David Duke at CBS in Ireland were interested but they didn't have sufficient budget to sign bands to albums deals. Then an A&R scout called Chas De Whalley at CBS London picked up on it. He came up with some demo money and came over and produced some tracks.

ADAM: Chas was nice enough. He was relatively young and I don't know if he'd done much production work before but he was quite keen, he wanted to sign the band. I suppose it was a smart move on Paul's part to get him involved because it meant he might be loyal to us and help get a record deal.

BONO: I don't remember those sessions as going great. We were crucified by self-consciousness, it was hard to get the rhythm section tight, and the vocalist sounds like he is having an identity crisis. But the songs we recorded were strong enough to withstand our weaknesses.

LARRY: 'Out Of Control' has some timing flaws in it. One part of the song was meant to have a one bar break. For whatever reason, it turned out to be three and a half beat break in a bar, which is a little strange. The recording session went something like this: 'Larry's not playing the same part / it's a different tempo / it's speeding up and slowing down.' I was told much later that a CBS record executive said the band was great but the drummer was crap and should be fired a.s.a.p. How right he was.

EDGE: It wasn't a fantastic recording and we weren't terribly impressed with the original mix that Chas did. We recorded in Keystone but ended up remixing in Windmill with Robbie McGrath who had been Horslips sound engineer. I'm not sure if it helped.

ADAM: CBS in the UK passed on it.

EDGE: CBS were umming and ahhing for ages. In fact, they suggested that if we drop Larry they'd give us a record deal. We told them to stuff it. That was head of A&R, Muff Winwood, or Duff Windbag as we called him after hearing that suggestion.

PAUL: I suggested that we release the track as a single in Ireland only and in return CBS would have the right to release U2 records in Ireland even if we signed to somebody else. For that reason U2 records came out on CBS Ireland for a number of years, which was actually a bit of an embarrassment to CBS, because it was a constant reminder to them that they missed the boat. CBS Ireland put out a one-off three-track EP with the songs from the demo: 'Out Of Control', 'Stories For Boys' and 'Boy/Girl'. We had a competition on the Dave Fanning show to choose the A-side and I think every single person who phoned in picked 'Out of Control'. So in September, the 'U23 EP' was released as a seven-inch with a picture bag and a limited edition numbered twelve-inch.

EDGE: It was an amazing feeling, to actually have your first record and hear it being played on radio. I was also frustrated – I knew that we could do better. But at least it was something.

LARRY: Pat Kenny had a morning radio show on RTE and there was a debate on about new Irish music. Bono was on the programme. I was working in the oil exploration company. I slipped off into a vacant office and tuned in to hear the programme. And then it happened for the first time. They played thirty seconds of 'Out Of Control'. It sounded amazing.

BONO: I never liked the sound of it. I liked holding it in my hand, but it kind of spoilt it when I put it on the turntable. But at this point I think my father knew that this whole rock-band business was serious. So that was good.

ADAM: It was just amazing to hear your own song on the radio. But we still didn't have a record deal, that was the really scary bit. We knew the single would sustain us for three or four months, and then what?

EDGE: I had made a commitment to go to college if we hadn't got a deal after a year, and now my time was up. I had to make the call. I applied to Kevin Street Technical College. I got into the Natural Sciences programme. It was really just out of a sense of obligation. I was so sure we would get a record deal that I didn't buy any text-books, I borrowed from other people when I needed to read them. I just didn't want to waste any more of my parents' money on stuff I wasn't going to use. All my books of notes were full of lyric ideas, songs, set lists, logos for the band. McGuinness used to laugh when I'd show him something I had been working on because it would be in a book supposedly dedicated to science. There would be two lines of chemistry and the rest would be U2.

ADAM: We were at an impasse and conscious that in terms of keeping our momentum in Ireland we had to create another stepping-stone in our career. The idea was to do a club tour in England, and we were going to finance it through a publishing deal. Bryan Morrison was the publisher and he came to see us rehearse in the garden shed at Edge's house. We jammed into this tiny space and made him listen to us thrashing out some stuff. He didn't mention much about the music but, because Edge's parents were away, he did complain that the house was a little bit mucky and suggested we should do the washing-up.

PAUL: Bryan Morrison was an independent publisher. At one time he was manager of Pink Floyd. He had been around for years, indeed he's still around. He had been alerted to U2 by his scout, Mark Dean. He offered us a publishing deal, without very much money. It was, I think, three grand but we were so desperate that we accepted in principle. We were going to use this money to play gigs in London that were being set up by an agent called Ian Wilson. Then two days before we were due to leave, Bryan Morrison called up and said, 'I've been thinking about this deal and I've changed my mind. I'm going to pay you an advance of fifteen hundred.'

EDGE: We were going to sell our publishing rights for a pittance for the next twenty years or something. It was a pretty crap deal and at the very last minute, knowing that we had this tour booked, he made it worse. So we basically told him to stuff it up his arse.

ADAM: We had a band meeting and decided to approach our parents and ask them to fund it for us. My relationship with my parents had broken down to such an extent that I couldn't ask them for money. They were still saying: 'get a job'. So I think Edge's parents, Larry Mullen's dad and Bob Hewson put up five hundred pounds each.

BONO: Five hundred pounds was a lot of money back then. So this is where, in my case, the Big Bad Wolf turns into Little Red Riding Hood and arrives with polished apples. My dad came through for me. I'm sure it was after a torrent of abuse, but he did come through.

LARRY: The request was greeted with a mixture of amusement and disbelief. But, in fairness to him, my old man came up with the money.

PAUL: I borrowed some money from Seamus Byrne and Tiernan MacBride, two film colleagues. Between us, we scrambled together just enough to make the trip. Bryan Morrison came to see the band a few weeks later. It was the first time he'd seen them do a show and I remember him saying to me, 'I suppose that was a bit of a mistake, wasn't it? You'd never make a deal with me now?' And I said, 'No.'

ADAM: On the day before we were supposed to be leaving for London we had a bit of an accident. I had my parents' car and I was driving Edge and the equipment to a rehearsal in the Stardust in Artane, and we were involved in a small collision.

EDGE: It was a very undramatic car crash which happened at probably fifteen miles per hour. We were dragging down the road in an old, clapped-out Austin with no rubber on the tyres and suddenly, right in front of us, a massive lorry was blocking both lanes. We jammed on the brakes (what brakes there were), and it went into a bit of a skid and hit the truck. We didn't have insurance, we were in real deep shit in some respects, the last thing on my mind was that I was injured, even though I was bleeding from a head wound and my arm didn't feel so great.

I left Adam there, grabbed my guitar and boarded a bus to the Stardust. I told the guys, 'We had a car crash, Adam's not going to be coming to rehearsal.' Whereupon one of them said, 'I think you might be bleeding. And why are you holding your hand that way?' I suddenly realized, 'Oh shit, yeah, I've been in a crash. I should probably seek some medical help.' So I went to the doctor and got patched up. I explained we were due to go to London the next day and he said, 'I think you'll be OK.'

The next day I woke up in agony. I think I'd sprained all the tendons and muscles in my left hand.

ADAM: Edge was in real pain. He spent the whole journey to England with his hand in a bucket of ice. My parents weren't too pleased either when they realized they were down a car and I was heading off. Oh God, my poor parents. But we had rented a van and I made good my escape. We were off on an adventure, we were cocksure and convinced we would get a record deal.

EDGE: All the way over on the car ferry I was in agony. When we reached Liverpool we stopped off at the General Hospital. They gave me a bunch of morphine tablets and sent me on my way. We had one day to settle in and then the next day we were doing a gig. So I took out the guitar and found that even though I couldn't move my wrist at all, I was actually able to use my fingers. With a giant plaster and arm brace, I sat in the apartment we rented and tried to figure out how to play the songs with my damaged hand. There were a couple of things I couldn't do but mostly I was OK, so we went ahead with the shows and for dramatic effect I actually went on with the sling. I took my hand out of the sling, carefully placed it on the guitar neck and off we'd go.

LARRY: There were stories about bands going to London and living in squats. In fairness to Paul, he rented an apartment in Collingham Gardens in Kensington. Bono and I shared a room, as did Edge and Adam.

ADAM: We were on a *per diem* of two quid each a day. We would pool our money and go to the local bad Italian restaurant, exotic stuff for us in those days.

PAUL: Getting from A to B and not running out of money was the priority. But I used to have an expression – 'It is important not to be scared of the money' – either scared of having too much or too little. Money was really like diesel, to get you to the next point.

BONO: Paul McGuinness took us to Poon's, which is a famous Chinese restaurant up in Chinatown. It was all new to us. We walked in and there were all these Chinese waiters shouting at us. We sat down at a table and tried to get an order in. And they were saying: 'Hurry up, what do you want?' And I remember Larry replying: 'Hold on, we're paying for the food here. You don't shout at us, we shout at you.' Paul explained to Larry that in really posh restaurants you let them shout at you. You pay more for abuse. Larry didn't quite buy the concept … then, or ever.

Larry's a very cautious character. I think he wasn't sure about being away from home in a city like London. I was just entranced, my eyes were the size of saucers, and I was walking around London with songs in my head.

LARRY: We were in London, we were actively looking for a record deal, that was the goal. So the gigs were very important. There was much discussion about what's cool and what's not and how we should look on stage. I remember Bono's frustration at some of the gigs because we were so crap. And Edge just *kept on* breaking guitar strings – at every gig guitar strings would break. We had to develop a bass, drum and vocal tune while Edge changed strings. That tune became an important part of our set.

ADAM: On the one hand it was exciting because we seemed closer to the heat of where things were happening. But London was also a very scary place for us, and continued to be for quite a long time. It seemed ages before we started to play good gigs there, because it was so foreign and alien to us.

LARRY: We were like fish out of water to a large degree, very unsure about what we were doing. We'd reached a certain level in Ireland, so it was like going back to scratch, playing to nine or ten people who just couldn't be arsed. The sound in the clubs wasn't very good, we couldn't hear ourselves playing, it seemed like everything was stacked against us. I couldn't help thinking that maybe it had all been a big mistake.

EDGE: Some of the shows were really good, some were a bit of a mess. We did the Moonlight Club, The Hope and Anchor, The Rock Garden, Dingwalls, the Electric Ballroom supporting Talking Heads, and we saw a lot of record companies.

BONO: On that tour they were going to decide whether to sign us or not. This was a make-it or break-it situation. On the good nights they didn't show up, on the bad nights they did. At the end of the week, all the record companies had passed on us. Even with the press interest that we'd aroused, we ended up going home red-faced, without the recording deal that we'd promised our fans and fathers.

ADAM: We were coming home for Christmas in a state of shock. London was a huge city, and the venues we had heard of as legendary gigs were really kind of toilets ... and we weren't able to fill them. Every record company came to see us and still we hadn't managed to set London on fire. We'd run out of money. I had two bass guitars and, at the end of that week, I had to sell my Rickenbacker bass to pay for our boat ticket back. It was pretty grim because we really had failed; we were penniless, we owed our parents money, nobody wanted to sign us. The only way to go was up.

BONO: We had one last idea, which was based on the sense that the Irish press has a history of colluding with Irish people who cause a bit of a stir in the outside world, and fanning those little sparks into a forest fire. We started to work on the concept of 'U2 breaking the UK'. Rave reviews, it's all happening. We were on the cover of *Record Mirror* in the UK, and that meant a lot. We had the cover of *Hot Press* in Ireland. So forget about playing third on the bill to ten people, the way we were telling it two hundred people turned up to see us in the Half Moon in Herne Hill. We then booked an Irish tour which climaxed at the National Stadium in Dublin, which no junior act had ever done before. It was a place that only the greats played, the boxing stadium in Dublin. And people were aghast. 'Have U2 really broken that big?' 'Yes, they're that big.' They are!

ADAM: We persuaded CBS Ireland to release another one-off single, which was a new demo of a song called 'Another Day', not one of the greats in the U2 canon, it has to be said. But it was an interesting track, the best recording of our latest demos, it had a choppy, modern, New Wave feel. We did a tour of wherever we could play in Ireland that was a big gig. The culmination of that tour, which only took about a week, was the National Stadium. It held two and a half thousand people, and at the time it was the gig where the biggest of the foreign bands would play. It was a real international venue in its day. Booking ourselves in there was considered pretty cheeky.

EDGE: We were world-famous in Dublin. Just having gone to London was almost as good as having a record deal in people's eyes.

LARRY: The tickets went on sale, and people were buying them. There was real excitement about that show – it was as if we had come back as conquering heroes. I remember arriving at the stadium, doing the soundcheck, there was a proper PA system, there were lights, we could hear ourselves onstage. After all the problems of London, this felt right.

ADAM: It was definitely the biggest gig we had played at that stage in our lives. But one thing we noticed was whenever we played a big gig, it always felt better than being in a club. I think this is true of every time we've moved up into a bigger venue, it's always been a very comfortable shift for us. It's almost as if the smaller places are just too small.

LARRY: Family, friends, friends of friends, everybody came to that show. My dad was there, a lot of parents around. We had a really good gig, the audience reaction was special.

BONO: And at that concert arrives an A&R man from Island Records who answers to the name The Captain, Nick (sometimes known as Bill) Stewart, who couldn't get along to any of the shows when we were in the UK, saying, 'Oh, my God, this is a band playing a place called The Stadium. They're that big.' And he arrives to find it's not exactly a stadium but it's a large venue, it's not sold out but it's busy. We play well. This is our homecoming gig, and all our families are there.

LARRY: Nick Stewart came backstage after the show and offered us a record deal. It couldn't have happened at a better moment.

BONO: Ball in back of net. Last minute of extra time.

INTO
THE HEART
1980 - 1981

Adam

WE ACTUALLY SIGNED OUR RECORD DEAL IN THE LADIES' TOILETS AT THE LYCEUM IN LONDON. IT'S A LONG STORY …

BONO: The Captain was six-foot-two, had a chin like a piece of Wedgwood and the creamy voice of Empire. Somebody told us he had been in the British Army and served in Intelligence as an undercover agent in Northern Ireland during the Troubles. I remember thinking: 'The Captain pretending to be a Paddy? Not a chance.'

EDGE: Nick Stewart really does look like your absolute central casting British Army officer. When asked what he was doing in Northern Ireland, he said, 'Impersonating a tall Irishman. Which is extremely difficult, because there aren't any!' He was a complete toff but somehow ended up being A&R man for Island Records.

BONO: I liked Nick enormously. He was very funny, loved music, and he had a sense of drama. He knew he'd found something special, and he wasn't fully fessing up to the fact that he hadn't yet swung it with Chris Blackwell, who owned Island.

PAUL: I went to London to negotiate properly, which wasn't easy because if there's only one person offering you a deal it's very hard to haggle. Fortunately Nick wasn't our only supporter at Island. The Press Officer, Rob Partridge, was friendly with Bill Graham and they used to have conversations about U2. He was also very close to Chris Blackwell, who owned Island, and there was another press guy, Neil Storey, who was crazy about U2. Really, the credit for signing U2 goes to all those guys along with Anne Roseberry from the publishing arm of the company, Blue Mountain Music.

LARRY: Just when we thought the deal was in the bag, Nick said he needed to bring some other record executives down to see us. Luckily we were added to the bill of a small festival in London promoted by the Irish Chamber of Commerce called 'A Sense of Ireland'. We played at the Acklam Hall, in Notting

Hill, with two other bands, Berlin and the Virgin Prunes. It wasn't up to the standards of the Dublin stadium show but it was enough to get us our deal.

BONO: We were on the cover of *NME* before we had the record deal. That may even have helped swing it.

EDGE: Paul Morley of *NME* had come to Cork to see us playing in the Arcadia. Somebody poured a beer into the back of my amp from the top balcony so it exploded. There was smoke pouring out. I'm thinking, 'Oh shit, we've got the *NME* here, the audience is going to get restless, this is our worst nightmare.' And Bono just went into one. He said, 'OK, I want a hundred people up here.' And he stood on top of a PA speaker and said 'We're going to play the rock and roll adulation game. I want you to worship me!' He went on and on like this. Eventually I found a spare amp and we started the show again. We were in the dressing-room afterwards and Paul Morley came in ranting about 'metaphysical peaks!' He loved it! He loved the show for the sheer audacity and chutzpah that Bono had, and he gave us a fantastic write-up.

LARRY: Hanging on in London, waiting for the deal, we all went to a gig one night at the Lyceum. Paul turned up with Nick Stewart and said, 'I have the contract.' So we went into the girls' toilets and signed our names.

PAUL: We needed somewhere we could see what we were doing, and the ladies' was a little bit nicer than the gents'.

ADAM: I guess signing your record deal in the ladies' toilets has a certain kind of rock'n'rollness to it. It was pretty ridiculous, but I don't think it affected the quality of the document.

LARRY: The Sense of Ireland people put us up in the Tara Towers Hotel. It was really plush by our standards but because we had to stay on a few days we didn't have enough money to pay the extra hotel bills. So Bono asked Paul to ring Nick Stewart to try and get some cash.

EDGE: Nick said, 'Look, I'll talk to the financial department. We have the deal done but it hasn't gone through yet. But I'll see what I can do.' To his credit, he came round a few hours later and said, 'Well boys, here we have the loot.' And he dropped a bag of cash on the bed.

LARRY: There was a few hundred quid in the bag. I thought: 'This is amazing!' You ring a guy at the record company, ask him for money – he comes over to your hotel with a bag full of it. Welcome to the music business!

EDGE: It really was a bag of cash. There were no paper clips or rubber bands involved. It looked as if he'd done a convenience store on his way up. We later found out he had raided the petty cash in every department of Island Records, and that's how we paid for the hotel and got home.

ADAM: It wasn't the greatest deal that any band had ever signed but it was enough. It was a commitment for a couple of singles and an album and a little bit of money.

PAUL: Island Records started out in the late Sixties and still retained some of its hippie character. We were very lucky to be signed to Island in fact, because even though they were short of resources and somewhat disorganized, it was our opportunity to become good at stuff. Island treated us perfectly honourably but what I thought was respect was, in fact, a certain amount of chaos. They let us get on with it and, pretty quickly, the sort of things most bands expected their record company to do for them, we were doing for ourselves. We wanted to keep the initiative and that meant making our own plans, particularly with regard to touring.

Many friendships developed over the years. We tried to treat people fairly and remember that people who work in record companies, even if they become a bit jaded over the years, signed up originally because they like music, and you can usually tap into that. You are competing for their time; are they going to give their attention to that Bob Marley record or are they going to work on your U2 record for the next couple of hours?

Chris Blackwell was very smart, very worldly, a great ally for U2. He picked up on the intelligence of the band, and the commitment they showed. He quotes back to me something I apparently said to him in those very early days: 'We're not in the record business. We're in the U2 business, which is different.' And he agreed – he saw the bigger picture.

ADAM: Quite soon after signing the deal we started making plans for recording an album, singles, finding a record producer. Nick was very keen that we work with Martin Hannett, which was an inspired decision.

BONO: Martin Hannett was a genius. He had worked with Joy Division, who were our favourite band at this time. It would be hard to find a darker place in music than Joy Division. Their name, their lyrics and their singer were as big a black cloud as you could find in the sky. And yet I sensed the pursuit of God, or light, or reason ... a reason to be. With Joy Division, you felt from this singer, beauty was truth and truth was beauty, and theirs was a search for both. In amongst the squalor of everyday life, they were building with their music some kind of cathedral. As I look back now, this was a very religious point in music. We were a long way from pop music. At that moment, what was going on everywhere was politics as an alternative. There was a cultural revolution, stirred by the polemic of the almost Maoist-like music press. The theme was: 'Music's not a matter of life and death, it's much more serious than that.' No wonder people died.

LARRY: We met Martin in London while he was recording with Joy Division. It was an odd meeting. There was a kind of creative intensity in the room. They seemed quiet and disengaged. Unlike us, they seemed to be focused on what they should be doing in the studio. There was no chit-chat, we didn't come away saying, 'Good laugh, aren't they?' They were respectful and cool.

EDGE: They were actually recording 'Love Will Tear Us Apart', so we were in on that session. There was an atmosphere in the building, like something amazing was happening, plus a kind of stifling hipness – it was a very intense vibe. I think they might have been listening to some Wagner. It was not your common rock 'n' roll session by any stretch of the imagination, but it did sound great.

BONO: Here was Ian Curtis, this guy with the big, haunted, hunted voice, in person. We were looking through their records and they had Frank Sinatra records, *The Wee Small Hours, Songs For Swinging Lovers*. This was post-punk, they were listening to Wagner. They had the most incredible collection of music I had ever seen in my life, which had more in common with Bob Hewson than his son. They blew it right open for me.

EDGE: We played Martin a demo of '11 O'Clock Tick Tock'. He wasn't impressed with the demo, but he said he liked the song.

BONO: The title came from a note Gavin Friday put on my door in Cedarwood Road. We were going to meet at 11 O'Clock Tick Tock – it's the end of the night. The idea for the song came from standing on the balcony at the Electric Ballroom watching The Cramps, an extraordinary rock 'n' roll band. This was the peak of Goth and the gig was filled with candles. Voodoo was the order of the day, there was the atmosphere of a Black Mass, and I was thinking it was the night of the tragically hip. There was a lostness in the looks on their faces. It was that sepulchral make-up, white face, dark eyes, stuff my mates in the Virgin Prunes were up to their painted eyebrows in. But it felt like the end of the world. To a very young boy, nineteen years old, from the suburbs of Dublin, it seemed there was no life here at all. There might have been more humour than I was capable of spotting at that time.

EDGE: We were really scornful of the fact that a movement which, in our eyes, was all about smashing the former hegemony of boring Seventies metal groups and replacing it with something that was all about individuality and raw expressiveness, was somehow having the life drained from it by this kind of codified, fashionista element that was creeping in. To be hip you had to dress a certain way and act accordingly and write a particular kind of song. So we wore it as a stubborn badge of pride that we weren't prepared to fall into line with every other group and take the fashionable stance of the day, which was the proto-shoe-staring, no stage movement, jaded act, with lots of songs with completely impenetrable lyrics that probably don't mean anything. We were uncool because we were hot, we didn't keep our cool, we just erupted as a live band.

I remember Bono getting on stage at the Lyceum, a bit later that year, and we were playing with Echo and the Bunnymen and three or four northern English groups who were all part of this new psychedelia, acts who hardly broke sweat on stage. We just launched at the audience, and in the middle of 'Electric Co', Bono took a quite extravagant jump off a PA stack and his pants split wide open. And it was all press, record companies, everybody from the business was there. And Bono went into a rant. It was like, 'I'm wearing these for you! I'm wearing these for you!' pulling his clothes off with disgust at having even attempted being hip. He completely lost his cool. And it became a feature, occasionally, where Bono would be so keyed up that he'd just go into overdrive and you never quite knew what was going to happen, there was a real sense of jeopardy. This particular night it went a bit wrong, but definitely that was coming from a place of frustration and anger at the way the business had become so codified in the UK. We really didn't feel part of what was happening in England, and this was the moment when they, and we, realized that there wasn't going to be a happy end to this love story. There would be blood on the walls, probably ours and theirs.

PAUL: Martin Hannett came over from Manchester to make that first record in Windmill Lane studios in Dublin. He didn't think much of the facilities and there were some special pieces of equipment he made us rent from London and ship over.

BONO: He looked like Dr Who, and he was into technology. He had harmonizers and things we had never heard of. We were always attracted to sound scientists, and before Brian Eno there was Martin. He put a harmony guitar part on '11 O'Clock Tick Tock' and made it sound other-worldly. That's what he obviously learned from Joy Division, how to take the suburbs and make them feel like the furthest edges of the Milky Way.

ADAM: Martin was a bit like a big, cuddly garden gnome. He was very laid-back but, with hindsight, I think he was probably out of it all the time – there was a fair amount of smoking of dope.

EDGE: We'd never been in the studio with a proper producer, so we were a little nervous and that affected everyone's playing. We had a really hard time getting the backing track, we just couldn't seem to settle on a tempo. We would start off at one tempo and after about sixteen bars it'd be up three or four BPM (beats per minute), and we'd just keep getting faster and faster and faster throughout the song.

ADAM: I don't think he thought much of the rhythm section. It was really hard to get a backing track, and we were at it for hours. Eventually he said to Edge: 'What are we going to do? It's three in the morning and the rhythm section can't play in time together!'

LARRY: He was asking me to use a click track, which is a metronomic time reference. I told him I had never used one before and that I wasn't sure if I could play in time with one. I was trying to get comfortable in a new environment, and do what I thought was best. I must have really done Martin's head in. The track is not quite in time but it does the job. He listened to the track over and over again, constantly playing it back. By the end of the session I couldn't bear to hear it any more. I think he was highly medicated and as the session went on he became more and more incoherent. Despite his condition, he did a great job.

PAUL: Martin was pretty moody. I remember him coming out of the bathroom in my flat in Waterloo Road with a bottle of some kind of cough medicine. He said: 'Is this stuff legal in Ireland?' and promptly drank the whole bottle.

EDGE: Once we finished the backing track there was great relief. It was such a struggle I think Martin was ready to do a vocal and get to the mix. I thought

WE JUST LAUNCHED AT THE AUDIENCE, AND IN THE MIDDLE OF 'ELECTRIC CO', BONO TOOK A QUITE EXTRAVAGANT JUMP OFF A PA STACK AND HIS PANTS SPLIT WIDE OPEN. BONO WENT INTO A RANT. IT WAS LIKE, 'I'M WEARING THESE FOR YOU! I'M WEARING THESE FOR YOU!' HE COMPLETELY LOST HIS COOL.

EDGE

we could do a bit more so I said, 'What about a few overdubs?' He looked at me like I was from Mars and said, 'Like what?' I said, 'How about another guitar?' 'Off you go then,' he said, as I recall without much conviction. When I went in to the recording room, I had no idea what I was going to do. The engineer started the tape and I just began playing. I hit on a harmony part to the main hook. Martin suddenly got excited, declaring: 'God, it sounds like brass. I love it!' I know he had been a producer for a long time but I actually think it was the first time he had ever overdubbed a guitar. The mix took a while, as he had his own trademark drum sound, which was made by putting the snare drum through a period effects unit called a Time Modulator. I remember he carefully turned all the settings to zero after he'd finished so our engineer wouldn't see what he had done.

BONO: The record sounded more like him than us in the end, but it's brilliant and better for it, I think.

PAUL: '11 O'Clock Tick Tock' drew some attention but it was by no stretch of the imagination a hit single. But we were always inclined to make plans pessimistically, so that if something didn't happen we would not be defeated. We bought a van. It had a bulkhead and I had it fitted with a bench seat. It wasn't very comfortable but it was at least a van and it carried a certain amount of equipment in the back, and it would just about take the four members of the band and one or two others in the front. Probably the most comfortable place was actually lying on the floor and I remember that's where Bono used to spend most of his time. We took that van all over England and Ireland and had some fairly hairy moments in the middle of the night when whoever was driving was tired.

BONO: We did get the van, finally! We lived in that van. I remember it very well. It had a brown carpet, which I spent many hours contemplating. Rather than stay in Manchester or Birmingham or Liverpool, we used to drive back after the gig and save the money that we'd spend on hotels on eating once a week in a nice restaurant. This was instigated by Paul McGuinness. We may have been impoverished, but he would rather sleep in the van and have one good bottle of wine. We came to know more about wine than guitars. But there I was, in a confined space with all these men – it was like being at home in Cedarwood Road! But this time I had to make this family work. Sitting in the van you get to know everybody backwards. It's just hours and hours and days and days, listening to music, sleeping on the floor, because I can sleep anywhere. I can sleep standing up, on the street, in the cold. I would sleep on the floor right over the prop shaft. And I could feel it turning and the heat would come up from the engine. It was a kind of jungle sleep you'd get, which is when you're half-awake, half-asleep, all the way home from Manchester, and your head was filled with music, and your voice was sore from singing. And then you'd wake up in London.

EDGE: Rather than stay in a hotel, which would have been exorbitantly expensive, Paul found us a house to rent, which, in typical McGuinness fashion, wasn't some dingy little place in Clapham, but was actually just off Hyde Park next door to Jeremy Thorpe, former leader of the Liberal Party. I think there were only three rooms, and we were all bunking in one bedroom. But it was a feature of McGuinness's management that we might have no money but we always seemed to find a good restaurant to eat in. He was of the Oscar Wilde school of thought: the necessities I can do without, but don't touch my luxuries.

PAUL: There's a grain of truth to this because we did for a while make a point of not spending very much on hotels; we would go to good restaurants, and Ian Flooks, our agent, was something of a *bon viveur* and he certainly encouraged this practice. Our first agent, Ian Wilson, left to manage a band and I started working very closely with his boss, Ian Flooks. He had a great agency called Wasted Talent and they had the Police, The Pretenders, The Clash and Talking Heads, all the cool bands. Ian was very smart and I think he could see how big U2 were going to be.

He and I started to get into really close contact, planning tours in fine detail, thinking about what the gigs would be, what shape the room was, how many people to play to. We had a very conservative booking policy. We always wanted to sell out, so we were playing venues that were slightly too small for the band, and we wouldn't book a second day if we thought it would be only half-full. That was something we did consistently through the years. We always wanted to leave every town knowing that you couldn't get into that U2 gig, it was sold out.

LARRY: We were playing a lot of polytechnics and universities around the UK, slowly building our own audience. Money was always tight but at least we could afford to get a good PA, and a monitor desk. This made it easier but it didn't guarantee the band would be on form every night. We travelled the length and breadth of the UK, stopping occasionally to eat in motorway cafeterias and satisfying our growing addiction to Space Invaders. We stayed in bed and breakfasts ranging from the sublime to the ridiculous. The final straw was the nylon sheets with little grime balls on them. It was time to buy a sleeping bag. If this was the glamorous rock'n'roll lifestyle I'd been promised, I wanted my money back. Sometimes by the time we went on stage everyone would be trashed. The travelling and hanging around all day was the most difficult part for me. I was excited about playing but I had too much time on my hands. I wasn't much of a drinker back then. Looking back now, I could have done with one. Adam, on the other hand, was having a blast. This lifestyle seemed to suit him. He'd taken to doing silly things, like making his escape from the odd bed and breakfast late at night by climbing down sheet ropes he'd thrown out the window. He was mad for it.

ADAM: Fun is a very relative thing. If you're finished at eleven o'clock, there's a few hours left to go out and play. And, yes, I guess I would have been out most nights in bars and clubs; I suppose it was fun. It's what people that age normally do – the hotel wasn't much to go back to in those days.

I remember it as a very competitive time – 'Who's doing what, where, and how well are they doing it?' It was really about figuring out where we were in the pecking order and how to improve our situation. It was not about being *laissez-faire* and just seeing what happens tomorrow. The feeling was, 'We've got to be on that TV show. We have to get that magazine coverage. We must keep moving forward, maintain the momentum.'

PAUL: Martin Hannett would have produced the U2 album but he was committed to mixing the live sounds for Joy Division in America. Then Ian Curtis killed himself and that tour never took place.

EDGE: Martin cancelled at the last minute. I think he was completely devastated, and recording with U2 was something he just wasn't up to at that moment. Steve Lillywhite's name came up. He had done Siouxsie and the Banshees, XTC, great groups we really admired, and we had a chance to road test the relationship with Steve with our second single, which was 'A Day Without Me'.

ADAM: Martin was very laid-back and late-night. Steve was much more bright, morale-boosting, keeping things moving along. He empowered us, made us feel good about ourselves. The way he mixed a record was to make the most of what was there. Martin tried to close down the sound of the band to its bare minimum, whereas Steve kind of blew the sound up. 'A Day Without Me' was not an obvious single but it showed off the use of echo and gave Bono something to sing against.

BONO: Steve was such a breath of fresh air. He was like a children's television presenter: 'OK everybody, take out a box of Cornflakes and get an old container of orange juice and chop the top off it. If you glue them together you can make a phone!' He was that side of Britain, very positive and practical: 'All right, we can find a way to make it. Larry and Adam, you can't play in time. OK, right, I've a few ideas!' And, of course, Larry would be sitting there scowling at him as he tried to help him. But he bonded with Adam. Adam's the quicksilver in the mix. If Adam's going off, we're all going off. And if he's not, no one's going anywhere. That's really what it's like being in U2 – he sets the pace. And he found a friend in Steve.

ADAM: There was a level of excitement, Steve felt like the right guy. We knew we had the tunes to make an album, which was recorded in Windmill Studios. I don't think anyone particularly wanted to decamp to London, that would have been a big jolt. We were very young, still living at home, and there wasn't much spare money around. When we did our record deal we were taking out maybe twenty-five pounds each a week. That wasn't going to cover many taxis, you still had to take the bus. Windmill was the best studio in Dublin and it was owned by contemporaries of Paul's and he was able to agree a very good deal with them.

BONO: Steve had come straight from a Peter Gabriel session and so he was at his most experimental when he worked with us. There was incredible fun being had recording the album because we would try out everything. We turned a bicycle upside-down and used the wheels for percussion, playing them with forks from the kitchen. We'd smash bottles for sound effects, bring in a glockenspiel. It was a very creative approach to recording a rock band. Steve deserves full credit for that. Adam and Steve would stay up experimenting on themselves, and experimenting on us the next day in the studio. Those backing tracks were great – we recorded the drums in the bottom of the stairwell and had microphones all the way up to the very top of the ceiling, four storeys up. I used to go to sleep on the couch when they were doing the drums. I just wanted to listen to that; I would have had an album of just drums.

EDGE: Steve had a great way of pulling the best out of everybody. Nothing was a hassle, the sessions were very positive. I think it was particularly great for Adam and Larry to work with somebody who was able to understand that we were not incredible musicians. We did what we did.

LARRY: Steve was like Dr Feelgood, a tonic for the troops. I don't think he thought I was up for the job though, so I never really connected like the other guys did. Steve was used to working with some great drummers, professional musicians. I was eighteen when we recorded *Boy* and wasn't confident at all about my playing. I was hampered by my inexperience and my inability to loosen up. I had good ideas, I just couldn't play them like everybody else. I was focused and conscientious but unsure about using things like the click track. It was Steve's idea to record my drums under the studio stairwell. If felt strange at first. We were just getting used to recording together and the next thing I'm under the stairs. And then there was overdubbing. I was asking, 'What the hell's an overdub?' Steve would patiently explain: 'That's when you play on top of something you've already recorded.' I had no idea how these things worked, I was out of my depth. Steve was a great producer, he had his tricks and he knew how to use them. The big drum sound, that was his.

EDGE: We didn't have much time so we recorded all the songs we'd written as quick as we possibly could. We might have a few hours to do some overdubs on each song and then we'd be on to something else. Bono was finishing off some of the lyrics as we were wrapping up guitars and percussion. The whole thing just went really quickly, because it had to.

BONO: I found I didn't really like writing lyrics. I didn't listen to songs for their words, particularly. I was interested in ideas and I couldn't concentrate on the details. It was always annoying for people, because they kept saying: 'Why has the lyric changed from yesterday? And why can't you record it? Because you want to change it again!' To be so good conceptually and so poor in terms of finishing, I'll never understand.

EDGE: When we were gigging, knowing the album was coming up, we'd occasionally ask Bono how the lyrics were going, and he'd say, 'No problem. I've basically finished them, you know.' But it was the last minute, as usual with Bono – things get done only when they absolutely have to be done, so there were still quite a few outstanding couplets by the time we started recording.

But that was a period when so many lyricists were getting away with completely vacuous nonsense, lyrics that were so pretentious with very little real attempt to communicate. So I wouldn't have been that interested, as long as they sounded OK, that was fine. But Bono obviously wanted them to be good, and even though he'd been singing these sort of half-lyrics for such a long time, he sat down and really had to clarify what he was trying to convey. Some of them have stood the test of time, some have not. But it was the beginning, I think, of his becoming the lyric writer he now is. It was his first foray. I think the lyric writing was influenced by the choice of album title, *Boy*. It was Bono's suggestion, without actually offering a full explanation. *Boy* had a strength and clarity about it.

BONO: Myself and Guggi had made a pledge as kids that we would never grow up. We didn't want to be like adults, which is a fairly common experience of childhood. But we meant it, and in a certain way we pulled it off, both of us. You can be so powerful for the things you don't know. I probably had a hunch then that we might lose some of our uniqueness, and our first album was perhaps trying to lay claim to the power of naïveté.

I had a very clear idea of what the cover should look like, a child's face coming out of white, like a photograph before it's fully developed, which is really an amazing metaphor. I had a sense that this was subject matter no one else in rock and roll had ever explored – the end of adolescent angst, the elusiveness of being male, the sexuality, spirituality, friendship. It had a huge gay following, that album. I really couldn't fathom it at the time. But I look back now and see that it's full of homo-eroticism: 'in the shadows, boy meets man'. I was just approaching it thematically and wanting to look at that moment when you're developing, to go back to the photographic metaphor. It's U2 in development.

EDGE: When 'I Will Follow' came through, I recognized that we'd actually cracked something special.

BONO: 'I Will Follow' came out of a screaming argument in the rehearsal room. I remember trying to make a sound I heard in my head, and taking Edge's guitar from him and hammering away. It was literally coming out of a kind of rage, the sound of a nail being hammered into your frontal lobe.

It's a song about unconditional love, which is what a mother has for her child. If you walk away, I will follow. No matter what you do, you cannot separate yourself from my love. Which echoes the scriptures: 'nor height, nor depth, nor any other creature, shall be able to separate us from the love of God.' It's an amazing thing, but there's a chill in it. I'm singing from a mother's point of view. I know that's mad but I have done it a few times. But if you step out of that for a second and think it's a song about my own mother, it becomes a suicide note – 'If you leave me, I'm coming after you.' This is mind-blowing to me looking back. What drugs were we on? None!

Many of the songs were from the set we had been building over a couple of years and they are played very confidently. The sequence that blows my mind is 'An Cat Dubh', the black cat, to 'Into The Heart'. It's astonishing. Just the violence of Edge's guitar playing, this image of temptation, a cat sleeping beside a dead bird in suburban Dublin, and playing with it, the way they do, cat stalks the bird, kills it and then shakes it about. And somehow knowing the sexual side of that, desire and innocence, and the way it can play with you. And the beautiful lyrical guitar, Edge breaking the rules of punk rock and playing a kind of guitar theme, a solo almost, that went on for an age. That's amazing. And then the comic megalomania of 'The Ocean'. 'I felt the world could go far if they listened to what I said.' The future is laid out in that record! There's some beautiful writing, musically rather than lyrically, full of arcing, aching melodies. It's one of the best debut albums of all time, I think.

LARRY: I think *Boy* was recorded in just over a month. As it turned out it was the quickest album we were ever going to make. And then the touring really started.

BONO: I loved playing in the north of England. I loved being in Manchester, Liverpool, Newcastle, Scotland. People started following us around. We had a very short set, and we used to play a few songs twice. We'd start and close the show with '11 O'Clock Tick Tock' and 'I Will Follow'. I didn't talk so much. I only developed the rap because they were tuning up all the time – now we had someone tuning up for us.

EDGE: I got hooked on Space Invaders. We would call into the motorway service stations to have something to eat, spend ten minutes eating some dodgy sandwich then spend the rest of the time in the arcade playing Space Invaders. We were really kids, and we suffered the rough end of UK guesthouse accommodation. We checked into a place in Leeds in the middle of the night and through bleary eyes I noticed the garden was in full blossom in the middle of winter. I thought that was a little strange, only to discover when we left the next morning that the entire garden was filled with plastic flowers.

WE DID FOUR MONDAY NIGHTS: FIRST NIGHT IT WAS HALF-FULL, SECOND IT WAS FULL, THIRD IT WAS QUEUES AROUND THE BLOCK, FOURTH NIGHT THE STREET WAS BLOCKED. AND WE WERE OFF. BONO

PAUL: We weren't exactly out from under the cosh but we had a little money and were working with a professional road crew, and could at least make decisions about whether to buy a guitar. We had a very good relationship with Island; the press guys Rob Partridge and Neil Storey used to come to an enormous number of gigs, far more than their job would have required, and they helped stir up early support in the London music papers. We decided to attempt to break London by playing four consecutive Mondays in September. No one wanted to play on Monday, so it was easy to get booked.

BONO: Monday nights in the Marquee club were amazing. This was the ground The Who had walked before us, and we were developing an audience. We did four Monday nights: first night it was half-full, second it was full, third it was queues around the block, fourth night the street was blocked. And we were off.

PAUL: It was a way of building an audience but doing it visibly, so that people would know they were part of something that was growing. It was the same thing we had done at the Dandelion, because it was always clear to me that if somebody turned up at a gig and there were fifty people there, and they turned up for the same gig a week later and there were only twenty-five people, they'd be disappointed. And they certainly wouldn't ever come again. Audiences want to be vindicated when they make a choice about a band, they want it to be confirmed by other people. There's a herd mentality to any audience and building a following has a lot to do with that. This was when people realized there was something happening, and we were bringing that about by playing live, not having hit records.

EDGE: We went to Europe for the first time on that tour. We played The Milkyway in Amsterdam in October 1980. That was a great show. It was really a wonderful feeling to discover the language barrier was not a barrier at all, and to realize that music really did what we'd always imagined it could do, cross over and connect in a way that transcended any cultural or linguistic differences. There were certain little places that really caught fire for the band early on. Outside of Ireland and the UK, Holland was the first country that really went off for us.

PAUL: The idea of doing a preliminary tour in America cropped up, even before the album came out there, just to get everyone thinking about America and experiencing it before there was any pressure. During the recording of *Boy*, I had gone out to New York for the first time in my life to meet Frank Barsalona, who was the biggest and most important agent in America in the Seventies. It was a rather hopeful venture on my part, but my father died suddenly, the day after I arrived, so I had to turn around and go straight back to Dublin without completing my mission. The loss of a parent is obviously very affecting and a major change in anyone's life. The band all attended the funeral, and I was grateful for their support. Bono and Larry had both had to deal with such losses already. Mortality seems to be one of the elements that underpins U2 and perhaps has helped cement relationships. When I returned to New York a few weeks later, Frank Barsalona had no option but to meet with me, really, given the tragic circumstances under which our last appointment was cancelled. In fact, we went on to become good friends and the working relationship with him and Barbara Skydel, his number two, was the basis of U2 breaking America as a live band. The same goes for our agent in the rest of the world, Ian Flooks.

ADAM: Frank Barsalona was a classic case. He would tell us stories about The Beatles and The Who and Led Zeppelin, because he'd been their agent in his day. We thought he was the Don of America.

PAUL: In the Sixties, he had been The Beatles' booker at GAC (General Artists Corporation) and he later formed his own agency, Premier Talent. He had been the agent for the British Invasion and then brought in all the big rock bands. He established a network of promoters around America: Bill Graham in San Francisco, Don Law in Boston, Barry Fey in Denver, Michael Cohl in Toronto, Arnie Granat and Jerry Michaelson in Chicago. That network was expected to play Frank's bands at every level.

So Frank would call them all and say, 'I have a new band and they're called U2. I want you, Don, to play them in the Paradise' – which was a little club in Boston – and the understanding was that the promoters would keep the band as they rose through different levels of capacity. And that's exactly what we did from 1980 all the way through to the Zoo TV tour in the Nineties. And it started off with a little tour of the north-east in a van.

BONO: Paul had been filling our heads up with America. He rather cleverly figured that rock bands in the classic sense – The Beatles, The Stones and The Who – were out of fashion in Europe but they were still adored in America. We weren't really writing singles in the pop sense and Paul had more confidence that we could get played on US college radio than on Radio 1 in the UK. So he sent out early copies of our album to some college radio stations and they really got into it. We headed off to play in America on the strength of that.

EDGE: The Irish are on the fringe of Europe, and there is quite a sentimental attachment to America by virtue of the shelter it's given to the various waves of emigration that have left Ireland. It is almost the promised land, so going there was a chance to explore this mythic place. But also it is the dominant culture of world media, with its TV shows and movies and music, and my first impression was that it's exactly like it is on the TV. In some weird way I suspected that the America of TV programmes and films was something of an exaggeration. But you walk down the street and it's like you're walking through any number of TV shows. It was all there. I was fascinated by the different accents, the architecture, and even the trivial things like the coffee.

BONO: I wrote about it in a song. 'Angel Of Harlem'. We landed in JFK and we were picked up in a limousine. We had never been in a limousine before, and with the din of punk rock not yet faded from our ears, there was a sort of guilty pleasure as we stepped into the limousine. Followed by a sly grin, as you admit to yourself this is fun. We crossed Triborough Bridge and saw the Manhattan skyline. The limo driver was black and he had the radio tuned to WBLS, a black music station. Billie Holiday was singing. And there it was, city of blinding lights, neon hearts. They were advertising in the skies for people like us, as London had been the year before. And it was snowing. We pulled up at the Gramercy Park Hotel and everyone went in.

EDGE: We got out of the car and walked straight into the lobby. I looked out of the window and saw the two guitars, in their cases, just sitting there on the sidewalk where we'd left them, and two guys walking across the street about to grab them, so I ran out and got there first. But we were so close to being taken out by a sucker punch: bunch of kids from Dublin arrive in New York and immediately have their guitars stolen. It would have been too sad.

BONO: I just couldn't get enough of New York. I didn't want to actually go into the hotel because I'd stop seeing it, so I went out on to the corner and just continued to look around. My black, fake-fur coat was turning white with snow as a gentleman pulled up beside me in a car and offered to have sex with me. I ran back into the hotel and told everyone what had happened. They looked at me as if to say, 'What do you expect? You were in a fucking fur coat, you pansy!'

New York, I still can't get over it. Every time I go there, I have a deep intake of breath. No one talks at a normal volume. Taxi drivers, people in the restaurants, they're twenty percent louder than everybody else in the world. It has a Third World energy.

LARRY: I had never had jet lag before. I was completely disorientated. For me, going to London felt strange, but New York was something else. I was overwhelmed. There was so much to take in. I wish I'd enjoyed my first time in NYC more.

ADAM: I had been to New York with my family. I'd gone on the Staten Island ferry and I knew all about hot chocolate with whipped cream on top and pancakes and all those kind of things that you first experience – American TV, the static you get from the carpet – so I felt like I'd done America.

BONO: Michael Deeny, who'd managed Horslips and really taught Paul all he'd known, met us in New York and tried to get us into a club where Basquiat and all the great American artists of the era used to hang out with all the great musicians. I think it was called the Mud Club. Michael was a Northern Irish Catholic. He had been educated at Oxford and he had a posh accent and a stammer. He was wearing a beautiful cashmere coat and was knocking on the door of this building in New York – the club was two flights up – saying: 'I've organized ev...ev ... everything. Don't wo...wo ... worry, you can get in.' Of course, no one was letting us in. They'd obviously looked at us through the keyhole. We weren't cool enough. So Michael said, 'There's been a mis...misunderstanding. Stay here, I'll be r... r... right back,' and went off. We were standing outside this place for twenty-five minutes, not knowing where he had gone, until there was the sound of somebody falling down the stairs inside, and a big door opened and Michael Deeny, his hair dishevelled and with a bloody nose, was pushing back security, shouting: 'I've shown them!' He'd climbed up the fire escape at the back of the building, broken in through the kitchen and come down behind the security men to try to let us in.

This is the man who had chained himself to the wheel of the South Africa rugby team's tour bus during apartheid. And, of course, all these big South African white rugby players beat the shit out of him as the bus hopped down Piccadilly in the wrong gear – really an amazing character. A lot of Paul's bolshiness, his kind of effrontery when dealing with the rock 'n' roll circus types came from Michael, I think. You know – 'Would you mind not talking to me during Edge's solo, please.' That kind of thing. Perfect manners but more dangerous than a dig in the head.

LARRY: Our first American gig was in the centre of NYC at a place called The Ritz. Unfortunately, it wasn't a great debut. We were very nervous and the vibe wasn't with us. Bono would get very anxious in the run-up to an important show and that anxiety was infectious.

EDGE: We played a few shows on the East Coast. We did the classic thing, up and down the highways of America in a small van with two rows of seats and the gear in the back, staying in the cheapest hotels we could find. The sound engineer was driving, the lighting engineer was in the seat next to him and the band were in the back, it was that simple.

ADAM: We would just drive and drive and drive. It was the middle of winter, there was not a lot going on, but we were still young enough that we could sit in a station wagon or a van for hours on end, looking out the window, stopping at truck stops, goofing around trying on cowboy boots. Everything was built on such a large scale, it felt like driving through a movie. I liked Americans from the start. They could be loud and brash but were essentially very friendly people. One thing that struck me is that the minute you mentioned you were a musician, people were very interested in you, which was certainly not the case in Britain or Europe. You got more acceptance in America.

EDGE: Our show in Boston was the real surprise for us, because we opened for a band called Barooga Bandit at a crammed little club and noticed that we were getting a particularly good reaction. In fact, we played 'I Will Follow' three times because we opened the show with it, closed with it and used it as an encore as well. We left the stage feeling incredible because the audience was so enthusiastic. Then we all went back down to check out Barooga Bandit, only to find that the venue was deserted, everyone had left. It was then we realized that they had come to see us. We found out that one of the local college stations had been playing our album as an import, and we were actually quite a big band in Boston as a result. That was another moment of real encouragement.

I'D COUNTED IN A SONG AND LARRY HADN'T COME IN. I COUNTED IT IN AGAIN AND HE STILL DIDN'T COME IN. I LOOKED AROUND; TO MY PSYCHOPATHIC EYES HE LOOKED LIKE HE WAS HIDING BEHIND THE DRUM KIT. SO I PICKED UP THE KIT AND CHUCKED IT INTO THE CROWD. THERE WAS A TOTAL MESS ON STAGE – I THINK EDGE TRIED TO KNOCK ME OUT. BONO

LARRY: There was a guy called Carter Alan at WBCN, a rock radio station in Boston, they were banging U2's music from the very beginning. So when we went to Boston, it was a bit like a homecoming. It was a big deal for us. You could say we broke out of Boston.

BONO: Every night had to be the best night. If it wasn't, there had to be a reason, and we had to get to the bottom of those reasons. We were the furthest you could find from chilled-out. It was very combative, sometimes with the audience and sometimes between us. We played a little club in New Haven and I wound up throwing Larry's drum kit into the audience.

LARRY: It was one of those gigs, things weren't going terribly well. Bono was ready to start the song, but I had a problem with my drum kit. There are two spikes on the front of the kick that are meant to dig into the floor. But the drums were on a piece of carpet and during the gig the whole kit started to move. As Edge was starting '11 O'Clock' I was attempting to pull the runaway drum kit back to a place where I could reach it. I didn't even have the drumsticks in my hand.

BONO: I'd counted in a song and Larry hadn't come in. I counted it in again and he still didn't come in. I looked around; to my psychopathic eyes he looked like he was hiding behind the drum kit. So I picked up the kit to show the audience the drummer hiding behind and chucked it into the crowd. There was a total mess on stage – I think Edge tried to knock me out.

LARRY: He chased me around the drum kit, wanting to kill me with a mike stand. I ran to the dressing-room, running for my life. Edge jumped in and got a slap while trying to save me.

EDGE: I was hanging on to the back of Bono's shirt trying to restrain him from hitting Larry, and he hit me instead. So I wound up in a fight with Bono.

BONO: Edge smacked me. It was actually a full-on rumble with all members of the band whacking at me and me whacking at them. It was pure pantomime, Laurel and Hardy. But Edge packs a punch. There's a lesson here: never pick a fight with a man who earns his living from hand to eye co-ordination.

LARRY: I always knew the potential for danger. In some ways I was surprised it hadn't happened earlier. With the pressure and surging adrenaline that comes during a gig, he believed that I was not playing just to piss him off. As soon as I explained what happened, he said, 'Oh, OK.' Bono could be unpredictable, back then he was always ready for a scrap. He was a terrier and had no fear, you always had that in the back of your mind. No matter how upset you became with him, the only way to deal with it was to run for your life.

BONO: As I try to warn people, you couldn't get further from the songs than the singer. But I do my best!

PAUL: We did our first dates in Germany, which in those days was a divided country, with Berlin an isolated outpost of the West. To get to Berlin you had to drive through the corridor, which was a sort of wired-off motorway through East Germany. The very next night we were playing Munich, so we drove through the night to get there and the border came up and next thing we knew there were dogs and guns and searchlights and shouting. The band were in sleeping bags behind the bulkhead and the East German guards thought we were smuggling people out of the country. It was a very nasty altercation.

BONO: Our sleeping bags were wet from the condensation, because it was freezing outside and it was wet inside. We were sleeping. There was all this noise and shouting, 'Open the back of the van! Open the back!' Paul was trying to explain to them in English and they were poking rifles around, 'What are you smuggling? Open the van!' And they opened the back of the van and there's a rock band asleep. The officers made us get out, which we were not happy about. I remember just looking at these border guards and realizing they were the same age as us, but with short cropped hair – it's all in the song 'Stranger In a Strange Land'. That was really a song about our own alienation. We were a rock band but we weren't living like a rock band. We were fish out of water.

PAUL: That was the most basic kind of touring. We moved up a little after that into a really stupid school bus. It didn't have any bunks, it just had picnic tables. Sometimes I would be in my car. I had a Lancia that gave a lot of trouble.

EDGE: Paul's Lancia was of a particular vintage that was notorious for breaking down. It died on the *périphérique* outside Paris, in a huge explosion of steam. Paul took the radiator cap off before it had cooled down, so this thing blew about twenty feet in the air. Paul just completely lost it, he almost did the Basil Fawlty act of spanking the car. Then he went for the petrol cap. We suddenly realized he was taking out his cigarette lighter, and the four of us had to grab him, because he was actually going to try and torch the car there and then on the road outside Paris. We physically restrained him and dragged him off and we had a cup of coffee. He was a member of the Automobile Association, so they showed up at some point and towed us to the car ferry.

ADAM: We went back to America for three months, March, April and May 1980. Paul put a lot of work into spending time with Frank Barsalona and Chris Blackwell, trying to figure out what you did between record company and agent and promoters to get maximum impact across the entire country. In America, every city is a vastly different market, it's like being in a different country. It's different radio, media, TV and print. So it's a hugely contrasting process to getting your song played on radio in England. You have to go in there and make an impression to get everyone behind you. That's why the traditional and effective way of getting on in America is touring. It takes basically three or four months to cover the country and you just drive and drive and drive. I don't think you can do it after a certain point in your life. But we were in our early twenties and we were prepared to sit in a van for hours on end, looking out of the window. Our recreation was to go a truck stop and goof around and buy cowboy boots – it was that simple back then. For the *Boy* tour we were renting a proper tour bus and playing some pretty decent club gigs.

EDGE: The difference between our approach and that of many UK bands of the time was that we went in with a real determination to conquer America on a business front, and that meant Paul making all the right connections. We really had to hustle to get the money from the record company to go in the first place.

PAUL: Warner Brothers Records was a famously artist-friendly, Californian, slightly hippie organization in those days, and it was through them that U2's records were being put out in America. There was a young product manager there called Tim Devine, and he was my first really significant helper and put a great effort into getting U2 launched in America. Bob Regehr was the head of Artist Development. He was a big old cowboy from Wyoming or somewhere but he famously signed Prince to Warners. It was from him that you could get money to finance tours and I got to know him and told him I wanted to put the band on the road for three months, cover America, and go everywhere twice. Each of the major cities we would play once then come back at the end and play them again. And he said, 'Island Records' deal is up next year, there's millions of dollars un-recouped, and you want a hundred and fifty grand. 'Where will I get it back? How can you ask me for this money?' I said, 'Well, I don't know anyone else to ask.' So he gave us the money. Our other important allies at Warners were George Gerrity in radio promotion, Carl Scott in artist development and Bob Merlis and Donna Russo in press. Mo Ostin was like the president of a kind of music university. We used to think of Warner Brothers as our Harvard. Mo was always very kind to us and gave us the launch pad that other labels eventually benefited from.

In the early years, '81, '82 and '83, we were probably doing about three months on the road in America each year, and it wasn't self-supporting until I think '83 or '84, and Regehr supplied that cash. Sadly he got cancer and died, but he was the first really committed American executive who had a budget that I could tap into. The people at Warner Brothers taught us an awful lot. Ellen Darst worked for Bob Regehr in the New York artist development office and she had experience in radio promotion and sales, she had quite a broad grounding in the business and was very smart. Sometime during that first tour she asked me for a job. I said, 'How can I possibly afford to hire you?' She replied, 'No, you can't afford to hire me yet. But I'd like to come and work with you when you can.' Eventually she ran Principle Management's New York office, taking care of U2's American activities and other clients right up until 1997.

BONO: We went back to The Ritz in New York, and it started to go off for us. There was a balcony and the tables there would be taken by the music industry. They'd sit while everyone else would be jumping up and down. I stopped the show and made them stand up, and Paul McGuinness told me later: 'Lucky they did. Because if they don't, that's another matter.'

LARRY: We had a great reaction in America, even when the gigs weren't great. There was a real generosity, not only from our audience but from the people in the business and some journalists. Everywhere we went the attitude towards us was really positive.

BONO: In Chicago, the venue had tables in front of the stage, which we wanted to move. We said: 'We don't do gigs with tables in front of the stage.' Then this big Chicago scene unfolded, with them telling us in no uncertain terms: 'No, *we* don't do gigs where there's *no* tables in front of the stage. You get it?' We said: 'OK, we get it!' So during the gig, I walked out along the tables, jumping from one to another, and made them into a stage. It was a great moment.

LARRY: Bono would dance with girls in the audience. We played a place called J.B. Scott's in Albany, New York, several times. During one show there he picked a girl out of the audience and danced with her. The next time we played in Albany that same girl came to the show with her mother, who was insisting that Bono put the wedding ring on the daughter's finger and make an honourable woman of her.

BONO: We played Portland, Oregon. Two girls came into the dressing-room. We'd never met real groupies – we'd heard about them. We were rather disappointed that we didn't attract any, just so that we could look at them up close. We weren't interested in any sexual relations, it was just curiosity, we were flattered by their attention. We were talking to them, and, you know, wanting to kind of poke them and look into their eyes and ask them to fill out a few questionnaires. After they left, I went crazy trying to find a case of mine with all the lyrics I had prepared for the second album, which was due to be recorded as soon as we returned from the tour. I think there were three hundred dollars in it as well. So in addition to the kind of injury to wallet and notebook, pride took a bit of a pummelling. Boys mesmerized by girls shock! That's the story and it is one I have been telling for years. As it turns out, I am not sure they were groupies. It may well be that I just lost the case, as I am wont to do, and pinned the blame on bystanders. Twenty-five years later two honest girls (not, I must stress, the ones in the dressing-room) returned the contents of the case to me without even asking for a reward. Decency is alive and well and living in Portland. And I hate to have to admit this to my long-suffering band-mates, who had to listen to me bemoaning the loss of my treasure chest of lyrics and using it as an excuse for not finishing any new songs, but the notebook really contains little more than obscure hieroglyphics.

EDGE: Bono had lost this little case with lots of couplets and bits and pieces he had written. And I thought, 'Oh, this is bad,' because we were going in to work on the next record. But it has to be said we didn't really have any music either. We were heading for a big problem, but at that point everything was going our way and we just did not see it coming. As a band, suddenly finding yourself in New York, Boston, Chicago, then on the West Coast, Los Angeles, San Francisco, it was all a lot to take in. It was such an eye-opener and such a thrill for four kids from Dublin.

THERE WERE SOME LATE NIGHTS AND HANGING OUT WITH PEOPLE WHO YOU THOUGHT IN YOUR WILDEST IMAGINATION MIGHT BE GROUPIES, PROBABLY SMOKING THE ODD BIT OF KILLER GRASS AND DRINKING WINE. ADAM

LARRY: The East Coast has a slightly European feel to it, it has the Irish connection and the weather is sometimes not unlike the weather at home, so it was easy enough to get used to. The West Coast felt like a world apart. It was very hot at the time, and the people we met in the music business seemed to have a very different vibe. Everyone was tanned and improbably healthy. They talked a lot about swimming pools and girls.

BONO: I remember an electrical storm in Florida and thinking, 'Everything's bigger over here. The sky is bigger, the weather is wilder.' We had some days off and we went out to the beach and stood there, with no tan and no surfboard.

LARRY: I was starting to notice more and more pretty girls just hanging out. There were drugs being consumed openly, lines of cocaine on mirrors in our dressing-rooms. I had no experience of drugs and judging by the people offering them to me, it was an experience I could do without.

As for the girls, it didn't seem right that our people take advantage of U2 fans. In fact, a lot of them were groupies and not necessarily U2 fans at all, and the whole point of hanging around was to be taken advantage of. Anyway, I felt they were our groupies and they shouldn't really be messed with by these heathens. As a band, we had a policy that backstage passes for sexual favours was a fireable offence. A little harsh maybe, but that's U2 life.

ADAM: I don't think it was wild and crazy in any way. There would be a lingering tiredness you'd get from sleeping on a bus and travelling, driving, doing gigs, meeting the Press wherever you were. Then you'd be up early and on the move. There were some late nights and hanging out with people who you thought in your wildest imagination might be groupies, probably smoking the odd bit of killer grass and drinking wine. You would occasionally end up going to weird parties. I'd hang out with Paul quite a lot. He would always find something to go on to after the show. And maybe the guys were beginning to have prayer meetings on the bus and in their rooms. Paul and myself would be down the front of the bus; generally with loud music, people smoking drugs, having a couple of beers. And Bono, Edge, Larry and Pod, who had been the drummer with the Virgin Prunes but was now part of our road crew, they would be down the back of the bus. I don't really know what they were doing because I didn't go down there very often.

EDGE: Adam probably felt a little bit like the other three had lost it. Suddenly, from being in a rock 'n' roll band, he's with a bunch of guys who have got religion and are carrying Bibles in their luggage and occasionally getting together for a meeting to pray. It must have actually been very distressing for him. Paul was probably a little puzzled as well. But there was no tension, just a little bit of disappointment. It's certainly not what you would have expected when you thought of a rock 'n' roll band during that time. We were, I suppose, unique.

LARRY: The prayer meetings were a safe haven because they brought us together through some of the ups and downs of being on the road. Except for Adam, he was off having a really good time. There were many things that we didn't feel right about doing. Looking back now, it was very extreme and led me to misjudge too many situations. We were learning to distance ourselves, we were training to be separatists.

ADAM: There was a controversy about the album sleeve in America. I didn't really know what the word 'paedophile' meant. That was probably the first time I'd heard it. And I didn't understand the concept of homo-eroticism, for that matter. It was explained to me that there were people who liked to have sex with children, and that the picture of Peter Rowan (Guggi's brother) on the cover might be construed to be sexual. So obviously when people put it that way, it was a fair enough point. So we changed the sleeve to a weirdly abstract photo of us, put through a photocopier and stretched.

LARRY: In San Francisco, there was a gay activist journalist working for a magazine called *Mother Goose*, he was a big fan of U2. I think it was him that mentioned that many of the gay community believed that the boy on the cover had some gay connotation, and that the little boy was me. So when we went to San Francisco there was quite a bit of heat on me. I was seriously wigged out. It was very hard to be comfortable with that kind of attention. My first reaction was to be very pissed off. I was being described as a gay icon. 'What's that?' Eventually, I woke up and thought: 'That's brilliant. I'm really flattered.'

ADAM: Somewhere in the middle of that tour, we had a break in the Caribbean, staying at Chris Blackwell's house. It was ostensibly a working

SPRINGSTEEN HAD FILLED MY HEAD WITH ALL KINDS OF IMAGES OF AMERICA, AND PARTICULARLY NEW JERSEY, THE SHORELINE, ATLANTIC CITY, ALL THAT KIND OF FUNFAIR, BOARDWALK AMERICA. BONO

holiday, though I don't know how much work really got done. We recorded a single, 'Fire', with Steve Lillywhite. It was a new song that was going down quite well live, although as usual it didn't have any lyrics until the final recording. I think we only spent a day in the studio. The weather was too nice for recording! That was our first summer vacation in a way. It reminded me of those pictures when The Beatles were in the Caribbean, all very 'boys go water skiing for the first time'. That was the idea but we didn't actually manage it. I think Bono nearly sank the boat. He was definitely involved in a boating incident of some kind – I think he got it stuck on a reef.

BONO: I have a history of borrowing boats, and I like to think I always put them back. But hot-wiring boats is a bit of a speciality. I'd never been in water that wasn't below zero. I remember the turquoise sky and turquoise sea. We were all over there with our girlfriends and just like a bunch of children playing in the sand, running around. It felt like there was no one else in the world that interested us. We were a little community but really a tight one, and it was a lot of laughs and fun.

LARRY: It was a special place. Bono's better half Ali came over, as did Edge's girlfriend Aislinn O'Sullivan, who later became Mrs Edge, and my girlfriend Ann.

I met Ann in our first year in Mount Temple. She was the popular girl and I was the moody kid holding up walls. It was one of those things. We were opposites, yet we just sort of hit it off. We became friends. It was very innocent. My parents used to say to me: 'Don't you think you're a little young to have a girlfriend?' It seemed perfectly normal to me.

Travelling with the band had real peaks and troughs. On the one hand, I was living every musician's dream, on the other I missed Ann and what was left of my family at home. Strange because after my mother passed away, myself and my old man didn't talk much. There was too much water under the bridge, too many things left unsaid, we disappeared into our separate worlds and didn't reconnect until many years later. Even so, I still missed him and the occasional heated debate.

The girls would come out every once in a while, thankfully. They were close. We had to make a real effort to stay in touch. We'd skip meals just to have enough money to make a short phone call every four or five days. Girlfriends were a reminder of home and in some ways became your compass, there was a lot of temptation out there.

BONO: 'Fire' was not a very good song. I always had this faith that we could make it up as we went along, but sometimes we couldn't, and that was a case in point. When you are in a place like Nassau, you don't really want to go in and work. You realize why all these great groups make crap records when they go to record there – who wants to go to the Bahamas and sit in a studio?

EDGE: I don't really remember the sessions. I do remember the Bahamas, so that probably puts it into context. 'Fire' was one of those songs that we had very high hopes for, because we thought it was innovative and different, with the echoes being used in a new way. The problem was it was high in potential but actually not very high on content. But it did get us on *Top of the Pops* back in the UK for the first time. This was the show that we'd watched religiously for so many years. And finally, to get to go to the studio and see it all, it was a little bit like: 'Is that it?' It was very well put together but there was nothing sacred whatsoever. It really was one notch up from *Youngline* in terms of production. But the bands were all giving it everything. It's kind of the Coliseum and you are the Gladiators. You go out there and you've just got to make it work. And we were spectacularly bad. We were the only band who played on *Top of the Pops* whose single went down the chart the next week.

BONO: We weren't exactly mingling with the stars in America. There had been maybe somebody from Blondie and Talking Heads at The Ritz in New York. Joey Ramone might have been there. But then, at a gig in the Hammersmith Palais back in London, we met Bruce Springsteen and Pete Townshend. That was a great moment. Springsteen had filled my head with all kinds of images of America, and particularly New Jersey, the shoreline, Atlantic City, all that kind of funfair, boardwalk America. My brother had brought home *The Wild, The Innocent and The E Street Shuffle* and played it to me when I was fifteen. And I wasn't interested in brass-playing bands at that point, I really wasn't, but it just got under my skin. And then, of course, Townshend had written the book as far as we were concerned, because U2 wanted to be The Who. We didn't want to be The Beatles or The Stones. We didn't really want to be any other band. But if we had chosen one band, it would have been The Who. So to have these two superheroes come down and hang out, without any fuss, was very impressive. Bruce Springsteen is a lesson in modesty in terms of the way he carries himself when he goes out.

EDGE: We just couldn't believe these two guys walked into our dressing-room. It was quite overwhelming. They were the first bona fide stars we had ever met, really. Pete Townshend was a very special figure to us. I remember blurting out something stupid like: 'God, if I could ever write a song as powerful as "My Generation", that would be it. That's what my ambition is in this life. That would mean so much to me!' And he turned round and said: 'Yeah, you know, you'd earn a fucking fortune as well, mate.' But that was the self-effacing dryness of Pete. He was very complimentary. He really went out of his way to make us feel great. I always remember that – he didn't have to come back and say anything. He was excited about our band, and I think he just wanted us to know that he reckoned we were something special. We were on a high for a few weeks afterwards.

LARRY: Bruce became very important to us. When it came to making decisions about the size of venue we should play, we referred to Bruce and what he had done in our position. He had conquered America, with a certain amount of style and class. And although musically we come from different traditions, there was a special connection with him. What he was doing live was something we aspired to be able to do. His shows were legendary. We learned a lot from him.

PAUL: We returned to Ireland in the summer to start work on the second album. There is a saying in the music business: you get your whole life to write your first album and three or four weeks to write your second; there was a great deal of pressure.

LARRY: We had just come back from touring the United States, everything had gone well, and all of a sudden it was time to get our new album together. We got off to a ropey start. Money was still tight and we didn't have a place to rehearse, so we ended up back where it all started, Mount Temple. Don Moxham saved the day by allowing us to use a room at the school for a small price. Lunch every day was a Chinese takeaway; I haven't eaten Chinese since. The whole experience was pretty sobering after the euphoria of the tour.

ADAM: I suppose my attitude, naïvely, was you go in there and you make it work. The way we used to write was laborious and time-consuming because we would play for long periods of time and argue for even longer, then go back to the tape-recorder to check that what we were arguing about was actually right. And then whoever had the higher ground in the argument, we'd hang on to that bit and then we'd play for another half-hour until we could

WE WERE RUNNING OUT OF STEAM, RUNNING OUT OF ENTHUSIASM FOR THE WORLD. STEVE LILLYWHITE WOULD KEEP SAYING: 'COME ON. I MEAN, HOW LONG'S THE SONG, BONO? WHAT IS IT, THREE AND A HALF MINUTES? YOU CAN WRITE ENOUGH WORDS TO FILL THREE AND A HALF MINUTES'. BONO

duplicate it. It was very haphazard and it was labour-intensive, and we just didn't have the time to do it properly. So we took what ideas we had and sort of stuck them together with glue.

EDGE: With the confidence of youth we came off the road, went into a rehearsal space and assumed the songs would come. We worked up a bunch of ideas very quickly. Much of it was improvised; we'd take a guitar riff or a drumbeat and build a song around it. So we ended up with a lot of musical bits and pieces, and Bono had the job of trying to find melodies to sit on top of these things. And then the real panic set in when we realized it was getting close to when we were supposed to record the album and there were literally no lyrics for anything. I don't think the enormity of the problem struck us until we were in the studio. Bono was really panicked and usually upstairs in another part of the building trying desperately to get his ideas together. It was a really dark time. Island Records may have been behind the band but we hadn't sold a lot of records at that point. *Boy* didn't make the top fifty in either the UK or the US. We'd done respectably but it was not a big phenomenon. We all knew that the second record really had to be good. Those sessions were really tough at times, particularly on Bono. And out of desperation, I think, the lyrics for 'Gloria' arrived – that was really what he was going through. It was almost journalistic, that was where we were at, we were desperate and could see the whole thing falling apart.

BONO: We were running out of steam, running out of enthusiasm for the world. Steve Lillywhite would keep saying: 'Come on. I mean, how long's the song, Bono? What is it, three and a half minutes? You can write enough words to fill three and a half minutes. That's not much, is it? You know, how many songs do we need? Eleven, that's all.' And he wasn't wrong. But I'd be there scratching away.

But I believed – and I still do – that the way to unlock yourself, creatively and spiritually and pretty much every other way, is to be truthful. It's the hardest thing to do, to be truthful with yourself. And if you've nothing to say, that's the first line of the song: 'I've nothing to say.' So I started to write about that. The song 'Gloria' is about that struggle. I turned it into a psalm. *I try to stand up but I can't find my feet. I try to speak up but only in you am I complete: Gloria in te domine.* Wild thing for a twenty-two-year-old. Gregorian chant mixed with this psalm. It was a stained-glass kind of a song.

Really, these aren't lyrics. Carl Jung talks about a kind of shared consciousness, the collective unconscious, images that we all have from dreams that make us who we are. And what you get when you don't write are these images that kind of come up to the surface. So there's some strange things. There's a song called 'Rejoice', and it's exactly the same image as 'I Will Follow', it's a house tumbling down. It's bizarre to me that I would write two songs using that image. We've just been out playing it twice a night, and there it is again, 'it's falling, it's falling, outside the buildings are tumbling down. Inside a child on the ground says he'd do it again'. It's like a recurring dream. Looking back on those early songs, where language really is not as important as these unconscious images, I might have stumbled onto something out of my untogetherness. It's the kind of thing a lot of people relate to, but it's not intellectual.

'Tomorrow' was unconscious rambling. Years later I realized it was a narrative account of my mother's funeral. 'Don't go to the door, there's a black car outside.' I guess a hearse is what I was thinking about. It's all this kind of rambling. I'm tempted to just say to myself, 'Get over it!' But these things that happen to you in your life, if you don't deal with them properly at the time they do have a way of surfacing, they find holes.

'I Threw A Brick Through A Window' is a song about not liking yourself. It's seeing your reflection in the window and wanting to smash it. I don't know where that's coming from. I try not to major on self-loathing but it does creep in every so often. Guilt to me is a very useless emotion. You make a mistake, you try and rectify it, you apologize, and you get on.

LARRY: I had real difficulties with 'I Threw A Brick Through A Window' because of the tempo. Sometimes, after spending days writing and re-writing, recording and re-recording, it was hard to keep in time, and I wasn't helping by not using a click track. My drum parts started to suffer because I was spending all my energy just trying to keep time. The real wake-up call for me was after a long day getting nowhere on 'I Threw A Brick'. When I came back to the studio the following day, Edge had overdubbed a great tom part. I was so pissed off he had come up with a better drum part than me. It was the kick in the ass I needed.

ADAM: We managed to get the music together but the pressure was on Bono to come up with something and to perform. He was at his wits' end. And we weren't mature enough, or wise enough, to say: 'Hold on a second, let's step back from this, we'll take time out and do this properly.' We were all at fault here, believing that we had to pursue that particular schedule, at a great cost to ourselves.

BONO: Then in the middle of making this album we play Slane Castle with Thin Lizzy, the biggest open-air gig in Ireland, and we decide to play the new songs that we're working on that we've never played before. But not only that, we decide to play them first. We walk on to the song 'Tomorrow', with uillean pipes playing – and we were shite. We failed spectacularly.

EDGE: That was one of the worst shows we'd ever played in our lives. We'd come out of the studio, one of the most traumatic recording experiences of our lives, straight into this show, without any time to rehearse. Some of the songs we'd never performed together, because Bono might have sung on top of something that we'd recorded as an instrumental, and no one had really figured out how they would translate live. So we were really a shambles. To make matters worse there were some technical problems with guitars and equipment, so there was a whole kind of stop-start, broken-up momentum to the event.

ADAM: I think it was an attempt to recreate the environment where Bono would perform at the mike. So in the interests of helping him with his writer's block we thought he'd feel jolly good if he was in front of an audience. Absolute bloody disaster. But we were naïve and we were fearless, we would give anything a try, and I guess that's to be commended in the end.

BONO: It's a recurring theme, all the way through the band's life. We will always find ourselves in a corner so we have to fight our way out of it.

LARRY: The recording was hard graft. We also had a problem with the Christian meetings hanging over our heads. Some in the Christian meeting felt we should give up the band and go and do something more spiritually edifying. Edge in particular was questioning everything. I felt that the meetings were starting to get scary, people were becoming really radical. Myself and my father had come to blows over the whole thing. He had studied theology and thought we were simplifying something that was complex. We would go at it for hours. So we just stopped talking about it. Shalom continued to get more

EDGE LEFT THE BAND. BUT HE DIDN'T TELL THE BAND, HE JUST TOLD ME. HE WAS FEELING AT THIS POINT IN TIME THAT HE COULDN'T SERVE BOTH GOD AND MAN. I DECIDED I COULDN'T EITHER, SO WE BOTH QUIT. BONO

and more intense, there were frequent prayer meetings and considerable pressure to attend every one. It was as if you were awarded stripes for being there, and if you didn't show up, somebody was asking why. It was starting to feel all wrong.

EDGE: It was a little bit of a difficult time as we tried to reconcile completely contrasting imperatives. On one level to try and be as true on a spiritual front as we could be, and then on the other level to be in the best rock 'n' roll band we could ever be in. So there was an element of uncertainty going forward.

LARRY: The idea was to create a Christian community, where people would live and work under strict Christian standards. When you're young and impressionable it all sounds ideal. But there was something terribly wrong with the concept. It was a bit like the bigger the commitment you made, the closer you were to heaven. It was a really screwed-up view of the world and nothing to do with what I now understand a Christian faith to be. There was huge pressure to follow that path and what made it even stranger was that rather than it coming from the church leaders, it was coming from our friends. I learned a lot though and I also gained a faith I didn't have before, and that's still with me.

BONO: Edge left the band. But he didn't tell the band, he just told me, and I wasn't interested in being in the band if he wasn't. He was saying: 'This is great, what we're doing, but there is another world out there and that's what I want to be part of. And the real cure to the world's ills does not lie in a post-punk rock band but in developing yourself spiritually and finding your place and finding God's purpose for your life.' He was feeling at this point in time that he couldn't serve both God and man. I decided I couldn't either, so we both quit.

EDGE: It was a very, very clear fork in the road really. I wanted to take stock, to find out if what we were doing was in fact going down the wrong road. We were listening to all this negativity from people who were supposed to be our friends, telling us we can't continue in this band, it's not right. I said to Bono, 'Look, I'm quite happy to give this up if it's not the right thing for us but I need to find out. Are these people a little nuts or do they have an insight that I've been missing?' Bono understood my position and thought this was the right way to deal with it, hit it head on. He wasn't interested himself in going ahead if it wasn't the right thing. So I took a bit of time to get it straight in my own head who was to be trusted. I thought that the answer would become very clear, and it did.

LARRY: Edge left the band, I left the meetings.

ADAM: Bono and Edge turned up and said they were having real difficulties coming to terms with what was going on for them spiritually in their Christianity and what being in a rock 'n' roll band meant. That was a bit of a shock to Steve Lillywhite, myself and Paul, and so we did what we always do in a crisis: we had a meeting. And it's not that anyone talked them out of it but I guess Paul put an interpretation on what they were saying and said: 'Is this really what you want? Do you really think you're going to be more effective by going back to your kind of normal lives? Or do you think taking this opportunity to be in a great rock 'n' roll band is, in the long term, going to have more value?' I guess whatever went on after that, it gave Bono, Edge and Larry enough resolve to feel that they could finish the record.

PAUL: I took the position that I would respect anyone's beliefs and I would expect them to respect mine, even if they weren't the same. And that's pretty much been the basis on which we have worked ever since. When they told me that there wasn't going to be a tour and they were going to stay in Dublin and do God's work, whatever it was, I was really shocked. I said, 'Give me time to think about this.' I went out from Windmill Lane and walked around the block. I came back and I said, 'Look, quite honestly, if God had something to say about this tour he should have raised his hand a little earlier because, in the meantime we've booked a big crew and made commitments to people and, in my view, you're obliged to follow through on them.' So that was kind of the end of it. They accepted that, and it never happened again.

BONO: Giving up the band was very hard to do, because we both loved what we were doing. But something very powerful happened there. Sometimes you have to let go of what you love to really have it. Without being too melodramatic, it's like Abraham waits all his life for a son, and then God tells him to go down and sacrifice Isaac. It's one of the wildest episodes in the scriptures. But it seemed that when we got it back it was going to be even more powerful. The sort of spiritual ideas that were going around at that time were very profound but very heavy. Christ saying: 'He that loves his life shall lose it.' I mean, this is pretty extreme. This suggests that if you really want to live, you can't hold on to your life too tightly. You have to let go, you have to surrender. I'm not sure I understood that back then but, in my zealotry, I didn't want there to be anything in my life that came between me and God, including music. Because, of course, you can make anything an idol; it doesn't have to be money or it doesn't have to be fame – anything can get in the way. Smugness, for instance. Years later, I had a better understanding. You can hold on to something so tight it's like you've already lost it. And that's one of those deep spiritual insights that took me a long time to discover. It makes you very weak to want something so badly. When you let it go you're much more powerful. And something happened around that time, where we let go of the thing we'd wanted all our lives, the thing that had given me a way to face the world again, that made sense of me. That album, in a way, was where U2 said: 'We will go wherever we have to go. We will break all the rules of hipness. We will be as raw emotionally as we have to be, in order to be honest.' Even after that, we were giving up the band. It was really pushing it as far as we could to prove that we couldn't be bought off by our ambition. And I think it's an amazing thing, we nearly succeeded in derailing the band, but at the same time we regained it more fully.

EDGE: I felt very clearly that this band had something unique and special, and it was completely bogus to suggest that you couldn't have a legitimate spiritual life *and* be in the rock 'n' roll business. That was a dangerous piece of nonsense. That's not to say that the people involved in Shalom were in any way bad people, it's just that, in a group dynamic, ideas sometimes gain credibility when they really shouldn't. It was a necessary thing to get through. It was the beginning of our extricating ourselves from that system of peer support. I'm sure it was a big relief to Adam when we started to drift away from that very close-knit group and trust our own counsel.

BONO: We had this notion, early on, that we didn't want to be the band that talks about God, but then we made an album that spoke of little else. Patti Smith was dealing with some of this kind of subject matter, as were Bob Marley, Marvin Gaye, Bob Dylan. But there weren't many people who wanted to lift that stone and see the creepy-crawlies that were underneath. Your spiritual life can be as messy as your other lives, so if you are going to sing about it, own up to your frailty and vulnerability.

ADAM: I didn't really have a difficulty with the lyrical direction. I understood that rock 'n' roll was soul-based, that it was spiritually-based. What I wasn't sure about was whether that was acceptable from a New Wave band, which is kind of what we were, we were part of that collective. I just wasn't sure whether that was going to work. But I was enthusiastic about the music, it was a rock record and it had some very interesting stuff on it.

EDGE: Whatever he could come up with that sounded close to the spirit of the music, Bono would just have to accept that's all we could achieve. I don't think he was under any illusions at the time. He was kind of heartbroken on some levels that we had to finish the record under those circumstances. But that said, there's something very powerful going on. I think it's the absolute honesty that comes through, because it really is people in a desperate situation. It has a power by calling out for divine intervention, for help, for anything to try and deal with the situation we were in.

BONO: I wanted to call the album *October*. The title came before the song. It was the idea that we were born in the Sixties, a time when materialism was in full bloom. We had fridges and cars, we sent people to the moon and everybody thought how great mankind was. But the Eighties was a colder time, materialism without any idealism, the sun without any heat, winter. It was after the fall, after the harvest. I had the line, *October, the trees stripped bare of all they wear*. Here I am, aged 22, with a head full of gothic dread, looking around at a world where there's millions of unemployed or hungry people, and all we've used the technology we've been blessed with is to build bigger bombs so no one can challenge our empty ideas. Christendom is telling us that God is dead, but I'm thinking Christendom is dead and our little combo has been hired to play at the funeral. Mad stuff. Those Joy Division albums had really gone to our heads. October is an ominous album title. The song itself is a really gentle, meditative piece of work. Edge at the piano coming up with these beautiful icy notes, and this picture of loss of innocence, the fall, the leaves falling from the trees, and you're left exposed. I was amazed during those sessions when Edge played piano. I didn't know he could. And he didn't really know either.

EDGE: I hadn't really played piano since I was a kid. I'd abandoned it aged twelve to take up the guitar, but I did remember some elements. I really don't know where that October piece came from, other than just sitting at a piano and that's where it brought me, into this quite stark, quite grey but beautiful European place. After going on tour through Europe, seeing Paris, Amsterdam, Berlin and Hamburg in winter, I never felt so European. It had a profound affect on me, as much as seeing New York city for the first time.

LARRY: The album turned out a lot better than I thought it would. I felt that the songs were good, we just didn't know how to finish them.

PAUL: That was probably the roughest patch for the record company, because they didn't much like the record, and they didn't like the sleeve either.

BONO: The cover was my fault. I had this very strong feeling about Docklands, Dublin. Windmill Lane was on the docks, and this particular area on the docks I used to walk to during recording, and look into the Grand Canal dock for clues. It felt very special there, there was a sort of industrial aesthetic. There was something in the water for us. Of course, this is now where Hanover Quay is, where our studios are and now it's the centre of the new Dublin. But then there were no signs of life whatsoever. Just a dog called Skipper and a guy called George who operated the lock. I think the instinct was right to shoot it there, but it just didn't come off.

LARRY: Although it's not a particularly ingenious or clever album cover, there's no pretence. It's a picture of four guys with funny haircuts.

ADAM: We hadn't a clue how to be art-directed or stylized for something like that. It was just very naïve, put the four lads together and shoot the photograph. At the time, Bono was very keen on that Sixties presentation of putting a big border on the photograph and having the track listing on the front. A lot of people tried to dissuade us; representatives from Island Records came over and told us, 'The cover stinks.' But we were so much up our own arses that we didn't have the sense to listen to what was being said.

EDGE: This is where U2's artistic control theory really came out and bit us on the arse. It's really not a great sleeve. But when the guy from the Island art department came over to talk us out of it, to us the issue was not really the sleeve, it was artistic control. We were desperately trying to prevent a take-over of all of these creative controls by Island. So we sent him back to London and told them it was in the contract we could have the sleeve we wanted. I have to say, he was absolutely right and we would have been much better off listening to him. But, then again, we wouldn't have held on to the control that we had, so in the long run maybe we were right.

PAUL: There was an important change in the dynamic between the band and myself around that point. Adam and I had operated almost as a tag team, getting the other members of the band to do things. We were, in a way, practical people and there were times when the other three needed to be brought round to something for professional reasons. I tried to exploit this relationship one too many times, asking Adam to get them to agree to something, I can't remember what it was. And Adam, said, 'No. And stop asking me to do things like that. I'm a member of the band and you're the manager, and let's just remember that.' It was absolutely true and quite an appropriate thing to say. And I stopped doing it.

ADAM: It was a period of great uncertainty on many levels. The record didn't do particularly well. The deal that Island Records had done with Warner Brothers in America was coming to an end, so there wasn't much of a push being given to their product and it was hard to get tour support. There was no radio play, so we were depending on word of mouth, and it wasn't really happening.

EDGE: It's our most awkward album in some ways, the most confused, and it came out to mixed reviews. It did OK in the UK but in a lot of countries it didn't do as well as *Boy*. That was a setback. At that moment, I think Island were considering dropping us. But I believe it was Chris Blackwell's instinct that maybe there was more there, that this band, if given the chance, could go places, and that we hadn't actually been dealt a fatal blow. So on that instinct they said: 'Let's give it another go.' That's something that probably wouldn't have happened at a bigger label, and certainly wouldn't happen today, when bands are dropped at the first sign of trouble.

PAUL: If we'd been with a different label I think they might very well have decided to drop us. That didn't happen, but we knew we had to raise our game if we were going to survive.

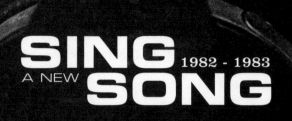
SING 1982 - 1983
A NEW SONG

Bono

WE MADE OUR FIRST VIDEO, FOR 'GLORIA', ON A BARGE ON THE DUBLIN DOCKS. IT TURNED OUT TO BE VERY IMPORTANT.

PAUL: I think because of my background in film the band were at first rather gloomily assuming that I would want to direct them. But they were clients and not an opportunity for me to experiment as a director. We have always used the best directors we could find.

LARRY: I had no idea about videos, none of us did. I had just bought a brand-new pair of red Doc Martens boots which cost me fifteen pounds, a lot of money back then. There was a scene where the director, Meiert Avis, asked me to splash through a puddle. I said, 'I'll get my new Docs wet.' He said, 'Yeah, well that's what we want for the scene.' I told him, 'Forget it.' I wasn't getting the boots wet.

BONO: When we went on tour in America, something strange happened. In some cities we would still be playing clubs. 'Gloria' was not getting on the radio, and things were looking a bit wobbly. But in other cities, there would be a thousand people there, or two thousand. We were being booked into theatres to cope with the demand. We played the Hollywood Palladium in Los Angeles, to over four thousand. It turned out these cities were test markets for a new idea, which was music television, MTV. There weren't many music videos around but one of them was 'Gloria', and they played it all the time. We became the first MTV band and they started to help break us.

PAUL: We knew the people who started MTV quite well. It was a very innocent and much less research-driven business than it is now. You made a video and took it round there and you could play it to one of their executives and three hours later, if they liked it, you'd see it on air.

BONO: In LA, we stayed at a hotel called the Sunset Marquis. It really was just a fantasy for us, from the north side of Dublin, to be sitting by the pool watching famous figures walking behind yucca trees.

EDGE: Paul hooked up with somebody at the Sunset and we were invited to a party at a big record producer's house. I remember walking in and realizing that everyone was off their heads. For a nineteen-year-old from Dublin, going to this party was like going to Mars. The perspex grand piano struck me as being quite something, and then it started playing all by itself. The décor was high Seventies and the open-plan living space featured about an acre of white carpet, white sofas, containing a lot of very white guests who had obviously been at the white powder. The record producer seemed to have a girlfriend and a wife, the latter of whom introduced herself as his manager, so I was instantly confused. The wife took a major shine to me and offered to show me the 'gold discs'. I was a little green, I have to admit, and I didn't quite understand what was going on, so I accepted. She dragged me off into the garden saying things like, 'Yoji normally comes to rake the Zen garden on a Tuesday' and, 'Over there is Elton John's house, the one on the left is Dudley Moore's.' My head was completely blown. Not only because I had just been transported into a real-life Hollywood movie but also because I hadn't been taken by the hand for a walk by a grown woman since I was about four years old. I genuinely wasn't sure if she was just being friendly or if she thought I might fall into the Koi pond. The penny finally dropped when we got inside this darkened studio with gold discs on the walls and she was still holding my hand. I made my excuses and left.

She was a gorgeous lady but I was like a rabbit caught in the headlights. It felt as if I was about to experience everything that anyone had ever told me about what happens to rock 'n' roll bands when it all goes horribly wrong. We ended up going back to the main house, and the first thing I saw when I walked in the door was a woman walking over, slapping Dusty Springfield across the face and walking out. The hostess was crying, 'Oh my God! Oh my God!' The girl was Dusty's 'significant other', and she had freaked because Dusty was chatting up Paul McGuinness. After the initial shock had subsided, our hostess said to Paul, by way of an explanation: 'Oh Paul, I'm so sorry, Dusty always goes hetero on Quaaludes.'

BONO: The Midwest was very conservative in those days, but we loved it. On the outskirts of Detroit we stayed in a very famous rock 'n' roll hotel. I was wearing tartan pants and my hair was turning into a cross between a badger and a mollusc. This guy cruising the street called me a 'fucking faggot'. Without thinking, I stuck my head into his car and was reaching for his throat when I realized he was a six-hundred-pound gorilla with two big dogs and a shotgun in the back. He was a monster of a man, and he just pushed open the door and came running for me. At which point a film crew,

ANTON CORBIJN WAS A PERSON WHOSE OWN VISION WOULD SERIOUSLY IMPACT THE BAND'S. HIS PICTURES ARE OFTEN VERY MONUMENTAL, WHEREAS THE BAND CERTAINLY WERE NOT. WE WERE VERY STOIC, IT WAS A VERY AESTHETIC TIME, ANTON TOOK PICTURES THAT LOOKED LIKE THE MUSIC RATHER THAN THE MUSICIANS. BONO

who had been following us round, spotted this and started filming the incident: Irish rock star's death live on camera! This man was saying, 'I don't mind ripping your head off on camera, son. I don't mind ripping your head off with the police watching. I don't mind going back to jail just for the pleasure of ripping your faggot little head off.' I tried to talk the gentleman down and explain that tartan pants weren't necessarily an indication of sexual preference, it was just bad taste.

You see, the look was still a problem for us, because people sometimes couldn't hear the musical ideas and intelligence of the band because we looked crap. Then we met a man who would help change that.

LARRY: In New Orleans we did a gig while sailing down the Mississippi on a boat called the *President*. The *NME* was there with a very tall Dutch photographer called Anton Corbijn. He made a big impression on us and not just because of his imposing height. He had done a lot of cool shots of Joy Division and others so we were slightly in awe of him. There was an instantaneous bonding between us, and it's a relationship that has lasted all these years. He's one of the great photographers.

BONO: We were all very struck by him because he bought us and the record company a round of drinks. Anton went on to become one of my better friends and a person whose own vision would seriously impact the band's. Anton recognized the spirit of the band and educated us in our ability to take risks in photo sessions. We've done everything for Anton, we've been photographed naked, we've worn frocks and makeup. But strangely the fun we always had with Anton was rarely captured in his photographs because he has a very different take. He's not trying to capture you as you are, he's trying to portray what you might be. The pictures are often very monumental, whereas the band certainly were not. That was his thing – he found the right images for those songs. We were very stoic, it was a very aesthetic time, Anton took pictures that looked like the music rather than the musicians.

I'M A BIT OF A STRAY DOG. I WOULD NOT HAVE BEEN IN THE QUEUE TO GET MARRIED HAD I NOT MET SOMEONE AS EXTRAORDINARY AS ALI. I ALWAYS FELT MORE MYSELF WITH HER THAN WITH ANYBODY. BONO

EDGE: Back in Dublin, we recorded 'A Celebration'. It wasn't bad but it wasn't good enough to get us out of trouble. We were still reeling from the whole album debacle, recording without having songs. At that point we needed a hit. 'A Celebration' wasn't one of those.

PAUL: We went back to America to support the J. Geils Band. It seemed like a good way of covering parts of the country where we hadn't made an impact and also to see how the band worked in arenas. They were playing to between five thousand and ten thousand people. The Geils Band were at their peak with their big hit 'Centerfold' and were enormously hospitable to us. They taught us our arena manners.

BONO: A good-time blues band might not have been the obvious match for your humble post-punk rock band. I think Paul was testing out his theory that the Irish had enough salt to keep themselves preserved in hillbilly country. And he had enormous respect, as indeed do I, for Peter Wolf, the main man in the J. Geils Band. This was an extraordinary DJ, a very gifted commentator on pop music, who happened to be a singer.

LARRY: Peter Wolf was really kind to us. He was friendly, very supportive, anything we needed he made sure we had, but the gigs themselves were tough. The J. Geils band had a very different audience to us and we had to work hard to get their attention. Bono had a particularly tough job getting through, although it didn't take him long to find ways to make himself heard.

BONO: We were warned by the promoter that the last opening act had been bottled off, Tom Petty receiving one beer bottle to the forehead, big gash, lots of blood, because they didn't want any of that kind of punk stuff going on in the Midwest. So we had an idea, I think it was mine, to finagle our way into the hearts of their fans. We had seen them play, and I noticed that when the screen surrounding the stage lifted, people naturally thought the J. Geils Band were about to go on, so they stood up and applauded. But in fact the support act would walk out and be bottled off. I thought that's a mistake, if the support act were already there when people were standing and cheering there was an opportunity to accept the applause as yours – so that's what we did. We hid behind our amplifiers. The screen was pulled up, the people stood up and started cheering, and I walked out from behind the amps with my hand in the air going, 'Thank you!' The crowd kept applauding, and we started into our set with the faces of seasoned and much-appreciated local heroes – and got away with it. It was a great moment.

LARRY: However tough is was, it did give us the chance to play cities we would have had difficulty playing on our own. So from that point of view it was a good exercise.

ADAM: There was very little support from the record company and by the end of that tour in America we were way out of money. I think we could just about cover air fares to get people home. That was a bit of a brick wall, to realize that we'd come this far, we had two records out, we'd put a lot of work into it, and we couldn't even afford to pay the crew. At the end of that period, there was a firm resolve to come out of the box fighting with the next record.

PAUL: We actually had run out of cash. We finished the tour on my American Express card, and when we got home I couldn't pay the bill and they took my card away. That was a really low point. Of course, everyone in Dublin thought I was some kind of rich English person who had loads of money to subsidize U2's activities. The reality was there was no money and I didn't even have a credit card any more.

EDGE: We had let things drift a little bit and it was time to get back to the original vision that we had for the band. We were determined the next album would be more to the point, tougher and more hard-hitting.

BONO: A few things had been happening on the *October* tour. Bobby Sands was dying, on hunger strike in Ireland, and people were shouting his name at us while we were on stage. There were a few 'up the IRA' contingents, who felt we were Irish in America; there was some kind of Provo-mania happening. I could not but be moved by the courage of Bobby Sands, and we understood how people had taken up arms to defend themselves, even if we didn't think that was the right thing to do. But it was clear that the Republican Movement was becoming a monster in order to defeat one. Those were very dangerous times in Ireland – Nationalism was turning ugly. So we rather turned against the tricolour (the Irish flag), and when they would be thrown on stage, I would dismantle them. I'd take off the green and the orange and be left with the white bit in the middle, and that became the white flag. A simple statement but powerful at the time. So when we were preparing for the *War* album, we started thinking about what it was to be Irish. We had to examine some of those questions. Do you really believe in non-violence? At what point would you defend yourself? They're not simple issues to resolve.

EDGE: We rented a little place on the beach in Howth, on the north side of Dublin. As soon as we got off the road we started going there and working up ideas. The band were basically sponsoring a little house for Bono and Ali that we could also use as rehearsal space. No one minded, because they were skint and, like the rest of us, either living at home or in some dodgy flat.

BONO: It was an old mews house, it might once have been a stable. It had three rooms, the band took the living-room, myself and Ali took the bedroom and we all shared the kitchen. It was an idyllic spot with the waves crashing on the walls of the house. I remember it as a really great time, songwriting and just being in a band.

ADAM: What must it have been like for Ali to have us in there? Amazing that she put up with us.

BONO: In the interests of decorum, I would like to point out that Ali and I did not move in until we were legally wed. You know, I'm a bit of a stray dog. I would not have been in the queue to get married had I not met someone as extraordinary as Ali. I always felt more myself with her than with anybody. I met a beautiful couple on that tour and I was talking to them about the love of my life, and they were saying, 'Are you going to get married?' I said, 'Well, gosh, I never thought about that.' And they told me, 'If you've got that sort of thing, you should never let it go.' And I took their advice.

Adam was my best man. For all the crackle and pop of his lifestyle, Adam always had a kind of wisdom. He was the perfect gentleman, who believed in love, but at the time he seemed to believe in love with a lot of people. But I'd been having conversations with him about it and he always seemed to suggest that if you can find everything in one person, then you should seize the day. I also asked him because maybe I didn't feel as close with him as I did with the others.

ADAM: I thought it was an incredibly brave thing to do. At that point there wasn't really much money around and we were going to be away often, so I didn't really know how he was going to pull it together. But I'd known Alison for as long as I'd known Bono. It's been a very beneficial union. I think Bono without Ali would unleash an energy upon the world that might have as much negative effect as it has positive.

BONO: We didn't have a stag night, which is just as well. Aged 22, I was more than a little earnest, not really interested in drinking, and I'd fallen out a little bit with the Village. The Virgin Prunes had gone their own sort of guerrilla, arty way. We were on the same festival at some point in France and somebody wrote in the programme: 'If U2 are God, the Virgin Prunes are the Devil.' We really had become the antithesis of each other and our close friendship started to come under strain. I was probably coming back from tour and talking about America and what was happening for us and how we were becoming a big rock band, which they thought was a bit uncool. As a sort of art event, they used plaster of Paris to make a parcel out of my car and wrapped it up in paper and eggs. And then when I woke up in the middle of the night to discover them throwing eggs at my bedroom window, a row broke out ... I think there might have been some violence involved. It all just got a little bit out of hand for a couple of years, and only really came back when I rediscovered my sense of humour.

ADAM: I hadn't a clue what best men did. But I was happy to get him to the church, basically on time.

LARRY: Although Bono had left the Christian meetings, he still had a lot of friends involved, who were invited to the wedding. It was a mix between a traditional Protestant wedding and a born-again Plymouth Brethren Baptist ceremony, so you could say it was a little unconventional. Our parents had been invited and they were seeing and hearing for the first time some of the things that went on at the Christian meetings. I think it confirmed what my father already thought. But it was a great day, and it meant two weeks off while the happy couple went on honeymoon.

BONO: It was a very eccentric affair. We had the wedding in a small chapel in Raheny. I arrived late and there were so many people outside I couldn't get into the church. There was a choir singing and lots of tin whistles being played out of tune. It was an occasion we weren't quite prepared for, myself or Ali, but we were carried away with it. Then we went up to Sutton House Hotel, where Van Morrison shot the cover of *Veedon Fleece*, and that was wonderful. The band got up on stage and blew all the fuses in the building so we spent our wedding night in the dark, crawling round on the bedroom floor looking for each other. We were children, very young in the head and very young in the heart.

We went to Jamaica on our honeymoon, to a house called Goldeneye owned by Chris Blackwell. It was incredible. Ali still laughs about how, on our honeymoon, I was writing an album called *War*. I was working on the lyrics, Edge was at home working on the music.

EDGE: I had the room to myself and I was working on a four-track cassette recorder. Those two weeks were something of a breakthrough for me as a writer. I made a lot of progress with 'New Year's Day', working with a great bass line of Adam's, and got rough demos of 'Seconds' and 'Drowning Man'. The first draft of 'Sunday, Bloody Sunday' came during one particularly depressing day in that little house by the sea. I was alone, nothing was going right and I had a big fight with my girlfriend because I was working when everyone else was on holidays, and it was looking like maybe I should be on holiday too and not wasting my time trying to become a songwriter, since I was obviously no good at it. I did the only thing I could think of, which was to channel all my fear and frustration and self-loathing into a piece of music. I picked up the guitar and let it all come out. It was just a sketch, an outline, I didn't have a title or a chorus melody, but I had a line of lyrics and a theme. If I remember rightly, my opening line was *Don't talk to me about the rights of the IRA, UDA* … It was a full-on anti-terrorism song.

BONO: I had the idea to contrast the actual event known in Ireland as Bloody Sunday – when innocent protesters had been shot by British Army paratroopers – with Easter Sunday, the central event of both denominations – Catholic and Protestant – that were at war in our country. It's provocative but I don't think we really pulled it off. Many of our songs were great ideas, but we hadn't yet the chops to execute them in all their complexity, so we just hinted at this. It was a song whose eloquence lay in its harmonic power rather than its verbal strength.

LARRY: The songs, rather than meandering, seemed to be a little more concise. Edge had really taken on the role of musical director, and Steve Lillywhite knew the form and seemed more assured as a producer; which is not to say it was easy. On 'Sunday, Bloody Sunday', Edge had the guitar chords, Bono had some of the lyrics, so we went into Windmill. We always seemed to begin recording before we had finished writing, so we would rehearse, then the red light would come on and we would start recording. It wouldn't be right, we'd go back and rehearse some more. 'OK, we're ready now.' And on it went.

I remember doing a drum pattern and Bono saying, 'No, it's not what you did earlier.' And I said, 'No, no, it's the same.' And he insisted, 'No, it's not,' and a row broke out about whether the drum part was the same as the one I'd done three times earlier, and it went on and on. It reminded me of the famous Troggs tapes. Bono remembered it sounding like one thing and I remembered it being something else and, of course, there was no way either of us could have known because we hadn't recorded it. But we spent hours arguing about it. Everything was recorded after that.

BONO: In a U2 song, the hook is not necessarily the guitar, or even the melody. It can be the drums. And on 'Sunday, Bloody Sunday', it was definitely Larry's drumming that brought the song together.

LARRY: That's the marching band influence. The military drum beat. My year in the Post Office Workers Band finally paid off.

EDGE: I borrowed a Fender amplifier which provided some quite icy and tough sounds. We wanted the music to be more grounded, bring it back to earth, so it was a conscious decision to lay off the echo.

ADAM: We wanted something that was more abrasive, a bit more in-your-face, more street rather than stadium. I think because of the way we were performing, people were already beginning to get a whiff of stadium off the band, of those big gestures. I guess it was an attempt to underplay it.

LARRY: Steve really wanted me to use a click track. I was definitely not keen. I had taken the naïve position that any drummer worth his salt should be able to play in perfect time. I was fortunate to run into Andy Newmark, a drummer I liked a lot, on a trip to London. I told him about my situation and how I felt I was being asked to betray 'my art'. He smiled broadly and said he never played without a click. That was it. I went back to Dublin with my newfound knowledge. Recording suddenly became a lot easier.

EDGE: One morning, on my way to rehearsal, I was standing at a bus stop with my guitar. A guy came over carrying a violin case. He was probably about nineteen. He said, 'You're from U2. Have you ever thought about having violin on your album?' Three days later Steve Wickham was in Windmill Lane with his violin. I think it was his first recording session but he was absolutely fantastic to have around because his energy was so positive. He was only in the studio for half a day, but we did 'Sunday, Bloody Sunday' and 'Drowning Man'.

BONO: 'Drowning Man' is an Edge backing track and an Adam bass part. It's some obscure time signature, like 5/8, and it's me improvising *à la* Van Morrison, wailing away in the manner of the scriptures. The lyrics were still a struggle. I wasn't really enjoying writing in a notebook. I would wake up in bed in the foetal position, and Ali would say: 'What's wrong?' I'd tell her, 'I don't want to get out of bed.' And she'd say, 'You don't want to write is what you mean.' I still hadn't fallen in love with the written word. I was forcing myself to write but not doing a very good job, kind of rebelling against it. Ali was literally kicking me out of bed in the morning, putting the pen in my hand.

It was very lonely writing lyrics. I was always encouraging Edge to write, but he wasn't very interested. But he wrote some of 'Seconds', he might even have come up with the line *It takes a second to say goodbye*. 'Seconds' is particularly pertinent today because it's about the idea that at some point someone, somewhere, would get their hands on nuclear material and build a suitcase bomb in an apartment in a western capital. It was twenty years early but I wouldn't call it prophetic, I'd just call it obvious.

EDGE: I sing the first verse, probably because I wrote the lyric for that section. I actually imagined Bono would always sing it. But he said, 'You sing it, I'll do another verse.' So he wrote the second verse and sang that.

BONO: I love Edge's singing. People mix up our two voices.

ADAM: 'New Year's Day' started as a soundcheck jam. I was basically trying to play 'Fade to Grey' by Visage, and trying to find the right interval. Sometimes your mistakes are your best bits. We spent a lot of time trying to connect that with the piano part and then combine those chord changes with the melody. In terms of songwriting, it's kind of a bass part still searching for a melody.

BONO: It's just a killer bass line, and Adam's haircut is really the clue to it. He had been to London and considered himself vaguely sympathetic with the New Romantic movement. So listen to 'Fade to Grey', the Steve Strange track, and you'll get a little glimpse into 'New Year's Day'. But it's a much better bass part than anything that was going at the time.

LARRY: When I hear 'New Year's Day' on the radio, I can't help thinking, 'What a great song. What happened to the drum part?' It's so uneventful and straight. With a little more time spent on that song, I might have been able to come up with something more inventive. I remember once sitting somewhere and the song came on and I overheard two guys talking (obviously drummers), saying, 'Those drums are so boring, Duh – duh – duh – duh.'

BONO: The lyric is all over the shop. I'm thinking about Lech Walesa, the Polish Solidarity leader. A picture of him standing in the snow, a sense that having given up the band for God, we wanted to start again. And we would begin anew, afresh, repeating a theme that would continue for the rest of our lives. *'I will begin again. I will begin again.'* Snow as an image of surrender and covering and these little glimpses of narrative, which are really just excuses for the overarching theme, which was Lech Walesa being put in prison and his wife not being able to see him. Then, when we had recorded the song, they announced that martial law would be lifted in Poland on New Year's Day – incredible. I did five or six verses for that song without writing lyrics, different tracks filled up with different verses, and Steve Lillywhite chose the ones that are there. But they were made up completely on the mike. It was all about speaking in tongues, 'Open my lips, and my mouth shall show forth thy praise.' That's where we were at. We were like the Quakers, sitting around until the spirit moved us. We were a bunch of lunatics – but we weren't wrong.

ADAM: Kid Creole and the Coconuts were seasoned New York musicians who were in town. We invited the trumpet player down to work on a song called 'Red Light'. We thought it might freshen up the sound of the band.

BONO: The singers came too. Three Coconuts. They were so hot. Everyone started to perspire, the temperature in the studio was at an all-time high. We had the studio lit red for effect, and one Coconut took her top off and sang in what looked like a ballerina's bra. The boys from Ireland had difficulty breathing.

EDGE: On the last day of our session, we worked all through the night, it's six in the morning but we still felt we were a song short. And then, to our horror the next session arrives. It's a band called Minor Detail and they are booked into the studio at eight o'clock. They arrived early just to hover about and get ready for their eight o'clock start. And we were saying: 'But we haven't finished our album. You know, we've been in here for the last eight weeks. This is our last morning. You're starting at eight? You're kidding! Can you give us some more time?' They weren't hearing it. We had two hours and that was it. So we said: 'OK, we've got one more song to do. What's it going to be?'

There was another number we had worked up and eventually abandoned. It had a great bass hook but a slightly unwieldy arrangement with lots of strange sections and time changes but we had failed to pull it together as a coherent song. Someone said, 'Let's dig out that tune and see what we can do with it.' We decided to chop out the bits that weren't working – literally, so Steve did some very quick multi-track edits and took out any section that just didn't seem to be part of the main idea. So then we had this slightly unusual piece of music and we said, 'OK, what are we going to do with it?' Bono said, 'Let's do a psalm.' Opened up the bible and found Psalm 40. 'This is it. Let's do it.' And within forty minutes we had worked out the last few elements for the tune, Bono had sung it, and we mixed it. And literally, after finishing the mix, we walked out through the door and the next band walked in.

BONO: Beautiful bass part, and another powerful idea. At this stage I wasn't aware that the psalms were the blues really and that we were connecting with a deep well of ideas. But the chant from it *How long, how long must we sing this song?* was taken up by crowds all around the world, reaching a kind of peak at Live Aid. All through the day, after Queen or David Bowie died down, you'd hear 'how long, how long' coming out of the crowd. I'm sure some people think: 'How long till they finish the fucking song?' But it just became a theme of exasperation at the world. 'How long must we sing this song?'

LARRY: We knew there was something special there. We felt we had finished the songs and done as much on the album as we could possibly do. There was a sense that we'd achieved what we'd set out to achieve.

BONO: I had bought a car while we were recording *War*. My first car, a secondhand Fiat Uno 127. This was a major step in my life – I was off the bus! One night I was driving round the corner from Cedarwood Road. It was raining. I was going to a party, I had a bottle of wine in the back of the car and I was wearing a fake fur coat and cowboy boots with Cuban heels. I turned the corner. I realized as I was turning that I wasn't wearing my safety belt, so I started struggling to put it on. This was a bad idea. When I looked up, I was heading at speed towards a telegraph pole, so I tried to slam on the brakes, but my heels were wet and my foot slipped and I hit the accelerator instead. I realized, in that moment, that high heels were not ideal for driving. I smashed into the telegraph pole, at speed, just as I got my safety belt on. I obviously hit it an incredible whack, because I felled it. This large pole was lying across the road, and it was an electrical pole as well as a telephone pole, so it cut off all the phones and a fair amount of electricity in the neighbourhood. I got out of the car. I was completely unhurt and not even a little shaken. It was odd. But I had been hit by the wine bottle, which had smashed on the back of my head and was now trickling down my coat. So all the old dears who had been on the

MILITANT FOR PEACE WAS OUR IDEA, HENCE THE BOOTS AND THE QUASI-MILITARY GARB – AGGRESSIVE NON-VIOLENCE. WE WEREN'T REALLY SEEING IT AS ANY KIND OF CRUSADE. BONO

phone and had heard the crash, came outside their hall doors, and started to crowd around the car with the pop star in the fur coat with the Cuban heels, reeking of wine – a very simple story from their point of view. And the more it dawned on me what they were thinking, the more I realized I'd better get my arse out of there to a police station and get breathalysed. So I left and went round to my friend Reggie Manuel's house and asked him to take me to a police station. It took a while because a few police stations wouldn't have me – strange. But when Reg dropped me back, something awful was unfolding; there was a crowd around now, police, ambulances, and they were lifting the telegraph pole up. And under it was a couple, Mr and Mrs Corless. Oh my God! I didn't remember seeing them there. Maybe I was suffering from shock.

Only it turns out they weren't there when I hit the pole. In fact, ten minutes after the accident, they had been standing around the car, talking about what happened, with the telegraph pole down and all the wires lying across the road. Another vehicle passed by, a guy driving really slowly, looking at the scene of the accident, and his wheels got caught in the wires. So he ended up resurrecting the pole and slamming it down on poor old Mr and Mrs Corless. I wasn't there but that didn't stop them suing me, because they knew what I didn't, that you should never leave the scene of an accident. You will be happy to hear they survived.

ADAM: We made a video for 'New Year's Day'. We needed snow, so the director suggested northern Sweden. It was very basic, us performing in the snow, just kind of wrapped up, so you couldn't really see us. I think Bono sussed that to be in a video you had to look like yourself, so he wasn't wearing woolly hats or anything. I don't even think he was wearing thermal underwear, just the same clothes he had on when we got off the plane from Dublin.

EDGE: Bono's mouth almost froze solid; if you watch him lip-synching his mouth won't quite work. But the video has an epic quality, there was something about that song that seemed to conjure up images of Dr Zhivago and European winterscapes. People always ask me: 'Was it difficult riding the horse in the video?' And I have to tell them that was shot the day after we left. Apparently the four figures on horseback were all women, dressed similarly to ourselves.

PAUL: 'New Year's Day' was a top-ten hit in the UK in January 1983. Then in March, *War* came out and went straight into the English charts at number one. And we were flying.

BONO: There's nothing like being at number one, there really isn't. It's just better than number two. We were staying in the Portobello Hotel in London. I loved that place. It was after one of our London shows; people were drinking wine, Paul McGuinness's voice was booming through the din, he was on the phone to America. And he was calling out the radio stations that had added 'New Year's Day' to their playlist, on heavy rotation, we were having a hit in the US! We had a number one in England and we were off in America. There's no feeling quite like it in the world. Everything terrible that ever happened to you in your life was no longer terrible in that moment.

EDGE: When we started talking about what we were going to do for our production of the *War* tour, we really felt we had to try and do a bit better than previous tours, which had been pretty bereft of anything close to what you might call design or visual coherence. So we found a stage designer and outlined some of our ideas. He came back with a simple but very elegant scheme featuring three white flags.

ADAM: I couldn't quite understand the white flag concept – militant pacifism. Maybe it said more about us than we thought: we are the do-gooders of the music world, and we believe so much in what we're doing we're going to stand up in front of a white flag. That must have been going on in it somewhere. I just loved the flag as a piece of theatre and the fact that it would flutter in the wind.

EDGE: I have to take some responsibility for the flags. We were playing some European festivals on the *October* tour as one of the junior acts, and Bono was doing his usual thing of diving into the crowd and all the stuff that terrified Paul McGuinness. On one occasion he grabbed this flag and started waving it around, and everyone went nuts. I said to him afterwards, 'That was actually quite interesting. It's such a strong visual.' The white flag seemed like a beautiful symbol with a connection to the album, 'Surrender' being one of the songs, and they became a big feature of the tour.

BONO: The set had flags and the video had flags. It was cheap production values but with real resonance. We couldn't afford much of a light show, but we were always looking for ways to describe ourselves a little differently and the flags were a great visual hook. I think we might even have had a wind machine. As the band grew bigger, some people found it a bit much. They attributed a kind of Onward Christian Soldiers aspect to it, and if you look at it that way, perhaps it was a bit overdone. But it wasn't intentional. Militant for peace was our idea, hence the boots and the quasi-military garb – aggressive non-violence. We weren't really seeing it as any kind of crusade.

EDGE: We played Belfast not long after we'd finished the album, and we were a bit nervous about singing 'Sunday, Bloody Sunday' there. Bono, without saying a word to us beforehand said: 'We're going to do a song for you now. If you don't like it, we'll never play it again. It's called "Sunday, Bloody Sunday".' And we really didn't know what was going to happen.

ADAM: I guess that was how he felt. He was the singer. He was on the line.

EDGE: The place went nuts; it drew a really positive reaction. That was an important moment. When playing those songs live there was a kind of tangible, physical reaction from everyone present, including me. It was like: 'Oh shit!' Realizing we had something very heavy on our hands. It took me quite a while to get over it; I remember I would be shaking like a leaf coming off stage. There were some very powerful shows on the tour. Bono was out there most of the time, really throwing himself into the crowd.

LARRY: Bono's whole thing was: 'Unless I go after it, I can't expect the audience to go off. If I have to go in and beat them into submission, I will. I am going to get this crowd on their feet and I'm going to get them to respond to me, and I will do whatever I have to do.' In some ways I would have preferred to have him on the stage and actually get through the songs and try and let the music speak for itself. The truth is the band weren't good enough for that, we needed Bono to do his thing.

ADAM: Nobody asked him to go out there in such a big way but when he did, you could feel the effect of it. It was very powerful. But he was not the world's most likely contender for scrambling up scaffolding. His sense of direction and balance were not those of an athlete.

BONO: The funny thing is I'm afraid of heights but when the music is on I'm not, and I've done some really stupid stuff. 'Electric Co' was the big number where we would go into a free-form improvisation, I'd sing bits and pieces of other people's songs and just disappear off

THE LEGEND OF ADAM'S PARTYING MAY BE A LITTLE
EXAGGERATED. THE TRUTH IS ANY INDULGENCE AT
THAT TIME WOULD HAVE LOOKED OVER THE TOP
COMPARED TO THE REST OF US. I MEAN, THE BAND
WEREN'T EVEN DRINKING. CAN YOU IMAGINE? YOU'RE
IN A CANDY STORE AND THESE GUYS DON'T EVEN
WANT TO SMELL THE SWEETS. LARRY

somewhere. It was a way of getting people at the back of the crowd, who
were probably just drinking beer, eating a hotdog, talking to their girlfriends,
trying to focus on a few ants on stage. 'Looks like he's about to take
his own life! He's climbed up the very top of the scaffolding, he's running
along the roof now. Look!'

ADAM: There was this suspense: 'He's off, is he going to make it?' And it's
dark. This is ironmongery he's clambering over. You just didn't want anything
to happen to him. You didn't want him to take a fall, to be hurt or paralysed.
You didn't really need him to take that risk for the band, but there was
absolutely no talking to him.

BONO: I loved those blue buses. I loved doing a runner from the gig and
sleeping on the bus overnight, hurtling down the American freeways, stopping
off in truck-stops in the middle of the night for coffee, the closeness with
our crew.

EDGE: Route 66 culture is alive and well, and we had a great time. Going
through dry counties, with no alcohol – that blew our minds, coming from
Dublin: 'Wow, there's still parts of America that have Prohibition!' There's stuff
you just don't know about; for example, you go through another county and
every second corner of the road there's a billboard advertising fireworks. In
many areas of America fireworks are illegal, so there are these little pockets
where they're sold. When you start touring in that fashion you find out how
diverse the United States really is. The idea that it's a homogeneous culture is
so inaccurate. It's hundreds of cultures. The kind of homogenization of
America that Europeans often sneer at is, in a weird way, actually a kind of
celebration of the opposite. It's the triumph of finding a commonality between
so many diverse ethnic, religious, geographical entities that make up this thing
called the United States of America. It's far more diverse, I think, even than

Europe, because it covers tropical Florida to the deserts of the west to the frozen northern areas. One of the great things that Paul McGuinness figured out was that to break America you needed, more than anything, just to be there and go to these places. And so we did. We would go to parts of America that had never seen any European bands, certainly none of the bands from our set. We really started from the bottom. The first time we played in Texas, we opened for a wet T-shirt contest in some terrible little bar attached to a shopping mall in Houston. It was a great learning curve. We learnt about playing live, and we discovered that America is a place with so many different visions of the world.

PAUL: In the days before the cell phone, bus life was completely different. Hours and hours would pass in more or less complete silence. There was no endless chatter with friends and loved ones, no ongoing negotiations, business would have to wait until you got to a truck-stop and while the bus was refuelling you'd make the two or three phone calls that you had to make then get back on the bus. Phone calls were precious.

BONO: We were on the bus one night, I think it was somebody's birthday, it might even have been Adam's, and we had all fallen asleep except Adam, because he'd eaten the cake and whatever else. In the middle of the night I was woken up by the bus driver screaming. Adam was standing there naked, off his trolley, trying to get out of the bus at 70 mph. Adam just wanted to take a piss, not realizing where he was. It was quite something.

LARRY: I think the legend of Adam's partying may be a little exaggerated. The truth is any indulgence at that time would have looked over the top compared to the rest of us. On a level of one to ten, what he was up to wouldn't even get on to the scale. If there was a problem, it was that Adam didn't have any partners in crime in the band, so some of the people he ended up hanging out with were dodgy, road warriors who had been around the block. But Adam didn't have anybody else. I mean the band weren't even drinking. Can you imagine?! You're in a candy store and these guys don't even want to smell the sweets. Strange days indeed.

BONO: We were in a very different orbit. Drugs, sex, you had a sense occasionally that they were there but they just weren't a part of our world. We met, really, the best people. And the worst you could say about them was they were wearing silk jackets with radio station numbers on their backs.

EDGE: At that point I started to think about the whole rock-star thing, and there was a part of me that thought: 'No, I don't think I'm going to buy into this.' I didn't trust that way of seeing yourself or the world, the cult of celebrity or whatever you want to call it. I loved what I did, but I didn't like that particular label of being a star. I was happy just to write songs, play music and really think more in terms of the work than anything else.

LARRY: Success to me was not having to carry or set up my own drums any more.

PAUL: We wanted to be big everywhere, not just in a few places. We had no misgivings about playing to big crowds if we could get them. It was just a matter of getting there as quickly as possible. Red Rocks in Denver, Colorado was going to be our biggest gig to date, a seven-thousand capacity outdoor arena.

ADAM: Denver is in the middle of the country and it's quite hard to get to. So once you are there, if radio's on your side, the audience can be quite enthusiastic. We had a really good gig there on the *Boy* tour, in 1981, and a promoter called Chuck Morris said he'd take us to this site called Red Rocks that was up in the mountains. It was a great natural amphitheatre. From the moment we saw it, we were thinking, 'Some day we will play here.' It was very photogenic. So now that we were finally going to play Red Rocks, in 1983, we decided to put whatever cash we had into making a film, not that there was much cash around.

PAUL: We brought over a British production team headed by Malcolm Gerrie, who produced *The Tube*, a really groundbreaking music show made in Newcastle that had been supportive of U2. It was crucial to have a real rock and roll director and cameraman because the species did not exist in America. If you wanted a live video, you got a guy who shot football, and it looked like it.

LARRY: Only in America would you find this beautiful place at the top of a mountain where you could put on rock concerts. There was a lot of money riding on this, all the money we'd made from the tour, everything that was in the bank, basically. We felt we were well organized, camera crews set up all over the gig. We had brought extra lighting equipment from Hollywood, searchlights, all kinds of stuff. Then on the day it started to rain.

ADAM: Red Rocks is a mile high, so it's more often than not in the middle of a raincloud, which none of us had really taken into account. But the weather could

RED ROCKS WAS FREEZING COLD. THERE WAS STEAM COMING OUT OF OUR MOUTHS. EDGE WAS FINDING IT HARD TO PLAY GUITAR BECAUSE HIS HANDS WERE FROZEN STIFF. BONO

be very changeable up there, and this was one of those periods where it just rained and rained. We'd spent the money, we had the film crew there, and all the lights and cameras and equipment. Our production people were saying there's so much water about that the lighting rig is live. We can probably use the back line and perhaps run the PA but it's just not safe. Our concert promoter was going on the radio saying, 'The gig is cancelled, we'll reschedule it for another time,' but that wasn't really an option. We didn't have the money to reschedule it – this was a one-shot for us. So we did radio interviews, saying: 'We know it's raining now but we're sure it won't be when the show starts, so please come.'

LARRY: Those were nerve-racking, nail-biting times; many of the crew were advising us to pull out, but in true U2 style we carried on regardless.

EDGE: Our one concession was that we would do a second performance indoors in Boulder for anyone who really did not want to brave the elements, but we were going ahead for whoever did show up. Our promoter, Barry Fey, could not believe it. I don't think he'd ever heard anything quite so crazy in his life, going on with an outdoor show in the worst kind of weather, rain and wind in the mountains. He thought we'd lost our minds completely. But, as luck would have it, the rain stopped about two hours before we went on, and instead of a downpour there was this kind of drizzly, misty, hazy thing going on in the air. It was like God's dry ice. The atmosphere visually was incredible.

LARRY: In the end, the rain actually helped us. It made it look really extraordinary.

BONO: It was freezing cold. There was steam coming out of our mouths. Edge was finding it hard to play guitar because his hands were frozen stiff.

EDGE: You might notice if you watch the Red Rocks video, there are very few crowd shots. The reason for that is the place was only a third full. But those who were there were real die-hard fans and they were just so relieved that we were going to play, and we were so pleased to be able to play, and that helped make it a truly amazing show.

BONO: After Red Rocks, the band went into overdrive, because everyone saw us playing these giant concerts in America. But there was only really about two and a half thousand people there. It was pissing rain and there was a cloud over the mountain and people weren't sure if the concert was cancelled, so they didn't come, so it was less than half full. But the way it was filmed, it looked like an enormous crowd. Where would we be without a wide angle lens?

At the end of the concerts on the *War* tour, when the band left the stage, there was this phenomenon of people singing the refrain from 'Forty': *How long to sing this song? How long to sing this song?* It was very moving and it had marked all the best shows on that tour. But no one was singing it that night. They were all too cold and there weren't enough of them. We were backstage and we were kind of disappointed. We had pulled off this concert that no one thought we could, it would have been so nice to hear the crowd chanting. And as we were having this discussion, I remember hearing a little soprano voice pipe up: 'How long to sing this song?' I was thinking, 'What's that?' 'How long…'

Dennis Sheehan, our tour manager, had got the mike and he was hiding down beneath the barrier, trying to get the crowd to sing, without being asked. And slowly they started singing it. It was a very funny moment. The edit made it appear a little less organized. I guess that's what I really love about rock 'n' roll, the spontaneity and the spirit of it, but also I love the strategy, the illusion, the smoke and mirrors, the shamanistic aspects. It's just such a big bag of all kinds of motivations, and you end up with magic. Telling that story might spoil it for other people but if it wasn't on the *Under A Blood Red Sky* record no one would have known, because that was the record of that tour, and the crowd singing was the highlight of the tour.

Filming Red Rocks cost us thirty grand. That was all the money we'd made. This was the first tour we were going to make any money at all, and this is where we put the money, so there was a lot riding on that night.

ADAM: It was a benchmark. We could now say: 'Right, we've got to a point where we're contenders. We're at the starting gate.'

EDGE: Los Angeles Sports Arena would have been the biggest show we'd ever done up to that point, and it went slightly out of control. I think one of the problems for us was dealing with suddenly being a bigger band, playing in larger venues. And I think, as a performer, Bono had a slightly unrealistic sense that he had to somehow reassure everyone that although we were playing these big venues nothing had changed. One of the ways he tried to cope with that was by throwing himself into the audience even more and really making a point about the physical connection with people down in the hall, trying to break down the barrier between stage and auditorium.

On that night it involved climbing up part of the PA and then on to the balcony that went around the whole auditorium. So he clambered up and he was still singing and reached the very end and realized there was nowhere else to go. He built up this quite dramatic journey and there was no finale for this little trip into the audience. Impulsive as Bono can be at the best of times, he's never ever more so and more unpredictable than when he's playing a show, and all kind of good sense goes out the door and he's capable of really bonkers stuff. The only thing he could think to do at the time was jump off the balcony and hope the people underneath would catch him. And it was a long drop, about a full storey up – you're not talking about a stage dive. There was maybe twenty feet between him and the deck. I couldn't believe it. He just jumped.

BONO: There were pictures in the *Los Angeles Times* of me coming off, twenty feet up. Robert Hilburn did a review where he said it was the most exciting thing he'd ever seen – and the dumbest.

EDGE: And fair enough, he did get caught by the people underneath. It was quite an impressive sight. A very memorable moment, I'm sure, to see a singer doing something obviously so dangerous but involving so much trust. The only problem was there were another two or three people behind him who decided to do the same thing, and I'm not sure they enjoyed quite as good a landing as Bono did.

Luckily I don't think anyone was seriously hurt. But it seemed to underscore something that I think has always been true, which is that Bono will do anything to make the event come together. That performer's instinct is so strong in him, he will stop at nothing. The physical connection with our audiences is a big part of what makes our shows special. It's personal, it's not just about us showing up and playing to whoever arrives. There's a deep understanding between the band and U2 fans and getting in amongst our audiences has always been a big thing for Bono. We were into it but we just thought you've got to have some level of common sense about it, some instinct for self-preservation, which at times he seems to lack. I mean, he's not a naturally athletic character but I have to say, when he performs, the shit he does you just wouldn't credit. Of course, we were terrified of Bono killing himself in some stupid fall, but the idea that somebody else might get hurt was paramount in people's minds. As far as our crew were concerned, he was out of control. So there was a frank exchange of views, as they say.

WE HAD A SERIES OF SESSIONS WITH OUR PRIEST TO
MAKE US AWARE OF THE BASICS: ANY CHILDREN WOULD
BE RAISED CATHOLIC, AND IF AISLINN APPEARED TO BE
OVERSPENDING ON GROCERIES I WASN'T TO GET MAD
AT HER. THUS EQUIPPED FOR LIFE TOGETHER WE WERE
DULY MARRIED ON JULY 12TH. EDGE

BONO: Those kind of moments would always be reported to the police, and the band and management would sit down and suggest this wasn't the way to go. But I'm very physical and not at all passive and not comfortable standing behind the microphone in my proper place. I was interested in a different kind of cabaret; so I would feign guilt – 'Never do it again, Your Honour.'

PAUL: He did promise. But he didn't give it up completely, I'm afraid.

EDGE: We had a month off in July '83 so Aislinn and I decided to grab the opportunity to schedule our wedding. We had no money so Aislinn's dad paid for the reception. We went with tradition and opted for the bride's church, the Catholic church in Blackrock. This involved a series of sessions with our priest, since I was protestant, to make us aware of the basics: any children would be raised catholic, and if Aislinn appeared to be overspending on groceries I wasn't to get mad at her. Thus equipped for life together we were duly married on 12 July. We went on our honeymoon to Sri Lanka. We had a wonderful time at first and then civil war broke out. We spent a very nervous few days trying to get back to our hotel from a road trip, forced to drive along deserted roads after the midday curfew, only to discover it had been evacuated of all foreign guests. We had to wait for a few days to get on a plane home. All of this was unfortunately portentous of how the marriage would go.

On my 22nd birthday, in August, we played Phoenix Park Race Course in Dublin, twenty thousand people, with Simple Minds and Eurythmics supporting, an amazing bill. It was really a 'returning-heroes' show, coming home having conquered the world. We'd never played anything close to that size before. It was just one of those fantastic nights playing to the home crowd and you could do no wrong. Everyone we'd ever known was there. Jimmy Reilly, the drummer from Stiff Little Fingers, was backstage, still reeling from the death of his brother, shot by a paratrooper as he ran away from a patrol in catholic west Belfast. Our tour manager at the time was another Northern Irishman, a protestant called Tim Nicholson whose brother was in the British Army. It struck me that in our dressing-room Tim and Jimmy were chatting away about music but if their brothers had ever met they would have been sworn enemies. Music unifies people like nothing else.

BONO: Those homecoming shows are like big weddings, where you're always going to forget to invite some auntie or uncle, and they're never going to speak to you again. Somebody is always going to have a row, someone is always going to drink too much, a child is going to be conceived – and I'm only talking about backstage, not the great outdoors. They are great tribal events. I pulled my dad onstage, and he was beaming. I think he was proud. I was doing what he didn't. I had been fortunate enough to live off my gift rather than just the sweat on my brow. That was really a very, very proud moment for me.

ADAM: We did our first tour of Japan, which was the most alien place I had ever been. Japan was the closest thing to realizing what Beatlemania must have been like. The excitement that the Japanese were exhibiting seemed incomprehensible; we were being pursued through railway stations and hotel lobbies by Japanese teenagers. It seemed out of all proportion to the music. But Japan is such a foreign culture, I sometimes think they view Western music and culture rather like a cartoon.

BONO: I couldn't believe my eyes. We weren't always a 'man' band, we were a boy band in Japan. When we left the airport there were screaming fans, and wherever we went there were shrieking girls: in the hotel, waiting outside the lifts, when we arrived on the bullet train in Tokyo. We were on this extraordinary speeding chrome and plastic supertrain from the future, we came into Tokyo and all the lights blacked out. We couldn't see anything, and the screeching of the wheels was unbelievable. And then I realized it wasn't the wheels that were screaming, the noise was coming from the thousands and thousands of fans who were waiting for the train and now had their faces pressed up against the glass, so we couldn't see out. And I remember hearing a sound, something like, 'Rarry'. I mean I heard 'Bono' and I heard 'Edge' and I heard 'Adam' but mostly I heard 'Rarry'. When we emerged from the train, myself and Larry took fright and started running, with all these teenage girls running after us. We ran down the steps of the train station, and they were rolling down the steps behind us. Some of them were tumbling over each other, it was a terrible scene. We ran out, saw a taxi, and climbed into it. The taxi was surrounded by fans banging on the roof, the driver just staring at this scene. Larry turned round and started screaming at him: 'Go, go, go!' The taxi took off; about a mile down the road the taxi driver began speaking to us in Japanese, and I looked at Larry and he looked at me. 'Do you know where we're going?' 'I don't know where we're going. Do you know where we're going?' It was Laurel and Hardy. Then the taxi driver started putting his hand out for money, but we had none. So he began to get very cross and tried to stop the car and throw us out. But somehow, after the promise of a large sum of money, which he seemed to understand (or perhaps it was the threat of violence), he did bring us back to the train station.

LARRY: OK, there was a little bit of screaming. There may have been twenty girls outside the hotel. Hardly in the boy-band league. But there was some sort of girl action going on and it made a big impression on the other three. I was a little embarrassed, although flattered at the same time. Just being in Japan was a mind-bending experience. It felt like we had arrived on the set of *Bladerunner*. It was so expensive, we couldn't afford to eat in the hotels or restaurants. We had to take food out of the dressing-room to live. Our girlfriends and wives were on the trip, and I remember schoolkids stopping Ann and myself in the street to have their photograph taken with us. It was nothing to do with U2 but because we were both blonde. I think we were part of an anthropological study.

BONO: We went to Hawaii on the same trip and did a show there. I had never been in a place so exotic. It was a long way from home. At the Kahala Hilton there were bottles of wine on the menu for ten thousand dollars. Ronald Reagan had just stayed there. I remember thinking, 'Why are dolphins jumping past my window?' The hotel was set up with dolphins swimming through channels. As an unreconstructed Calvinist, to me it was the end of the world. This was about as far as you could go wrong, and I was reaching inside of myself and trying to ask, 'Why am I not enjoying this? Why do I feel so bad? This should be fun.' I suppose it was just the cultural bends, not really being used to how preposterous success is and trying to find my answer to it, which was to stay on track and write a song about Martin Luther King, which we did. 'Pride in the Name of Love' came out of a soundcheck in Hawaii, the melody and the chords. Around about that time I met a journalist from *Rolling Stone* who had been really pivotal in breaking the band in America. His name was Jim Henke; he had given me a book called *Let The Trumpet Sound*, a biography of Dr King, and another on Malcolm X. They were covering different sides of the civil rights discussion, the violent and non-violent. They were important books to me. The next album started there in Hawaii, with thoughts of man's inhumanity to his fellow-man on my mind, and dolphins swimming past my window.

IN
THE **NAME** OF
LOVE
1984 - 1985

Adam

WE WERE BUYING OUR FIRST HOUSES. I BOUGHT A
LITTLE HOUSE IN RATHGAR WHERE I LIVED WITH MY
GIRLFRIEND, SHEILA ROCHE, FOR ABOUT TWO YEARS.

Sheila went on to work for Principle and became Paul's right-hand woman. It
was just an ordinary house but it was great to have a place of your own,
somewhere you could sleep late without your parents complaining.

EDGE: I really was living quite a different life to everybody else. Aislinn and I
had a place in Monkstown. And then we got pregnant. I remember telling the
rest of the band about this momentous event. It wasn't easy and the news did
place a bit of a strain on relations for a while. It wasn't part of the script, and
the others must have felt like their future had been thrown into doubt. They
got over it, and the band continued without any major problem, but starting a
family certainly kept me very grounded. During those heady days of our rise to
fame, I think it was probably quite a good thing that somebody had their feet
on the ground.

LARRY: I was still living at home. I didn't want to get a house and a mortgage
and be in a situation where the bank might take it off me. At the back of my
mind I thought this might not last for ever. Also, I wasn't in a position to move
in with Ann. I felt I could stay at home for now, I was happy enough and rarely
there anyway. It was just myself and my dad, not much to say to each other,
carrying on our separate lives. It was probably a pretty normal Irish
relationship. I decided I was going to wait; so I did, until my father remarried.
I bought my first house on the north side of Dublin, and I have lived there
ever since.

   It was around this time I became known as Larry Mullen Junior. My dad
received a tax bill from the revenue, saying he owed six hundred quid over a
three-month period for income he had received. He had a hard job convincing
them they had the wrong Larry Mullen. He said to me, 'There has to be a
change. You either have to put Larry J Mullen or Laurence J Mullen or do
something else.' So I decided to add the Junior, so my dad wouldn't continue
to get my tax bills.

BONO: Ali and I bought a house in the Victorian seaside resort of Bray in south County Dublin. Only it's not a house, it's what's called a Martello Tower, a sort of round turret built for coastal defence in the early nineteenth century. The walls are seven-feet-thick granite. The bedroom is at the top of the tower in a lighthouse-like glass structure, the kitchen is at the bottom. It's an extraordinary place to live. And the band even rehearsed there, like we had in the little house by the sea. We worked up some of the songs there, 'Pride', 'Unforgettable Fire', 'A Sort of Homecoming'. We knew that the world was ready to receive the heirs to The Who. All we had to do was keep doing what we were doing and we would become the biggest band since Led Zeppelin, without a doubt. But something didn't feel right. We felt we had more dimension than just being the next anything, we had something unique to offer. The innovation was what would suffer if we went down the standard rock route. We were looking for another feeling.

EDGE: We had done three albums with Steve Lillywhite, and both he and we had come to the conclusion that it was time to move on. We were absolutely adamant that we were not going to repeat the same formula; it seemed far too predictable, so we started talking about who we were going to get to work with us.

ADAM: We were looking for something that was a little bit more serious, more arty. Roxy Music was a name that kept coming up, with a sense that this was the sonic territory of European pop music as opposed to American rock. Rhett Davies had produced Roxy and we had a meeting with him which didn't really go anywhere. Then we started thinking about Brian Eno, who had been the keyboard player in Roxy Music and had gone on to produce Bowie and Talking Heads.

EDGE: Bowie obviously was a big influence for all of us but I'd also been listening to Eno's solo records, his ambient music and other weird works. 'Before and After Science' was a particular favourite.

LARRY: I thought it was a great idea to get someone to come in to help us develop in a different way. It seemed we had done very well on three chords and the truth but we needed someone who could take our songs in a different direction, add new textures and explore new ways of using the studio.

PAUL: Steve had a theory that bands should change producers often, which didn't really work in his favour but he sort of talked himself out of a job. They asked me to contact Brian Eno, who was very unforthcoming and said he

WE KNEW THE WORLD WAS READY TO RECEIVE THE
HEIRS TO THE WHO. ALL WE HAD TO DO WAS KEEP
DOING WHAT WE WERE DOING AND WE WOULD BECOME
THE BIGGEST BAND SINCE LED ZEPPELIN. BUT
SOMETHING DIDN'T FEEL RIGHT. WE FELT WE HAD MORE
DIMENSION THAN JUST BEING THE NEXT ANYTHING, WE
HAD SOMETHING UNIQUE TO OFFER. BONO

wasn't really a record producer any more, he was a video artist and he wasn't interested in producing records. I remember Bono getting quite irate about this and saying, 'Get him on the phone, I'll talk him into it.'

BONO: I rang him up. He said, 'I'm sorry, I'm not really interested in production any more. I'm about to retire.' I said, 'You don't understand. We want to make records the like of which have never been made before. We don't want to make them in a studio. We want to make them out of the places where we live, like a Martello Tower in Bray.' And he replied, 'It's funny you should say that. I'm so bored of being in a studio. I'm looking for a new way of making records.' And I told him, 'Well then, make them with us.' He said, 'No, I can't, I'm about to retire. You know I'm a visual artist and I've got other ambitions for my life.' 'You can't turn us down without meeting us,' I insisted.

PAUL: So Eno agreed to come to Dublin and there was a big pow-wow over lunch. Brian had brought his engineer Daniel Lanois with him, clearly with the intention of passing the gig to him.

EDGE: Brian told us later that he had already decided he was not going to do it. The only reason he came to Dublin was out of a sense of obligation. But Danny Lanois was interested, so Brian was going to help Daniel land the gig and find a way to bow out afterwards.

BONO: We described what we were about. We played him *Under A Blood Red Sky*, the Red Rocks show, and his eyes glazed over. I now realize how awful the sight of a rock band in full flight was to Brian. But he caught something in the spirit of the band that perked his interest.

EDGE: We were talking about different recording approaches, about ambient recording, in the sense of trying to capture not just the performance but the sonic interaction of the people in the room. I think Brian became very interested in this. We also discussed trying to find a really great-sounding space and use the acoustics of the room as a natural characteristic of the recordings.

PAUL: By the end of lunch, Brian and Danny had both agreed to work together on the album. Brian's girlfriend, later wife, Anthea Norman- Taylor represented the two of them and we established the principle at that time that you shouldn't have to pay twice as much for two producers. So they would work jointly on it, represented by her, and whatever the split between the two of them would be we might never know. At that point, Chris Blackwell, who had always been pretty silent on such matters, got in touch and started trying to talk us out of it.

EDGE: Chris Blackwell said, 'Are you sure you want to work with Brian Eno?' There were stories about him going to Island Records with one of his art projects. I think it was a song called 'Bird List', which was a recording of some very obscure beat over which Brian was reciting the names of birds. 'Osprey ... Seagull ... Thrush'. Chris was terrified that Brian was going to take this band that were poised to take over the world and bury them under a layer of avant-garde nonsense.

PAUL: Chris was persuaded by the band's enthusiasm and we went ahead and made the album with Brian and Danny. They came to Dublin and lived like the odd couple in the mews at the end of my garden in Monkstown for a few weeks. Windmill Lane, where we had recorded the first three albums, was a very difficult place for a band to work, because while there was plenty of space for instruments there was hardly any room for people. I was looking around for a place for the band to rehearse, and the best I could come up with was the Church Hall in Ranelagh. It was rather overpriced and I mentioned this to Lord Henry Mountcharles one day and he said, 'Well, fuck that, I'll give you somewhere to rehearse and I won't charge you half as much.' Lord Henry lived at Slane Castle, where the band had played with Thin Lizzy, and he had become a good friend of Adam. He made Slane available to us to rehearse and he would feed us too, because he had a restaurant on the premises. He could give us beds if we wanted to sleep over. There was a kind of honour system whereby we would count up the number of people who had stayed the night and pay a fiver for each sleeping body. The band decided this was such a great environment to work in that we brought recording equipment in to do the album. The Gothic ballroom in Slane was originally built for music, and turned out to be a very good recording space. We brought in some portable equipment from New York and made the album on that.

BONO: The sound is magnificent. If Phil Spector was going to lie in state, it would be here. And we have this thing in our head: we're going to make the big music. That's who we are. We're not Indie, we're not miserable, we're full of joy, and we are going to take over where Phil Spector left off. Big ideas, big themes, big sound. We're going to take risks, and prove just how elastic a rock band can be. And we have Brian Eno as our producer. Brian arrives, looking how you might imagine an architect of the Eighties to look, leather tie, leather jacket, his chrome dome of a head, piercing eyes, and something we didn't see an awful lot in him, but it was there: humility. And he put himself at our disposal. This great artist and superb strategist went to work for these rather uncouth Irish musicians. He had his friend at his side, Daniel Lanois, who had more music in his little finger than Brian had in every appendage. A truly funk soul brother, the skinny white guy in every funky band, a guy who reeks of music.

The combination was deadly. Larry and Adam, as insecure as they were in the studio, suddenly started to warm to this Canadian, this Danny Boy, who just brought the best out of them. Myself and Edge, who were more cerebral, were attracted by Brian's big ideas. Every great rock band in the British invasion went to art school. We never did, we went to Brian. And his was a great act of generosity. Those arpeggiating sequences you hear in 'Bad' and later on *The Joshua Tree*, they're him. He catalysed our songwriting, allowed us to get away from the primary colours of rock into another world where we could really describe ourselves in what was going on around us. It was monumental.

EDGE: I think we were very generous with Brian, in that we didn't object to him taking liberties with what we had achieved up to that point. We were eager to learn and not precious at all about our sound or the way we worked. We threw ourselves wholeheartedly into this different approach. We had some good songs pretty much in the bag beforehand, so we felt confident enough to just see where it went.

We came into the studio one morning and Brian and Dan had slowed down the backing track of 'A Sort of Homecoming' and presented it as a starting point, and Bono got on the microphone and just improvised lyrics and melodies. 'A Sort of Homecoming' was probably about four minutes forty in its normal length. This was half speed, so the total track was around nine minutes long. It was great, Bono had conjured up some fantastic moments but it was all a bit longwinded. So I edited it down and cut it into reasonable shape to be put forward for the next phase, as it were. And Brian listened to it and said, 'You know what? This is finished. I don't think we should do anything more. OK, it doesn't have any real lyrics. It's improvised stream of consciousness but it's pure performance and we should just accept it as a moment that has been captured.' And that became the track 'Elvis Presley In America'.

BONO: This is more like fine art or perhaps just pretentious art. Here was this beautiful harmonic portrait, a song slowed down till it sounded like the brain of somebody loaded with Valium, who can't touch the things in front of their face, somebody so wrapped in the cotton wool of painkillers, someone very like Elvis Presley. So it's a blur, it's a mumble, but how dare you call a song 'Elvis Presley In America' and not explain yourself? I agree with Dave Marsh, the great rock critic, who said it was the greatest song ever squandered.

The album was really good, but it was uneven. The lyrics weren't really up to much because Brian, Danny and Edge weren't very interested in lyrics. They wanted to preserve my Bongolese. 'Why write lyrics?' they said to me. 'Why bother? I'm getting the feeling from this. Imagine you're Japanese, imagine you're Italian, imagine you're Welsh, imagine you're from the west of Ireland, you hear it with your heart, you don't hear with your head.' And I, like an idiot, went along with it, and so I never finished great songs like 'Bad'. Classics like 'Pride In The Name of Love' are left as simple sketches.

EDGE: Brian wasn't in any way constrained by the thinking that was prevalent in music at the time. His points of reference were very wide. They included contemporary art and philosophy and thoughts and ideas that were really outside the envelope of rock 'n' roll. We appreciated that because the arguments were very interesting, but we certainly had our moments of disagreement. The more conventional the song, the less interested Brian was. He didn't take a huge interest in 'Pride' or 'Unforgettable Fire' but Danny was there to cover for him, so they balanced each other out very well.

Brian was far less precious then I had imagined he would be, but grumbled a lot, particularly about the food. Onions were a kind of subplot during our Slane Castle sessions. Brian kept stressing 'no onions in my salad pleeese'. I think the kitchen started messing with him after about the fourteenth complaint, because suddenly there were onions in everything, even the breakfast cereal. Rule one of recording in a residential studio: don't piss off the kitchen.

If Brian was a grumbler of the highest order of Suffolk grumblers Danny brought an intensity to the record that maybe even surpassed our own. He wanted desperately to be around something great and he would react explosively to any technical interruption of the creative flow. Various parts of Slane Castle felt the rough end of Danny's boot on those occasions, and there were times we all feared a piece of recording equipment might go through one of the Castle's eighteenth-century stained-glass windows. It was good to have somebody working with us who was as determined and focused as we were. It was also a relief that he seemed to like onions.

Studios can be very technical and clinical, but with Danny you could simply take the technical side as given and instead focus on capturing something amazing in performance – a moment, a sound, a part, some kind of unique and special event. That was Danny's thing.

LARRY: I had been quite frustrated with earlier recording sessions. I felt I wasn't getting enough time to work through my drum parts. Adam's bass playing was always inventive, largely because of his jazz timing. The down side for me was having to concentrate on keeping time rather than trying out different parts. When we started working with Danny and Brian, things changed for me. Danny liked to work from the bottom up, so there was a lot of focus on the drums and we worked together on developing my playing. I am not technically proficient, so Danny encouraged me to find new approaches and gave me the time I needed. He also got me much more involved in what everybody else was doing. I enjoyed his way of making music very much. Brian was impatient, he wanted to move quickly, and he had little time for our dogged quest for the song that would get us on the radio. He spent a lot of time coming up with genius keyboard sounds and textures, adding them to our music and taking songs in new directions, so between the band, Brian and Danny there were some very inspiring days in the studio. The only problem was that I thought we were creating interesting music but we were struggling to find hit singles.

ADAM: A bit of panic started to set in that we didn't have the goods. Steve Lillywhite was visiting Dublin and came up to see us. We played him a few things, and he said, 'As long as you've got "Pride", you'll be all right.'

BONO: Pride is really one of the most unworthy human traits. Strange to call a song 'Pride'. And it's such a great non-violent anthem. 'Early morning, April four, shot rings out in the Memphis sky' is a factual inaccuracy because Dr King was shot in the late afternoon.

EDGE: One of the inspirations for the album was the Peace Museum in Chicago. There was an exhibition called *The Unforgettable Fire* showing paintings and drawings by survivors of Hiroshima and Nagasaki. Painting was part of the therapy to help these people purge themselves of their internalized emotions. The image of that catharsis, coupled with the insight it gave into the horror of nuclear holocaust, stuck in Bono's mind. That was just one thread of the record. It became the title later on when we were trying to figure out what exactly the record was about.

BONO: The theme of the album was a flirtation with death, nuclear fission, the raw material for a power plant or for weapons of total destruction. The title track is very rich harmonically and very evocative of a city, in this case Tokyo. We met this guy, he was our publisher in Japan. His name was Tatsui Nagashima. He remembers the fire bombing of Tokyo and told stories of the heat of this inferno and his friends and relatives running to get away from the fireballs as they engulfed what was in many places still a city of paper and wood. He escaped with his wife but many in his family were barbecued. Later, Tatsui would work as an interpreter at an American base. I asked him, 'How could you do that if the Americans had killed your whole family?' He said, 'It's not part of our culture to think about the past, we think about the future.' I thought grace was a Judaeo-Christian idea but he really did mean it. He had brought The Beatles to Japan. He embraced everything that was American and European. But it's worth remembering that the Japanese are the only people on earth that really understand the voodoo in $E=mc^2$ and know what it is to have entire cities evaporated. Tokyo, coming like a Phoenix out of the ash, is really worth celebrating. It's also worth remembering that in the etiquette of the Samurai, the vanquished take on the colours of the victor. You adopt the philosophy of the person who has humbled you. And if Japan hasn't kicked America's arse in the area of commerce and the free market I don't know who has. I am not sure how much any of that is actually articulated on the album. It's sketches really, the songs build up pictures, but they don't tell you anything.

EDGE: Adam was just playing a little bass figure during a break in a session. I started playing along, totally unaware that Brian was listening in the other room. He happened to have some treatments set up for a vocal Bono had been doing and he applied those to the guitar. He recorded it straight to stereo tape and we kept it as a live instrumental. We called it '4th Of July' to commemorate the birth of my daughter, Hollie, Bono's godchild, who was born on that date, right in the middle of making the album. Being at the birth was such a monumental and profound experience: seeing a new life, your own flesh and blood, entering the world. It was miraculous and terrifying all at the same time. I remember just hoping that Aislinn and I were going to make good parents. It was also kind of a weird time. I definitely felt I was on my own; not because anyone wanted me to feel that but simply because no one else had a clue what I was going through. Rather than trying to explain, I just tried to deal with it and not burden anyone else, they weren't going to get it anyway. So it was very hard.

ADAM: Brian would get bored easily; he is great if he is doing something but if he hasn't anything to do he loses interest.

LARRY: Brian's impatience with the process was apparent. But in fairness to Brian, it can be excruciating watching U2 work.

ADAM: When we moved back into Windmill, supposedly to start the mixing, there was considerable tension between the production team and the band, really because we weren't at a point where we could finish anything. 'Bad' was something we had done with Brian as a sort of 'impro' piece, and he wouldn't let us replay it or change anything, so the improvisation stands pretty much as is.

BONO: 'Bad' is just a huge promise of a song. A friend of mine, about as close as you can get, squandered his intelligence and his gifts to heroin. Dublin in the late Seventies and early Eighties was a capital for smack. The Shah of Iran had been deposed, and people smuggled their money out of that country in white gold and pearls, by which I mean heroin. It was cheaper than weed, it was cheaper than smoking spliff, and a lot of sweet teenage kids, who just liked to smoke a little bit of ganja, were offered this cheap high, something beyond their imagination. So they'd smoke heroin. They'd smoke it once a month, then once a week, and they became slaves. They gave up everything they held sacred to this drug. I tried to describe that with the song, 'Bad', what it was like to feel that rush, to feel that elation, and then to go on to the nod, the awful sleep that comes with that drug, and then scream: 'I'm wide awake, I'm wide awake, I'm not sleeping!' I can see what's going on. That is potentially a truly great song … if I had finished it. And in a way I do finish it every night, live. I change the lyric. Poets have no problem with revising their work. Songs shouldn't be set in stone. If they are any good, they are living, breathing organisms.

LARRY: Bono was now caught in the situation that I had been in. He was getting less and less time on his lyrics. While recording, we seemed to do our best work when we were in the room together. We depended on Bono to be there, every step of the way. He had to be singing something, anything, to get the song finished. When Bono came in and strapped on a guitar or started to sing, the band responded. He'd be throwing shapes, waving his arms in the air, a thumbs-up for something good, a scowl for average and a dejected look when it was crap. He was conducting the orchestra. A song recorded in the room with Bono and a song recorded without him could be very different animals altogether. By the time we had finished the songs, he was scrambling to get the words together.

BONO: 'MLK' was the last track on the album, just a great lullaby. In the scriptures they talk about the blood crying from the ground. And with 'MLK' you have just that, the blood crying from the ground – but not for revenge, for understanding. I had a conversation with Bob Dylan at that time. He said, 'We associate three kings with Memphis. Elvis, the King, of course. The great B.B. King. But then there's Martin Luther King. Where's his Graceland, where's his monument?' The city had plans to tear down the motel outside of which he was murdered. That struck a chord with me.

I met Bob Dylan while we were making *The Unforgettable Fire*. He played a concert at Slane Castle, July 1984. *Hot Press* magazine heard that Dylan had been speaking very well of U2 and so they asked me would I like to interview him? I, in my innocence, didn't realize they were then going to tell Dylan that Bono wanted to interview him. We all went to Slane, where I was to be presented to the great poet. It meant an awful lot to me. What I wasn't expecting was that it would mean anything at all to him, so when he asked me if he could have his photograph taken with me, I was a little taken aback. But that was the measure of the man: his humility and his humour.

Myself, Van Morrison and Dylan sat around backstage talking about the origins of Irish music. He recited all eleven verses of Brendan Behan's 'Banks of the Royal Canal'. It was a great occasion. I was very thrilled to be in his company, and indeed Van's. They were the two masters and I was the student. However, student or not, I was still appalled by Dylan's band and I told him so. 'With the exception of Carlos Santana, a bunch of extras from the Seventies,' I think was the phrase I used. He indulged the young pretender and, in a funny kind of way, we became the sort of friends who might keep an eye out for each other, not that Bob Dylan ever needed me in that role. But years later, I did try and make his recording life a little easier by introducing him to Daniel Lanois. Easier is probably not the adjective Bob would use but two of the best albums he made in the Nineties were courtesy of Daniel. I love Bob above anyone else in what you could call pop music. He is the guy whose suitcase I'd carry, whose taxi I'd call, whose drinks' bill I'd swallow and whose grave I'd dig. He is the Picasso of pop music to me. He's Dickens, he's Shakespeare, he's

Thackeray … with a smidgen of Charlie Chaplin thrown in.

I've learnt a lot in the little time I've spent in his company and I'm very grateful for the access I've had. He's been very generous with my own rather uneven education. But it all started on the Boyne Valley, just across the way from the castle where we'd done *The Unforgettable Fire*. He asked me to sing 'Blowin' in the Wind' with him. He imagined that, as a great fan, I would know the words. Little did he suspect that I don't even know the words of any U2 songs, let alone Bob Dylan songs, and that I'd be inclined to make them up as I went along, to more than the chagrin of the entire audience who, if they could have, would have bottled me off the stage. Sometimes I'm lucky, that day I was unlucky. I apologized to him later. I said, 'Sorry I made up some more lyrics for "Blowin' in the Wind". Yours were probably better.' He said, 'I do it all the time. I can't remember them either.'

EDGE: Brian left before we finished the album, but Danny was there to hold the whole thing together and deliver the mixes.

LARRY: I hoped this record would change people's perception of the band. This was U2 evolving and really opening up, bringing light and shade and experimentation to the music. Taking risks, I suppose.

EDGE: We spent a couple of days driving around the west coast of Ireland with Anton Corbijn finding some very interesting locations. There was a book that Steve Averill had found that he thought was a good starting point, and we took pictures in front of some ruined castles. It was suitably ambiguous, and had a certain Irish mysticism that we liked. Something about decay, history, bad builders, questions about where we had been, where we were going, the end of something and the beginning of something else. It was all there in that shot of the castle. Unfortunately people assumed that this burned-out hulk on the cover of our album was Slane Castle. I heard that Henry lost a lot of wedding receptions that year.

PAUL: Anton's photograph was basically completely copped from somebody else's photograph (a picture of Moydrum Castle, County Westmeath featured on the cover of *In Ruins: The Once Great Houses of Ireland* by Simon Marsden). Anton had put his camera in exactly the same spot and used the same kind of solarized filter technique, the only difference being the four members of U2 were in the picture. So that cost us a few bob – Anton promised never to do it again.

My job with U2 was beginning to change, mainly because we were able to start renegotiating what had originally been quite a poor record deal. Our deal with Island was too close to its end for their comfort and other major labels were starting to approach us with better offers. But what Island could give us, which nobody else could, was the return of our copyrights, so that first renegotiation basically turned on their tearing up the publishing deal and giving us back our songs, extending the record deal, upping the royalty and improving terms generally. I think that arrangement was a very wise thing for us to enter into. The band showed great restraint at the time because clearly one of the other major companies could have written a very large cheque for us. But the band knew by then how important it was to own their songs and so that was the policy that governed that renegotiation.

We embarked on a tour of Australia before *The Unforgettable Fire* was released and that was sort of a glimpse into what was coming. It was the first time we had gone to a country effectively as a big band, benefiting from everything that had been achieved in advance. We were far more popular than we had expected and had to extend the tour. We were selling out arenas, and we did five shows in the Sydney Entertainment Centre, playing to sixty thousand people in all.

You can't go into those ten-thousand-seaters with the same show you would play a theatre with. It was exciting and interesting, not just for the band but also for the crew. Willie Williams was with us by then as a lighting designer and he was starting to expand his horizons and get involved in stage design. I think it would be fair to say there was a change in the whole live music business at the time and people were looking for higher standards of lighting, sound and production. The traditional kind of roadie of the cartoons with the big tummy and the main requirement that he'd be able to lift heavy weights was no longer relevant. Crew people tended to be cleverer and more professional and less likely to be stoned out of their minds.

BONO: That tour was the beginning of a love affair with Australia and New Zealand. It was almost a twenty-four-hour flight into Auckland. I arrived at the hotel, went to bed and at two in the morning I was wide awake again. I went down into the lobby and saw some people sitting in the bar who looked kind of interesting. I sat down beside them and introduced myself. They recognized me as being in the band. I told them I didn't know anybody in Auckland and so they took me out, and we were out all night. They took me up to the top of a place called One Tree Hill, where a single tree stands at the top of the mount, like some stark Japanese painting, and we looked around at this city that's made by craters of volcanoes. I remember it so vividly, I think, because it meant something to me about my own freedom. I liked being on my own. I

'BAD' WAS ALMOST AN IMPOSSIBLE COLLISION OF CULTURES FOR US. IT WAS A DIFFERENT KIND OF SONGWRITING, LIKE VAN MORRISON CROSSED WITH GERMAN ELECTRONICA. WE WERE STRUGGLING SO HARD TO FIND THAT SONG. BONO

liked being away in that moment from home, and in a way I also liked being away from the band. I was on my own. No one knew I'd left my room and the hotel. It felt like anything could happen. I've been doing that all my life – disappearing into other people's lives for a few days. And people let me do it. They take me home, they feed me; I've met some special people through that.

The next day we went down to the gig, and I noticed this very helpful fellah running around the place, a striking-looking Maori. Lithe, quick on his feet, sharp and with a real light of intelligence in his eyes. His name was Greg Carroll and he was working on the gig as a local stage manager. We became very close friends. He came on the road and became the band's assistant. He was very close to Ali. He used to take her out when we were away, a real gentleman. He would take girls dancing and really look after them and spoil them, and they all loved him, including Paul McGuinness' sister Katy who became very special to Greg. When he died a couple of years later, I thought of the night that I had met him and that journey. So it was a love affair with New Zealand, with the Maori people and Greg and on to Australia. I love touring, being on the road. It's so hard now to leave my family and my friends but I'm just a natural traveller.

PAUL: That was an interesting time; the band had to address the problem of recreating Eno's rather broader sonic landscape live. I remember walking into the studio once during recording of *The Unforgettable Fire* and saying, 'Does this mean we're going to have a keyboard player and brass section?' It became pretty clear that no one wanted this to lead to the expansion of the band.

ADAM: We'd booked the tour and thought we would open in Australia and by the time we got to Europe and America we would have it together. But it was a disaster, the material just did not work, so before Europe we had emergency rehearsals.

EDGE: That's when I discovered sequencers. I would program keyboard parts and let them run and then I was able to play guitar on top. We ran a click track off the sequencer for Larry and we suddenly had a keyboard player in a small black box. Magic!

BONO: I met Mick Jones recently and he was talking about the first time his band Big Audio Dynamite played with U2 on that tour. They opened for us in Nantes in France and he watched our soundcheck and said, 'I've never seen a band just play one song over and over and over again so many times. What was going on?' It was the song 'Bad'. It was very difficult to do, almost an impossible collision of cultures for us. It was a different kind of songwriting, like Philip Glass meets *Astral Weeks*, Van Morrison crossed with German electronica. You have sequences which are rigid and metronomic and then you have a bass which is improvising all the way, and the voice too. We were struggling so hard to find that song. Larry hated click tracks and felt it was interfering with the free-flowing side of the band. And now he hates playing without them.

One of my favourite singles was 'I Feel Love' by Donna Summer with Georgio Moroder. What struck me was that her voice sounded more soulful set against the electronica than it did set against a live disco band. I thought, 'That's interesting. The human voice works by contrast. It actually becomes more human in comparison with the electronica.' I had this idea that Kraftwerk were Europe's finest soul group. They didn't have big voices but their small voices really moved me, I responded to the pathos of their music. We were starting a love affair with electronic music, which I suppose reached its apotheosis with 'Pop'.

ADAM: 'Pride' was our biggest hit to date, at that point, and the album had been really well reviewed. We were just getting into arenas in America, so that would have been fifteen- or twenty-thousand-seaters, whereas in Europe we weren't quite at that point. At the start of that tour we played a lot of tents in Europe, which were big temporary venues that could take maybe eight thousand. They were horrible. You'd get condensation on the inside, which would affect the equipment, and we were just starting to use sequencers and computers, and playing to clicks and trying to work with these new structures, so that side of it was more important than at any other time but it was always going wrong. The start of that tour was hard.

BONO: We had a guy working with us at that point called Ian Flooks. He was our agent but he was much more important than that. He was really a great guide through the UK and Europe, where to play, how to play and who to play with. He was one of Paul McGuinness's best friends. They were partners in crime when it came to food and alcohol. I remember on these tours, thinking: 'Why are we playing, say, three nights in Lyon but only one night in Marseille?' And it would turn out there'd be a really great restaurant in Lyon and no great restaurant in Marseille. It is one of the more bizarre sides to this band that we have always celebrated any success that we've had by going to a restaurant and opening wine. If Paul McGuinness and Ian Flooks were there, it was always very expensive wine and they would go through a whole song and dance about it, talking about the nose and the bouquet. Then a strange thing happened. We started to notice that when anyone else gave us a bottle of wine it didn't taste the same; in fact it became really hard to drink plonk, and the penny slowly dropped that this pretentiousness might actually amount to something.

PAUL: Playing a better venue to more people, staying in a grander hotel, maybe going to a finer restaurant, these were part of the pleasure of touring. Throughout the band's career, I have been to nearly all their concerts. Sometimes I would be back at base, so to speak, I might go to New York to get something done, but essentially we went everywhere together. I thought it was pretty pointless being the manager of U2 if you didn't get to see their shows. I didn't regard it as a burden so much as a privilege. I would have my own criticisms of the show and would be part of the debrief that we have every night. It probably sounds rather Calvinist but I have to say it's what keeps them sharp.

EDGE: Touring didn't change really. There are small things that might make the experience that little bit easier, like having your own room in the hotel, a nicer tour bus, there might be limousines taking you to the airport. But at its core it is about the shows and trying to get into the zone and give a performance that does the material justice and really creates a special event. And that is absolutely the thing that gets us through a tour, because we can't go through the motions as a band, it's just not in us. I would say that is true of Bono particularly, but all of us generally. Whether it's because we can't afford the luxury of taking it easy, because it would be so patently obvious, or whether it's just because on a psychic level the band can only operate on total commitment, I don't know. But, for whatever reason, there's always a sense of jeopardy – in a good sense and to some extent a bad sense – about our shows. It's an intense thing but it's something we love, because when it goes off it really can go off. The biggest change for me was having a young family, because no one really had an idea what that might involve, not even our tour managers. There were lots of times when it was very frustrating to realize that hotels had been booked without taking into account that we have a baby on the road with a nanny, so we needed to be in adjacent rooms. Stupid stuff, but there was a big learning curve for everyone, not least me. It was like, from being just one of the guys, suddenly I was a parent and trying to maintain my family and hold up my end in the group. That was tough; it was hard to keep everything going along smoothly.

BONO: We were somewhere in Germany and Bob Geldof called. I didn't know what to make of the call at first, because Bob was Irish, and we looked up to him and respected him, but all I remembered was having rows with Geldof about how he thought pop music and rock 'n' roll should stay away from politics and agitprop, be sexy, fun, mischievous. The Boomtown Rats were a long way from The Clash. So it was odd to get a call from Geldof to talk about Africa. But he spoke so well, he talked like no one else can, and I put down the phone and thought: 'How am I going to get the band to agree to this?' They were aware that the tragedy unfolding in Ethiopia needed a response but they knew their schedule and it was going to be very hard. So I agreed and the band didn't. Edge couldn't make it, he had a family situation, Larry had stuff to do. Adam said, 'OK, well, I'll come and help you out.'

ADAM: We went to Basing Street Studios in West London. When we arrived, we realized it was an absolute media circus: Press, TV cameras, photographers. Everyone was there, and to be thrust into that world of London pop stars was mind-boggling. I was really quite aware of being an outsider. These people all seemed to know each other and have a level of comfort in this bizarre situation. I just didn't know where to go or what to do, where to sit or whatever. I remember overhearing George Michael having a conversation with Boy George about how he kept losing his credit cards and it was a real pain in the arse. I didn't really know what was going on. I was always a little bit frightened of Geldof anyway, because he was big and gruff and Dublin, so I kept my head down. I knew I was there to chaperone Bono and to contribute in any way I could. Bono was the person that had been invited there to sing and I understood that he didn't want to go to something like that on his own.

BONO: I felt awkward; at that point we were feeling very self-conscious. These were London's pop cognoscenti in the era of bad hair. Seriously, it was like a blow-drying convention. And we were an Irish rock band who had broken America. People didn't quite know what to make of us, they were just staring at us, as if to say, 'You don't look like pop stars.' That's how it felt. Let's say they didn't work very hard to make me feel another way, except for one person. Simon Le Bon spotted me feeling awkward and out of place, and came over. 'Do you want a drink? Are you OK?' Duran Duran were super-pop stars at this point and I thought he had some grace and a sense of humour. I mean, I had mine in an inside pocket at that point. Then there was the moment when I read the lyric to 'Do They Know It's Christmas' and thought, well, it's a really good lyric, but the only line I'm not going to sing is that one: *Tonight, thank God, it's them instead of you*. It's the most biting line, and actually reveals how selfish a mindset we all have underneath. I think Bob was trying to be honest and raw and self-accusatory. Rather than sing, 'We're lucky it's not us' he was saying: 'Well, when you say that, you mean "lucky it's them". Now look at it. Now look at yourself.' So I walked up to Bob and he said, 'Listen, I want you to sing this fucking line here.' I said: 'Just please don't tell me it's this line.' He said, 'That's the very line.' 'I can't sing that, Bob.' 'Can't sing the fucking line? What do you mean you can't sing the line?' I told him I didn't want to sing the line. He said, 'This is not about what you want, OK? This is about what these people need.' I was too young to say, 'This is about what you want.' But it was his show and I was happy to be in it. I knew it needed some force, the line. I kind of did an impersonation of Bruce Springsteen, that was really what was in my mind.

ADAM: I'm not really a singer but I was in the chorus line. There's a photo of everyone in the studio singing the choruses, so it was nice to be a part of that. The song went to number one. It was an amazing time. Maybe it was a reaction to the years of Thatcherism, when you knew that a Conservative government wasn't likely to take much interest in the plight of Africans – I don't know. But it did seem that, when Geldof came along, suddenly the power of music, or the power of that generation, could actually do something. Perhaps we felt we could solve the world's problems – I don't think the same is true nowadays. It's interesting that, in Bono's work, he's able to achieve more by going into the political world rather than encouraging people to form mass protests in the streets, which hasn't seemed to be all that effective in recent years.

PAUL: We went to America, where we were just getting into arenas in our own right for the first time. That was the first time we had a plane, which was very exciting. It was an old Vickers Viscount. Even in 1984 it must have been quite an age. We used to travel around America quite slowly in this creaky plane, looking out of the big windows.

EDGE: We were on the cover of *Rolling Stone* as 'Band of the Eighties', which was a massive thing for us in America.

FORGET ABOUT A BAD-HAIR DAY, I WAS HAVING A BAD-HAIR LIFE. YOU SHOULD NEVER LOOK LIKE YOU'VE HAD YOUR HAIR IRONED. I LOOK AT PICTURES FROM THAT PERIOD AND I AM THE PRINCE OF MULLET, AND THE ONLY THING THAT'S KEEPING THAT MULLET AWAY FROM POP HISTORY IS A HAT DESIGNED FOR A TALLER MAN. THERE'S STILL PEOPLE WHO CAN'T LIKE US BECAUSE OF THAT HAIR-DO. BONO

BONO: *Rolling Stone* had a big impact on our lives, both the journalists and the culture of the magazine. They took the music very seriously. They spell-checked, they fact-checked. We weren't used to people checking your quotes, we were used to people making them up. *Hot Press* in Ireland had a great culture of taking music seriously. The magazine was shot through with idealism and a kind of funky, guerrilla, 'let's stay afloat at all costs' mentality that we always loved. And my affection for *Hot Press* migrated to *Rolling Stone*. So being on the cover was a very big deal for us but I remember not liking the photograph much.

We arrived at the photo session and there seemed to be thirty people there. Now we were used to Anton, who doesn't even have an assistant. This was like a movie set; it was the Eighties, and money was just being splashed around. We were hugely flattered that *Rolling Stone* were throwing all this money at us, but the idea for the photo session was so shite. Very Seventies Led Zeppelin, *Houses of the Holy*, and we really didn't want to be part of that. We had different ideas about what we should look like and we felt a little bullied by the scale of the operation. I think I grumbled and might have mouthed off to a few people. In the end I don't think it was a very good cover.

EDGE: But still it was the cover of *Rolling Stone* and you don't look that sort of gift horse in the mouth.

BONO: U2 have had two really rotten fashion phases. One was the *October* tour, where I had a skunk on my head. It looked like a badger, actually; early experiments with peroxide, and it didn't work. We were so involved with whether we even wanted to be in a band or not, we really weren't thinking that much about what we looked like. The second was the *The Unforgettable Fire* period. That was pretty rough because I'd taken to wearing military boots that were knee-high. You should never draw attention to your legs if you don't

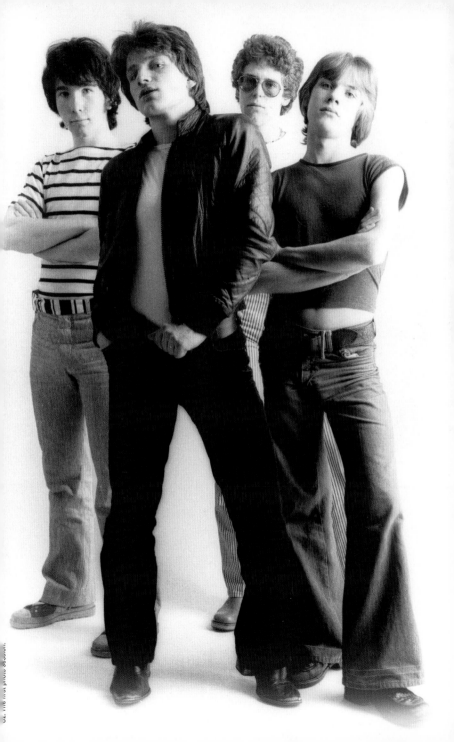

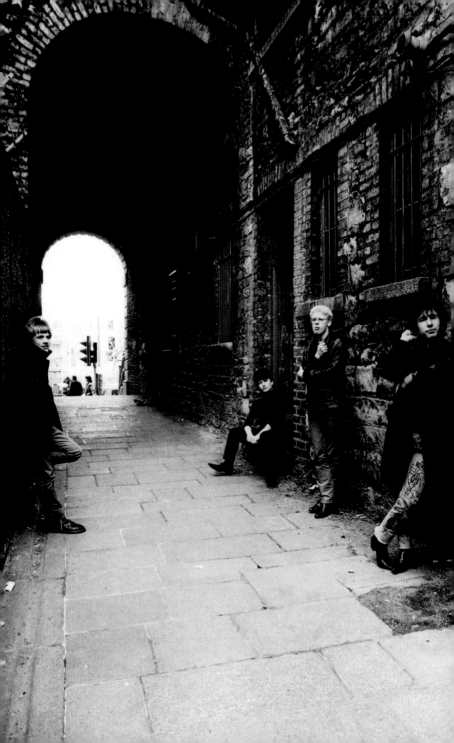

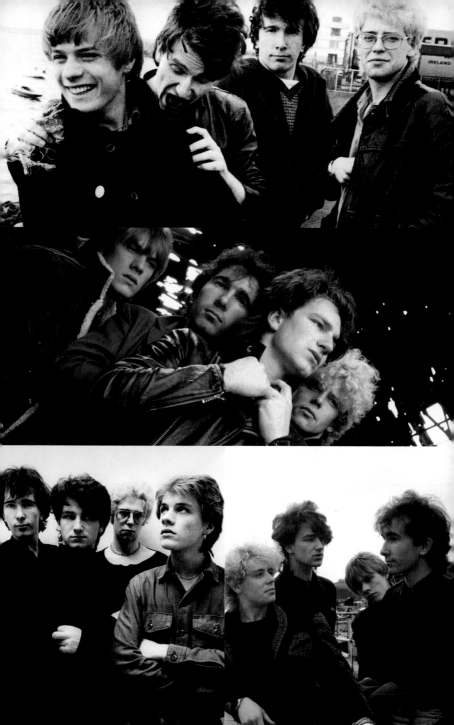

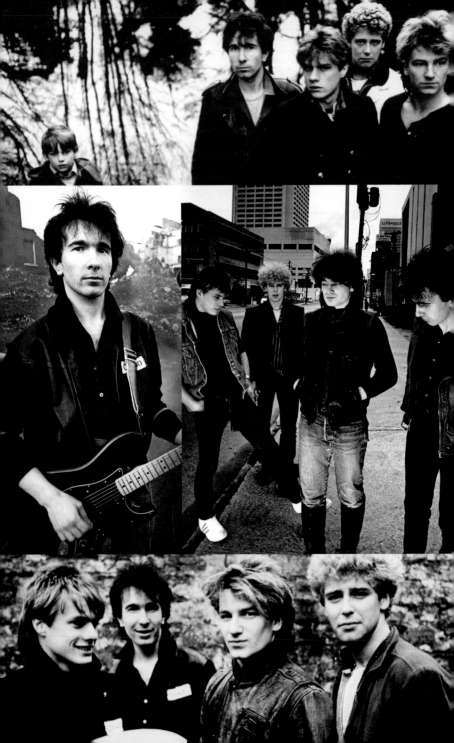

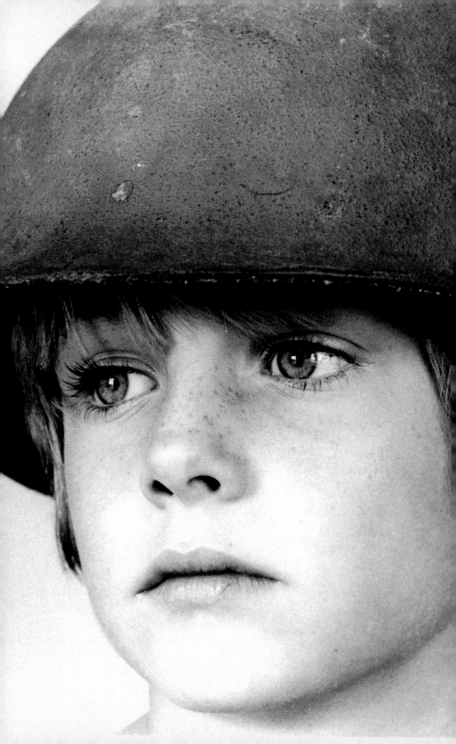

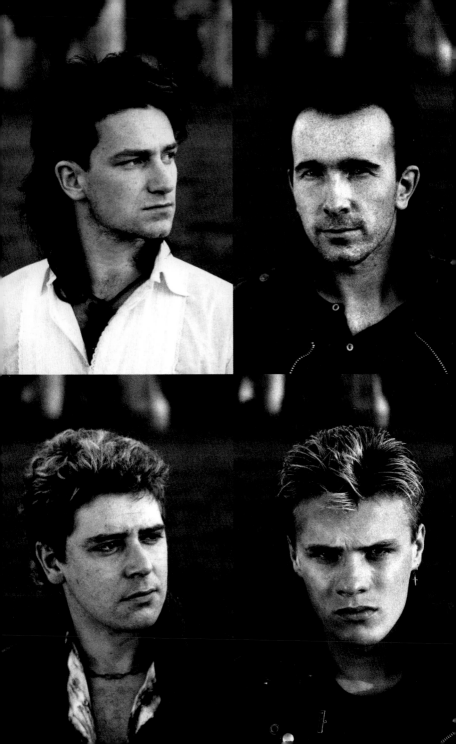

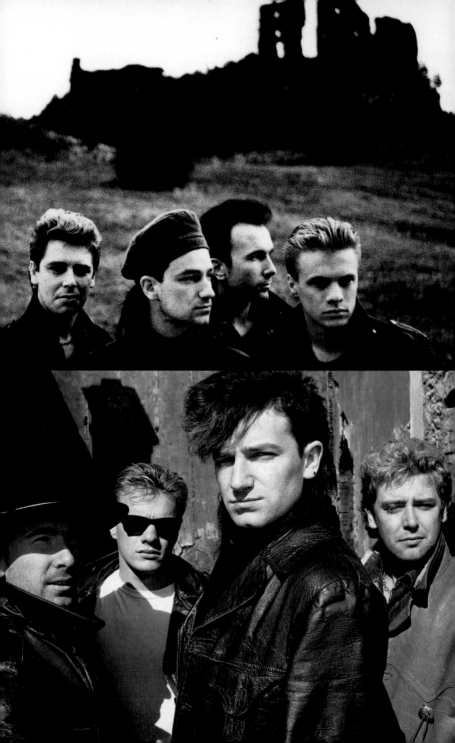

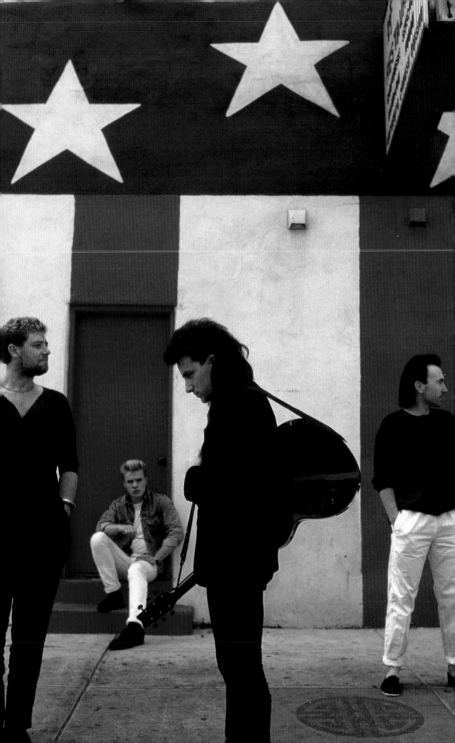

have any. And forget about a bad-hair day, I was having a bad-hair life. You should never look like you've had your hair ironed. I look at pictures from that period and I am the Prince of Mullet, and the only thing that's keeping that mullet away from pop history is a hat designed for a taller man. There's still people who can't like us because of that hair-do.

EDGE: Looking back at photographs, we did ourselves no favours at all. The lack of style is astonishing.

ADAM: We were really trying to be a little bit looser and not quite so buttoned up to the neck and military-looking. It was more Eastern European, something like that – refugee chic.

BONO: We played Madison Square Garden in New York for the first time and that felt like some sort of landmark. You heard about Led Zeppelin playing at Madison Square Garden, and The Who performing there. The building felt like home the first time we played there and it still does. It's the most expensive hall to play but nowhere else feels quite like it.

EDGE: The first time in the Garden was a bit special. All the big names play there, so if you show up for work and you're not like Barbra Streisand the staff would go: 'Who the fuck are you?' So it was kind of intimidating but at the same time a fantastic feeling to be playing in what must be one of the greatest venues in rock 'n' roll, certainly in terms of its history. I remember we saw the Stones there in 1981 but the sound was really bad. I don't know whether it was just where we were sitting but you couldn't distinguish anything. It almost put us off ever playing those venues. We'd just got in from Dublin and we were a bit jet-lagged and Bono fell asleep in the middle of their set. He was sitting next to me and about twenty minutes later they started playing 'Jumpin' Jack Flash' so I gave him an elbow to wake him up. He woke up and listened for about a good minute. Then he turned to me and said, 'Have they played "Jumpin' Jack Flash" yet?'

BONO: I had an amazing moment with my old man on that tour. I brought him over to the US to see us play. It was his first time in America. I picked him up at the airport in a limousine. He wouldn't get in it. So we had to take a taxi. It was in Atlanta and at soundcheck I organized with the lighting people to put a Super Trouper spotlight on him during the encore. I said, 'I wanna introduce you to somebody, it's their first time in the United States.' Holler! 'It's their first time in Atlanta!' Bigger holler! 'This is the man who gave me my voice, this is Bob Hewson!' The light came on, twelve thousand southerners hooting at him, and he stood up and he just waved a fist at me and mouthed an expletive followed by the word 'off'.

After the show, usually I'm left on my own for a minute to calm down, but I heard footsteps behind me and I looked around and it was my dad and his eyes were watering and I thought: 'This is it! This is the moment! Finally, he's going to tell me something!' This is a moment I've waited for all my life. My father was going to tell me he loved me. And he walked up, he put his hand out, a little shaky, a little unsteady, he'd had a few drinks, looked me in the eye and he said, 'Son … you're very professional!'

There is a band from Atlanta, who U2 became very close to, and that is REM. They were very, very hot at the time, extremely hip, better reviewed than us in the UK for their albums and starting to really happen. We tried to go and see them in Los Angeles on that tour. There was a fellah called Charlie McNally, a tall, skinny, Dublin promoter who used to look after U2. Charlie had left Ireland with some sort of cloud, saying he wouldn't be back until he'd made his first million. So some crude observers said, 'Looks like we won't be seeing Charlie again.' Next thing he had a limousine company in America, and Paul McGuinness was anxious to use it, because he'd been very good to us. So he was driving us to REM and an amazing thing happened on the way, the reason I never saw REM until much, much later. We ran out of petrol. We actually had to get out of the limo and push it. We had to push it for ages just to get off the highway. It was one of the great moments. There's always a little bit of Paddy just to remind you of home.

We did finally get to see REM when Ian Flooks put together an amazing bill for The Longest Day concert, in Milton Keynes in England. It was a festival pretending to be our gig, really, with some of the best bands ever all in one day. U2, REM and The Ramones. The band that made us a band – and they're guests of ours. How could this be? Maybe there isn't a God. I remember walking backstage and I saw this odd-looking bohemian with tiny little plaits in his hair, scribbling on a piece of paper. He looked like Lucky from *Waiting for Godot*, with a striking, tragicomic face. I sidled up beside him and said hello and he had a beautiful, mellifluous, southern twang, with perfect manners. That was the moment I met Michael Stipe. He was reading something and so was I, I can't remember what we were reading but it was a mine's-more-interesting-than-yours moment, and there was that dance when two contemporaries kind of work around each other. That began a relationship that is one of the most important in my life. Michael Stipe's friendship means more than I can ever tell you. He's one of the most consistent people you can have as a friend. I consider myself very loyal but unreliable. He's very reliable.

That was a great day, the Milton Keynes Bowl, fifty thousand people stretching up the slope of a hillside. I always loved that gig. I don't like playing flat fields because the people at the back can't see.

ADAM: Then we came back to Ireland to play Croke Park in Dublin for the first time, a huge outdoor show, fifty-seven thousand people. That was a pretty special moment. It was one of those celebrations of Irishness, with a lot of public drunkenness and people throwing up and that kind of carry-on. Playing at home is often nerve-racking but that was one of those days when everything just went well, it was a good gig. My parents were there, things had moved on between us. Supportive would be the wrong word, but they were in the loop, they knew what was going on and they could see it and feel it. So it wasn't so important to prove myself any more.

EDGE: That was probably the high point of that tour because we really had done it. This wasn't a band that was doing OK, this was a band that was topping the charts and had broken America and the world, coming back to play in their home town, in the centre of their city. There was an entire stadium jumping up and down in time to 'Pride'. Making a stadium into a club gig is the way I remember it. Just incredible!

PAUL: Live Aid was at the end of *The Unforgettable Fire* tour. Geldof called me up somewhere on the road saying, 'Look, I know I said there wasn't going to be a gig but now there is.' I said, 'Bob, tell me where it is and what time we're on and we'll be there.' And it did turn out to be a very special day for U2.

LARRY: I was nervous about it, it was such a huge gig. People were queuing up to do it because of the exposure, they were talking about the amount of TV coverage and whatever. It was hard to convince some people that we were there for the right reasons.

ADAM: Live Aid was absolutely terrifying but tremendously exciting as well. Terrifying because you only had your fifteen minutes and everything had to work, there was no rehearsal, no soundcheck. The environment was a little bit out of control, there being numerous cameras around, and a lot of people generally in the backstage areas. So you were always exposed, always vulnerable. We were going on in daylight, which was not a great situation to be in, but we were underdogs at that stage and we had to make those fifteen minutes count, given that it was a bill filled with enormous talent and we just didn't want to get lost in that list.

BONO'S DIVE INTO THE CROWD WENT A BIT WRONG BECAUSE HE HAD SO MUCH STUFF TO CLIMB OVER TO GET TO THE FRONT ROW. WE LOST SIGHT OF HIM COMPLETELY. HE WAS GONE FOR SO LONG I STARTED TO THINK MAYBE HE HAD DECIDED TO END THE SET EARLY AND WAS ON HIS WAY TO THE DRESSING ROOM. EDGE

EDGE: It was an extraordinary scene backstage. Everybody and his uncle was part of this thing. We met Muhammad Ali before we went on, being photographed by David Bailey. These were names to conjure with.

BONO: I remember standing beside Pete Townshend, before The Who went on, asking, 'Do you get nervous before you go on?' He gave me a drop-dead look and said, 'Nervous? Nervous about playing live, in front of people? I'll be nervous when I meet God. But nervous in front of you or anyone else out there? Never.' Oh, wow! That is why I will always stay an apprentice. I never want to miss that.

People were very good to me. I was walking with Ali and Freddie Mercury pulled me aside and said: 'Oh, Bo-No ... is it Bo-No or Bon-O?' I told him, 'It's Bon-O.' He said, 'Come over here with me. We've all been talking, myself, Roger and Pete and David, and we all agree, there's no singers any more, everyone is shouting these days, but you're a singer.' I was up against a wall and he put his hand on the wall and was talking to me like he was chatting up a chick. He had me laughing but I was shifting nervously at the same time, with Ali and myself exchanging glances. I thought, 'Wow, this guy's really camp.' I was telling somebody later and he said: 'You're surprised? They're called Queen!' But I was really amazed. It hadn't dawned on me.

David Bowie came over to me. And I was like: 'David Bowie just came to talk to me!' And then we started walking together and I turned to ask him something, and I was wearing that ridiculous hat with the wide brim, and I nearly took his eye out. This is the Elvis of the UK! This is the man who, more than any other, set fire to my vivid imagination. If John Lennon lit the fuse for my political point of view as a performer, as an artist it was David Bowie. And to have a moment with this God-like genius and almost take his eye out with the brim of your hat, it wasn't a great result. Paul McCartney came over and said nice things to us. I couldn't believe it. So it was very important to go on and do well. But it was panic stations back there, changing sets every five minutes.

LARRY: Jack Nicholson introduced us. I could see an Irish flag flying. I proudly said, 'It's amazing, we're the only Irish band playing here today.' Geldof was standing behind me and started to splutter. Of course, the Boomtown Rats had played earlier.

ADAM: We were supposed to play three songs, 'Sunday, Bloody Sunday', 'Bad' and 'Pride', which was our hit. But then Bono went missing.

LARRY: In the middle of 'Bad', he went on a wander trying to pick out some girls to dance with. It felt like he was gone for ever. We were quite jittery as it was and when Bono went missing, a certain panic ensued.

EDGE: Bono's dive into the crowd went a bit wrong because he had so much stuff to climb over to get to the front row. It was a massive stadium show with multiple barriers and camera tracks and a level difference between the stage and the floor that must have been twenty feet. We lost sight of him completely. He was gone for so long I started to think maybe he had decided to end the set early and was on his way to the dressing-room. I was totally thrown, and I'm looking at Adam and Larry to see if they know what's going on and they're looking back at me with complete panic across their faces. Next thing I spot him way down below clambering over the last of the barriers to get to the people. We're still playing away, giving it loads. So after he has a little cuddle with a girl down the front he starts to make his way back to the stage, which takes another five minutes. I'm just glad the cameras didn't show the rest of the band during the whole drama, because we must have looked like the Three Stooges up there: Curly, Larry, and Moe.

PAUL: I was on the side of the stage with my heart in my boots because I thought he'd completely fucked it up. I couldn't see him, I didn't know where he'd gone. All I knew was that we weren't doing the set that we'd agreed. He went into that extended version of 'Bad' and never got to the third song, which was going to be 'Pride'. The band were on stage feeling a little lost because they didn't know where he'd gone either and he was down at the front treating it for what it was, a TV show, and in some kind of inspired way he understood that. But I didn't know it on the day and afterwards we all thought he had completely blown it.

BONO: We didn't do the hit because I'd gone AWOL to try and find a television moment and forgot about the song. The band were very, very upset – they nearly fired me.

PAUL: I think it is fair to say there was a bit of a row afterwards.

BONO: There were all kinds of mixed emotions. It was a great day but I thought I had fucked it up. I went home and turned the TV on just in time to watch Bob Dylan and Ronnie Wood and Keith Richards walk out on stage in Philadelphia. These are three people I hugely admired, Bob Dylan was the lightning rod in my spiritual quest as a musician, and they looked like they were out of it, all of them. They were mumbling all kinds of stuff. It was the end of a very long day and I just saw my hero as a man, as a frail, vulnerable fellah who had quite obviously bitten off more than he could chew in the hours coming up to the performance. I felt very sad, because of all the prophetic utterances out of that mouth, all the references to scripture in his versification, his ability to take it on the nose from the critics, to stand up and say simple, proud, upright things. And here he was, just looking confused, addled.

I thought, 'I hope he's OK.' I worried for his health. I didn't know what he was doing but I knew he was close to some kind of edge. He didn't fall off, in fact, after a few stray comments about American farmers he catalysed Farm Aid, but something really disturbed me. There was just myself and Ali in the room and I got out of bed and down on my knees. It was a very real moment, the end of a very big day.

My own depression continued for a few days. We went back home, down to Ali's mother and father, who lived in Wexford. I was in a very dark mood, depressed and still upset with myself and I met this sculptor called Seamus Furlong, a friend of Ali's family, an old man, in his sixties. I walked into his little forge and he was working on a piece. It was a person in mid-air. I said to him:

'What's that?' 'It's called "The Leap".' I said, 'What's the leap?' 'It's about the leap of faith. That's you.' 'What?' 'That is you.' 'What are you talking about?' I asked. 'We saw you at Live Aid.' He said, 'You did a leap.' 'What do you mean?' 'Do you remember when you went into the crowd?' 'Oh, I remember it all right. I've thought of little else for the last couple of days.'

'You were getting out of your skin,' he told me. 'You weren't happy on the stage. You wanted something more. You made a leap of faith, you got something, you touched it. And I did this because I was inspired to.'

It was just complete coincidence, but it really encouraged me. Two days later, I got messages to call Paul. I phoned him and he said, 'You're not going to believe this but everyone's raving about U2 on Live Aid. Radio stations and TV have been asking people what the highlights were, and a lot of them are picking U2.'

I said, 'That's great.' And he said, 'I think they're mad.' Because he thought that we were crap as well.

PAUL: That was the end of that particular tour and I went to the South of France the following day with my friend Michael Hamlyn, who used to produce all our videos. I really just thought what a great opportunity and what a big mess Bono had made of it. Then we went into Antibes to buy the English newspapers the next day and it was such a huge story and it seemed to have been popularly decreed that Bono and Freddie Mercury had stolen the show. It gradually dawned on me what had happened. All of U2's albums went back into the charts and their status took a huge jump. Nothing was really quite the same again because now everyone knew who Bono was.

EDGE: It really took us by surprise when people started talking about U2 as one of the noteworthy performances of the day. I thought they were joking, I really thought we were crap. But looking back, as I did a week later, I started to see what it was. It was the sense of real, total jeopardy, which is always very exciting for a live event, and Bono's complete determination to make physical contact with the crowd and eventually getting there after two minutes of struggling over barriers. I think there was something about the amount of effort he had to put in to do it that somehow made it even more powerful.

ADAM: Bono's journey really meant something, it carried the emotion of the day to people. So his performer's instinct was right. Again.

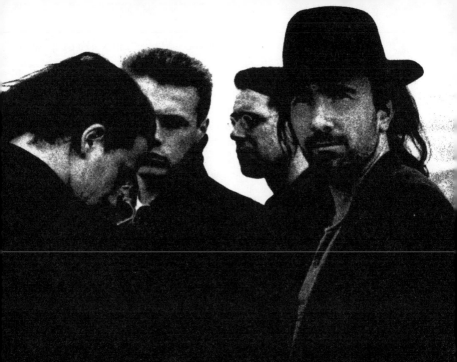

1986 - 1987

LUMINOUS TIMES

Bono

A CALL CAME IN FROM MERRILL WEALE FROM A
GROUP CALLED WORLD VISION. HE SAID: 'WOULD
YOU LIKE TO SEE AT FIRST-HAND WHAT'S GOING ON
IN ETHIOPIA?'

I thought it would be a PR thing but he said: 'No, if you want to come out, I'll
set it up, that's all.' He didn't ask for anything in return. That appealed to me,
going under the wire, working as regular volunteers. Ali agreed, so we set off
on an adventure that would change our lives.

We were put in charge of an orphanage in north Ethiopia, in a feeding
station at Ajibar. I was known as the girl with the beard, I guess because I had a
beard and an earring. After a while, it seemed to Ali and myself that there was
a lot of waiting around in the camps, not just by the children but also by the
adults. So we developed a repeating educational programme with various one-
act plays and songs to spread information on health, hygiene and other issues
affecting the locals in an entertaining way. One was called *The Labour Play*, it
was about giving birth and we worked on it with a nurse. It was a programme
that would repeat every three weeks. We would teach the kids a song and they
would go round the camp singing it and educate their parents on a couple of
things. I learned some of the language and wrote simple songs. For instance,
people were eating the seeds that were being brought in for next year's crop.
So the children would sing *We can't eat the seeds because they're for next
year / If we plant them right there will be no more tears.* It wasn't poetry but
it sold the idea. I still remember the tune. I have heard that some of the ideas
lived on after we left. I hope that is true.

It's a truly shocking sight to wake up and look over a hill, the early
morning mist hanging, and see thousands and thousands of people in rags,
who've walked all night to come to our feeding station, only to stand outside
and not be let in, and watch the other Ethiopians eating their food and yet
have no malice. I thought that they should have been enraged, not at the
other Ethiopians but at the world. They should have been angry, yet they
never seemed so to me. I was really humbled by them.

At one stage, a man came up to me with his little boy and said that I should take his boy with me. I said I couldn't. He asked me where I lived and I told him I live in Ireland, near the United Kingdom. He said, 'You can afford to take this boy. You can look after this boy.' 'I can't,' I said, 'I can't take him with me.' He told me, 'If you don't take him he will surely die.' And I didn't.

I don't know whether he made it or not; but in a certain sense I have always taken that boy with me, and if the rage rises up inside me, as sometimes it does, it's usually him I'm thinking of.

I remember a child being put in my hand, not much more than a few inches long and white as snow. Malnutrition in a newly born child leaves the skin completely white. I had this tiny baby in my hand and I remember saying my prayers and thinking, 'Well, there it is.' I thought there was no hope but the nurse was saying, 'No, no, this child can make it.' I heard years later that she did make it, which is lovely. It's something to think about when you're watching TV and somebody asks you for money and you think: 'Oh, I can't do everything.' Of course you can't, but in this kind of area your contribution has real impact. It is so beyond 'value for money'.

The thing I came away with in the end was a sense that there was a structural side to this poverty. There had been a civil war in Ethiopia as well as the natural calamity that had caused this particular famine but the story of starvation and poverty in Africa is not always war and natural disaster. A lot of it is corruption, as I discovered later, and not just theirs but our corrupt relationship with Africa – trade agreements and the like, old debts we keep making them pay. My awareness of this all started on that trip.

I'd brought a camera and wanted to record what I saw but I couldn't photograph people in the state they were in, it just didn't feel right. Then on the last few days I started to photograph the people who were well, those who had come through. It was nice to look at the rather regal faces of the Ethiopians in a different light. They say Ethiopia was the Garden of Eden, and you certainly can see the Queen of Sheba in those faces. I put it out as a book called *String of Pearls*.

When I arrived back from Africa, material for *The Joshua Tree* was developing, the emotional germs of a kind of lyric approach and big ideas and big questions. Then I was asked to participate in Steven Van Zandt's anti-apartheid single, 'Sun City'. It was one of those things where I couldn't get the band to do it and so I had to go on my own. I always hate doing that. People look back and say: 'Bono's right out in front on these things. Shouldn't he bring the band with him?' But Edge, Adam and Larry, very understandably, wanted a life. This was my life for me, this was how I could justify being in a band, in a certain sense. The life it was giving me brought responsibilities with it was my rather pious, if true, mindset.

A MAN CAME UP AND SAID THAT I SHOULD TAKE HIS BOY WITH ME. I SAID I COULDN'T. HE TOLD ME, 'IF YOU DON'T TAKE HIM HE WILL SURELY DIE.' I DON'T KNOW WHETHER HE MADE IT OR NOT; BUT IN A CERTAIN SENSE I HAVE ALWAYS TAKEN THAT BOY WITH ME, AND IF THE RAGE RISES UP INSIDE ME, IT'S USUALLY HIM I'M THINKING OF. BONO

So I went off to New York where, at the same time, Steve Lillywhite was recording with The Rolling Stones and he invited me down to the sessions. He said that Mick and Keith weren't getting on very well and maybe it would be good to have a distraction. So I dropped by and they were very good to me, all of them. At one point Keith started playing the piano and Mick was singing country songs. They seemed to warm to each other as well as to me. I saw this rich back catalogue of other people's music they were familiar with. Then they asked me to sing a song. I said, 'I don't know anyone else's songs.' They laughed and asked, 'What do you mean?' I said: 'I don't know anyone else's songs *at all*. And, by the way, we tried to play a couple of your songs as kids and you really wouldn't want to hear that.' They said, 'You must know something!' I asked them, 'Do you know The Ramones' "Glad to See You Go"?' It really wasn't going to work out. That is when I realized that U2 had no tradition, we were from outer space. There were no roots to our music, no blues, no gospel, no country – we were post-punk. Our starting points were the *NME*, Joy Division, Kraftwerk, Penetration and The Buzzcocks. It was a strange situation. Keith said, 'You don't know the blues?' I said, 'Not only do I not know the blues, I object to it.' He was taken aback. 'What do you mean?' I told him, 'Anyone who ever played the blues, where I came from, it was just twelve-bar laziness and it meant they were fresh out of original ideas.' He replied, 'Then you haven't heard the blues. When you hear the blues you won't be bored, you'll be frightened.'

Sometime over the next few hours, Keith got hold of some vinyl and put on some John Lee Hooker and Robert Johnson. I was already in awe of Keith just as a songwriter and as a rock figure; that he was taking time out to turn me on to the blues was something I was never going to forget. He played me these records and it sounded like the end of the world – more punk rock than anything I'd grown up on. I was listening to one John Lee Hooker track and I asked, 'Who's playing the drums?' 'That's his foot,' Keith said. 'He was just kicking at the floorboards.' I was blown out of it. I left with my head in a spin and I went back to my hotel room on my own and wrote 'Silver And Gold' and tried to apply what I'd just heard to the project at hand, which was an anti-apartheid record. I called Keith the next day and said, 'Can I come round, I've got a song I'd like to play for you? Maybe you'd like to play on it?' Keith said, 'Sure.' So I recorded an acoustic version of this, my first blues song, with Keith Richards and Ronnie Wood. Ronnie played slide with a flick knife, he's really one of the greatest slide players there ever was. A journalist called Robert Palmer, one of my favourite writers, who has since passed away, played clarinet. So that was 'Silver And Gold'. The next day we did 'Ain't Gonna Play Sun City'. I shaved the top of my African beard off. I looked like a mental, punk-rock Abraham Lincoln. When we did our little gig in Washington Square in downtown New York, Bruce Springsteen was there, the king of New York, but I remember noticing there were a lot of U2 fans there. They were really active, and that's when I realized our audience are more get-up-off-their-arse than most. There's a difference between agitprop in the sort of nihilistic, anti-everything sense and the concept of constructive protest that I believe our audience was wholeheartedly embracing. At Live Aid, there was a huge amount of U2 people there. They were in America and they were everywhere. When we went on the Amnesty International tour later, they doubled their membership from our audience. I think it was recognized that there was a new mood amongst music fans to effect change in the world, and our audience was at the forefront of that. Whether it was Live Aid, the anti-apartheid movement or Amnesty International, music was now seen as a unifying force, a kind of glue to make a new political constituency. And that is really worth voting for, because that hadn't happened out of punk. We were gathering force on very clear, achievable goals – some would say easy targets. Some would say we were avoiding the hard fights. But, in 1985, who could tell that apartheid would fall? Who could predict that Amnesty International could be so effective? It is true that we weren't narrow, we were broad; that was our power, and still is.

EDGE: I had some time before everyone else got back to work and decided to find a project that might bring me into some new areas of music composition. Paul put the word out and we got an offer to do the soundtrack for a little English movie called *Captive*. The script was great although the finished picture didn't quite live up to it. I asked Michael Brook, a Canadian technical guru whom I met through Eno and Lanois, to collaborate with me. I worked on demos at home and then Michael and I spent a couple of weeks in Windmill Lane recording, mixing and putting music to imagery. We recorded one song with a very young singer called Sinéad O'Connor. It was a welcome change from working with the band, and I made some discoveries that I brought back with me, one of which was actually a Michael Brook invention, the Infinite guitar, which was to become a very important part of the next U2 record.

BONO: I recorded a collaboration with Clannad, 'In A Lifetime'. I am the man who can't say no, but I loved Maire Ni Bhraonain. I think she has one of the greatest voices the human ear has ever experienced. And I had a great time making the video. I was driving a Humber Super Snipe at the time, which was a big old bus of a thing, and I'd bought a hearse version for spare parts, so before we carved it up, I thought I'd take it for a spin in the video.

I used to meet my father on Sundays for a drink and he'd pull me aside and say, 'I've a crow to pick with you.' He always did have a crow to pick. I hated the expression. A crow to pick – I don't know what it means. A crow to pluck? I've no idea. All it means is trouble. He'd say, 'Apparently, you went in to Grafton Street to get some discs and you asked for an album from somebody – I don't know who they were, some new-fangled group – and they said they didn't have it. And you said, "Do you not know who I am? Get me it!" Now you can't be going around doing that.' I'd say, 'Do you really think that I would carry myself like that?' He'd say, 'That's what some fellah said in the office. This was in the papers.' I had to tell him: just because it's in the papers doesn't mean it's true, and after a while he started to accept this. Then one day, after we made the Clannad video, he said, in a conciliatory tone, 'You're always telling me not to believe what I read in the papers. I heard there was a good one there the other day. Apparently, you were seen driving around in a hearse. What will they think of next?' I just didn't have the heart to put him straight.

ADAM: When a tour ends, you have a period of evaluating the tour, holding business meetings, closing it all down, being around for various things. Then you might take a month or six weeks of not answering the phone. After that it really is time to start writing again; that's the process. When there are four of you trying to make the thing work, it can be very time-consuming and unwieldy.

EDGE: My daughter Arran was born on the 15 October 1985. It was an amazing time but we were already starting to work on the first stages of a new album, so there was little time to reflect. I just had to run very fast to keep up. Larry had bought a house very close to our old rehearsal cottage. We moved out there for a couple of weeks to work up some of the ideas we'd generated during *The Unforgettable Fire* tour. There were some very rough versions of what became 'With or Without You', 'Red Hill Mining Town'; a song of Bono's called 'Trip Through Your Wires' and a song called 'Woman Fish' that mercifully never saw the light of day, other than on an Irish TV show that we

WE HADN'T SHOT OURSELVES IN THE FOOT FOR A WHILE, SO WITH TWO SONGS HALF WRITTEN WE DECIDED IT WAS THE PERFECT TIME TO GO TO THE NATION TO SHOWCASE OUR 'NEW DIRECTION'. IT WAS DREADFUL, THE WORST IN A LONG LINE OF ROPEY TV APPEARANCES. EDGE

agreed to do in a moment of dementia. We hadn't shot ourselves in the foot for a while, so with two songs half written we decided it was the perfect time to go to the nation to showcase our 'new direction'. It was dreadful, the worst in a long line of ropey TV appearances. The idea, if there was one, was to try out the new material in front of a live audience. We found out instantly that we had a long way to go. We tried later to bribe the staff of RTE to give us the tapes, but it turned out they had shared our opinion of the performance, and hadn't thought it worth keeping.

It was a hard period, which it often is to begin with, it felt like we were going nowhere with the music. Bono, at least, had a strong sense of the tone and colour of the lyrics. He wanted to get into America. I'd written off roots American music as an area for exploration back when we were starting out because all I knew of it was the watered-down 1970's FM version. I had become kind of inoculated against the white blues. But during *The Unforgettable Fire* tour I discovered an amazing US institution: 'Public radio.' For the first time I heard the music of Robert Johnson, Howling Wolf, Hank Williams, Lefty Frizzell and other seminal blues and country singers and players. Suddenly I knew it was time to take another look.

ADAM: We were really trying to make energetic new music that was based in early rock 'n' roll. In a sense it was something of a return to basics, only they weren't our basics.

BONO: We were starting to hang out with The Waterboys and Hothouse Flowers. There was a sense of an indigenous Irish music being blended with American folk music coming through. The Hothouse Flowers were a big influence on us because they were really the first Irish dance band. They were sexy, they spoke Irish and the singer sang blue eyed soul. Then The Waterboys were around us, bringing that sense of a more mythic muse. Mike Scott was the best songwriter in the world at that time, but, you know, Irish music tends to end up down the pub, which really diluted the potency of the new strains.

The muse got drunk, the clothes got bad and the hair got very, very long. But we were affected by this, it pushed us down the road of looking for roots. My conversations with Bob Dylan and Van Morrison and Keith Richards were all pointing me to look back.

EDGE: Working up some rough sketches, we went into STS, a little studio with a really great team, led by Paul Barrett, a very talented keyboard player, producer and engineer. There was little to be excited about at that point. 'With Or Without You' was really just a chord pattern, it didn't have melodies or guitar parts. We tried all kinds of permutations but it never seemed to get any closer to sounding like a record. The first musical idea of real interest to come out of STS was a magic jam. I was playing around on a guitar part and Adam and Larry started playing along. At first I was thinking, 'What the fuck are they doing?' It was such a bizarre angle they were taking, I was almost going to stop the jam and get everybody back on track. Eventually we ended the take and I explained that they had been playing on the wrong beat but when we listened back in the control room it was absolutely brilliant. That was the beginning for 'Bullet The Blue Sky' and it is a perfect example of why bands are such a great creative concept. There is no way any of us would have been able to get to that place on our own.

BONO: We started out with a riff and then Adam began playing bass in a different key, as the jazzman is wont to do. A riff is a riff – the bass is the genius bit.

ADAM: Everything in that jam was in a completely different space but as a whole it really worked together. From that one moment, we were able to develop the contour of the song.

EDGE: 'With Or Without You' still sounded awful. 'Red Hill Mining Town' was a bit better. That was probably the sum total of what we had at that point. We played those demos to Brian and Danny, who thankfully agreed to do this record with us. It was just at that point we got word of the Amnesty International tour.

PAUL: Jack Healey was director of Amnesty's American division. He was an impressive guy, a former Franciscan monk and Catholic priest, who was very taken with U2. He came to see us at Radio City Hall in 1984 and asked us to do a tour for Amnesty. Bono and I gave him an IOU for a week of the band's time, whenever he needed us, with the idea he could use that to get other people involved.

EDGE: It couldn't have been worse timing. We were building up to go into the studio and I was worried all the focus and concentration would be lost. At the same time there was no way we could not do it, it seemed too important. We put back Brian and Danny's arrival, and decided to go for it.

PAUL: I said to Jack Healey: 'The first thing you need if you're going to do this tour is a promoter, and the only promoter with the authority to pull this off is Bill Graham.' (That is the American Bill Graham, of course.) So I introduced Jack to Bill. Next thing, I get a call from Bill saying, 'You have to get on a plane and come and work with me and get the other artists.' We phoned every artist in the world and none of them would do it. It taught me quite a lesson actually, because in any of these situations the contact must really be artist to artist. So Bono hit the phones, and Anne-Louise Kelly, who worked for me at the time, and Ellen Darst, both became heavily involved. Our own small infrastructure proved very effective.

BONO: Myself and Anne-Louise Kelly stayed late every night trying to get people to go on the tour, ringing everybody we knew, Paul McCartney, Mick Jagger, Prince. Prince was at the height of his popularity and his manager said, 'Well, just ring this number between seven and eight.' I said, 'Oh, great, is that his home phone number?' He said, 'No, it's in the studio.' 'Will somebody pick it up?' I asked. He said, 'Well, we don't know but he sometimes walks past between seven and eight.' I said, 'Can I have an appointment to speak to him?' He said, 'No, he doesn't take appointments. But if he's passing and the phone rings, he'll pick it up.' I remember thinking: Success is not heavy, it's weightless. Without gravity, you're just left to spin. I guess everyone spins out for a while. Many people were very nice but Peter Gabriel was the first to commit. It was my first taste of the real in-the-trenches type work that I do a lot of now. It was a thrill when people would eventually say they'd do it, after a few phone calls.

In the end it was U2, Peter Gabriel, Sting, sometimes with The Police, Lou Reed and a few others, Jackson Browne, Bryan Adams, The Neville Brothers and Joan Baez. That became The Conspiracy of Hope tour.

Lou Reed really helped us out. I had a strange moment with him at the first Press conference. Every time I turned to talk to him he would look the other way. I wasn't expecting that kind of cool, the cold kind. His wife at the time was there, Sylvia, a gorgeous girl. I said to her, 'Has Lou got a problem with me?' She said, 'A problem with you? No, not at all. He's actually just a bit shy. It meant so much to him that you sang his song during Live Aid.' Apparently no one asked him to do Live Aid and he was sitting at home like everyone else, watching, and suddenly I started singing 'Satellite of Love' and a little bit of 'Walk On The Wild Side' in the middle of 'Bad'. Sylvia said, 'He just doesn't do small talk about serious stuff, and he takes you very seriously.' We became very good friends, Lou Reed and I. He is to New York what James Joyce was to Dublin.

EDGE: To get a collection of artists like that all travelling together on the same plane doing Press conferences and concerts in every major US city was fantastic in every sense. There was very little ego management necessary, the atmosphere in the camp couldn't have been more positive. Every Press conference started with Aaron Neville singing 'Amazing Grace' *a cappella*. Seeing Aaron, who is the sweetest gentleman, but who looks like he could rip your head off, singing that melody in his falsetto voice usually softened up even the most cynical journalist. Then Jack Healey would hit them between the eyes with one of his sermons. When he spoke about the plight of the prisoners of conscience he summoned up an intensity of moral outrage that only a true believer could achieve. After that it was all over, they would completely cave in.

We headlined the tour on a couple of occasions, Sting played before us. In New York, The Police were headliners but at the very last minute they said they wanted us to end the show. So there was a kind of ceremonial handing over of guitars. We played with their instruments after their set.

BONO: When The Police played, you realized this was one of the great groups ever. When they gave us their instruments I took it as an incredible act of generosity on their part, because we were the young brats, bullish, with that awful snotty-nosed thing you have to people who've come before you. When they handed over their instruments, it was very emotional for them. I think it was clear in Sting's eyes that he was not going to be in a band any more. They had come together for this tour and that was it. It was a very big moment, like passing a torch.

EDGE: Meeting Bob Dylan for the first time was a momentous occasion for me. He played the Los Angeles show, and he came up to me in the corridor backstage at the Forum and said: 'Love your work, it's incredible. It's great to play with you, man.' I was walking about a foot off the ground for the rest of that week.

BONO: The person whose spirit lit up the place every night was Peter Gabriel, in my opinion. His generosity as a man, his humour, his spirit as a

THE AMNESTY TOUR SHOWED US WE WERE RIGHT TO BE PURSUING THIS KIND OF RAWNESS AND CONTENT, TRYING TO HAVE SONGS THAT DESCRIBED THE BLEAKNESS AND GREED OF AMERICA UNDER RONALD REAGAN. ADAM

performer. He was right up there. His song 'Biko' was the most articulate on the subject of Amnesty. Steve Biko was an anti-apartheid campaigner who was beaten to death in captivity. The song became an anthem for that tour.

ADAM: There was a core of maybe eight artists who all travelled on a chartered plane and checked into the various hotels together. It felt like something that happened in the Sixties. It was quite a sober affair; I think there was a pillow fight one day on board but that was about it. People turned up, did their stuff. I think they were very clear as to why they were on the tour. It's hard to have an ego when you're dealing with prisoners of conscience as an issue.

LARRY: After the shows we would go back to the hotel and maybe somebody would sit at a piano and there might be a bit of singing but it all was pretty low-key. Wild and crazy rock stars.

EDGE: One of the triumphs of the tour was that we managed, through influence and media pressure, to get the great Nigerian band-leader Fela Kuti sprung from jail. He was being held by the Nigerian authorities on some trumped-up charge of suspected tax evasion. Effectively they were trying to silence him and eventually, before the end of the tour, they let him out and he played on the tour. It was the starting point for our association with Amnesty and that was the first of many prisoners of conscience who succeeded in gaining freedom after our fans made a big fuss about it.

There was something about being on the road with all those people doing this thing for Amnesty that really did focus us, so when we came back to Dublin, the album sessions had an extra intensity and power. I think that the tour, rather than taking away from the record, actually helped us enormously to home in on what it was we wanted to say that really mattered to us.

ADAM: I think the tour showed us that we were right to be pursuing this kind of rawness and content, trying to have songs that described the bleakness and greed of America under Ronald Reagan.

BONO: I took a break in Los Angeles with Ali. I was interested in what was going on in Nicaragua and El Salvador, which was the big political issue of the time. There was a group called Sanctuary, supporting peasant farmers who were caught in the crossfire of what was essentially a civil war in El Salvador. There were guerrillas and government troops torturing these people, covertly backed by US forces who feared the Nicaraguan socialist revolution would spread. We were involved in some small way helping Sanctuary through a friend of ours called David Badstone, who is now a professor of philosophy in the University of Oakland. At some point he said, 'Why don't you go and see for yourself?' So Ali and I went for a week's holiday to war-torn Central America. The plane was bargain basement, if there weren't chickens and goats on the seat beside you, then you could certainly hear them cackling and bleating somewhere nearby. There was some trepidation as we settled down.

I had an extraordinary time in Nicaragua, and fell in love with this very musical, very cultural place. The ideas of the revolution were, from my point of view, a coming together of many of my interests: Christianity, social justice, artists in power. The powers that be felt the Sandinista revolution had to be squashed because it had the potential to catch fire, and had that happened in Mexico, the United States would have felt very unsafe.

We went up to see our peasant farmers, who were trapped in the crossfire of this revolution, and we got caught in the crossfire ourselves. I'd never been shot at before. I remember the really dull sound of bullets zipping over our heads. It was somewhat inglorious, not at all what I was expecting. A group of soldiers had seen us going into a rebel-backed area and were attempting to frighten us. They certainly succeeded – we just froze and I was wondering: 'What do we do here? Why have I brought my young wife to this dangerous country?' David kept a completely cool head. 'Just keep walking, don't look around, don't do anything,' he said. They fired off a few more rounds over our heads and we kept walking and that was that. We got further up the hills and there was mortaring going on and the ground was shaking. The government troops would inform a rebel-sympathetic village that they were going to destroy it and everyone had to leave, but people wouldn't leave their homes, so there were many fatalities. It would be fire-bombing followed by mortaring. I remember watching this horror happen on another hillside, in another world, next door to where we were but not so far away that we couldn't feel it. And then meeting these beautiful farming communities, who were grateful for the help they were getting from the American-based group, Sanctuary. That was El Salvador.

When I returned to Dublin, I rekindled my friendship with Gavin and Guggi. We would paint together and listen to music and then go out drinking afterwards and just be silly. I was fresh out of silliness at that point and I knew I needed some of that back. I remember Ali saying to me: 'I didn't fall in love with this righteous person. I fell in love with somebody who had much more mischief in them.' We had great laughter in Africa, and in El Salvador. I may have been taking these trips in order to get away from being a pop star. In those far-off places people had no idea who I was and it felt great. I was self-conscious as a pop star in the Eighties. It happens to people in the first flush of fame and I'm way over it now but back then it felt oppressive. So I used to love going away and, of course, in heightened fear and anxiety you are at your silliest. We would do the stupidest things, we'd behave like children. We had a lot of laughs. Back in Dublin I wanted the same thing, I needed to regain a sense of fun and I found it with Gavin and Guggi. It was great to be back with these people I'd grown up with – I felt alive.

EDGE: After The Conspiracy of Hope tour, we were still short of a few songs. We spent a lot of time talking about what this album was going to be. Bono had been reading Flannery O'Connor and Truman Capote. I was reading Norman Mailer and Raymond Carver. We had all fallen under the spell of America, not the TV reality but the dream, the version of America that Martin Luther King spoke about. The language of the American writers particularly struck Bono, the kind of imagery and cinematic quality of the American landscape became a stepping-off point.

BONO: I'd been travelling widely, so travel was a huge theme. I'd been listening to the blues, and immersing myself in American writers, from native American writing through to black writers like James Baldwin, Ralph Ellison and poets and playwrights like Tennessee Williams, Allen Ginsberg, Sam Shepard, Charles Bukowski. I had this love affair with American literature happening at the same time as I became aware of how dangerous American foreign policy could be in the countries around it, with the brutal crushing of the Sandinistas. I started to see two Americas, the mythic America and the real America. It was an age of greed, Wall Street, button down, win, win, win, no time for losers. New York was bankrupt. There was a harsh reality to America as well as the dream. So I started working on something which in my own mind was going to be called *The Two Americas*. I wanted to describe this era of prosperity and Savings and Loans scandals as a spiritual drought. I started thinking about the desert, and what came together was quite a clear picture of where I was at, as a person a little off-kilter in my emotional life but very much waking up as a writer and as a commentator on what I saw around me, my love of America and my fear of what America could become.

EDGE: The idea of making a 'cinematic record' where each song would conjure up a physical location came out of one of the first discussions we had with Brian. The landscape of the American southwest and the desert become recurring lyrical themes. We had a few clues to the general feel and texture of the music, some beginnings from here and there, and a determination get to some unique place, but no finished songs. We started trying to knock our rough ideas into some kind of shape, mostly by experimentation. Progress was in fits and starts and we relied far more on instinct than craft. It didn't seem like there was any point in being methodical, which was hard on everyone, but being uncertain and, in some ways, out of our depth, created a tension and sense of jeopardy that kept us all very focussed.

LARRY: In July, Greg Carroll was killed in a motorcycle accident in Dublin. He was a very special guy, a Maori from New Zealand. We hooked up with him in Auckland during our tour. He was working as a stagehand and made a big impression on us all. He'd never been outside of the country before so we got him a passport and he came to Australia and, later, America with us. Then he came to Dublin to work for us on day-to-day business. He made a new life for himself and was very popular around town. His death really rocked us – it was the first time anyone in our working circle had been killed.

EDGE: It was an absolute tragedy because he was a very young guy and the circumstances of his death were really avoidable, just one of those freakish things. Greg was a very beautiful character, a bit naïve but a great soul, and physically a great athlete. He always wanted to know what was going on and would go out of his way to figure out new technologies, new ideas, anything that was happening that would be of interest to us. His job on the road was to look after Bono when he was performing; he would be the guy with the knee pads and elbow pads, jumping down to make sure that if Bono went climbing his mike lead wouldn't get snared on a piece of scaffolding. If Bono was about to dive into the audience, Greg would be there to make sure he didn't break his neck. You can see him shadowing Bono's every step at Live Aid during his walkabout.

   His death was as a result of a terrible motorbike accident but it came from his instinct to push life to the extremes. Greg was like a member of the family, but the fact that he had come under our wing and had travelled so far from home to be in Dublin to work with us made it all the more difficult to deal with.

ADAM: It was a very sobering moment. His body was taken back to New Zealand. Bono and Ali, Larry and Ann and Paul's sister Katy McGuinness, who

Greg had been close to, went down and saw him off in a traditional Maori way. It was a very sad business.

BONO: I guess the problem with dealing with death, for me, is that it's always the same death. It's always my mother dying, it's always the centre of the universe disappearing and having to find another one. It just brings me back to that moment every time. It was a very big event in the life of a small community here. The big subjects seem to be things that we always have to be reminded of. That's what our band seems to be about, and that just sort of set it off, it brought gravitas to the recording of *The Joshua Tree*. We had to fill the hole in our heart with something very, very large indeed, we loved him so much.

EDGE: My family was expanding and we had just bought a new house. While Aislinn and I were house-hunting we had seen an amazing estate in the hills. We decided it wasn't for us but later I had the idea that the owner might rent it to us to record in. The house was called Danesmoate. So we set up in this big old Georgian house in the foothills of the Wicklow Mountains, about half a mile from Columba's College where Adam had been infamously expelled. Adam ended up buying the house, perhaps to get up the noses of the establishment next door although he would never admit to that. We set up a studio with Flood engineering. Flood had been involved with some of our favourite records of that period, with New Order, The Associates, Nick Cave & The Bad Seeds. So that was a great additional asset to the team.

ADAM: We wanted to do the backing tracks live as a band. Danesmoate was a Georgian house in the country but there had been an addition to it which produced this very large drawing room that had double ceiling height, which was great sonically. When you hear that big drum sound on *The Joshua Tree*, it's the sound of that room.

EDGE: Danesmoate had a very creative atmosphere but sonically gave us a few problems. The drums were at ear-splitting volume and we just couldn't settle in. To make matters worse, the *Captive* soundtrack project had gone awry and I was on the phone to lawyers in London trying to sort out the mess. Right in the middle of all of that drops Robbie Robertson. Danny Lanois had agreed to produce his first solo record and Robbie was looking for some clues and decided Dublin was as good a place as any to look. We were big fans of The Band and honoured to help out. Danny and Robbie recorded two backing tracks with us in as many days. We wished our own sessions were going as well. Things began coming into focus as Bono started getting a grip on the lyric

THE PROBLEM WITH DEALING WITH DEATH, FOR ME, IS THAT IT'S ALWAYS THE SAME DEATH. IT'S ALWAYS MY MOTHER DYING, IT'S ALWAYS THE CENTRE OF THE UNIVERSE DISAPPEARING AND HAVING TO FIND ANOTHER ONE. BONO

to 'Bullet the Blue Sky' – that was like a cornerstone. The guitar playing was informed in some ways by the lyric; the STS demo was much more bare-boned, like a heavy funk track, but it eventually became more of a haunted blues.

BONO: I wanted something biblical. My understanding of the scriptures were the psalms of David and the lyricism of the King James Bible and I tried to bring that in, to give it a religiosity. Then a picture of this face comes up to me, red like a rose on a thorn bush. It was Ronald Reagan, which I never told anyone at the time. Brian Eno said, 'You'll ruin it for people if you give them images.' Then it talks about money versus idealism. Reagan is now deified as the man who ended the Cold War by playing a game of chicken with the Soviets and winning. All credit for that, but I wish we had found a way to rapprochement without playing nuclear chicken.

I was angry with what I saw as the bullying of peasant farmers by big aeroplanes, supported by American foreign policy and dollars. In Nicaragua, seventeen families ran the country before the revolution; all of the wealth was in the hands of those seventeen families. In Salvador it had been similar. In Chile, a democratic choice had been overthrown by a CIA-backed coup to impose a killing machine called General Pinochet. There was a lot to despise about America back then, there was shameful conduct in the defence of their self-interest. And whilst communism turns out to be one of the worst ideas the world ever came up with, idealism turned in on itself; to support everything that's anti-communist was a really bad idea. It ruined Africa. They were bad times. I described what I had been through, what I had seen, some of the stories of people I had met, and I said to Edge: 'Could you put that through your amplifier?' I even got pictures and stuck them on the wall. I brought in film of the horrors and put it on a video and said: 'Now, do it!' It was more, more and more. He was asking, 'How much fucking more?' I wanted it to feel like hell on earth, because from the demon seed comes the flower of fire. All these images of fire-bombing, it's a demented song. And outside it's America. Who's bombing these villages? The peasants didn't even blame their own people. 'Who is making us feel this way? Who is shattering our lives? Who is shaking the walls of this house? It's the Americanos.'

That is when I started to realize that the lyrics on the first four albums are not really lyrics at all, they're sketches. I wasn't a writer really, I was a painter, or an emoter or a shouter, I seemed to have almost a fear of writing; it was an advanced form of procrastination. I'd had it in my school work. You'd do anything but the thing you have to do because doing it brings on judgement – fear of failure, probably. So just don't try. Live off your wits, which I'd be good at. Scat, create pictures and then justify it as the first brush stroke. After 'Pride (In the Name of Love)', I looked at how glorious that song was and thought: 'What the fuck is that all about?' It's just a load of vowel sounds ganging up on a great man. It is emotionally very articulate – if you didn't speak English. With *Joshua Tree*, I decided I'd better write some lyrics. I was reading more anyway, so I was more awake to the word. I discovered a love for writers and started to feel like one of them.

EDGE: Fairly early on we got a basis for 'One Tree Hill', a song for Greg Carroll, but after that progress was difficult. It was really bits and pieces where you just get a glimpse of what might be and slowly piece it together. We kept recording and each time we felt like we had run out of road there would be a breakthrough. Some were total accidents. One very important moment was the breakthrough for 'With Or Without You'.

ADAM: The chord sequence came from Bono but, in early versions, it sounded very traditional because the chords just went round and round and round. It was hard to find a different take on it or a new way into it, it was just a promise of a song. We started playing with a drum machine and having it build up with a big fat bass.

EDGE: I was sent a prototype of the Infinite guitar by Michael Brook. It arrived during the sessions with elaborate instructions on how to hook it up: one wrongly placed wire and you could get a nasty belt of electricity. This piece of gear would have failed even the most basic of safety regulations. When it did come on the road with us, my poor guitar technician would regularly electrocute himself. It was homemade technology, but very effective. It gave me infinite sustain, like a violin. I had just taken it out of the box and was playing around with it in one room while Gavin Friday and Bono were in the control room listening to the backing track of 'With Or Without You'. We were really at an impasse in the search for the right arrangement, and were just at the point of leaving the song to one side. Then, through an open door, they heard the sound of the Infinite guitar combining with the bass and drums and just went: 'That's it! But what the fuck is it?'

BONO: Gavin's involvement in *The Joshua Tree* can't be underestimated. He personally rescued 'With or Without You'. He pulled it out of the wastepaper bin, organized it, structured it and was the one who believed it could be a big hit when Brian and Danny had passed on it. It's my chord sequence but what makes it special is Brian Eno's sequencer; he did for 'With or Without You' what he'd done for 'Bad', which was to create a keyboard arpeggio. Then, having sketched it out and improvised, Edge was working on his Infinite guitar, which makes a beautiful haunting ghost of a guitar sound, and it was going on in one room while the bass chords were going on in another, and I heard them in stereo working together. We brought Edge in and started recording immediately.

The lyric is pure torment. One of the things that was happening at that time was the collision in my own mind between being faithful to your art or being faithful to your lover. What if the two are at odds? Your gift versus domestic responsibility? I had always been the kind of person who would sleep on everyone else's floor, the eye of a travelling rat, a natural tinker. I would just wander off and be very happy. So now I have this person in my life whom I love more than my life but I'm wondering if the reason I'm not writing is because I'm now a domesticated beast. I'm wondering if I'm house-trained? If I meet somebody and I want to go off with them, to find out what their world is like, I can't because I'm a married man. It's not even about sexual infidelity, I just remember thinking: 'Is this the life of an artist? Am I going to have kids and settle down and betray my gift or am I going to betray my marriage?' It was a very difficult time in my head. I had met a couple of people on the way who had taken advantage of my naïveté, is the best way I can put it, and I realized I knew so very little about this world and now, the future looked like I was going to know even less. You can learn about politics, culture, but your emotional life also has to be developed. I think in some senses mine wasn't, and I was going through all this kind of uncertainty. I was at least two people: the person who is so responsible, protective and loyal and the vagrant and idler in me who just wants to run from responsibility. I thought these tensions were going to destroy me but actually, in truth, it is me. That tension, it turns out, is what makes me as an artist. Right in the centre of a contradiction, that's the place to be. There I was. Loyal, but in my imagination filled with wanderlust, a heart to know God, a head to know the world, rock star who likes to run amok and sinner who knows he needs to repent. All of those things were going on but I didn't understand at the time that is actually it.

If I had cut loose, what would have become of me? I remember looking at Shane MacGowan with awe not just at his talent but his unflinching pursuit of truth, wherever it led him. He was one of my favourite singers and songwriters and there he was out pursuing the muse with no holds barred. All the people whom I looked up to as writers, they'd all done the same. Nothing had stood in the way, they had acted with abandon, and had lost marriages, bands, friendships, all in pursuit of the muse. But the muse is taciturn and can abandon you, leave you with nothing. My muse makes different demands. If I'd gone that route many of our best songs would have gone unwritten. Or if I'd taken the other road, which is straightforward, given myself over to the domestic side of life, the songs would have been lost. It's the tension between the two that keeps me sharp. You don't have to resolve them, just don't go too far either way.

So that song is about torment, sexual but also psychological, about how repressing desires makes them stronger. The most important line is probably, 'And you give yourself away.' It just flipped it and it releases all the mental tension, which is when the 'Aah-aah' comes out. That is what giving yourself away is, musically.

ADAM: 'I Still Haven't Found What I'm Looking For' started out life as something completely different, a jam called, for some mysterious reason, 'Under The Weather Girls'. It was a bit of a one-note groove but it had a great drum part, so we kept the drums and this whole new melody came and all the music changed to fit around that melody. It was quite traditional rhythm and blues, which wasn't somewhere we had gone before, but it was exhilarating.

LARRY: That song wasn't as arduous as most, even though it had its moments, and we knew it was going to be our trophy. Danny was very focused on the rhythm section and was able to make sense of my weird drum pattern. Rather than me changing the part, which would have happened in the past, he encouraged me to continue working on it. In the end, he mixed quite a bit of the drum pattern out and left the basics, and it became even more unusual but less fussy than it was originally. Danny's musical genius is all over that record.

EDGE: It was kind of an interesting jam, an odd backbeat from Adam and Larry. At first I wasn't so convinced. It sounded to me a little like 'Eye of the Tiger' played by a reggae band. Then Danny and Flood put up this great mix and we got ready for Bono to try and find a top line melody. There are only a few moments of full-on electricity-in-the-air creativity that I remember from the making of that album, but the birth of 'I Still Haven't Found What I'm Looking For' is one. Bono started singing, and as usual there are a lot of signals and a few helpful suggestions coming his way from the floor, but then he just nailed this fantastic melody that came out of a classic soul tradition.

THE SEVEN TOWERS WERE AN ATTEMPT BY IRELAND TOWARDS MODERNITY IN HIGH-RISE LIVING – JUST AS EVERYONE ELSE IN EUROPE HAD FOUND OUT TOWER BLOCKS WERE NOT A GOOD IDEA, WE STARTED BUILDING THEM. WE USED TO GO UP AND DOWN IN THE LIFTS, BECAUSE WE WEREN'T USED TO HAVING LIFTS. THEN THEY STARTED TO BREAK DOWN AND THE STAIRS BEGAN TO STINK OF PISS. BONO

And as I listened to this incredible song emerging out of the fog, I remembered something I had written in a notebook, a possible song title that I had actually stumbled upon that morning. I tried it in my head as Bono sang, and it scanned so perfectly that I wrote it on a piece of paper and handed it to him as he sang. It was like hand in glove. From then on, when anyone came to visit, that was the first thing we would play them. That's how you find out the best song. It's down to personal taste but when the record company or your mates come around you want to blow them away and you are going to instinctively choose the best song every time. I hadn't figured out what the title was about beyond maybe the idea Dylan expresses in 'Idiot Wind', that 'You'll find out when you reach the top you're on the bottom.' Bono took it in a different, more gospel direction.

I have to credit Bono for spotting the guitar hook of substance. One day, in amongst all the other stuff I was trying out, he heard a couple of notes that worked for him. He was right, without the chrome bells it wouldn't have had the counterbalance to its muddy shoes. In fact, the track only came to sound like a record in the final mix. Everyone chipped in on that one, but the final mix was made in my home studio with Danny and myself on the board, working on top of an earlier Steve Lillywhite mix. We had a very unorthodox habit of mixing on top of a mix, adding a little of the same ingredients a second time to the blend. That is what gives it the weird phasing sound.

If 'I Still Haven't Found What I'm Looking For' took a long time to get right, some songs arrived almost perfectly formed. 'Running to Stand Still' was one of them. I was waiting to do a piano part on another song and started playing some chords to myself. Danny Lanois heard something in it, picked up a guitar and joined in. Pretty soon Adam, Larry, and Bono were in the room with us. The first improvised version of the tune had almost every important musical idea in it, vocal melodies and structure. I think we only played it once or twice more. It had such a strong identity, we just had to get out of its way.

ADAM: 'Running To Stand Still' was 'Bad Part II', really, the campfire version, Bono singing about the chronic heroin problem that was present in Dublin at the time, and personalizing it with his experiences of the seven towers in Ballymun. Phil Lynott had died in January 1986, which was hugely tragic. I heard rumours about what had been happening to him but I don't think I quite believed them. When you see someone up on stage, being vibrant, and then they're reduced to kidney failure in a hospital, it's hard to equate the two. I thought that was a huge loss for music. I had made contact with Phil back before we ever had a deal, I used to see him around and I had been in his house a few times for parties but it was hard to actually feel at ease with him. There was a bit of darkness around, that is really all I can describe it as. That was heroin.

BONO: My brother was running a business and things weren't going well. I asked him how it was going and he said, 'It's like running to stand still.' It's a phrase I hadn't heard before, and it seemed to sum up the experiences of people I had known who had heroin habits. Guggi had lived in the seven towers in his bad years; they were an attempt by Ireland towards modernity in high-rise living – just as everyone else in Europe had found out tower blocks were not a good idea, we started building them. I had played in the foundations when they were being built. We used to walk over the fields and climb up them and then later we would go up and down in the lifts, because we weren't used to having lifts. Then they started to break down and the stairs began to stink of piss. Communities were moved out from the inner city to this social experiment; people who had been neighbours all their lives suddenly lost contact with each other. There were wonderful people living in the seven towers, but there were too many dysfunctional lives gathered in one place. There was a couple living there, both of whom were junkies. The guy used to pay for his habit by doing what was known as a run to Amsterdam, where he would pick up the heroin and strap it to his body and bring it back. If he was stopped he would go to jail for ten years but if he made it, he'd be able to afford his and his wife's habit.

The tragedy is he was a decent man at the heart of it, made a slave to his drug of choice. His wife was at the back of my mind. *She walks through the streets with her eyes painted red / under a black belly of cloud in the rain / in through a doorway she brings me white golden pearls.* White gold, from Iran, to Amsterdam, to Holyhead, to Dublin, and into the vein and oblivion. They used to do it by boat, these all or nothing runs.

ADAM: 'In God's Country' was a difficult song to record, although it's actually quite a simple, throwaway piece. I guess because we're not trained musicians, it's almost laughable how hard it was sometimes for us to play together and make something that sounded good while just playing in time. Making it work and then making it interesting were the two jobs at the time – sometimes we made it work and sometimes we made it interesting. That one definitely fell between two stools. In fact, I could never quite figure out why the chords for the two choruses were actually completely different, but there you go. The choruses were different, so I guess that means they weren't really choruses!

EDGE: I don't think 'In God's Country' was ever going to be one of our best tunes but we needed a few up-tempo songs, so it was useful at the time. Some songs are just better than others.

BONO: I was frustrated trying to get a bit of rock 'n' roll out of The Edge, and the only way I could get him to do this was to pick up the guitar myself. It used to so annoy him to see me with a guitar that he would start playing. So I wrote it really quickly just to demonstrate how swiftly you could write a rock song. I was saying, 'Look Edge, I'm not a guitar player, OK? I don't know all the chords but just try this. A-minor to D. Just like that.' He would say, 'It's not very good.' He's told me it was crap. Now I'm going to have to make sure it's good! What I really want him to do is to come up with something better, I don't want to have to be depending on this. The lyric was really good, the tune is pretty good, and the hook is pretty average – thanks to The Edge.

LARRY: Surprisingly, Edge is extremely competitive, always has been. He can endlessly listen to other guitar players and stay with it until he has figured out what they are doing. Sometimes he gets lost in his sound issues. His fascination with soundscape and the sounds of guitars, frustrating as it can be to listen to, is obviously a vital part of what U2 is. However, when it comes to actually just banging out a three-chord trick or putting some rock emphasis on things, he will shy away. He always felt that was the easy road and he wasn't comfortable with it, so the only way to get Edge to actually rock out was to annoy him with Bono's appalling guitar playing. Bono would thrash it out and Edge, being competitive, would say, 'Well, feck it, I can do that.' Then Bono would insist he was a better guitar player than Edge, and off he'd go. Being the one normally getting into trouble, these moments give me particular pleasure.

ADAM: 'Trip Through Your Wires' has that lovely loose, sloppy, throwaway side of the band that we can sometimes capture. Bono's harmonica playing is very expressive, with a nasty, aggressive sound. That harmonica first made an appearance when we were trying to cover Neil Young's 'Heart of Gold' back in our schooldays.

LARRY: Bono always took out the harmonica, right back from the beginning. Bono uses the harmonica to see if he can conjure up some backing vocals or new melodies, anything to make the songs better. He's actually not a bad harmonica player.

BONO: I've never practised harmonica in my life, ever. The only time I have ever played harmonica has been as we were recording or live on stage. I quite like it – I'm not very good at it but I'm in a line of not very good harmonica players, as I see it. 'Trip Through Your Wires' was another demonstration of how easy it is to write a song ... or not, as the case may be. I wrote it in a few minutes. It had a nice jaunty feeling that I thought might balance some of the other things. It was inspired by a series of phone conversations I had with somebody, who might have meant well and who was fascinating in their own right, it's just they were pretending to be somebody else.

LARRY: 'Red Hill Mining Town' is one of the lost songs. It was over-produced and under-written, one of those great ideas that never quite got there. Bono had a very clear idea about how he wanted it to sound but I don't think anyone was quite sure where he was going with it. What we ended up with was neither one thing nor the other. During improvisation things happened that were amazing but because of a lack of confidence in our ability to repeat the idea, we tended to hang on very tightly and perhaps not push forward as much as we should have. So sometimes we ended up with a bunch of great ideas as opposed to a fully developed song. In my view, that's part of the genius of U2 but it can also be part of the problem with our songwriting.

ADAM: If you try and dissect a jam and then reconstruct a jam, you can get to the point where you've killed it. But if you can capture the moment and edit it into some kind of a shape where people overlook any timing or tuning discrepancies, then you don't lose the inspiration and momentum and you kind of capture the pearl. 'Exit' came out of the band jamming. It was quite a long piece originally and we just played it once and then Eno cut it down into that shape. The problem is when you're in a touring situation you have to learn numbers that were never actually written so much as spontaneously created.

BONO: I had read Norman Mailer's *The Executioner's Song* and Truman Capote's *In Cold Blood*. This was my attempt at writing a story in the mind of a killer. It is all very well to address America and the violence that is an aggressive foreign policy but to really understand that you have to get under the skin of your own darkness, the violence we all contain within us. Violence is something I know quite a bit about. I have a side of me which, in a corner, can be very violent. It's the least attractive thing in anyone and I wanted to own up to that.

ADAM: 'Mothers of the Disappeared' came out of Bono's trip to El Salvador. Larry had a drum loop that Eno put a treatment on which is just so eerie and foreign and scary. I think the Spanish guitar melody came from a song Bono had used in the camps in Ethiopia to teach African children some very basic hygiene. The keening that he does in that is kind of prehistoric, it connects with something very primitive. He was inspired by this strange, almost silent protest of the mothers of people who had disappeared without any trace but were assumed to be victims of torture and kidnap and murder. Bono had met with them and understood their cause and really wanted to pay tribute to it.

BONO: Driving along the motorway in Salvador we saw a body on the road, a body that would have been thrown out of a car. People would just disappear. If you were part of the opposition, you might find an SUV with the windows blacked out parked outside your house, just to let you know they were watching you. If that didn't stop you, occasionally they would come in and take you and murder you; there would be no trial. The mothers wanted to know where their children were buried. The same had happened in Chile, the exact same thinking to inspire terror and with identical support: the United States of America. That song means as much to me as any of the songs on that album, it's right up there for me. I wrote it on my mother-in-law's Spanish guitar for these beautiful women with pictures of their missing sons and daughters.

It gave us a beautiful end to the album and 'The Streets Have No Name' was the perfect introduction. It is one of the most extraordinary ideas, only matched by The Doors' 'Break On Through To The Other Side' as a throw-down to an audience. Do you want to go there? Because if you do, I'm ready to go there with you, to that other place. Call it what you like, a place of soul, a place of imagination, where there are no limitations.

EDGE: 'Where The Streets Have No Name' came together in a bit of a rush the evening before we were due to start recording again. We were starting to get close to the end game and it dawned on us that we were short a certain kind of song. We knew we had some great ideas but there is something that happens when you start thinking about playing your songs live. In some way it's the ultimate test of your belief in your material. There is nothing you can hide behind on stage. If you don't have the goods, it's obvious. You really don't want to be up there playing a tune that almost came together.

Bono was off on a trip with Ali to write some lyrics, so I had some down time to go after the music. By then we had left Danesmoate and set up in my newly acquired house, Melbeach, which the family had not yet moved into. I took a room upstairs and set up a few keyboards, a bass, a guitar, and a drum machine. At first nothing came. I was recording onto a four-track tape machine, working alone, sequencing keyboards to the drum machine. I was starting to get desperate and thinking about the next tour. I imagined being at a U2 show and tried to dream-up what I would want to hear. It was my attempt to conjure up the ultimate U2 live-song. It was a strange feeling when I finished the rough mix, because I thought I had just come up with the most amazing guitar part and song of my life, but I was totally alone in a big house with no one to share it with. I remember listening to the complete silence of the house for a few seconds after the music had stopped and then doing a dance around the room punching the air. Then I went home.

LARRY: It took so long to get that song right it was difficult for us to make any sense of it. It only became a truly great song through playing live. On the record, musically, it's not half the song it is live.

ADAM: The demo always sounded great but we could never play it as a song. At the time it seemed almost like a foreign language, whereas now we understand how it works. I suppose it was something completely new for us, it was complex with frequent chord changes and time shifts. We would rehearse it and play it and rehearse it and play it ad infinitum and never get a finished version. In the end, the version we've got was cobbled together from a few different takes. The third verse is probably the best section, where it really works. It caused so much difficulty that Brian actually tried to wipe it at one stage.

EDGE: It was very difficult to get a performance we liked; it was taking so much time that Brian attempted to erase the multi-track. He was sick of trying to take this performance and somehow bring it up to scratch. His idea was that if we had to start again we might actually end up saving time. Pat McCarthy (who has since produced REM and Madonna) was tape-operator on the session, and managed to persuade Brian not to erase it – I think there may have been some physical restraint involved. We persevered with that backing track and actually, with Steve Lillywhite's help, we got a great mix of it. Even in those days we were pretty dogged. We would really keep going with something and our producers could get worn down by that process. From the very beginning there was a sense of elation in the music that we were holding on to, and finally it came through.

PAUL: As the band were getting to the end of the record it seemed they couldn't quite get it over the line. At that point I suggested we get Steve Lillywhite over to see if he could help out. I don't think Eno and Lanois were very happy about that. Steve came over and basically picked out the singles and mixed them all and became a royalty participant in the record. There was a certain amount of bad feeling about this guy coming in at the end and just putting a little polish on things. Personally I think he did rather more than that and he's done it ever since with nearly all the records, coming in like the cavalry to save the day.

LARRY: Danny and Brian brought very different things to U2. Danny brought his musical knowledge and his ability to take something ordinary and make it extraordinary. Brian was great on keyboards, on mood, on sketches and concepts. But neither of them really understood rock 'n' roll or, more importantly, how to get rock 'n' roll on the radio. We needed to be on the radio, we had always wanted that. Steve has 'pop ears' and understands what's necessary to get your songs on the radio.

EDGE: Steve brought his wife Kirsty MacColl over, and it was Kirsty who came up with the running order for the record. We were all working flat out trying to finish mixes, Kirsty said, 'Give me something to do, for fuck's sake, I'll work on a running order.' It has to be said, Kirsty was not a massive U2 fan. We told her to put 'Streets' first and 'Mothers' last but that was all the guidance we gave her. So she starts listening to the other songs and she was saying, 'OK, that's good, like that one, put that second. Mmm, not sure about that one … Yeah, I like that … Really like this one.' When she finished listening, she wrote out a sequence in about ten minutes, based purely on putting the songs in order of her favourites. We thought this was funny but then when we listened to it, it really did sound like a great sequence, so we went with it.

The album cover idea came out of the imagery, and the cinematic location of the record. It felt right to follow the music and lyrics into the landscape we had tried to conjure up, and shoot our cover in the desert. So we talked to Anton about different deserts, and it seemed obvious it should be somewhere in the United States. So Anton went off to look for locations.

ADAM: The record wasn't finished, so there was a little pressure on. We travelled to Los Angeles and headed off into the Mojave Desert on a coach with Anton, Steve Averill and a couple of crew. Off we went into the desert for a few days, staying in little motels, with Anton taking photographs. They were long days.

LARRY: That was a real road trip – it was an education, certainly for me. The America I had known before this came from being on buses, travelling from gig to gig, city to city. I enjoyed it but I knew there was another America out there, the movie America of old, the desert, the cowboys, all that kind of good stuff. So there we were, travelling through the Mojave Desert, through old gold-mining towns that had been closed down for a hundred years, standing at Zabriskie Point and realizing the magnitude and hugeness and beauty of America. That was the first time we got to see that side of America, just open spaces, no fast food outlets. It was amazing.

EDGE: We drove as far north as San Francisco, where we found a ghost town called Bodie, and down to Death Valley, Zabriskie Point, and loads of other little places along the way. During one trek between two locations we started talking about the different plants and asked the driver, 'What are those weird cactus things we're seeing all the time?' He said, 'They're Joshua trees.' I think it was Bono who said, 'That's a very interesting name. Let's do some photographs with some Joshua trees.' It was all fairly spontaneous. We kept driving along the road until we saw this big open hillside of these prehistoric-looking plants. We poured out of the coach, went down, Anton found a good one, and snap, snap. We shot for twenty minutes or so, climbed back on the coach and on we went.

LARRY: I remember Anton saying, 'Oh there's the Yoshua tree.' He couldn't pronounce the J. So we stood there having our photograph taken by the Yoshua tree. We wanted to laugh but Anton would get very upset if people laughed, or even smiled. It was all very funny, not that you'd know by the facial expressions on the album cover.

EDGE: People still remember very clearly the image of us with that Joshua tree but it wasn't, as most people thought, some sort of allusion to Gram Parsons and Joshua Tree Monument Park, which is quite close to Los Angeles. It was really just a reference to that whole desert southwest and the experience of being out there. The desert is a transitional place. It doesn't have a kind of right or wrong, nor any kind of strong personality. For us, it was like a journey through this neutral ground to get to where we were going. The names of these places were given by people in covered wagons literally heading west, going through Death Valley, enduring real hell to get to their promised land. 'Truth or Consequences', 'Hawkmoon', 'Telluride' as in T' hell you ride, 'Yankee Blade', 'Death Valley Junction'. Or the ever fun 'Whiskey Town'. You could sense the history and the struggle these places had witnessed.

ADAM: The look the band was going for was a displaced European immigrant arriving in the desert. When you get to Death Valley, you do wonder what was it that drove people to travel from east to west without really knowing what they were going to find on the other side. There was no guarantee they were even going to find land that was habitable, but they kept going and eventually found California.

LARRY: There was a love/hate relationship with America. A lot of that album reflected Bono's feelings coming back from El Salvador and The Conspiracy of Hope tour and seeing the brutal face of US foreign policy. But calling the album *The Joshua Tree*, was in some ways an acknowledgement of the influence that American culture had on U2. America was having a bigger impact on us than we would ever have on it. Coming from Ireland, the only show in town was the one happening in America. It was not only the biggest album sales market, it was the touring market. America was the centre of the world and we were being successful there and that's what we wanted more than anything else. America embraced us in a way that we never expected, so the title honoured that, in a sense. For me, it represented the other side of America – the open space, the freedom, what America stood for. It's not a metaphor, not even a concept. It's a kind of tribute. It wasn't like we went looking for *The Joshua Tree*, *The Joshua Tree* came looking for us.

EDGE: I think we knew we had something very special. There was a certain moment of it all making sense, when the music seemed to come from nowhere. It didn't have any references to anything else that was going on in the Eighties, it seemed to be coming up from the ground. The band also looked different to everything that was happening. We didn't really design our look, we were just trying to find clothes that were suitably neutral and would fit the record and the imagery we were playing around with – it was a non-look. There was a certain simplicity to it. I had taken to wearing a hat by then. It covered a multitude, so to speak.

ADAM: We definitely thought we had made a record that went somewhere other records didn't go. It was an exciting time.

PAUL: Island Records was still an independent and I think there were a total of nineteen different licensees around the world, a different company in every territory which meant they all had to be worked individually. In America it was Atlantic but in Canada it was MCA, Sonet in Scandinavia, Ariola in Germany, Phonogram in France, Dischi Ricordi in Italy, Festival in Australia. Phil Cooper, who was a bit of a genius, was the head of Island's own international department and he and I used to go around the world together to see all these different licensees. I think part of the process was collecting the money that they owed Island for last year before he would let them have the new U2 album. That was the way I really learnt about the record business internationally, by going to each country and meeting the people there. It was a huge relief two years later when Island was taken over by Polygram and there was an extensive international system to plug into, but I wouldn't have missed the earlier experience, it was very educational. I remember gathering all those licensees together at Midem (a music industry trade fair) in Cannes in early 1987 and playing them the music and they all lit up. They could see that they were going to have a huge year. When *The Joshua Tree* was released on 9 March 1987, we were in Dublin rehearsing. Over the course of that week, chart returns were coming in from all around the world, and *The Joshua Tree* went to number one in pretty much every country. We were on our way.

LARRY: From my perspective, everything was going along really nicely, we were making progress by degrees, sometimes small increments, but always moving in the right direction. Suddenly *The Joshua Tree* was number one in America, for nine weeks. Then 'With or Without You' went to number one. We were on the cover of *Time* magazine. We were no longer trying to conquer America. One moment you are on one side of the fence, the next moment you are catapulted to the other. This was something most bands only dream about; we were the band.

BONO: I remember going to Las Vegas. We were filming a video for 'I Still Haven't Found' and there was a big fight on at Caesar's Palace, Marvin Hagler and Sugar Ray Leonard, and we had seats. We were then brought around to see Frank Sinatra, who was playing a big charity do. Everyone was there, the A-List of old Hollywood. It was like twenty-five grand a table. We were brought in and given a table for free; we were expecting some seats around the back but we were brought right up in front of the stage. Best seats in the house, five yards from Sinatra's feet. It was spectacular. Sinatra came on, the Chairman of the Board, this twentieth-century musical legend, singing all these incredible songs, and he stopped the show, pointed to our table and said, 'Hey, I just want to mention some people who've come here tonight. They've come a long way. They've come from Ireland. They're number one. They're on the cover of *Time* magazine. They're called U2.' And we had to stand up and do a kind of celebrity wave in the spotlight. As we did that, Frank looked down, aghast. He could not believe the state of us. Frank was such a natty dresser. We looked like a bunch of gypsies. He said, 'Wow, you may be number one but you haven't spent a dime on your clothes.'

Afterwards he invited us back to his dressing-room. We hung out for ages. Larry and Frank were talking about Buddy Rich, the drummer, who had just died. Frank and Buddy were roommates on tour, great friends who occasionally descended to fisticuffs. Larry and myself were roommates when we started in the band, so we were all laughing together, this was something we understood. People kept knocking at the door, saying, 'Gregory Peck to see you.' 'Joan Collins to see you.' He wouldn't go out and he wouldn't let us go. Most of his friends were actors but I realized he so much wanted to talk about music. It really was such a big deal. Of course, everyone was muttering, 'Why isn't Frank coming out?' 'He's in with U2.' So we went to that gig feeling like U2, Dublin, Ireland, and left feeling like the number one group on the planet.

OUTSIDE
IT'S AMERICA
1987 - 1989

Paul

THE JOSHUA TREE TOUR STARTED IN THE US DOING MULTIPLE NIGHTS IN ARENAS AND EVENTUALLY BUILT UP TO STADIUMS, WITH SOME HUGE OPEN-AIR SHOWS IN EUROPE IN BETWEEN.

We toured throughout 1987, we were on the cover of *TIME* magazine, got Album of the Year at the Grammys, had a number one album and two number one singles in the US. It was a dizzying period.

LARRY: Everything changed really quickly. The fan action took a massive jump, and the media attention went off the scale. Before *The Joshua Tree* there was a certain degree of planning, and if there was chaos, at least it was organized chaos. After *The Joshua Tree* came out the scale of what was unfolding sent the whole organization into a tailspin. We were excited but taken by surprise by what was happening. It was clear that we were no longer underdogs.

EDGE: It's all a bit of a blur. I think we probably did go a bit mad at the time. Even before the album was finished we were on a roll. The atmosphere we were working in was very charged, and many of the people who were around at the time really got drawn into the excitement. It was an incredible team of people operating at their peak, or close to it. We hit a moment. We were taking America over. The record was just doing so well, it was a runaway train and we were just hanging on and doing the best we could.

BONO: At the start of the tour, during rehearsals in Tempe, Arizona, I cut open my face falling off a light. I've still got the scar on my chin. I was lost in the music and at the start of any tour you're just getting to know the physicality of the stage, the geometry of it, and you're overestimating your own physicality. You think you're made of metal yourself and you're not. Cuts and bruises, that's what I remember from *The Joshua Tree*. We were playing bigger and bigger shows and it was not always working. When things aren't going right and I'm feeling like we're not communicating, I go through terrible things on stage. In my head, a big blackness descends like a cloud. Sometimes

I would be able to purge it through songs like 'Bullet The Blue Sky' or 'Exit' but at other times I couldn't get out of the dark moods, they'd stick on you. Music is so powerful, it carries you to some places you'd rather not have been.

LARRY: We were always inconsistent live and Bono would get frustrated with the band. There was a certain amount of discomfort at being elevated to this level and not being able to deliver, because I never felt I was that great anyway. When all you have is the band, the idea that you might not be able to stand up to scrutiny is scary. It was hard to appreciate the moment, with that in your head.

BONO: I remember that whole era as being a little self-conscious, in the sense that you fall for it a bit, you take fame a little bit seriously by pretending that you didn't want it and that it's an intrusion and that it won't change you. They're all lies. We did want it. It doesn't have to be an intrusion. And it should change you. Why would you want to stay the same?

EDGE: I think what was going on through that whole period was suddenly having to really figure out what and who we were. Suddenly being right in the midst of all this mainstream media madness made us quite uptight in a weird way. There was a weight of expectation and a certain responsibility not to fuck up. We were always quite self-critical. It's not an effortless thing for U2 to make a record or do a show. At times the difference between getting it and blowing it is quite fine. When you're in that much of the spotlight, it can turn into an almost paralysing fear of failing.

BONO: There was a beautiful night in LA when Bob Dylan joined us on stage for 'Knocking on Heaven's Door'. He sang beautifully and the crowd went ballistic. I think he was surprised. It was the Eighties and he wasn't sure where he was at this point in his life and times. I think that night reminded him just what a feeling there was for his music. We then went back to the Sunset Marquis Hotel. We had stayed there since we were twenty years old but this time there were crowds. The whole street had been blocked because people had gone to the hotel after the show, waiting outside, hoping to catch a glimpse. There were thousands of people outside and they wouldn't leave. Bob said, 'It's really going off for you. How are you doing?' I said, 'I think we're doing pretty good. It's a bit of a mindbender.' He looked at me, in a very still way, and said: 'Imagine going through this on your own.' A band of equals is a very powerful thing because you can keep an eye out for each other. Bob Dylan never had that.

EDGE: T-Bone Burnett, Bob Dylan and I ended up going back to my room at the Sunset Marquis for a few drinks. Then T-Bone suggests that we all write a song together. I had a sketch for a song called 'We Almost Made It This Time' so I got my guitar and played it to everyone. Bob thinks for a second and says, 'I like the idea of secrets, how about *I was listening to the Neville Brothers, it was a quarter of eight / I had an appointment with Destiny but I knew she would come late / She tricked me, she addicted me, she turned me on my head / Now I can't sleep with these secrets, they leave me cold and alone in my bed...* We almost made it this time...' Now I don't know if Bob had those couplets stored away for a rainy day, or if he just came up with them right there on the spot, but I was winded, I think Bono was too.

T-Bone just kept on going as if that kind of stuff would happen around Bob all the time. Maybe it did, but for me it was like getting a punch from Muhammad Ali. It wasn't so much embarrassing as sobering, to realize how far we had to go. I couldn't even try and respond. I don't think Bono offered up very much either. It was such a reverse of what we had imagined. We had become a very successful band, we were hanging out with Bob Dylan, but our success wasn't bringing us a sense of artistic validation, it actually made us feel worse. We could see the flaws, the areas where we hadn't delivered. We were really trying to live up to the respect and the opportunity we'd been given through our fans, to take on this position of being such a big group. So it was tough going at times. Bono, particularly, went through really intense doubt about himself and the group as a whole.

In the middle of this, Aislinn and I were trying to keep our family together. We had two daughters during a period when U2 had recorded two albums and embarked on two world tours. It was tough on Aislinn and I really found myself desperately trying to keep band and family working in parallel. It was a strain and I can't say that at all times both got the attention they deserved. The touring was really the most difficult time because it's not an ideal situation to have to go away for a couple of months when you have a young family. I was really kind of on my own. They were difficult times.

BONO: There was some strain there just trying to keep our heads. When you're going through it first time, you don't know what fame is. It is as if all the molecules start vibrating at a different speed, there's a bit of freak energy in the air. But it wasn't all fear and loathing. There was a lot of drinking on this tour. Margueritas, tequila and a lot of laughs at times. It was a period of thawing out for the more uptight side of the band, U2's personal Glasnost.

LARRY: We were flying around America and that was great. I wasn't sorry to see the back of the buses. Our plane was like a flying brothel, in terms of décor as opposed to activity.

ADAM: It was very challenging but I did enjoy being on those big stages. It is a bit more difficult to get over that physical size and distance but we were a hot ticket, it was all going off. The plane and the limos actually made touring much easier. Sure, it was chaotic, but it has always been chaotic. I don't know that there was a whole lot of real difference, certainly not from my perspective.

LARRY: By the time we came back to Europe we had sold seven million albums and had made the decision to move into stadiums. That was an experience. As much as the indoor gigs were fraught with difficulties just from a musical competency point of view, the outdoor shows brought on a whole new set of problems. We were in these huge open spaces with no video reinforcements, so the band looked liked dots and it was hard to have any physical contact with our audience. The sound was always an issue, there were so many elements to consider – weather, atmospherics and so on.

BONO: At the Stadio Flaminio in Rome, Brian Eno was standing at the side of the stage. He has his emotional temperature turned down as a general rule but he had tears running down his face as he heard thirty-five thousand people in Rome singing the 'Ha la la la de day' refrain from 'Running to Stand Still'. He couldn't believe it, people who spoke a different language singing one of the songs we'd put together. And we had an amazing night in Bernabeu Stadium in Madrid. We were supposed to have a hundred thousand people but a hundred and twenty thousand showed up. People climbed over the doors, it was impossible to keep them out. We had never seen a crowd this big and it wasn't a festival, it was a U2 show. In the encore they started shouting: 'Torero, torero, torero, torero.' A hundred thousand people singing 'torero' is quite a sound. Somebody said: 'They're saying you are the bullfighter. It's the biggest compliment they can pay you.' So I went back on. I got the local promoter to translate something for me. I said: 'We are not the bullfighter. We are the bull!' The Spanish loved that.

EDGE: We played two shows in Wembley Stadium, 144,000 people, and we played Croke Park again. We had some time off during the summer too. It was a relief to be back in Dublin after the whole experience of America and Europe. It was great to see the kids. I had a little bit of difficulty getting my head around home life. You come home from the tour exhausted and a little

THE ORIGINAL IDEA WAS THAT WE WOULD FINANCE
OUR OWN ROAD MOVIE AND INCLUDE LIVE FOOTAGE.
IT WAS ALL GOING WELL AND THEN ALL THIS OTHER
STUFF STARTED BEING ADDED TO THE SCHEDULE
BECAUSE IT MIGHT LOOK GOOD IN THE MOVIE. IT
BECAME A MONSTER. I BLAME THE MADNESS OF *THE
JOSHUA TREE* TOUR. WE LOST TOUCH
WITH REALITY. LARRY

freaked out, and the house has been running along fine without you. Then you get a dig in the head for all the times you were missed while you were away, and you have to try to get back into the domestic routine. At that point we were the biggest band in America, probably the biggest band in the world, and we're coming back to Dublin and life as usual. It was quite low-key, we're not talking private planes and fancy cars. We had nice houses but it was still a regular lifestyle. Aislinn made sure that the grand madness was kept outside the front door.

Actually the first the sign of grand madness was the idea of doing a Hollywood movie. I think it was Paul McGuinness's idea. He had been in the film business before he became involved with us and it was probably always part of his plan to get back into it. A film featuring the band was the perfect vehicle.

PAUL: I get a lot of the blame for this and I'll take it because I was up to my neck in it. I was very keen on the idea of going wide at a time like that, just seeing how big this thing could get. I had always admired Colonel Parker and Brian Epstein for realizing that music could capture the imagination of the whole world.

EDGE: The original idea was to make a low-budget film and release it in a limited number of theatres, and make it a kind of fan-based event. We talked to quite a few directors, Jonathan Demme amongst them. We loved *Stop Making Sense*, which he had made with Talking Heads. Phil Joanou was the youngest director we talked to, with the least extensive CV, but he was a bit of a technical wunderkind who knew so much about the band, and his enthusiasm was inspiring. We didn't really put much of a plan or script together, we just thought we would start documenting the tour in 16mm black and white and see where we would get to.

BONO: Joanou was such a great guy: tiny head, big brain, very technical. He could tell you how every shot in any movie was accomplished, what lights they used, what camera, what lens. We wanted to make a film about our journey through American music and try to mythologize the tour.

LARRY: The original idea was that we would finance our own road movie and include live footage with the money we'd made from *The Joshua Tree* tour. It was all going well and then all this other stuff started being added to the schedule because it might look good in the movie. It became a monster. I blame the madness of *The Joshua Tree* tour. We lost touch with reality.

EDGE: We were playing one of our early US stadium shows, the Robert Kennedy Stadium in Washington DC, we had the documentary crew with us and the show was not going well. In those days, when a U2 show went badly, it could go very badly indeed. It could be just a sequence of mistimed moments and songs that fell flat, and the mood on stage could go very sour. On this particular night, in an attempt to try and get something going, Bono ran full pelt out on to one of the side wings. In the rain that was slowly falling, the side wings, which were covered in vinyl, became like an ice rink and his feet went from under him and he landed bang on his shoulder and separated the joint.

BONO: The song was 'Exit' and it had taken me to some ugly place. I slipped in the rain and I came down on my left shoulder and severed three ligaments from the clavicle. I was in terrible pain. Of course, they never healed back. My shoulder has come forward now, so I have to train my shoulder to go back. But it was rage that caused it. That was when I realized rage is an expensive thing for your general well-being.

EDGE: He actually finished the song, left the stage and went straight to hospital. Phil Joanou is such a consummate film-maker he got into the car that brought Bono to hospital and was filming the whole way as this tormented singer was raving in agony. It is not pleasant but it just typified the level of angst and intensity that was prevalent in the group.

LARRY: We had to take a nurse on the road to take care of Bono's shoulder. His arm was in a sling for about a month. We were living in the Hamptons on Long Island, New York and we would fly back and forth to gigs in the same day. We had houses on the beach, it was during the wintertime and it was freezing and miserable. There was nothing open, there was nothing going on.

EDGE: There were two houses. I had the family, so I had one house. Then two doors up there was the U2 compound, which had Bono and Ali, Larry and Ann and Adam. Paul was down the road with his family. Aislinn didn't really want to be there and I can't blame her. It was not the most interesting place to be on your own with a couple of young kids in September / October, when the weather is starting to get a bit colder and no one else is around. It seemed like a good idea at the time to fly in and out from Long Island to all the shows on the East Coast but it was a miscalculation really.

ADAM: It was kind of weird going back to houses at night because there was no room service. I preferred staying in hotels.

BONO: The contrast between the crowds and the joy of a U2 show and then this kind of silence the next day and family life slightly freaked me out. I hadn't yet figured out the psychology of this, that you empty yourself onstage so there is a hollowness that follows a big night like that. I began to understand how Keith Richards became a junkie. He said it was after tours, that is when he turned to heroin. If they were playing every night he was fine, it was when they stopped playing the void had to be filled.

EDGE: There were a lot of light moments amidst the drama. The Dalton Brothers made their debut in Indianapolis. We were getting ready for our show when Paul McGuinness came in and said: 'Los Lobos have missed their plane, they're not going to make it.' We were just goofing around and the idea came up to support ourselves.

We all got into full western gear and went out and played a set of country tunes. We were truly crap but in those big venues only the first five or six rows could really see our faces. Some of them sussed us and after about three songs word started to spread and at the front of the building there was quite a lot of excitement and laughter but everybody else was off buying popcorn. Virtually no one further back than that was paying any attention.

ADAM: We did get booed a little. I think that was part of the fun.

BONO: Alton Dalton, Luke Dalton, Duke Dalton and Betty Dalton. Adam made a great Betty. We played a few times. I remember meeting Mr Udo our Japanese promoter, who hadn't seen us for a few years. He didn't know that we had dressed up as anybody, he just thought: 'My, how you've changed. Is this what it takes to be big in America?'

BEING FAMOUS, YOU LEAVE YOUR PRIVACY BEHIND
BUT THE LIFE OF THE IMAGINATION BECOMES THE
REAL MANSION. THERE ARE MORE ROOMS YOU CAN
GO INTO. FRANK SINATRA, JOHNNY CASH, ALLEN
GINSBERG, I WENT AFTER ALL THESE PEOPLE TO SEE
WHAT I COULD LEARN. BONO

ADAM: There were a couple of country songs in the canon that could be pulled out to play on acoustic guitar. We could just about get through The Eagles' 'Tequila Sunrise' from our Mount Temple days and Edge knew some Hank Williams songs, things like 'Lost Highway'. It was part of what was going on throughout that tour, an element of looking for the authentic American music. In a way that became *Rattle and Hum*, the album.

BONO: We played two nights in LA. I woke up one morning with a song in my head, 'Love Rescue Me'. Lots of songs arrive in a dream state. At first you think it must be somebody else's song, because it's there, verse, chorus, melody. I had been dreaming about Bob Dylan and I thought it might be a Bob Dylan song. It's about a man people keep turning to as a saviour but his own life is getting messed up and he could use a bit of salvation himself. I wrote a couple of verses out but I didn't really know what to do with it. Then I thought, 'I've got Bob Dylan's number. Why don't I give him a call?' He invited me to visit him. He had a place out on the Californian coast, way outside Los Angeles, really low-key, you'd never find it, never imagine there was anyone so famous living there. I was really happy to be there, hanging out with my hero. He was always very kind and gentle to me. I told him I woke up with this song and I thought it might be one of his. He said: 'Well, play it for me.' I played what I had and said: 'Is this one of your songs?' He said, 'No, but maybe it could be.' So we finished it. He just sings fantastic stuff off the top of his head. He came up with the line: 'I'm hanging by my thumbs, I'm ready for whatever comes, love rescue me.' Hanging by my thumbs! Best image in the song.

I've learned a lot from Bob Dylan, just by writing with him. I learned about writing. 'Love Rescue Me' is really about self-loathing and the phrase 'the palace of my shame' was an interesting idea. Part of the rock star disease is stewing in your own juices. All writers think their feelings are important but a great writer realizes that though his feelings may be important, they're not all important enough to share. 'The palace of your shame' describes how people build their lives into a monument to self-pity. Irish people love the melancholy; it's that bitter sweetness that we do better than anyone else. I always reckon it's the rain.

I have a history of finding masters and making myself a student. Really my life has been that of an apprentice. That's why I'm a better writer this year than I was last year and I'll probably be a better writer next year. Everybody has a few things they've figured out and I will always be ready to humble myself in front of somebody who knows more than me. I said to Lou Reed once: 'If you've got one piece of songwriting advice for me, what would it be, Lou?' He looked at me, took a few beats, and said, 'Don't be afraid to break rhyme.' Great. But again it took a couple of years before that penny dropped.

Being famous, if you're smart, gives you a route to more knowledge, as opposed to stopping there. You have the opportunity to meet people whom you're interested in, to explore ideas that you might not have been able to explore otherwise, to go to the source. So you leave your privacy behind but the life of the imagination becomes the real mansion. There are more rooms you can go into. Frank Sinatra, Johnny Cash, Allen Ginsberg, I went after all these people to see what I could learn. In the UK and Ireland, these people are treated like old ghosts but in India and other cultures, when people hit sixty they just start getting their power. That's when the real wisdom is upon them. Whereas in rock music, you're supposed to be dead after twenty-seven years.

EDGE: We were trying to get some new material together for the record that became *Rattle and Hum*. I started work on some music down in a little house in Connemara in the west of Ireland, before we went back on the road. We were definitely on an American roots-trip coming off the US tour. I was listening to the Dylan compilation, *Biograph*, which had just come out, and I had the Stooges' first couple of records and a great box set of Lefty Frizzell, a hugely impressive country singer from the Fifties. Bono came down for a couple of days. Out of the music I had, we worked out 'Desire' and 'Angel Of Harlem' as rough outlines. I started a couple of other things, which became 'Hawkmoon 269' and 'All I Want Is You', and Bono came up with 'When Love Comes To Town'. Bono thought the song was too traditional for us. We had been to see B.B. King a few weeks before and after the show B.B. said 'I would love it if you guys would write me a song', so the idea came to cut the tune with B.B.

BONO: B.B. King was waiting for us to present him with the song. Of course, I hadn't finished it. I wrote the lyrics in the bath in about ten minutes, while he was waiting downstairs. Got out of bath, dressed, went down and gave him the song.

There was a deeply humbling moment as I watched the great man read the lyrics. It's talking about the soldiers rolling the dice for Christ's robes, it's betrayal at every level. He said to me: 'You're kind of young to write such heavy lyrics.'

EDGE: We ran through the song with him a couple of times at soundcheck and got him to play it that night with us. He is just an incredible, gracious, big-hearted character with an amazing soul, one of those people for whom everything is music. Standing up on stage next to him as he sang was really thrilling. The guitar playing we knew about but we didn't quite realize what a singer he is.

We actually cut the backing track for 'When Love Comes To Town' in Sun Studios in Memphis. We had a gig in Tennessee and we managed to get Sun to open up for a couple of days. We had Cowboy Jack Clement come in, the original engineer Sam Philips used to record Elvis. We dragged out some of the equipment that had been in mothballs since the Sixties, since the place had stopped being a working studio. It was incredible because the sound was right there in the bricks and mortar. It wasn't trickery, it wasn't anything other than the feeling and the acoustics of the space itself.

BONO: The mikes were still there that Elvis had used. The room was small. The floor was linoleum over stone, the walls had some kind of acoustic panelling but real Fifties stuff. There was a beautiful crack-off sound, real crack and smack. We invited The Memphis Horns down and recorded 'Angel Of Harlem'. I thought I would lighten the session up, so I sent out for a case of Absolut Vodka. I was giving it to the horn players and we were all having a little laugh and Cowboy came up to me. Cowboy was a guy who knew how to get into trouble but he also knew when not to get into trouble. He said, 'Bono, how long you been doing this?' I said, 'Ten years, nearly.' He said, 'Ten years and you don't know not to give the horn section Absolut Vodka? You can give it to anybody else but you can't give a horn section Absolut.' I asked, 'Why, particularly, the horn section?' Cowboy said, 'Listen, stupid, you try playing a horn when your lips won't work.'

ADAM: The idea was to record these songs as little vignettes to break up the live footage in various places along the tour. We didn't know the album was going to turn into a double album at that point. It was really just a way of setting up things for the film.

BONO: Something strange happened towards the end of *The Joshua Tree* tour. We had campaigned for Martin Luther King Day in Tempe, Arizona, where the tour opened back in April. There was a Governor there called Mecham who was holding out against it and we had got involved in local politics there and took a stand. We went back to Tempe at the end of the tour, in December, to play the Sun Devil Stadium. I was getting death threats throughout the tour. One in particular was taken very seriously by the FBI. This character was a racist offended by our work, he thought we were messing in other people's business and taking sides with the black man. One night the FBI said: 'Look, it's quite serious. He says he has a ticket. He said he's armed. And he said if you sing "Pride (In the Name of Love)", he's going to shoot you.' So we played the show, the FBI were around, everyone was a little unnerved. You just didn't know, could he be in the building? Up in the rafters? On the roof? During 'Pride', I was singing the third verse, *Early morning April 4, a shot rings out in a Memphis sky*. I just closed my eyes and sang. And when I opened my eyes, Adam was standing in front of me.

EDGE: The tour was a big success and the record was continuing to do really well; it ultimately sold twenty million copies. It looked as if we could do no wrong at that moment. In spite of our angst, everything had fallen into place. Then somewhere along the way we started getting word back regarding the costs of shooting our movie and suddenly realized, 'Shit, we don't have a business plan together for this.' We really did things backwards. We had hired a director, started shooting film and, because it was a documentary, we had all the actors and locations in place before we even had a deal. That may not be the best way to do things. It started to become obvious that the only way we were going to be able to afford to get the money we'd spent was to start talking to the major studios. So almost by default we had a meeting with Paramount Pictures and it was a classic case of lighting the touch-paper and standing back.

PAUL: We spent five million dollars of our own money making the movie and we sold it to Paramount for the same amount. That was a bit of a relief because we were quite seriously in the hole for a while.

LARRY: When Paramount Pictures got involved we were no longer making a road movie for ourselves.

EDGE: Instead of opening in twenty theatres, we were talking about one hundred and twenty. We were just shooting documentary stuff and kind of hoping that in amongst all of it there would be some kind of thread that we could weave into a story. The tour finished in America and we went home to

Dublin. Phil was working away in LA, editing and trawling through all the footage. Basically he had hours and hours and hours of us hanging out, going out, blowing our noses, whatever. No one had any idea what it would amount to. Then we started hearing from Phil that we needed an explanation for it all, it lacks form, so he came to Dublin to shoot interviews and a few other pick-up bits and pieces.

ADAM: We had been demoing some songs in Dublin, 'Desire' had come together, so Phil shot a version of 'Desire' in The Point Depot, which was then a warehouse, before it was converted into a concert theatre.

EDGE: I was working in a small house in Rathgar. Aislinn and I had bought a big place in Monkstown but we hadn't moved in yet. Anyway, I'm at home working and the doorbell rings. I've got this great rhythm going but I couldn't find a tape-recorder. So I just kept playing, went to the front door, opened the door playing the riff. It was the postman. He gave me two letters. I took them, threw them on to the hall table, still playing the riff, said, 'Thanks mate. Goodbye', kicked the door closed, still playing, walked up the stairs, found the tape-recorder next to my bed and recorded the riff. And that was the beginning of 'Desire'.

BONO: 'Desire' is a little classic, a little 45. Edge took the beat from *The Stooges' '69*, which was their take on the Bo Diddley beat. The rhythm is the sex of the music. I wanted to own up to the religiosity of rock'n'roll concerts and the fact that you get paid for them. On one level, I'm criticizing the lunatic fringe preachers 'stealing hearts at a travelling show' but I'm also starting to realize there's a real parallel between what I am doing and what they do.

ADAM: In June 1988 we moved to LA to finish the sound mixing for the film and do what had now turned into a live album plus some new studio tracks. Initially it was just going to be five or six new tracks that were featured in the film but it kept expanding and we ended up with nine new tracks in all, which is pretty much a new album.

BONO: Any other band would have probably put out the live album and gone home but we were determined to do something more original. We wanted to make it an album of the tour, both on and offstage, by putting in the middle of these *Joshua Tree* shows our learning curve on American music.

BONO: Myself and Edge went over before everybody else and sat with Phil while he edited the live footage. Then the band came. It was an incredible time. We found a house that was like an army barracks, a quadrangle with a pool in the middle of it. There was no air-con and it was about to be knocked down. This was its last lease. It was enormous but it was cheap. It was in Bel Air in the Hollywood Hills area.

LARRY: It was like the Brady Bunch, four separate bedrooms in this huge house that had been deserted for quite a while. We had to rent everything, furniture, carpets, posters for the wall, TVs. It was a mad place.

EDGE: By the time we got to Los Angeles a certain giddiness had entered the camp. I rented a house with my family, the others lived together in a compound. I was having quite a fraught time in Beverly Hills. They were having a wild time in their hippy commune up in Bel Air. The contrast was quite abject. I threw myself into working on the album, and overseeing the movie audio post-production. It would be nice to say that through my single-mindedness and supreme focus I saved the record, but I think in truth I was not at my best either and the schizophrenia of the record reflects the weird time we were all going through.

BONO: We really did live the life. I got the Harley-Davidson, and went to work on a bike. We were starting to live by night, spending our time downtown, away from the high altitude in every sense. Over the years the heart of LA shifted west and downtown was left behind to become a banking and business centre, with just the ghost of its party past lingering on in jazz clubs and dance venues. It is a strange, schizophrenic place, where you find people in suits stepping over junkies and drop-outs on their way into their glass towers. LA is not really a party town; after ten o'clock people would be in bed so they can get up bright and early and jog to the corporation, but we would head down the 101, down the freeway and into the belly of the beast. There was a club called The Flaming Colossus and it was just an extraordinarily imaginative place to hang out. There would be gypsy music one night and Arabic music the next, live bands, belly dancers, a sword-swallowers' conference. All kinds of colourful people who lived in the night, collected there. I was just starting to let go of being looked at, I was beginning to become uninhibited. I was going out dancing, being silly. I developed a taste for whisky. Whisky does not make me sleepy, unlike wine which I drink now, so I didn't want to go to bed. I'd be swinging out of the rafters. I could drink a lot of it and it didn't seem to make me drunk but I was thumping the odd punter, so I put that away. 'Oh gosh, the bloke that wrote the song about Martin Luther King, is that the bloke that just tried to break my nose?' I put a stop to that.

ADAM: I went to a party in the Playboy Mansion. Our producer Jimmy Iovine's wife Vicky offered to take me to look around with one or two of her girlfriends. Most of the bunnies or ex-bunnies I saw there would have been older than me, they definitely were from different vintages. I was twenty-eight at the time and I think I was probably one of the youngest men there. Berry Gordy was there, Tony Curtis. I looked in the grotto and wandered around but it is not a world of eroticism that Europeans would relate to. I didn't actually get to meet the legendary Hugh Hefner. There were a lot of limos lining up and he would have been pretty busy dealing with the real VIPs. The bass player of U2 in 1988 wouldn't have been on his radar.

BONO: Los Angeles is a city built on people's imagination. What Boeing and Microsoft are to Seattle, the movie business and the music business are to LA. If you're a star it's like you're a captain of industry. Cop cars would sidle up to you, lights flashing, and hail you through the loudspeaker on top of the car: 'Love the new album.' I remember being stopped once. I was driving a vintage 1963 Chevy and I was pulled over by the cops. They said, 'Have you any ID?' I said, 'I've no ID.' They said, 'Anything? You must have something on you.' So I pulled out a picture of myself and Bob Dylan. It was like: 'Sure. Go right ahead, buddy.' Bob might as well have been the mayor.

I saw more of Bob in that period. He means more to me than anybody living in music or art. I don't see him as a songwriter, I see him as an artist. To me he's Goya and Shakespeare in one person, and he was tolerating his young acolyte's naïveté. I felt he saw something in me but it wasn't fully formed. As Van Morrison said around the same time: 'That Bono fellow, he'll be great when he's finished.' I took that as a compliment because I felt the same. The fact that we were selling ridiculous multi-platinum amounts of records wasn't what was important. I was growing, we were getting better, and that was what mattered.

LARRY: We were recording in the A&M Studios. Jimmy Iovine was producing. Jimmy had a particular way of working. He would come in, have a listen, and say, 'Well, you need to work on it more,' and he'd take off. We didn't have the sort of input we were used to from Brian or Danny but what we did have was a reality check: 'It's not ready, I can't help you, you need to do this yourselves.' It was a bit of an eye-opener. However, as far as the songs are concerned, I think there's some really good work on that record. Jimmy was very clear about what the songs needed, he just wasn't around enough to push them along, so it relied heavily on the band, particularly on Bono and Edge, to really focus in. There are no songs from that period that feel unfinished. They are as they should be.

BONO: Sometimes the most important thing for a producer to say to you is that the song isn't there yet, or point to the moment in the take where it is. You would play Jimmy a song and he'd say, 'I like the chorus.' You'd say, 'What, you think we should rewrite the verse?' He'd say, 'No, I think the chorus is the verse. Now go write the chorus.' He has an enormous IQ but he's not a player who can get in the room and pick up an instrument and improvise with you. We were really a punk rock group trying to play Bach. Our limitations are our strengths but really we need keyboard players around, we need the experimentation around us sometimes to get to new terrain. If we were more complete as a combo, he would have been the perfect producer for U2. Jimmy Iovine has been one of the most important influences on this band's life and mine in particular, as a close aide and a friend. He especially challenged me as a lyricist, because in conversation he always had the better lines. If I look back at all the work in the Eighties, I needed to be challenged more.

EDGE: I was the guy who ended up trying to pull the record together, when it seemed to me Bono and the others were off basically partying harder than ever before. Jimmy Iovine did not know what to think. Here is the band that wrote about civil rights and God going 'native LA' before his eyes. I was holding on to the record as a kind of lifeline. I was going under, personally, and my marriage was disappearing up in smoke very fast. I think I was probably the only one, although maybe Larry as well, who wasn't really going for it in a party sense. I mean, there was quite a lot of partying going on in my Beverly Hills house but not while I was there. I think if I had gone for it, I wouldn't have come back. It became so bad there were times when I would sit outside the house in the car, thinking: 'Well how much cash have I got in my pocket? How far would that get me?' Literally contemplating heading off, getting out of there for a bit of oxygen. I threw myself into the record and that probably didn't help the situation at home. I think Aislinn felt abandoned because I was so completely caught up with what I was doing that I just wasn't there in any kind of meaningful way. We're not talking about a small road bump, we're talking about fundamental problems that probably had always been lurking and just being in the pressure cooker of the music business and the success we'd had, it all unravelled spectacularly.

LARRY: Los Angeles was a litany of crises, one problem after another with the record, the movie, with life. I started to feel really homesick. There was nowhere to go, the place shuts at nine o'clock. I borrowed some motorcycles and rode around LA. on my downtime. Working in A&M Studios was OK but there was another studio, Ocean Way, it was underground, subterranean, no daylight. I just couldn't cope, I was desperate to leave LA.

BONO: 'Hawkmoon 269' was recorded in Sunset Sound, with all that shit that happens around there going on. Search-and-destroy choppers looking for drug busts. Sunset Strip, hookers. Every neon sign advertising sex in some shape or form. You could feel all that coming through in 'Hawkmoon'.

EDGE: Hawkmoon is a place in Rapid City, Dakota. We passed it on The Conspiracy of Hope tour. The 269 comes from the number of mixes. We spent three weeks on that track.

LARRY: It shows you where we were at. We had lost the ability to make good decisions.

ADAM: At some point Bono and I rented a Jeep Cherokee and headed off from LA to New Orleans. Bono allegedly did the navigating, I did the driving. I wouldn't trust Bono behind the wheel of a car.

BONO: We started the drive on Highway 10, a road that links the west coast to the east. You drive out of LA and you leave one America and enter another. It is the real America, an America I love. We filled the car up with Johnny Cash and set off, headed out to the Painted Desert, out through a town called Truth and Consequence, through New Mexico, Arizona, Texas, diverted to Tennessee. We didn't know exactly where we were going, we were making it up as we went along. It was an adventure.

ADAM: It was about two weeks of driving. We would drive, book into a motel on the edge of town, have something to eat and then get on our way the next day.

BONO: At some point we lost our car. I think it might have broken down and we were thumbing a lift. A Corvette, driven by a young man, pulled up. The guy kind of blinked and said, 'Are you who I think you are?' We said, 'Yeah.' So we got in and he was dropping us wherever we needed to go and he said, 'You're not going to believe this, I was just listening to your tune and then I see you on the road.' Then he put on 'Where The Streets Have No Name'. It was the last minute of the song and we listened to it through his gigantic sound system and attempted to be bashful. At the end of the song something happened that blew my mind. It sounded like the end of the world, it sounded like Godzilla was stomping along beside the car. There was the most incredible bass drum and snare sound I'd ever heard. I thought, 'What is this?' It went, Boom-boom-whoo! Boom-boom-whoo! I looked at Adam and Adam looked at me. We had never heard anything so loud. It was Def Leppard's 'Pour Some Sugar on Me' and it sounded about twice as loud as 'Where The Streets Have No Name'. We took note! Because, in the end, people choose music that makes their sound system sound good, which is one of the things that musicians don't like to admit. I think we both made a mental note that next time we had better go after a more sonic experience on our records.

ADAM: At that point we could still go places without people instantly recognizing Bono, so it was a kind of free time for him. We hung out for a few days in Santa Fe in New Mexico, which is a great artistic town. We didn't stop off anywhere in Texas because it was such a big state. We were in Memphis for a bit, where we hooked up with friends.

BONO: We met up with Robert Palmer, the esteemed *New York Times* critic, who had written 'Deep Blues'. The blues was so beloved by him that he lived in Memphis. I think he had some serious health problems and had had a bruising with drugs earlier in his life but he was just the most beautiful of men and truly in love with the music. He had a band, in which played the clarinet, and he had some very brilliant friends. He said, 'If you're interested in the blues, I'll show you the blues.' And we went out of Memphis, travelled into the country, into the cotton fields, to a Juke Joint, which was the only place you could get liquor on a Sunday. They were drinking gin and juice and making music.

ADAM: Because they're a long way from a town and don't have enough money for transport, at the end of the week the agricultural workers club together and somebody's house becomes a venue for a dance. All the local musicians gather, it's very rough and authentic, similar to the kind of thing that happens in the West of Ireland, only black.

BONO: Robert Palmer said, 'Not all the great blues men left for Chicago. One of the greatest of them is a fellow called Junior Kimbrough. He still plays here occasionally.' We were in this place where the whole basement was the bass, whatever they had down there it was reverberating through the building. There were people playing, sharing instruments, people talking while they played the drums, amazing songs. At this point a friend of ours, a girl called

Lian Lunson, had been with us for a day or two on our journey. Eventually the guests from out of town were brought in to the bedroom to meet Junior. He must have been in his seventies. He put his hand up for us to shake. We curtseyed and pretended we were familiar with his material. We waited for an hour till the sun came down. Then Junior came out and the crowd of fifty or sixty people were parted like Moses and the Red Sea. He just walked up, took a guitar and let out this blood-curdling howl and started into a little pop ditty called 'I'm Going to Rape You, Little Girl', which immediately alarmed our travelling companion, Lian, and indeed all of us. I think he was just stirring it up for a bit of fun. But powerful, powerful music was made. Then things started getting a little crazy, liquor was going to people's heads. Robert Palmer said, 'I think you should go now.' We said, 'Are you not going?' He said, 'No, *I'm* safe here.' So off we went.

There was another moment in Memphis. Maybe the car had broken down but at some point we found ourselves a driver. We were just looking for a taxi when this girl turned up with a limo, dressed like a regular limo driver except with a leather mini-skirt. She was a great girl and was driving us around various places. It was a Sunday and she overheard us talking about trying to find the church that Al Green sang in. She said, 'I can sort out the church.' So we went to this church. Al Green was not there, presumably he didn't preach every day but we stayed for the service. The preacher was working up a bit of a head of steam. He couldn't see us, we were sitting at the back of the church, but he started saying, 'God sees you, God sees you. Even if you're hiding, He can see you. It doesn't matter where you come from, He knows where you're headed. You may have taken Highway 10. You may have been headed to New Orleans and you take a by-road into Memphis and you may meet the Lord. You don't know when you're going to meet the Lord.' Adam was looking at me and I was looking at Adam. The preacher said, 'And you can be on that Highway and you can have your SUV and you can be on automatic or you can be on cruise control, you may not even have your feet on the pedals. But I want you to know on the path of life there are no guard rails and you don't know when you're going to spin off. If there's anybody here tonight who can feel the Lord speaking to them, stand up.' Adam whispers, 'He's talking about us.' I'm thinking, 'How does he know this shit?' So we're wondering, should we stand up? I'm always the guy who wants to stand up, put my hand up, just in case there's a blessing going. I give my life to the Lord at any opportunity but Adam's saying, 'I'm feeling a trifle uncomfortable. How about you?' After the service I said to a couple of the parishioners, 'So when does Al come here?' They said, 'Al who?' I said, 'Al Green.' They said, 'No, Al doesn't sing here. Al Green sings in another church, the other side of town.' We said, 'Well our driver, Melissa, she brought us here.' They said,

'Oh yeah, that's the preacher's daughter.' She had become a fisher of men herself and set us up. It was beautiful.

ADAM: We went on to Nashville and hooked up with Cowboy Jack Clement. He took us around to meet various people. We had a good time hanging out in the studio with John Prine and we went to see Johnny Cash.

BONO: Johnny Cash had us round to lunch. There was a giant French Oak table laid out with enough food for a hundred people. We were a party of five. Johnny's wife, June Carter Cash walked in and said, 'Don't you be worrying about having to eat all this, I'm just doing a photo shoot for my new cookbook. We're eating in here.' So we followed her into another room with a more modest spread. Johnny was a prince of a man. He had brain-power and talent and machismo but leavened by humility. He said Grace with this beautiful meandering prayer, thanking God for everything on the table and the four walls, the roof and all that was outside. I was very moved. Then Johnny opened his eyes, turned to me and said, 'Sure miss the drugs, though!' We talked about Irish poets, we talked about the scriptures. I asked him did he know where the name Cash came from? He said, 'Yes. We're a baronial family from Scotland. The House of Cash.' I said, 'I might have to disagree with you, Johnny. The Cash are a horse-loving, travelling people from County Wexford in Ireland.' He only half-guffawed when I broke the news.

ADAM: In New Orleans we hooked up with Daniel Lanois, hanging with the Neville Brothers and all that crew. Danny had just finished making an album with Dylan, *Oh Mercy*. Bono had put the two of them together and that was the album that really brought Dylan back from where he had been languishing.

BONO: New Orleans had the sweetness of a rotting vine, when the grapes are just on the turn. I loved it, the noble rot as wine lovers call it. There's some dark colours, violet and purple. It was raining when we arrived. Danny had this baroque château in New Orleans, a beautiful house with an amazing stairwell. It was a magical place. The Neville Brothers blew my mind. Aaron sang like an angel but looked like he was the Devil's bodyguard. Danny Lanois had found a world of people as lost to the music as he was; there was dizziness in the air. That was such a great journey and a great time spent with Adam. I'll treasure it for the rest of my life.

'Heartland' came out of that trip. That is the story of myself and Adam. *Mississippi and the cotton wool heat / Sixty-six the highway speaks / Of deserts dry, of cool green valleys / Gold and silver veins, shining cities … Freeway*

THESE SONGS, IF THEY'RE ANY GOOD, ARE USUALLY AS MUCH BIOGRAPHY AS AUTOBIOGRAPHY. THEY CONTAIN THE PERSON YOU WANT TO BE SOMETIMES MORE THAN THE PERSON YOU ARE. BONO

like a river cuts through this land. The song is full of little bits of travelogue from my journal.

There are some beautiful songs on *Rattle and Hum*. 'All I Want Is You' is probably the best. Jimmy Iovine always says, 'It's a great song but we never made it a great record.' He felt if we'd gotten it right it would have been a number one hit. It never was.

BONO: I sing this song to Ali. I met this most private person, she's just impossible to know. And she doesn't want to be known, which is the intriguing thing about her. As a performer who attempts to connect to audiences all the time, I'm fascinated by people who are not interested in other people's opinion of them. She's interested in my opinion but that's about it. Ali is a force of nature. She is like a current that you don't see until you're in the water. She has a very strong pull but you don't feel it immediately. These songs, if they're any good, are usually as much biography as autobiography. They contain the person you want to be sometimes more than the person you are. I wanted to be more the kind of man in the house than she wanted me to be. She doesn't need me to be anything other than the person I am. I would think, 'Gosh, I wish I was more this way, I wish I was more that way.' She would always look at me and say, 'Actually, I like you the way you are. Lighten up.' She's got that kind of belief in who I am at the essential level. It's an amazing thing.

EDGE: Van Dyke Parks came into the studio, listened to what we'd done, went off and wrote this absolutely gorgeous and incredibly haunting arrangement which lasts two and a half minutes. It was a great way to end the album. 'All I Want Is You' is probably the best of what we were trying to do with that album, in that it has a traditional basis but it was a truly U2 song. Looking back, I think the flaw at the heart of *Rattle and Hum* was that it lacked innovation. It was our own fault, because we were in America, in the middle of Hollywood, making a movie with a big studio and it wasn't really about experimenting and finding the next musical jumping-off point. It was more about expressing ourselves as fans, absorbing the atmosphere and allowing ourselves to explore the roots of the form, which was not necessarily the best recipe for an original album.

BONO: At one point I chickened out of the retro nature of the songwriting on *Rattle and Hum*. I woke up with this mad riff in my head. I explained it to Edge and he played his version of it, which of course made it a lot better. I'd been reading Albert Goldman's book on Lennon and it so offended me. It was one thing Goldman taking on Elvis with that kind of East Coast sneering voice; his Elvis book was a portrait of white trash from an intellectual's perspective and telling the world what was really going on in the court of the king. In a way his book on Lennon was an abject failure because Lennon had already told us everything about himself. There were no surprises. He had described his own bad habits, his nervous breakdowns, his dalliances with eccentric ideas and verbal incontinence. The book seemed completely unnecessary to me. I thought, 'He can't reply, so I'm going to.' And that became 'God Part II', in homage to Lennon's beautiful song 'God'. I appreciate all of this looks like megalomania but show me an artist who wants to take on the world who doesn't have a little bit of megalomania. The title was supposed to be biting humour rather than just being fatuous. As I may have said before, this is a band that needs an editor. There is a verse in there, *Don't believe in the Sixties, the golden age of pop / You glorify the past when the future dries up*. This is on an album in which we are exploring roots music. That might be a little close to the bone. The whole song came out of a moment where I was worried about what we were doing. That song doesn't actually belong on *Rattle and Hum*. It is really the first song on *Achtung Baby*. I'd come to the end of nostalgia, that's the clue.

EDGE: At the eleventh hour, we were trying to get something together with a bit more of a contemporary feel. It had a kind of venom that the album lacked. The original ambition for the record was that it would be a memento of this great tour, a combination of new songs, live songs, a few odd bits and pieces. Then, right at the end, the penny started to drop that we were just too big to get away with that kind of oddball release. We began realizing it was going to be held up against everything else we had produced, it was not going to be treated as a scrapbook. Really it was too late to change the nature of the record.

PAUL: I think something went wrong in the post-production of the film, where it became a bit too self-reverent. The point of view of the film-maker disappeared and every shot was kind of approved by the band.

LARRY: That movie was made by committee, the Politburo, which was us. In fairness to Phil Joanou, the live stuff was extremely well done. A lot of the incidental moments were more difficult; we were trying very hard not to be

EVERYTHING CHANGED FOR ME WHEN JORDAN WAS
BORN. EVERYTHING. YOU UNDERSTAND WHY WARS
ARE FOUGHT, YOU UNDERSTAND WHY MEN WANT TO
OWN LAND, YOU UNDERSTAND WHY WOMEN ARE SO
SMART, BECAUSE THEY HAVE TO BE. BONO

exposed. We wouldn't allow the cameras into the dressing-room and stuff like
that. We didn't know what we wanted. We made a lot of mistakes during that
time but we were learning a lot as well.

BONO: I think it was a moment when hubris was the next logical step in our
development and we walked into a sucker punch. The performance stuff in
the film is amazing. It's shot by Robert Brinkmann and Jordan Cronenweth. No
rock 'n' roll band had been shot like that. The black and white footage is like
Raging Bull at times. And then the other stuff is us being self-conscious in
front of the camera. Self-consciousness will turn the prettiest face ugly and
make the most vivid personality dull grey. No matter how long Phil spent with
us, as soon as the lights went on we froze. The hardest thing to do is to be
yourself. When somebody says 'just be yourself' what do you do? Especially if
you don't know who you are.

EDGE: I think Phil did a great job. More than anything it is a kind of
snapshot of the state of mind of the band, it shows how fast and loose we
were, playing with the U2 thing, and how close we probably came to
completely blowing it and how we just managed to scrape by and keep it
together. Rather than using *The Joshua Tree* as a springboard to something
even greater, we made a road movie and almost ran out of road.

The album suffered because it was attached to this massive movie
marketing campaign, so it was heralded as if it were the Ten Commandments
coming down from on high. When it came out, there was a general sense that
it was a confusing collection, neither fish nor fowl. I think it has some great
moments but it probably represents a momentary lapse of judgement. For a
while there, instead of us chasing success, success was chasing us.

PAUL: The plan was to release the album first and get it to number one all over
the world, which we did. The movie was released shortly afterwards and it had
the strangest opening weekend profile of any movie before or since. It had a
huge Friday and everyone in the industry thought we'd absolutely struck pay-

dirt, it had a very disappointing Saturday, which is the opposite to what normally happens and then by Sunday there was nobody going to see it at all. We opened the movie very broadly, on twelve or fifteen hundred screens across North America, which is a very wide release. So everyone who was passionate about U2 went to see it on the same night and by Sunday it was all over and we were all starting to feel slightly foolish, particularly me.

EDGE: I don't think Paramount lost money but it didn't catch fire in the way they thought it might. It was kind of a strange time, reality smacking you in the mouth after this incredible run of good fortune. We went to a series of premières and then went home to try and pick up the threads of our normal lives. Aislinn was expecting our third child, and Blue Angel was born on June 26 1989.

PAUL: *Rattle and Hum* is perceived as one of U2's failures. We sold twelve million copies of the record, so that is the kind of failure I can live with. But it received some pretty savage reviews. John Pareles of *The New York Times* accused U2 of bombast and pretension and basically trying to pilfer from American music rather than develop from it. I think that criticism struck home.

ADAM: There's a limit to how big an audience a rockumentary like that plays to but I'm glad we did it. It's there for posterity now and it did capture something of what was going on at the time. I liked the album very much. I thought the live tracks were great and I liked what Jimmy Iovine did with the studio tracks. I didn't really buy into the criticism that it attracted.

LARRY: The criticism wasn't unexpected. We had reached the point where something had to give. Some of the reviews were extremely harsh but that's show business. Criticism is a hard station for anybody and I think you can take it when you do something crap. But while the movie may have been a mistake, it wasn't crap. And I'll stand over those songs any day. Any day.

We should have done our small road movie. We should have disappeared for a couple of years and reinvented ourselves. But for all of the pain of seeing your work being described as pompous, arrogant and out of touch, it did inspire us to go and chop down *The Joshua Tree*.

ADAM: Throughout 1989, there were singles being released from *Rattle and Hum*, videos being made, remixes, a lot of promotion. There were a few little side projects throughout spring and summer. Bono and Edge wrote a song for Roy Orbison. I played with Maria McKee, the singer from Lone Justice, who had moved to Dublin and was doing some fantastic solo stuff. I am happy to be involved in extra-curricular activities as long as there is an opportunity to rehearse and work things up, rather than just hanging on by the skin of my teeth. I went to the Glastonbury rock festival and camped on site, which was good fun. I have always been able to move pretty anonymously. Being the bass player in U2 is not nearly as visible as people might think, particularly when you are hidden behind a singer like Bono. There was a whole raggle-taggle bunch of us at Glastonbury, because The Waterboys were headlining one night and Hothouse Flowers and Maria McKee were around as well. I did join the Hothouse Flowers for one of their tunes. That was the first and only time I've played Glastonbury. We tried to do some recording in STS but I don't think it came to anything. Babies were born – Edge and Aislinn had their third daughter, Blue Angel, and Bono and Ali had their first, Jordan.

BONO: Jordan was born on my birthday, 10 May, 1989. What a great gift she has turned out to be. U2 were in STS at the time. Ali picked me up from the studio to go to the hospital. She was having contractions. I said, 'Are you sure you should be driving?' She said, 'It would be better for my nerves if I drove.' She had packed a little flask of whisky and some reading material ... for me! I brought a tape-recorder with me from the studio. I don't know what I was thinking. I had half an idea that I would mike up the baby's heartbeat. I was very stressed out, trying not to show it, being Ali's drip roadie, wandering around trying to be useful. I like to be in control of things that are potentially dangerous, so it was very hard for me to let go of that. My natural instinct would be, 'Somebody I love is in pain. Who do I hit?' You can't hit doctors and nurses who are trying to bring your firstborn into the world. Ali told me to have a little lie-down. There was another table in the theatre, so I got up on it and started reading. I had the tape-recorder attached to Ali and I noticed that the heartbeat was getting lighter and slower. I got up and said to Ali, 'Should the heartbeat be getting slower?' She said, 'I'm sure it's fine. The baby is just relaxing.' I said, 'Ali, this isn't right.' She said, 'Would you RELAX! Get back up on the table. Have a drop of whisky!' So I'm lying there and I heard the heartbeat getting slower again. I got off the table, went out, found a nurse and said, 'Look, am I imagining things or is this heartbeat getting slower and is that a good thing?' She said, 'Oh my God, that heartbeat's far too slow!' She called the doctor. And little Jo Jo was in trouble. So there you are ...

She was very small when she arrived, five pounds five. She used to sleep on my chest. The doctor said, 'It's good if they sleep on your chest because they can hear your heartbeat and the baby thinks it's inside you.' We are very close, Jordan and I. Everything changed for me when she was born.

Everything. You understand why wars are fought, you understand why men want to own land, you understand why women are so smart, because they have to be, they have to deal with so much more stuff than we do. I was left in awe of women. It really did turn my life upside-down.

PAUL: After all the criticism for *Rattle and Hum*, we decided it might be a healthy thing to do a tour without an album, just to go out and play for the fun of it, and not play America or Britain but cover some territories we hadn't been able to get to on *The Joshua Tree* tour.

BONO: We hadn't taken *The Joshua Tree* to Australia. Our Australian audience meant an awful lot to us and we didn't want to lose touch with them, so we concocted a tour that would start in Australia, then move on to some dates in Europe, and end on New Year's Eve in Dublin. I think I talked the band into it.

ADAM: On the back of *Rattle and Hum* we were wondering whether we could perform with a large expanded band. It was looking at U2 post-*Joshua Tree* and thinking what are we going to do next time around? How are we going to tour? Now that we are a big stadium act, do we draft in extra players and put more people on stage? We were trying to loosen up, to see if we could be unstructured and play a more varied set every night.

PAUL: As a result of *Rattle and Hum* there were a few U2 songs that had brass. B.B. King had a brass section. He had a bit of a hit with 'When Love Comes To Town', so we approached B.B. and put it to him that we would do a three-month tour of these territories together. He would play support and he and his brass section would join U2 for a couple of songs. It was a strange deal to make for B.B., because he was used to playing as many as nine shows a week. He would often do a couple of shows a day. He was flabbergasted at the very idea of being on a tour where you only played three or four shows a week. Rehearsals started in August and there was a slightly uncomfortable moment when Adam was arrested.

ADAM: A couple of members of Hothouse Flowers and other friends were all gathered in a pub in the Dublin mountains where, on nice days, people hung out in the car park looking over the view of Dublin. We were all sitting around outside having a pint. There may have been a joint being passed around, as there often was in those days, quite probably in every car park in every pub in the country. These two characters came up who said they were undercover drugs officers. None of us really took them very seriously. They set about searching us but nothing was found but then they went into my car and had a poke around and found some hash. I was arrested and taken down to the local police station and charged with possession. It was not very pleasant. I was foolish to allow myself to be in that situation, seeing as hash is an illegal substance, but I think there were more serious problems in Dublin in terms of drug culture than me smoking a joint. In the end it was quite a minor offence that some individuals tried to blow up into something quite serious. There was concern in the U2 camp that it would affect my eligibility to tour abroad. When it went to court the judge 'invited' me to donate IR£25,000 to charity in return for having no conviction on my record. I accepted his invitation. If the judge's intention was to make an example of me, I am not sure if that was the right way to do it, since the message it was sending out was just confusing. It was certainly confusing to me. I doubt you would get fined as much as that if you were dealing heroin. It made it look a lot more serious than it was. I'm sorry that I was foolish enough to be caught breaking the law but the money went to the Dublin Women's Aid Refuge centre, and I was very happy to help them out.

EDGE: Bass Player from Rock and Roll Band Gets Found With Small Quantity of Hash was never a headline that was going to shock the world. So off we went on tour, with B.B. King and his brass section. It was a strange kind of beast. We thought it could be an elegant way of introducing brass into our set. That was the musical identity of the tour.

I enjoyed some of what we were doing but it really did feel like an excursion down a dead-end street. There are certain things that we've done over the years that have borrowed heavily from the blues but as a general rule we'd be coming to the blues through a very different kind of filter to someone like B.B. King, so it was a challenge to play in that idiom and make it fresh. I'm not sure we actually pulled it off, to be honest.

LARRY: B.B. King is a legend and I'm very proud to have played with him. There was a lot of fun on that tour but it compounded the criticism of the movie and album, which was basically 'U2 go to America and discover the Blues and are telling us all about it, as if we didn't know.' Although audiences were clapping, you felt people were confused. There was a sea change due. Everybody knew it.

BONO: If I'm honest, this was the end of a journey that Bob Dylan had sent us on. In 1985, sitting backstage at his concert in Slane Castle, he said to me, 'You've got to look back. You've got to go back. You've got to understand the roots.' I think we wanted to ground all the electricity that was going through us and to understand the past better. And it really did help us. Listening to black music helped us get the groove ready for *Achtung Baby*. Listening to folk music helped me to develop as a lyricist. But this was a work in progress; gauche and awkward as it might have been, I think it was a necessary part of our development.

EDGE: We went to Australia and New Zealand, then came back for a couple of European stops and ended up in Dublin at the end of the Eighties, 31 December 1989, playing The Point Depot. We were pretty exhausted at that time. It wasn't the weariness of the tour, it was the combined effect of the tour, the movie, the other tour and basically having been running at full speed for a very long time. Bono hadn't said anything to us before he stumbled into a kind of half-confession, half-speech at the end of 'Love Rescue Me', telling the crowd this was a going-away party. He was very tired and emotional. It felt like the end of an era but that was the mood in the camp – we had run out of steam.

BONO: New Year's Eve, home town, what could be better? We're the biggest band in the world. These are the people who've made it so. You walk out on stage, you're ready for the roof to lift off, but you can't get the roof off. The weight of expectation has it locked down. The magic was gone, we couldn't see the stars. Outer space, the Milky Way, all the high-minded, other-worldly ideas that made us special didn't seem to be present that night. It was just the roof and the walls trapping us and our audience. And I realized that it was either over or else we'd have to go back to square one and dream it all up again.

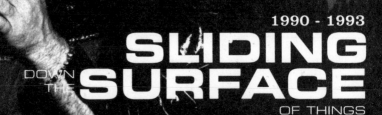

1990 - 1993

DOWN THE **SLIDING SURFACE**

OF THINGS

Paul

IT WAS THE FIRST TIME WE'D DRAWN BREATH REALLY SINCE THE BEGINNING OF THE BAND. SO THERE WAS A CERTAIN AMOUNT OF TIME FOR PEOPLE TO GET THEIR DOMESTIC AFFAIRS IN ORDER.

Although Bono and Edge immediately threw themselves into another piece of work, composing music for a stage production of *A Clockwork Orange* by the Royal Shakespeare Company in London.

BONO: The Barbican Centre, where the RSC were based, was to be a cathedral of highbrow British opera and theatre. Edge and I were treading these hallowed boards, writing music for Anthony Burgess's classic story of a dystopian future. We had ideas about sound as a plastic thing we could play with and bend its shape. Looking back now, it's clear that this early experimentation was preparing the ground for *Achtung Baby*.

EDGE: As research for *Clockwork Orange*, I was listening to a lot of industrial music, noisy and abrasive sounds built around drum machines and clangorous sonic distortion. I was really quite getting into these harsh recordings by bands such as KMFDM, The Young Gods and Einstürzende Neubauten.

BONO: We worked on some stuff in STS Studios in Dublin. It was a very small place, over a record store for traditional Irish music, full of dusty carpets and bright minds. A lot of our best songs have been demoed there.

EDGE: We would go in and brainstorm and try out different ideas. Beethoven's 5th is a central part of the *Clockwork Orange* story, so we were cutting it up and re-using it. Bono has always been more than just the lyricist in U2. He is great for musical ideas, melody lines and concepts. Occasionally we would come up with things that weren't appropriate for the play, it might be a guitar riff or a keyboard pad, and we would put those aside for U2.

BONO: The melody has always been the part of songwriting that I don't have to think about. Orchestration, cello parts, string parts, it all comes very easily to me. Tying it all together into something coherent and cohesive, that's not easy. Or having the clarity of thought and turn of phrase to complete a lyric, that requires work.

In the end, there were some great things about the production and some not so great. The set designer was incredible. Phil Daniels, the lead actor, was excellent. But the RSC was bureaucratic and hard to work with and Anthony Burgess turned out to be an extremely cranky old sod who had written music himself and wasn't at all pleased about our involvement. Nobody wanted to tell the great man that he was a better writer than musician.

PAUL: Burgess was a mad old bugger. He was a musician and composer as well as being a novelist. At the interval, I went out to the bar and found him engaged in conversation with five or six journalists, telling them how much he hated the music. And this was the first night of his own play.

BONO: We enjoyed the experience. I think we will return to the musical theatre. It is still a wide open terrain run by fairly dull minds. I'd love to have a go at it.

LARRY: Edge and Bono were working closely during that period. Myself and Adam felt a little separated from what was going on. There was a sense that the way we approached songwriting had to change. Edge and Bono moved very quickly to discover new things. Edge in particular was spending a lot of time listening to dance music and goofing around with drum machines.

EDGE: I had my own studio in the basement of my house. I was doing a bit more engineering, actually working the mixing desk and getting more in tune with the technical side of recording. I was working to escape, that is the sorry truth.

Leading up to *Achtung Baby*, Aislinn and I finally decided that we needed to separate. We weren't functioning as a couple, so I thought it best if I moved out, leaving Aislinn with the kids in the house. I stayed with Adam for a couple of weeks and then moved into a little cottage up from his main house for another few months. It was a grim period for me, finally looking failure in the face and seeing this was something that could not be redeemed. We tried. We went to counselling. I think it had gone too far. So making the record was a welcome distraction but inevitably it started to reflect what was going on in my life, partly because my own creative instincts were overwhelmed by it, but I think it also infused Bono's contribution.

BONO: Edge and Aislinn splitting up caused havoc in our little community. It was just too much to bear. These were two beautiful souls in agony. Edge was really in a very stressed place. I hadn't seen him like that before. Then there was a domino effect, and all of us went through difficult times.

EDGE: There is a process of osmosis when you work so closely together. What I was going through was obviously written all over my face and I think it focused Bono's mind. There were other parallel stories woven into some of the songs, because other people were going through something similar. Love, and love gone bad, is the eternal subject matter, so it was inevitable it would become a big part of that record.

BONO: I was going back and forth to the south of France, falling in love with the country, trying to find a house to live in. I was enjoying my new baby and writing *Achtung Baby*. We had never allowed the band to use the word 'baby' in a lyric. It did not exist in the U2 vocabulary. It is on *Achtung Baby* twenty-seven times, which is one of the reasons for the title. No one has ever made this connection although it is obvious from my point of view: enter the child! Life had changed utterly. Ali was pregnant again and our second daughter was born during the making of *Achtung Baby*, in July 1991. She arrived on the seventh minute of the seventh hour of the seventh day of the seventh month. So we called her Eve, which is the centre of the word seven. The babies are right there in the very first song, 'Zoo Station': *I'm ready to say I'm glad to be alive / I'm ready, I'm ready for the push...*

I had written a great deal on the Australian tour, surfing the jet lag. I spent the summer organizing it all. There was plenty to draw on. We recorded some demos in STS. 'Who's Going To Ride Your Wild Horses' sounded promising. We had the beginnings of 'Until the End of the World', 'Even Better than the Real Thing' and 'Mysterious Ways'. So then we went to Berlin thinking, 'Well, even though the songs aren't all written, we've got some bits and pieces and they'll come together.' Wrong!

ADAM: We started with a very sketchy idea of what *Achtung Baby* was going to be. We wanted it to be forward-looking and forward thinking and a complete about turn – yet we didn't really have any idea how we were going to achieve that. It was the beginning of the Manchester baggy scene in the UK, Stone Roses, Primal Scream, Happy Mondays, and it was confusing for us to figure out how to fit in. Those groups had a retro thing going on, which we were trying to stay away from, but they also had looped percussion and rhythm tracks and everything was becoming loose as people were getting turned on to Ecstasy. We didn't understand that culture.

Bono had the idea that if you took Brian Eno, Daniel Lanois, Flood and U2 and decamped to Berlin for a while something interesting was going to happen. It is not a bad theory but as always we were under-rehearsed and under-prepared.

PAUL: There were some U2 proverbs floating around. There's one in particular I remember: 'Domesticity is the enemy of rock 'n' roll.' How can you possibly play a great guitar solo if you are then going to pick up the kids from school or do the shopping? There was an idea that to make a good record you needed to get away from the wife and kids. It was a difficult time for Edge, too, rock 'n' roll perhaps also being the enemy of domesticity. So the idea of going away to record was floating around. We didn't want to go to New York. The American road had been well travelled by other bands. I suppose there was a sense of the new Europe emerging. The idea for Berlin may have come from Eno, because at one time Eno had lived in Berlin with David Bowie and Iggy Pop, the three of them in one squabblesome apartment in Kreuzberg. I remember Eno saying there was constant fighting about socks. It's a fantastic image, the three great men screaming at one another: 'You took my socks, you bastard!'

The Berlin Wall had come down the previous year, November 1989. I drove to Berlin in June 1990 in a splendid new Jaguar convertible to see Hansa studio, where Bowie and Eno recorded *Low* and *Heroes* and Bowie and Iggy Pop recorded *The Idiot*. It had an extraordinary location right beside what was left of the Wall. Berlin was the largest, Westernized city that far east, so the reconstruction of former Soviet countries after the fall of communism was being mounted from there. Every hotel was full of people selling things but they weren't carpet salesmen, they were touting vast projects such as airports and building schemes. So actually getting rooms in decent hotels became a problem for U2.

BONO: We arrived on the night that Germany officially reunited, October 3 1990. We were on a British Airways flight, the last flight to touch down in East Germany on the night East Germany ceased to exist. There were celebrations underway, so we thought we should have a piece of that and headed over to the West. The streets were full and we were wandering around in a giant crowd of people, who all looked like they were not having a very good time. We thought to ourselves, 'these Germans don't know how to celebrate. They're a bit grim! This is supposed to be the best night of their lives.' Then we realized we were at the wrong party. In fact, we had joined a protest march by the Communist Party. That would have made a great headline: U2 arrives in West Berlin to Protest the Pulling Down of the Wall!

I THOUGHT THIS MIGHT BE THE END. WE HAD BEEN
THROUGH TOUGH CIRCUMSTANCES BEFORE AND
FOUND OUR WAY OUT, BUT IT WAS ALWAYS OUTSIDE
INFLUENCES THAT WE WERE FIGHTING AGAINST. FOR
THE FIRST TIME EVER IT FELT LIKE THE CRACKS
WERE WITHIN. LARRY

Dennis Sheehan, our beloved tour manager, had found us guest houses that visiting dignitaries to East Berlin used to stay in. We were in the Brezhnev villa. I was sleeping that night in the former president of the U.S.S.R.'s bed. In the middle of the night, I woke up and went down to look for the kitchen to get a glass of water. There was none, because the kitchen was across the road and so I was just wandering hopelessly around the house, naked as a jay bird, when I heard voices in the hall. I put my scruffy head around the corner and there was a family of Germans standing there. I asked what were they doing here? To which a very irate elder gentleman replied, 'What are you doing here?' I said, 'This is my house.' He said, 'This is not your house. This is my house!' I said, 'It is my house. I'm renting it.' He said, 'Where are the people who own the house? You do not own the house.' I said, 'Look, what are you asking me? This is our house. I think you're going to have to leave now or I'm going to call the police.' To which he replied, 'This was my father's house, this was my mother's house. This is MY house!' I realized that he had come over the border to find the house he was born in, which had been seized by the communists. Oops! I said, 'I'll tell you what, I think I've got the picture and if you come back later I can show you around. But right now I'm naked and everyone else is asleep.' It was a very surreal start to *Achtung Baby*.

PAUL: U2 moved into the MPs' hotel for the East German Parliament, which was opposite a rather nasty parliament building called the Socialist Palace. That was a very strange hotel. The bellhops had to disconnect the KGB security cameras and sweep the room for bugs. There were prostitutes hanging around the lobby, which seemed to be a centre for currency exchange. It was rather bleak. And Berlin in the winter is pretty inhospitable.

ADAM: Hansa studios felt like it had been preserved in mothballs. It wasn't exactly a vibrant, happening place. It was an old SS ballroom, which is a bit of a bad vibe really. The collapse of the Berlin Wall seemed to result in a general state of malaise within Germany. It was depressing and intense and dark and gloomy.

LARRY: Berlin was starting to make Los Angeles look like a holiday camp. It was particularly depressing because of the separation within the band. It felt confrontational. It seemed like I was out of the loop and I was having difficulty getting back in. There was some alarm, on my part, at the extensive use of drum machines. I felt my input was being diminished. Even before we went to Berlin, there were tensions. It was the start of the chopping down of *The Joshua Tree* but it was also the dismantling of U2 as we had known it. People's roles changed and responsibility became an issue. Which was absolutely fair enough because it had to change. I had been quite content experimenting in the studio and going along with whatever was going on, being in the room when Edge was throwing ideas and joining in. Now it was, 'When you go into the studio, what is your approach going to be?' I wasn't quite sure what was being asked of me. Dance music was not something I was particularly interested in whereas Edge was listening to a lot of club mixes and going out to discos and really focusing in on drum beats and the BPM (Beats Per Minute), which was something we'd never even paid attention to before. When we set up to play, he would say, 'The drum box is going to do this, and could you play around it?' Danny was uneasy with the way it was going, because Danny felt that there were four people in U2 and we should all work this through together. We didn't approach it the way we'd approached our records before – or since, it has to be said. That was the first and only time there had been a communication breakdown. I was shell-shocked. After *Rattle and Hum* I had been thinking about what was I going to do playing-wise. I'd really started to listen to other drummers, thinking, 'that's a good drumbeat, that's an interesting way to do that.' I remember distinctly getting into Ginger Baker and John Bonham. I had started to focus in on drum parts and learning to play differently. But while I was going one way, Edge was going the other. I was trying to find out what more I could do. Edge was going, 'what less can you do?'

EDGE: We went to Berlin with a lot of ideas but most of them were very skeletal and undeveloped. They were directions and hints that we hoped would become fully-fledged songs when we kicked them around in rehearsal but unfortunately, since a lot of them started out from unusual origins, sometimes drum machines, sometimes just strange sounds, they didn't sound very good when the band tried to play them. There was an awkward phase where things weren't working out and there were two ways to analyse it. Adam and Larry were convinced the song ideas were crap and Bono and I thought the fault lay with the band.

LARRY: I thought this might be the end. We had been through tough circumstances before and found our way out, but it was always outside influences that we were fighting against. For the first time ever it felt like the cracks were within. And that was a much more difficult situation to negotiate.

BONO: What we thought were just hairline cracks that could be easily fixed turned out to be more serious, the walls needed underpinning, we had to put down new foundations or the house would fall down. In fact, it was falling down all around us. We were running up hotel bills and we had professional people, the U2 crew, staring at our averageness and scratching their heads and wondering if maybe they'd have been better off working for Bruce Springsteen. We came face to face with our limitations as a group on a lot of levels, playing and songwriting. When you're at sea the smartest thing to do is to find some dry land as quick as possible. So I think Larry and Adam were just anxious: 'Stop messing around with all this electronica, let's get back to doing what we do. Because all this experimental stuff isn't working very well, is it? And, by the way, *Clockwork Orange* was shite.' There was a bit of that going on. 'Did somebody say we were a rock band?' As you'd be walking down the corridor, you'd overhear that kind of remark.

LARRY: In the past, when we were writing music, we would be in a room playing and the discussion was always along the lines of: 'I don't like that particular part, try something else.' There seemed to be consensus. We were starting on a blank page to a large degree, perhaps with just a guitar melody or a riff or a vocal idea. So we started at the same place and ended at the same place. This time around, it wasn't a blank page. The parameters were already set, by drum machines, loops and synth pads. And it's kind of hard to embrace new rules when you don't understand them.

PAUL: I don't think it is easy being in U2. Obviously the rewards are very considerable, both artistically and financially, but for Larry and Adam, in particular, there seems to be a lot of sitting around. Yet their critical judgement is crucial and is very highly regarded.

ADAM: We weren't getting anywhere until 'One' fell into our laps and suddenly we hit a groove.

BONO: Maybe 'great' is what happens when 'very good' gets tired. We kind of out-stared the average, it blinked first and 'One' arrived.

AT THE INSTANT WE WERE RECORDING 'ONE', I GOT A VERY STRONG SENSE OF ITS POWER. WE WERE ALL PLAYING TOGETHER IN THE BIG RECORDING ROOM, A HUGE, EERIE BALLROOM FULL OF GHOSTS OF THE WAR, AND EVERYTHING FELL INTO PLACE. EDGE

EDGE: I was trying to take one of our half finished ideas and give it some inspiration. I went off into another room and developed a couple of different chord progressions, neither of which actually worked where they were supposed to. Danny Lanois said, 'What happens if you play both of them, one into the next?' I was playing acoustic guitar and Bono got on the microphone and started improvising melodies and within a few minutes we had the bones of the song, melodically, structurally and even lyrically.

BONO: The words just fell out of the sky, a gift. We had a request from the Dalai Lama to participate in a festival called *Oneness*. I love and respect the Dalai Lama but there was something a little bit 'let's hold hands' hippie to me about this particular event. I am in awe of the Tibetan position on non-violence but this event didn't strike a chord. I sent him back a note saying, 'One – but not the same.'

EDGE: At the instant we were recording it, I got a very strong sense of its power. We were all playing together in the big recording room, a huge, eerie ballroom full of ghosts of the war, and everything fell into place. It was a reassuring moment, when everyone finally went, 'oh great, this album has started'. It's the reason you're in a band – when the spirit descends upon you and you create something truly *affecting*. 'One' is an incredibly moving piece. It hits straight into the heart.

LARRY: It was similar to the way we had recorded in the past. In some ways it was a sign that the blank page approach was still valid. Everything was not broken.

BONO: There was melancholy about it but there was also strength. Brian wanted to rid it of its melancholy and so talked us into taking off the acoustic guitar, which is perhaps the obvious accompaniment, and went to work with Dan and Edge to try to undermine the 'too beautiful' feeling. Hence those kind of crying guitar parts that have an aggression to them. Great songs tend to have some kind of tension at the very heart of them, the bitter and the sweet balanced perfectly. 'One' is not about oneness, it's about difference. It is not the old hippie idea of 'Let's all live together.' It is a much more punk rock concept. It's anti-romantic: *We are one, but we're not the same. We get to carry each other*. It's a reminder that we have no choice. I'm still disappointed when people hear the chorus line as 'we've got to' rather than 'we get to carry each other'. Because it is resigned, really. It's not: 'Come on everybody, let's vault over the wall.' Like it or not, the only way out of here is if I give you a leg up the wall and you pull me after you. There's something very unromantic about that. The song is a bit twisted, which is why I could never figure out why people want it at their weddings. I have certainly met a hundred people who've had it at their weddings. I tell them, 'Are you mad? It's about splitting up!'

EDGE: The lyric was the first in a new, more intimate style. It's two ideas, essentially. On one level it's a bitter, twisted, vitriolic conversation between two people who've been through some nasty, heavy stuff: *We hurt each other / Then we do it again*. But on another level there's the idea that *we get to carry each other*. 'Get to' is the key. 'Got to' would be too obvious and platitudinous. 'Get to' suggests it is our privilege to carry one another. It puts everything in a different perspective and introduces the idea of grace. Still, I wouldn't have played it at any wedding of mine.

BONO: It never did get to number one, although it did get voted the greatest song of all time in a Q magazine critics poll, which meant a lot. It's a slow burner, like a lot of U2 songs.

EDGE: I think Berlin was a worthwhile experiment. It was an inspiring place in an odd way, even though the results weren't necessarily there to be seen. It took us out of the familiar and gave us a certain kind of texture and cinematic location which infused a lot of what we were doing. But it was actually going back to Dublin when things fell into place.

BONO: We rented a house called Elsinore in Dalkey, on the sea, which came to be known as Dogtown. It was a great place to work, just a mile down the road from where Ali and I lived in Killiney. I would walk to work and back. And I remember it coming together. The nights were getting warmer. The summer was coming in. One day, Flood had a different look in his eye. It started to feel good. We recorded 'The Fly'. Edge's guitar sound was literally like a fly had broken into your brain and was buzzing around.

Fintan Fitzgerald, who was running our wardrobe, had found this very Seventies superfly set of blaxploitation sunglasses. I would put them on whenever we hit a problem and make everyone laugh, running off at the mouth and describing the visions I'd see. I quite liked being this character, a barfly, a self-appointed expert on the politics of love, a bullshit philosopher who occasionally hits the nail on the head but more often it's his own fingernail he leaves black and blue. I thought I could get a whole song out of him.

ADAM: I don't know which came first, the glasses or the tune, but as soon as Bono found the glasses he knew what the character should be and how he should sound. The voice is over-driven which suits this quite demented and almost psychotic delivery. At that time, it was impossible to know whether U2 fans would follow Bono down this particular path, so that was a real leap of faith. The whole track is a high-energy sonic barrage but with an angelic chorus. It's a classic example of U2 and Eno interfacing.

BONO: The fly on the wall is a really insignificant image outside of voyeurism. *A man will rise, a man will fall, on the sheer face of love like a fly from a wall.* It's saying: 'Scale this rock face at your peril. Lots have tried before you and have been left on the fly paper.' And the *Shine like a burning star* part I sang in the Fat Lady voice, which is really a kind of Jaggeresque, campy falsetto.

EDGE: Bono's greatest gift is his imagination but it's also sometimes his worst enemy, in that to tie himself to one idea can be torture for him. He'd sooner have ten ideas in one song. I suppose the list of truisms in 'The Fly' is pretty close to following the device from beginning to end, although he does it in character. There are these characters, certainly in Dublin and I'm sure everywhere else, who sit on stools by the bar all day and they know everything. They seem to have moles in the White House and spies in the Kremlin. They're bar-stool philosophers, with all these great theories and notions, on the edge of madness and genius.

BONO: I started to realize that rather cracked character could say things that I couldn't, because I was getting hemmed in as Bono, earnest young man. It was the Shakespearean idea of the fool that I played with in my teenage years. Now I knew enough to be serious about it. I was also influenced by New York artist Jenny Holzer. She worked with illuminated boards on which all sorts of truisms are written, like 'Protect me from what I want'. I wanted to put a few of those aphorisms in a row to get a certain effect, so I was looking for a song that could build up in single lines: 'ambition bites the nails of success', 'a friend is someone who lets you help', 'every artist is a cannibal, every poet is a thief, all kill their inspiration to sing about the grief'. I just love him on the phone at the end: *Listen, I got to go, I'm running out of change. There's a lot* *of things, if I could, I'd rearrange.* The way I saw 'The Fly' was like a crank call from Hell … but the guy likes it there.

David Bowie was with us one night. We were all such students and fans of his and we asked his advice on 'The Fly'. He said, 'Do you really want my real advice?' We said, 'Of course!' He said, 'Re-record it.' He was right but we had run out of time. It took us fifteen years to really get it right live. It did go to number one in the UK though.

EDGE: There was a song called 'Lady With The Spinning Head' which we were really struggling with. It eventually ended up as a B-side. But we tried and failed to develop it so many times, it actually spawned three different songs, 'The Fly', 'Ultraviolet (Light My Way)' and 'Zoo Station'. If you ever listen to 'Lady With The Spinning Head' you will hear elements of all those songs. 'Zoo Station' was a version that we took in a more industrial direction. Danny provided an incredibly mad intro which sounds like a keyboard but is in fact guitar on which I'm creating strange textures.

BONO: One of the striking things about Berlin is that they have a zoo in the middle of the city. It was bombed during the war and there's a story that when people got up the next day to wander through the rubble of their lives, there were giraffes and lions and elephants roaming around. That story really stuck with me. There was a subway station called Zoo Station, because it stopped at the zoo. And the subway line that went in there was the U2 line. It was written as an opening track, the beasts breaking out of their cages. Really it's a riff rather than a song. Flood, Danny and Brian and the whole production team came together on that. You get to see what we were all capable of. There is humour and playfulness and curiosity in the lyric. A sense of lifting stones, no matter how many creepy crawlies might be underneath. It is subterranean but not homesick and not the blues. A platinum guitar part from The Edge comes in at the chorus like daylight through a crack in reason's ceiling, cutting through the murky sub-lows.

EDGE: It is a song that finally came to life quite near the end, when Flood was mixing and started to introduce heavy distortion on the drums. It was just so exciting, the sound of a band falling apart. We were really having a lot of fun in the studio and Flood was the perfect guy for the job. The lyric came through like a manifesto: *I'm ready, I'm ready for the laughing gas, I'm ready for what's next …*

ADAM: When people put on the record, we wanted their first reaction to be either 'this record is broken' or 'this can't be the new U2 record, there's been a mistake'. So there is quite a dramatic extended intro where you just don't know what you are listening to.

EDGE: 'Even Better Than The Real Thing', was a chorus riff that I came up with in LA. It is about as close as we could or would ever want to get to The Rolling Stones.

ADAM: We demoed that the year previously but it sounded deeply traditional, with a Stonesy groove. Then Edge got a new whammy pedal which created a kind of double octave sweep and it really turned the track around.

BONO: It was originally called 'The Real Thing', which is a dumb title for a song. 'Even Better Than The Real Thing' is much more reflective of the times we were living in, when people were no longer looking for the truth, we are all looking for instant gratification. It's not substantial as a lyric but it suggests a certain sexual tension and desire to have some fun playing in the shallows. *Sliding down the surface of things.* There is a moment when you want to read a magazine, not a novel. It was nice to take some of the more fun bits of rock 'n' roll. We really needed that playful thing to balance what was at the heart of the album and make the bitter pill a little sweeter to swallow.

EDGE: 'Until The End Of The World' was built around a Bono guitar riff from 'Fat Boy', an idea from one of our brainstorming sessions in STS. These demos later became the Berlin Bootleg when a tape fell into the wrong hands and ended up all over the world. It didn't seem to be going anywhere but I loved the riff. We met German film-maker Wim Wenders in Berlin when he shot a video for our cover version of Cole Porter's 'Night and Day', recorded for the *Red Hot and Blue* AIDS charity album. Wim was working on a movie called *Until The End of the World* and he was looking for music. Back in Dublin I got something going using the Fat Boy riff and cut a backing track with Adam and Larry. Bono started working up ideas and it was so exciting that I said, 'You know what, we have to put this on our record.' So we told Wim, 'You can have it but we want it too.' He was cool with that. Then we said, 'By the way, we're borrowing your title!'

BONO: The lyric was written very quickly in Wexford in my father-in-law's house. I woke up one morning and it was in my head, a conversation between Jesus and Judas. 'That'll be a hit!' Ali thought to herself. It is not the usual pop fare.

I was looking to find a key for my voice. Because we tend to work out of improvisation with guitars, certain keys continually turn up: D, E and A, because they are the keys guitarists go to. They're actually not great keys for

WE HAD A DEEP-SEATED BELIEF THAT THE SPIRIT OF THE BAND WAS TRUE ENOUGH AND STRONG ENOUGH AND IMPERISHABLE ENOUGH TO NOT RELY ON ANY OBVIOUS GUITAR SOUNDS OR SIGNATURES TO COME THROUGH. IT WOULD COME THROUGH ANYWAY. IT WOULD COME THROUGH A THICK PRISON WALL. BONO

me to sing in. I sing much better in B flat, which is why I tend to sing so many songs a little bit too high or a little bit too low. I was trying to find a combination of low and high for this song but I never did. The only melody that felt comfortable was really conversational and that led me to be able to write a lyric. 'The Fly' was the same. When I sing down low in that conversational tone, my lyric can be more like your prose writing.

The song was written at the same time as one of Ireland's greatest poets, Brendan Kennelly, was writing his great 'Book of Judas', a series of poems about the betrayal of Christ. It was an epic coincidence, because I was given the poems to review after the album was finished. The whole Zoo TV tour that followed owes much to one of Brendan Kennelly's great lines: 'the best way to serve the age is to betray it.' That became our theme for the next couple of years, to do everything U2 weren't supposed to. We had a deep-seated belief that the spirit of the band was true enough and strong enough and imperishable enough to not rely on any obvious guitar sounds or signatures to come through. It would come through anyway. It would come through a thick prison wall. What we were trying to say was: 'We exist as a band. It's our chemistry, not a formula.' And so we threw out all the sounds and themes that were associated with our band. I started to write about the hypocrisy of my own heart and the way I saw relationships around me and, to paraphrase Oscar Wilde, how 'each man did kill the thing he loved'. I was reading all the great poets: Keats, Shelley, Byron. 'Until The End Of The World' was a kind of vision, it was ecstatic in a religious way, a song about temptation. The temptation is not the obvious. The temptation is anything that will keep you from your destiny. But, hey, in the end, it is all about the riff ...

ADAM: It took quite a lot of work to get it into the state that it is now. Flood came up with a fantastic sweeping guitar sound that seemed to go between the speakers. It turned into a very seductive rock tune. There were some nice percussion loops that Larry added to. It's one of my favourite songs, it has such great atmosphere and drama.

EDGE: Every album is notable for a certain effect unit or series of effect units that are around at the time. A particular sound can often become the starting point for a song. I'm fascinated with how sound can be sculpted by using or often abusing the technology of the day, finding ways to make it do things it wasn't really designed to. I spend a lot of time playing around with effects and chaining them up and seeing what could happen if you put one effect through another. That was what was so great about working with Brian, somebody who was also really interested in how to use sound as part of the creative process, as a tool to facilitate song-writing and arranging rather than just tagging it on for effect.

BONO: Most lead guitarists practise scales. They do their homework on the fretboard. Edge will spend hours every day twiddling knobs on amps and pedals. Edge's effects pedals often represent the difference between ordinary and extraordinary, they are the alchemical ingredient that makes gold out of base metal. 'Mysterious Ways' was a bass line in search of a song. Adam came up with it while we were working on 'Night And Day' but it was never much more than a one-note groove for a long time. Edge got a new pedal he was playing around with, making this envelope of sound which would turn a guitar chord into the funkiest of jackhammers. I heard it from another room and ran in. I said, 'What's that sound?' He said, 'I don't know, I've just come up with it.' I said, 'We need it for "Mysterious Ways".'

EDGE: 'Mysterious Ways' was built from the groove up. It started as an experiment with rhythm, Adam, Bono and myself jamming away over a beat box. Adam had done a great bass part and the key to the song was finding ways to mess around with chords on top without having to change the bass. It took quite a while to really find itself melodically, Bono seemed to come in from a different angle to everyone else but that helped him find something truly original. I think it's a great song because everyone really shines on it. Larry came in at the end and demonstrated the difference between a drum machine and a real drummer by coming up with a much groovier beat. It has all of the personality of the band with the sensibility of rhythm that we were going for.

BONO: It is U2 at our funkiest. Sexy music. Sly and The Family Stone meets Manchester baggy. We came up with a few different verses but Edge really liked the nursery rhyme feel we ended up with. *Johnny, take a walk with your sister the moon / Let her pale light in to fill up your room.* It's a song about a man living on little or no romance. We were going to call the album *Fear of*

Women at one point. Edge came up with the *It's all right, it's all right* coda. He wanted to prove a point. He said, 'We've never had a song that says it's all right.' So I said, 'All right.'

'Trying To Throw Your Arms Around The World' was another song that broke the U2 mould. It's a drinking song and, of course, we weren't a band known for our imbibement of alcohol, although that was changing fast. Things other people had done at 18 or 19, like getting loaded and being irresponsible, I didn't get around to till I was in my late twenties living in LA. Ali was really good about it, she recognized it was a stage I needed to go through. It's a song about drunk ambition but in the funniest sense, not so much megalomania but just the ambition to get home in one piece. It was written in Australia, staying up all night and missing my baby. We had been listening to Serge Gainsbourg and there's a little bit of 'Je T'Aime' in that.

EDGE: 'Trying To Throw Your Arms Around The World' is light relief in the middle of a very dark piece of work. It is a nice mood to have on the album because the sound of *Achtung Baby* is really desperation and resignation and all sorts of worrying tones inbetween.

BONO: 'Ultraviolet (Light My Way)' was a little disturbed. *There's a silence that comes to a house when no one can sleep* is a great line, and I can say that with all modesty because I stole it from Raymond Carver. My apologies. It is an epic U2 song but again the key of it left my voice in a conversational place and allowed a different kind of lyric writing. It has almost a Motown chorus: *Baby, baby, baby, light my way*. This was the peak, the mountain top of babies. But it disguises very dark content: *Your love is a secret that's been passed around*. Jealousy. Infidelity. Love rears its ugly head again.

EDGE: That was another song that came out of 'Lady With The Spinning Head'. It's an epic, no doubt about that, with some gorgeous aspects, but it's quite unwieldy to play. It's never going to become a busking standard, put it like that. I once said to Bob Dylan, 'People are going to be playing your songs for thousands of years.' He said, 'Man, they're going to be listening to your songs too. It's just no-one's going to know how to play them.' Sometimes, I might add, that includes us.

ADAM: 'Who's Gonna Ride Your Wild Horses' was a very rough demo that we could never really improve on, so we kept going back to the original demo. There's something magical about it. It's a great torch song, with melody and emotion but I don't think we ever captured it again and we have never really

I SAID TO BOB DYLAN, 'PEOPLE ARE GOING TO BE PLAYING YOUR SONGS FOR THOUSANDS OF YEARS.' HE SAID, 'MAN, THEY'RE GOING TO BE LISTENING TO YOUR SONGS TOO. IT'S JUST NO-ONE'S GOING TO KNOW HOW TO PLAY THEM.' SOMETIMES, I MIGHT ADD, THAT INCLUDES US. EDGE

been able to play the song live. Sometimes you get songs like that. They have so much promise but it's as if you can't open the tin, you can't get in at them.

EDGE: It is not that we *can't* play the song live, it's more that it doesn't come alive. I remember Bono playing the original STS demo to Jimmy Iovine. Bono was explaining to Jimmy about House music, this new dance movement that was taking off at that time. Jimmy heard the demo of 'Who's Gonna Ride Your Wild Horses' and said, 'You're banging on about House music? That's house music! You write a song like that, you get to live in a house like this!'

BONO: 'So Cruel' is mostly my song. I picked up a guitar late one night in Dogtown and started singing. People thought it was too traditional, one more attempt at writing a song for Roy Orbison but Flood found a way of making it feel like it was on the same album.

ADAM: 'So Cruel' was lifted up by studio trickery. It started out as an acoustic tune. I was playing acoustic bass, Edge was playing acoustic guitar and Larry was playing a bodhran (Irish drum). It wasn't something one could imagine being on the record but overnight Flood did a couple of treatments to the track that utterly transformed it. He keyed my bass part off Larry's bodhran, which gave it a much more bubbly, off-beat feel and then we overdubbed a few things and the drum part went on.

BONO: The more I think about it, that was one incredible trinity at work: Brian Eno, Danny Lanois and Flood. No one has a keener feel for music than Danny, he's sensitive to it ringing true and being believable and touching the heart. Brian also demands that music reaches his heart but has the head to be hard on ideas that he felt he has seen and heard before. Then there's Flood, who at that point was Scottie in the Engine Room, actually just getting us to the right galaxy. 'You know the Dilithium Crystals were breaking up, Captain!' And he loved it that way.

EDGE: In amongst the dark romance, 'Acrobat' has a bit of venom about it. It's in the bitter, John Lennon tradition of 'Working Class Hero', slightly snarling and cynical. It never became a live favourite, maybe because I don't think that is what people come to U2 for. But I really like it.

BONO: 'Acrobat' is one of my favourite U2 songs although it doesn't quite get off the ground the way I'd hoped it would. It has a kind of manifesto in there somewhere. *Don't believe what you hear, don't believe what you see, if you just close your eyes, you can feel the enemy.* It is a song about your own spleen, your own hypocrisy, your own ability to change shape and take on the colours of whatever environment you're in, like a chameleon. *I must be an acrobat, to talk like this and act like that.*

EDGE: We were always suspicious of irony, hiding behind a wink, clever-clever lyrics at the expense of soul. U2 followed more in the line of the direct passion of artists such as Van Morrison or Bob Marley. But, in retrospect, I think we followed that idea through to the end and actually discovered that irony is not necessarily the enemy of the soul.

BONO: 'Love Is Blindness' ends the album in some style. There was some reference to the little death, which can be taken to mean a faint during orgasm but also works as an image of terrorism. I was mixing up the personal and the political. *A little death without mourning, no call and no warning ... a dangerous idea that almost makes sense.* There's nothing more deadly than an idea – or a person – that's almost right. You know, it took the 20th century a hundred years to get over communism. There's another dangerous idea that almost made sense. The song has images of terrorism, bomb-building, clockworks and cold steel, parked car. In a personal sense, I have observed the phenomenon of a person planting a kind of landmine that years later they will accidentally tread on and blow their lives to pieces. You can watch people doing it, wilfully getting involved in actions they will pay a very heavy price for later. Trajectory is everything. One inch out as the rocket launches and you miss Mars and end up on Venus. If you're lucky – and I have been – you discover it was always where you wanted to go.

EDGE: 'Love Is Blindness' is a great end to the album and probably one of Bono's finest lyrics. Bono wrote it on the piano, not an instrument he is noted for playing. His first idea was that he was going to send it to Nina Simone. That low end bass throbbing effect was a real stroke of genius from the production team and then the combination of percussion and drums is extraordinary. Eno

TRAJECTORY IS EVERYTHING. ONE INCH OUT AS THE ROCKET LAUNCHES AND YOU MISS MARS AND END UP ON VENUS. IF YOU'RE LUCKY – AND I HAVE BEEN – YOU DISCOVER IT WAS ALWAYS WHERE YOU WANTED TO GO. BONO

and Lanois are the best producers in the world, I think. And with that album they really proved it.

LARRY: It's the drum pattern from something else. I think it might even be from 'I Still Haven't Found What I'm Looking For', slowed down.

BONO: Brian, Danny and Flood did extraordinary things on 'Love Is Blindness'. The bass sounds like liquid at the centre of the earth, a kind of molten lava bass sound. And Edge's solo, his whole life just came out of him when he played. He played until the strings came off. I was pushing him and pushing him and pushing him. 'One more time, please Edge, one more time.' Finally, when we went for the take, one string broke and he just kept playing harder and harder. Another string broke. And he has such a light touch, ordinarily, he's so gentle. All that left him for a kind of rage. And yet there's not one bum note in there. It's incredible.

EDGE: The end of the album was quite tough. We had decided 'The Fly' was going to be our first single way before we'd finished the album but when it came to delivering it we weren't happy with the mixes. So at that point we did something which would make studio professionals laugh. We put the mix on a two-inch multi-track tape and subtly added extra vocal and guitars. Danny and myself actually did the final mix live, mixing on top of the mix, and I think part of the reason why that song sounds so dynamic was because it was a real hands-on performance mix. The guitar sounds which open 'The Fly' were achieved because there was extra guitar being mixed in on top of an existing guitar, so there's a really crazy natural phasing effect happening. This is completely unorthodox. That sort of technique went out with four-track in the Sixties.

BONO: It was a very emotional last night in the studio. We stayed up all night, as is the U2 tradition. It had been an exhausting few days. Chris Blackwell had gone home two days previously because he thought there was no way we'd finish when we said we would.

EDGE: Right at the end, when we were mixing 'One', I had an idea. I walked in literally as the boys had completed the last mix and said, 'I've got a great guitar part for the end of "One".' It was like telling them someone had died. I had to really get forceful to convince them to allow me to record this guitar part. I said, 'OK, I'll do it in one take and you can mix it right after that.' I ran in, put the amp up, plugged it in, played the guitar part once, they mixed it ten minutes after and it was done. The very last night, we were trying to sequence the album upstairs at Windmill, experimenting with different running orders before taking it to LA to get mastered and we just ran out of time, so I had to grab all the tapes, which were all in different formats, DAT, half-inch and quarter-inch tape, stuff was all over the place, there was a taxi waiting outside, I jumped in the taxi and headed straight off to the airport.

BONO: We all looked out the window and cheered and clapped Edge as he departed.

EDGE: I basically slept all the way to LA, got off the other side and spent four or five days in the mastering room trying to make sense of it all, hoping I wasn't fucking up the album. By the end I was just completely toast. I don't think I was making any sense.

ADAM: It was a bloody difficult album to make but a lot less difficult than the alternative. If we hadn't done something we were excited about, that made us apprehensive and challenged everything we stood for, then there would really have been no reason to carry on. We were at a watershed. If it hadn't been a great record by our standards, the existence of the band would have been threatened.

LARRY: I thought it was a great record. I was very proud of it. Its success was by no means pre-ordained. It was a real break from what we had done before and we didn't know if our fans would like it or not. I remember conversations between the band about how it didn't matter if it wasn't successful or if people didn't like it, we thought this is great. And if this is the last record we make, it would be a great way to go.

BONO: Our sound mixer and guru, Joe O'Herlihy, used to use the expression 'Achtung Baby!' all the time. When I asked him about it, he said it was his favourite line from *The Producers*, a movie the road crew used to frequently watch on tour buses as we were travelling through America. I thought it would make an ideal title for the album, it was attention-grabbing, it referenced

Germany where the album began, and hinted at either romance or childbirth, both of which were on our minds, but it had a lightness to disguise the heaviness of the album. There were other titles, *Man* – as opposed to *Boy*, obviously. We were thinking of calling the album *Adam* at one point, that's why we shot Adam naked for the sleeve.

ADAM: Anything that the U2 of *The Joshua Tree* wouldn't do, this new U2 would do. Bono volunteered me to be photographed naked, as I recall. I was still a young man and the idea of doing a nude photo shoot appealed to me because I'd been looking at Robert Mapplethorpe's work and following that whole New York photographic art scene. I felt that in a permissive society, if one could view a naked female and not suffer any kind of inhibition, then one should be able to look at a male body in exactly the same way. I knew there might be repercussions but this was a one-shot opportunity for me. This was the right record for such an expression.

BONO: This photograph began the legend that Adam is the most well endowed member of U2.

ADAM: That is indeed what legend would suggest but I'd have to say that within the U2 camp, I would definitely be the most diminutive of all the members.

EDGE: Adam is the most well endowed member, no contest, but he wouldn't know because he's blind.

BONO: Some people think U2 should be hung. All I am saying is that we are, in fact, particularly well hung.

ADAM: We do also appear in drag on the *Achtung Baby* sleeve. Again, that was born out of a desire to confound expectations. I don't think these symbols, these pieces of clothing, change you fundamentally, they just change the way other people look at you. I certainly had no difficulty with it, except that my dress was rather tight. I think one thing you learn when you wear women's clothes to the full extent is that there is quite a severe fashion masochism being expressed through women. Really, to wear those clothes and look that good you have to contort yourself in to some pretty weird shapes. You have to balance a lot of things. To move and be elegant in some of that gear is really hard. And, of course, you get backache from the heels.

BONO: It's still my favourite U2 artwork. Often with Anton, we keep looking for a single image and we can't get them. The success of this is it's 16 different images and they're all great sleeve ideas. I came up with the grid system as a solution and it has become associated with our band. I keep seeing it now in commercials and on internet sites. We didn't invent the square squared but I think we own it for our era.

PAUL: There was a lot for me to do in the build-up to releasing *Achtung Baby*, because it was during that period that Island Records was acquired by Polygram. This was a process I was very actively involved in, because we were not only the label's biggest act, we were actually part-owners of Island Records. This came about before *The Joshua Tree* basically because Island couldn't pay us our royalties for *The Unforgettable Fire*. To cut a long story short, we ended up taking part of the company instead. It was a very good thing to do, as it turned out. Chris Blackwell was preparing to sell the company anyway. So when Polygram started to run their slide rule over Island they needed to know that U2 were going to support the new environment. He certainly didn't want us bad-mouthing the deal or saying, 'We want to be with an independent.' We had number one records in every country in the world, so I knew how to work the independent distribution system worldwide but the opportunity to work with Polygram had enormous attractions for me as a marketing person and as a business person. The new head of Polygram, Alain Levy, had turned it into the smartest multi-national of all time, pulling in very clever people from all over the place. David Munns had an international marketing budget, run out of London and personally controlled by himself, it seemed. They doubled their size by acquiring independent labels such as Island, A&M, Def Jam and Motown. It was a way of setting up a record within an international organization that I hadn't experienced before. In America, they set up the Polygram Label Group, which was a team of independents utilizing the same marketing unit run by a very smart guy called Rick Dobbis, who was great fun to work with, and a promo guy called Johnny Barbis who was a genius. The calibre of people we were working with suddenly improved, which was tremendously exhilarating. There were several false starts with *Achtung Baby*, because like most of U2's records it was never finished at the time we expected it to be finished. So I used to go to sales conferences, which usually took place in exotic locations like Hong Kong, and tell them about the new U2 record and play snippets. It was a way of working that I hadn't experienced before and I greatly enjoyed. Chris Blackwell remained to run Island. Chris had ambivalent feelings about whether he really wanted to be in a corporation but it was a bit late for that. But he had cannily made a deal

ALL THROUGH THE EIGHTIES WE TRIED TO BE OURSELVES AND FAILED WHEN THE LIGHTS WERE ON. WHICH IS WHAT SET US UP FOR ZOO TV. WE DECIDED TO HAVE SOME FUN BEING OTHER PEOPLE, OR AT LEAST OTHER VERSIONS OF OURSELVES. BONO

whereby if Island succeeded sufficiently, Island basically ate the Polygram Label Group and Chris became the boss rather than one of its clients. That eventually happened, in large part because of the continued success of U2, but I didn't think it was a great result because the unit started to disintegrate and there was lots of trouble afterwards within Polygram. Within a few years this remarkable group of people had all departed and Universal, a smaller company, acquired Polygram. But it was the golden age of corporate record companies, and I certainly enjoyed it.

BONO: The tour was being conceived at the same time as the album. Zoo radio was a phenomenon before reality TV, with so-called shock jocks such as Howard Stern. It was aggressive, raw radio, the precursor to the *Jerry Springer* Show. The world was getting tired of fiction. The pantomime and parade of real people's lives was where the media was going, celebrities shot by flash photography, where you could see how many fillings they had in their mouths. We wanted to make a tour that referenced this zoo/reality phenomenon. I had an idea of taking a pirate TV station with us on the road, making programmes and broadcasting them.

ADAM: Bono's concept for an audio-visual video show was that we could intercut into what was on the screens with live action and pre-recorded footage and jumble it all up. When we had been in East Berlin, the only English TV channel at the hotel had been Sky News, so at the end of the day, when we came in from our own war of attrition in the recording studio, we were able to watch the first President Bush's war on Saddam Hussein, the liberation of Kuwait. They were dropping laser-guided missiles and bombs and you could see very accurately what they were doing. It was a horrific inferno live in your hotel room but you could always switch channels and watch bad German soap operas and car ads. That was the root of it. Politically it was a very troubled time. In the course of Europe becoming united, it was beginning to fall apart with the war in Bosnia Herzegovina. There was fragmentation occurring and we had the idea that with Zoo TV we could pull everything into it.

EDGE: It really started with 'The Fly', Bono writing that lyric from the point of view of a different character. He had never explored irony before, or the freedom that comes in writing about something serious in an indirect or apparently flippant way. The junk shop shades gave him a clue to a whole different persona, role playing in a way that we hadn't touched on since our early shows in McGonagles in 1979. That playful aspect of U2 had been lost. I think we were drawn to anything that was going to give us a chance to get away from *The Joshua Tree* earnestness, which had become so stifling.

BONO: We couldn't be ourselves. All through the Eighties we tried to be ourselves and failed when the lights were on. Which is what set us up for Zoo TV. We decided to have some fun being other people, or at least other versions of ourselves. That's when we bumped into that great line of Oscar Wilde's: 'The mask reveals the man.' It's like people at a fancy dress party – they're free.

It was fun to break out of being Bono and go back to the more theatrical conventions of our very early shows. Gavin was a real help, because he's so dramatic in that way. We had Brian Eno helping out with some video art. The scattering of small TVs was his idea.

EDGE: We got connected with some very interesting directors who had worked on *Buzz TV*, which was an experimental show with a really novel, cutting-edge approach to television. We put together a think tank that included the band, Eno, the *Buzz TV* directors (Jon Klein, Mark Pellington and Mark Neale), Willie Williams our tour designer, who was absolutely inspirational, Kevin Godley, who was doing a lot of our videos at the time and Cathy Owens, a friend who helped find a lot of unusual talents out there in the world of the visual arts. It was a very interesting team of creators. It was such a new way to go that really there was no shortage of ideas, the only limiting factors were what was practical and what was going to fit within our budget.

LARRY: We really wanted to do something that had never been seen before, using TV, text and imagery. It was a very big and expensive project to put together. We allowed ourselves to be carried away by new technology.

PAUL: Everyone was talking about the new Europe and the new democracies. It was a time of great political imagination. Also satellite television was new, people were talking about concepts such as 'new media' and 'convergence'. It was being predicted that computers and satellites would bring information to everyone and borders would disappear because of information. A lot of it was nonsense but technically what you could do on stage had changed. There

WE HAD BECOME GLUM ROCK'S LEADING LIGHTS. ZOO TV OPENED UP ALL THE POSSIBILITIES OF THEATRE; ROLE PLAYING, IRONY, SATIRE AND FARCE, AND FINALLY KILLED OFF THE OLD IDEA THAT WE WERE A BAND OF PAINFULLY EARNEST PEOPLE WHO DIDN'T KNOW HOW TO HAVE A GOOD TIME. EDGE

were big screens being introduced by Philips, who were the owners of Polygram. I sensed a huge commercial opportunity here that would give Philips the chance to demonstrate what they were always going on about, which was synergy, and have Philips' hardware and Philips' software on a tour by a Polygram artist. I thought I might even legitimately get them to sponsor the tour. They had a particularly interesting product called Night Star (actually, being Dutch, they'd spelt it wrong and it was called Nit Star), which was a big screen which could be used in a modular way, so you could put four of them together and have an even bigger screen. I went to them and said, 'Look, can we have some of these and we'll build a production around them?' They went off and had a lot of meetings. Meanwhile, we bought the screens anyway. Eventually they came back and said, 'Sorry, you'll just have to pay for them the same as anyone else.' I was furious. The guy who ran Philips at the time was Jan Timmer, the father of the CD. He came to a U2 show in Rotterdam on that tour and saw all this stuff and Bono really attacked him, saying, 'This is ridiculous. Look at your technology all over the stage but Philips name is nowhere because you wouldn't get involved in the tour.' And Timmer said something very strange, he said, 'You have to understand that in a company as big as Philips even the boss cannot always get his own way.' A pathetic thing to say. To be fair to Alain Levy, he was very embarrassed and he chipped in a few hundred grand of Polygram money. But years later Philips sold Polygram from under his feet without even telling him. So it's rough out there.

LARRY: Despite all the technology and design aspects, the biggest difference for me was Bono and the glasses. He had been so open before, the idea that people wouldn't be able to see his eyes through his glasses was huge. Bono was embracing his inner rock star. However, my job didn't change.

PAUL: The Trabant cars became one of the enduring images of the artwork and the tour. These cars were made of compressed wood pulp and smelt like wet cabbage. Somehow they became part of the imagery representing the fall of communism. We saw them everywhere in Berlin. There was tremendous racism between the West Germans and the East Germans. The West Germans used to call them the Ostis and regard them as lame-brained, stupid and lazy. So when the Wall came down, the feeling in the West was: 'Oh, they're coming over here in their stupid little cars.' We played with them on stage and hung them from rigs with their lamps turned into spotlights.

EDGE: There was a great sense of excitement in the camp at the start of the Zoo TV tour. We knew we were doing something no-one had ever done before.

PAUL: The tour started indoors, in the Lakeland Arena in Florida in February 1992, and it just grew and grew, moving outdoors in Europe and then returning to the stadiums of America.

ADAM: We were in Lakelands for a few days doing dress rehearsals and getting to grips with the equipment. I remember the moment the clothes arrived and we finally saw Bono as The Fly.

LARRY: We notified the media when the band would arrive for rehearsal. We drove up in a white stretch limo with police outriders. Bono was sticking his head out of the sunroof, flashing the victory sign, wearing The Fly shades and a black leatherette jacket. While there were times when you might need escorts to get in and out of gigs, usually it was done very discreetly. Now we were allowing the press to see it, and basically saying, 'Yeah, we are rock stars, we have police escorts, we travel around in limousines and, you know what, we're not embarrassed about it any more.' There were certain things about it that made me cringe but there was something refreshing about saying, 'Yeah, this is the shit, this is what goes on, and it's a lot of fun.' The honesty was a huge relief. And those gigs were great. The music was challenging. The spectacle was astonishing. The audience reaction was amazing. I think a lot of people had been afraid that U2 had lost its conscience, because it was dressed up to be flippant and kitsch with all this rock star flamboyance. People thought we had abandoned the past. Really, we had abandoned our own insecurities. This was maybe the most political thing we'd ever done.

ADAM: Bono phoning the White House was a nice touch but he would only ever get through to the operator. In the course of the whole tour, I don't think he managed to strike up a relationship with the operator. If you know Bono, that's got to be some tough cookie.

BONO: Operator Two and I had a great relationship. She tried not to show it but I could tell she was very amused, as we rang her night after night. We'd have twenty thousand U2 fans leaving a message. 'Tell the President to watch more TV!'

We were trying to make a point about using everyday technologies as part of our art installation: televisions, radios, telephones. It's always a thrill when you realize how powerful a simple object can be. It is incredible what you can do with a phone if you think about how to use it. You can call the President of the United States or you can call for a pizza. One night, just for a laugh, I did call for a pizza. I ordered ten thousand pizzas from Speedy Pizzas in Detroit. They could only do a thousand but we bought them and distributed them around the audience.

Another thing we did was create a Video Confessional. When our audience arrived every night, some of them would get into a queue to go into a tiny leopardskin telephone box and tell their deepest secrets. It was randomly edited, the sublime and ridiculous hard cut together, and displayed on huge screens before the encores. There would be people genuinely making confessions about things they'd done in their past, confessions of love to somebody in the audience who didn't know how they felt, confessions of abusive behaviour, occasional flashing of breasts (although we tried not to put a lot of that in), a couple kissing. It was amazing and included some very emotional stuff. One guy confessed to his brother that he had been involved in a drunk-driving accident, where people got hurt. Though we laugh at Jerry Springer and these trailer park confession shows, there is a positive, psychological benefit to saying something in a public arena. It somehow makes it real. It was amazing what went on in that little telephone box where you got to be as honest and intimate as you wanted in front of 20,000 people you don't know at all.

EDGE: Bono was definitely on a bit of a roll as The Fly. Some people said at the time, 'Can he come back from this?' It was such an all-encompassing thing, he was playing the role of 'the rock star' but the question lingered, was the rock star playing with him? I think it was just an aspect of why he'd wanted to get into rock and roll in the first place that was suddenly given the chance to be fully exorcized. It didn't indicate a change in our core values, just an attempt to redress the balance. No one knew we had a sense of humour, we had become glum rock's leading lights. Zoo TV opened up all the possibilities of theatre; role-playing, irony, satire and farce, and finally killed off the old idea that we were a band of painfully earnest people who didn't know how to have a good time.

I THINK A LOT OF PEOPLE HAD BEEN AFRAID THAT U2 HAD LOST ITS CONSCIENCE, BECAUSE IT WAS DRESSED UP TO BE FLIPPANT AND KITSCH WITH ALL THIS ROCK STAR FLAMBOYANCE. PEOPLE THOUGHT WE HAD ABANDONED THE PAST. REALLY, WE HAD ABANDONED OUR OWN INSECURITIES. THIS WAS MAYBE THE MOST POLITICAL THING WE'D EVER DONE. LARRY

If you put on *Achtung Baby* now and tried to tell somebody this is where we discovered humour they would think we were bonkers, because it's such a heavy record. It's tortured. But in amongst all the intensity there is a little element of humour and lightness and a certain throwaway quality, where not every single thing sounds like your life depends on it, which is the way *The Joshua Tree* and *Unforgettable Fire* sounded.

LARRY: I was really enjoying working with the technology, being able to use percussion as a time reference gave me a lot of room to operate as a player. All the things that had concerned me about making Achtung Baby were really resolved during those live shows. I suppose it was the proof that we had gone down the right road, that this was the future for U2, the mixture of technology and band, although I think later on we may have pushed that envelope just a little too far.

PAUL: Zoo TV was perceived worldwide as a new category of presentation. It was the dawn of video as a creative element rather than what we call i-mag, image magnification. We were being written about by architectural critics and art critics. It was great fun. Psychologically, it took U2 into a very elite group that really only included Pink Floyd and The Rolling Stones. I remember watching one of the shows with Mick Jagger. He turned to me and said, 'This is going to be like Star Wars. If you do one as big as this, we have to do something even better.' In a way he was right, because from then on audiences were not going to accept a band on a black box with a bit of steel and tarpaulin over their heads and a couple of big white sheets at the side of the stage with pictures. Those three acts, Pink Floyd, The Rolling Stones and, most of all, U2 raised the bar for everyone.

I remember that whole tour as a triumph, although it didn't actually make any money. Frank Barsalona, Ian Flooks, Barbara Skydel and myself all implored the band to let us put the ticket price up by five dollars. I think it was a 25-dollar ticket price and it was too low. They were very sensitive about ticket prices generally, far too sensitive I felt. If we had put on another couple of dollars it would have been not just a creative but also a huge financial success. I suppose it was an investment in the future, which is what we always used to say to make ourselves feel better about the money.

BONO: On the first American leg, we created a character called the Mirror Ball Man, a kind of Showman America. He had the confidence and charm to pick up a mirror and look at himself and give the glass a big kiss. He loved cash and in his mind success was God's blessing. If he's made money, he can't have made any mistakes. I would preach the gospel of prosperity in my mirror ball suit and end with the line: 'I have a vision! I have a vision! Television.' The Mirror Ball Man would call the White House, where, much to his bemusement, Operator Two regularly declined to put him through to the President. There's a film somewhere of Mirror Ball Man in Times Square driving a Trabant. I got Winona Ryder to help me out. She dressed up as the Mirror Ball Man's side-kick, a tiny Fly, all in leather with the black glasses, we called her The Flea. She was such a great girl to go along with it but I'd forgotten that she was a very big star at the time and she kept getting mobbed. I was saying, 'This is not Winona Ryder, it's The Flea' but I couldn't convince them. People were grabbing her, screaming, 'It's Winona!' All through that tour there were little performance-art things going on around the globe for no particular reason. You could file all of this under grand madness... costing about a grand a minute!

EDGE: We had a belly dancer during 'Mysterious Ways'. Sex and U2: the combination was unheard of. It was a piece of happenstance really. Christina Petro was a dancer who was a fan of the band and she turned up outside the venue in Miami in full belly-dancing outfit. For a bit of light relief, the crew arranged for her to dance onto the stage during the final dress rehearsal. It was actually really effective, sexy but cool and a reference to the video of the song. So we asked her to come out on the road with us.

ADAM: We had the ability to beam stuff in and out via satellite, we could do link-ups and live events with other places. There was a U2 competition where the winner had the whole show on their own TV at home.

BONO: The energy of television has a lot to do with its ability, at the touch of a remote control, to make extraordinary hard cuts from Daffy Duck on the Disney channel to a preacher telling the congregation they're going to go to hell tonight if they don't keep the show on the air with some donations, from an ad for the new Buick to real news of real lives being exploded in far-off places. We put all that on stage. The really extraordinary thing about modern media is the way they play havoc with your emotions. Channel-hopping, if we were really sane, would be much more upsetting than we let it be.

EDGE: Zoo TV wasn't a set piece, it was a state of mind. It was constantly evolving and changing and taking on new ideas as it went. If you compare the opening indoor leg in America in February 1992 to the end of the outdoor tour in Tokyo in December 1993, it's hardly recognizable as the same show. We changed it consciously for each new area of the world.

LARRY: We started indoors in America and continued in Europe, where we got involved in the Stop Sellafield protest. That was interesting. People may have thought we were no longer involved in social or human rights issues but we were actually doing more than ever before.

EDGE: Greenpeace has been something we've supported for many years and they were running a campaign to protest against the building of a second nuclear plant at Sellafield in Cumbria in northwest England, where they reprocessed nuclear waste to make plutonium for atomic weapons. Just as the rest of the world was ending the arms race and starting to think about ways of reducing their nuclear stockpiles, Sellafield had the brainwave of building a multi-billion pound reprocessing plant to create more weapons grade plutonium.

BONO: It was high comedy. We stormed the beach and recreated the cover for The Beatles' *Help*, using semaphore, except we were dressed in protective clothing. It's a memorable shot if not very flattering. It made our point that the locals lived in some real danger. Even a hundred miles away on the east coast of Ireland, there were reports of increased illness that might have been attributed to some of the leaks from the reactor at Sellafield. It was suggested that the Irish Sea had become the most radioactive sea in the world. Some fishermen swore they'd seen two-headed fish – I'm sure there were a few two-headed fishermen involved. But even on an economic level, the Sellafield reprocessing plant was making no money and no sense for Great Britain.

EDGE: The event was a big success from a media point of view but they eventually did open the second plant despite all the complaints. So I don't know whether our protest made any difference but I'm sure it didn't do any harm.

BONO: After years and years of protest, including a campaign led by my own dear wife, Ali, who (with her partner, Adi Roche) organized a million and a half postcards from Irish people protesting to Tony Blair, the British government have finally concluded Sellafield has to be closed down. That's what I always tell people: These things take time.

PAUL: We went back to the US in August for the start of what we called *Zoo TV – Outside Broadcast*. Nobody else had ever attempted to do such a large-scale outdoor production. It was quite something.

BONO: Catherine Owens found this piece by Emergency Broadcast Network – EBN. They had reorganized George Bush Senior's State of the Union speech over Queen's 'We Will Rock You'. They used all his own words but re-edited them in a different order. So you had the President of the United States rapping, 'Some may ask, why rock out now? The answer is clear: these are the times that rock man's soul. I instructed our military commanders to totally rock Baghdad. And I repeat this here tonight … We will, we will rock you!'. It was a magnificent opening to the show and unlike anything anyone had ever seen before. We were, however, now involved in an election campaign and were looking like we had taken the side of Bill Clinton, the young Governor from Arkansas. It was a potentially divisive opening for our audience but they seemed to take it very well. Ironically, the band had made me promise we wouldn't get involved in the election. They'd say, 'We're not going to get involved in this election because we're not American, are we Bono?' 'No, we're not,' I used to say,

'We're Irish. I'm not going to get involved in the election.' 'So why are we calling the White House?' 'It's a bit of mischief!' 'Why are we taking a call from the challenger?' 'It's fun!' 'Does that mean we're going to be involved in the election?' 'No.'

But it did. And we were.

ADAM: Bill Clinton phoned up a radio show when we were doing an interview and there was an exchange of pleasantries. That became another little subplot running through the tour, because he later turned up at a hotel we were checked into in Chicago and had to take a smaller suite because Bono was in the presidential suite.

BONO: Myself and Edge had been up all night, writing a song called 'Two Shots of Happy, One Shot of Sad' for Frank Sinatra. He never recorded it, though his daughter Nancy has done a beautiful version. We were in Edge's room when we heard that Bill Clinton, the presidential challenger, was in my room waiting to meet us. My room, I should explain, was completely trashed from a party there the night before. Such was the gaiety at this party that some of our crew had tried to wake the then Governor up. The Secret Service sweetly explained that 2 a.m. is a little late to be calling but when the great man from Little Rock found this out, he evidently thought otherwise and came looking for us. I'm sure that when his handlers saw the state of us and our room, they must have regretted this meeting of pop and politics. The Governor was completely relaxed, laughing out loud at the empty bottles, pizza boxes and very full ashtrays. I remember I was still wearing a crushed velvet suit from the night before. We talked about everything from the troubles in Ireland to the place of the saxophone in rock and roll. He is very easy with people and has enormous curiosity for what could make the world a better place. A new kind of politician had entered the world stage, the first of our kind, meaning someone who grew up listening to rock 'n' roll rather than Mantovani. Real brainpower, real charm, a real sense of humour. What more could you want? He ended by inviting us to go along with him to see the Chicago Bears play that night. It's fair to say that though we had the bigger suite in the Ritz Carlton, he had the bigger motorcade.

EDGE: A little romance came back into my life during the *Outside Broadcast*. It is sometimes erroneously reported that I married the belly dancer. Well, that's not quite true. My wife-to-be, Morleigh Steinberg, came on the tour as a choreographer/show critic but later started to perform the belly dance in 'Mysterious Ways'. We had known each other for a while. Morleigh's first connection with U2 dated back to 1987. Although I didn't know her at that time, she is actually in the 'With Or Without You' video. She was shot by Matt Mahurin in a very abstract style and projected over the band as we perform the song.

BONO: Morleigh has the most beautiful armpit in the world. If you see that video you'll know what I mean. She was a modern dancer and a choreographer with an avant-garde dance troupe called ISO, which was an offshoot of a more well known group called Momix. I had become a real fan of theirs.

EDGE: I met Morleigh in person during *The Joshua Tree* tour. When we played LA, she was having a party in her house and I went along for an hour, just sitting on the stairs enjoying a really nice conversation with Morleigh and her sisters, having no idea how our lives would connect later on.

Morleigh stayed in touch with Bono over the years. When we were putting Zoo TV together, Bono thought it would be good to have a choreographer to critique what he was doing. So Morleigh came along to give him some feedback and worked with us on pre-production. Our original belly dancer, Christina, had literally dropped everything and run away with the circus but she couldn't do the European tour, so Morleigh said, 'I'm not a belly dancer but you need more of a performance than a straight belly dance, so, if you want, I'll do it.' So Morleigh came out for the rest of the tour. During her time on the road, our friendship evolved into something more.

BONO: All of us had fallen in love with Morleigh, she has a very easy way about her. She is Californian in all the ways that you love California, a bright light in a very low-key way. Edge fell for her. It was that thing that often happens when people fall in love, they were friends before they were lovers.

PAUL: It was the supermodel era. Because the fashion business tends to be located in particular centres, New York fashion week, the Paris collections, London fashion week and so on, the top models tended to be in the one place at the same time and occasionally those places would coincide with the U2 tour. It was great fun to have the show suddenly descended upon by these beautiful creatures, all of whom were pretty independent and didn't need to be transported around. They were particularly delightful guests because they are professional travellers themselves and have their own support infrastructure. We're used to dealing with famous guests but most of them don't even know how to get from the car park to the hospitality room. The supermodels are completely expert at that kind of thing and very practical. We liked them a lot.

BONO: I'd agreed to be on the cover of *Vogue*. I was told I would be the first man on the cover in 20 years. During the session I was introduced by the photographer, a lovely man called Andrew Macpherson, to the person he described as the most beautiful girl in the world: Christy Turlington. And there began a friendship that we still have to this day. When the supermodels started coming to concerts the thought did occur to us that these girls – Kate Moss and

Helena Christiansen and Naomi Campbell and Christy – were much more fun to hang out with than musicians. And they all had impeccable taste in music and always knew what was happening next. Helena actually does DJ gigs. I met Naomi on a plane when I was seated beside her and couldn't wait to get off the plane to tell Adam, because Adam had harboured a crush on Naomi for years. So I set them up on a date. And the rest, as the fellah said, is not history.

ADAM: Naomi came to a show and we met. It was a very strange, frenetic time, the beginning of the outdoor tour and we did become involved quite quickly. That relationship brought with it the dubious pleasures of the paparazzi. On the one hand that can be a lot of fun and not to be taken too seriously but it can be a little invasive as well. Despite being in a world-famous rock band, I'm not someone who particularly lives in public. I think there are people who do and they can manage it and it's no great difficulty for them but it was a difficulty for me.

The bigger you get, the smaller your world becomes in a strange way. You can get cabin fever. Your routine is actually very unnatural, to know where you've got to be at any given time. You're constantly exposed to the public, no matter how you happen to be feeling, you're dealing with people all the time and they are expecting you to be one thing or another thing. This was not a good time for me. I was heading for a crash, everything was spinning out of control. I definitely wasn't prepared for it and I wasn't really able to deal with everything that came with Naomi. Relationships are hard enough without that kind of extra pressure. All I can really say is that in the end it didn't work for me and that's a wisdom I've acquired in retrospect. When I look back now and look at what went wrong, it wasn't the right place for me. But you don't know that until you try it.

BONO: Adam and Naomi did suit each other in a certain way, they really did. But I think Adam was spinning out at that time and he just fell in love too quickly for it to ever grow and mature. But they had good fun.

Adam is a romantic at heart. There have been times in my marriage when I thought about those conversations I missed, those nights out, those great girls that showed such promise. Now, with a little experience, I think I know what that night would have looked like and where that conversation would have taken us and it is not a place that is particularly interesting. But it's not easy to deal with money, it's not easy to deal with fame, it's not easy to deal with women throwing themselves at you, even being married, perhaps especially being married. No matter how strong you are, no matter how upright, these are real hurdles that you have to figure out how to get over. I will never forget the time Adam saw me in a headlock with some starlet and said to me, 'It's fun. It's exciting having sex with someone you don't know. Don't let anyone tell you it isn't. It's a great adventure getting to know somebody. But as rare as it is to fall in love, it is not as rare as real love, I will die for you love, I will be there when you're sick and when you're frail love. Now that's rare. I would give everything, all these experiences that I'm having, all these different and extraordinary women, I'd give them all up for what you have.' I remember Adam telling me that. And if there was one reason for having him as best man at my wedding, that was it, that one conversation.

EDGE: Rock stars and supermodels, it is a little bit of a cliché but we were happy to live with the cliché because the supermodels we got to know are great people and we still count them as very close friends.

LARRY: That whole supermodel, club-going, paparazzi thing was not really my scene. I found it a little uncomfortable. They were all nice people and I was very fond of them. But some people don't do Christmas, some people don't like beaches, some people don't like the wind, some people don't like the sun. The fashion world is not my natural habitat.

BONO: How can you claim to be uncomfortable with public attention and then spend your life playing in a rock band? There are some things about our drummer that I have never figured out. Larry actually had a solo spot during those outdoor shows and I am not talking about a drum solo either. This is a man who would sing 'Dirty Old Town' and other Irish drinking songs *a cappella* nightly in front of 50,000 people and then tell you he doesn't like attention.

LARRY: It was awful. Bono had to do a costume change. The question arose, 'What are we going to do?' I said,

'I don't know. Why are you looking at me?' Bono said, 'Well, somebody's got to do something. How about you getting out and doing an Irish traditional song?' 'I can't do that!' 'Oh go on, give it a try.' 'There is no way!'

Bono said, 'Look, I'm stuck, there's nothing else to fill it. This'll help me out.' I did it for him because he already had his arse so far out the window that I felt it was only fair to do something to help him out. It was excruciating. It is part of that tour that I don't particularly like to be reminded of.

BONO: The presidential election took place at the end of the American tour. George Bush Snr, who had never taken any of my calls, lost to the challenger, a self-declared U2 fan. The Mirror Ball Man had one last opportunity to consummate his relationship with Operator Two. I said, 'Hi, can I speak to ex-President George Bush, please?' She told me he was not available. She was all business, that Operator Two. I do like that in a woman. I said, 'But it's our last night! Can I leave a message for George?' She told me I could. I said, 'I just wanna say I won't be bothering him from now on. I'm going to be bothering Bill Clinton now ...'

ADAM: The American tour ended in November, then the outdoor leg in Europe was starting in May, so we had a gap of a few months. We were invited to Clinton's inauguration on 20 January, 1993. Bono and Edge couldn't make it but Larry and I went along to show our support. There is a whole jamboree and party circuit that goes on in Washington the night before, thrown by all the various people and groups who funded or supported the President's electoral campaign. The President goes to each of the parties and says a few words. Rock The Vote MTV had been a significant contributor and they were staging the hippest and hardest to get into party, so we went to that. Actually, we were considering attending Senator Teddy Kennedy's bash but Michael Stipe and Mike Mills from REM were in town and we had hooked up with them the night before. They had very publicly supported Clinton and they wanted to perform on stage for the new President. So the idea came up to have half of REM and half of U2 perform at the MTV party. Their album at the time was *Automatic For The People*, ours was *Achtung Baby*, so for one night only we became Automatic Baby. We played a very stripped-down, acoustic version of 'One', which really is a song for any occasion. Mike Mills played guitar, so it was easy for us to slot in, with Larry on bongos and me on bass. I don't know if it can rival Marilyn Monroe's 'Happy Birthday Mr President' as one of the great presidential performances but it was fun to do, and Clinton seemed to appreciate it.

PAUL: Kathy and I went to D.C. for the inauguration. The night before, I got a call to say my younger brother, Niall, had died suddenly in Ireland. It was a tragic echo of what had happened with my father the first time I went to New York, back in 1980.

EDGE: We were going into our second year on the road. The thought came up, 'We've got a bit of time off. We've got some ideas hanging around from the last record, let's do an EP, maybe four new songs to spice the next phase of the tour up a bit. It'll be a fan thing. It'll be cool.' So we went into The Factory studio in Dublin for a couple of weeks in February 1993. But halfway through the process of working on the material, Bono, the eternal optimist, said, 'If we're going to all the bother of making an EP, let's push ourselves and see if we can make a full album.' I was struggling at the time to try and get some shape on the music, so I was not enthusiastic at first. But I saw it as a big challenge, a bit of throw down. Can U2 make a record in twelve weeks, which is all the time we had, or have we become so spoilt by endless record budgets that we need a year to make an album?

PAUL: Right from the beginning of that campaign, from when *Achtung Baby* started to materialize as a fully formed album, Bono and I used to talk about the so-called one-two punch, which meant two albums in one campaign. When you've got people paying attention, why not hit them again quickly? And that was where *Zooropa* came from.

BONO: I thought if momentum is a creative player in the making of great albums, maybe we should just see what happens if we try to earth all this excitement and lightning that was striking all around us. It was a good plan but it nearly killed us.

EDGE: We had Eno and Flood on board, so that was a great help but because of the time problem, we really just had to go for it. There was no opportunity to mess around or second-guess ourselves, we had to write and produce and record and that was it. Some of the material was left over from the *Achtung Baby* sessions, a verse melody that became 'Stay', and an instrumental backing track of a completely different song that became 'Numb'; some stuff we originated on the spot, such as 'Babyface' and 'The Wanderer'; and some stuff was taken from little ideas that had happened on the road. 'Zooropa' was two separate pieces of music I found listening back to cassettes of jams at soundchecks. I grabbed them, found they fitted together and we ended up making a song out of these completely disparate elements. We were on a roll. The songs came together very fast. The problem was we hadn't finished by the time we had to go back on the road and Brian and Flood went off to do other projects they had already arranged, so were in a little bit of a quandary. Everyone was telling us, 'Well, it's an EP. You did good but there's a lot more work needed to finish some of these songs.' But they weren't counting on the absolute dogged determination of this band.

ADAM: Our enthusiasm ran ahead of us. We just kept going. The European tour started up in May and we spent the first month flying back to Dublin after our shows and going into the studio to do a few hours' work that night or the next morning. So not only was it a very long tour but we recorded an album in the middle. It was about the craziest thing you could do to yourself.

LARRY: The show would finish at 11. As soon as we left the stage it was straight down into the cars, straight to the airport, take off. Because the shows were in Europe, normally they were an hour or two ahead, so we'd arrive back in Ireland about midnight, go straight into the studio, do a couple of hours' work, go home, go to bed. There were often a couple of days between shows, so we'd go into the studio in the afternoon, work into the night, get up the next day, head to the airport and fly to the next city. There was a month of that. It was mad, but it was mad good as opposed to mad bad.

EDGE: It was remarkable the lengths we went to actually pull it off. But we did.

BONO: It was a thrilling, very creative time. We were lost to our work and our art and life all seemed to blur into one. The plastic pants were becoming harder and harder to get off after the show. I'd started out trying to parody a rock star and discover what it felt like. By now I was dangerously starting to enjoy it. But there was another interesting development for the *Zooropa* leg of the tour. It was time to put the Mirror Ball Man in mothballs. We wanted a more Eurocentric character, more decadent, more old world, rather than the brash Yankee salesman with God on his side. I started to think about what The Fly would be like when he's old and fat and playing Las Vegas. U2 conjured up the Devil!

EDGE: In January 1993, myself and Bono went to Hamburg to take part in a Festival Against Racism at the Thalia Theatre. It was a concert performance, press conference, theatrical event and debate on the subject of anti-racism. This was a time in Germany when there was a lot of right-wing activity. I suppose the negative economic effect of the East and West joining together created a certain social tension.

BONO: There were a lot of things happening in Europe at the time. In Germany, Turks were being brutalized by skinhead gangs. A child had died in a house that was burnt down. All over Europe, fascism was becoming a bit cool again, which was terrifying. In France, there had been swastikas painted on synagogues. Jean-Marie Le Pen, the ultra-right-wing *Front National* party leader was enjoying huge support. So we decided to have a little go at that.

EDGE: We saw a performance of *The Black Rider*, which was a musical play by Robert Wilson, William Burroughs and Tom Waits. It was based on a German folk story about making deals with the Devil, who was a Mephistolean character called Pegleg. So when Bono started thinking about another character, we thought of the Devil. We thought about what he might look like, how he might act. Bono made a speech at the conference saying, 'Mock the Devil and he will flee from thee. Fear of the Devil leads to Devil worship.'

Another inspiration was a character we had observed in Madrid. Madrid is one of the few places where it feels normal being on the road because most people stay up later than you and are partying far harder than you. We ended up one night in this noisy dance club in the wee small hours, watching this guy walking through. He was probably in his early sixties and impeccably dressed, a dapper Spanish gentleman wandering about a House club, ignoring everybody but kind of waving in the air at an imaginary audience. It was quite extraordinary. I don't know whether he was on some weird psychotropic drugs or whether he was just an eccentric or a mime artist but we watched him for a good twenty minutes and it really gave us so much material.

BONO: For this character, MacPhisto, we came up with a sort of old English Devil, a pop star long past his prime returning regularly from seasons on The Strip in Vegas and regaling anyone who would listen to him at cocktail hour with stories from the good old, bad old days. There was a certain pathos to him. Gavin Friday said to me, 'If you want to make a Devil you should have horns.' I said, 'Yeah, well I'm not wearing horns. I'll look ridiculous.' He said, 'You need proper red horns.' And he got them made up. I put them on and it was the maddest-looking thing but it helped, because when you're dressed as the Devil your conversation is immediately loaded, so if you tell somebody you really like what they're doing, you know it's not a compliment. We used to ring up fascist politicians like Jean-Marie Le Pen's office and flatter them live in front of audiences of sixty or seventy thousand. I rang Alessandra Mussolini, the Italian dictator's granddaughter, who was getting into politics, and we'd have seventy thousand people singing, 'I just called to say I love you' on her answer machine. I called the Archbishop of Canterbury and told him I loved what he was doing and that it was great that the Church didn't seem to stand for anything. It was death by cup cake, darling! During our Italian dates, in a performance-art moment, I had myself filmed walking across the square at the Vatican. MacPhisto had developed a limp at this point so I had a walking stick, and I was shooing the birds, dressed as the Devil, walking across the Vatican Square, muttering under my breath, 'One day, all of this will be mine. Oh no, I forgot, it is mine.'

EDGE: That character was a great device for saying the opposite of what you meant. It made the point so easily and with real humour. Every town presented a new set of possibilities and options, so there would be a general discussion about what we might do, with a lot of planning between Willie and Bono. One highlight was calling The Minister of Fisheries in Norway, Jan Henri Olsen, to congratulate him on whaling, which was forbidden by the European Union but legal in Norway. He actually took the call and invited Bono to come and have a whale steak with him.

PAUL: *Zooropa* was released on 5 July, 1993, while we were on the road. From Polygram's point of view, it was a gift from God because they were not expecting a U2 album for another couple of years. If *Achtung Baby* was the first course, it was the perfect time to bring our audience something rather more experimental and esoteric, which was *Zooropa*. It is still one of my favourite U2 albums because it's so loose.

LARRY: *Zooropa* is the sound of U2 becoming comfortable with a new recording environment. After the attrition of *Achtung Baby*, it was clear that this technology stuff was OK, it's not the Devil, it's not the enemy, we can work with it. Edge was still exploring dance and hip-hop culture, club mixes, all that kind of thing. He was experimenting and U2 were his guinea pigs.

ADAM: It's an odd record and a favourite of mine. It was kind of quirky, it didn't have any of the big U2 anthems on it, it was very much a record that grew out of the studio sessions. I think the opening, 'Zooropa' itself, is absolutely mesmerizing.

BONO: It was our attempt to create a world rather than just songs and it's a beautiful world. The opening was our new manifesto, *I have no compass, I have no maps, and I have no reason to go back*. Brian Eno was in his element here. The studio became an instrument, a playground, lots of plastic attack from his DX7 keyboard, lots of raised eyebrows from Larry and Adam. The opening was the audio equivalent of *Blade Runner*'s visuals. If you closed your eyes you could see the neon, the giant LED screens advertising all manner of ephemera.

I wanted to get away from the weight of where I was going. I wanted to fly. There was enough melancholy around. *And I have no religion, I don't know what's what*. There is a line in the New Testament which says that the spirit moves and no one knows where it comes from or where it's going. It is like a wind. I have always felt that about my faith. Religion is often the enemy of God because it denies the spontaneity of the spirit and almost anarchistic nature of the spirit.

The counterbalance of that freedom is 'Numb', which is the sound of the inside of somebody's head, with a great lyric and performance by Edge. It is a relentless portrait of what he was feeling at the time and what a lot of people were feeling in the wider world about media. He was in that spot but it became a great metaphor for the media overload generation incapable of feeling anything for the pictures you see.

ADAM: 'Numb' was a left-over from *Achtung Baby* called 'Down All the Days'. The song didn't really work but the instrumental backing was interesting. Brian added some fantastic keyboards. Then when we were trying to get a final running order together for *Zooropa*, we had this backing track but we didn't know what to do with it. Edge took it off into another studio to demo a few ideas and, within a few hours, had worked out this way of almost rapping over it. I think it is a sonic masterpiece and Edge's delivery is fantastic.

EDGE: It was a few hours' work and a lot of editing. The lyric came very quickly and tapped into many of the ideas behind Zoo TV, the sense that we were being bombarded by so much information that you find yourself shutting down and unable to respond. I wrote so many verses I had to cut two out. The mix was the easiest thing in the world. You just put up the faders and let it go. That was the joy of making that album, the sense of immediacy.

'Lemon' came late too and became one of the album's standout tracks. It was something I worked up with a drum machine and bass, very rhythmic, but it was hard for me to find guitar parts until I used an unusual gated guitar effect which worked with the rhythm. Bono came up with the lemon. When he's improvising over a piece of music he is at his most creative. Often you're scratching your head, thinking, 'What psychedelic substances is he on that he would even dream up something like that?'

BONO: I have very few memories of my mother because my father never talked about her after she died. So it was a very strange experience to receive, in the post, from a very distant relative, early Super 8 footage of my mother, aged 24, younger than me, playing a game of rounders in slow motion. This beautiful, young Irish girl, with a narrow waist, curvaceous figure, dark gypsy hair. The film was early colour and it looked extraordinary. It was a wedding, where she was the maid of honour in this beautiful lemon dress.

I sang in my Fat Lady voice but there's a poignancy to the lyric. There were two things going on, memory and loss, a portrait of a girl in a shimmering lemon dress that kept it sexy and playful and the pathos of a man separated from the things he loves.

I really felt for Edge at that time, because he had to move house. His first wife, Aislinn, was really a very special girl and he was so close to his family. 'Lemon' is about leaving home, versus not leaving home.

EDGE: A few songs came out of jamming, all of us in the room with Brian. 'Daddy's Gonna Pay For Your Crashed Car', 'Dirty Day' and 'The First Time', which we recorded live. There are some great songs on *Zooropa* but some songs are not all there, it is as if they still have their promise in them, you can hear their potential, and I actually like that about the album.

ADAM: 'Stay (Faraway, So Close!)' was a song Bono and Edge had been working on for some time. Bono used to say it was for Frank Sinatra but we needed songs for *Zooropa* so we thought we would have a go. It was hard to figure out how we would do it. I mean, no one is going to mistake us for Frank Sinatra's backing band. A very humble little combo sound is what we ended up with and that really worked.

EDGE: For me 'Stay' is the stand-out track on the record. It came to us in instalments. We got the verse back in Berlin while working on 'Achtung Baby'. Then during the *Zooropa* sessions we heard Wim Wenders was looking for a song for his new movie, so I had a go at finishing it for Wim. I was playing around on piano with some old-school chord progressions trying to summon up the spirit of Frank Sinatra. It's definitely not from a rock and roll tradition. It stands outside of any particular item, like it always existed.

BONO: 'The First Time' is a very special song. It just seemed right that in the middle of all the chaos and blinking lights of the futurescapes there would be a very simple, poetic moment. It's the story of the prodigal son but in it the prodigal son decides he doesn't want to return. It is about losing your faith. I hadn't lost my faith but I'm very sympathetic to people who have the courage not to believe. I've seen a lot of people around me have bad experiences with religion, be so badly abused they feel they just can't go there any more, which is a shame.

'Dirty Day' is a father and son song. 'It's a dirty day,' was an expression my dad would use and there is a lot of him in there but it was also influenced by Charles Bukowski, the great American writer and drinker. His nickname was Hank and I use his phrase at the end of the song, *Hank says the days go by like horses over the hills*. The song is about a character who has walked out on his family and, years later, meets the son he's abandoned. So it's not about my father but I used some of my dad's attitude in it. 'I don't know you and you don't know the half of it.' 'No blood is thicker than ink.' 'Nothing's as simple as you think', they are all things my dad would say. 'It won't last kissing time,' that's another one of my dad's, the way he would dismiss something he thought was transient. Like U2 when we started. The thing that makes that song is the middle eight, when the voice goes up: *From father to son, in one life has begun a work that's never done.*

I have had a lot of father-figures in my life. What a list that would make! But somewhere up the top of them has got to be Johnny Cash, who we wrote a song for and persuaded him to come in and sing it with us, to close the album, 'The Wanderer'. I wrote the lyric based on the book of Ecclesiastes in the Old Testament, which in some translation is called The Preacher. It's a story of intellectual wanderlust. The preacher wants to find out the meaning of life and so he tries a bit of everything. He tries knowledge, educates himself, reads every book, but that doesn't do it. He tries travel, sees every sight, but that doesn't do it. He tries wine, women and song, that doesn't do it. All, he says, is vanity, vanity of vanities, striving after wind. As you read this book you think, 'I can't wait to hear what does do it!' And the most extraordinary line is: 'There is nothing better for a man, than that he should eat and drink, and that he should make his soul enjoy good in his labour.' Love your work. That's what it is. It is good to love what you do. I think there's a lot to that.

The song is the antidote to the *Zooropa* manifesto of uncertainty. Even if the album begins with *I don't have a compass, I don't have a map* – in other words, I don't know but I accept this state of uncertainty – 'The Wanderer' presents one possible solution. Overall on the album, the key is learning to live with uncertainty, even allowing uncertainty to be your guide. I remember trying to sort out some phrasing problems with the lyric and Johnny stopping me, saying, 'No, I like it when the rhythm's uneven. I get to do the unexpected.' Another lesson from a master. But hearing the voice of an ancient mariner singing over electronica was quite a juxtaposition and one of the best things we've ever done.

EDGE: The songs are not classics but they are more experimental and interesting than most classic pop songs. This is something we don't necessarily care to do anymore. We don't go down the road with a piece of music just because it's unusual. That's not enough for us now. We want something that's potent and some of these songs are not particularly potent. But sometimes my favourite records are not the ones that are made with big broad strokes. I like people's more subtle, quirky stuff.

BONO: I thought of *Zooropa* at the time as a work of genius. I really thought our pop discipline was matching our experimentation and this was our *Sergeant Pepper*. I was a little wrong about that. The truth is our pop disciplines were letting us down. We didn't create hits. We didn't quite deliver the songs. And what would *Sergeant Pepper* be without the pop songs?

EDGE: I never thought of *Zooropa* as anything more than an interlude ... but a great one, as interludes go. By far our most interesting.

BONO: The very same week *Zooropa* was released, a young American writer/film-maker called Bill Carter came to see us at our concert in Verona in Italy and asked would we do an interview for Sarajevo Television. Because at the time that Europe was pontificating about the single market and single currency and what we'd all be capable of if Europe got together, right on the edge of Europe, in the nation of Bosnia that had emerged from the post-communist Yugoslavia, there was a city like no other, a symbol of Christian and Muslim tolerance, where three ethnic groups – Croats, Serbs and Bosnians – lived together in peace. And this great old city of Sarajevo, whose library was one of the great treasures of the world, was now involved in the most intractable conflict, where the very tolerance that the city symbolized was being challenged in an appalling siege by Serbian forces. It was not a battle over territory, it was a deliberate attempt to raise ethnic tension. And it was a turkey shoot, women and children on the way to the market were being targeted by snipers just to cause terror. Sarajevo had become a running sore on the body of Europe ... but not a gaping wound in the heart of Europe, because it was not really being let in. It was only page eight or nine in the newspapers. The political response was uncertainty and prevarication. The English couldn't agree with the French on what to do. The UN were there but their role was only to observe. Things were getting worse and worse and nobody was really talking about it.

During the course of the interview with Bill Carter, he described everyday conditions. He described how, in makeshift bomb shelters, people were listening to U2, playing rock and roll and dance music at deafening levels to drown out the sound of the shells landing. Young people were watching MTV, seeing bands and presenters who looked just like them, and wondering why no one was talking about what was happening to them, how ordinary young people were being murdered on their way to school in a city just a short drive across the border from the clubs and concert halls of Italy and Germany.

EDGE: Bill's idea was that U2 should go to Sarajevo and that would create a lot of publicity and help maintain the press profile of the siege, because it seemed that a certain media fatigue had set in and people were just getting a little tired of the story. People were dying every day but it was no longer really being reported.

BONO: So I agreed in an emotional moment to do a gig there. And after I've agreed on Sarajevo Television, I then have to explain to the band why putting our lives at risk is going to help the people of Sarajevo. Larry is immediately sensible: it looks like a publicity stunt. Adam would quite like to see Sarajevo. Edge thinks, 'What would we play?' We don't even tell Paul, because we know what his reaction is going to be.

PAUL: There was a mad idea to dash off to Sarajevo and do a concert during the shelling. There was even an attempt to do that without telling me. But it would have been very foolhardy and dangerous and would have probably got a lot of people killed.

EDGE: We looked at our schedule and tried to work out how to fit in Sarajevo. We thought about trying to get in on a UN plane. Logistically, it would have been impossible and when Paul got wind of it he pointed out that not only would we be risking our own lives, we would be endangering our crew and our audience. But we said, 'Maybe there's something else we can do that might maintain attention on this terrible situation.'

BONO: We decided to put our TV station to work for them and offered them unmediated airtime so they could speak to our audience every night.

PAUL: Bill Carter went back to Sarajevo where he managed to get together a little video unit. The European Broadcasting Union had a satellite link out of Sarajevo which we bought time on. And we started to do live satellite connections between U2's concert and Sarajevo every night. Most of the Zoo show was scripted and highly rehearsed. The Sarajevo links were not.

EDGE: It was flying by the seat of your pants. There was no script, no clue as to what was going to happen or who was going to be there or what they were going to say. Some nights it felt like it was part of the concert but a lot of nights it felt like quite an abrupt interruption that was probably not particularly welcomed by a lot of people in the audience. You were grabbed out of a rock concert and given a really strong dose of reality and it was quite hard sometimes to get back to something as frivolous as a show having watched five or ten minutes of real human suffering. But at a time when it seemed like the nightly news was just becoming a form of entertainment, this was the opposite. This was a form of entertainment presenting some real hard news where there was no editor involved, no way to soften the harsh reality of what you were seeing. We don't normally see that kind of cold hard news. We get a very sanitized, editorialized take on everything, be it the atrocity of Rwanda to the siege of Sarajevo. When you watch the television news, you are getting something palatable, whereas this was really quite unpalatable most of the time. And for that reason I think it affected people very much, including us.

BONO: Live by satellite every night you had the extraordinary spectacle at a rock gig of reality trampling all over art. And then the band would try to recover.

PAUL: Larry was pretty much against it. He thought we were exploiting other people's misery for entertainment. Bono definitely felt that we were shining a light on something important.

LARRY: We were playing a rock 'n' roll show and it was lots of fun, and although the political stuff was serious it was done with a smile. Then suddenly seeing video footage of people being bombed and a satellite link-up with people in Sarajevo saying, 'We're being killed, please come and help us.' That was really hard to watch and hard to listen to. I was worried we would be accused of exploiting these people. I remember saying to Bono, 'I don't know if I can handle this any more, it's really hard up there.' He just pushed through. He said, 'I want to do this and I'm going to do it.'

PAUL: The worst night was Wembley Stadium, when three women came up on the screen and said, 'We don't know what we're doing here. This guy dragged us in. You're all having a good time. We're not having a good time. What are you going to do for us?' Bono started to reply but they just cut him off. They said, 'We know you're not going to do anything for us. You're going to go back to a rock show. You're going to forget that we even exist. And we're all going to die.' Right in the middle of the show at Wembley. And the show never really recovered.

BONO: It was very upsetting. But the next day Brian Eno was inspired to get involved with the War Child project and a lot of great things came out of that. So some people were inspired to take action and some people were just horrified.

Salman Rushdie came on stage at the same concert. Again, tolerance was the subject we were playing with. Freedom of expression was a real issue in music and you had people trying to stop the stories of the street coming out as hip hop. But what Salman Rushdie had gone through was a truly appalling moment in the history of censorship, when the Ayatollah Khomeini had issued a *fatwah* against his life for supposedly blaspheming the Prophet Mohammed in his novel *The Satanic Verses*. Islamic Fundamentalists were trying to kill him and Salman had been living in hiding since 1989. So freedom of speech was the reason we asked Salman on stage in front of 70,000 people. No one wants to offend another's religious convictions. I have enormous respect for Islamic culture but I would encourage extremists to consider the murder of a novelist as sacrilegious to *my* faith. God does not need us as His bodyguard. Surely it's the other way around. We tried to leaven the situation with some humour. I was dressed as the Devil at the time and I whispered in Salman's ear, 'It's inevitable that one always falls out with one's biographer.'

PAUL: We did four shows at Wembley Stadium on that tour, playing to 240,000 people. We headed out to Australia, where it became the *Zoomerang* tour and *New Zooland* in New Zealand. Bad puns aside, there was a sense of expectation everywhere we took the show. Audiences were never disappointed. It was very much a creative high point. People who work for me still refer back to Zoo TV as the most enjoyable campaign they ever worked on.

BONO: During a little break in the tour, I recorded a duet with Frank Sinatra. I may not have been the most obvious choice to sing the classic 'I Got You Under my Skin' with the 77-year-old Chairman of the Board but I was more than flattered to be asked. Scheduling was difficult and we recorded our vocals in different countries. I did mine with producer Phil Ramone in STS Studios, Dublin. I remember Sinatra's people visibly wincing when I changed the line 'don't you know, you fool, you never can win' to 'you know, you old fool, you never can win'. They looked around at each other afterwards and said, 'Hey, he'll laugh…won't he?' 'Yeah, yeah, yeah, he'll laugh.' *The New York Times* put the song on the cover of the entertainment section and said it was the best thing on his *Duets* album. I was very proud of it. Then someone suggested we should make a video. We asked our friend Kevin Godley to direct. It was set up for one of Frank's favourite bars in Palm Springs. Kevin had the idea to capture on film the first encounter between Frank and me that day.

EDGE: I happened to be in LA so Bono said come along, just for moral support. We drove up to Palm Springs, met at the bar where the video clip was

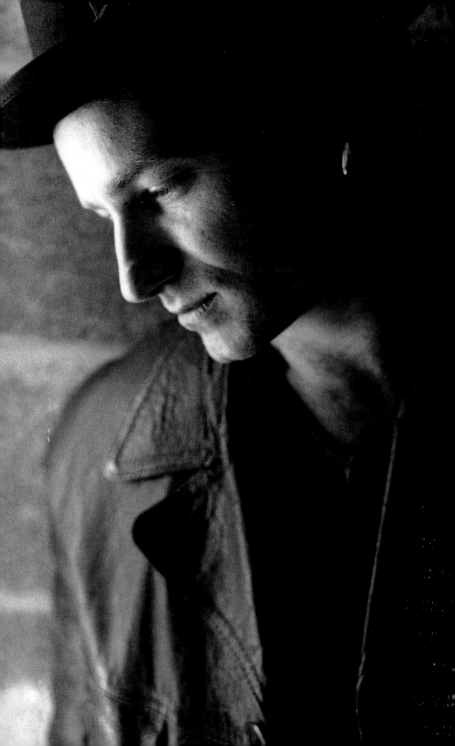

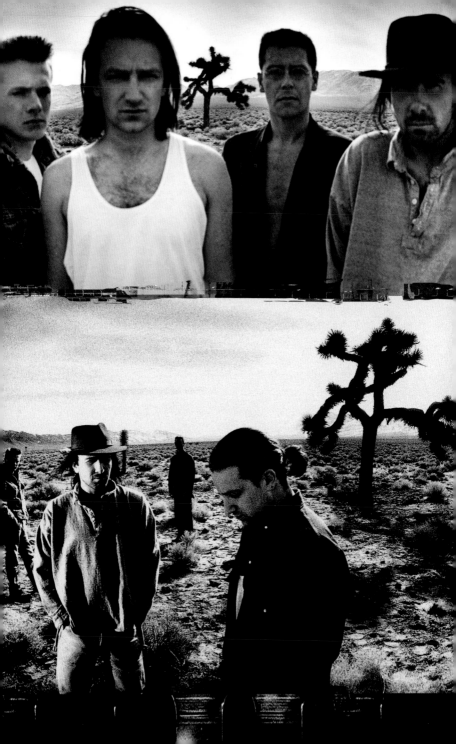

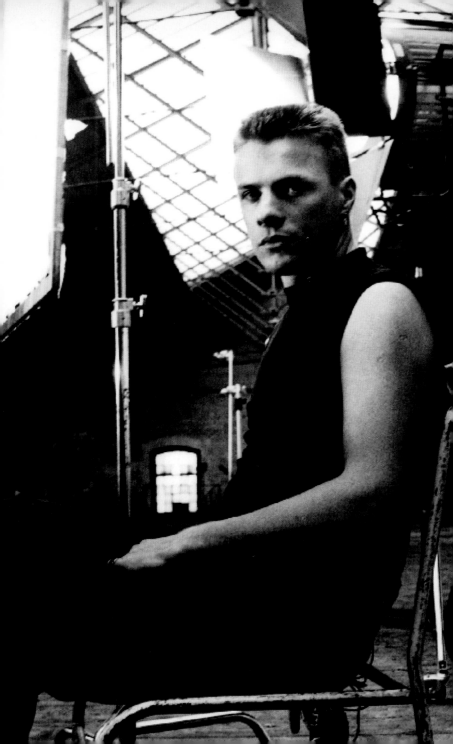

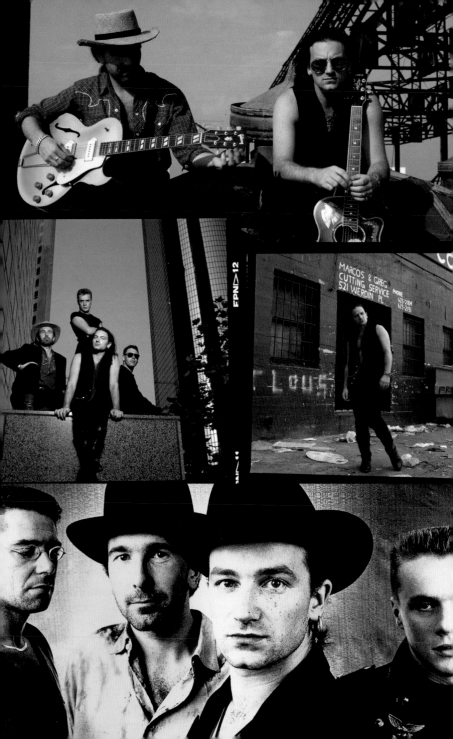

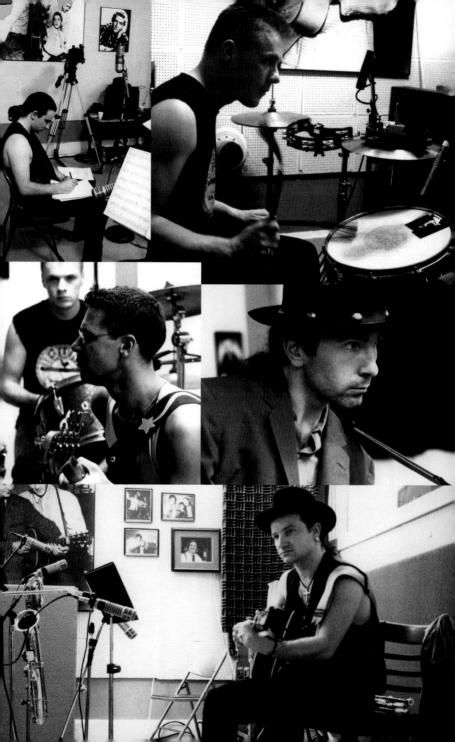

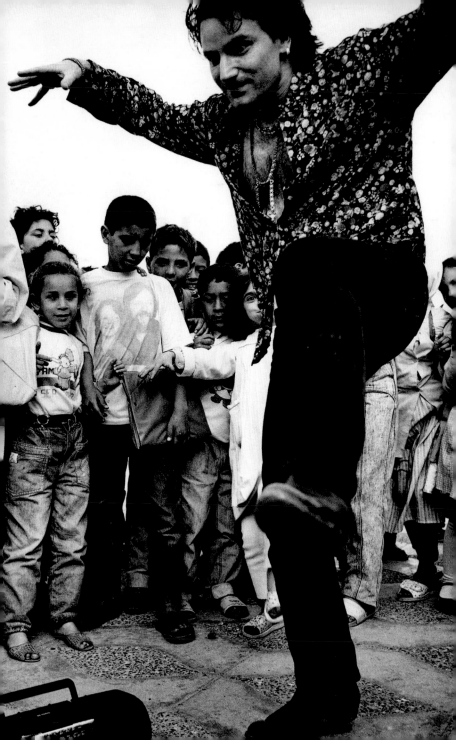

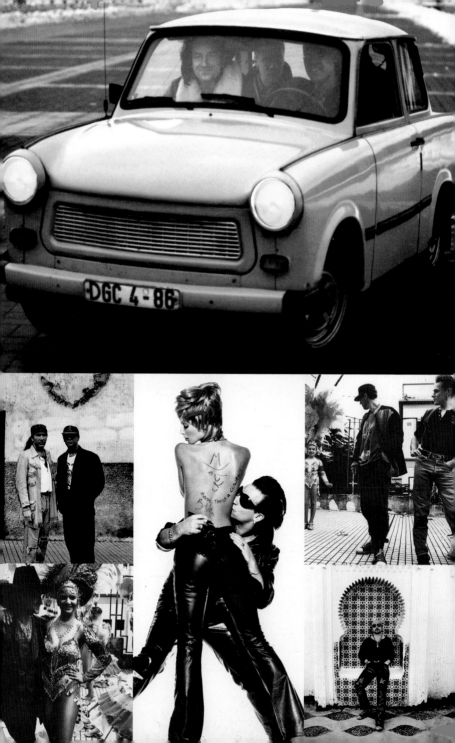

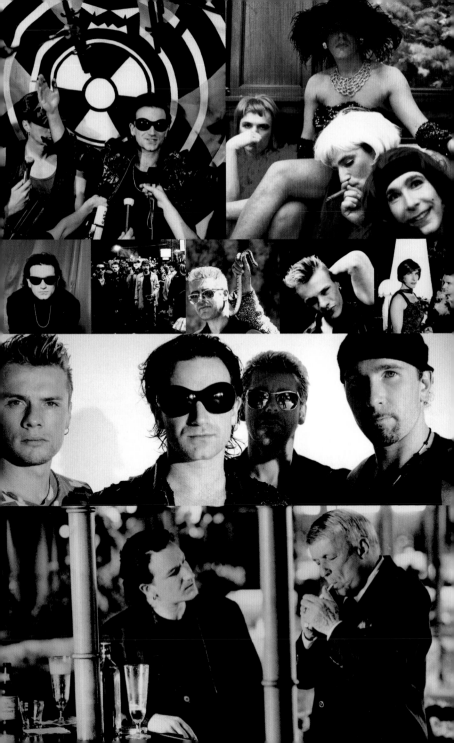

supposed to be shot. Simple idea. Bono walks in and sees his 'old mate' Frank at the bar. Frank was incredibly charming and smart and witty and everything you would expect him to be but it was obvious that he was starting to suffer from some kind of lapses of his full grasp of reality. You would suddenly see this look of confusion cross his face as he lost his bearings for a second. Everything went fine until Kevin, our director, asked Frank to do it again.

BONO: So Kevin made me wait outside, cleared the room and left Frank standing at the bar, waiting for me. This was not a good idea, because Frank started to get agitated. He wasn't sure what exactly was going on. He may have had a bit of a panic attack. I was waiting outside the door when there was a sound of confusion and I overheard the great man shouting, 'George, Schlatter, get us out of here! What are we doing?' They tried to calm him down by telling him he was shooting a video with Bono. To which he replied, 'Sonny Bono? What am I making a video with him for?' He started to leave. They tried everything but they couldn't stop him. He'd had some kind of short-term memory loss. His people were all very embarrassed. My people were all very embarrassed that I wasn't Sonny Bono!

EDGE: I like to think he was just affronted by the very idea of being asked to do something a second time, because I imagine Frank was the kind of guy who didn't do second takes. He got it right the first time.

BONO: He called later on to apologize. He said, 'Listen, I don't like to do a lot of takes. And when I'm hanging around sometimes I just get uncomfortable.' So we got together and shot some footage in the back of his limousine. They put a camera in the front passenger seat and at the end of this long, white limousine the two of us were sitting there, chatting about Dean Martin, when he leaned over to me and said, 'Turn down the window.' I said, 'I beg your pardon?' He said, 'Turn down the window about an inch.' I just did what I was told and looked at him. He said, 'You look better like that.' He was lighting me. Old school Hollywood, key and fill. Amazing.

Afterwards we all went out for something to eat in a Mexican restaurant. His wife Barbara was there. She walked in wearing a beautiful red trouser suit, upon which Frank remarked, 'Jeez, Barbara, you look like a blood clot!' He was on great form, telling stories, drinking a giant tequila in a fishbowl-sized glass.

EDGE: I was sitting beside him and I watched as he picked up the blue napkin that was in front of him, stared at it, folded it up neatly and under his breath said, 'I remember when my eyes were that blue.' It was not for anyone else to hear, he was really kind of muttering to himself. And he put the blue napkin in his inside jacket pocket to keep.

BONO: I sang, unaccompanied, 'Two Shots of Happy, One Shot of Sad' and told him we'd written it specially for him. He seemed genuinely touched. He asked us back to his house, where a few more drinks were taken. There was a classic shtick going on between him and his barman, lines like 'Am I a boy or a man?' when the barman gave him half-measure. 'Make it worth my while to pick it up.' He was brilliant. We watched a movie in his screening room, where all the beautiful fittings were done in snow-white. The film wasn't very good and trying to keep up with Sinatra's intake had gone straight to my head and so I fell asleep. When I woke up, I had this extraordinary sense of dampness between my legs and thought the impossible. 'Oh, my God, could this really have happened? On the snow-white couch? It couldn't be! What a monumental defeat, Ireland versus Italy.' But I had just spilled my drink. Phew!

Frank was very generous. At some point in the evening he showed me some of his paintings and I commented upon one in particular. The next week, the painting arrived at my house. He sent me a beautiful Cartier platinum and sapphire Pasha (CK) watch, inscribed from Francis Albert to Bono. A very generous man. One of my favourite stories about him involves tipping. He apparently gave the biggest tips in the world. One night he gave a doorman a hundred bucks for just opening the door. The doorman hardly even reacted, which stopped Frank in his tracks. Frank looked back and said, 'Is that the biggest tip you ever got for opening a door?' To which the doorman replied, 'No, I've had bigger.' Frank, irritated, wants to know, 'Who would give you more than a hundred dollars for opening a door?' 'You gave me two hundred last week,' said the doorman. He was a mythic figure.

LARRY: By the time we got out to Australia, the tour had been going on for two years and people were really starting to go a little off the rails. I started to notice that Adam was drinking more and that he was drunk in the early afternoons. It never seemed to affect his gig, so no alarm bells were ringing. Adam was such a great drunk, he was great fun and not morose at all, at least not in public. It may have been different in private. It was only much later, when we talked about it, that I started to understand the demons he was fighting. But he was very discreet. On the face of it, he looked like he was just drinking a little too much and having a really good time.

EDGE: Being on the road is very hard. Being on the road for a long time is even harder. The most difficult thing is to have your own sense of space and identity within the touring community. It is a lifestyle that leaves you with little time to call your own but simultaneously it's quite lonely. People tend to take the opportunity to do something on their own when they can. I think in Adam's case, unfortunately, on that tour he got into a very self-destructive, private habit, which was all sorts of forms of indulgence and self-abuse in terms of alcohol and probably other substances and other activities. There had been a few episodes over the years when Adam would have a blow-out, although not before a gig so it was just seen as a way of blowing off some steam. It took us somewhat by surprise when it suddenly became a massive problem. I was a little blind-sided. I didn't notice him going down.

ADAM: Life was pretty chaotic. I don't really like that kind of intensity, I don't like that sort of activity, so whilst I was able to go along with it, I wasn't really in control, it would be fair to say. Every night was a party, but I don't think I felt much contentment or peace, that's for sure. I'd be fine during the day, I'd be fine for the gig but afterwards it was too easy to go out all night or just keep drinking in your room. I was beginning to realize that every time I drank, I couldn't really be sure of the result. And it always made the next day worse. So I decided to lay off and stop drinking during the final leg of the tour. We were filming the concerts in Sydney Football Stadium for the big tour video. It is still hard for me to actually figure out what happened. All I can say is that I remember the night before thinking, 'Mmm, it might be nice to have a glass of wine.' The next thing I remember it was about 7 o'clock in the evening of the next day and people were trying to wake me up and see if I could go down and do the gig. I don't really know what happened in the intervening time, other than that I'd been out for a bit and I'd gone through the mini bar in the room.

LARRY: The shows in Sydney were a big deal, David Mallet was the director and he had 25 cameras set up. Adam didn't turn up for the sound-check. He was in his room and he wasn't coming out. I called him on the telephone and eventually got through. I said, 'What's up?' He said, 'I can't do the gig.' I said, 'Look, you have to just get yourself together and come down to the venue and we'll talk about it.' But he just couldn't do it. In a million years that was the last thing I would have expected.

ADAM: I was so wobbly and shaky and emotionally all over the place, just in complete meltdown, there was no way I could stand on stage for two hours.

EDGE: Obviously the timing was drastic because it was the big video that we were going to release of the Zoo TV tour. There was a huge amount of our own cash riding on this. I think it was probably the pressure that tipped him over the line. He was in a terrible state but if you were to look at the weight of responsibilities that Adam was carrying versus, say, Bono, or even me, it would have been pretty low. But everyone deals with stress and pressure in a different way. This was the straw that broke the camel's back for Adam, the culmination of the tour and this TV show.

LARRY: It was the first time that somebody hadn't turned up for a show. We were in shock but we had no time to stop and take it in, we just had to scramble and we rehearsed with Adam's bass technician Stuart Morgan during sound-check. Stuart had been working with Adam for two years and knew the parts. He ended up doing the gig.

EDGE: We took the decision not to cancel the TV event but to use a stand-in. It was a tough decision but I think it was the right one. I think it helped Adam put everything in context. Because although he missed that show he could actually hear it in the distance, and for the first time he heard the band play without him. I think that brought everything into focus in a fairly major way for him.

ADAM: It was an extraordinarily hard thing to face up to. In the big picture, missing a gig is not necessarily the worst offence in your life but, for me, it was the first time as a member of U2 that I had really let my band mates down for whatever reason. And this wasn't sickness or personal tragedy, this was self-inflicted. It appeared to be out of my control, which was very scary. Even the fact that 12 hours later I was still kind of shaky and fucked up, that wasn't good. Plus the fact that the band had a lot riding on it. It was a spectacular calamity. That gig was filmed but I have never watched it, I don't really want to go there. It was a watershed moment. It was abundantly clear that I had a problem with alcohol. I understood this was for real, it was serious, and I needed to get myself together.

LARRY: There was a meeting with Adam. We said, 'Let's just finish out the tour and deal with this when it's over.' Adam was as freaked as we were. I think he got himself into a state and just couldn't find his way through it. There was a lot of sympathy but we were very clear about what we needed him to do. We are a band and we need each other. It wasn't going to be possible to continue like this. Some harsh words were spoken.

ADAM: They were pretty concerned and a bit pissed off as well. But they supported me in the decision that I made at that time, which was to say to them that I had a problem with alcohol. It was then that I officially stopped drinking.

BONO: Adam was a great person to be around but unhappy in himself, I suppose. We were playing at being rock stars, he was actually living that life. My feelings were not that he had let us down, more that he had let himself down. In a funny way, Adam is the most professional person. Not turning up for a gig would just be unthinkable for him. To have his guitar tech stand in for him was something that was going to take him a long time to recover from. Our first thoughts were for him: 'How are we going to get him through this?' He had bitten off more than he could chew and it bit him back.

PAUL: I suppose I might have seen it coming and tried to ignore it. But sometimes people come unstuck under pressure. I certainly wouldn't want to condemn him for it. It was terrifying at the time because we had this enormous film production and to do those video specials you really need to shoot them over two days to get something worthwhile. What this effectively meant was we only got one day. It was a disappointment and a wake-up call. And I'm no angel, but I don't have to go on stage. There are people who drink in the band and there are people who don't particularly drink in the band. Adam certainly doesn't any more. I think as we all get older we start to realize how dangerous it can be.

BONO: We lost the first night's filming because Adam wasn't there. So we had one night to get it and he was still in a bad way. But he looks amazing in the film and there is a real boldness to his playing, against the odds. I don't know how he kept it together. We all thought it might be the end. We didn't know if we wanted to go on if somebody was that unhappy. But the performance of 'One' defined what the night was about and maybe what the band is about. We are one, but we are not the same. We get to carry each other.

LARRY: The tour ended in Tokyo. People needed to let off steam and Tokyo was just the place. We slipped off into the underbelly of this incredible science-fiction city. Things went a little crazy.

EDGE: Tokyo felt like the capital of Zoo TV. It was as if everything we were playing around with and using as material for this exposition of the end of the 20th century was even more evident in Tokyo, a glittering hi-tech city of the future. Everyone got a bit giddy but that was good. It was the end of three years' work and there was a festive last week of school feel in the camp.

BONO: I had always loved being in Japan but I was now head over heels, I wanted to go out all the time. Of course, we often had a lot of Japanese carers to accompany us. But one night I slipped out the back entrance of a bar to avoid our security and took off in the company of Fighting Fintan Fitzgerald, our head of wardrobe. We were joined by another good friend of ours from the music world, who I didn't know at the time was battling with heroin addiction. The three of us went down side streets, alleyways, all in the pursuit of the perfect bar or club, to meet locals unencumbered by an entourage, to go exploring off the beaten track. We ended up in some girl's apartment, a small, traditional Japanese place, drinking some beers and chit-chatting. Some people started smoking a spliff and, though I don't smoke spliffs, I did know that in Japan it was a ten-year prison sentence for doing so. So I enquired of our hosts if this was a sensible thing to be doing. It was explained to me that the police did not come here. This was a house run by the Yakuza, the Japanese mafia. 'Well, that's great,' I thought to myself. 'I really feel safe now!' I guess our friend had led us back to this place to score some dope. I knew there was something untoward going on. This wasn't harmless fun but I was tired and fell asleep on a bunch of coats. When I woke up I thought my drink had been spiked. I thought I was hallucinating. There was a six-foot boa constrictor crawling up my leg. I completely froze. I didn't know what to do until I heard Fighting Fintan Fitzgerald saying, 'Don't panic. My mother used to work in a zoo!' He picked up the snake and put it round his neck. Fintan knew no fear but the same could not be said of the snake. There was the sound of a glass of water being poured onto the ground and the cry went up from our brave wardrobe man, 'It's pissed all over me!'. It turns out snakes take a pee if they're disturbed. One of the girls performed in some kind of burlesque revue and the snake was part of her act. To use the old cliché, we made our excuses and left.

LARRY: I went out every night and stayed out all night, which was something I had never done before and haven't done since. We were hanging out, exploring the underbelly of a city. I also went off on my own, which I hadn't done before either. I found myself in all kinds of weird and wonderful situations, and though I avoided getting into serious trouble I did get into some. I had become so used to being away from home, so caught up in U2 world, the idea of coming back to any form of normality was making me nervous. I didn't know if I was ready to go back to Dublin and sleep in my own bed and get up and deal with my family and friends. Normal life looked alien to me.

BONO: Jimmy Iovine used to say, 'Rock stardom is wasted on you.' But I think we got quite good at it in the Nineties, although it was always a part-time job. We were play-acting but it's fair to say it was getting harder and harder to get those goggles off. There was a certain freedom in just letting people down.

PAUL: Everyone gets a little nutty for quite some time after the end of a tour. You have physiological reactions that continue for months afterwards. Around about 9 o'clock you suddenly start going, 'Where's the show? Where's the show?' When you come off a tour, you should be given the kind of warning a doctor gives his patient after prescribing Valium: Don't take any important decisions or drive a car for a while.

LARRY: I remember Edge saying, 'Hey Larry, how about you and me buy a bus and travel around America and just do it for another year?' I looked at him and for a split second thought, 'Oh yeah.' Because the alternative seemed too hard. Thankfully, good sense prevailed. We went home.

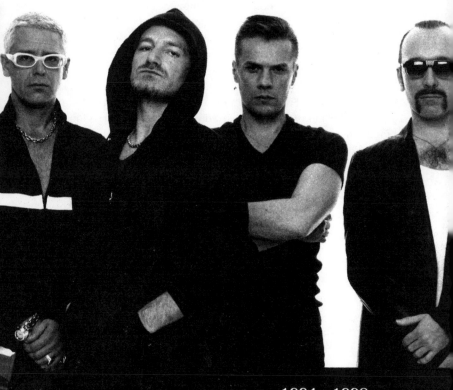

1994 - 1998

SOME **DAYS** ARE
BETTER
THAN OTHERS

Bono

1994 WAS THE START OF THE BIG THAW. THE STRAIN OF RISKING BANKRUPTCY ON A NIGHTLY BASIS TO PUT ON ZOO TV HAD PUSHED OUR CREATIVE SELVES TO THE LIMIT, TRYING TO MAKE ALBUMS IN THE MIDDLE OF A TOUR, HAD LEFT US EMPTY AND EXHAUSTED.

When I came home from tour, I realized I had no routine in my life at all, so I called Willie Williams, our show designer and one of our closest friends, and asked did he know any routines that I could use. He knew what I meant.

He said, 'I like going to the café in the morning and reading a newspaper.' I said, 'Really? What's that like?' He said, 'Well, you pick a café that you kind of like and get to know people and they say hello to you and nod in the morning and you order your cup of tea and read your newspaper.' I said, 'That sounds great. I'm going to try that. Any other ones?' He said, 'Let's see. On a Monday you could write letters or respond to them.' Wow, this is fantastic! Sundays he had a church that he liked to go to. He said, 'You meet people after church and sometimes you go back to their house.' 'No way!' I said. 'OK, Sundays I'm going to do that.' That began the tradition of the Sunday lunch chez Bono and Ali. Our house is like a train station on Sundays. People come and go and we eat and drink wine. It was relearning how to live as civilians. The South of France played a huge role in teaching us how to relax.

EDGE: Early in the Nineties, Bono hatched this idea that the band would try and buy a huge house in France and create a small compound with enough space for us all to spend time there together. An estate agent called to say he had found a fantastic place right on the sea and we all went down to view it. Adam and Larry took one look and said they thought the whole idea was completely mad. But at that point I was on my own, I'd moved out of the family home and it felt like something that had potential to be the next phase of life. So Bono and myself bought this house together and started making plans to renovate, because it was in such bad condition. We are only just finishing it, over fifteen years later. It's two houses on a single piece of land

and we swap houses every couple of weeks. When I tell people 'I go on holidays with Bono' they look at me a little funny but it has actually worked out really well. We bought it in 1992, it was at least another year before one of the houses was habitable and we spent a lot of time there during 1994. That was our summer of love, as Bono calls it. We had a rare old time.

BONO: They're so respectful of privacy in the South of France. I could go down to the village and get the bread in the mornings, play with the kids, swim in the sea, nobody would bother me. At nights, people would come over, we'd eat pasta and listen to music. There'd be house parties, lots of dancing. The Big Girls (supermodels) were around, they were now better friends with Ali than me. It was striking how much in charge of their own lives these women were. Their power is that no one hears them speak – they're like silent movie stars.

I became very close to Michael Hutchence, who was dating Helena. He was great fun to hang out with, you could be silly or serious with him. We'd be sitting at the table from one o'clock in the afternoon to one o'clock in the morning, talking and laughing. Occasionally Michael and myself might run amok, we slept on a few beaches coming home from the clubs in Cannes but it rarely got completely out of hand because there were young kids around. It was just a very warm time. There was one particular place on the beach front called The Morea, with live salsa music and calypso, owned by a fantastic family who had a completely unique approach to commerce: they wouldn't let us pay for anything, ever. We used to bring gifts and barter with them. Occasionally the joint would turn into a scene from an Elvis movie, because one of us would misjudge our drink and we'd end up on stage and have the whole beach singing along. It wasn't completely rarefied because our friends from Dublin were with us. It was as if we'd set up our own little republic in the midst of the French one.

The thing I particularly remember from this period was that Edge and myself fell back in love with music. We listened to it day and night, everything that was new, everything that was fresh.

EDGE: It was a lost weekend that went on for a year. It was a time to reconnect with family and friends and live a little bit, having been so focused on the band for so long. It was so much fun and it gave us a chance to enjoy music and really listen to it and get thrilled again. There was a lot of great stuff happening right then, amazing dance music, the Chemical Brothers, Leftfield, Underworld, the Britpop scene was taking off, the whole Oasis phenomenon was unfolding. I was able to approach those records as a pure fan and I loved them.

LARRY: I was having a slightly different kind of a summer. I was restless in Dublin. I needed to get away, figure a few things out. I decided to go to New York.

ADAM: It was my idea to relocate to New York for the year off and start a new life as a non-drinker, which is commonly known as 'doing the geographic'. It was surprisingly easy to stop but it was difficult to stay stopped. I ended up smoking a lot of marijuana, which is not exactly a solution. It stops you getting drunk but it stops you doing just about anything else.

Having made the decision to go to New York, Larry and I both individually arrived at the conclusion that it was an opportunity to improve ourselves and do different things of a musical nature. Larry decided that he wanted to figure out programming and between us we bought a little studio set-up. The idea was that we would get more user experience, although I have to say I still don't really operate recording equipment any better than I could in the past. I have come to the conclusion that there are two parts of the brain, one is creative and the other practical and I may be sadly deficient in the latter. I actually took singing lessons, because I was interested in whether I could find my voice, although it proved somewhat elusive. Through the course of the singing lessons I met a bass guitar teacher, a guy called Patrick Pfeiffer who has written a book called *Bass Playing for Dummies*. It's a good book and I'm going to try and pay more attention to it.

I wanted to know how to apply the rules of scales and different time signatures. Patrick was really good at making it simple and spelling it out but in the end I realized that everything he was teaching me I was already doing instinctively. It was a regime for a session musician who wanted to be able to go into any musical situation and do the gig, which is not particularly relevant to the rather unique way U2 operate.

LARRY: I hooked up with David Beal, a session drummer and programmer who ran a small studio downtown. He took me through drum machines, sequencers and the basic operation of a studio. I also took the opportunity to see Gary Chaffee, a drum doctor in Boston. There were things about my playing I wasn't happy with. I was also feeling the wear and tear of two years on the road, my back was sore, so were my hands. Gary specialized in taking broken drummers and retraining them to play better and do less damage to themselves. Adam and I did some playing together and we reworked the theme music for the first *Mission Impossible* movie. Recording and producing that track was the highlight of my time in New York.

EDGE: We were interested in the idea of getting warmed up to make a U2 album by taking on a more experimental project that would throw us into new areas that might inform our own work. I did that with the soundtrack album before *The Joshua Tree* and Bono and I had done *Clockwork Orange* before *Achtung Baby*. So we talked to Brian Eno about doing a film soundtrack.

PAUL: There has always been a bit of tension between U2 and Brian Eno, because Brian regards himself as a creative force. I think he finds it frustrating that within the parameters we've set, he is not a writer, he is one of the producers and he comes into the studio with all that he's got, his talent as a musician, his judgement, his voice. And if Brian whistles something and it ends up on the record, then that is what producers are supposed to do. For that they get a fee and percentage points, they participate in the success of the record just as the artist does. The question of songwriting credits and royalties has been debated over the years. We have a collaborative music-making process that's been established from the beginning and I couldn't possibility permit a situation where Brian Eno was making more than a member of U2. Brian is a genius but so are the band. I would think that it's a privilege and an education to work with U2 as a producer. It was against this background that U2 decided to have a go at making a record with Brian as a full partner. It wouldn't be a U2 record, it would be a side project.

BONO: We saw Brian as a great catalyst but the thought did strike us that it would be nice to formally write with him, the way he had with Talking Heads and David Bowie. We asked Paul to find us a movie project to work on. At one stage it was going to be the soundtrack for Peter Greenaway's *The Pillow Book*, a great avant-garde film set in Japan.

EDGE: *The Pillow Book* project fell through and by the time we were in the middle of making the record there was still no movie. We were quite excited about what we were doing, so at that point Brian said, 'The movie is just a vehicle to give us something to work off. So let's continue and we'll just make soundtracks for imaginary films.'

BONO: Brian even came up with film titles and rough plot-lines. We didn't want people to get confused and think it was a U2 album, so we formed another group. That became *Original Soundtracks 1* by Passengers. Brian thought of the group name, I still like it.

ADAM: Larry and I arrived back for those sessions. And instead of not having touched an instrument for six months, which would have been a possibility, we were already up to speed and went into those sessions very confidently.

I MET A BASS GUITAR TEACHER, A GUY CALLED PATRICK PFEIFFER WHO HAS WRITTEN A BOOK CALLED *BASS PLAYING FOR DUMMIES*. IT'S A GOOD BOOK AND I'M GOING TO TRY AND PAY MORE ATTENTION TO IT. ADAM

They were very free-form, not unlike jazz. I suppose I had enough musical knowledge to be able to feel relatively comfortable in that environment. The idea was to make a record that would define itself. Brian had always felt we were good at improvising and wanted to work in a way where there was no pressure to produce formally constructed radio-friendly songs. We had videos of films we like and we played to them for a couple of weeks. Brian then selected material that was cut down and became the basis of further sessions the following year. It was a very easy record.

PAUL: There were some fairly heated exchanges in the course of making it. Brian had a slightly different idea of what they were doing and found it frustrating that the band did not take it quite as seriously as him and would turn up to sessions late. It was supposed to be a fun, relaxed project, with no big deadline but in the end it probably didn't work out the way everyone intended. Larry is not a big fan of that record, which he has made abundantly clear.

LARRY: It was a little self-indulgent. I thought we might be pushing our audience too far. I think there are some great songs and a couple of interesting ideas on that record but, for me, it didn't go anywhere.

EDGE: I love it, because it's so different to our normal work. I've always had an interest in more experimental music. It doesn't necessarily fit into a conventional envelope of songwriting. I think the moods of the pieces are very strong, the themes are effective. A lot of film-makers and dance companies have made use of the music. It suits applications where you don't want too much foreground, you want music with a certain transparency, where it really is a mood setting.

BONO: There are some beauties on there. 'Your Blue Room' is one of my favourite songs, which was actually used in the Michelangelo Antonioni and Wim Wenders film *Beyond The Clouds*. The song is based on the idea that sex is a conversation of sorts. On one level it's purely carnal but on another it's a prayer. It's an incredible thing to say to your lover or your maker: 'Your instructions, whatever the direction.' 'Miss Sarajevo' is another song that has got to be right up there. That was a trip, to write a libretto for a voice like Pavarotti's. To get into the right frame for that I was impersonating my father singing in the bath impersonating Pavarotti.

He had been asking for a song. In fact, asking is an understatement. He had been crank-calling the house. He told me that if I didn't write him a song, God would be very cross. And when I protested that we were in the middle of our own album, he would say, 'I am going to speak to God to speak to you. It's Easter. When I next call you, you will have a song.' One of the great emotional arm-wrestlers of the age.

The song was our response to the surreal acts of defiance that had taken place during the siege of Sarajevo. One woman refused to go to the shelter and used to play the piano when they were being bombarded. Another woman organized a beauty contest. 'We will fight them with our lipstick and heels,' she said. All the most beautiful girls in Sarajevo walked out on stage with sashes saying 'Do they really want to kill us?'. It was pure Dada and it deserved to be celebrated in song.

'Miss Sarajevo' was premièred at the annual Pavarotti and Friends concert in Modena, Italy on 12 September 1995. Edge and I brought our parents along, who were big opera fans. Pavarotti picked us up from the runway of the airport in a white Mercedes. We drove fifteen miles to his house, through the gates, up a hill, round a corner, round a bend, past the house and up to a table. He got out and bellowed, 'Pasta!' A beautiful woman walked out with the food and we sat down and ate. It is at the table that friendships are really made. He is an extraordinary individual, big in everyway – big heart, big voice, big girth, big appetite.

EDGE: Backstage was amazing, because instead of the usual rock 'n' roll crew, there was Princess Diana and various dignitaries and Italian politicians. And, in the midst of it all, Bob Hewson and my mum and dad, all big opera fans and all singers too. That was the occasion of my dad's legendary duet with Pavarotti. It was Brian's wife, Anthea's birthday and so we asked Pavarotti to sing 'Happy Birthday' to her, which he very graciously agreed to. My dad joined in at the end, which I thought was funny at the time. Later, when I started to hear the dinner party story of the great duet between my dad and Pavarotti, I realized what was behind it. But my dad is a tenor and he takes it quite seriously. It was a big moment for him, even if it was only 'Happy Birthday'.

BONO: Edge came up and asked me, 'Would your father like to meet the Princess of Wales?' Edge's family are Welsh, of course, and they were dying to meet her. And I knew the answer, actually, but I asked anyway. My dad just looked at me. He said, 'Fuck off! That's like asking me do I want to meet the winner of the Lotto!' And off he went: 'What has the Royal Family ever done for anybody? They were born into all this wealth and power!' He was a bit of a Republican and the whole thing went off, and I just laughed and left it there. But we were in the dressing-room and a short while later Princess Diana walked in. She was beautiful, in a canary yellow dress, and she put out her hand to my father and he put out his and she said, 'How do you do?' And he went, 'Oh! Very pleased to meet you!' And I swear, 600 years of history disappeared. 'Very, very nice woman,' he said as she went out. 'Gorgeous girl!'

LARRY: When I went to New York in 1994, I needed to reassess where I was going. By the time I came back, Ann and I had decided to try and start a family. We'd been together since our teens. It was time. And so my first son was born in October 1995. Three weeks later, I was in hospital having surgery on my back. I had been carrying an injury since *The Joshua Tree* tour but it had been getting worse and required urgent attention. The band started working with Howie B., a DJ and producer who had worked with us on Passengers. They were playing to drum machines and loops and records that Howie was mixing in the studio. I must confess I was upset when they started without me, because there are things that happen early on in a record, key decisions are made. Eno actually sent a note to the other band members asking them to wait. But, for whatever reason, they were very keen to get started.

EDGE: The thinking was that we were going to further experiment with the notion of what a band was all about and find new ways to write songs, accepting the influence and aesthetics of dance music. We were in an experimental frame of mind, so because Larry wasn't really in a position to play with us we thought, 'Let's just start with Howie mixing drum beats and see where that gets us.'

ADAM: Club music was absolutely dominating everyone's musical taste at that stage. Bono and Edge had bought and revamped The Clarence Hotel in Dublin and opened a nightclub beneath called The Kitchen. We felt there was some kind of connection between what we did and what was happening in the clubs, a couple of our tracks had been big remix hits, notably 'Even Better Than The Real Thing' and 'Lemon'. We wanted to make a record that fused rock and pop with the tightness you could get with sequencing and rhythm loops. So much club music is instrumental and we thought if you could get something that hard and tough and atmospheric with great melodic vocals the

WE WANTED TO MAKE SOMETHING THAT REFLECTED THE LIFE WE WERE LIVING, THAT HAD SOME OF THE JOY OF FAMILY AND THE HEADINESS OF LATE NIGHTS AND BRIGHT LIGHTS. BUT JOY IS A VERY HARD THING TO CONJURE AND HAPPINESS WON'T DO. BONO

result could be really amazing. Brian wasn't particularly interested in making those kind of records and so he chose not to get involved but Flood was a good collaborator, who had some experience in this area with Depeche Mode. Howie B. was a great musical engineer and sonically very progressive. He establishes very creative energy in the room and acts as an inspiring catalyst. He's not necessarily a guy who knows how to get tunes that radio will play but that's not really his job. And Nellee Hooper was originally a part of that production team, a hugely talented British producer who had made amazing records with Massive Attack and Bjork and helped us put together 'Hold Me, Thrill Me, Kiss Me' for the *Batman Returns* movie soundtrack. It was quite a gang of people and it can be hard to accommodate that many different views.

BONO: We were really enjoying our lives and maybe slowly, subtly, forgetting how hard you have to work to make a great record. It's like catching lightning. It takes a relentless pursuit of it. It takes spontaneity. It takes attrition. It takes hours and hours of relentless focus. And you can forget that if you've not been doing it for a while.

ADAM: We worked in our new studio, which we had developed from an old warehouse building on Hanover Quay in Dublin. It was designed more as a rehearsal space and music workshop than state-of-the-art studio. It was rough and ready.

BONO: There was confusion about who was producing it. Howie had an indomitable spirit and was always in good form. You just had to laugh around him, he was so sharp. Nellee Hooper was bright, funny and very well dressed. He arrived on the first day of the sessions with a beautiful striped orange and yellow Charvet shirt for me and a Peter Blake lithograph for the studio wall. We converted a van into our own Disco Bus, fixed it up with big bass woofers, speakers and microphone and we would go out clubbing *en famille*. We wanted to make something that reflected the life we were living, that had some of the joy of family and the headiness of late nights and bright lights. But joy is a very hard thing to conjure and happiness won't do. We just couldn't get the fun onto the album. The songs weren't good enough. The themes were there. Some of the melodies were there. But it couldn't seem to get airborne. I think those sessions might have caught us just at the end of that arc of fun and frolics. We were probably starting to re-enter earth's atmosphere and the lyrics were beginning to bring dark colours to the canvas. Nellee was decisive: 'Put me in charge and I'll go down with the ship. If you don't, I won't,' he shouted as he jumped overboard. Flood had more stamina than he should have and stayed on.

EDGE: The great synthesis between songwriting and dance didn't happen. It was like mixing oil and water. The two approaches were actually pulling us in opposing directions. In some ways the earliest improvisations that we were doing with Howie were the best: fresh, different and very exciting. But when the songs started to emerge from the mist, we missed the personality of the band. The songs were resting on drum machine beats and sequenced bass and had a little bit of a sterile quality. What makes a great U2 record is the sense of four personalities working in accord, in a particular moment in time. So during the course of recording, we tried to change direction.

BONO: *Pop* is the sound of U2 trying to make an ode to club culture without using the tools of dance music, which were loops and drum machines and pro-tools. The rhythm section had objected. I thought we could have both, but they didn't really want any electronica. They rightfully pointed out that this wasn't what made us unique or extraordinary. I hate it when common sense gets in the way of a good concept. At one point, listening back to some very long and average jamming session, Nellie turned to me and said, 'This isn't *Thriller*, is it, Bono?' The thing to do would have been to have stopped, re-organize and continue with the songs at a higher level. But we didn't. And, worse than that, our manager talked us into that most heinous of crimes: booking the tour. Deadlines were looming ominously. *Pop* never had the chance to be properly finished. It is really the most expensive demo session in the history of music.

LARRY: I expected to be out of action for a while but I thought I would be able to go into the studio and work for a couple of hours every day for a few weeks to slowly build myself up. As it happens, I was back in the studio after three weeks, playing seven or eight hours a day, not great for my back, I needed a little more time to recover. But we were struggling with some of the material and for the project to move ahead I had to put a lot of time in. We were dismantling songs and restructuring them. I had to replay sampled loops that Howie had used without permission. I was scrambling to try and get fit and scrambling to get my parts completed for the songs.

BONO: *Pop* opens with 'Discotheque'. We wanted a setting for the album. 'Discotheque' is a riddle about love. Once you know that, it changes the way you hear the song. *You can reach but you can't grab it / You can't hold it, control it, you can't bag it.* One of my definitions of art is the discovery of beauty in unexpected places. Looking for the baby Jesus under the trash as I sing in 'Mofo'. This was really the theme of *Pop*: big subjects for the basement. But it is not enough to have a good lyric or a great idea. If the tune or the musical location aren't right then you might as well be standing on a soap box at Speakers' Corner.

EDGE: 'Do You Feel Loved' was a great thought that never really became a great song.

BONO: We wanted to make a sexy, groovy song. And we nearly did. The whispered voice in the verse doesn't quite take off. The truth is, I was in a bit of trouble. At first I thought it might have been the smokes. Rather stupidly, in my early thirties, I'd moved from smoking cigars on *Zoo TV* into smoking Camel cigarettes. But I don't think it was just that. I think I had damaged my voice.

PAUL: When I started managing the band, Adam and I smoked but none of the other three did. Now they all smoke except for Adam and me. Bono came to tobacco late in life. I was an ex-smoker by then and I remember saying to him, 'I can't believe you've started smoking. Aren't you worried that you'll damage your voice?' He said, 'That's the problem. I like what it's doing to my voice.' It was giving it a rougher timbre but it was subject to change. It was starting to come and go.

ADAM: Bono would have a few good days and then a few bad days. Sometimes his voice was there and it was great and other times it was raspy and gone for no apparent reason. Personally, I think the problem might have been the studio. We were quite close to a concrete factory and if you left something sitting out for a couple of days it would be covered in dust. I suspect that if you've got sensitive vocal cords, concrete dust is probably not a great thing for them.

EDGE: 'Mofo' is really the dance aesthetic done fully. There is no pretence there about trying to maintain the band format, we're embracing the dance culture in that song and I think it works. Great lyric and great production. Maybe we should have had the confidence to make the album more clearly one thing.

BONO: It was as if my whole life was in that song. Electronic blues death rattle. It takes the cliché insult 'motherfucker' and turns it into something raw and confessional. It went through some bizarre titles, 'Mothership', 'Oedipussy'. It contains the most exposed moment in the hardest song on the record. It was extraordinary playing 'Mofo' live. The song would come to a shuddering halt and there I was, just speaking to my mother in front of fifty thousand of my closest friends. Some nights it would really surprise me what an emotional place I would get to. *Mother, am I still your son? You know, I've waited so long to hear you say so. Mother, you left and made me someone. Now I am still a child but no one tells me no.* It is a device you can imagine in theatre or cinema but you rarely see in songwriting, where you stop time and the character turns to the camera and explains himself. It's Hamlet's soliloquy but I never saw any ghosts. I'm looking forward to meeting my mother. I'm fully expecting to, in the proper place and time. I hope I have a backstage pass.

EDGE: The full-on sonic assault between dance and rock only lasted for three songs. By the time the album gets to 'If God Will Send His Angels' we were back on more familiar U2 territory. It is a nice tune but the chorus doesn't quite connect.

BONO: If we could sing and play like Prince that would have been top ten. It's a song of quiet anger at the way the world is and God's failure to intervene. A few people around me had experienced some awfulness that they just couldn't forgive God for. Personally, I don't look at the world as a place where God is in charge of everything that happens. I think it is up to us how much we let God into our lives. It's a world of wild and unexpected winds, earthquakes, and tsunamis where accidents can happen. I don't blame God for them. I think this is what happened when we threw God out of the garden, which is my own interpretation of what happened in Eden!

There are a lot of arguments with God on this record. He makes his biggest appearance on a U2 album since *October*. It should have been called *Shouting At God*. But it does not chart my loss of faith. I think even the most mediocre minds can figure out that if you're rattling on and on about how much you don't love somebody, it is evidence of passion. You can't be having an argument with God if you don't believe there is one.

There has been some very serious and scholarly work done on Pop Art and what it meant in the world. Someone described *Pop* as the death of God, suggesting that if there's no eternal, all we had left was the moment, the snapshot, the surface. So it is an album about the death of God. I'm just allowing myself to express those big questions. Even though they weren't particularly mine, I felt they were in the minds of a lot of people around me.

EDGE: 'Staring At The Sun' was another great tune that never became a great record, for whatever reason. I don't know why we didn't quite nail it. In the end, when we were playing it live, we just sang it with acoustic guitars and the song came through much better.

BONO: I think it nails a certain mood, where you actually don't want to know the truth because lies are more comforting.

EDGE: 'Last Night On Earth' had more of the band aesthetic. It was a good tune but is it up there with 'New Year's Day' or 'Sunday Bloody Sunday'? Obviously not, or we would still be playing it live.

BONO: The chorus came to me at the very end of the sessions on *Pop*, which were getting a little turgid and tiring. It was four o'clock in the morning of the last night in the studio. We had people mixing who hadn't been in bed for a week. Paul was waiting to take the tapes to New York to master the record. I started singing the line: *You've got to give it away*. Don't turn it into work was the message. Which was exactly what we were doing. We were supposed to be making an uplifting expression of what happens when rock 'n' roll meets club culture. Instead, it felt like a load of men on an oil rig in the middle of the North Sea. My voice was completely shot, which is why we put so much echo on it and Edge sang along with me to cover it up.

EDGE: 'Gone' is another one I had high hopes for but it always sounded better on acoustic guitar.

BONO: 'Gone' is a portrait of the young man as a rock star, trying to cut himself free from responsibilities and just enjoy the ride, the suit of lights, fame. *You change your name, well that's okay, it's necessary. And what you leave behind you don't miss anyway*. But I think what this album tells you is that some things you can't leave behind. That's really it. It's like the university professor who just can't dance. Deep down we weren't as shallow as we'd like.

ADAM: We had been in the studio, slugging it out over the record for months. I think we all needed a bit of fresh air. So we went to Miami and had a very

THE TRUTH IS, I WAS IN A BIT OF TROUBLE. AT FIRST I THOUGHT IT MIGHT HAVE BEEN THE SMOKES. BUT I DON'T THINK IT WAS JUST THAT. I THINK I HAD DAMAGED MY VOICE. BONO

good time. We went out. We met a lot of very serious people and some very superficial people and enjoyed both. We were introduced to the art of smoking cigars in a sort of late-night Mafia place, none of your spit 'n' sawdust here, this was shag-pile carpet all the way. We came, we saw, we conquered – it is all in the lyric of the song 'Miami'. Our eyes were wide open … some of the time!

BONO: Bill Graham died when we were in Miami, of a heart attack in May '96. He was only 44. That was a black moment in a very brightly coloured year. We came back for his funeral, and Edge, Gavin and I were pallbearers. Bill was the man who discovered us, really. The first writer to write about us and encourage us to be the band we were. He was more than a bit of a genius and his conversational style really suited my own, he was improvisational and took flights of fancy, you would be talking to him and disappear for an hour down mad tangents then somehow end up back where you started, seeing the world in a whole, new, different way. Bill was priceless.

LARRY: Bill was a real champion of U2 but he also criticized the band. You miss people like that, you could always trust his honesty and value his perspective. He had a big heart and a real feel for music. We could have used some of his advice on *Pop*, I think.

BONO: So many of the songs on *Pop* are almost but not quite there. 'The Playboy Mansion' was originally called 'Hymn to Mr Universe'. It was supposed to be a Pop Art anthem but its contemporary references work against it. Jokes about Michael Jackson and O.J. Simpson just aren't funny any more. The original lyric was much more emotional. I am not sure the best version ended up on the album. The same could be said of 'If You Wear That Velvet Dress'. It wanted to be a lounge classic. It ended up in an airport lounge as background noise.

'Please' was written with somebody in mind, who shall remain nameless. Some of U2's best songs are conversations, even if you don't know who's on the other end of the line. It's not an exact portrait, it's a certain kind of person you'd meet in middle-class Dublin suburbs, who are very sympathetic to the IRA paramilitaries and provide the intellectual support base for militant Republicanism. It's people who think ideas are more valuable than

SOME THINGS YOU CAN'T LEAVE BEHIND. IT'S LIKE THE UNIVERSITY PROFESSOR WHO JUST CAN'T DANCE. DEEP DOWN WE WEREN'T AS SHALLOW AS WE'D LIKE.

BONO

other people. *Love is hard and love is tough, but love is not what you're thinking of.* It is a song about terror really. Are there ever any excuses for it? *September, streets capsizing, spilling over, down the drains. Shards of glass just like rain* ... It was the Docklands bombing in London that it referred to and the breakdown of peace talks in Northern Ireland but after 9/11 it became impossible to sing. But the recording is a little unfocused, a little unclear, and didn't resolve. I'm not sure we've ever really done the song justice.

ADAM: The bass is in a different key to what Edge was doing and there was a lot of argument about which notes were in the key and which ones weren't. That's probably why it's so unresolved because it's straddling a couple of different keys without really committing to either. But sonically it's an amazing piece of music and the melody is fantastic.

LARRY: It is a great song but I don't feel it was finished. Like the rest of that album. A few extra weeks would have made all the difference to those songs.

ADAM: 'Wake Up Dead Man' was something Edge had from the *Zooropa* sessions. It was a big Gothic rock song, which didn't seem right for this album. Towards the end of the sessions we dusted it off, stripped it down and did a very sparse, electric version of it. It's a very hard-hitting song.

EDGE: That was really where I was at, at the time. That was one of the lower points of my spiritual faith, I would have to say. The 'wake up dead man' phrase was borrowed from a chain-gang song. I came up with first verse and chorus. Bono wrote the rest.

BONO: Really, this is in the tradition of the psalms of David, which offer an honest dialogue with God. I always wondered why was David so beloved of God? I think it was probably honesty. Because in a lot of the psalms he's really giving out: 'Where are you when you're needed? Call yourself God? Look, I'm surrounded by my enemies. You got me into this, get me out of here!' It's so direct. I think it's very important that people feel able to address God from whatever state they're in, whether that's devotion or anger. Both are present here.

EDGE: An album that starts with the bright promise of 'Discotheque' ends with the dark night of the soul that is 'Wake Up Dead Man'. That's the story of the making of the album, actually. It began as an escapist concept and then slowly, almost like the coming up of the dawn, the morning after, it ended with the realization that there is no escape and you're back to the grim realities. The first line of that song was written in my car at dawn as I arrived back in the driveway of my house in Dublin, about to walk into the house on my own. *Jesus help me, I'm alone in the world and a fucked-up world it is too.* That is really the truth of our lot. You are on your own, even in a crowd. Whatever you're doing, ultimately it's about you and your Maker.

BONO: We wanted to make a party record but we came in at the end of the party. The dancing was over and there were a load of broken bottles and young people sleeping under tables and the odd row in the garden between lovers who've imbibed too much. It starts in the 'Discotheque'. 'Do You Feel Loved' was our attempt to stay in the night but, very quickly, it's the morning after and what can only be described as the 'Mofo' of all hangovers. And it pretty much stays there.

The title of the album was a piece of deliberate disinformation, and a spectacular own goal as far as the rock audience were concerned, because they don't like pop. It is amazing what you can do with a title. It becomes the lens through which people see everything. This made you think about pop art and the moment. We'd been down there with *Achtung Baby*. It's the same argument but with a different person. *Achtung Baby* is a lovers' row. This is an argument with love itself, if you believe, as I do, that God is love. That is the continuum. We should have called the album U2 *Lighten Up*. That is a serious piece of work but you need to be at the peak of your powers, across a few disciplines, to hit the mark. It's not enough to write a great lyric, it's not enough to have a good idea or a great hook, lots of things have to come together and then you have to have the ability to discipline and screen. We should give this album to a re-mixer, go back to what was originally intended, so that 'Mofo' is on top of the stickiest groove with a proper plastic attack, 'Do You Feel Loved' is done as a liquid bass line hook that carries the intimacies whispered on top of it, 'If God Will Send His Angels' should be diamonds and pearls.

LARRY: The tour was booked before the album was finished, a pretty strange thing to do after being in the business as long as we have. Imagine having to schlep your arse around the world promoting a record you don't feel is finished. If we had two or three more months to work, we would have had a very different record. I would like someday to rework those songs and give them the attention and time that they deserve. It is a sort of U2ism, being unable to let go, and I am unable to let go of that record.

EDGE: We finished the album with Flood producing, scrambling to change the character of the record with neither the resources of time and in some ways material to do the job properly. It was a compromise project by the end. It was a crazy period trying to mix everything and finish recording and having production meetings about the upcoming tour. We were burning our candle at both ends and in the middle too. 'Discotheque' was chosen as the first single and the mixing went on for days. If you can't mix something, it generally means there's something wrong with it. We mastered in New York and Howie was adding effects to 'Discotheque' and I was recording extra backing vocals on top of the mix of 'The Playboy Mansion' in the mastering suite, which is completely unheard of. It's a sign of absolute madness.

PAUL: *Pop* is always described as the album that didn't get enough time to get finished. It got an awful lot of time, actually. I think it suffered from too many cooks. There were so many people with a hand in that record it wasn't surprising to me that it didn't come through as clearly as it might have done. And there were a lot of distractions. It was also the first time I started to think that the technology was getting out of control. When people are trying to choose between mix 26 and mix 27 of something, the sheer range of possibilities becomes a form of paralysis.

I didn't like the album title personally. I wasn't sure how ironic you could be in rock 'n' roll and I suspected that you couldn't be very ironic at all. Calling it *Pop* carried the wrong message. It wasn't a pop album, it was a modern album, but U2 were still a rock 'n' roll band.

EDGE: We did the 'Discotheque' video dressed up like The Village People. It was a joke. I had some misgivings because sometimes that kind of joke can backfire. I think we got away with it but it was another point of departure between the band and some of our US fans. I guess if you are a seventeen-year-old rock fan from the Midwest you just don't want to see your favourite band acting like disco troupers. I like to think we were dangerously ahead of our time. It is a great video, and has been copied many times since.

BONO: It was tricky getting Larry into the Village People gag. But he's comfortable and amused by his gay icon status and almost ready to laugh at all of this. The emphasis being on 'almost'.

LARRY: It was a bit of a struggle. And that's an understatement. I liked the name *Pop*, the cover and the packaging, even if it didn't bear any resemblance to the content of the record. We recognized that to continue as a band and to move forward we had to explore new ideas and follow new directions. You have to listen to what's going on around you. We were crossing into unknown territory and it felt like skating on thin ice but I think the instinct was right. I just don't think the execution was all it could have been.

PAUL: We had enormous ambitions for *Pop*. We wanted the production to beat *Zoo TV*. The band were also going to let the ticket price meet the market for the first time. We had parted company with our agents, so we would be touring in a different way. It was a painful process. We had to tell my very good friends Ian Flooks and Frank Barsalona, great men who had supported us from the beginning, that we no longer wanted to work with them. Not that we were getting another agent, we just weren't going to have an agent at all. We constructed a new paradigm for touring, where we would sell the whole tour to a single promoter in an arrangement where we shared the profits of the tour but they would underwrite costs and put up a guarantee. We invited bids based on the assumption that it would be an outdoor-only, stadium tour worldwide of about a hundred shows. We went with Michael Cohl and Arthur Fogel out of Toronto, who were at that time called TNA. Later on, they sold their company to Clear Channel, an enormous corporation who are in the radio business and lots of other businesses as well. Arthur stayed on to run Clear Channel Touring, who we now tour with. We are actually working with a lot of the same people, because most of the key promoters in America and Europe were bought by Clear Channel in the late Nineties. What it all means in business terms is very fundamental: if you are doing a very big tour with high overheads (and we were running *PopMart* at a daily overhead cost in excess of two hundred thousand dollars) then if one show falls out, or one promoter fails to pay, it can knock the figures for the whole tour sideways. In this new arrangement, we are no longer taking that risk ourselves. The whole world tour is a single transaction.

PopMart was a spectacular production. We were prepared to buy into whatever new technology we could lay our hands on. Willie Williams came up with this huge asymmetrical screen, which was developed by some geniuses in Montreal who made giant illuminated maps for railway networks and nuclear power plants. We had a mirrorball lemon spaceship, inside which the band would arrive on stage. The giant cocktail stick and yellow McDonald's-style arch were all supposed to be poking fun at the earnestness of rock 'n' roll and ironically mocking the superficiality of pop culture. We were having our cake and eating it, I suppose. All those things which were supposed to be funny went over the heads of a lot of the members of the audience, many of whom, to this day, probably think McDonald's sponsored the tour.

EDGE: We were really out of step with America and I think that became clear when the tour went on sale. This was the height of grunge, the Seattle heavy rock scene, which (apart from real innovators such as Nirvana) I must confess I found insufferably boring. We were exploring different musical ideas but what we didn't appreciate was how difficult it was going to be for anyone in America who loved rock music to get to where we had got to. Dance culture existed on a very underground level in the US. Musical genres don't really mix, because radio is extremely polarized. You've got R&B stations, rock stations, alternative stations, dance stations, whereas listening to UK or Irish radio, you will hear any combination of these different forms on a minute-by-minute basis. So, in terms of imagery and aesthetics, we were completely moving outside our American fan base. *Pop* is, in fact, a rock 'n' roll album but it's certainly not a grunge record. When we actually put the record out in March 1997 and put the tickets on sale, the cracks started to show. We weren't getting quite as much support as we were used to from radio. Reviews were mixed. The word was out that this wasn't our finest hour. To make matters worse, in an attempt to reach for even deeper levels of irony, we did a press conference to launch the *PopMart* tour in K-Mart in New York, a low-cost supermarket chain.

BONO: Very Andy Warhol of us, we thought. How clever, how funny. But our music is not at all disposable, common denominator, cookie-cutter or off the rack. Years later, some intelligent people I know were talking about how K-mart had sponsored our tour. People really didn't get the joke and thought this was U2 selling out.

EDGE: There was an obvious lack of excitement in America. I don't think we had to cancel shows but we certainly weren't looking at sell-outs. Suddenly we knew we were going to have to work our arses off to get the momentum back.

PAUL: We were fighting an uphill battle from the beginning. And when the first show took place in Las Vegas, it was severely under-rehearsed and a lot of the technology wasn't working properly.

ADAM: The technology for the screen (which involved 3D light diodes) was only just becoming available. We thought if you moved the LED's further apart you could double the size of the image, so it was a mathematical gamble that we could create the world's largest screen. It was 150 feet across and 50 feet high, ten times larger than the *Zoo TV* screen. There was a big Andy Warhol, Claes Oldenburg and Roy Lichtenstein influence on the staging, really playing with the notion of pop music and pop art and pop culture. The McDonald's arch was actually a way of supporting the PA. In a normal show you have the PA on either side of the stage, but here it was right in the middle. It was an elaborate piece of engineering that maintained the sense of fun, referencing the supermarket, shopping mall concept. The lemon was a tremendous toy, it would spin and open up and we'd walk out of it. It was a piece of crazy kitsch but a real show-stopper. And it literally did stop the show on one occasion, when it failed to open and we had to exit by the emergency escape hatch.

BONO: We thought, let's open in Las Vegas, with its monuments to consumerism, the most day-glo city on the planet. Of course, if we had thought about it for a bit longer, it might have occurred to us that this was also the one place in the world where a giant forty-foot lemon space ship would not look striking, it would look normal.

PAUL: As we were to somewhat belatedly discover, there is something called Desert Throat that professional Vegas singers know all about. Of course, you don't get it if you're in the cabaret room of the Golden Nugget with the air-conditioning turned on. You can get it if you're out in the football stadium in the desert. Bono got it.

BONO: It turns out I'm allergic to a desert weed. So I was out running in the desert, wondering why my voice problems were getting even worse.

ADAM: The actual screen arrived very late in the day. The costumes arrived the night before the show. We were still figuring out how to play the songs. This was material that had been generated in a studio environment and we really hadn't a clue how to make these songs work live. At the same time we were wrestling with a new PA concept that was above our heads, which produced all sorts of other physical sound problems, because you get weird resonances. We were trying to figure out how to use that stage. The first show was pretty bad. We really did stumble through the set.

BONO: You could almost hear our balloon being burst. It was not without humour. During 'Discotheque', having emerged from our mother ship and descended the stairs like four alien pop stars, Edge couldn't see his effects pedal through the smoke. 'I'm over here,' he shouted as Adam nearly walked off into the barrier.

YOU'VE BEEN FIGHTING WITH ALL KINDS OF FEARS JUST TO GET ON A STAGE SOMETIMES. YOU JUST DON'T THINK YOU HAVE IT IN YOU TO HIT THOSE NOTES, TO VISIT THE PLACES YOU NEED TO FOR THE SONGS TO COME ALIVE. BONO

PAUL: One of the problems about our business is that your first night, no matter where it takes place, is going to be reviewed by the world's press. You don't have the privilege they have in the theatre business of out-of-town try-outs or previews before the reviewers come. You just have to take it on the chin. I don't look back on that whole campaign with much pleasure. There was a lot of bad temper associated with the tour. As it got tougher, people's manners deteriorated.

ADAM: We spent a lot of that tour playing catch-up. We rehearsed whenever we could. We went into studios to remix and re-record songs for singles. We worked very hard to turn that around.

EDGE: It took us till about halfway through the tour to figure out how we were going to work the show. But as it came together it was truly amazing. We rearranged a lot of the songs. We dropped 'Do You Feel Loved' quite early on. 'Discotheque' got heavily restructured. 'Staring at the Sun' was stripped right down to just an acoustic duet. 'Gone' had a new guitar part. 'Velvet Dress' was higher and more direct. 'Mofo' became almost a heavy rock song. 'Miami' got much darker. The only ones that survived in what you might call their album arrangement were 'Please' (although that had a new ending) and 'Last Night On Earth'.

BONO: When you're playing something live, there's no time for whimsy. It either works or it doesn't. Your decision-making is made so much simpler, because you can tell when you're losing people. The studio often leaves people with their head up their arse. And that's the reason you need to go out on the road, so you can get it back down.

PAUL: We thought we had an ace to play whenever we needed it, which was 'Staring at The Sun'. We thought it was a solid gold number one hit. It clearly wasn't the song we thought it was. Plus we made a really terrible video. Chris Blackwell has said the problem was there was no procedure for the record company to tell U2 to stop. He certainly told us he didn't like it. I don't think I liked the video much but we gave ourselves no alternative other than to put it out. It wasn't a hit. The rest of that campaign was spent trying to drag that elusive hit out of the album that would revive its fortunes. We all loved 'Please' but that summer Edge, Howie and Bono spent weeks in a recording truck in a hotel car park in France between gigs trying to get a mix that would turn it into a hit single. They never did.

LARRY: Had the album been finished, we could have got away with doing K-Mart, having a bad opening show, having a lemon on stage, all those things. The difficulty was that the record wasn't able to support all these new, bright ideas.

BONO: When that show worked it was mindblowing. Its neon nature was a fabulous thing to behold at a time when rock music was so white bread and suburban angst. Oasis came out and played with us in San Francisco. They were in their full glory. Noel Gallagher had always been a great advocate for U2 if the music press was getting too precious. Oasis didn't really need to play support with U2, they were one of the biggest bands in the world. In fact, when I mentioned the gig, Noel said, 'You sure you want to support us?' They were funny. They got the big S4 speakers at the side of the stage turned around so that they could get the full hit of the sound system. They just loved it. I don't think they were remotely interested or concerned if anyone loved them back, which was very endearing.

PAUL: There was an accident at that gig, when a piece of the rigging chain fell on the stage beside Bonehead, the Oasis guitarist. We would have found out how bony his head was if it had been a couple of feet closer.

EDGE: After the show, we went out for the night with Oasis. We were talking about songs and Noel, not for the first time, was saying how much he loved 'One'. Lo and behold, the song came on the radio at that very moment. Without any hint of embarrassment, everybody started singing, Noel and Liam and Bono and I, *We are one, but we are not the same.* That was one of those legendary nights. We ended up until dawn at Tosca's, a very funky little café bar that had stayed open for us. Bono stood on the bar and sang operatic arias. Oasis legged it before us. So Bono, not slow to pick up on an implied victory, took it as U2 seeing off the Oasis challenge in the drinking Olympics.

BONO: I remember watching the sun come up over the San Francisco Golden Gate bridge. When it goes off, a night like that is hard to come down from. So you stay up because you can't go to bed, your pulse rate is too high. You've been fighting with all kinds of fears just to get on a stage sometimes.

You just don't think you have it in you to hit those notes, to visit the places you need to for the songs to come alive. I feel sick with nerves, on occasion. But when you've finished and it's come good, there is an easy laughter amongst everybody and a sense of camaraderie that can create the best nights of your life. The truth is, I can't go out unless we've got two days off after a show because of my voice. Edge can go out. He's a dark horse. He probably goes out more than anyone knows. He just wouldn't tell you.

EDGE: I love dancing. I got into it in the early Nineties, Berlin period. When we are on tour, it was one of the fun things to do, find a great club, generally with Fighting Fintan Fitzgerald, who picked up his nickname because after a few drinks he was just dying to find someone who he could have a row with. Anton Corbijn is also a bit of a mover and shaker on the dance floor. And Morleigh is a professional dancer. So if we ended up out together, we'd have a great time.

There were some great nights on *PopMart*. But there were some I would like to wipe from my memory. It's a bit of sobering experience to play to a half-full stadium ... or less! Certain problems you can ride out with bluster and bluff but there's no way of bluffing your way out of that, it's there for everyone to see. The worst of all was Tampa Florida, 20,000 people in a stadium built for 75,000. The deep South was particularly bad for the tour, because that is heavy rock territory. Some critics were complaining that U2 had gone disco and to a lot of Americans during that period disco was the enemy. We had the same problem in Germany. The European dates were fantastic, 91,000 people on two sold-out nights in Rotterdam on the opening shows. And then we got to Cologne and there's 29,000 people in a 60,000-capacity stadium. Obviously, 29,000 is a lot of people but it doesn't look like it when they all crowd down the front and the stadium seats are empty. Germany actually does have a huge dance movement but the idea of a rock band being influenced by the dance movement was against the law as far as a lot of German fans were concerned.

ADAM: The album had done better in Europe, possibly because people understood the sonic territory better. We had some great shows.

EDGE: Having said to our friends in Sarajevo 'we shall return!', like General MacArthur to the Philippines, when it came time to plan the *PopMart* tour we insisted that we play Sarajevo. The war was really only coming to an end as we were putting the plans in place. There was still a lot of ethnic tension, although it was starting to stabilize. So a show was put into the schedule and we took the financial hit of going there. It meant driving all the equipment through war-torn

Bosnia. The crew, particularly the truck drivers and coach drivers, did a very heroic thing in getting the equipment to the stadium. And when the first trucks arrived, they were cheered as they entered Sarajevo. It was almost like a symbolic liberation for a lot of those people of Sarajevo, because it was the first real sign that some semblance of normality had returned.

LARRY: There were hundreds of NATO peace-keeping soldiers everywhere. The stadium was old and battered. We were led down into a very dark, underground concrete bunker, which was now our dressing-room. The atmosphere was weird. It turned out that the stadium had been used as a morgue during the siege. On either side of the stadium there were graveyards, including a huge children's graveyard. As the day went on we were hearing stories about this place and it just became more and more horrifying.

Showtime arrived and we went out on stage. There were hundreds of soldiers on the left side of the stadium. The rest of the crowd was made up of Croats and Serbs who had travelled to the show on trains that hadn't run since the start of the war. People travelled from all over the region to see the gig. These people were killing each other only a year before. Here they were together at a U2 gig. What an amazing thing.

EDGE: Unfortunately, on the morning of the concert, Bono woke up without a voice. I don't know if it was laryngitis or just the stress of the previous couple of months of touring. Cancelling was out of the question, so the concert went ahead and I have to say that it didn't really matter that our lead singer was under the weather because every member of the audience seemed to join in on every song. There was a mass chorus for the whole concert.

LARRY: The crowd had to sing for Bono, so it was a very emotional night. At the end of the show the audience didn't leave. They turned around and faced all the peace-keepers and started applauding. It was a moment I will never forget.

BONO: The next day, there was an editorial in the newspaper saying 'Today was the day the siege of Sarajevo ended'. Even still, people talk about the war as lasting from the end of the Winter Olympics to the U2 concert. The amusing thing was that for all the talk of achievement in bringing this giant pop spectacle to the beleaguered city, not one person I spoke to mentioned the drive-in movie screen or the mirrorball space ship. I'm not sure we were as big a part of the show as we thought. I think the show was really about the city of Sarajevo. And at the end they weren't just applauding us or the UN peace-keepers, they were kind of applauding themselves for getting through it.

LARRY: We went back to our hotel, the Holiday Inn where reporters had stayed during the siege. It had been shelled and part of the hotel was missing. I was in a room with mortar shrapnel embedded in the walls and bits of the floor missing. Nothing could have prepared me for this.

EDGE: We were there for a day or so, wandering around the city, seeing the devastation. Being in the place that we'd seen so many times on TV really brought home a different sense of the horrors that must have occurred during the siege. There was a real sense that another potential genocide had been narrowly averted, albeit a little late in the day and not without a lot of casualties. But Sarajevo was still standing.

LARRY: I went for a walk with the Bosnian Ambassador to the UN, Mohammed Sacirbey, who'd helped arrange our gig. He brought me to all these areas that I'd read about, where people had been queuing for bread early in the morning and been picked off by snipers up in the mountains, places where rocket-propelled grenades had been fired into crowds of people. On every footpath, where there were craters and marks from explosive devices going off, they were filled in with red concrete, representing all the death and destruction these people had endured. It had an incredible impact on me, being confronted so graphically with man's inhumanity to his fellow-man but also contemplating the qualities of ordinary heroism and sense of community it must have taken to survive.

BONO: I've been a few times to Sarajevo. I was made a Citizen of Bosnia for my support of their cause during the war, which is about the biggest honour I've ever been given. I was introduced to President Izetbegovic, who lived in very humble lodgings at the top of an apartment block. There was a bicycle outside the door. He was a scholar who had written some important books. A religious man without being a zealot. We took off our shoes, and he and his wife brought us into their house. They made a gift to Ali of a beautiful silk scarf with little gold threads in it, and made us tea. It was a very special time. He talked about the siege and the everyday acts of heroism and the cruelty of the targets chosen by the invading army. Sarajevo was home to one of the great libraries in the civilized world, housing lots of priceless Islamic, Christian and Jewish manuscripts. He told us, with tears in his eyes, that days after it was fire-bombed words were falling through the sky, falling on people's heads, falling on their hands, falling into prams as women pushed them down the streets, falling into people's cups of tea, falling in front of them as they walked the cobbled streets, words raining down days later, rare pages and not-yet-petrified pieces of vellum. It was a very moving story. I visited the ruins later.

EDGE: My first child with Morleigh was born during *PopMart* on 1 October, 1997. Morleigh was in Los Angeles at the end of her pregnancy. We had a month-long break in the tour and I was set to arrive ten days before her due date. Unfortunately, babies being no respecter of tour schedules, she went into labour while I was in transit between Israel and LA. I arrived a few hours after Sian was born. But just the sight of her made up for the disappointment. Sian has been such a joy to us.

BONO: We were in America for the second leg of the tour, on a plane on our way to Arizona, when the news came in that Michael Hutchence had taken his life in a Sydney hotel room. I couldn't believe it. Of all people, he really loved life. And it loved him back. We had gotten quite close, and Ali and he became great friends.

EDGE: It really was the most painful blow of all, because Michael was such a good friend of ours. We got to know him during the *Zoo TV* period, when he had been living in Paris with Helena and we were in the South of France a lot. When they split up, we tried to keep in touch as much as possible but it was difficult. He wasn't around as much and he was involved with Paula Yates, who was married to Bob Geldof, another good friend of ours. So it was a much more difficult situation. There were other complications because it transpired that he and Paula were involved with substances that maybe made them less social. That was very sad to find out afterwards. When somebody who is close to you dies like that, you inevitably wonder what you might have done. If we'd made more of an effort to be around, we might have been able to make a difference. It's still a dreadful feeling that he went the way he did. To this day, no one really knows what his intention was. I know that he was quite down around that period. Was it a cry for help that went too far?

BONO: Ali had seen him a month previous and thought he looked a little disturbed. He was very upset about the way Paula had been treated by the British Press and he couldn't understand why Bob so loathed him, and was not remorseful at all about having had a relationship with Bob's wife. Something was eating him, she said.

You know, there's a moment when laughter turns to cackle, when the party balloons start to pop and you're the last person left standing and maybe you should have gone home an hour earlier. It's happened to me a few times. It was happening to him a lot. I asked him a couple of times was he OK. I remember he talked a lot about Kurt Cobain's suicide. Michael said to me, 'If he'd had a chance to just experience how good things can be when you're in a band rather than the drag of being a famous face, that would never have happened to him.' They say it's a pattern in people who take their own lives that they've been thinking about and even talking about it over the years. But I'm not sure, I think maybe with all the abuse he'd given his body and his mind it was a spur of the moment thing, to end the horrors he was going through coming down. He'd got into a very big black hole and just couldn't see a way out of it. That is the only thing I can think of, it was just a black dog that was savaging him. I know someone he had talked to on the phone that night, and Michael was very upset, he had wept, told this friend he was very unhappy. So I'm not sure it was death by misadventure. I'd love to think it was. I miss him. Especially when I'm in the South of France, I miss his company. He would have been very good at getting old, very debonair, and his rascal side would have kept the place on its toes. He was a charming, deeply sensitive soul, who would always check in to see if you were all right. I wish I'd checked in more with him to see if he was all right.

At the next gig we played 'Gone' for Michael. The middle eight goes: *You're taking steps that make you feel dizzy/ Then you get to like the way it feels / You hurt yourself, you hurt your lover / then you discover what you thought was freedom was just greed. / Goodbye ... no emotional goodnight / We'll be up with the sun / Are you still holding on? / I'm not coming down.* Some songs are like premonitions and that's certainly one of them.

EDGE: *PopMart* really came into its own when we went south of the border, down Mexico way. Everything started to make more sense down there.

BONO: When we arrived in Mexico, the national radio station changed its name to *Pop Radio*. There was a feeling in the country that's hard to describe. Everybody knew that we were filming the show, that this was the moment when it was going to be recorded for posterity.

LARRY: Mexico was exciting and crazy at the same time. The band played well and the crowd was fantastic. Then we came off the stage and the security guys were flipping out, saying, 'You need to get in a car and go – now!'

EDGE: We heard there was big trouble, people had been hurt. It took us a while to finally piece together the story of what had happened. It seems the Mexican President's three sons had got a small group of their secret service bodyguards and just shown up at the venue, without tickets or passes. They hadn't even simply made a call to say they were coming. The Mexican guys on the door weren't about to argue. They drove in backstage in a van and went and saw the show. They left towards the end, the secret service guys rather unceremoniously pushing their way through the crowd, and took a shortcut through a cordoned-off area. It was closed for safety reasons to accommodate the camera cranes, which have a counterbalance of half a ton or more swinging at high speed. If it hits you, you're in serious trouble. This small group of people started wandering through this area, the camera-operator rushed over to tell them to stop, whereupon there was an altercation with the secret service.

BONO: The road crew then went into overdrive. So when the secret service attempted to get out, the head of our security, Jerry Mele, lay down in front of the car. The crew had no idea, of course, that these were the President's sons. They just knew that there had been an incident and they were trying to keep the car there until the police arrived. The car ran over Jerry Mele. He suffered horrific back injuries that he has never fully recovered from.

We went apeshit when we heard. Paul McGuinness got a call to say, 'The President is very sorry about this. Please don't go to the papers. Would you like to come round to the house and discuss it tomorrow?' So we thought about it and decided the best thing to do was to make our case to him personally. When we arrived the next day it was a very strange atmosphere. Our road crew were separated from us and we were brought in to meet President Ernesto Zedillo. We were arriving to make a complaint. He was standing there, smiling, with his three sons, who had albums to be signed. We were not very happy and the more he tried to placate us by pointing out the paintings on the walls and making small talk, the more angry I was getting. He said, 'Let's all forget about the past.' I said, 'On the contrary, we're here to talk about it.' He said, 'Look, this could have been a lot worse. You took on the secret service. They're trained to protect their charges.' We said, 'Are they trained to mistreat our audience and people who are there to protect our audience? If we'd even known that we were going to have guests, we would have looked after them. They don't need to storm in unannounced with a security detail.' To which he replied, 'My sons like to keep a low profile.' Obviously, the Mexican President's idea of low profile is a little different from most people's.

It was a very ugly incident. It won't stop us loving Mexico. One of the things I'm most proud of in my life is *PopMart Live* from Mexico City. It really is extraordinary and illustrates everything that was exciting and worthwhile about the whole *Pop* adventure.

EDGE: We brought *PopMart* to Brazil, Argentina and Chile. If Tokyo was the capital of *Zoo TV*, then Rio was probably the capital of *Pop*. The audiences in South America were so passionate, the shows were unbelievable.

BONO: When we played Chile, the most extraordinary thing happened. The tickets were too expensive for everybody, so we agreed for a live television broadcast. We thought, if we've got the whole country watching then we should play 'Mothers of the Disappeared' and actually invite the mothers on stage. So all these women who had lost family to the excesses of General Pinochet and his security forces came on stage. And we took five minutes as each woman held up a picture and called out the name of her missing son or daughter. Our audience immediately divided. There was booing and hissing and cheers. Some people in Chile believed that General Pinochet was a necessary monster to hold back the bigger monster, which was communism. Some people did not want to rake up the past. But I said directly to General Pinochet, as if he were listening, 'General Pinochet, God will be your judge, we will not. But at least tell these women where are the bones of their children?'

It was quite a moment and it sent shock waves through the country. Two months later they held the same protest in the Chilean Parliament, where they brought in the pictures and said the same thing: 'We want to know where the bones of our children are buried.' Subsequently, the Opposition parties came to power, and the new Chilean Ambassador sent word to us that the televising of our concert had put the protest idea in their heads. Amazing thing. Oddly enough, people say, 'Were you disappointed that your audience booed and hissed?' And I say no, because it's proof to me that a rock 'n' roll audience are not lemmings, they're not going to just follow you off the cliff, they're not going to vote how you tell them to vote. If they don't agree with you, they will let you know – but that doesn't mean they're not fans. I'm all for it. I was flattered that we weren't just playing to people who agreed with us.

EDGE: The tour went to Australia and Japan before ending in Johannesburg in South Africa, so there was a crazy few weeks of traversing the southern hemisphere.

PAUL: The tour got out of hand and it was never scaled down. We had two Andropovs, which are very big planes, and we air-freighted everything, even scaffolding. We had planes full of steel bars. I would say, 'Haven't they got steel bars in South America? Can't we rent steel bars?' Steel bars seem like a thing you don't air-freight. We'd been doing things our own way for such a long time that we thought we were invincible. My view was that *PopMart* lacked logistical and financial control. I knew things were getting out of hand when I got a call in the middle of the night saying that the two Andropovs were insufficient to take all the equipment and was it all right if they hired a 747 as well?

BONO: We had been the first band invited by the ANC to play the new South Africa at the end of Apartheid but had been unable to take them up on their invitation. It was great to get out there. We spent very precious time with Archbishop Tutu. The introductions were fantastic because his people call him The Arch and there was a moment when The Arch was introduced to The Edge. All kinds of people come through his offices and the way he deals with it is really quick and efficient. 'Let us bow our heads,' he says. We had only been there five minutes. We all bowed our heads and in this beautiful prayer he reminded us why we were there. They paid a very high cost for their present freedom.

After leading us in prayer, he asked would we like to meet some of the volunteers? We said, 'Sure.' He brought us into a room where six hundred people were waiting, sitting down. 'Ladies and Gentlemen,' he announced, 'U2 are going to play for you.' And not an instrument in sight – let alone in hand. We just looked at each other and attempted a rather feeble *a cappella* version of 'Amazing Grace', which is actually not a bad choice considering what he was doing was really grace in action. He is a great man.

EDGE: Having started off so difficult, everything ended on a high note, which was a great feeling.

LARRY: I was happy enough with the way it had gone. I was even happier that it was over.

ADAM: It was actually a very successful tour. We made the Guinness Book of Records for having the largest ever audience, almost three million people at 93 shows. We sold seven million albums. Which is not bad for something that is regarded as one of our low points.

PAUL: There were the inevitable Post Mortems and we came to some conclusions. Mine would have been: Don't bite off more than you can chew.

THE **LAST** OF THE **ROCK** **STARS**

1998 - 2001

Bono

WE GOT BACK TO IRELAND IN APRIL 1998. WE HAD
BEEN FOLLOWING WITH GREAT INTEREST WHAT
WAS HAPPENING ON OUR HOME TURF. JOHN HUME
WAS NORTHERN IRELAND'S ANSWER TO MARTIN
LUTHER KING.

He was fighting for the Catholic minority, not with petrol bombs and Armalites
but with a clear voice and a well-thought-out argument.

His main point was that the real border was in people's hearts and
minds and that would be the hardest one to tear down.

The peace process was the first real breakthrough in my life, the first
sense that all this bad blood might now have found a tourniquet. The Good
Friday Peace Agreement was a great work of compromise. It wasn't giving
everybody what they wanted, all parties were going to have to swallow some
foul-tasting medicine. Parity of pain was how it was described to me. But
compromise is a great word when you think about it. In May 1998, there were
to be separate referendums in Northern Ireland and Southern Ireland on this
agreement, painstakingly brokered between John Hume's SDLP and David
Trimble's Ulster Unionist party in the face of much resistance from the forces
of bigotry and the men of violence. We wanted to see it succeed but the signs
were not good. We offered to help in any way we could.

EDGE: The polls were looking very tight and while it was obviously going to
be a massive Yes vote in the Republic, there was a good chance the No vote
would win in Northern Ireland.

LARRY: We all have views on what our Irishness means to us. Two members
of the band were born in England and were raised in the Protestant faith.
Bono's mother was Protestant and his father was Catholic. I was brought up
Catholic. U2 are a living example of the kind of unity of faith and tradition that
is possible in Northern Ireland. We all agreed the Yes vote was the only way
forward. Getting involved in domestic politics is always dangerous but these
were exceptional circumstances.

BONO: We were asked to take part in an event with David Trimble, the Protestant Unionist leader, and John Hume, the moderate Catholic voice. I said we'd agree if they would appear on stage together. Such was the antipathy in this situation that these two senior politicians, who were both campaigning for a Yes vote, had never appeared on a stage together and never shaken each other's hand. They were in a desperate situation, facing defeat, so with raised eyebrows and furrowed temples, they agreed to the showbusiness at hand.

LARRY: We were hijacking an event that was already going on in Belfast. Northern Ireland's finest rock band Ash were appearing at a concert on 18 May to appeal for a Yes vote. We asked if we could use their gear and play a couple of numbers.

BONO: On the night there was some nervousness. I had some time with Trimble and Hume in a room together, just the three of us. I said, 'I'm going to ask you to do something that is very difficult for politicians. I'm going to ask you to walk out onto the stage and not say anything.' They looked puzzled. I told them this was a photo opportunity and the most important thing was that they shake hands for this photograph. They agreed. And as a mark of respect to all those that had lost their lives over the years to Sectarianism, we decided we'd ask the crowd for a minute's silence, which I'm not sure has ever happened at a rock show, least of all in front of one of the loudest audiences on earth. But the crowd did keep quiet. And we got the shot.

LARRY: It was quite the moment seeing Bono standing between David Trimble and John Hume with their arms raised to the sky.

EDGE: That was a great moment, for all those who had struggled for so long to bring peace to Ireland, but also for music. As Jake Burns from Stiff Little Fingers said back in 1978, the solution to Northern Ireland's problems is a thousand punk bands. We played The Beatles' 'Don't Let Me Down', which was a bit cheeky but appropriate for the moment. In the days after the event there was a distinct swing back to the Yes vote. In the end it was won by a very small margin, two or three points. I think there was a lot of courage shown by the politicians involved, particularly David Trimble, in getting involved in the event and it certainly was crucial to the peace process.

BONO: Extreme militant Unionists and militant Republicans didn't like the word compromise. Some of these militants broke away and a dissident Republican group known as the Continuity IRA decided to try and destroy the peace process, which was just taking baby steps, by letting off a car bomb in the tiny town centre of Omagh on 15 August 1998. It killed 29 people and injured 220 men, women and children just out doing their Saturday shopping. It was the most low-down act of cowardice in a history of cowardly acts carried out by both sides. I remember looking at the television in complete disbelief. There were no words you could say. We couldn't speak. Everyone in Ireland was in deep shock. When they read out the names of all the people who died on RTE, the country came to a complete standstill. People were weeping in cars, on O'Connell Street, all over the place. It was really a trauma for the entire nation, because not only was it the destruction of so many lives, it seemed it was a destruction of the peace process, which had been so painstakingly put together with sticky tape and glue and a lot of faith. It would be hard to describe to people who were not Irish what it felt like that day. It was the one of the lowest days in my life. Maybe because we felt we had a stake in the peace process, I could not comprehend how people could do something like that. The closest I ever came to a crisis of faith happened after that. It was hard to be a believer at that moment. We wrote the song 'Peace on Earth' after that, which is as bitter and as angry a song as U2 have ever written.

There was some particularly heavy stuff going on in my own personal life. My father had been diagnosed with cancer. He was in his seventies but still cut a strong and imposing figure. He had often talked about getting cancer, such was his sunny disposition. He always figured that would be the way he would go. So when he told me, I said, 'Oh, you must be really pleased with yourself now.' He laughed and then glowered. But it's a sinking feeling. Even though a third of people who are diagnosed with cancer survive nowadays, it's about catching it early and we weren't sure how far it had gone. My brother really took the lead role in dealing with this, and my father let him. Whereas he didn't really let me in, in the same way, which I completely understand. I think it was very difficult for him to let even one person into this place where he was so vulnerable.

I had a few concerns of my own, in that respect. My voice problems hadn't got any better. There was a swelling on my vocal cords, which was not a nodule, and wouldn't go away. I had been seeing specialists but there was some uncertainty about what it was. It was suggested it was my lifestyle, the smokes, drinking too much, on the phone all the time, never going to bed. I was trying to make changes but it was difficult. We were talking about making a new album and I had come up with the idea that I wanted to make a singer's record. I kept saying it to people, almost to make myself have to do it. But my voice was not strong, and I knew it. Doctor Maurice Collins, a very gifted Ear, Nose and Throat surgeon, said, 'Look, we're going to have to take this

THERE IS NOTHING LIKE A BRUSH WITH MORTALITY
TO PUT THINGS INTO PERSPECTIVE. EVERYTHING
COMES INTO SHARPER FOCUS, YOU REALLY
APPRECIATE WHAT YOU MIGHT HAVE LOST. IF YOU
THINK YOU MAY NOT BE ABLE TO SING AGAIN, WELL,
THEN YOU'RE NOT GOING TO MESS AROUND. BONO

seriously. I want to put you out. And when I get down and can really have a good look at this, if I'm worried, I need your permission to do the biopsy.' I said, 'Biopsy? Isn't that what you give people when you think they might have cancer?' So there it was, the thing I had been trying not to think about. A throat biopsy would have really put me out of action, it would have meant not being able to sing at all for three months. I said, 'No way. I can't do it.' He said, 'I just want to go in and have a look with the microscope. I will know within ninety per cent certainty if it is a cancer. But if I see that, you have to let me operate.' So I finally agreed. I didn't tell anyone, I didn't tell Ali, didn't tell the band, I just went through it on my own.

I remember sitting in a ward being prepared for theatre, wearing the blue apron, I had the curtain around me, I couldn't see anyone but I could hear people down the corridor, moaning and groaning having come out of surgery. I was thinking, 'I really don't want this. I really would like to sing.' My mind rambled to thoughts of losing my voice forever, if it was cancer, how would you beat it? I'm not afraid of death but I would hate to put my family through it and I knew the band had a few more albums in them. How inconvenient this could all be.

So I went in to the operating theatre, lay down and they put me out. Next thing I know, I'm half-conscious, groggy, and the good doctor comes into view and says, 'I'll be back in an hour when you wake up.' I just grabbed his arm and shook it. He said, 'Oh! You're OK! You're fine.'

So I was lucky but there is nothing like a brush with mortality to put things into perspective. Everything comes into sharper focus, you really appreciate what you might have lost. Ali was pregnant again not long after that, so whether it was my dad having cancer, or Michael's untimely death or whether it was a fresh image of a new life and how vulnerable that child is when you first hold it in your arms, it seemed like the moment to make an album about the essential things. I wanted to make a very emotionally raw record about real life and the responsibilities that come with that life and the joy of just being alive, being awake, being able to do what you love, spending time with your friends and family. If you think you may not be able to sing again, well, then you're not going to mess around.

EDGE: We bought ourselves a bit of time by doing *The Best of U2 1980-1990*, which came out in November 1998. We had always resisted doing anything that might look like we were winding up but thought if we isolated it to the first ten years then it would be more like a bit of housekeeping, tidying up the past. It was a nice excuse to re-master some of the earlier recordings, technology having moved on quite a bit with CDs. But we were already starting to think about the new album.

ADAM: We were a bit bruised and bloodied after the *Pop* experience. Because even though audience and sales figures were in the millions, it didn't catch fire the way we had hoped it would. We came away feeling that we hadn't quite dotted the 'i's and crossed the 't's and we needed to re-group and get back to work quite quickly. We all felt that it was a good idea to talk to Brian and Danny and see if they would be up for working with us again.

EDGE: One thing that had emerged at the end of *Pop* was that we'd really taken the deconstruction of the rock 'n' roll band format to its absolute 'nth degree. We felt we wanted to hear the band again, to hear guitars, bass and drums as discrete elements of an arrangement. We said to Brian and Danny, 'Look, we don't have any songs for this album, really. Give us a few months to get things together and we'll make a start.' But Brian said, quite strongly: 'No, let's not do that. Let's go in and work very fast and develop a lot of material really quickly and then just pick the best bits.' So we went into Hanover Quay with Brian and Danny and spent about three weeks all together just jamming, Brian on synthesizers, Danny on rhythm guitar or percussion. Unfortunately this experiment didn't produce many great ideas so I started bringing in bits and pieces to work on. 'Kite' had its origins in a little string loop I made. Everybody started playing along and the song kind of jumped on us. That was amazing. In one long improvisation in which the melodies, guitar parts, different sections of the song, drum parts, the whole thing came together.

BONO: My voice returned in that moment. When I sang, 'I'm a man, I'm not a child' everyone in the studio almost fell over. I went: 'Wow!' It was like the blind man when the scales fall off his eyes. It was almost comedic. Where did that come from? I want some more of that!

I think I can have that note when I'm worthy of it. It's really bizarre. Because I would never sit down at a piano or at a guitar and come up with a note that high, because it's too hard to hit. You would never write it. But I stepped into it. In ten years there hadn't been a note like that hit in U2, full voice.

ADAM: It was a memorable moment. I don't think we had heard that voice for a long time.

EDGE: Unbelievable. Singing like a bird.

BONO: We were finally getting to the bottom of what was wrong with my voice. It is an allergic thing that affects my nasal system. I had to take all these allergy tests. The guy doing it was laughing and said, 'I'll tell you one of the things you're really allergic to is the desert weed, but luckily you're from Ireland, you don't have too many deserts there.' I said, 'No, we don't.' And he said, 'But if you're ever in Las Vegas you better watch out!' Of course, we launched the whole *Pop* tour in Las Vegas, when my voice was at its worst. So it was a great relief to find out these things but it was very hard for me to accept that I have allergies, it seemed more of a Woody Allen condition. I've had a tendency to ignore it, which doesn't always help. The medication I was taking was drying up my throat, smoking certainly wasn't helping, so it was an ongoing struggle, which is why I took to wearing the permanent sunglasses because my eyes go red. Over the years I have more or less got it under control by becoming more aware of what affects me and changing my diet.

But I think there is more to it than that. It seems to be that when I sing from a certain place, I can hit certain notes. I think it's a B flat, it might be a B natural. Next stop is a C. A great tenor will hit a high C once in a night, maybe three times a night in some of the harder operas. So I'm down just one tone from that. Go back and look at when that note turns up in any U2 song. You can actually count them. You find it in 'Bad', 'Pride (in the Name of Love)', 'I Still Haven't Found What I'm Looking For'. They are the notes when you just leave, the notes that you disappear into, and you don't know where they come from but it is some other place. When I sing them, I'm transported. I'm certainly not conscious as I'm doing it. If I was, I'd have more sense than to try them. Because then I have to go through the pain of singing them every night. So usually if they come up it's because the material has thrown them up.

The most important thing is I found my voice after some difficulty over the years and the record was made with a certain kind of freedom and boldness.

ADAM: When we started demoing in 1998 we genuinely thought we'd have the record ready within a year but then it ran over to take up 1999 and into 2000. After the Pop experience we weren't going to set deadlines.

LARRY: Edge took some time out and worked by himself on a lot of the songs. We then got back together in Hanover Quay and played with those ideas. It was the way U2 had recorded in the past: the band in a room playing together. I think everyone enjoyed the process although, as always, there were moments where it was very tough. U2 sessions can be excruciating. One day things are going well and the next day things are falling apart. It had been made clear that this record wasn't coming out until we had eleven great songs. We didn't even think about artwork or titles or anything like that until we were well down the road. It was a great way to work.

EDGE: Sometimes it seems the way we work is like building a house from the roof down. We find an idea, a rough outline for a song and start getting sounds and creating the sonic identity and the feel for it. Then we start recording and in the same process discover what it needs in terms of arrangement. The production approach almost comes before the song itself – and the lyrics are the last thing. So you start with a sound and end with a song. The process can be time-consuming and this album consumed even more time than usual. We were still doing everything that we had always done before but we weren't doing quite as much playing in the room with Bono.

PAUL: Jubilee 2000 approached Bono and he felt inclined to get involved. Jubilee 2000 was a coalition of more than 90 NGO's (Non-Governmental Organizations), churches and trade unions, quite a broad group, looking for something to mark the millennium in terms of world poverty. It was a campaign for the cancellation of Third World debt, with specific proposals to write off some $376 billion owed by 52 of the world's most impoverished countries to the IMF, the World Bank and the wealthiest nations of the West. I think Bono found it embarrassing to be in the photograph but not on top of the issues. Once he decided to get intellectually involved there was no stopping him.

BONO: Ali and myself had been to Africa in 1986 and had our hearts broken by the everyday tragedy that was life on that shining continent, the waste of lives and opportunity. We had a sense, even then, that a lot of Africa's problems were not just natural calamity or war and warlords but that some of the poverty problems were structural. Corruption was a big problem, obviously, corrupt leaders and tinpot dictators who were staying on for third and fourth presidencies and not looking out for their people. But there was also corruption on the part of the developed world. The West, for its own strategic reasons, had loaned huge sums of money to African nations during the Cold War, often to very mad and bad men, just because they weren't communist. These people, like Mobutu of Zaire, had squandered the countries resources on personal enrichment, and now the western world was holding to ransom the children of these choices made years and years before.

This was obscene and not acceptable. In Europe, in the 19th century, if somebody failed to repay a debt they put them and their families in debtors' prisons. Not very fair and not very efficient, because there is not much chance of getting your money back if the whole family is in prison. So that was soon abandoned as a concept. But still, in the 20th century, we were keeping entire countries in debtors' prisons. The injustice of it really struck a chord with me. It wasn't a charity-based idea, it was a justice-based idea. It made me think there was something solid we could do to change the lives of the people we'd met years earlier.

Jubilee 2000 had the coming millennium as a dramatic hook to hang the campaign on. We wanted to encourage a one-off opportunity to drop the debts of the poorest countries in the world to the richest, an historic act of grace that would provide a fresh start for a billion people living on less than a dollar a day. The idea had a force of its own but it became my job to make it louder.

Rock 'n' roll bands are good communicators. We use PA systems, video, song lyrics and T-shirts to get our message out. The message may just be a musical one but it can also be something more substantial. I'd been on other campaign trails for Greenpeace and Amnesty International so I first thought my job would be to engage our audience as a kind of grass-roots movement to get behind this project. I did some of that but where I really came in handy was in America, working behind the scenes. Jubilee 2000 was already up and running in Europe but in America it was not as recognized. It would be too late in 1998/99 to grow a big enough grass roots movement. So I had to just go straight to the decision-makers and try to pitch them the ideas.

As I've said before, I come from a long line of travelling sales people on my mother's side. I've no problem selling ideas if I believe in them, but these ideas brought with them a weight of responsibility I had not experienced before. I did not want to screw up. My first call turned out to be the most important call of the lot. Top 10 phone calls of my life, even. Not just because Eunice Shriver was one of the most extraordinary women in America, founder of the Special Olympics, JFK's older sister (could have been President herself). But because she catalyzed a relationship between me and her son, Bobby, without whom I would have spent years, rather than months, finding my way around Washington DC. Bobby Shriver had a keen sense of civic duty, a passion for social justice and enough modesty to know when a Kennedy should attend a meeting or hide in the corridor outside. I'm not kidding. A bright light Democrat, he was the one who counselled me to find his counterpart on the right. Through his brother-in-law, Arnold Schwarzenegger, he connected us to tough-talking Republican congressman John Kasich. This advice and these connections proved crucial. He was the peeler of the onion. The man who more than any other knew, from his family's experience, just how many layers of body armour we would have to get through to find a beating heart in America's body politic.

The first person I visited was Bill Clinton. I pitched him the idea by asking him to imagine New Year's Eve, 1999: the drum roll, the fanfare, would all be dumb parade unless hitched to a big idea like this. He was totally on board but even the President needed support in his cabinet and support from Congress to get it through the political process in DC. There began a series of meetings with twenty, thirty, forty, eventually hundreds of people at the ground floor, staffers, Congress people from the right and the left, people like Pete Peterson at the Council of Foreign Relations, everyone from David Rockefeller to Larry Summers, the Secretary of the US treasury, whose signature was on every dollar at that time. Anybody who could put obstacles in our way, we met them before they could try. Economists, macro-economists, journalists, religious groups, popes, priests, evangelists. It is absurd, if not obscene that celebrity is a door that such serious issues need to pass through before politicians take note. But there it is. Jubilee couldn't get into some of these offices but I could. And I knew that the idea could catch fire if it was given a chance.

There were all kinds of surreal meetings on this road. I swapped a pair of blue Fly shades for a rosary with the Pope, forty thousand Jubilee supporters surrounding the city of Cologne during the G8, Bob Geldof splattering the British Prime Minister with a raised voice and *fusillade* of expletives. And having Tony Blair dodge the spittle by enquiring in his perfect Oxford accent, 'Have U2 a *Greatest Hits* coming out?' Geldof also attacked dogged Jim Wolfensohn, the President of the World Bank, a very elegant man and, indeed, the person who started the heavily indebted poor countries initiative, known rather unpoetically as HIPC. Obviously not a songwriter. In a meeting with him, Sir Bob was in full tilt, pinning the President of the World Bank to his own chair in his own suite in a hotel in London. Trying to dodge the abuse, the President said to me, 'So when were you made a knight?' I was puzzled at first. Then I realized that, in Jim Wolfensohn's mind, there was no way a Sir could be treating him this badly and that, in fact, Bob must be Bono and I must be Sir Bob.

This kind of stuff was going on every day. I remember Horst Koehler, later President of Germany but then Chairman of the IMF, sitting down beside me and opening with, 'So, you're a rock star. You make a lot of money and then you find a conscience,' and having to explain to him that I had a conscience before I was a rock star. And one very Southern Congressman referring to me as Bonio and refusing to look at me in the eye, telling me, 'Everybody's lookin' at me like I'm Scrooge but this money's goin' down a rat hole. You'll just be buyin' more gold taps and Gulf streams for tinpot dictators. I'm tryin' to stop you but I cain't get people on my side, they have one drink with Bonio in the midnight hour and they roll me. You expect me to sit here and smile at you?' In the end that particular Congressman became an advocate. I almost preferred the curmudgeons, they never lied to you.

I went to see Jesse Helms, who was a right-wing Republican Senator in the US. If you just mentioned his name to Democrats they would start twitching. I went into his office in the Senate to find out why they were blocking debt cancellation and after talking for some time to really get under the hood of the issues, he became quite emotional, even tearful about Africa. It was clear beneath the tough skin of this old cold warrior was a heart that could be moved. It was front page of the *Wall Street Journal*: Jesse Helms Brought to Tears by Stories of African Children. People couldn't believe this had happened. As I was leaving he wrapped his arms around me and gave me a blessing like an ancient Jewish patriarch to his son. I was very moved … God was on the move. I do have a fascination with older people. There is a certain authority that age gives you and in the scriptures the giving of a blessing from an old man was a big deal.

PAUL: At first gradually, and then thoroughly, Bono got involved in the Jubilee campaign. We were scheduling Bono's political activity out of Principle Management in New York and Dublin. It was sometimes very difficult to do that at the same time as being fair to the other members of the band. There were times when they were left waiting because Bono was busy meeting the Pope. It could be irritating for them, as much as they supported him in what he was doing. He was sometimes a little careless of other people's time and there were certainly strains on Principle Management and strains on the band.

BONO: It was trying for my bandmates but they were well up on the arguments as to why I should be doing this and knew the risks. They feared the blows that would land on me and, I suppose, on them, although I don't think that was uppermost in their minds. There was a sense that it could demystify and devalue U2. It wasn't very glamorous work. A rock star looks much better on a barricade with a handkerchief over his nose and a Molotov cocktail in his hand than he does with a bowler hat and briefcase full of World

Bank reports. It should have damaged us … but it didn't. There was some kind of blessing to be had there.

I think the rock audience had grown up since the Sixties. There was a kind of acknowledgement that revolution was not around the corner and that real changes were going to be made by increments. So the more committed individuals started to educate themselves about the issues and that is what I had to do too. I became a student of Jeffrey Sachs, one of the most outspoken and highly regarded economists in the world, an extraordinary man and a great ally of the world's poor, who not only understood the hard science of debt relief but had enough moral outrage to demand it be done. I piggybacked his classes in the John F. Kennedy School of Government at Harvard. Rock star on campus, what a laugh, but in the process I discovered (to my surprise) I'm quite a rational thinker, even if I appear to behave irrationally or emotionally or spontaneously. I enjoyed communicating great ideas. And great ideas have a lot in common with great melodies: a certain clarity, a certain instant memorability, a certain predictability.

ADAM: When we first heard about the Jubilee 2000 campaign, we were all on board. We recognized that this was something worth fighting for. We sat down and talked about what we could do as a band but it quickly became apparent that it was a job for one person and the best man for the job was Bono, without a doubt. He could command the ear of whoever he wanted to talk to and he could bridge the gaps between politics, nationality and religion. When you weighed up what was at stake against the needs of a rock 'n' roll band, the scales came down pretty heavily on one side. Jubilee 2000 had the potential to change the world in a way that made U2 seem like light relief. But Bono was just as committed to the band. He is an extraordinary person who is able to have a foot in these very different worlds and somehow maintain his balance. I'm sure it has its difficulties. At times I am sure he feels he is stretched too thin, and maybe his family would like to see more of him, but he does seem to be able to handle the pressure without melting down.

LARRY: Bono was spending more and more time on the phone, talking to world leaders, arranging to meet the Pope. There was some grumbling about the amount of time it was taking up, and Brian and Danny were very frustrated. The big question was whether it was having an impact on the band's music? The answer was a resounding no. Was it having an impact on the way the band was functioning outside the music? The answer is yes. But nobody could argue with what he was doing, it was clearly too important. And believe me, if we could have, we would have.

EDGE: I don't think that Bono's work on Jubilee 2000 had much of an impact on the record, although there were times when Brian felt his concentration was affected. Brian essentially has a very simple approach to making records. He thinks that you have to give it your complete attention to get into the zone where the best of what you are capable of can occur. So he views any distractions as a big problem.

Bono is always moving at very high speed, doing more than one thing at any one time. He gets engaged with things very quickly, tries to make a difference, and then will get on to something else. He's not a long-distance runner, in that sense. But it does take U2 a long time to make a record. There is a lot of time that might not be wasted but it's not particularly productive, nothing seems to be moving forward. So it demands a lot of patience. That's also not one of Bono's strong points. Bono creates in bursts. So this new arrangement, where he was around less often, did not necessarily mean he was less productive. For instance, a song like 'In A Little While', the vocal for that really came together very quickly, in one or two improvisational takes. It was after a very big night out on the town, Bono coming back into the studio after two hours' sleep, hungover and with no voice and suddenly just bang, it all happened. And you can't get to that kind of a moment by increments. It's a sort of total thing. You hit or you don't. And that's how Bono works.

ADAM: I think Bono is as important to the creative process of the band as he always was, he just doesn't have to be there as much. It gives us breathing space and time to focus on detail. The way things have changed over the years, it probably takes the band longer to realize its potential, because you have to set it up right, you have to deal with mundane issues of monitoring and sound and comfort and familiarization and practising and trying it in different keys and trying it at different tempos, a whole host of things before you arrive at the best musical platform for Bono to sing. Then, when you do arrive at that platform, within a very short period of time you might discover you have built the platform in the wrong place. Usually he'll come in and let you know that pretty quickly. So then you have to shift the platform and move it somewhere else and those are the bits of the work that his temperament isn't particularly well suited for. So it kind of works out quite well that we get to take care of our stuff and then, when we have our shit together, he gets the benefit of us having worked out the problems.

EDGE: On the early U2 records, Bono had to be in the room. To get the right arrangement took quite a while, with a lot of discussion about everyone's part and we all worked together but really Bono was the one with the objective eye. But around the *Joshua Tree* album that started to change, because we spent a long time working on songs to no avail, really. Our old approach no longer seemed to be working for us so we had to find new ways of creating music. This was just another development. The material on *All That You Can't Leave Behind* took a long time to come together. And actually there was a break for two months when I was working on U2 songs and Bono went into the studio with Danny and Hal Wilner to record the soundtrack to his film *Million Dollar Hotel*.

BONO: One day, during time off from the making of *Rattle and Hum*, myself and Edge were hanging out on top of the Million Dollar Hotel, which was just around the corner from our favourite club in downtown LA. We were at the top of one very tall building and Edge reckoned, if he really had to, he could jump to the roof of the next. And he was getting far too close to the ledge for my liking. That's where I came up with the idea.

Spending time in this city of the imagination, I was bitten by the movie bug. I met a screenwriter called Nicholas Klein at a party in the Hollywood Hills. He said, 'Have you got a story?' I said, 'I don't. But I've got an opening scene: this guy jumps off a building trying to get to the next.' And he said, 'Well, I've got the perfect line for you.' I said, 'What's that?' He said, 'After I jumped, it occurred to me...'

So I wrote the story with Nicholas Klein and, over ten years later, Wim Wenders made it into a film. It was a story about unconditional love. Really, that was it. It was about a beautiful girl who had never really been loved that way because her beauty just brought her bad luck and abuse. Until she met this beautiful, simple boy who loved our heroine, Eloise, perfectly and, in the end of the film, he finds out that she loved him back. It was also a whodunnit, where the narrator was the murderer, which we thought was very clever. I don't think anyone had tried that before. It was also a heist film, so you can see what I mean when I say we might have needed more than 34 days to shoot.

I wasn't on the set very much but I loved doing the soundtrack album. It was produced by Hal Wilner, who is an American national treasure and an old friend of U2. He's an archivist and sonic activist and he put together the Million Dollar Hotel Band with such incredible talents as Brad Mehldau, probably the greatest jazz interpretative pianist in the world, Bill Frisell, the inspirational avant-garde guitarist and Jon Hassell, amongst the greatest living jazz trumpeters. I always feel like I've only one leg when I'm not in the studio with U2 and I especially lean heavily on Edge. Without Daniel Lanois, who I roped in to write with me, I'd have been in big trouble. And without Hal to fly the spaceship, I don't think I'd have wanted the ride.

EDGE: A couple of our B sides ended up going into the project, which was fine. No one begrudged Bono that.

ADAM: There were a couple of U2 songs there, and a couple that might have become U2 songs, but they were the kind of atmospheric, mid-tempo pieces that we come up with quite easily. They can be quite pretty but they're a different kind of music to the rock 'n' roll records that we like to make that can really jump out of the radio and perhaps change your life. *Million Dollar Hotel* had been such a long time coming, it was really great for Bono that it got made and it got seen.

BONO: *Million Dollar Hotel* was premièred at the Berlin Film Festival, where it won a Silver Bear. Steven Spielberg rang Wim to say he thought it was Oscar material. Not everyone was so enthusiastic.

I went to the Sarajevo film festival, where the movie was shown at eleven o'clock at night in the town square. It was an extraordinary evening in this city I had come to love, watching *The Million Dollar Hotel* with three thousand people. It was warm at first but then, as the night went on, it got kind of chilly. And more than a few people left. I was in a café afterwards and a guy came up to me and said, 'Bono, some people they left the film before it was finished, these people are shit, they don't know nothing about film, about Wim Wenders.' I said, 'Listen, it's a long film, it was a long night, it was getting a bit cold, I might have left myself to be honest with you.' He said, 'No! Bono, these people, they weren't even in Sarajevo when there was a siege, they only come back, these people are shit, they don't know film, they don't know Wim Wenders, they don't know Bono.' I said, 'What did you think of the film?' He said, 'I don't know, I left halfway through!' That is pure Sarajevo. But he said it to my face.

LARRY: It wasn't like we were sitting around in the studio, waiting for Bono to come in. The songs were getting pulled and pushed and dragged in different directions. Songs were being recorded, dismantled and put back together again in search of that elusive something. It is an almost never-ending process of adding and subtracting. We were also getting our family lives together, spending weekends at home trying to get some order in our lives. Ann and I had a second child. U2 was part of our lives, a huge, central and vitally important part, but it wasn't all we had any more.

Adam and I bought places near Bono and Edge in the South of France. We did some recording and mixing down there during the summer. There is a lot to do to finish a record and we all need to get stuck in. We're involved in every facet of our business. In the past, when recording was finished, we

IRISHNESS HAS ALWAYS BEEN A TRICKY ONE FOR ME, BECAUSE I AM WHAT THE IRISH WOULD CALL A BLOW-IN. GROWING UP IN IRELAND, I DON'T KNOW IF I FELT ENGLISH BUT I DEFINITELY FELT DIFFERENT TO EVERYONE ELSE. ADAM

would go our separate ways. It was hard to get decisions made. Bono felt we should find a place to work and play. France was perfect. It can be a pain when you only have two weeks off and you get called in for a meeting at an hour's notice. But that's U2. It makes sense for us to be in the same place when we're working.

BONO: Ali gave birth to our first son, on 17 August 1999, Elijah Bob Patricius Guggi Q Hewson. A few names that are important to me there, possibly a few too many. Ali is incredible. Sometimes I think she has built a home to work without me. I'm not quite sure how I feel about that but all I can point to as evidence of my own role are these amazing children. She definitely could not have done that without me. It felt like the beginning of a whole new family. Whenever there's death there is no greater comfort than new life.

EDGE: It's always a good sign when babies start arriving. My boy Levi arrived 25 October 1999. It was in LA. And this time I made sure I was there for the birth.

ADAM: We were given the Freedom of Dublin City at a ceremony in March 2000. It genuinely meant a lot to us. Irishness has always been a tricky one for me, because I am what the Irish would call a blow-in. Growing up in Ireland, I don't know if I felt English but I definitely felt different to everyone else. As I went through my teens, partly as a rebellion against my parents, partly just through assimilating the culture, I progressively thought of myself as Irish. Then when U2 started to play in England, I thought I might respond to my British roots, but in fact that was when I realized I had effectively become Irish. I was never sure that the Irish would agree with my personal assessment of nationality, there is a lingering trace of Englishness in the way I talk, but I have the freedom of the city of Dublin and I guess, whatever else, that makes me a Dub!

PAUL: It was an enormous honour for me that I was included when the band were given the Freedom of Dublin City. I'm a bit like Adam in that I had never been to Ireland until 1962 when I was sent to Clongowes Wood College, a Jesuit boarding school. Then I went to Trinity College where I met most of the close friends I have to this day, particularly my wife Kathy. This made me feel like a real Dubliner.

LARRY: I was genuinely honoured. So honoured, I completely messed up my speech. I wanted to say something like 'Dublin has done more for U2 than we have ever done for Dublin' but said the opposite. I am not the world's greatest public speaker.

EDGE: It was very moving to see our close friends, families and a large crowd of other Dubliners all gathered in the cold night air to mark the occasion. I thanked the crowd for the previously granted, and even more precious, privilege that they had afforded us – a life.

One of the ancient privileges of being a freeman of the city is the right to graze sheep on open ground. So the next day Bono and I borrowed a couple of sheep and took them out to eat the grass on St Stephen's Green. It seemed like a good idea at the time.

BONO: I'd trade my right to graze sheep on Stephen's Green for parking my car on a double yellow line any day.

EDGE: It was really a great honour to be given the Freedom of the City. And at the same ceremony, a Burmese academic named Aung San Suu Kyi was honoured in her absence. I wasn't particularly aware of her before but we made an effort to find out who she was. And that was how we learned the incredible story of this brave Burmese academic based at Oxford University in England who felt that she had to return to Burma to oppose the brutal military regime of her native land, even though she was risking her life and leaving her husband and family behind. She became leader of the National League for Democracy and, although she was arrested and kept in isolation for years, she won over 80 per cent of the vote in Burma's democratic elections in 1990. She has been under virtual house arrest ever since. She became the subject of our song, 'Walk On'.

BONO: It's a song about nobility and personal sacrifice, about doing what's right, even if your heart is telling you otherwise. The spoken intro gave us the title for our new album: *And love is not the easy thing / The only baggage you can bring / Is all that you can't leave behind.* Love, in the highest sense of the word, is the only thing that you can always take with you, in your heart. At some point you are going to have to lose everything else anyway. There's a passage in Corinthians that uses the image of a house going through a fire, and it seems to suggest that when, in death, we eventually face judgement (or inspection, as one translation puts it) all that is made of straw and wood will be burned away, only the eternal things will survive. For me, those things are family and friendship, abstract things, they're not the things that you make. So at the end of the song, there is a litany of ambitions and achievements. *You've got to leave it behind / All that you fashion / All that you make / All that you build / All that you break / All that you measure / All that you steal / All this you can leave behind* … It is a mantra, really, a bonfire of vanities, and you can throw anything you want on the fire. Whatever it is that you want more than love, it has to go. That's a really interesting question to ask: What are the things you want more than love?

EDGE: *All That You Can't Leave Behind* was an album that acknowledged our own past, which we had never really done before. It was really during the writing and recording that this aesthetic started to emerge, so that it wasn't just rushing headlong forward, jettisoning the past as we went, which had been the approach to previous records. I remember there was a big debate about the guitar sound on 'Beautiful Day'. I was playing the Gibson Explorer. This was really the sound of U2, the sound we had made our own and then abandoned as far back as *War*. Whether or not we should bring it back became a real talking point. Bono was particularly uncertain about it. But when I played it, it stood up. It was unarguable really.

PAUL: Bono has one of the most distinctive voices and Edge has one of the most distinctive guitar sounds in rock 'n' roll history. And yet people hadn't heard either of those two things very much for years. It seems like common sense to make a virtue of your biggest strengths.

LARRY: People thought *All That You Can't Leave Behind* was a return to the U2 of old. The truth is we were still using the studio in a similar way. It was not the end of the drum machine, 'Beautiful Day' has one all the way through the song. Technology is a big part of what we do. I think on this album, we were a little more subtle with it.

EDGE: It was because we were coming up with some innovative music that I felt a license to use some signature guitar sounds. There are a lot of new ideas on *All That You Can't Leave Behind*. Even though the word on the record was 'a return to the traditional U2 sound', 'Beautiful Day' is actually quite complex.

IN YOUR TEENS YOU FEEL YOU CAN DRIVE THAT CAR AS FAST AS YOU CAN AND YOU WON'T COME OFF AT THE BEND. IN YOUR TWENTIES, YOU HAVE SOME NEAR-MISSES. IN YOUR THIRTIES YOU REALIZE YOU ARE IN DANGER. AND IN YOUR FORTIES, I THINK YOU'RE JUST REALLY GLAD IF YOU WAKE UP IN THE MORNING. BONO

The song started in the small room at Hanover Quay, all of us playing together, but it didn't sound particularly great at first. As a straight rock song, it was pretty ho-hum. Brian's electronification of the chords with a beat box and string part (which is what you now hear at the beginning of the song) was a breakthrough. It is the combination of all the contrasting elements, the backing vocals, which happened very spontaneously one night (I heard a part and Danny jumped in on the same mike) and the more machine-age arrangement ideas, plus the chemistry of a band that end up making it what it is. It took two weeks to mix that song, because it just wasn't ready. Bono added a simple line, playing the chord pattern on guitar to double the bass, and that solidified everything. But there was still something missing. I changed the bass chords in the chorus and Bono remembered a little keyboard thing that he thought was a clue. I found a way of putting that into a guitar part, which gave it a sour quality that stops it being too positive. The chords on their own are so bright and cheerful the song could have very easily sounded insipid. So there is a bit more to 'Beautiful Day' than meets the eye.

BONO: 'Beautiful Day' has a directness reminiscent of early U2 but with Edge bringing a dizziness and futuristic quality so that it doesn't feel retro. The guitar chords were nothing special but they were my attempt to get the album airborne, the way a rock band like The Buzzcocks would. The lyric expresses amazement, really, that whatever situation you find yourself in, as uncomfortable and upsetting as they can be, if you're alive and you are awake, then you have perspective on it. I was influenced by an Australian preacher I know called John Smith, who was a pastor for the Hell's Angels at one point and who is a very eloquent speaker with a brilliant mind. I remember him talking to me about how depression is a nerve end. Pain is evidence of life because it reminds you there are things in your life that aren't right. So you should be thankful for it really and celebrate that there is so much to live for.

Mortality was the big subject-matter of the album. In your teens you feel immortal, you feel you can drive that car as fast as you can and you won't come off at the bend. In your twenties, you have some near-misses. In your thirties you realize you are in danger. That is when you really no longer feel immortal. I remember my father saying the same thing. Actually, of course, I was just about to turn forty. And in your forties, I think you're just really glad if you wake up in the morning.

'Stuck In A Moment You Can't Get Out Of' was written about Michael Hutchence. Edge was working on a gospel-influenced chord progression on the piano and he had a beautiful Motown-style melody. It was very pop, so I was looking for a phrase that would balance that, that was almost awkward. I remember Larry saying the verses need to be much tougher and that is when I came up with the opening line: *I'm not afraid of anything in this world*, which is just a throw-down. A pop song that starts with that, you have to back it up. I thought Michael deserved a lyric that wasn't mawkish or sentimental, the way two friends would talk to each other: 'What is going on here? There's nothing to be afraid of.' It's got that attitude of when your jaw sticks out, like before a row: *I'm gonna stand up straight, carry my own weight, these tears are going nowhere*. It is like somebody's in a stupor and you're trying to wake them up, the cops are coming and they're sitting at the wheel and you're trying to get them out of the car 'cause they're gonna crash it. Because I just knew that if Michael had hung on an extra half an hour it would have been OK. That's the thing. When you're in that moment you don't believe you can get out of it. You think this blackness that surrounds you will never pass. But it does pass.

ADAM: That is really classic Edge songwriting. It was the first time I've heard Edge perform a song that didn't really need anything else, just a lyric. It could just be him and the piano, it's all there. A great gospel song.

EDGE: 'Stuck In A Moment' was a new thing from U2, in terms of structure, tempo and even chords. Brian set the piece off beautifully. I performed the piano into a sequencer, and he took it and eliminated the first and second notes and just kept every third note, which he set into a different keyboard with a heavy treatment on it, so you get an otherworldly effect over what is quite a traditional gospel piano sequence.

With U2 it is so often the sound that sets the tone of the song. 'Elevation' was one of those songs. It started with a really cool guitar sound that I got with a vintage pedal that Danny brought in. It sounded like some mad funkadelic thing. I hit on a great guitar part almost immediately, so I programmed a quick beat box rhythm and we all started playing against that. Adam really came into his own on 'Elevation' because he is the hip-hop man in the band and there is a real hip-hop attitude in the rhythm section. And then Bono got on the mike and improvized.

BONO: It is fun and frolics but the goal is soul. It is about sexuality and transcendence, a playful piece about wanting to get off, or, in this case, to literally get off the ground. I can't actually remember writing it. It was all over in minutes, which is probably not the greatest admission to make in a song about sex.

EDGE: 'Elevation' is almost light relief in a very heavy sequence of songs. 'Stuck In A Moment', 'Walk On' and 'Kite' are all farewell songs of one kind of another. We worked on the lyric of 'Kite' together, and Bono was convinced he was writing about his kids but I could see that it was more about his dad. He was going, 'No, no, I don't think that's it.' He couldn't see it, but I could. I suppose it's just when you know someone so well, you can see things they won't admit to themselves. I think he was struggling to figure out how to deal with it, because his dad was a very dry person who found emotions difficult, and Bono is such an emotional and open character, so there was an incredible mismatch. I think it was a tough thing in terms of communication or the lack of it.

BONO: That is the thing about songwriting, sometimes you're the last one to know what you're on about. It was a reference to an absurd moment of parenting, where I took a kite up on Killiney Hill with Jordan and Eve. I'd been away, and wanted to do the dad thing but the kite blew off the line and smashed to smithereens on the first flight, and Eve asked if they could go home and play with their Tamagotchis. So the song is about letting go but when I was singing it, suddenly I was back in a caravan site when I was a kid, in Rush or Skerries, and I remembered that my dad had tried to do exactly the same thing with a kite, and it had gone equally badly. I realized I wasn't singing from quite as theoretical a place as I thought. I felt the goodbye aspect of the song was not from me to him, but from him to me.

There is a little journalism at the end, which is *the last of the rock stars / when hip hop drove the big cars / at the time when new media / was the big idea*. That was just setting it in time, saying that's the moment, and then leaving it behind. One of the things about having kids is that if you were concerned you might not be around to see them growing up, what would you do? It is a phenomenon that people on aeroplanes, when they are told to prepare for a crash, they write notes. For whatever reason at that point, I felt the aeroplane was going down. Everywhere I looked, my father was sick, Michael Hutchence was dead, I wasn't sure of my own well-being. I just wanted to have some songs that would, in a way, tell my kids something about who their father was.

'In a Little While' is clearly addressed to the Mrs. *A little girl with Spanish eyes, when I saw her first in a pram they pushed her by / Oh my, my how you've grown*. They used to call me a baby-snatcher in the mall at school for dating a girl from the year below. They say a year is a lot in showbusiness. In high school, it's a lifetime. It is sung in a voice that was up all night.

EDGE: Bono had been up till six in the morning, got two hours sleep, came into work, got on the mike and just hit this incredible improvised lyric and melody.

ADAM: It is sung in a broken voice. And believe me, Bono was broken that day.

BONO: I may have misjudged my allocation of units the night before. I had this idea of writing about the temporal nature of being, but setting it in a hangover gives it some comedy and earthiness that balances the philosophical pretensions. It is really an apology. *In a little while, this hurt will hurt no more, I'll be home, love*. I'm good at apology songs. I've had to be.

There is a beautiful tangent in the midst of this. *A man dreams one day to fly / A man takes a rocket ship into the sky / He lives on a star that's dying in the night / And follows in the trail, the scatter of light*. It's the divine comedy. Christ described the assembled gathering as sheep, which I think is one of the best metaphors for mankind. There's such comedy to that. Have you ever watched a flock of sheep? No one is in charge. They change direction without any seeming logic. I love the idea of human beings (and don't take this personally because I'm one of them) believing they are in charge of their own destiny. For all the progress and all the enlightenment we have had, I do see us kind of stumbling around. There's a sort of audacious side to human beings that puts himself at the centre of the universe. I'm capable of it in lots of ways, reasoning with the Almighty, doing deals. The big question, for me, is not if we believe in God but, much more importantly, does God believe in us?

In the Sixties and Seventies, we were putting a man on the moon, we were creating medicines that would extend people's lives, and everything was possible through progress. By the Eighties and Nineties it was clear that we hadn't dealt with the big issues and it was harder to be optimistic about progress. We could fire rockets into space but we were destroying our own environment. We have the medicines but we won't give them to people who are suffering a plague like AIDS. At the end of the 20th century, people should be really humbled by what we are capable of, but it is still not enough. We have to find new answers to these questions. The world's problems are not going to be all sorted by science. These huge problems come down to poverty and depression and ultimately to the human heart and its greed. Which is really clear at this point. I'm sure that in fifty years, when historians are looking at this period, they will say, 'Oh, that's when the 20th century ran out of gas, right on cue, at the end.' It's a new game in the 21st century. All this stuff was in my head as I was writing a beautiful little pop song. That tangent makes the song for me. It should be called 'The Pilgrim and His Lack of Progress'.

EDGE: 'Wild Honey' breaks up the album, in a way, before the darkness of 'Peace On Earth'. It may have been a misjudgement. I always thought of it as a bit 'Ob-La-Di, Ob-La-Da'.

ADAM: There was quite a lot of debate about whether or not that would be included. It was a bit of fun and frivolity, which is not something U2 are noted for.

BONO: Brian Eno loved it, he thought it sounded like a Van Morrison song. I really did want it on the album, because it was playful and broke the mood. Call it a sorbet between courses. I am not sure if Larry felt the same way.

LARRY: It's a playful side to U2 you rarely get to see. But it wasn't one of my favourites.

EDGE: 'Peace On Earth' is a real pour your heart out song. It's a bit bleak but it's real. It came together very easily. I had the music and Bono got on mike.There is one line I was never sure about: *I'm sick of hearing again and again that there's gonna be peace on earth*. It's too negative. I thought it should have been *I'm sick of hearing again and again that there's never gonna be peace on earth*. Which turns it completely around. Cynicism has it's place but it's often a self-fulfilling prophesy. The notion that we only have a few short years on planet earth so we all better 'get real' and live life to the hilt is just an excuse for total self-centredness. That said the reliance on the fairy tale, pie in the sky when you die aspect of religion is as dangerous, because it excuses so much. I don't think either are right. Our stance as a band is that we believe in heaven but we live as if we didn't.

BONO: I tried to bring it back to growing up on Cedarwood Road and my own violence: *Where I grew up / There weren't many trees / Where there was we'd tear them down / And use them on our enemies*. There's a vanity in there. I put in a couple of my own aphorisms as if they are part of the wisdom of the world: *they say what you mock / Will surely overtake you / And you* *become a monster / so the monster will not break you.* It's a terrible cheat as a writer but I'd love to get one of them off.

I was very shaken by the Omagh bombing but the reason my faith survived it, the reason it can survive any awfulness the world can throw at it, is that I am not surprised by evil. To me, we live in a jungle and I'm expecting at any moment that something will try and eat me. I'm on tenterhooks. I'm more surprised when the punch isn't thrown. But that does not make me cynical. In fact, rather the opposite. I'm amazed at people's ability to sacrifice for each other. I'm amazed at how people can show love where it's not expected and how love can conjoin disparate groups. I'm just amazed at human beings. But I'm never surprised when the weather turns nasty and I try to plan for it. I love it because the sun is up, and I am ready for the moment when it's not.

Not everyone around me feels the same. I have seen people's faith rocked by tragedy, some people very close to me. That is what the song 'When I Look At The World' is about. It is a tender song but also quite tough. I have heard it suggested that it is a portrait of Ali. I have certainly been guilty of putting Ali on a pedestal in the past, which can be dehumanizing because it rids people of their complexity. But here is a confession, on this song, I have put myself on the pedestal. It is written from the point of view of someone who is having a crisis of faith looking at someone who has built their house upon the rock. *When there is all kind of chaos / And everyone is walking lame / You don't even blink now do you ? / Or even look away / So I try to be like you / Try to feel it like you do / But without you it's no use / I can't see what you see / When I look at the world.* The last image is quite cold. It is almost annoyed with someone for their faith. *I'm in the waiting-room / I can't see you for the smoke / I think of you and your holy book / While the rest of us choke.* I don't know why it is set in a hospital waiting-room in the days when people could smoke in such places. It is so heavy, I can hardly think about it. It could almost be the voice of my father, looking at me. The glower. The put-down. But that is the thing that runs right through that album, that gives it its cohesiveness, the ring of truth, connecting with what was going on in my life, connecting to my father and to my mother, which is probably what it all really comes back to, because I haven't been in a waiting room filled with smoke since I was fourteen years old. I am always amazed when stuff like that comes out.

EDGE: Adam, Larry and myself recorded that track on our own very quickly and then I overdubbed some guitar parts. At the end of the album sessions, everyone said, 'Great guitar sounds, Edge. How did you get them?' and I couldn't remember because it happened so quickly. So I was left thinking, 'Shit, how am I going to play that live?' I had no idea. And actually, I don't think we

IF IT WAS A SIMPLE, PAINLESS PROCESS THEN I DON'T THINK THE RECORDS WOULD HAVE THE SAME INTENSITY OR RESONANCE. YOU HAVE TO GOUGE AWAY AND OPEN THE VEINS AND FIND THE SHIT THAT REALLY MATTERS TO YOU, AND TO DO THAT YOU HAVE TO GO TO SOME DARK PLACES. EDGE

ever did play it live. But I like the lyrical idea of seeing the world through someone else's perspective, and their perspective being the thing that makes the world seem OK. I certainly can relate to that. As you get older there is a danger that you can become so negative about everything because your disappointment starts to overwhelm your sense of the possible. One of the great things about having kids is that the possibilities start to become larger again.

ADAM: 'New York' was a performance jam piece that came together as edits. It started with a drum pattern of Larry's that Brian and Danny were working on while we were all having a meeting.

LARRY: There can be a lot of hanging around in a studio. We spend a lot of time finding the right guitar riffs, the right vocal lines, the right bass part and the right drum part. It can be tedious. Often during the down time between writing and recording I get a chance to record drum patterns. 'New York' is a good example of a pattern I had been goofing around with, trying to perfect. I asked the engineer to record and loop it.

We had to take a break for one of those long meetings that go on right through the recording process. When we came back, Brian and Danny were playing around with my loop.

ADAM: It was a very frustrating meeting, as it happened, and we were itching to get back to the studio. We walked into this groove of Brian and Danny's, with a big foghorn sound on Larry's drums loop, and all joined in, Bono got on the mike and it all unfolded very quickly. Of course, as always happens with these jams, we had to cut it up, edit it and learn to play it later.

BONO: I just can't get over New York. It feels like the centre of the earth. Which is, I'm sure, why Osama Bin Laden singled it out. It's certainly the city of our times, as Paris and London have been in the past, the centre of Western culture. I have an apartment there, and I'm lucky to be able to live in it, walk around in it and experience the intense heat of New York summers. There have been times in my life when I have gotten lost there … and it is a great city to get lost in. But there's a darkness in the song. It is an ode to New York but in the background you sense danger. It is about a mid-life crisis. *I hit an iceberg in my life / But you know I'm still afloat/ You lose your balance, lose your wife / In the queue for the lifeboat / You've got to put the women and children first / But you've got an unquenchable thirst for New York.* I was trying to own up to that part of every man that wants to run from life and its responsibilities. And I can do that in a song – it's much better than doing it in real life. As a songwriter I tend to release the bats and follow every wild thought. So the character is me in a parallel universe, the person who would just give in to his own wanderlust. Ali never holds me to account for these songs. She knows that the weaknesses of the human heart is one of my favourite subjects. I don't want to leave any stone unturned, including my own. Ali has great grace. It can't be easy being married to an artist who insists on exposing his own hypocrisies. But she knows it's not an autobiography.

The album ends with 'Grace'. There are a couple of my favourite people rolled in to that lyric but the most important thing is that they personify my favourite word in the lexicon of the English language. It's a word I'm depending on. The universe operates by Karma, we all know that. For every action there's an equal and opposite reaction. There is some atonement built in: an eye for an eye, a tooth for a tooth. Then enters Grace and turns that upside down. I love it. I'm not talking about people being graceful in their actions but just covering over the cracks. Christ's ministry really was a lot to do with pointing out how everybody is a screw-up in some shape or form, there's no way around it. But then He was to say, well, I am going to deal with those sins for you. I will take on Myself all the consequences of sin. Even if you're not religious I think you'd accept that there are consequences to all the mistakes we make. And so Grace enters the picture to say, 'I'll take the blame, I'll carry your cross.' It is a powerful idea. Grace interrupting Karma.

ADAM: It was a beautiful way to end the album.

EDGE: It wasn't an easy album to make but then none of them are really. I mean, if it was a simple, painless process then I don't think the records would have the same intensity or resonance. You have to gouge away and open the veins and find the shit that really matters to you, and to do that you have to go to some dark places. And that doesn't necessarily happen easily or quickly.

LARRY: There was a lot of painstaking work. When you hear a song like

'Beautiful Day' on the radio it sounds so effortless but to get that song to that place was hard, days and days of trying to put this jigsaw together. Edge went after this song like his life depended on it. It was important to prove that we could write great songs and get played on radio. We need to prove to ourselves that we were better than we were on our last album. I think we did that, and it felt good to be in U2 again.

BONO: The cover is aesthetically low key, with none of that kind of Mount Rushmore iconography some people associate with U2. We're just in an airport, kind of hanging out. I like Larry's playfulness. He's kind of looking out from behind my back and I'm fiddling with my passport. It's the Roissy terminal in Charles De Gaulle airport, designed by French architect Paul Andreu, who I am a fan of. I have a thing about airports, rather like I have a thing about hotels – I spend most of my life in them. Airports are the first thing you see when you come into a city. When you come into the Roissy terminal, with its kind of velvet concrete, you see the difference design makes to people's life. It's an ode to an airport. And it fits with the title perfectly. What's the destination? The future. And then, just because advertising pays, I thought I'd put God's phone number up in the airport's digital clock. J33.3. That's Jeremiah 33:3. The Scripture is 'Call unto Me and I will answer you'. It's celestial telephony.

The video for 'Beautiful Day' was shot on the runway, which I couldn't believe we got permission for. The Concorde had recently crashed and they were very sensitive about the runway. But it was a beautiful day, literally. I had a character in mind, who was just a little half-cocked, a kind of uber-Bono. My favourite scene, which was done spontaneously, was getting on the luggage rack and being taken through that black hole where the bags go. Everyone wants to go through the hole, don't they?

ADAM: 'Beautiful Day' came out and got a really strong reaction. It seemed everyone kind of loved it, they hadn't heard the band sounding that way since maybe *Joshua Tree* or certainly *Achtung Baby*.

PAUL: I think it was a very good idea to make a record that actually sounded like U2 again. The album came out on 31 October 2000 and went straight to number one in thirty-two countries.

ADAM: We were due to perform at the Grammy Awards in Los Angeles in February 2001. We had three nominations for 'Beautiful Day' but we didn't really think anything would come of it. We just thought we would turn up and perform our song. But we won all three Grammies that night. That was an amazing way to start the year.

LARRY: We had received many Grammies before and it was great to get them but this was different. After *Pop*, America kind of lost interest in U2 and felt we had pushed the boat out too far. We felt vulnerable and slightly shaken by what had happened. So when *All That You Can't Leave Behind* did so well and 'Beautiful Day' won all those Grammies, it felt like a real endorsement. For the first time in ages, I remember feeling grateful for the gongs. I was embarrassed that I hadn't appreciated them before. Since then, I value awards and I value people's applause in a very different way.

EDGE: Bono came up with this line about reapplying for the job of best band in the world. It was a good line … at the time. I mean, it's never really that simple. But I think we felt we had blown it to some extent with the 'Pop' album but this record was very strong and direct and it was going to be the basis for a great tour. We had the goods.

BONO: There's great humility and arrogance in that line. The humility is admitting that you've lost it. And the arrogance is imagining you can have it. But it got everyone talking and that's part of my job. Are they? Could they? How dare they? That's all good.

And part of reapplying for the job was a reappraisal of what was cool and uncool for rock 'n' roll bands to do. For the last fifteen years, we had maybe done a half-dozen interviews a year. We were still following a kind of Seventies punk rock model. The idea was that you should keep a mysterious distance, don't go round selling yourself.

Well, we decided to sell ourselves on *All That You Can't Leave Behind* and we've continued to this day. And the reason is the world had changed for rock 'n' roll. We weren't just fighting for the band's life, we were fighting for the format. And you're up against people who work very, very hard. Hip hop was all over the place. So if you don't do those TV programmes, other people are going to do them. I was thinking about our first couple of albums, when we would do anything we could do, every interview, every radio station, any TV show. In fact, it's how any rock 'n' roll band starts off, whether it's The Beatles, The Sex Pistols or U2, before the mysterious distance turns into a pompous distance, where you think you don't have to do this kind of promo, that it's somehow beneath you. It's amazing how lazy rock 'n' roll had become. Hip hop artists have videos selling their songs and in that same video they're telling you about the next song that's coming or the next artist signed to their label. They've got clothing lines and fashion labels. They're just so industrious. It's the way music was in the Sixties, when The Rolling Stones would be on a TV show in between Engelbert Humperdinck and a magic act. You have to find the energy of your era and ride it.

PAUL: Learning from the *Pop* experience, we decided to start with a very controlled, indoor-only show. Those American arenas are just right for U2. I wish there were one in every city in the world. Bono likes playing stadiums, he really does. There's something gladiatorial about it that excites him. But it is very difficult to do a show in a football stadium. It has to be a great spectacle and it's very hard to make the listening experience as good as it would be in, say, Madison Square Garden.

LARRY: I was happy to be back in arenas. This record was about letting people know that the *Pop* experiment was over, and the essence of U2 was still the four members of the band. Arenas seemed the right place to do that. We actually did some club gigs leading up to the tour, something we hadn't done since the early days, The Man Ray Club in Paris, The Astoria in London and Irving Plaza, New York. Playing in front of fifty thousand people is easy in comparison to playing in front of two and a half thousand people, when the audience can see the whites of your eyes, they can see your fear, they can see everything. It was scary. Our music is suited to bigger places. We spent our early career trying to get out of the small places.

ADAM: It was really great to be back indoors because, musically, it's a much easier performance space, being on a smaller stage in a small building. Granted, not everyone thinks of arenas as small buildings, but if there's 20,000 people there, you can see them as well as they can see you, so there's a connection. Once you get into anything bigger than 20,000 you can't really see the audience and they can't really see you.

EDGE: The record was hailed as being back to basics, which it wasn't. And the tour was described as a minimalist production, which, of course, it really wasn't. It is all relative, and compared to *Pop* anything would seem back to basics.

LARRY: The Elevation tour was a great design. I liked it straight away, when Willie Williams, Bono and Mark Fisher came in with the original drawings. The use of the heart as a runway to get out into the audience, and the way the heart itself filled with people, was great. It was almost like a club gig within an arena.

YOU BECOME FAMILIAR WITH THE ENVIRONMENT
AROUND DEATH WHEN YOU WORK IN AFRICA, A
CERTAIN STENCH, A CERTAIN DEVASTATION, THE
RUBBLE OF IT. BUT IN MY OWN FAMILY IT WAS
BRINGING ME BACK, CLOSING THE CIRCLE, BRINGING
ME BACK TO MY MOTHER'S DEATH. I THOUGHT I HAD
ESCAPED IT, BUT I WAS WRONG. BONO

PAUL: We met Willie Williams when he was a punk and he was lighting man for Stiff Little Fingers. He came up to us and said, 'I want to work for you.' At first he was a lighting operator and then he was the stage designer. Our stages weren't particularly complicated back then but he grew as an artist with the band. His contribution to the productions over the years has been immense. He is an artist, his canvas is the rock 'n' roll stage.

EDGE: The idea of opening with the house lights on came in the last week before we did the first show in Miami. And it really worked. In a very subtle way it made a huge statement about the nature of the show and the nature of the relationship between the band and the audience, stripping away artifice back to something that was very personal. It was a great opening gambit.

BONO: We had done a few small gigs. Started off in Paris, playing to a couple of hundred people. We were really going back to the very beginning. Forget clubs, it was like going back to the Dandelion Market. The humbling bit was that we weren't very good. And then we started improving. We did one in New York to a thousand people. It still wasn't as transcendent as it needed to be. By the time we got to London we were getting rave reviews, but we weren't firing on all cylinders. It was like sex with the lights on. Which, of course, can be very exciting … but not that night. We had been the champ, we had been knocked down, we were standing back up but we were not super-steady on our feet yet. It was a return to the ring but not world-class. The title fight was Miami, 24 March 2001, the first night of the Elevation tour. There was a DJ conference going on in Miami, every DJ in the world seemed to be there, but they all bailed-out to come and see U2 play. And that was a big compliment for us, being fans of club culture. And they saw what rock 'n' roll can do when it does get off the ground. It really went off. Miami was great. I love that city. It was hot and humid in every way that night.

LARRY: The new songs worked with the older songs. It was kind of seamless. It felt like we were reconnecting with our audience and they with us.

ADAM: Bono went walkabout, just like in the old days. We were playing 'The Fly' and suddenly he was gone. All you could see was a ripple through the audience as he ran to the back of the hall.

EDGE: That is what a live show should be. It should have a sense that anything could happen.

BONO: I tried to leave and get a taxi. But I couldn't get a taxi, so I had to come back around. I ran through the audience to the back of the arena and then I had to run all the way around the perimeter to get backstage, pursued by security and what seemed like half the audience. Of course I wouldn't tell the band that I was planning something like that because then they'd petition to stop me.

I really believe it is my job to attack the distance between performer and audience. From climbing speaker stacks to stage diving, it is all the same thought. And, if I may be immodest, U2 have reinvented the rock show with that in mind several times, from the B-stage for Zoo TV to the heart on Elevation. Now the B-stage is ubiquitous but I had been trying to do that since the mid Eighties. The thing that made it possible was in-ear monitors. When you have your sound monitoring on a wireless earphone it drowns out the time delay that occurs from being out in front of a big PA. So technology changes the shape of a rock concert, if you want it to. The heart was fantastic. The only problem was some of our most ardent fans were following from gig to gig. So whatever city we'd turn up in there would be the same people in front of us, which was a little disorientating. And when we tried to make sure that locals got into the heart, there was a mutiny. They all sat down in Boston, in the middle of the heart, because they knew we were filming the show. They thought they weren't telegenic enough and that's why we were trying to keep them out. It was just that we wanted to play in front of a fresh audience. So there's still trouble over that.

EDGE: Joey Ramone died on April 15. We played The Ramones' 'I Remember You' in his honour that night in Portland. We had played it at our New York warm-up show at the Irving Plaza before the tour began. There was an element of nostalgia for us playing a club in New York, it took us back to where we had started and the Ramones reference was to acknowledge the influence they had on us. Joey heard about it and later, when we were playing

BONO'S RELATIONSHIP WITH HIS FATHER WAS
COMPLICATED AND NEVER EASY. THEY WERE VERY
ALIKE. ALTHOUGH HE WOULD NEVER SAY IT, I THINK
HIS FATHER WAS ENORMOUSLY PROUD OF BONO. I
DON'T KNOW WHY HE COULDN'T TELL HIM. PAUL

on Saturday Night Live, there was a knock on the dressing room door and there he was. He obviously knows people who know people. We were blown away that he would come down to see us. He looked a little rough, you could tell he wasn't in the best of health. So we hung out with Joey and had a great time talking to him and telling him the stories of the early days, about playing Ramones songs and pretending they were our own to get on TV. We told him that we couldn't afford the ticket price to see The Ramones when they played Dublin in 1978 but one of our friends got in and opened up the emergency exit so we could all see the second half of the show for free. And it was just the greatest show we'd ever seen. Joey loved all those stories. A couple of months later we found out Joey was terminally ill. We were devastated when he died because we were huge fans and having just met him, he was very much on our minds. We heard through a close friend of his that 'In A Little While' was his favourite U2 song and during the time he was really going downhill fast, in hospital, he would asked for it to be played. So it obviously meant a lot to him. And so, for the rest of the tour, we dedicated 'In a Little While' to Joey.

BONO: Ali and I had our fourth child, a son, John Abraham, in Dublin on May 20. I had a five-day break in the tour, which was nerve-racking. If the baby came early or late I'd have missed John's arrival into the world. But he came right on target. So there was birth and there was death too, the whole shebang. Joey Ramone died. My dad was dying. It seemed like this is where we came in, well, Larry and myself anyway. This is the furnace in which U2 were forged.

EDGE: Bono's father's health had really become a major issue by the time the tour relocated to Europe in July. It became clear that Bob was actually slipping away quite quickly. It wasn't a case of whether he was going to be around at the end of the tour but just how long he had.

Bono was faced with a very difficult decision to cancel shows or not. You're talking about the opportunity to spend time with somebody who is not going to be around any more. That's what was in my mind. I was open to the idea of Bono saying 'I need these couple of months with my dad.'

LARRY: It was the first time for many years that we were facing a situation where somebody within our family was dying. It was hard to know what to do. Everyone rallied round. Bono put his head down and went at it. For those of us who know him, we could see the strain and the stress and the upset in his face, but to those outside it appeared he was just carrying on as normal. And that's essentially what he did, he buried his head in the work to stay afloat.

BONO: I was allowed to wail and keen, as the Irish call it, on a nightly basis. Most of the problem of grief is that people bottle it up. But I could use these songs to keep myself sane. I was having conversations in these songs that maybe I couldn't have with people.

EDGE: He decided he was going to work around the tour and spend as much time with his dad as he could. So there were a lot of flights home to Dublin after the European shows to be at his dad's bedside. He would spend a couple of days in the hospital and then come back out on the road. It was very hard on Bono. I really felt for him. I think the shows almost became his opportunity to release emotion. In some ways it's where we've lived for so many years that it's almost a natural process to deal with all of those feelings through music and performance. We were ready to do whatever he wanted to do. What was nice is that he did get a lot of time with his dad, one-on-one. And I think that, as much as was possible given the character of his father, there was a sense of closure and peace and things being brought to some kind of understanding between them. They had a deep love for each other but at the same time their ways of communicating were worlds apart. Generations apart.

BONO: I felt close to him towards the end, even though we weren't conversing. He had Parkinson's, so all he could do was whisper, so he had an excuse. I could tell he was happy about that. He was a wily character and he would dodge a conversation better than anyone.

I was coming back from those gigs and sitting next to him. I would draw him in the hospital room, all the wires and tubes. Sometimes I would read to him. He loved Shakespeare. If I read the Bible he would just scowl. I would lie beside him at night on a roll-up bed. It was really wonderful to be able to sleep beside my father. And, you know, I think my father was very proud of me.

I came out with an enormous respect for my brother, because he was so good at all the stuff that I wasn't. It's strange, you become familiar with the environment around death when you work in Africa, a certain stench, a certain devastation, the rubble of it. But in my own family it was bringing me back, it was closing the circle, bringing me back to my mother's death, and lots of things were going off. I thought I had escaped it, but I was wrong. My brother was doing the dirty work, the real rolling up your sleeves stuff, as nobly as only he could. I was just there, trying to help out in other ways.

I was there for his last words. It was a last 'Fuck off!' I was lying beside him in the middle of the night and I heard a shout. So I called the nurse. He was whispering something, so we both put our ears to his mouth. She said, 'Bob, are you OK? What are you saying? Do you need anything?' He said, 'Would you ever fuck off and get me out of here. This place is a prison cell. I want to go home.' Not very romantic, but revealing. I really had a sense that he wanted out not just of the room, but out of his body. It was not long afterwards that he exited, stage left.

ADAM: We were doing four nights at Earls Court in London. Bob passed away in the early hours of Tuesday, 21 August. We played our third show that night. If Bono had wanted to cancel the show, of course we would have. But knowing Bono's character, I assumed he would want to play. He believes in including people in whatever's going on. I think he believed the right place for him to be was on the stage, revealing his grief in the music and having it witnessed by an audience. I don't think he knows another way. I don't think having a quiet night, keeping vigil, would have been Bono's way.

EDGE: It was a very powerful show. Obviously, my main concern was Bono and how he would be able to cope with it. But he managed to get through it really well. And I think it did help actually. I think he knew that and that's why he wanted to do the show.

LARRY: Obviously people were concerned about him but he was in control. We were just watching his back as much as we could. Bono is a very complex individual and a lot of people would not have been able to do what he did. It's a sign of his strength and character that he was able to carry on. And I know that's what Bob would have wanted. I think Bono knew that.

BONO: The songs were keeping my head above water. I was holding on very tightly to those songs.

ADAM: In a situation like that, it's not really about words, you just do the best you can and give your friend as much support as possible. It was a case of being happy to be of service. I think it was a relief for all of us to be playing the shows rather than sitting in a hotel room contemplating what had just happened.

BONO: We buried him ourselves. My brother and I put him in the ground and we physically covered him, we didn't let the undertakers do it. There were some nice things at the service. Everyone sang 'The Black Hills of Dakota'. *Take me back to the black hills, the black hills of Dakota*. That was nice. I sang a song I was working on, 'Sometimes You Can't Make It On Your Own'.

PAUL: It was very affecting. The band have been at the funerals of both of my parents, as it happens. It takes years to get over anything like that, and maybe you never do. Bono's relationship with his father was complicated and never easy. They were very alike. Although he would never say it, I think his father was enormously proud of Bono. I don't know why he couldn't tell him.

LARRY: I was very fond of Bob. He had a dry sense of humour and he liked to laugh. When the opportunities arose, I would sit with him and chat and have a drink. He was a very Dublin man, a tough nut, a real working-class Irishman. He loved drama and the opera. In the last five years of his life he became quite dandy. He started to wear cravats with his shirts. He was very dapper, with a real sense of pride in himself. Having heard all the stories of life in the Hewson household, when you saw the two of them together it was kind of funny. He always saw Bono as his kid. He didn't see the rock star. It was like, 'He's my son, he deserves a clip around the ear.' That's the way he behaved around Bono. And although he may not have said it to Bono, he took real pride in what the band were doing. But he also really enjoyed sticking the boot in, just because he could, with a snigger. I enjoyed that about him and I miss his humour.

ADAM: It was very difficult burying Bob and then playing at Slane, I have to say. We were back in Dublin to play the biggest shows of the whole tour, two nights at Slane Castle, over 180,000 people. The day before the first show, August 24, we attended the funeral in Howth and we gave Bob a real good send-off. But I found that still lingered as a kind of hangover into the next day and into the show. I think maybe we'd been on a roll, there'd been a lot of momentum, and when Bob was finally buried it was a bit of a full stop. And, in myself, I felt I needed a bit of contemplation, a bit of quietness away from everything. And that wasn't to be. It was straight into a show the next day, and it all had to be dealt with in a very public way because it had obviously been a big story within Ireland, so everyone at the show knew what had happened. I'm a different kind of a person to Bono, my chemistry is different. I felt very vulnerable. I didn't feel that I had my armour on and so it was a difficult show. But it must have been a lot more difficult for him.

BONO: In a place like Slane, where you have a crucible of people, a gig can be a sacramental event.

LARRY: It was twenty years since we'd played Slane. And it was thrilling to go back to our home town and play to that many people. But Bob's funeral really felt like the end of an era and it took the edge off a huge occasion. The second show, a week later, was completely different. The Irish football team were playing a World Cup qualifier against Holland in Dublin. I went to the match at Lansdowne Road and afterwards helicoptered to the gig. It was quite a trip, and quite a day. The football game was shown on the screens at Slane, so if Ireland had lost there might have been trouble. But Ireland beat Holland 1-0, a team with so many star players no one really believed that Ireland could possibly win. Jason McAteer scored an amazing goal. It all made for a great gig. After the sadness of the first show, this was a celebration.

EDGE: It was pretty mind-blowing. The energy from the audience was astonishing. You could feel it, physically.

ADAM: We filmed both those shows, as you do when you are going to make a live video. But we only ended up using footage from the second show. They were just so different.

BONO: We had a month's break in the tour. I was on holiday in Venice, walking with my little boy and I got lost in the back streets. We went into the American Hotel, looking for directions. There was a television on, showing the news. A plane had just flown into the twin towers in New York. Everything changed that day.

PAUL: We were about to put tickets on sale that very week for the final leg of the tour, October and November in North America.

ADAM: And then September 11th happened. And it was a very confusing time. Emotions were running high. Nobody really knew what was happening in America. A lot of people cancelled shows.

PAUL: The whole world seemed to change. We drew a deep breath, put the tickets on sale anyway, and the shows all sold out.

LARRY: We wanted to be in the US. It was where we belonged.

ADAM: That was when the record had a whole other lease of life. Radio started to play it in a way that it hadn't been playing it before. It became very important to people.

EDGE: I think the album has a certain tone which seemed to connect with people after 9/11. It has an ache about it, and it's asking some big questions and dealing with loss and the stuff of real life. In the aftermath of 9/11, America was in massive crisis, and the album seemed to strike a chord with people.

PAUL: In a strange way, the U2 tour became a sort of emblem of what America was. The shows after 9/11 were just completely different in their mood, they were transformed by what had happened. Americans are very inward-looking. And they went through a convulsion then that the rest of the world may be paying the price of for the rest of time. Those shows were like religious ceremonies and truly great rock and roll shows. An extraordinary loop of energy and emotion passes through the band and through the audience and through the material, people live vicariously through those songs and through the people performing them, and that became very explicit in the months after the twin towers. It was fascinating to watch it happen, night after night, to see songs suddenly transformed and bursting with new meanings.

LARRY: 'Sunday, Bloody Sunday', 'New Year's Day', every song seemed to have a new meaning, the audience laughing and crying, all at the same time. It was an extraordinary experience to be on a stage with everybody going through an emotional rollercoaster, including the band.

BONO: It was a different country, and it still is. It's a country that had never been invaded. It was suffering from shock. The first shock was the attack on the towers and the Pentagon. The second shock was the aftershock, realizing that so many people around the world hated America, seeing people jumping up and down in Indonesia and elsewhere, celebrating the twin towers turning to dust. They were just completely traumatized. And so were we. These are our friends. This is a country I love. And they were wailing in shock and grief and loss. And the same process of keening that I had used for myself, singing these songs, they were starting to use, and we became very close with our audience.

LARRY: U2 have always had a special relationship with New York. It was the first city we played in America. There was the Irish connection, there was the magic of the city itself. Myself and Adam have had apartments in New York for over ten years. Bono recently got a place there. We have always seen it as a second home.

EDGE: When we got to New York it was like the shows had taken on this completely other aspect. They were no longer just rock 'n' roll concerts, they were a kind of group therapy session.

ADAM: New York was a shaken city. Playing Madison Square Garden, it seemed as if people were coming out of their apartments and homes and being prepared to let their guard down for an hour and a half. They were amazing shows.

EDGE: The level of emotion in the building was unbelievable. I don't think there was a dry eye in the house, including the band. It was an unbelievably moving thing to be part of it.

ADAM: Catherine Owens had come up with this piece where, during 'Walk On', we rolled the names of all the people who were missing after the 9/11 attacks and that was a powerful, cathartic moment and an amazing thing to be a part of. The wounds were still raw and an audience has to really trust you to let you push certain buttons. And those audiences did, they trusted us and they went there with us.

BONO: In Madison Square Garden, the lights came on during 'Where The Streets Have No Name' and there must have been ten thousand people with tears running down their faces. And I told them they looked beautiful, which became the line in 'City of Blinding Lights'.

EDGE: At the end of the show members of the fire service came up on stage. They just happened to be there, it wasn't planned. A lot of them had lost brothers and close friends.

BONO: U2 have always been a favourite of firemen and police in America, because so many have Irish roots. I remember this one guy grabbing the microphone. He says, 'This is for my brother, John. We had a rock band. Cheers, John. I always told you we'd make it to Madison Square Garden.' And then he shouted out: 'And New York, you'll know where to find us if you need us, you just dial 911.' That was the moment I realized the great irony of that date. SOS dial 911.

EDGE: It was a very New York event. Really, we were just the soundtrack to a city that was going through mourning and coming to terms with great loss. And somehow the music was a salve of some kind. We were just happy to be there and try to be of service. So they were very special concerts for reasons that are incredibly regrettable.

BONO: I was sitting in Balthazar's, a kind of brasserie, one of my favourite places in New York. My car was outside and the police had come to move it on and my driver had rather inelegantly said, 'Can't I stay here? Bono's inside.' And they said, 'Bono? We need to speak with him.' So these two police officers came in. And they said, 'Is that your car outside?' I said, 'I'm really, really sorry.' They said, 'Oh, you can park wherever you want. We want to talk about what you're doing with Africa.' This cop said, 'I was in the twin towers when they came down.' He was there with the Franciscan priest who was killed when he was struck by falling debris after removing his helmet to administer last rites to a fallen firefighter. He said, 'I just want you to know that America has got to show the world who we are. We've got to show people that we want to help them and that we're not their enemy.' It struck me that a police officer who had lost friends in 9/11 would be the last person you'd expect to come out with such a comment. That was a real moment for me. There was a lot of anger in the air, too. I think that's OK. People were right to be angry. And I wanted to give them a place to vent that anger. But it was important at that moment to talk about tolerance and to be able to remind people that the Muslims in America were not to be tarred with the same brush as these extremists. I hope we performed some function.

EDGE: We did the roll of names of the dead and missing during half-time at the Superbowl in February 2002. We played MLK but the list was so long it was still scrolling through for most of 'Where The Streets Have No Name'. That was really the last thing we did. It was the end of a great tour. And it was a kind of a bringing back of everything, re-establishing the centre and the core. I think, for everybody, it was a really important time.

BONO: The Superbowl was a big moment for U2, almost like our Ed Sullivan show, twenty years on. We had to build that stage in six minutes. I was on radio-controlled earphones and microphone. One error and you're off air. It was terrifying but all you can see is my usual expression when I'm terrified – a big smirk. But it was a great moment. That whole tour, we kind of fell in love with America again and they fell in love with us.

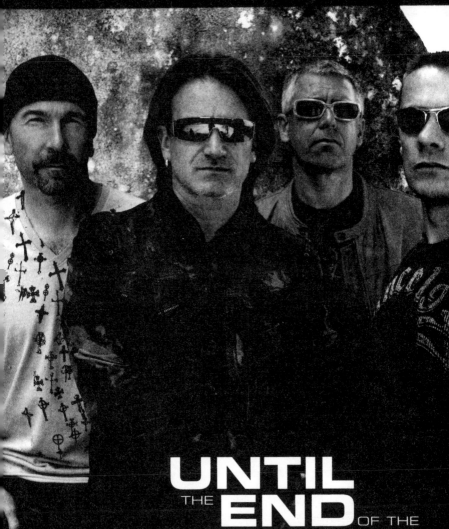

UNTIL
THE END OF THE
WORLD
2002 - 2006

Bono

WE CAME OFF THAT TOUR WITH REAL FIRE IN OUR BELLY AND THOUGHT, 'WOW, IF WE COULD BOTTLE THIS, WHAT MAD ELIXIR WOULD IT BE?'

So we sent our engineer, Richie Rainey, down to the sands of the South of France to look for a place where we could play.

EDGE: We took over this old, tumble-down Monte Carlo nightclub from the Seventies. The Monaco sessions, I think you could call them. It has a certain ring about it.

BONO: It was really a burnt-out basement. And it had the sound of a basement, which is quite a hard rock sound. The band were still flexible from being on tour and playing very well with each other and we wanted to capture some of that spirit, more sort of spunk than punk.

PAUL: There is always a lot of energy in the air at the end of a tour, and bits of unfinished music, people feel very disorientated, so I think the theory was it would be good to see if any of that could be turned into songs for the next album.

LARRY: Even though we were a little burnt-out after a long tour, we decided to spend three or four weeks in a makeshift studio throwing ideas around. It was time well spent.

EDGE: Running pell-mell from one thing into the next may keep the momentum going but you don't get a chance to come up for air. Part of what keeps the band still relevant is the fact that we do actually have a life, we do normal things, hang out with our friends, enjoy our families. Those are very important to the work, I think. These days we can take a little bit more time between projects. We're not financially under the hammer, so we can really try and get it right. But some of the stuff from Monaco ended up being the beginning of our next album, plus we worked on 'Electrical Storm' and 'The Hands That Built America', which became part of the next *Best Of*.

I DID FLASH A PEACE SIGN AS WE PASSED THE PRESS CORPS. BUSH WHISPERED UNDER HIS BREATH, 'THERE GOES A FRONT PAGE SOMEWHERE: IRISH ROCK STAR WITH THE TOXIC TEXAN.' BONO

PAUL: One of the great privileges of having a long career is that, to a certain extent, you get to write your own history. There was a lot of work putting together the second *Best Of* album, *1990-2000*. It was nice to see those big projects so well done. The mythological aspects of a great band are something we've always been aware of, as I think The Beatles were and The Rolling Stones are. I don't think it's surprising that U2 are protective of the way people regard them. So compiling something like that, deciding what goes on the record and what doesn't, remastering it, getting the videos up to release quality, all tends to take a long time.

LARRY: The *Best Of* albums give you an opportunity to look back at your work and appreciate it. Well, most of it. We had a chance to remix some of the *Pop* tracks which helped a bit but didn't quite lay the ghost of *Pop* to rest. I still have this probably mad idea that we might finish those songs one day.

ADAM: We had material left over from *All That You Can't Leave Behind* and the Monaco sessions, and Bono thought that we should forget the Greatest Hits altogether and put out a new studio album. I think that was kind of gratuitous. It took us three or four months just to complete two new songs, so we stuck with the *Best Of*.

BONO: 'The Hands That Built America' was written to order for Martin Scorsese's film *The Gangs of New York*. We have enormous respect for Scorsese, he has a genius for incorporating music in film, so when he calls, you pay attention. We worked with William Orbit, who's like another Brian Eno character, he loves textures and atmospheres, the spirit in the machine.

LARRY: We are always interested in experimenting with new producers. We liked what William Orbit had done on his own ambient work and with Madonna and Blur. He's a creative guy. We tried some things out with him in France. 'Electrical Storm' was an incomplete idea. It had a great guitar riff and some really beautiful melodic ideas. We worked very hard trying to put those ideas together. In the end we didn't quite nail it.

BONO: 'Electrical Storm' was an attempt to capture a sense of unease I was feeling around the world, especially in America, an air of nervous anticipation. It's really about a couple in a room, feeling a storm brewing in the sky outside and equating that to the pressure they feel in their relationship. It's a post-9/11 song but it is not an overtly political song. I had the feeling that if U2 made another big statement about peace, war would break out just to shut us up. A hardened terrorist is not going to put down his weapon because U2 says war is bad.

PAUL: In February, Bono made the cover of *Time* magazine again, this time without the rest of the band, with the legend: 'Can Bono save the world?' Bono was, if possible, becoming even more politically active than ever before but at least now he had his own organization, DATA, to look after that side of his affairs, which took some of the pressure and potential conflict away from Principle. He takes far too much on, I think, but it is hard to criticize him because his political achievements are very real. But there are times when it makes the rest of the band feel that they're taking second place. I suspect they think U2 should be more important to him than it sometimes is.

BONO: Jubilee 2000 had the Millennium as its hook, a window of opportunity to drop the debts of the poorest countries in the world to the richest. When the international campaign disbanded in 2001, we had a lot of momentum going, in the US especially, and thought it would be a mistake to let go of this extraordinary array of characters who had gathered around us. One third of all debts owed by the least-developed countries was in the process of being cancelled. That's fifty-six billion dollars. The United States cancelled all the money it was owed by the poorest countries in the world. The United Kingdom did. Italy did. France did. But this was mostly bilateral, country to country debt. We were still working hard on multilateral debt, which is the monies owed to the World Bank and the IMF. So Debt was the D in DATA.

As Bill Clinton left office, a very bright girl in Larry Summer's Treasury, chief of staff Sheryl Sandberg, pointed me in another direction. She said, 'A reform of trade would make an even bigger difference than a reform of the debt burden. If Africa had the same share of the global market that it had in the Seventies, it would be worth double the amount of aid the whole world gives it in a year, every year.' So Trade became the T in DATA.

The centrepiece was AIDS, the biggest pandemic in the history of civilization, bigger than the Black Death, which took a third of Europe in the Middle Ages. Seven thousand Africans dying every day of a preventable, treatable disease is not a cause, it's an emergency.

These were the three biggest issues facing the continent of Africa, the final A in DATA. But the acronym worked two ways. If you turned it round to focus on what the West wanted for releasing funds, it also spelt: Democracy, Accountability, Transparency for Africa. We founded DATA in Washington DC and London because we needed to formalize what myself, Bobby Shriver and Bob Geldof had been doing on the hoof for years now. Bobby found the money, Bob found the name and sitting in the kitchen of my house with two of the brightest lights of Jubilee 2000, Jamie Drummond and Lucy Matthew, we laid out some sort of manifesto. Geldof was still complaining that he didn't want to be in any organization, but was last to leave the room that day. He's been an advisor and a soul mate of ours.

Paul McGuinness has said to me all my life, 'Look, the job of the artist is to point out problems not to try and solve them.' But I have always seen creativity in places where you're not supposed to find it, in commerce and in politics. The same lateral thinking that works in the studio where you're pulling a melody out of thin air, I try to make it work for me wherever I am. I want to live the creative life not just do creative things in my life. And I think I turned out to be pretty good at this stuff.

I met President Bush in March 2002, which was interesting. I was seen as a Clintonite so we had to work with the new administration to convince them we weren't coming from any particular bias, politically. We worked both sides of the aisle in Congress. I developed a very good relationship with Dr Condoleezza Rice, who was the US National Security Advisor. She had let me and the DATA team in, in a refreshing way, and was passionate about Africa and the inequities of the developing world. We discussed ideas for a new kind of development assistance, one that would rout the old arguments about corruption and 'not redecorating presidential palaces for despots'. Because clearly a lot of foreign aid had been misused in the past, propping up tinpot dictators in ways that actually did more damage than good. We ended up working with Dr Rice on a plan to reward countries that tackled corruption, and where there was clear and transparent process in place, to give them an increase in aid. We were operating as advocates and activists and involved in hard policy work. I'm very proud of the work we did on this. President Bush asked me to be there when he announced the new initiative.

It was called the Millennium Challenge and it would, in effect, double aid to Africa, with an extra $5 billion on the table annually. So I had a photo op with President Bush, which led to criticism in some quarters, and some of my critics may have actually been in the band. I kept a straight face in the photograph but I did flash a peace sign as we passed the Press corps. Bush whispered under his breath, 'There goes a front page somewhere: Irish rock star with the Toxic Texan.' Bush is actually a funny guy. I think the swagger and the cowboy boots come with some humour. It was a tense couple of days, because I didn't want to be at that announcement of the Millennium Challenge unless they also committed to a historic AIDS initiative – a response that matched the scale of the crisis. They weren't prepared to publicly commit but privately they made a promise that they were working on something. There were a lot of people around me who thought I was very foolish to accept them at their word. But I did. And they did come through. In his State of The Union address in January 2003, President Bush announced fifteen billion dollars over five years to fight AIDS abroad. I was genuinely amazed. To put this into context, in 2001 if you had told anyone on Capitol Hill that a Republican Administration would get behind delivering anti-retro-viral drugs to people with AIDS in Africa, they would have laughed in your face. And they did laugh in my face. Bush and Rice deserve huge credit for this. And Congress, both Democrats and Republicans. So there was a sweep of activity dealing with all of this which took up about two years. It was pretty constant and very intense.

I do think at one point U2 wanted to get an album out really quickly. It is fair to say the DATA work derailed that. But some people in the band were relieved anyway.

EDGE: Morleigh and I got married on 17 June 2002. We actually married twice, at a small civil service in the Dublin register office and a few days later at a ceremony on the top of a mountain in the South of France. The Dublin ceremony was totally generic and I went to it thinking it was just a necessary formality, but something about the two of us saying our vows, even in the sterile environment of a register office, took me by surprise, it turned out to be a very powerful and emotional occasion. The only people present were my two 'best men', Bono and Chantal O'Sullivan. Our French wedding was a totally different affair, very well attended, held open-air in the most spectacular setting, a cactus garden at the highest point of the hilltop village of Eze overlooking the Cote d'Azur. Afterwards we had a big party down by the sea. It was a full moon and very magical. The actual ceremony was a kind of joint Christian/Jewish service. It was like when they play Gaelic football in Australia – I think they call it 'compromise rules'.

BONO: It was the hottest day on earth and they were at the top of that hill of theirs. Jewish people get married under a chuppah which is a sort of four-legged tent with no sides. Edge built his own chuppah himself, and he and Morleigh stood underneath it. Morleigh's father, Bob, sang old Jewish chants, which sounded Gaelic to me. Everyone had Japanese umbrellas because of the heat of the sun. It was very surreal and beautiful. And then people walked down the hill. It was a really great moment to see Edge whole again.

EDGE: It was really 2003 before we started work on the new album in earnest. 'The Hands That Built America' won a Golden Globe and was nominated for an Oscar. It didn't win the Oscar but we came over and performed at the ceremony in March, then I stayed in LA and did some work on my own, which turned out to be quite an interesting week. I had some loops Larry had made for this express purpose, and I was working with a very simple Pro-Tools rig in my house in Malibu. It was great fun not having to think too much about anything other than playing the electric guitar, working over grooves, working on riffs, not worrying too much about where it was all going. That was the birth of 'Vertigo'. It was really part of an experiment in exploring rock 'n' roll guitar, to try and find out what that means in the twenty-first century. Were there any new riffs left to be discovered? 'Vertigo' is kind of an eternal riff. It's like it has always been there. Once I had stumbled across it, that was a clue to where the album was going.

BONO: Edge doesn't take to rock 'n' roll lightly. And by rock 'n' roll I mean metallic, blood running through your veins adrenalized music. He doesn't like a lot of rock 'n' roll guitar-players, he finds them clichéd and blues-ridden. So for him playing rock 'n' roll, it's like it has to be a very special occasion. You know it's serious. He played me this riff and it was like watching Edge setting fire to himself. It's an extraordinary riff. And there were about ten of them. I thought, 'Whoa, I'd pay attention on this album, because the Edge is.' And it's not always a given that he would want to play guitar. He might be into keyboards this album, and then you have Larry and Adam going, 'Oh no, we'll never get a rock song out of him.' But this time I was very sure that he wanted to get into the ring and be very, very dangerous with his talent.

EDGE: When we got together in Dublin to start talking about the way forward, we felt the record was going to be a band record, kind of hard-edged, tough, maybe quite stripped down. I was listening to a lot of punk rock, The Buzzcocks, The Sex Pistols, The Who, really thinking about the sound of a band.

ADAM: On the Elevation tour we seemed to have reached a new plateau of being able to put across the material in a very simple way, without a lot of support from over-dubbing or electronica. We felt if we could go in with everyone playing to that level, we could make a tough guitar record.

LARRY: We wanted to make a harder sounding album than *All That You Can't Leave Behind*. We needed to focus on better songwriting and more up-tempo tunes.

BONO: There is no set way for a U2 song to begin but usually myself and Edge arrive with an idea. And Adam looks with one eye, enthusiastically. And Larry grumbles about how it isn't a rock song. It's hilarious, but Larry is just not impressed by the force of an idea. He's only impressed by its ability to engage him on an emotional level. Larry is not moved by anything intellectual, he's moved by something much higher, which is instinct. But it can be so annoying. Edge came in to a meeting about the new album with seven demos. No fixed vocals but just riffs and grooves and stuff in what you might call the rock tradition, which is something Larry and Adam have been bothering him about for twenty years. And after playing the seven demos, they just sat there staring at their shoes. Not a word. Not one fucking word. And when they left the room, myself and Edge started laughing. But you know what? They weren't wrong. It was a study in songwriting and it only becomes magic when they get involved. Edge humbled himself to the notion of a band kicking around an idea. It's very hard for someone as brilliant as Edge to put up with that.

ADAM: I can understand how they would have felt our silence as a slight but I think Larry and I are much more cautious than they are. Obviously we appreciate the work but when you hear stuff in rough form, you're going, 'OK, how is this going to work as a U2 song? There's no melodies here yet, there's still quite a lot of work to go but it's a good starting point.' In the past Bono has always had difficulty coming up with melodies over guitar-riff rock songs, they are almost so Neanderthal he needs more harmonic information. He is more of a soul singer than a rock singer. That is certainly the way I would have felt listening to the demos. Now I know Bono already thinks the album is finished because that's the way his head works, he's going, 'I can hear these songs, I can hear guitar parts, I've got melodies in my head, yeah, this is a hit!' So he thinks he's playing me a hit and I think I'm hearing some guitar riffs against a drum loop that need a lot of work. It is just a difference of perspective.

EDGE: We felt this was going to be a band record first and foremost. So we were thinking about producers who worked well with bands. Somebody different, new ideas, fresh blood. Chris Thomas's name came up. Chris had worked on a lot of records we really loved, notably *Never Mind The Bollocks* with *The Sex Pistols* and the early Roxy Music albums. He had engineered on The Beatles' *White Album* and mixed Pink Floyd's *Dark Side of the Moon*, all kinds of fantastic records.

BONO: The Sex Pistols and Roxy Music is a seductive combination. There's some punk rock energy here but also some experimental energy, and we wanted both.

EDGE: Chris came to Dublin, we gave him a bunch of stuff and he said, 'Yeah, this is interesting. Let's get in the studio and see how it works.'

BONO: Chris has a thing that we don't have a lot of in the studio – the gift of clarity. From my work outside the band, I was starting to notice that clarity was the mark of real cleverness. If I'm sitting with Bill Gates, he can explain the universal application of binary code. Whereas some supposed genius would just leave you puzzled. Somebody like Professor Jeffrey Sachs can unlock the mysteries of the free market and Keynesian economics. I became really attracted to clarity and to people who had it.

ADAM: Chris came on early in the process and had great rapport with Edge and everything guitar-wise was really working well. We started in March 2003 and the plan was to have an album out by the end of the year. But as the sessions progressed and the consolidation of U2's particular approach to songwriting started to happen he seemed less comfortable at guiding us through. Because we don't come from a schooled musical background, we really have to develop the arrangement and melodies and hooks simultaneously. It is very much a process of trial and error, where as you add more harmonic information to a track it affects the mood of the music, which affects the mood of the vocal melody and the lyric. I think Chris found it very hard to keep moving things forward. There were plenty of ideas around but we just couldn't seem to close the deal.

LARRY: We work in an unorthodox fashion and regularly drive producers, engineers, assistant engineers, studio managers and anybody else who happens to be around to distraction. Because it's not one person you have to deal with, it's four people and it takes an awful lot of stamina and a lot of understanding to work with us.

BONO: We wore Chris out. The same as we'd done with Flood and Nellie on *Pop*. We're like a virus that surrounds you with too many permutations and combinations till you just don't know where to turn.

PAUL: U2 work very hard, they're perfectionists, but work expands to fill the time available to do it. I still find it amazing they can concentrate for

WE WORK IN AN UNORTHODOX FASHION AND REGULARLY DRIVE PRODUCERS, ENGINEERS, ASSISTANT ENGINEERS, STUDIO MANAGERS AND ANYBODY ELSE WHO HAPPENS TO BE AROUND TO DISTRACTION. BECAUSE IT'S NOT ONE PERSON YOU HAVE TO DEAL WITH, IT'S FOUR. LARRY

such a long time on a record and I'm bemused that they don't write the songs before they record them. Chris Thomas came to see me one day and said, 'I've never worked with any artist where nothing is prepared, nothing is demoed, they just go in and wait for it to arrive. I feel I'm letting them down.' I said, 'This is the way it always is and actually it's going rather well.' But that was the writing on the wall. It was kind of gruelling and nobody seemed to be having much fun.

ADAM: We worked through the summer and coming into autumn 2003 we had recorded an album's worth of material. Jimmy Iovine had heard the tracks and was saying 'You've got a record, we're ready to release it.' But there was unease within the band.

LARRY: It just wasn't there. The songs had a lot of things going for them but they had no magic, that thing that separates the ordinary from the extraordinary. It's hard to put your finger on but the songs just weren't ready. It was a very difficult thing to say to Bono and Edge. Bono was really pushing for us to release those songs. He was unhappy when we didn't agree with him. This is not a conversation you have with your mates, who are working very hard, unless you feel sure you are right.

EDGE: It was like the air leaked out of the balloon and we suddenly hit the ground. We basically worked the guts out of nine months with Chris but the songs were getting nowhere, or in some cases getting worse.

BONO: The whole was starting to sound like the sum of the parts. That's the difference between math and magic. You start realizing wow, everything's in place but it's not special.

With U2 it's sort of songwriting by accident. We don't really know what we're doing ... and when we do, it doesn't seem to help. It's a strange process and I still don't understand it exactly but I know that the better we've gotten at our craft, the harder it has been for us to make magic. Years ago, we weren't good enough musicians. We didn't really know about how to write songs. We hadn't been in a bar band. We hadn't learned how to play other people's songs. And so we were just dependent on magic. It was all we had, that moment when it all went off. But as you get older you get better. You start to understand songwriting as a craft. You start to become aware of Cole Porter and Brian Wilson and they start to infect you with their virus. And the result is that you come down with something less original.

LARRY: We called Steve Lillywhite and asked him to listen to the songs and let us know what he thought. We explained that there had been some tense moments between the hats and the haircuts. He came a week later and stayed for over six months.

ADAM: Steve said the material was there but it needed reworking. Because he knew what we were capable of, he knew the quality of the performances wasn't there.

LARRY: It must have been soul-destroying to work so hard and put so much in and then have these two guys say, 'Well, actually it's not ready.' It took grace to respond by saying, 'Maybe you're right.' And that's all it is: maybe you're right. You take your chances. It says a lot about both of them that they were prepared to listen to a bass player and a drummer who have difficulty playing in time.

ADAM: It was not an easy thing to call a halt and put the album release back and start with a new producer but it was definitely the right thing to do.

PAUL: It was difficult for me to make the call to Chris, and it wasn't lightly done. I think it was hard on everyone to spend that many months working with someone and then have to admit that it didn't really work out. But he did a lot of good work and quite a bit of it is on the album but it was really Steve Lillywhite who came in, assembled it, cracked the whip and had the drive to get it finished. Steve's like a shot in the arm for any project because he's so infectiously practical and good-humoured that the whole mood of the sessions lifted.

There is no point in a big artist putting out a record any other time than in the fourth quarter of the year, when record sales worldwide are so big it is really equivalent to the rest of the year put together. So as we missed the deadlines for a fall release, the album then slipped not into early 2004 but into late 2004, which is an expensive option, to effectively add another year's work, with all the overheads that entails.

EDGE: I did a bit of work on my own before we got back into the studio. And then Steve moved to Dublin in January 2004 and suddenly things started coming through really strongly, we were writing new songs and old songs were taking on a new dimension. Some of the songs didn't change an awful lot, we just played them better. Steve's great talent for making records is perfectly allied to his huge enthusiasm and 'can do' attitude. The energy level went up several notches immediately and that seemed to affect Adam and Larry particularly, they really started playing so well. And so the whole project took off again. Everyone got their mojo back.

ADAM: Steve did quite a clever thing, he set us up in a different room in the studio. We had made all our records at Hanover Quay in the same small playing room, which was quite an enclosed space. He said why don't you move out into this bigger room next door, which was bright and open, with lots of windows overlooking the dock, and he said the sounds will be different and you'll play differently and you might like it. So there was a week when Bono was away on one of his trips and we went in there and cut about four tracks, 'All Because of You', 'Vertigo', 'Original of the Species', 'Crumbs From Your Table', and they became the new working templates. By the time Bono came back we were in really good shape.

EDGE: With Steve came Garret Lee, better known as Jacknife Lee, a very important person on the record. One of the things that had been missing as we were working with Chris was a kind of wild-card element, somebody who's going to throw a few spanners in the works as you go. We thrive on that. The songs were sounding good but a little ordinary, as if they were stuck. Jacknife Lee is an Irish DJ, re-mixer and musician based in London. In some ways he's a state-of-the-art producer, working on Pro-Tools and that type of digital, computer system rather than conventional studio recording. He is used to getting somewhere very fast, with very clear, strong ideas, and he was not in the least bit intimidated by us or what we were doing. We would give him a track that we'd recorded and he would throw back his version a few hours later, maybe having given it some new textures or changed the arrangement. Sometimes we loved it, sometimes we didn't. But it was always refreshing to have an objective opinion.

BONO: We may have set out to make a real rock album but, in the end, we're not a rock group, least of all a punk rock group. We're U2. We play with rock or punk or folk or soul or gospel music but it never owns us and we never own it. We just do our thing and our experimental side is as important as our songwriting side. So with Steve and Garret, we had the Yin and the Yang. And Flood came back in, who is also loud on the experimental side. The intro to 'City of Blinding Lights' is all Flood. 'Love and Peace or Else' really started to come out.

LARRY: You could argue that too many cooks spoil the broth. And then you can take the view that every broth needs some seasoning. It was a very productive time. Things were going off all over the place as you moved from one room to another, drums were being recorded in one spot, Edge was overdubbing guitar in another and there were vocals being laid down somewhere else. It was a very creative environment. Bono was heavily involved in DATA and wasn't around a whole lot but Edge, Adam and myself just went at it with Steve and Garret Lee. Everyone worked extremely hard and we got some real results. It was a great opportunity to deconstruct songs, take things out and add new things and really get to know the material. For me it was a thrill. I felt I really had enough time to work on those songs and play them in.

BONO: Everyone was delighted that I wasn't around so much because I drive them mad. I'm impatient and I'm grabbing people's instruments. At one point I was banned from drinking coffee. It's like I can't stand sitting around waiting for God to walk through the room. I want to go out and find God now. So I'm capable of drowning out people's voices, which is not an attractive trait. But with me off drowning out politicians, they could really get on with it. And when I came back to the studio there would be more inspiring stuff to hear, which would mean I could jump much further off it. It definitely suits The Edge having me out of the studio because he's very different to me. I jump on a melody quickly, I write words quickly. He's like one of these Zen masters who spend five years mixing the ink and five minutes on the script, writing the characters in these beautiful calligraphies. He's just a much more meditative person. It still gets intense and the creative friction is still there but there's more respect for different people's processes. And I was coming back into the studio really sharp. I was writing all the time. The music was really in me.

EDGE: There's really no typical way that U2 songs come into being other than this very instinctive process, where a piece of music will show promise and everyone will agree that it's worth working on. We then start trying to find the essence of the piece, whatever that might be. Songs often take very strange twists and turns in arrangement, style, and wildly different structures, sometimes different tempos, different lyrics and different melodies. But

EDGE IS A VERY CONSCIENTIOUS WORKER AND BONO WAS TRYING TO BE SUPPORTIVE OF HIM. IT MUST HAVE BEEN SOUL-DESTROYING TO HAVE THESE TWO GUYS SAY, 'WELL, ACTUALLY IT'S NOT READY.' IT SAYS A LOT ABOUT THEM THAT THEY WERE PREPARED TO LISTEN TO A BASS PLAYER AND A DRUMMER WHO HAVE DIFFICULTY PLAYING IN TIME. LARRY

there's always some core element that is common from the beginning to the end, and that is the thing we're trying to get to in its most pure form. 'Vertigo' is a particularly unusual case. My demo had a different vocal melody but pretty much all of the musical ideas that were in the original have found their way into the final song. Back in Dublin, the band started working on different melodies and rhythm ideas and it went off in various directions. It took quite a while of experimenting before we finally wrote the song to completion, recorded it, mixed it, the whole deal, but it was a completely different song called 'Native Son'.

`**BONO:** It's like cell division, our songs keep shedding their skin and a new song emerges. 'Native Son' was inspired by Leonard Peltier, the Native American rights activist, and it was an interesting idea for a song. On its way to becoming 'Vertigo' it stopped off at the mezzanine floor and turned into 'Shark Soup'. That's when we came up with the rhythms of it, singing in Spanish, and there is still a little bit of Spanish left over in the intro. I'd been reading Pablo Neruda, one of my favourite poets. He's dead now but I went on a pilgrimage to his house in Chile and I had a meal in the inn next door where I poisoned myself, I thought I was going to die. It was just me and Guggi, there was no one else in the inn, even the innkeeper had gone home. I was laying on the ground, throwing up at ten-minute intervals and Guggi was trying to get water but it was locked behind the bar. When the innkeeper came in, she found me on the ground. I said, 'Can you call a doctor?' She said, 'You really don't want to meet the doctor.' I thought, 'Okay, don't call a doctor, just call us a taxi.' Anyway, somewhere in and around there emerged a song called 'Shark Soup'.

ADAM: Bono might come up with three different melodies for a song and in order to know which is the right one he has to complete three different sets of lyrics because each set of melodies has a different lyrical logic.

EDGE: We really thought 'Native Son' was very close to being finished but Steve felt it was not a great performance. And he was right. 'Vertigo' is truer to the original idea that I had. It's just a great visceral rock 'n' roll song. Instrumentally, it's very simple, drums, one guitar, one bass and the vocals. There's really no overdubs until the last third of the song. It is a very straight-ahead performance.

ADAM: This record seemed to survive without overdubs. It really did seem that the tracks, once we'd worked them up, were very full and complete. I don't know if that's from twenty-five years of working together and knowing what you need in order to make the voice sound good but there's probably some truth in that, experience has moulded everything together.

EDGE: Rock 'n' roll is about capturing a moment, it's an instinct, it's not something you can sit down and write in the quiet of your study. Often when the band is in full flight words will start coming to Bono on the microphone, and it's very much inspired by the music. It is hard sometimes to write that kind of lyric. It's so much about the sound of the words and the rhythm of the words.

BONO: A lot of lyrics on this record weren't really worked out. I didn't have time to. I would get up very early in the morning with something on my mind that I needed to write about and out it would come.

In the case of 'Vertigo', I was thinking about this awful nightclub we've all been to. You're supposed to be having a great time and everything's extraordinary around you and the drinks are the price of buying a bar in a Third World country. You're there and you're doing it and you're having it and you sort of don't want to be there. And it felt like the way a lot of people were feeling at that moment, as you turn on the telly or you're just looking around and you see big, fat Capitalism at the top of its mountain, just about to topple. It's that woozy, sick feeling of realizing that here we are, drinking, drugging, eating, polluting, robbing ourselves to death. And in the middle of the club there's this girl. She has crimson nails. I don't even know if she's beautiful, it doesn't even matter but she has a cross around her neck, and the character in this stares at the cross just to steady himself. And he has a little epiphany and you don't know what the epiphany is. It's a song about a disused soul in a well-used nightclub. There really is a place called Vertigo, you know. It's in Germany.

EDGE: There are a couple of musical references in 'Vertigo' to our first album. That wasn't conscious really. As we were working on the song, trying different ideas, these things seemed to fit. It is reminiscent of those early recordings in some ways.

FOR OUR SONGS, YOU JUST TRY AND GET OUT OF THE WAY, TRY AND FIGURE OUT THE THING THAT YOU CAN DO THAT IS GOING TO SUPPORT THE MELODY AND MAKE THE SONG SOUND AS UNADULTERATED AS POSSIBLE. SIMPLICITY IS WHAT IT IS, FOR ME. EDGE

BONO: I remember thinking, 'This has got to sound fresh, like we're starting again.' It's taken us twenty-five years, but this is actually our first album. And 'Vertigo' is the first single from our first album. And, oddly enough, in that spirit, there's a quote from one of the three songs on our very first single. In 'Stories for Boys' there's a Vertigo-like line for the train-spotters. I didn't notice it myself till someone pointed it out. Hello, hello.

LARRY: 'Miracle Drug' was one of the new songs that appeared after Steve came on board. Every day we would have power hours, basically go into the room and jam and see what happens. Several songs came out of that improv.

EDGE: It was a rambling fifteen-minute improvisation. We chopped it up a bit with Carl Glanville, our engineer, and he found a guitar part that worked really well over Adam's bass. It was one of those things where all the elements were there, it just had to be rearranged. It came together really fast. Garret created that beautiful beginning with the keyboard and the low-end bass beneath the guitar, that really sets the mood.

BONO: I would play back the improvisations before they were melodies and I was moved to tears, continually. This is just guitars, bass and drums. Every time I listened to it, I'd have a new melody. It was like opening the door and words and melodies would rush out onto the street.

The character of Christopher Nolan was in the back of my head. He was a boy who came into Mount Temple just as we were leaving. He had been deprived of oxygen for two hours when he was born and developed cerebral palsy, so he was paraplegic. It's written from his mother's perspective. It's about her faith in her son when for nine or ten years she had no idea if he was a conscious, sentient being or not. The hospital, the carers, the doctors and nurses could not guarantee her that he was awake to the world. But she believed it. She saw something in his eyes that was the light of being. And she had enough faith in her instinct and in her love for him to teach him, to read to him, to talk to him as if he was there. And then, aged eleven, this drug appears on the scene which frees up one muscle, which is the neck muscle, and allows him to move an inch. And through that movement he was able to type out all the stories and poems he had in his head for all those years. He had a little unicorn device attached to his forehead and his first poem was called 'I Learn to Bow', which is about this mechanism of the head movement but it's also his poem of gratitude to God, who I think he felt had worked through science to free him up. Now, I don't know about you, but if I had been locked in myself for ten years and I eventually got out, I'm not sure I'd be so full of praise for my Maker. *Damburst of Dreams*, his first book, went on to win the Whitbread Literary award when he was fifteen years old. But the song is about his mother. *I want a trip inside your head, spend a day there, see what you can see.* Generally rock stars don't sing from an older woman's perspective. It's a song about faith, the faith that God can work through science, and in particular medicine. In a more oblique way, it is probably as much about AIDS and the drugs developed to arrest it.

Early on, I had the notion that the album would be highly political. The world is turning upside-down and there's a mad collision of cultures happening all around. You'd think this would be the time to comment. But it just wasn't where I was at. I get to use a soap box when I'm moonlighting, so I've become less interested in U2 as a soap box. All the stuff we see going on in the world we have in microcosm in the relationships around us, the deceit of your own heart and the brutality of everyday life. You don't have to take on these big scenes to get to the big subjects. I suppose with the passing of my old man, I just hadn't the stomach for it. You can't write to order. I have to write speeches and I write letters, which are polemic. But in songs you have to go where your heart is.

'Sometimes You Can't Make It On Your Own' was a song that had been around for a few years, even before my father died. And it was written about him even then. I sang a version of it at the funeral. Still it wasn't complete. It was just waiting there. It's annoying that. God isn't reliable. God will not come when you call, necessarily, unless you're in a very humble place, and maybe we're not there enough. It took years waiting on that song and then it just came together and it feels like the song always existed.

EDGE: Bono and I had been playing around with the song since the *Pop* tour but there was something that wasn't quite right. When we played it together as a band it was a bit cloying, so it didn't end up going on *All That You Can't Leave Behind*. We revisited it for the new album.

ADAM: It had a very traditional feel in its original form and so we spent a lot of time trying to find a different setting for it, a way of retaining the strong melodies but just changing the harmonic content to try and make it a little bit more special. I think it was on its third or fourth rewrite when Steve pointed out that it didn't really have a chorus, it needed an extra bit, a bridge to lift it to the chorus line, and Bono sang that falsetto piece on the spot.

EDGE: Suddenly everything fell into place. For our songs, you just try and get out of the way, try and figure out the thing that you can do that is going to support the melody and make the song sound as unadulterated as possible. Simplicity is what it is, for me.

BONO: The album turned out to be about family, intimacy, human relationships. There were some political subjects we were ready to have a go on but they fit with the album's theme, which is the loss of innocence. The title of 'Love and Peace or Else' is obviously heavily ironic, but the sentiment is straightforward. It's an argument between two lovers when the television is on and the sound is turned down and the troops on the ground are about to dig in, and I'm wondering: 'Where is the love?' That is the real moment in the song, for me.

LARRY: The drum part was originally done with Brian and Danny for *All That You Can't Leave Behind*. We set up a kit we bought from Hansa studios in Berlin. It wasn't a kit I was used to therefore I played it differently. We set it up in the room as the mixing console, as opposed to a sound-proofed recording booth, so it was very open and loud. I just sat down and started to play this sort of Glitter Band kind of glam rock drum beat, with Danny on maracas. It sounded great in that room.

EDGE: It was a wonderful groove, with Danny on shaker and Brian's incredible keyboard bass riff. That's all we had to go on. I made several attempts at writing it into a song, there are so many versions, using this sonic opening. We revived it for the new album and I managed to get a riff going that locked it all together. There are five producers credited on that track, Brian Eno, Danny Lanois, Chris Thomas, Jacknife Lee and Flood. The song got written in different stages and each stage there was a different producer around. You can't leave anybody out of the story but they weren't all there at the one time.

ADAM: 'City of Blinding Lights' was actually a track left over from the *Pop* sessions, although not in that form. There was a melody and a groove that ultimately didn't go anywhere and we kind of threw out everything, found chords that worked with that melody and built it back up, new drum parts, new bass parts, new guitars. It's turned out to be a bit of a killer.

TO BE SURPRISED BY JOY IS THE MOST WONDERFUL THING, TO BE REMINDED THAT YOUR HEART IS PUMPING BLOOD AROUND YOUR BODY AND YOUR EYES ARE AWAKE TO WHAT'S GOING ON IN THE WORLD AND WHAT'S HAPPENING TO YOU, AND TO GIVE THANKS. BONO

EDGE: It's an area of Bono's lyric writing that I really like, cinematic, conjuring up a place and time, New York, a city that really brings you to somewhere, a state of mind.

BONO: The first verse is in London and the chorus is in New York. The thing I had in mind was my first trip to London with Ali when we were teenagers, on the ferry and the train, walking into Piccadilly Circus and up Wardour Street and just discovering what a big city could offer you and what it could take away. And then, of course, New York, the scene in Madison Square Garden during the Elevation tour, where the lights came on and eighteen thousand New Yorkers were in tears, jumping up and down, and I shouted out to them, 'Oh, you look so beautiful tonight.' It is such a naïve and innocent line. That's what this song is about, remembering those times. *I miss you when you're not around*. It's not necessarily a curse, it's that part of us that is missing. It's about recapturing a sense of wonder, being in a city, and reminding yourself that you don't have to lose your soul to gain the world.

To be surprised by joy is the most wonderful thing, to be reminded that your heart is pumping blood around your body and your eyes are awake to what's going on in the world and what's happening to you, and to give thanks. I'm not a person to sit around and ponder my navel, I'd much prefer pondering somebody else's, preferably while they're dancing in front of me. But I need to remind myself of what I've lost occasionally, to reflect on why I am doing the things I do. I think that's what this album was about. The song ends with the line 'blessings are not just for the ones who kneel, luckily'. I thank God on a daily basis for endless amounts of grace and covering the cracks that I would have fallen through.

These are songs of innocence, songs of experience. The central theme of that whole album is that naïveté is a powerful thing, in the sense that you are more powerful sometimes by not knowing what you're up against in this life. Anton Corbijn had an exhibition in the Groninger Museum in Holland, where he is from, and I opened it with him in April 2000. He wanted me to go into this room full of Bonos, an idea I did not find particularly appealing. There were large photographs of twenty years growing up together, he and I. One of the photographs was probably my first time in a helicopter, I was twenty-one or something, and my life was literally just about to take off. And the eyes were so wide open, the face so wide open. I was utterly shocked. This Dutch journalist sidled up beside me and said, 'Hey, what would the Bono now tell the Bono in the picture?' I was a little stunned but my only half-funny reply was: 'I'd tell him he's absolutely right and stop second-guessing himself.' And I realized how much I'd lost. I'm not talking about lines on my face or a thicker head of hair but that way of looking at the world. There was such clarity to it, but it was so defiant in a way. Now I'm much slyer about achieving my objectives and much more strategic. So 'City of Blinding Lights' tapped into this. And you hear it on 'All Because Of You' as well, this idea that you can get back to that place, which I really do believe. One of the things that underpins our work is the idea that you can begin again and that you can reinvent yourself, but also that you can go back to the beginning, that you can be free of the mistakes that you've made. So in 'All Because of You' there are the lyrics: *I'm alive, I'm being born, I've just arrived, I'm at the door of the place I started out from and I want back inside.*

EDGE: The riff for 'All Because of You' came out of the now legendary Monaco sessions. We just wanted to make it a piece of great, raunchy, twenty-first-century rock'n'roll. It's probably the only real rock 'n' roll song we have ever written.

BONO: What we wanted from the music on this album was the same feeling we had on *Boy*, when the raw, visceral power of the music was enough. That's what we were doing with 'Vertigo' and 'All Because of You'. It was getting back to your sense of wonder. Maybe you can never be naïve again but you can see the world without sunglasses. 'A Man And A Woman' was about rediscovering a kind of flirtatious and romantic love, when you were younger and less sure-footed in the ways that love can take you. It's that dance around the subject, seduction, that beautiful flirtation, which is in the end the most sexual thing, the not knowing, the not going there. Men and women seem to want to trample that mysterious distance that lies between us. I'm intrigued by it, it keeps me interested.

EDGE: That's really the wild card on the album. Our engineer, Carl, was trying a radical mix of something we'd recorded, Bono came in, loved the sound of it, grabbed the bass guitar and started singing. The acoustic guitar,

WE ENDED UP GETTING THE GUITAR AND SINGING, OFF OUR FACES, ONE OF THOSE MOMENTS WHERE TWO MATES ARE NOT TALKING SENSE BUT THEY'RE DOING IT AT THE SAME TIME AND THEN, EVENTUALLY, IT SORT OF COAGULATES INTO A THOUGHT. BONO

which I'm playing, was actually from a completely different song, just chopped up and connected together. And it sent Bono off and really inspired him.

BONO: I think it's a little gift of a song. It's like a jukebox gem.

EDGE: 'Crumbs From Your Table' started with a chord pattern hit on in Hanover Quay studios. Bono and myself finished that one off in France, off our trolleys. It's the only time we've ever successfully written a song with more than a few on board. We're famously bad at that.

BONO: We were out, it was very late, the sun was coming up. I'm not a late-night person, I'd much rather get up early in the morning, but Edge is like an owl. He would just sit there and days could go by and he wouldn't need sleep. So he didn't want to go to bed and we ended up getting the guitar and singing, off our faces, one of those moments where two mates are not talking sense but they're doing it at the same time and then, eventually, it sort of coagulates into a thought and out came this beautiful song, words, title, melody, boom, it all arrived in the middle of this lunatic night. I knew then there was bitterness in it. *You were pretty as a picture, it was all there to see, then your face caught up with your psychology, With a mouthful of teeth you ate all your friends, and you broke every heart thinking every heart mends.* Whenever you hear a song where I'm giving out, it's usually myself I'm giving out about. But not in this case.

I'd been working, trying to get African countries proper political representation. I remember feeling angry about how the poor have to come to us in the West with their cap in hand. I thought, God does not see it like that. Whether you're the CEO of a giant corporation or a poor farmer in Africa, God doesn't see any difference. I just thought we should give the poor more respect. Why don't they have the same representation in Washington and London as the National Rifle Association or the tobacco industry? Because the beautiful, extraordinary people of Africa can't hit back. If you mess with the National Rifle Association, they will follow you to your pig roast in the middle of your constituency, they'll try and take you out of office. I want to have the kind of representation for poor people, where they don't have to go up begging for crumbs from our table. *And you speak of signs and wonders / but I need something other / I would believe if I was able / but I'm waiting for the crumbs from your table.* That line was a shot at the Church, because I felt at that time the Church wasn't doing anything about the AIDS emergency. The sleeping giant has since awoken, I'm happy to say.

EDGE: 'One Step Closer' started on *All That You Can't Leave Behind*. I thought the chord progression had promise. No one else did. I played it for Chris Thomas and he said, 'That sounds great, let's try and record a version.' Danny Lanois was in town, so we set up Danny playing pedal steel guitar, me playing guitar, Bono playing guitar and started recording. And lo and behold Bono launches into a completely different melody to the original. It started out kind of Velvet Underground and headed off into the country. But it came together really well and we didn't mess with it, although the original version was about fifteen minutes long. Bono seemed to have that many verses, which was incredible.

BONO: It was another song for my dad. *The heart that hurts is a heart that beats / Can you hear the drummer slowing?* When I was in hospital with him, I'd done all these drawings of the various equipment that he was living around, the apparatus that was keeping him alive. Jacknife Lee is really a master at making you know you're in the twenty-first century even if you're playing an acoustic guitar, and you can sense the technology in that song, blood moving through tubes, and his breathing. It's very intimate. The title came from a conversation I was having with Noel Gallagher. We were talking about whether my dad had his faith or not. I said I didn't think he did any more. I thought he had lost it. I wasn't sure he knew where he was going. And Noel said, 'Well he's one step closer to knowing, isn't he?' And so it began there.

EDGE: 'Original of the Species' went through all sorts of changes. I started on the music for *All That You Can't Leave Behind*. We recorded a version but didn't quite get it. Bono wrote the first draft of the lyric for my daughter, Hollie, but he reworked it and it became something a bit more universal.

BONO: I didn't want it to appear like a song to a child so I kept some sort of erotic tension. Again it's this thing about the difference between knowledge and wisdom. Beware of knowingness. You sense with teenage girls this incredible pressure to be beautiful and to do well in their school. It is as if every waking moment the whole world is telling them what they're not. I wanted to write a song about uniqueness. It's worth remembering that you probably have something the world really needs. Trying to discover what that might be is one of the challenges of life. But one way you will not discover it is by trying to be what you're not.

EDGE: The album closes with 'Yahweh', which was another one that came out of the LA sessions. It really came out almost complete. Bono heard it, grabbed the microphone, came up with some great melodies. It took us a long time to get the right arrangement but that actually was recorded with Chris. I think it's a beautiful song, so resonant.

BONO: I didn't want to offend anybody here. It's a big word. A name not written down in strict Hebrew circles. And even some not so strict just have it without the vowels, just YWH. And I understand that we should come towards God with a sense of awe. Because Christianity has allowed Christ to be a friend to us as well as Master and Lord, we may take that access a little bit for granted. But Yahweh was one of the names for God. When Moses spoke to the burning bush, he said, 'Who are you?' And the bush spoke back to him, 'I am Who am.' Yahweh. The Great I Am. I came upon it whilst singing without knowing really what I was singing, it's a sound I was making in my mouth that turned into a prayer. I hoped it didn't sound Sunday School or naff. I think every line in it is underscored by a desperate need for me to know what to carry, to turn off my very critical eye sometimes, to be fit for the shoes I've been given. I love singing it.

ADAM: The album was finished on the first weekend of July 2004. It took a year and a half to make, which seemed a long time, and it was very rough when we were in that middle period when it didn't seem to be going anywhere. However, once we got over that hump, the pace did pick up and it kind of galloped to the end. By the time it was finished, we were all excited by what we'd managed to create. We recorded a new song on the second-last night in the studio, which ended up as a bonus track in Britain and Japan. We had a kind of electronica track called 'Xanax and Red Wine' which included the line 'how to dismantle an atomic bomb', and we had done a couple of versions but couldn't make it fit together. Bono wanted to get that lyric back onto the record and we didn't have much time so the idea came to start from scratch, replay it with a sparse arrangement and adapt melodies and lyrics to fit that new format. It turned into 'Fast Cars'. It really ended those sessions on a high note. We were feeling we had made a great record, a record worth shouting about.

BONO: The last night we played the album back with everybody in the room, people were drinking and jumping around the place. It was an amazing night. After all that work, it was fantastic to hear it sound so fresh and exciting.

EDGE: I think it's our best album, although perhaps not our most innovative. We may have succeeded almost too much in making an album showcasing the band because I think some of the songs could have gone into a more experimental area sonically. But as a collection of songs, it's our best ever.

BONO: It is definitely the best songwriting. There's more great songs on this album than any other. There's no filler. And I think that's a triumph. In retrospect, it's missing sonic cohesion. The number of different producers was always going to be a tricky point because, while each of them did extraordinary work, you have to have a clarity of vision for the sonic architecture that creates the aesthetic of the whole album. And maybe the running order wasn't right. Maybe I didn't involve myself enough. I've been getting out of the way of the consensus rather than getting in the way of the consensus, which is my usual position. It's my job to disturb the waters. But I'd say it's as good a record as we have ever made, and a better record than anyone might have expected us to make after twenty-five years.

ADAM: I remember feeling really pleased with *The Joshua Tree* and thinking we'd really broken new ground and gone places I didn't think we'd be able to. I would say I was as enthused about this record, although it has a different kind of vitality and confidence to it. It is more mature and assured.

LARRY: I think it's a really good record, with some great songs. I'm not as emotionally attached to it as I am to *All That You Can't Leave Behind*. It just doesn't quite hang together as well as that album. It may be to do with the mix of personalities involved but it seems to be missing that same emotional thread.

PAUL: I love the record, it's wonderful, probably their greatest. Bono sings better than he has sung for years and so often in the work of the band the fact that his voice is the lead instrument gets forgotten. I'm delighted to see him back on top form, singing about things that matter to him. I wasn't so excited about the title. Indeed, I'm still not crazy about it. There was quite a bit of discussion about that. But it is a creative matter and though I will air my views, I don't expect to prevail.

ADAM: I thought the idea of calling it *How To Dismantle An Atomic Bomb* was challenging, it fitted the times. There was a bit of debate and I was aware we might be skating on thin ice if the release of our record coincided with a terrorist atrocity but I felt that was a risk worth taking.

LARRY: I understood where Bono was coming from with the title but I was concerned because at that time there was a lot of talk about weapons of mass destruction and dirty bombs. If there had been a terrorist attack of any type, the album may have been dropped from radio. As it happens, the title actually has more to do with Bob Hewson than anything else. As Bono says, we could have called it 'How to Dismantle an Atomic Bob'. Bono was emotionally attached to the title. In the end, his instincts were correct.

PAUL: The process of choosing a title would be that people air their views and then Bono decides. It's probably a bit more subtle than that, but that's what it feels like sometimes.

BONO: The nay-sayers were wrong, it's that simple. You just have to have a bit of bravery. The reason why corporate culture is in such a crisis, in America and elsewhere, is because of decisions by committee. No one wants to make a mistake so they don't do anything, which is the biggest mistake of all. I get into trouble because I'm always the one that's leading the band to the most criticism, so people are always bracing themselves on my behalf for the blow. And I appreciate that to a degree. But that's what rock 'n' roll is. You've got to grab the Zeitgeist and step into it. And that title made the personal and the geopolitical come together. It was the right title for that reason. People were worried it would look grandiose. What is rock 'n' roll if it doesn't dare to have big ideas?

EDGE: We thought we were going to make a political album but, in the end, it's a much more resonant record, reaching beyond the moment we're all living through to something very personal. There is a lot of family in these songs and that's probably what you are drawn to when times get really tough.

As Bono was putting the title forward, I was thinking, 'How does that relate to the album we have made?' and we began talking about this notion of 'faith versus fear'. To me the burning questions of the moment relate to how you cope with threat and fear. Are we going to be ruled by fear or are we going to attempt to transcend that and find a way of holding on to faith, be that faith in humanity, faith in some sort of higher power, or faith in the future?

If you look at what George Bush was up to, politically, everything he did was predicated on the idea that post-9/11 the baddies were out to get America and America has to be fearful of its position. And it seemed that gave him the licence to pretty much do whatever he wanted, whether it was throwing his weight around in the Middle East or clawing back freedoms and liberties that were written into the American Constitution. What was going on with the prisoners in Guantanamo Bay was so anti-American in many respects. So that was interesting. As we sequenced the album, a faith or fear arc started to make itself present, starting with Vertigo's sense of paranoia through to the spiritual surrender of 'Yahweh'. That to me is the theme of the album: how do you live in the twenty-first century when so much is up for grabs?

LARRY: It may well be the last album we record in Hanover Quay, our HQ for over ten years. The Dublin Docks Development Authority issued a compulsory purchase order as part of a plan to redevelop the whole area. We challenged it in court and they agreed that a replacement studio building would be constructed elsewhere. I'll be very sad to see it go. There are a lot of really great memories in that place. We made some good music and had a lot of laughs. It's irreplaceable, really. It's positioning on the water has a certain kind of tranquillity even through the chaos of studio recording. There is a real sense of creative space. I doubt we'll ever find anywhere as special.

EDGE: The end of the last week was quite crazy. We had been working very hard on the record, I was on the phone all the time to LA talking about edits and making sure they had the right versions of the songs to do their first pass at mastering, getting levels right and all that stuff. Then we went to France and did our first interviews and a photo session for *Blender* magazine. I had a rough assembly of the whole album on CD. Big decisions were being taken about singles and running orders, so it was important to be listening back and absorbing it as a body of work. So while we were spending the day being photographed at this big movie production facility with multiple sound stages, I was playing the CD through a little portable system. Towards the end of the afternoon, the photographer wanted to do one further set-up in a disused swimming pool outside. We just left everything, all the equipment, all the clothes and went outside for about forty minutes. We came back in and the equipment had already been dismantled, the lights were down and I was about to grab the CD. It was gone. So we searched everywhere. And it started to dawn on me that this was very serious. So then I hit the panic button. Everybody was asked to stay behind and within an hour the Nice police were down taking interviews, searching everything, all the trucks, every single vehicle, every interior. No CD.

It was a scary thing because if it had hit the Internet the next day that would have derailed two years of work and ruined all our long-term plans. Our record company was freaking out. They had Interpol on the case. The strangest thing was meeting members of a kind of secret music business, anti-piracy group whose job involves going around in a very cloak-and-dagger way to find out who's stolen tapes and who's behind big bootleg operations. They had all sorts of sophisticated ways of tracking mixes and had people scouring the Internet to see if they could find it. So it was a very dramatic few days. We never did find out who took it. It was probably someone grabbing a souvenir. My bet is that it was at the bottom of the Mediterranean within a few hours. It's the kind of thing that no one would have given a damn about a few years ago, but in this era of Internet piracy the potential financial damage is enormous.

BONO: I just thank God it was Edge who lost the CD. Because if it was me, there'd have been murder over it.

PAUL: The campaign started for me in early 2004. I was picking up on all this mobile technology and particularly the way in which telephone companies were likely to become distributors of music in the future. An old friend from the music business, Ralph Simon, was now chairman of the Mobile Music Forum. Ralph founded Zomba Music Publishing and Jive Records, he is a genuine music industry heavyweight, and he became my guide to this rapidly expanding area. Ringtones are really the thin end of an enormous wedge which will eventually be full spectrum sound and picture delivered through the air to mobile devices. In the past we had never worked with advertisers or sponsors. The only time we'd ever allowed U2 music to be used in a commercial way was in a movie. If we were able to attach a U2 song to a big-budget motion picture advertising campaign, it was like attaching a rowboat to an aircraft carrier. The music business markets itself by infiltrating other free media. It is very skilful at promoting its wares through radio, television and press rather than buying advertising space. I sensed there was a huge commercial opportunity with technology and information organizations, the sort whose machines we use in U2's work, to infiltrate their budgets and get our music on television in a dignified and honourable manner. So Ralph Simon and I spent most of 2004 talking to Vodafone, Nokia, Hewlett-Packard, Intel and T.Mobile, trying to find a way in which our brands could cooperate for mutual benefit without being embarrassing. I nearly pulled this off, but in the end I couldn't sell it to the band. Even though any of these deals could have been justified, they didn't want the accusations of selling out, and so, rather disappointingly, none of the deals on the table were consummated. Meanwhile, we were talking to Apple.

LARRY: There was a proposal for the band to take sponsorship from a telephone company and make large sums of money. I was opposed to the

THE RELATIONSHIP BETWEEN ART AND COMMERCE HAS ALWAYS EXISTED AND I HAVE NEVER FELT THAT WE WERE THE SACRED ARTISTS AND THE PEOPLE WHO SOLD OUR MUSIC HAD THEIR HANDS DIRTIED BY THE FILTHY LUCRE. ARTISTS ARE AS GREEDY OR AS SELFLESS AS ANYONE ELSE. BONO

idea. There were differing opinions in the band. There was enormous pressure to take sponsorship, because the record industry was changing and record companies were spending less and less money on marketing. It was a long hot summer for me. There was a real chance that those in favour of sponsorship would win the argument and I would be out-voted. Thankfully, it never came to that.

BONO: The relationship between art and commerce has always existed and I have never felt that we were the sacred artists and the people who sold our music had their hands dirtied by the filthy lucre. Artists are as greedy or as selfless as anyone else. We are in business, we are tradesmen who, in the Middle Ages, would wander from town to town selling our wares. Get over it. And we try to do the best deals we can for those songs. We try to protect them by not having people steal them. We try to get them on the radio so people can hear them. We try to get them on TV so people can hear them and see the visuals we've made.

PAUL: We already had a relationship with Apple. We were one of the first adopters of iTunes and encouraged other artists to support iTunes right at the beginning of 2002. So the opportunity arose to go into business with Apple selling U2 iPods, and they would use our first single to run their fall 2004 advertising campaign, for which they spent north of twenty million dollars for airtime around the world. They didn't pay us for being in the commercial but we were getting a royalty on every U2-branded iPod sold, which was kind of unheard-of in the history of the entertainment business, the hardware makers paying a royalty to the software suppliers, i.e. makers of the music.

BONO: The deal with iPod was fantastic. We got to make a video and have it on television. We got to put it on during the big sports games, the kind of exposure that not even a record company could afford, but a giant technology firm like Apple could. And they were a perfect partner. Steve Jobs, the co-founder and CEO of Apple, is the man who actually sorted out the problem of the music business and piracy. Stealing music is real. We make songs where other people make objects, and it's an expensive business. And despite what a few *enfants terribles* were telling people, music piracy was really changing the outcome of musicians' lives. Then along came this technologist who believed that if you made it easy and fun and reasonably cost-effective, people would rather buy songs than steal them. People can get water out of a tap but they buy it in a bottle, because they believe it's better quality and they like the bottle. The same with music. Added to that, he assembled a team that made beautiful objects. And it backed up a theory I have about how hardware drives the software. I knew it was coming, I felt it before it arrived. The iPod is the most beautiful object in music since the invention of the guitar. The bottom line is there's one deal you have with your fans: don't do anything embarrassing. And I don't think there's anyone who saw that commercial who thought it was embarrassing. It was really exciting. Selling out is bending over to do things you don't believe in, for cash usually. We turned down twenty million dollars just for the music. We turned advertising into a rock video. That was exciting.

LARRY: Apple made sense. It's the coolest company around and there was no money changing hands. We all agreed it was the right company to work with and we could both benefit from this relationship. Of course, there was grumbling from what you might call the militant wing of the U2 fan base. They accused us of selling out.

PAUL: *How To Dismantle An Atomic Bomb* was released on 22 November and shipped over five million copies worldwide, which was our biggest shipment ever. Within a month it was up to eight million,which made it our fastest-selling record. It was number one all over the world.

ADAM: 'Atomic Bomb' was treated as if it was our comeback record, even though *All That You Can't Leave Behind* had been a huge success. I think it takes a long time for the message to get through, and you can't really come back on one record, you have to follow it up with another action of commitment. We felt we'd made a record worth shouting about and when people heard it, they reacted in a similar way. When we released our first album, even the most moderate success was something to get really excited about. Twenty-five years later I still get excited but I also feel a huge sense of humility. This really shouldn't be happening. I would have been happy just to have had a record deal at this point.

EDGE: For us to get any kind of support from the rock 'n' roll counter-culture, which is obsessed by underground music, was extremely gratifying. And then to see it translate and capture the imagination of the current generation of record-buyers en masse was very exciting. The big prize for us has always been to stay relevant, so it felt like a vindication. We went on TV quite a lot. We wanted to get out there and meet people where they were, not where we had left them last time around.

PAUL: We had a big campaign planned. A year of non-stop touring, arenas followed by stadiums. Tickets would have gone on sale just after Christmas. And then something happened that put everything in the balance.

EDGE: In early December, we were shooting a video for 'Sometimes You Can't Make It On Your Own' in Dublin when I got the news that my daughter, Sian, was very seriously ill. I told the guys, 'I've got to go.' From that moment, my world changed completely.

BONO: Everything that we're about is community. The music comes out of the community. And so if somebody in the community has a trauma, all of us feel it. It threw everything. To see your mate with his heart broken and to see the bravery of this little seven-year-old girl … it was just an awful, awful moment.

EDGE: I don't want to go into too much detail. But my family went through some very intense times and Sian had to suffer through some awful experiences, which she continues to do with amazing fortitude for one so young. The strange irony is that when you spend a lot of time with your child in hospital you very quickly realize that there is always someone worse off than you. We always leave hospital with a strong sense of how lucky we are.

BONO: Your first instinct is to just down tools, focus on what's happening in the family and go into a supportive role.

ADAM: All our thoughts were for whatever Edge's family needed at that time. Everything was put on hold. As more information became available, and as we had more time to evaluate what was appropriate or conceivable, we started to do the calculations and see how everything could work together.

EDGE: After getting over the initial shock and the first three very intense weeks I started thinking about the year ahead and what, if any, of my U2 commitments I would be able to keep. The Vertigo tour had been announced

I WAS GETTING PHONE CALLS FROM ROAD CREW MEMBERS TELLING ME THEY WERE SENDING GEAR TO LONDON FOR REHEARSALS. 'WHAT REHEARSALS?' 'REHEARSALS FOR THE TOUR.' 'WHAT TOUR?' EDGE WAS IN LOS ANGELES, I WAS IN DUBLIN, I DIDN'T KNOW WHAT PARTS OF THE WORLD BONO OR ADAM WERE IN, THERE WAS A LOT OF CONFUSION. LARRY

but fortunately no tickets had actually gone on sale. There was a hell of lot of soul-searching and throwing ideas and dates around. Really, I wasn't sure whether I would be able to do it. I mean, the guys were great. They said, 'If you don't think you can do it then we understand, don't worry, we're behind you the whole way.'

LARRY: I would have found it very difficult to go on the road in Edge's position. The decision was his and Morleigh's alone.

BONO: Some people who had been through similar situations advised us that the most important thing for a family going through this kind of trauma is to keep doing what they're doing, that normality is important. And though you might say going on tour is not normal, it is for us and it is for Edge. Sitting at home staring at his beautiful girl nine to five would not be good for either of them.

ADAM: There was a point at which Edge had all the information to hand of what the treatment involved and what our touring cycle was likely to be, where he said, 'I think there's a way that I can commit to touring and also cover everything that I need to do for my family.' And that was a very brave decision but also a very generous one, because it allowed the band to function through that period. And Morleigh and Sian and their whole support structure was involved in taking that decision and knowing what the implications of that decision were. So I'm filled with admiration and gratitude that that was the way they decided to approach it and they had the strength of the family unit to evaluate the information and figure out that they could make it work.

EDGE: In the end it felt like the positive thing to do. To not, in a sense, become victims to this misfortune, but to actually, in a logical and reasonable and mature way, adjust your life so that life can continue. A new tour schedule was drawn up, built around Sian's needs, and in a strange way I think it honoured her. It was as if we were saying 'we're not going to lie down and just roll over, we're going to meet this head on and continue with our lives and make it work for everybody.' But it was a very tough decision for me to make and in the end it was Sian who gave me the strength to go ahead with the tour. I laid it out for her and said, 'I don't have to do it. I can spend more time with you if I don't go.' All I needed was her to say 'I don't want you to go' and that would have been it, I would have pulled the tour, but she ended up *reassuring me!* She said, 'Don't worry Daddy. It's going to be okay. I want you to do it.' Quite amazing.

BONO: The heroine of the day was, of course, Morleigh, because she had to take the extra weight, and she had to take the pain. Without her, the tour would never have happened.

PAUL: The tour was scheduled around Edge getting home at night, the core idea being that, certainly on the American leg of the tour, he would never be away from his family in LA for more than three days. So we had to completely reschedule at short notice, there were a lot of gaps built in and a lot less dates, with the result that when the tickets went on sale there were a lot of disappointed people, which I suppose is inevitable in a situation where we were underplaying worldwide.

LARRY: I was getting phone calls from road crew members telling me they were sending gear to London for rehearsals. 'What rehearsals?' 'Rehearsals for the tour.' 'What tour?' Edge was in Los Angeles, I was in Dublin, I didn't know what parts of the world Bono or Adam were in, there was a lot of confusion. And to add to the problems, our website, U2.com had been re-launched, guaranteeing new members tickets for the up-coming tour. Which was a mistake. You can offer a limited amount of tickets but you can't guarantee them for everybody. And this was before we realized the tour would be scaled down due to Edge's situation. People were joining just to get guaranteed tickets. There was a meltdown. They released a limited allocation of tickets on the website in January but many of them ended up going to scalpers who were re-selling them on eBay. Our fans felt cheated. Some thought they now had hard evidence that U2 didn't give a shit about them, and that we're only in it for the cash. They had a couple of journalists onside and suddenly it was all over the place that U2 fans were outraged. Sadly, I only learned of the problems through the newspapers. I immediately got on the phone to our friends at U2.com and got as involved as I could. I spent two weeks getting seating plans for each venue, personally trying to sort out problems, with limited success. The horse had bolted. I personally apologized on the website.

There are ways of managing these things, however you can never guarantee your audience won't get ripped off by scalpers. U2.com learned some hard lessons, and so have I. Had the militant fans been a little bit more understanding, it might have been easier to navigate our way through the problems. In fairness though, they had no idea the reasons why things fell apart. However, it makes you wonder why some people are fans of the group at all, if they think we would deliberately try and exploit them.

ADAM: We convened in Mexico for rehearsal in February. I would have to say the mood was sombre. People didn't have a sense of where it was going. We were quite behind schedule, it was a somewhat bleak environment, a little film studio in winter, set on the sea. It was grim. But within a short period of time, the music and the bones of the show started to come together.

LARRY: Mexico was close enough to LA for Edge to get home when he needed to. We didn't want to put any more pressure on him by expecting him to do all the musical things he would normally do, so we brought Steve Lillywhite, Carl Glanville and Jacknife Lee in to help. There was still a sense that everything was up in the air and from one week to the next we didn't know whether we were going to have to cancel the tour. It was very hard to see a mate go through something like this, and it's even harder when you know you can't do anything for him. There were times where I felt the decision to tour was a mistake.

BONO: The band were playing very well, even if we were very under-rehearsed. Oddly enough, there was a whole new level to Edge's playing. His guitar tech, Dallas Schoo, worked very hard on getting the sounds exactly right. There seemed to be no remove between Edge and his guitar. It was really extraordinary. He changed the set list and started putting in songs from the *Boy* album. And having him play 'Into The Heart', going into the heart of a child, that was a really eerie and beautiful moment, where the guitar had never been so expressive. The whole theme of *Atomic Bomb* was the loss of innocence, and the *Boy* album was about trying to hold onto it, so there was some symmetry in those songs. I don't know if that dawned on anyone but, for me, Sian seemed to be the pivot in the middle of this.

EDGE: My daughter's illness had the effect of reordering all my priorities. I found that I just couldn't be concerned about small details anymore. Knowing the extraordinary sacrifices and costs of putting on the tour, it made it all the more significant that each show should be really special, because it was the reason that I was there. And I had some very good reasons to be elsewhere. So those shows had a lot to live up to.

The album belied its title in that it was a lot more personal than political. So when it came time to tour, it occurred to Bono that this was how we could take things to the next level. We didn't see why there should be a separation between Bono the political campaigner, and Bono the artist. We made space for the politics in the show and they became the main theme, the undercurrent of the whole tour.

BONO: So we started to assemble the different pieces relating to what was going on in the world and in our lives, the cross-sections. A friend of mine, Emily B, had stumbled upon this piece of graffiti, COEXIST, with the Islamic moon as the C, the Star of David as the X and the Christian cross as the T. It turns out it was the brainchild of a Polish artist, Piotr Mlodozeniec. It seemed such a powerful symbol of tolerance. And then we had human rights abuses happening after 9/11, with the most hypocritical arguments being used for why we should forsake our sense of civilization. It was like 'it's okay to torture people because we're trying to save lives.' Basically, sell yourselves to save your arse. So we worked with the great video artist, Catherine Owens, on a piece where a head would appear projected on smoke and read out the Declaration of Human Rights, which was just so powerful. Well, you can imagine how this went down. The band, the management, they're all staring at their shoes, 'Oh God, here we go. And we haven't even got to the Africa piece yet. What's he got planned for Africa?' Willie Williams found this technology, Google Earth, where you can look down on the arena from a satellite perspective, beam out of the arena, watch it disappear under you, leave the town, the city, the country, go into space and pick a place in Africa and go visit it. We were going to do this on a massive scale at the show. More staring at the feet, more groans. And properly so, it was a little laborious. We discussed throwing 'Where the Streets Have No Name' out because it was so important to the last tour, we thought how can we top that? Larry and Adam quite rightly put a stop to that. But we had to find a new way of showcasing the song, so we came up with digital flags. And I was standing on stage the night before we opened in San Diego in March with all these African flags coming down, singing 'Where The Streets Have No Name', when I was reminded of something I had long ago forgotten – that I had written the lyrics for this song in a small village in northern Ethiopia on a scrap of paper, an Air India sick bag, I think. And here it was, nearly twenty years later, coming back to Africa, all the stuff about parched lands and deserts making sense for the first time. The hairs just stood up on the back of my neck. I could barely sing the song. And it was like that every night of the tour.

And then we put out this call and asked people to sign up to the One campaign, which was a DATA initiative we had launched the year before to try and rally Americans to fight global AIDS and extreme poverty. We'd ask the audience to bring out their phones and it would create this twenty-first-century moment where the whole arena turns into a galaxy of diode lights. And then we asked them, 'What do you want to do, call your mother, pay your gas bill or sign up to the One campaign to make poverty history?' It's amazing the roar that would rise up, because people want to be a part of that, and they feel they are a part of that, part of the generation that can actually turn the supertanker of indifference around. And so the show developed a very clear through-line.

After some initial doubts, the band came round. I mean, Larry would be looking at his watch whenever I started speaking at the opening of 'One'. He forgets he's on camera at all times, and people are watching him as he's watching his watch. He's timing me to see how long the speech would go on tonight. Priceless. In Washington DC, when we had all the politicians there, I went on for fifteen minutes. Larry was nodding off behind me, in full view of various Congressmen and women.

LARRY: It took a lot of work to make the speeches part of a rock show. It was a struggle to get the balance right.

EDGE: Some nights it would turn into a little bit of a lecture and they were not my favourite nights. I don't like it when Bono's coming over like a schoolteacher. But there were nights when it just blended perfectly with the music. It is amazing how new political ideas connect with old songs and give the songs a new perspective as well.

ADAM: Thirty years on, I trust Bono. That's his job. I think on a night by night, gig by gig basis, he's a pretty good judge of this stuff.

BONO: I don't get it right all the time. And fair play to our audience, there would be an occasional 'fuck off!'. But more people want to hear you talk because they know what you're talking about is important and that rock 'n' roll has always been more than entertainment. Some people just want you to hurry up. 'We'll give the fucking money, now shut the fuck up!'. I like both of them there. It's a balance. But Paul McGuinness, with the human rights piece, there was steam coming out of his ears. It was very funny. People were absolutely sulking backstage, but it came together.

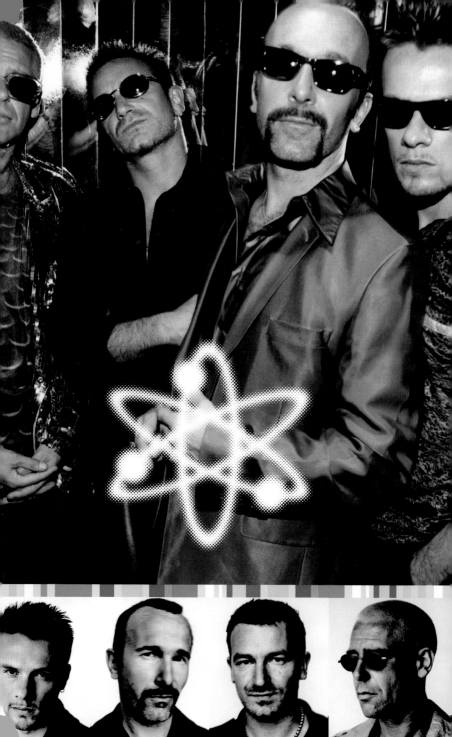

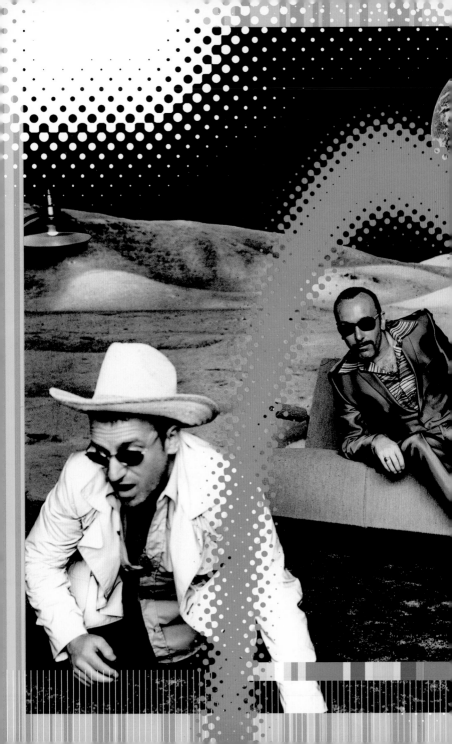

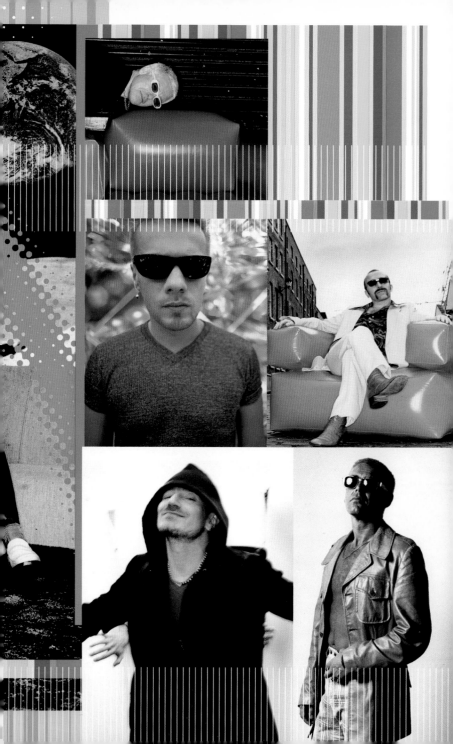

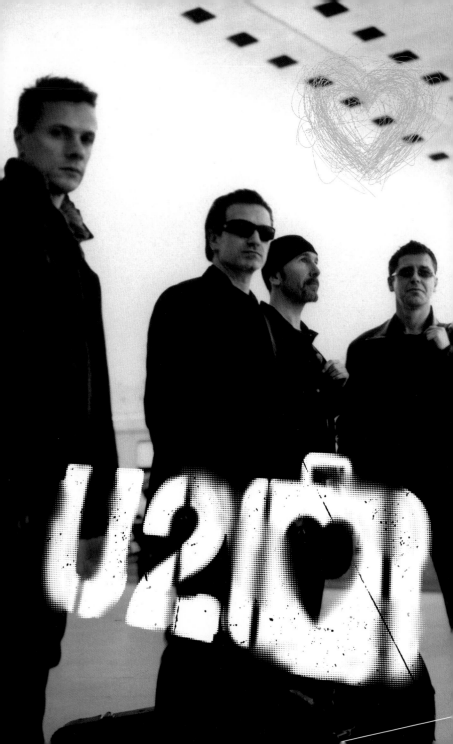

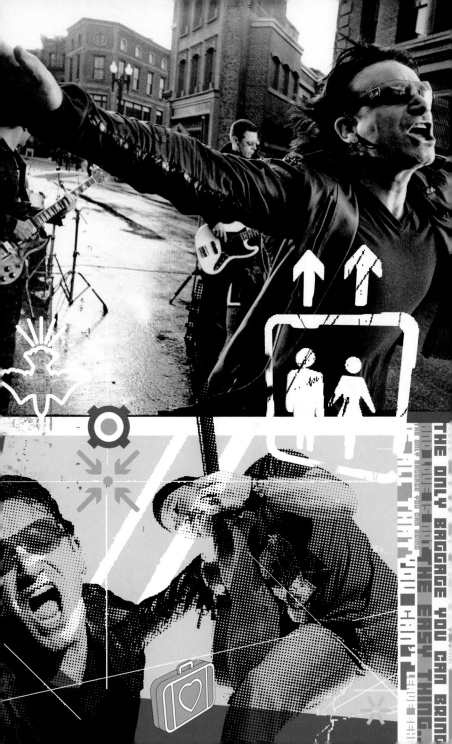

THE ONLY BAGGAGE YOU CAN BRING THE ONLY BAGGAGE YOU CAN BRING THE EASY THING ALL THAT YOU CAN'T LEAVE

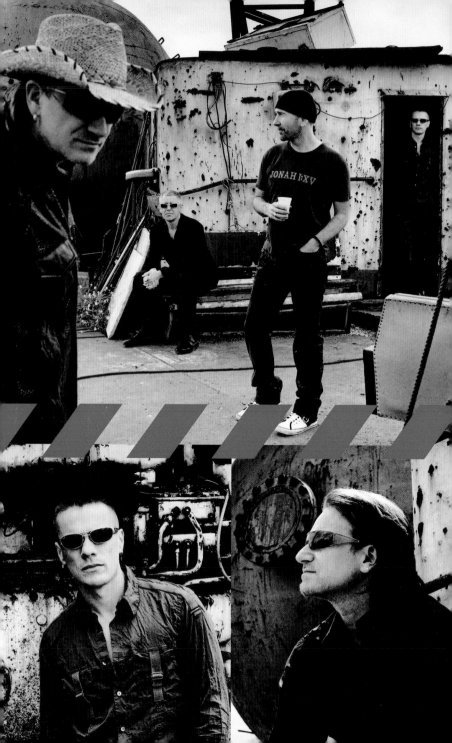

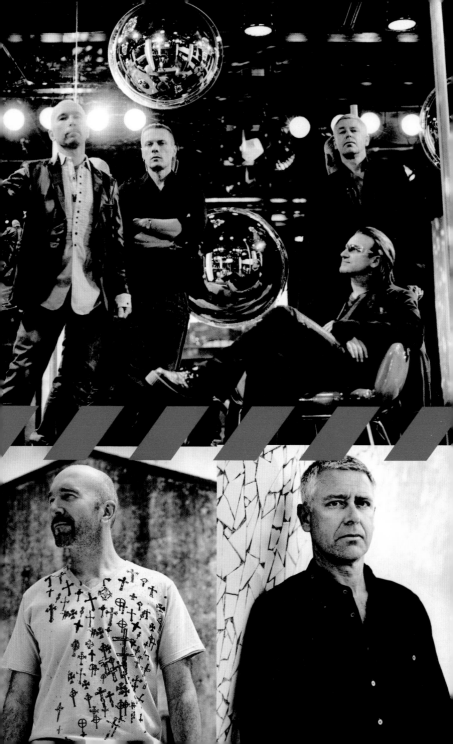

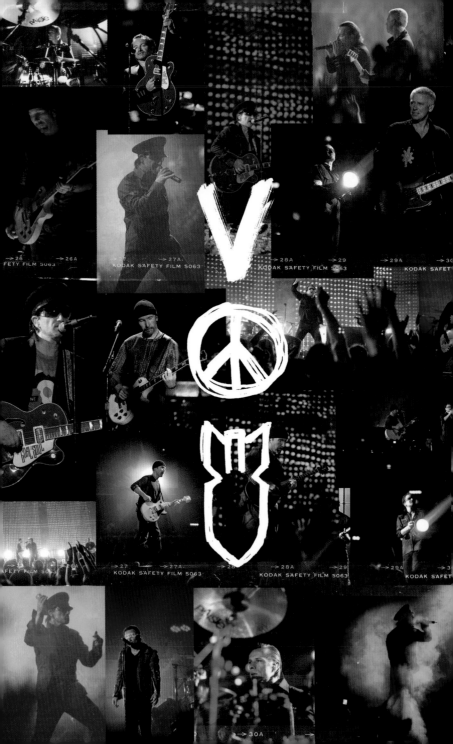

THE YOUNG MEN WHO SPENT THEIR WHOLE
CHILDHOODS WORKING UP TO MAKING *BOY* HAD
NOW SPENT TWENTY-FIVE YEARS OF ADULTHOOD
WORKING UP TO MAKING *ATOMIC BOMB*. I FELT WE
HAD SOMEHOW GOT BACK TO THE SAME POINT
AGAIN, REVISITING THAT PLACE OF YOUTH AND
INNOCENCE WITH THE MATURITY OF A LIFETIME. ADAM

ADAM: The set was challenging, and the audience really rose to the challenge. We had a couple of sets, which would change from night to night. We were playing seven or eight tunes off the new album and five or six songs from *Boy*, which only die-hard U2 fans might be familiar with. By the end of the tour we were doing 'Electric Co', 'An Cat Dubh', 'Into The Heart', 'The Ocean', 'Out of Control' and occasionally 'Stories For Boys'. It was inspired by a feeling that we had come full circle. The young men who had spent their whole childhoods working up to making that *Boy* record had now spent twenty-five years of adulthood working up to making *Atomic Bomb*. I felt we had somehow got back to the same point again, we were revisiting that place of youth and innocence with the maturity of a lifetime. I think it makes a very tall order for where we go next time.

EDGE: Those songs were speaking to us again, they felt relevant. What was interesting was how quickly they came back. A couple of rehearsals and we had them.

ADAM: That is the strangest thing. It was easier to remember songs you had written and recorded twenty-five years ago than it was to remember anything you'd done in the last fifteen. When you're going back to that place, you do bring to it a kind of a confidence, knowing that it's pretty good for what it is. Back then, you were concentrating so hard on creating it and performing it and making it work that you didn't necessarily appreciate the simplicity and directness of it. 'Electric Co' really stands up. There's some great things in there that you could only have come up with as an eighteen or nineteen-year-old. The elements were absolutely honed to the absolute minimum of what you needed to kind of get away with it. Later songs are a little bit more complex, sonically and production-wise, so when you play them as a three-piece-music section they don't always fit together as well.

LARRY: The early material was a bit of a challenge. Twenty years ago I played with little knowledge of what I was doing. And that is the beauty of those early songs, the parts are kind of obscure, simple and naïve. I wanted to play them again with new confidence but without losing their early magic. It was nice to rewrite a little history.

BONO: It gave me a chance to write some lyrics for the songs on *Boy*. We might have to re-record them, now that they are actually finished.

PAUL: In the early days of U2 there was a distinct lack of expertise and the songwriting was better than the playing. The musical imagination was there but the musical skill was not. But I remember how exciting it was at the time, and to hear those early songs played by U2 now is amazing. The material holds up and it does sound great when it's played well. But it was not a greatest hits show. If you added together the number of songs performed from the last two albums, well over half the show came from the twenty-first century. And that is a tribute to the real strength of the band. They have never been prepared to rest on their laurels. And the new material really shone through with its passion and power.

BONO: Sometimes I wonder if all art is prophetic. It tells you what's coming up in your life or what's happening in the world before it's happened. 'Miracle Drug' was one of those moments. It's a song about faith, the miracles that God can work through science, and in particular medicine. It supercharged the show on an emotional level. Every night. I could not look at Edge until he was singing. Then I would look at him, holding on to the words: 'I hear your voice it's whispering in science and in medicine.' And it always brought home what his beautiful daughter is going through, the most extraordinarily gifted girl whose humour and intelligence has helped her negotiate this ordeal. I always dedicated the song to doctors and nurses, people who spend their life looking after others, and know how fragile life is.

I started introducing Edge over the opening notes of 'Miracle Drug'. I would say something along the lines of: 'These four notes give me faith in the future. You know Edge is from the future.' And people look at me. I'd say, 'Yeah, he's from the future and he's come back to be with us here in the present.' Edge would be like, 'Don't.' So then one night I started to develop this theme: 'But he's not just from the future on this planet, he comes from a different planet. And in fact Larry, Adam and myself were all there when his space ship arrived on the north side of Dublin. And the space ship was making this sound.' The same four notes. 'And then the door opened, and out came

A SPACE SHIP ARRIVED ON THE NORTH SIDE OF DUBLIN. AND THE DOOR OPENED AND OUT CAME THIS STRANGE CREATURE. LARRY WENT UP TO HIM AND SAID, 'WHO ARE YOU?' HE SAID, 'I'M THE EDGE.' ADAM SAID, 'WHERE ARE YOU FROM?' EDGE SAID, 'I'M FROM THE FUTURE.' LARRY SAID, 'WHAT'S IT LIKE?' AND EDGE SAID, 'IT'S BETTER.' BONO

this strange creature. And Larry went up to him and said, "Who are you?" He said, "I'm The Edge." And Adam said, "Where are you from?" And Edge said, "I'm from the future." And Larry said, "What's it like?" And Edge said, "It's better." ' And then we go into the song. It was one of those moments, you laugh just before you cry. But, of course, I really believe that. The future is better. We were all believing for Sian.

PAUL: The first part of the Vertigo tour was extremely difficult for all concerned because Bono was leaving the tour quite frequently to do his political lobbying. He was heavily involved in the campaign leading up to the G8 conference of world leaders that inspired Live8. It meant that he was at times distracted. He was putting in very long days on the phone which is the kind of thing that would usually worry me. Most singers doing shows every couple of days don't go to meetings or talk to people or go to noisy restaurants or even talk on the phone in order to conserve their voices. Bono spent large parts of every day talking yet, quite remarkably, survived to sing some great shows without any perceptible falling off in quality. I'm deeply puzzled by how he managed this but, for the most part, he did.

BONO: There are moments when you hear the voice crack and you think: 'This has gone too far. I should be treating my voice with a bit more care.' But most of the time I would come back from those marches, rallies, meetings or conference rooms and arrive on the stage two feet taller. I'm floating because of what could come of all of this. And I feel God's blessing on it. You can't out-give God, I've noticed. I feel like I've been carried by people's prayers. And it hasn't hurt me at all. I'm in top shape. The gigs were brilliant. My voice has never been as strong. How could that be? It's crazy.

EDGE: Bono did seem to be everywhere at once. He was photographed with President Bush, and he appeared at the Labour Party Conference with Prime

Minister Blair, and these people were seen as the architects of the war in Iraq, which was a contentious issue for a lot of people, including our fans. But I think at this point Bono is almost immune to criticism about his motives and his judgement. He's earned that because after so many years of focusing on these issues, I think people pretty much know where he's coming from. And Bono will talk with anybody, meet with anybody, if he feels that by doing so he will further the cause.

LARRY: We understood that Bono's was a bi-partisan approach, and despite the war in Iraq he was going to talk to anybody who would listen and try and get the African issue on the world's political agenda. I marched along with thousands of other Irish people at an anti-war rally in Dublin. It's the first time I've ever marched against anything. I felt I had to do something. I have to admit it was weird then seeing Bono having his picture taken with Tony Blair and George W. Bush. The moral of the story is we can't afford to get the war and Africa confused.

ADAM: I just let Bono get on with it. His judgement of these things has proved to be pretty good. He works very well in these arenas and understands the language. I don't necessarily feel qualified.

BONO: With the UK about to begin a six-month stint as President of the European Union, as well as being chair of the upcoming G8 summit of world leaders in Gleneagles, Scotland, it seemed there was a unique opportunity to make this G8 the one that changes everything. Tony Blair and Gordon Brown had taken these issues very seriously and they were in charge of the agenda. Campaigners around the world were gearing up for it. In the UK, film-maker Richard Curtis had joined forces with the NGO's and coined the phrase 'Make Poverty History'. He and his partner Emma Freud were extraordinary. They did nothing else but work on this all year. But as the summit approached, we needed to create a sense of occasion. The idea of staging another Live Aid concert had been discussed many times, but Bob Geldof always insisted there was no way it was going to happen. And worse than saying no to us all the time, Bob publicly said it wouldn't happen, which was really not helpful. Because, if not a sword of Damocles, it was certainly a threat to governments, and particularly to the British Government, who would feel the full brunt of Live Aid. When Bob said no, you could feel the energy go out of the game. So we kept going back to him and trying to make the case that this could be part of the momentum to make G8 not just focus but actually deliver on the African agenda. Then, at what felt like the eleventh hour, Bob agreed, having dreamed up the concept of Live8 as a global lobbying event, with televised concerts in each of the G8 countries. But the stakes were raised in every sense, because if it's a failure, it would actually do damage. So Bob was working on it night and day, which meant so were we. Bob is not a formal member of DATA, he wanders in and out, but I would like to think we are his spiritual home, we're certainly his office. It takes a lot of manpower and back-up to do this stuff, so this meant chaos for an already stretched organization, particularly in America where the Live Aid brand didn't mean as much. We really had to scramble. We had six weeks and big stars don't plan six weeks ahead, they plan six months ahead. So there were a lot of dramas trying to get the right people on board. It was a very tense time. I adore him, he is my idol, but things were not easy. It was hard to watch him take all that on again and I feared we had pushed him too far but, in truth, no one else comes close at this stuff. People have described us as 'good cop, bad cop'. I am supposed to be more measured, applying a form of water torture, he is supposed to be aggressive, with fists and invective. The truth is we both operate by 'whatever means necessary'. It's 'ultimate fighting'. The only difference being I accept the only two rules of combat: no poking in the eye or biting. Bob does not.

PAUL: The tour relocated to Europe in June. Live8 was a month away, so there was a lot of organization still going on. Meanwhile, we had to transfer from arenas to stadiums, with a whole new production.

LARRY: The Arena audiences seemed controlled in comparison to the European stadium crowds, who were wild. They were some of our best shows ever.

EDGE: The show was actually better outdoors, which we weren't expecting. The first night in Brussels was pretty electric and from then it just seemed to get better and better.

BONO: There were so many highlights to that tour. Poland was probably at the top. We were in the middle of 'New Year's Day' and I'd completely forgotten that the song is inspired by the Solidarity Movement. Because with U2 songs, the original inspiration gets lost as the song evolves. I turned to find some water and when I looked back, the entire stadium, 80,000 people, had disappeared under a red and white Solidarity flag. They were gone. Somehow on the Internet and local radio it had been communicated that our audience should play a trick on us. They had brought cards and figured out who was white and who was red, and the whole stadium turned into a flag. I could

I WAS VERY EXCITED ABOUT PLAYING WITH PAUL MCCARTNEY, ALTHOUGH I WOULD HAVE BEEN JUST AS HAPPY PLAYING TAMBOURINE WITH RINGO ON DRUMS. LARRY

hardly speak let alone sing. It was a really emotional moment for anyone who was there. They felt we had stood by them in that moment when they went on strike for democracy and wanted to show us they remembered.

That began a new trend, which followed us for the whole tour. In Montreal, when we returned to north America, during 'Sometimes You Can't Make It On Your Own', the whole stadium turned violet and red. Everyone had brought these little lights. Obviously they had agreed they would all put them on during 'Sometimes'. So there's a new viral aspect to playing these outdoor shows where your audience are sort of taking charge and doing the art direction. It's bizarre but it's brilliant. It was a wonder, that tour. And, of course, there was Live8. Due to its late announcement, we were actually otherwise engaged. U2 had a concert scheduled in Vienna that night, but we opened the event in Hyde Park in London with Paul McCartney, and just hanging out with the Mac was a thrill.

LARRY: I was very excited about playing with Paul McCartney, although I would have been just as happy playing tambourine with Ringo on drums. We had one rehearsal in London the day before the show. McCartney was a gent. He brought his band with him, just in case we didn't know how to play the song. But I wasn't going to a rehearsal with Paul McCartney not knowing my parts. I had studied 'Sergeant Pepper's Lonely Hearts Club Band' over and over and over again. Thankfully his band weren't needed.

BONO: I came up with the idea of playing 'Sergeant Pepper' in order to persuade Bob that we could stage Live8 in a very new and dramatic way. Bob was going, 'Yeah, that's great, Sergeant Pepper.' And I said, 'But you do get it, don't you?' And it dawned on him: It was twenty years ago today. I knew he'd find that hard to resist.

The original idea was that we would have all the people of our time on stage, the way The Beatles had all the people of their time on the *Sergeant Pepper* album cover. So I wanted Bill Gates on the stage, actors, soccer players, philosophers, politicians, models, all the pop stars, tycoons, all the supporters of the Drop the Debt campaign posed in a tableau vivant, a living mural.

Maybe that was overly ambitious but, as it happens, Bill Gates was standing at the side of the stage when we played. And I thought we'd all be dressed up in Sergeant Pepper suits. We actually got them made up but McCartney rightfully said, 'Let's put the brass band in the suits and just be ourselves.'

PAUL: No one knew the brass parts, they had been long since lost. Sir George Martin was eventually tracked down in Canada and he went out to a record store, bought the CD, wrote out the parts and faxed them over the night before the rehearsals took place.

EDGE: Paul told us that he had never performed 'Sergeant Pepper' ever. He'd recorded it in the studio and at that point The Beatles had stopped touring, so he did the vocal once. When he came to rehearsals to play it with us, that was the only time in the intervening years he'd ever sung that song or played that guitar part. The whole experience was mind-blowing. He's still got a huge voice and he is an amazing musician. The rehearsals were a bit dubious at first. As the world's worst cover band, I just thought, 'Now is not the time for everyone to realize why we started writing our own songs.' But I was quite happy with it in the end.

ADAM: The Beatles had been a very significant influence on all of us, so to be in a rehearsal room with Paul McCartney playing one of his songs was like a dream come true. It didn't escape me that he was bassist in The Beatles. I certainly didn't want to play the part differently to the way he knew it. Edge coached me and we spent some time listening to the original and we had our ship pretty much in order when McCartney came on board. It felt like a bit of a master class. As long as he didn't single me out for not having my homework done properly, I was OK.

BONO: Paul is a much more dimensional character than people realize. He came into our dressing-room before the show to check out what we were wearing. He spotted a jacket at the end of the dressing-room. 'Is that a Christian Dior?', he says. Sharon, our stylist says, 'Yeah, well spotted.' He says, 'Stella just bought me one of them. Who's wearing that?' 'Bono.' 'Listen man,' says Paul, 'two of us can't wear the same jacket now, can we?' He was laughing, I was too . . . until I realized the Beatle had run off with my stage frock. The same man who probably invented the mop top and worked with his manager on those Beatles suits could spot a designer label by the cut of it, which is kind of amazing. Anyway, I did the big day in denim, looking like a mechanic. It was Paul's car, after all.

Then, as we were on our way to the stage, he came over and stopped us, in front of everybody, and said, 'Can we just pause for a second?' He put his arms around us and made a beautiful prayer up about how 'music is what we do and we give our music to Your service, Lord. On this day, use us.' We always spend some time in prayer before we go on, we pause and ask for a blessing on the show. Some people do it in a very showy, kind of theatrical way, like they want to get Jesus to play the tambourine. But this was a real moment for me. I thought, 'Wow, a blessing from the Beatle.'

I was doing backing vocals. Standing in John's shoes was quite a feeling. I couldn't get the smile off my face. And it was lovely to let off the doves in 'Beautiful Day' and see them circling overhead.

PAUL: After U2 performed, we helicoptered crew, equipment and band to RAF Northolt and flew back to Vienna just in time to do our own show. I mean, we have the resources and the manpower to do that, but it was exhilarating.

LARRY: We arrived about an hour and a half later. Not surprisingly, the gig in Vienna was not the best show we've ever done.

BONO: The next week was crazy because I had to go back and forth to the G8 Summit in Scotland, whilst playing concerts around Europe. So there was very little sleep for a couple of weeks. It was four hours a night. I sang with The Corrs at a final Live8 concert at Murrayfield stadium in Edinburgh. I love the Corrs. Andrea is right up there as a singer. Johnny Borrell, the great young frontman with Razorlight, gave me a rose on the way to the stage and I gave it to Andrea. It was a nice, flirtatious moment with a close friend in front of a million of my other closest friends. Meanwhile, the summit was going on down the road in Gleneagles. It is amazing that we got passes. The UK was hosting the event and somehow they let us run amok. There's eight of the world's most powerful men on a golf course in Scotland and myself, Bob Geldof, writer and director Richard Curtis and Emma Freud, and people from Make Poverty History. We were like a swarm of bees pollinating the different plants, moving from one camp to the other. We had breakfast with President Chirac, trying to get him to agree on a trade issue. And he was saying France wouldn't do it without the Americans. Then we go to see Bush and tell him that. We were able to speak to them directly, rather than through the civil servants who have been meeting for six months to negotiate these agreements.

One of the meetings I'm most proud of over that six months was where I gatecrashed a conference in 10 Downing Street. It was a meeting of the sherpas, which is the name for the negotiators. And the mood amongst the sherpas was really bad, they weren't getting anywhere. Through my relationship with Tony Blair, I was allowed to speak to them for twenty minutes. I told them what we believed was at stake and made them laugh, tried to move them, tried to make them aware that history was in their hands, not their leaders', and that the deals would be done or undone based on the small print. I asked them to look up from the numbers, look up from the statistics and try to imagine a different future where we didn't accept that a disease like malaria was with us and there was nothing we could do about it. There was everything we could do about it and it could be all but eradicated in five to ten years – if they enabled certain decisions to be made. I suggested that when they look back on their lives, this would be something they would be proud of and it was worth taking the pain.

That was a month before. So now cut to the G8 and they have gone as far as they can but it's still not far enough. And they're all not speaking to each other and it's very tense. I guess in a way we became a conduit from one leader to another which is kind of bizarre. We were late for German Chancellor Gerhard Schroeder because we were with President Bush. He was upstairs complaining, 'Where are these crazy people?' We meet him and apologize and he kind of chills out and we go off to a corner of the hotel, anywhere we can get a beer, because Schroeder likes to have a beer to relax. And we start going through it. He is in a really interesting predicament. Germany spends 4 per cent of GDP every year on the reunification of its country. Their economy is in a lot of trouble. They have the highest unemployment in decades and he is facing an election. How good do you think it's going to look on him to the majority of his voters that he might be about to give more money away, and not to Germans but to Africa? That takes a lot of courage. It is not applause they are looking for but these politicians need to feel there's popularity in the proposal in order to survive at home. And just as fate and faith would have it, U2 was on tour in Germany whilst we were having the negotiations. And I got to walk out on stage and say, 'Your Chancellor ...' and half the crowd cheer and half the crowd boo. I say, 'No, stop it, listen to me. Your Chancellor has been part of a historic move to give many of the poorest nations in life a new start by dropping their old debts.' So the crowd cheer for that. I said, 'If he comes back from Gleneagles, from the G8 summit, and he has signed up to that, you should give him applause.' So they give him applause. Then I say, 'If he comes home from Gleneagles, having signed up to 0.7 per cent and the $50 billion cheque that we're asking him to sign, we ask you to welcome him as a hero. If he doesn't, you can do what you like.' And, of course, Schroeder gets to hear about this. He starts to see that this subject gets a big cheer. He can see that we'll stand up for him if he does what's being asked of him. And he agrees to take the pain. He did the right thing, even though he was going into an election.

So we got to sit in on those meetings, and the mood was electric. As I've said, George Bush is a comedian. Whatever you feel about him I can tell you he's very personable in person. I walk down the corridor, he comes out and stands to attention. 'Here's the President,' he says. 'What do you want us to do this time, Bono?' Now this is a guy who knows where I stand on the war – a long, long way from where he stands – who knows there are so many things we could never see eye to eye on, and yet the leader of the free world lets us into the room and we're there for an hour, shaking the tree at the last minute, pushing malaria and pushing girls' education, making sure it ends up in the communiqué.

With Blair, we were saying, 'Could you get all the leaders to read out the communiqué? Is there something you could do to make it more poetic than the usual? Something like a declaration, a new beginning.' We didn't get that kind of language. It was too late for that. But he did get all the leaders to sign the communiqué in their own handwriting, something that's never been done before. Because the more their fingerprints are on the document, the more they are personally associated with it, the easier it will be to hold them to the promises contained therein.

We needed a fifty-billion-dollar purse, and right up to the last minute they weren't going to sign it. And even though signing it is a lot different from cashing the cheque, you can't cash it without them signing so that was a real breakthrough. Some people poured scorn on it. They thought fifty billion dollars wasn't enough. They are right. But that's what we were asking for. We felt it was the responsible amount, considering the economic climate. Had we tried for anything more, they simply wouldn't have signed it. It was a balancing act. Until we have a bigger movement of people in Germany and France and the United States, we have to balance our demands with the demand of these donor countries, who also need hospitals and schools. Of course they're not in a state of emergency like Africa and I don't think there's a comparison in need, but some of their constituents do. Until we educate them to the level of the emergency in the developing world, our demands have to be strategic.

EDGE: In Toronto during rehearsals for the second US leg I met up with Producer Bob Ezrin. We talked about the hurricane Katrina disaster that had devastated New Orleans and both resolved to do something for the musicians of the gulf coast area whose livelihoods had been lost. We put together the Music Rising initiative with Henry Juszkiewicz of Gibson guitars, and within two months had begun replacing instruments lost in the hurricane. I visited

New Orleans later in the tour to hand over some instruments in person. The last time I had been there was for our Superbowl performance in 2002. To see the city almost completely destroyed was so shocking.

For our second US leg we went back indoors. It probably should have been a stadium tour but because of shortage of tickets when the first leg went on sale we put the second leg up early, and in doing so made a commitment to playing the venues we had on hold at that point. So in hindsight we solved one problem but at a cost. We certainly could have sold the tickets. But more to the point, the outdoor show was working. We were playing some of the best gigs of our lives

PAUL: It was a pity America missed out on the stadium shows. We took it to the rest of the world and, I suppose partly as a matter of pride, I would like to take it to America, simply because I think it would knock people's socks off.

LARRY: Dates just kept being added. The tour extended into 2006 to take in South America. One thing about U2, too much is never enough.

ADAM: We went to LA for the Grammy Awards on 8 February 2006 to round out the year by playing 'Vertigo' and a version of 'One' with Mary J. Blige. We had picked up three Grammies the previous year at the start of this campaign, so this time around we were focusing on our performance as opposed to being there to collect gongs. It was a big surprise when we actually got five awards, including Album of the Year. That just blew us away. Between the two ceremonies, we've scooped eight Grammies. That is about as good as it gets. It was a confirmation that this record had been taken on board, it went into the culture and it did everything that you would want a record to do. There was a lot of rejoicing, a lot of vintage wine being drunk. The experience really recharged the band and, in a sense, gave us more of a reason to go out there and do more shows in Latin America. There was an enormous demand for tickets. At some of those shows, there were almost as many people outside the stadiums as inside. The fervour of the audiences in the southern hemisphere, where they don't get so many of these big productions, can be overpowering.

One of the things I loved about that tour is that you can really represent those songs with bass, guitar and drums and they sound powerful. There is a real lesson to be learned there. If we can make the songs work without too many overdubs, they're the better for it.

BONO: We're getting closer to the song that we hear in our heads but it's still not there yet. We've got to take it to the next level.

LARRY: You can only exist at this level through faith, blind ambition or the need for revenge. Or all three. We've had moments of great songwriting, great lyrics. There is no point if you are not trying to better your last album. We want to make an album that flows from start to finish, pays off musically, emotionally, lyrically. It has to have at least four singles that make it on Top 40 radio. We want it all and we want it sometime in the next five years! That's all!

EDGE: We really don't want to start making bad records. After all this time we know what a great record is. And that's tough at times because as eighteen-year olds you were immersed in music 24/7 and what we use to do instinctively we sometimes struggle to achieve now, because there are so many more distractions. But, in terms of songwriting, I'm better than I was, by a long way, I am smarter and I know what works. Larry's a better drummer, Adam is a better bass player, and Bono is a better lyric writer and singer. It just takes us a little longer these days, because we have to spend the time to get to where we want to go. There are more false starts, I suppose.

ADAM: It is hard to keep operating at this level, it takes tremendous commitment, but for as long as people are able to make that commitment, then it's worth doing.

LARRY: We're probably not good enough to repeat our best moments, although we try occasionally. I think we make better music and have better ideas now. No Greatest Hits tour just yet.

BONO: I don't think anyone thinks this is a job for life. I don't think it's healthy to imagine it's always going to be here. I always say two crap albums in a row and we're out. That, and a fat arse, can close this operation down. The price of admission is a level of commitment, and that might get harder and harder for some people, or even myself. We just may not want to go to the gym, they just may not want to have somebody else criticize their work. It gets harder. After you go home you return to be lords of your own domain. That is the way of males, in particular. They rid the room of argument until they've no one left except people who agree with them. It is understandable. But I like an argument.

LARRY: Bono was always larger than life. He brings a lot to those who know him. He's very generous and rather good company. He is also extremely complex. You don't know what is going on in that head of his and you might not want to. He has an explosive, unpredictable side to him.

He's got an insatiable appetite for adventure and he will do almost anything and go anywhere to satisfy that. Being as successful as he is has real downsides, the opportunities afforded him are mind-blowing, the responsibility that comes with it is immense. It is extraordinary how he can survive and thrive on it. His faith is his anchor and I think that's what enables him to navigate his way through and come out relatively unscathed.

The more successful and famous he becomes outside U2 the harder it is to get an opportunity to talk and hang out the way we used to, but that's life.

BONO: My gift is that I'm a singer, a songwriter and a performer. I just happened to have learned other skills to protect that gift, and those skills seem to suit political activism. But I am most excited about getting lost in the music again. In the near future, I am going to close the door on activism and commerce and other ideas that engage me, and I am going to shut it quite tight, for a little while at least, and focus on writing and making music.

I need this band. The truth is I need them more than they need me. That is the way I am wired. They raise my game. I would be terrified of being in a recording studio on my own, or just with people who are in my employment. That is my definition of hell on earth. You are as good as the arguments you get. I am a better person for being around these men. They're very dignified people. I'm sure I've given them all headaches, heartaches and anxiety attacks and a lot of sleepless nights. But I also like to think I've given them a few laughs and some adventure.

EDGE: I think we've been able to keep it together because we've all grown up with each other. We know how it works. We've all found our ways to contribute to the band. They're not necessarily equal but our four contributions are all crucial. For reasons that I couldn't even really fathom, it works as a four-piece, four voices, four intellects, four sets of opinion. Without that it wouldn't be the same. It's about a level of solidarity between four people who made a commitment back in the Seventies. And the reasons why it was a good idea at the time are still true. We still can, on our day, make great music together, come up with great ideas, and perform great shows. That is something we all value very highly. Knowing that you do your best work in that context gives you a real incentive to keep it going. If we were all capable of going off and having really successful solo careers, it might have made it more difficult to hold it together. But I think we all know, deep down, this is the forum in which we really excel. The day that U2 ends will be a sad day for all of us.

PAUL: It's very odd for the same five men to have been working together for nearly thirty years. It's been very difficult sometimes and there have been tears and anger as well as joy and exhilaration. I think we're good at being together and good at keeping our distance. Bono has a line that there are four people in the band and five on the board. I like working with U2 because it takes out of me every skill I have; there is art and commerce, politics and history. I was never a musician at all, frustrated or otherwise. I am a reasonable critic of material when it's finished or nearly finished. In the early stages of songs I don't think I'm much of a judge. I'm very proud of U2 and what they've achieved creatively over the years. I'm also proud of what we've achieved together in business. We always agreed that it would be pathetic to be good at the music and bad at the business.

BONO: It's a really efficient work unit, a band, because you have a bigger brain than most artists. Four brains is better than one. It's a lot less lonely and often much more fun. And especially in the rarefied air of fame and fortune, it's a rare privilege to be in the company of people who you started out with and who can see through you. We bring the best out of each other not the worst, which is what a lot of bands do. Human relationships have a tendency to crumble – marriages, families, friendships, it just seems there's a certain entropy that you can give in to which you shouldn't. And when you don't, you stand for that. And that's a lot to stand for. Sticking together is the hardest thing of all but the most rewarding.

EDGE: I don't think any of us begrudge the others. Adam and Larry would probably love to be more involved in the songwriting but, at the same time, no one is shut out of the process so when they do come up with something, it's taken seriously. There is no demarcation, no preciousness. If I'm working on a guitar part that's somehow not as good as it could be, Larry will let me know. It's a very open, healthy attitude. I suppose we've learned over the years that egos have to be checked in before you walk into the studio. You can have a band ego, in fact that's essential when you're determined to make something great happen. But don't get too hung up on your own personal side of it. No one frets about whether their idea made it to the final cut or not. It's the best idea that wins out.

LARRY: Edge is the unsung hero. On a musical level, he's got real insight, but he's not precious about what he does. Even though he might work twice as hard as anybody else, he accepts criticism and is open to discussion because he knows we all want the same things from the music. I have learnt never to underestimate him. He is dogged and relentless in the search for the perfect song, the perfect sound, the perfect idea, always looking for inspiration. Not many people know what's underneath that cool exterior.

BONO: Edge has the best nervous twitch of all, which is when things get really serious, he gets really comic. So he's always pulling the carpet out from under you if you start to take yourself too seriously. Larry, on the other hand, makes sure you do take yourself seriously in the times when you're being too flippant. Larry loves clarity. And so do I. So we're always looking for the top line, the melody line, what's really going on in the room. We are very similar in that sense, although he doesn't like chaos and I seem to enjoy it. It seems to be part of the creative process, for me. To get to clarity you have to be prepared to shake things up.

LARRY: I gave these guys their first job when I put the note on the school noticeboard. I have sometimes naïvely tried to bodyguard some aspects of the band. However, I am learning to let go. After thirty years it's a cool thing to be still making music with your friends.

BONO: You might think that people who have grown up together, worked together and played together and spent so much time in each other's company for all our teenage and adult lives would somehow end up the same, but we are all so different. And yet we have all shaped each other.

Adam was always different to me, he was different to all of us, and he had to walk such a separate path, because he was an individual in a band of God botherers. Yet Adam has made me think about my spiritual life more, to take care of myself better and to see things from a long-term perspective. He was born an old man. He was complaining about the lack of heat in school and our rehearsal room when he was sixteen. He wore slippers and a dressing-gown around the house when he was a teenager. But it was an early sign that a wise man was on the way. And maybe it was horrible for him to have to go through so many hard experiences to get to that place of wisdom but that was his journey, and he's there now. He's coming into something rather than out of something.

ADAM: I don't think I was destined for any kind of greatness in my life before U2. The best decision I ever made was to be part of U2 and I guess I haven't needed to make another serious decision since then. I am eternally grateful that this band came along when it did. It hasn't all been easy but then I probably made things harder for myself.

For a long time I believed the rock and roll mythology of acquiring

PERSONALITIES WILL NOT BREAK UP U2. MUSICAL DIFFERENCES WILL NOT BREAK UP U2. WE'LL BREAK UP BECAUSE SOMEBODY SQUEEZED THE TOOTHPASTE FROM THE WRONG END. LARRY

experience without responsibility. I chose to deal with being in the band in a very kind of singleminded way and I developed a lifestyle that I thought added up to what I was. I don't want to go back there again, so I enrolled on a twelve-step programme that gave me the tools to look at the way I was living my life and deal with things on a daily basis. I have learned a lot about myself but at the same time, I don't necessarily feel I've come a long way. I think I am pretty much the same person I have always been. I operate at a level that I'm comfortable with. I don't think I'd be comfortable meeting politicians or doing any of the stuff that Bono is so superbly suited to. And Edge is superbly suited to the technical area that he operates in. I don't feel I'm any better equipped in those areas than I was when we first met at sixteen. But I'm definitely more comfortable in my skin, and I suppose that's something.

BONO: I feel much more of a whole person now than I ever did. I seem to have resolved a lot of feelings for my father. Something happened last Easter. I went up to this little chapel in France and lit a candle and I got down on my knees and I wept but I thanked God for my father. And I thanked my father for all the gifts he gave me. That feels great. The reason why 'Sometimes You Can't Make It On Your Own' is not a miserable song is because it breaks open with the line 'you're the reason I sing, you're the reason the opera is in me.' He is the reason I have this life, or at least a very large part of the reason. So I certainly have got to a place of peace with him.

I thank God on a daily basis for my life in U2 because not only did this job put my talents to use, it put my insecurities and weaknesses to use. That's the miracle for me. So the emptiness that you're feeling through absence or the desire for meaning and purpose in your life, all that ache, it suits a performer, because you're trying to fill the God-shaped hole with the crowd, your audience.

I don't go to a therapist. If I had the time, maybe I would lie on a couch and pay somebody a thousand pounds an hour to tell me what my friends could tell me on a night out in Dublin. But in the meantime I'd rather stick with the nights out and the songs. For me, songwriting is the place where you can't lie. It's the place where you have to face yourself. U2's definition of art is breaking open the breastbone, open-heart surgery. I wish there was an easier way, but, in the end, people want blood, and I'm one of them.

LARRY: There is a lot of laughter in U2. Sadly, that rarely comes across. We are like a dysfunctional family, with all the laughter and tears that goes with that. Personalities will not break up U2. Musical differences will not break up U2. We'll break up because somebody squeezed the toothpaste from the wrong end.

EDGE: We are still a working band, and while this whole book has been a chance to look back, the truth is we don't really want to dwell too much on the past lest it gets in the way of where we are going in the future. We are still learning after thirty years and that's what it's all about. We are all still fascinated by music, what it means to people when it's great, and what it means to us. Having lasted this long, we don't want to go down without a fight.

If rock and roll is going to be around in five hundred years' time, it's going to be because people are still writing great songs. It is all about the songs and to get a great one is hard, very hard. By no means everything we do is great. Ever since we were a struggling punk band we have been recording all our jams and rehearsals, our improvisations and ideas, and if people heard all those unreleased tapes, believe me, it would confirm everything we have ever said about U2 being a dysfunctional band. If the work is great, it's great in spite of us, not because of us. I honestly still think of us as four chancers from north Dublin.

We have in fact promised ourselves that we will rig some highly sophisticated incendiary device to our tape vault, so if we all go down on the big plane it all gets burnt.

BONO: I'm waking up every day now trying to imagine what we can do next.

It is such an extraordinary thing, music. It seems to be how we communicate on another level. If you believe that we contain within our skin and bones a spirit that might last longer than your time breathing in and out, music is the thing that wakes it up. It certainly woke mine up. I wasn't looking for grace, but luckily grace was looking for me.

I used to think that one day I'd be able to resolve the different drives I have in different directions, the tension between the different people I am. Now I realize that is who I am, and I'm more content to be discontent. But I do feel I'm getting closer to the song I hear in my head. I mean that on every level. And when that distance between the song we hear in our heads and the one that comes out on the radio gets closer, I think this band's going to get much bigger. I actually don't think U2 is in any kind of mood to go quietly. If we get our songs right, I think we could really be very popular.

THIS IS THE STORY OF U2, AS TOLD BY U2, IN THEIR OWN WORDS AND PICTURES. THE TEXT WAS CREATED FROM OVER 150 HOURS OF EXCLUSIVE INTERVIEWS WITH BONO, EDGE, ADAM CLAYTON, LARRY MULLEN JR AND MANAGER PAUL MCGUINNESS, CONDUCTED OVER THE COURSE OF TWO YEARS ESPECIALLY FOR THE BOOK BY NEIL MCCORMICK.

Photographs, documents and memorabilia were supplied from personal archives by members of U2 and Principle Management. The book was art-directed by Steve Averill, the man responsible for U2's artwork from their very first poster in 1977.

Neil McCormick is one of the UK's leading music journalists. Neil attended Mount Temple School in Dublin with Bono, Edge, Adam and Larry and witnessed U2's first-ever performance. He has followed their career ever since, as a fan, friend and occasional critic. Neil writes a weekly newspaper column for *The Daily Telegraph*. He is a regular pundit on BBC television and radio. Neil is author of the best-selling memoir *I Was Bono's Doppelganger* aka *Killing Bono*.

Art Director Steve Averill has worked with U2 since their inception, firstly offering advice based on his role as a member of The Radiators from Space and then, in a more lasting role, as designer and art director of the band's graphic output, including all album sleeves. Now creative director of Four5One Creative he works with a design team that includes fellow long-time U2 designer Shaughn McGrath, who designed the initial concepts and Gary Kelly, the book's designer.

U2 AND PAUL McGUINNESS would like to thank everyone involved in creating this book: Super-agent Ed Victor for the grand plan; Publisher Trevor Dolby of HarperCollins UK for his patience and perseverance; Managing Editor Nicky Granville and Principle Management's Candida Bottaci and Steve Matthews for co-ordinating an immensely complex project; Steve Averill and Gary Kelly at Four5One for the outstanding design (and the long hours); editor Bill Flanagan for guidance; Jim Henke for inspiration and, of course, Neil McCormick, for his forbearance, sensitivity and patience, during long days and nights, working as our interpreter and scribe.

BONO WOULD LIKE TO THANK:
James, George and Niall; Derek Rowen, Donald Moxham, Maeve O'Regan, Mark Holmes, Skello; Reggie Manuel for getting me to the first rehearsal; my brother Norman, for teaching me guitar; Edge, Adam and Larry… for not letting me play guitar; Paul, for teaching me what the whole equation was; my babies for showing me how to grow up; Ali for love, friendship and patience; Bob and Iris, Terry and Joy for bed and never bored; Chris Rowe, Pod; the rest of the Hewson/Rankin clan for not disowning me; Gav, Guggi and Simon C, thanks for your ears, eyes and brains; dearest Michael Stipe; Q; Robert and Grace de Niro; Julian Schnabel; Lou Reed; Julie P; Heather G, Anne Madden and Louis le Brocquy; Salman Rushdie, Michka Assayas, Neil McCormick; Nicholas Klein; Thierry Klemeniuk, Sean Penn, Aislinn Evans, Dr Kevin Cahill; Kevin and Sue Godley; Pierce and Karina; Charlie Whisker and Mairead; Sugar O'Shea; Shaker; Chanty; Regina Moylay; all the Stankards; the Mayor and his Missus; especially Pat and Fran; Fergus the seed of Stankard himself with his magic Wanda; Claude and Moon; Cormac, Spiros, Paki; Christmas Stockings with Miriam; the poet Laureate, Gary Jermyn; Enid, Sybille, Ann Acheson; Lian Lunson and all the big girls, what bodyguards; Christy, Helena, Naomi, and the big Cat; the little ones aren't bad either… Anna, Gerry, the Android, Nathalie, Winona, Aurelie; Norman's little girls, Geraldine, Lorraine, Emma and

Leah; Ian and Siobhan's big boys, Malcolm, Ross and Duncan; Ruth and Barbara's little boys, Trevor, Michael, Scott and the amazing AJ; my idol Jack Rankin; my other Godchildren: Hollie, Baddie, Jessie, Shane, Noah, and Setsuko; Harumi, Hella; family Wenders, Iovine, Shriver, Geldof, Sachs, Buffet, Gates; Coleman, Devlin, McKillen, Sheridan, Clinton, Crosbie, McGuinness, Judd, Flanagan; T, Suzanne Doyle; Saoirse for freedom; Dawn Kenny, Rori Coleman, Catriona G for microphone technique; Lucy Matthew for light; Jack and Trish for making sure the house is not built on sand.

Bobby Shriver, my Lord Bob Geldof, Jamie Drummond, Zita Lloyd, Tom, Erin, Scott and Tom and all the DATA team; Sheila Roche, Melissa Jones, Tamsin, Helen and all the RED team; Roger, Marc, Fred, Bret, John and everyone at Elevation; the staff at the Clarence; Christian, Rogan, Scott, and everyone at Edun; eternally Pat; John; Theresa Dunne, Bernie, Ari, Jackie, Simon, Mark, Darragh, Sue, Ailbhe, Debbie, La Cooney, Niamh Kenny, Brian Murphy, all Temple Hill Billies; Richard Ford, Claire, Beta, Mark, Christoph, Lorna, Bruno and Serge for Les Roses; Peter Lacy, Marco Polo Coleman for all the above.

To all my musical idols, I could never repay you, nor have I tried. For the people I have not mentioned… there are three reasons: political, dementia and 45 minutes for 45 years.

EDGE WOULD LIKE TO THANK:
Bono, Adam, Larry and Paul for partnering with me on this wild ride; my father Garvin and mother Gwenda for their amazing foresight and belief in me; my brother Richard and sister Gill for being so understanding; my daughters: Hollie for keeping me honest, Arran for her quiet wisdom and Blue for keeping me young; Aislinn for three amazing daughters. My son Levi for all our shared adventures in nature; my daughter Sian for being my hero and for her unswerving belief in me; Chantal for friendship; Simon for all the laughs; Shivers and Marc for covering my back; Sammy and Liz for their dedication; all the Stankards for our community games; and everyone in my life for putting up with endless sessions listening to rough mixes and EQs. Finally, the person who makes it all possible, my wife Morleigh, for her encouragement, her lioness courage, but most of all for her love.

ADAM WOULD LIKE TO THANK:
Bono and Ali, Edge and Morleigh, Larry and Ann, Paul and Kathy, Brian and Jo Clayton, Sebastian and Sindy Clayton, Susie Smith, Aislinn Evans, Pete Townshend, Stuart Morgan, Carol Hawkins.

LARRY WOULD LIKE TO THANK:
Special thanks to: Ann, Elvis, Ava and Ezra, Cecilia, Becky and Sam, Steve and Iris Acheson, Alice Mullen, Joe Bonnie, John Wadham, Post Office Workers Union Band, Peter Martin, Paul, David and Adam, Donald Moxham, Dr Albert Bradshaw, Colin McKenzie, Eamon O'Neill, Eugene from Stryder, Larry Gogan, Dave Fanning, Steve Lillywhite, Brian Eno and Danny Lanois, Flood, Joe O'Herlihy, Sam O'Sullivan, Dennis Sheehan, Bob Koch, Dave Skaff, Paul McGuinness and Principle Management, Candida Bottaci, Keryn Kaplan, Steve Matthews, Bess Dulany, Jeremy Joseph, Regine Moylett, Sharon Callaly, Fintan Fitzgerald, Bret and Theresa Alexander, Jack Heaslip, Gavin Friday, Sharon Blankson, Chanty O'Sullivan, Dr Muller Wolfhart, Dr Brian Kennedy, Paul S, Carol Goldstein, Gaby Smyth, Mark Curran, Sean Murphy, Paul Russell and Lindsey Holmes, Anne-Louise Kelly and Ned O'Hanlon, Rob and Libby Frayne, JP and Suz Panaro, David Beal, Medhat and Paula Ibrahim, Suzanne Varney, Scott Nichols, David Guyer, Rocco Ancarola, David Toraya. This book is dedicated to my parents Laurence and Maureen Mullen, and to my sister Mary.

NEIL McCORMICK:
This tome was a mammoth undertaking for everyone involved. I would particularly like to acknowledge the support and help of Candida Bottaci at Principle Management, my conduit

to the band, unfailingly calm, sympathetic and resourceful under pressure. I guess you get used to it.

I would like to thank Publisher Trevor Dolby of HarperCollins UK for his encouragement, sympathy and good humour. Nicky Granville, project co-ordinator, helped pull all the strands of an incredibly complex book together with resourcefulness and energy. Steve Averill and particularly Gary Kelly at Four5one did an extraordinary job making these pages look so damn fine. Frances Angliss and Carolanne Adams were diligent and discreet in assisting with transcription and Richard Betts was a particularly painstaking proof reader. And I am immensely indebted to renowned American author and rock journalist Bill Flanagan, who stepped in as editor at the 11th hour to help me beat this book into submission.

I am grateful for the always friendly support of Susan Hunter, Steve Matthews and Nadine O'Flynn at Principle Management; Bono's unflappable assistant Catriona Garde (who somehow managed to schedule so much time with the most over-scheduled man on the planet); Ali Hewson (who helped me track her man down when it seemed he was determined not to be found) and Lucy Matthew (for a vital contribution to the DATA section). I would like to express gratitude to Paul McGuinness for his trust, and to his wife Kathy Gilfillan, for suggesting I might be up to this task in the first place.

Thanks go too to my agent Araminta Whitley at LAW; the team at the Arts desk of *The Daily Telegraph* for tolerating my divided attention and my better half, Gloria, for sharing her life with U2 for two years.

Last, but by no means least, thanks to Bono, Edge, Adam and Larry for their confidence in me and their candour. It was definitely a privilege and mostly a pleasure to be allowed such insight into what it is that makes a band I have always loved actually tick.

The McCormick family make cameos throughout this book. My brother, Ivan, was briefly a member of the greatest rock band in the world and my sister Stella provided backing vocals at that fateful Rat Salad gig. My little sister Louise worked as assistant engineer on many U2 recordings at STS. I would like to dedicate my work in this book to our father, Bill McCormick, who passed away during its writing, and to my mother, Marlene, who survives him. As the song goes, we get to carry each other …

U2 AND PAUL McGUINNESS would like to express their eternal gratitude to all those who have sailed on the good ship: Keryn Kaplan, Anne-Louise Kelly, Sheila Roche, Ellen Darst, Barbara Galavan, Steve Matthews, Cillian Guidera, Brigid Mooney, Caroline Ashe, Cecilia Mullen, Jackie Bennett, Eileen Long, David Herbert, Maria Duffy, Anne O'Leary, Liz Devlin, Candida Bottaci, Sandra Long, Aislinn Meehan, Tara Mullen, Gerry Watters, Trevor Bowen, Sharon Callaly, Susie Smith, Susan Hunter, Sally-Anne McKeown, Suzanne O'Dea, Alexa Smith, Eileen Osborne, Joy Warner, George Augusta, Sharon Gallagher, Jenn San Angelo, Avril Slevin, Delphine Esposito, Aoife McArdle, Nadine O'Flynn, Annie Fischer, Allison Finley, Debbie Bernardini, Robin Dunn, Gina Menza, Gene Kogan, Bess Dulany, Sheila 'Holly' Peters, Dee Vogel, Lisa Fischoff, Kathy Araskog, Donna Estes, Amy Schmalz, Shan Lui, Michelle Lieu, Missy Iredell, Joe O'Herlihy, Steve Iredale, Tim Buckley, Jake Kennedy, Dennis Sheehan, Tom Mullally, John Sullivan, Steve Rainford, Steve Witmer, Bill Spoon, AJ Rankin, Lance Stoner, Willie Williams, Dave Natale, CJ Patterson, Bob Moorbeck, John Clarke, Jim Singleton, Bob Wein, Mike Andy, Dave Wilkinson, Joe Ravitch, Dave Skaff, Peter Jennings, Peter Clarke, Steve Sunderland, Bob Koch, Bret Alexander, Theresa Pesco, Paul Barrett, Des Broadbery, Marc Coleman, Mary Gough, Marion Smyth, Greg Carroll, Fraser McAlister, Sam O'Sullivan, Rocco Reedy, Mickey Finlay, Fintan Fitzgerald, Dan Russell, Harold Hallas, Helen Campbell, Nassim Khalifa, Carol Dodds, Tim Lamb, Sharon Blankson, Stuart Morgan, Dallas Schoo, Rab McAllister, Suzanne Doyle, BP Fallon, Paul Oakenfold, Jack Heaslip, Jerry Mele,

David Guyer, Erik Hausch, Jerry Meltzer, Scott Nichols, Karen Nicholson, Helene Dean, Nick Levitt, Giles Baxendale, Rob Wachs, Mark Fisher, Catherine Owens, Ned O'Hanlon, Maurice Linnane, Mark Pellington, EBN, David Wojnarowicz, Keith Haring, Maria Manton, Vegetable Vision, Roy Lichtenstein, Run Wrake, Jennifer Steinkamp, John Maybury, Brian Wood, George Barber, Carter Kustera, John Bland, Image Now, Core Design, Adam Smith, Marcus Lyall, Michelle Yu, Noah Clarke, Joe King, Juan Delcan, John Leamy, Nick Hooker, Sean Fairburn, Tony Oursler, Sam Pattinson, onedotzero, United Visual Artists, Julian Opie, Ed Holdsworth, Jason Free, Monica Caston, Jake Berry, Rob Kirwan, Melissa Jones, Kaleen Lemon, Craig Sneiderman, Sue Iredale, Dave Rouze, John Sampson, Anthony Pittaro, Chris Heaney, Catriona Garde, Suzanne Varney, Ben Schwerin, Elizabeth Spencer, Terry Lawless, Philip Docherty, Brian Murphy, Jay Maskrey, Niall Slevin, Robbie Adams, Jim McCafferty, Cynthia Oknaian, Chris Blackwell, Carl Scott, Bob Regher, Tim Devine, Tom Hayes, Marc Marot, Phil Cooper, Ceri Nichols, Christine Atkins, Karen Yee, Jimmy Iovine, Rick Dobbis, Johnny Barbis, Dennis Fine, Nancy Sullivan, John Birget, Lou Maglia, Frank Barsalona, Barbara Skydel, Barry Fey, Dee Jamieson, Ian Flooks, Sally Morris, Jack Boyle, Brian Murphy, Don Law, Owen Epstein, George Regis, Bruce Slayton, Rob Partridge, Neil Storey, Nick 'Bill' Stewart, Annie Roseberry, Lionel Conway, Ken Ehrlich, Ron Goldstein, Michael Abramson, Bruce and Mary Moser, Regine Moylett, Amanda Freeman, Frances McCahon, Donna Schinderman, Paul Wasserman, Brian O'Neal, Karen Johnson, Alvinia Bridges, Desiree Gruber, Karen Bell, Audrey Strahl, Marilyn Laverty, Mark Satlof, Nigel Sweeney, Michael Cohl, Steve Howard, Eric Kert, Joe Rascoff, Jennifer Czin, Arthur Fogel, Craig Evans, Susan Rosenberg, George Gerrity, John Giddings, Dylan White, Fran Curtis, Roger Ames, Alain Levy, David Munns, John Kennedy, Max Hole, Pascal Negre, Zach Horowitz, Andrew Kronfeld, John Vlautin, Mika El Baz, Thom Panunzio, Steve Leeds, Howie Miura, David Saslow, Courtney Holt, Steve Berman, Candice Berry, Brenda Romano, Crispin Evans, Clive Fisher, Paul Kremen, Lori Earl, Bernadette Coyle, Lucian Grainge, Nick Gatfield, Claire Sugrue, Jason Iley, Naomi Beresford-Webb, Jon Turner, Dave Pennefather, David Renzer, Doug Morris, Bill Graham, Dave Fanning, Niall Stokes, Eamon Dunphy, Ian Wilson, Larry Gogan, Gerry Ryan, Martin Wroe, Dave McCullagh, Chris Westwood, Paul Morley, Steve Morse, Tom Moon, Gary Graff, Edna Gundersen, Dan Aquilante, Jim Farber, David Fricke, Joe Levy, Jenny Eliscu, Greg Kot, Anthony deCurtis, Robert Hilburn, Jon Pareles, Lisa Robinson, Sia Michel, Michael Elliot, Josh Tyrangiel, Gerry Mazoratti, Jim Traub, Elysa Gardner, Danny Eccleston, Gavin Martin, Sean O'Hagan, Stuart Baillie, Dave Henderson, Paul Rees, Conor McNicholas, Adrian Thrills, Mark Ellen, Andrew Muller, Adrian Deevoy, Michael Ross, Brian Boyd, Jeff McCluskey, Jeff Pollack, Jann Wenner, Tom Freston, Judy McGrath, John Sykes, Bill Flanagan, Bill Roedy, Van Toffler, Harriet Brand, Brent Hansen, Fleur Sarfaty, Carter Alan, Oedipus, Norm Winer, Annie Nightingale, Gary Davies, Mark Goodier, Simon Mayo, Neil Fox, Chris Evans, Jo Whiley, Zane Lowe, Cat Deeley, Ant 'n' Dec, Jonathan Ross, Chris Cowey, Malcolm Gerrie, Conor McAnally, Phil Mount, Suzi Aplin, Gavin Friday, Cheryl Engels, Arnie Acosta, Brian Eno, Steve Lillywhite, Daniel Lanois, Flood, Nellee Hooper, Howie B, Mike Hedges, Richard Stannard, Julian Gallagher, Mark 'Spike' Stent, Richard Rainey, Chris Thomas, Garret Jacknife Lee, Carl Glanville, David Mallet, Dione Orrom, Meiert Avis, Donald Cammell, Barry Devlin, Gavin Taylor, Phil Joanou, Michael Hamlyn, Kevin Godley, Richard Lowenstein, Anton Corbijn, Andrew Macpherson, Kevin Westenberg, Stéphane Sednaoui, Kevin Mazur, Wim Wenders, Richie Smyth, Jon Klein, Mark Neale, Jake Scott, Morleigh Steinberg, Jonas Akerlund, Joseph Kahn, Hamish Hamilton, Liz Friedlander, Alex and Martin, Fiona Dent, James Morris, Irene Keogh, Harry Crosbie, Denis Desmond, Jim Aiken, Robbie Wootton, Greg Feinberg, Ellie Shibata, Steve Averill, Shaughn McGrath, Candice Hanson, Allen Grubman, David Toraya, Eric Gatoff, Ted Harris, Gil Garson, Larry Shire, Jess Drabkin, Peter Grant, Stuart Fried, Ina Meibach, John Callaghan, Paddy Grafton Green, Euan Lawson, David Landsman, Fred Feingold, Mark Berg, John Gula, Nick Valner, Paddy Gardiner, Brian Murphy, Ossie Kilkenny, Gaby Smyth, Eva Thompson, Stephen Maltby, Owen 'Bo' Cooper, John Panaro, Jeremy Joseph and all at De-Lux, Sebastian Clayton, James Cooke, Adrian Kelly.

PHOTOGRAPHIC CREDITS

While every effort has been made to trace the owners of copyright material reproduced herein, the publishers would like to apologize for any omissions and will be pleased to incorporate missing acknowledgements in any future editions.

PLATES

1 © Evans family archive; 2 © Clayton family archive, © Hewson family archive, © Mullen family archive, © Evans family archive; 3 © Evans family archive, © Clayton family archive, © Neil McCormick archive; 4 © Tom Sheehan, © Martyn Goddard, © Paul McGuinness, © U2 archive; 5 © Colm Henry, © Paul McGuinness, © Tom Sheehan, © Evans family archive; 6 © U2 archive, © Evans family archive, © Colm Henry, © David Evans, © U2 Limited (Jacobus Van Hespen), © Rex Features; 7 © Star File, © Paul McGuinness, © Redferns (Richard E. Aaron), © Retna (Larry Busacca), © Retna (J. Blakesberg), © U2 Limited (Jim Rakete), © Clayton family archive, © Evans family archive, © U2 archive, © Andrew Macpherson, © Kevin Davies; 8 © Pavarotti International (Suzie Maeder), © Evans family archive, © NI Syndication (Neil Fraser), © Reuters (Damir Sagolj), © Reuters (Tony Gentile), © U2 Limited (unknown), © U2 archive, © Vatican press office (Arturo Mauri), © Alpha (Richard Chambury), © Empics (Ron Edmunds), © LA Times (Richard Hartog), © Pacemaker Press International; 9 © Phil Sheehy; 10 © Paul Slattery; 11 [top] © Colm Henry, [middle] © U2 Limited (Ian Finlay), [bottom left] © Paul Slattery, [bottom right] © U2 Limited (Ian Finlay); 12 [top] © U2 Limited (Anton Corbijn), [middle left] © Colm Henry, [middle right] © Adrian Boot, [bottom] © Colm Henry; 13 © U2 Limited (Ian Finlay); 14 © U2 Limited (Anton Corbijn); 15 [top] © U2 Limited (Anton Corbijn), [bottom] © U2 Limited (Kees Tabak); 16 © U2 Limited (Anton Corbijn); 17 © Stefano Giovannini; 18 [top] © U2 Limited (Anton Corbijn), [bottom] © U2 Limited (Anton Corbijn); 19 © Colm Henry; 20 © Terry O'Neill, [bottom] © Tom Sheehan; 21 © U2 Limited (Thomas Busler); 22 © U2 Limited (Anton Corbijn); 23 [top] © U2 Limited (Anton Corbijn), [bottom left and right] © U2 Limited (Anton Corbijn), [bottom middle]© Andrew Macpherson; 24 [top left] © U2 Limited (Anton Corbijn), [top right] © U2 Limited (Anton Corbijn), [upper middle] © Kevin Davies, U2 Limited (Anton Corbijn, Jurgen Teller), [lower middle] © U2 Limited (Jurgen Teller), [bottom] © U2 Limited (Anton Corbijn); 25 [top] © U2 Limited (Anton Corbijn), [bottom] © U2 Limited (Anton Corbijn); 26 © U2 Limited (Anton Corbijn); 27 [top] © U2 Limited (Kevin Davies), [middle left] Anon., [middle right] © U2 Limited (Kevin Davies), [bottom left] © U2 Limited (Kevin Davies), [bottom right] © U2 Limited (Anton Corbijn); 28 © U2 Limited (Anton Corbijn); 29 © Anton Corbijn; 30 [top] © U2 Limited (Anton Corbijn), [bottom] © U2 Limited (Anton Corbijn); 31 [top] © U2 Limited (Anton Corbijn), [bottom] © U2 Limited (Anton Corbijn); 32 © U2 Limited (Andrew Macpherson).

PAGES

iv–v, 156 © U2 Limited (Ian Finlay); vi © U2 Limited (Kevin Westenberg); viii, xii, xvi, xx © Kevin Westenberg; 1, 6, 22, 30 © Paul Slattery; 36 © Dick Evans; 72 © U2 Limited (Hugo McGuinness); 118 © Adrian Boot; 182, 208, 238, 350, 388 © U2 Limited (Anton Corbijn); 266, 320 © Kevin Davies.

*it*books

A paperback edition of this book was published in 2008 in the UK.

FIRST IT BOOKS EDITION PUBLISHED 2009.

Library of Congress Cataloging-in-Publication Data is available upon request.

ISBN 978-0-06-190385-4 (It Books edition)

09 10 11 12 13   10 9 8 7 6 5 4 3 2 1